The
OTTOMAN CENTURIES

Books by Lord Kinross

The Ottoman Centuries: The Rise and Fall of the Turkish Empire
Between Two Seas: The Creation of the Suez Canal
The Windsor Years
Portrait of Egypt
Ataturk: A Biography of Mustafa Kemal, Father of Modern Turkey
Within the Taurus: A Journey in Asiatic Turkey
Europa Minor: Journeys in Coastal Turkey
The Innocents at Home: A Visit to the U.S.A.
Portrait of Greece

The OTTOMAN CENTURIES

The Rise and Fall of the Turkish Empire

LORD KINROSS

WILLIAM MORROW AND COMPANY, INC.
NEW YORK 1977

In the gathering of illustrative material, the cooperation of the British Museum and of Nurcihan Kesim, Istanbul, is gratefully acknowledged.

The maps in this volume are based on a map of the Ottoman Empire drawn by K. C. Jordan, Royal Geographical Society, London.

MAP ARTIST DYNO LOWENSTEIN.

Printed in the United States of America.

4 5 6 7 8 9 10

Library of Congress Cataloging in Publication Data

Kinross, John Patrick Douglas Balfour, Baron, 1904-1976
The Ottoman centuries.

Includes index.
1.Turkey—History—Ottoman Empire, 1288-1918.
I. Title.
DR486.K56 956.1'01 76-28498
ISBN 0-688-03093-9

BOOK DESIGN CARL WEISS

To

Freya Stark

CONTENTS

LIST of MAPS

The OTTOMAN CENTURIES

PROLOGUE

WESTWARD ALONG THE HIGH EURASIAN STEPPE, FROM THE BORDERS of China across Turkestan and beyond it, there flowed through continuous centuries waves of nomad peoples. Pastoral, stock-breeding communities, living in tents, horsemen and camel drivers feeding and rearing the flocks and the herds which in turn were to feed and to clothe them, they moved in cycles between seasonal pastures, migrating onward periodically to seek better lands or to escape the pressure of kindred nomads behind them; sometimes trading their pastoral products for those of the townsmen and agriculturists; less frequently settling themselves by the way, in some watered oasis, to a life of cultivation. Obliged, for the maintenance of their pastoral economy, to wage a perennial war with the forces of nature, these nomads of the steppe, in loose federations of close tribal societies, developed their own especial energies, skills, institutions, and customs.

Widespread among them were a vigorous people who became known as the Turks. To the Chinese and other neighbours they were the Tu-Kueh or Dürkö, a belligerent race deriving the name (so it is said) from a hill in their region which was shaped like a helmet. Identified at an earlier stage with the Huns, the Turks were akin to the Mongols and to the people who were later to be known as Finns and Hungarians.

In the sixth century A.D. they conquered another people of their kind to rule over a land which became known as Mongolia. Thence they expanded over a wide area of the steppe toward north, south, and west, to establish a nomad empire, the largest yet known. Losing unity in dispersal, they nonetheless retained a distinct racial and linguistic character. Their sense of common identity was so strong that, in their pagan shamanist worship of earth, air, fire, and water, they referred to such elements of nature as Turkish. Soon evolving beyond simple pastoral barbarism, these Turks established, within their patriarchal clan society, a civilization of their own, with rulers who were more than mere tribal elders, and vassal tribes beneath their sway.

Early in the eighth century the tribes that went west, collectively known as the Oghuz, guided by a legendary grey wolf and led mainly by chieftains of the Seljuk clan, reached Samarkand, in Transoxiana, to establish their rule over western Central Asia. At the same time a new expanding race, the Arabs of the Islamic Caliphate, had swept northward and eastward from Arabia to conquer the Empire of Persia. Turkish power crumbled before them. But mercantile and cultural relations between the two peoples persisted. They traded along the caravan routes to their mutual advantage in the complementary products of cultivation and pasture. Moreover the Turks, from the ninth century onward, began to renounce their pagan beliefs and to embrace Islam.

The Arabs were quick to discern the martial qualities of these Turkish people. Apart from such moral virtues as endurance, self-discipline, and foresight, the nomadic way of life had bred in them a combative spirit, the habit of mobility, equestrian skill, and an unusual dexterity as archers on horseback. The armies of the Abbasid Caliphate thus began to recruit Turks into their ranks, Moslem converts with the status of superior slaves, free to rise through promotion. Hence by the end of the ninth century most of the military commands and many political offices of the Arab Empire were held by Moslem Turks. As the Empire waned in the eleventh century, their Seljuk dynasty filled the vacuum with an empire of its own, an Islamic state based on the traditions of the Abbasid Caliphate, which absorbed other Turco-Islamic principalities and, with the bow and arrow as its appropriate symbol of authority, extended its rule over Persia, Mesopotamia, and Syria. Thus did a nomadic people of the steppe come to rest in a static environment.

Unlike others of the nomad kind throughout history—the Huns and the Mongols, the ephemeral Avars—the Seljuk Turks rose, in a durable and productive sense, to the challenge of the sedentary life. Adapting their own traditions and institutions to the ends of a settled civilization, they emerged as empire-builders with a constructive sense of statecraft, making a positive contribution to history as the old Moslem world evolved into a new phase of social and economic, religious and intellectual advancement. These shepherds and warriors of the steppe became town-dwellers—administrators, merchants, manufacturers, artisans, holders and tillers of land, builders of roads, caravanserais, mosques, schools, and hospitals. They came to cultivate and encourage scholarship—the philosophy and sciences, the literature and arts in which the Persians and Arabs before them had set an example.

Nonetheless there remained, outside the settled, centralized life of the Seljuk state, a large and virtually autonomous population of Turks who still roamed over the uplands as nomads. Allied to other pastoral tribes, some of which remained pagan, they comprised in particular warrior groups, which had initially been the mainstay of the Seljuk fighting forces. They now harried the settled provinces and embarrassed the central government by their unruly, predatory ways. Forming in effect a separate society from that of the state, with a culture of their own and a dissident outlook, they became collectively known as Turcomans—a designation strictly applicable only to their Moslem elements.

Dominant among these were the products of an earlier popular movement, the Ghazis, holy "warriors of the faith." Recruited from a mixed crowd of volunteers, often vagabonds, fugitives, malcontents, and unemployed persons seeking subsistence, their allotted task was to fight the infidel and their predominant motive was plunder. Traditionally they fought as march-warriors, carrying out raids beyond the frontiers of Islam. In the eleventh century they came to operate in the west, on the fluid borders between the Seljuk and the Byzantine empires, in Asia Minor. Here they were confronted by groups of Greek march-warriors and raiders, the Akritai, so alike in their traditions of warfare and their isolation from any central authority as often to seem all but brothers-in-arms. Other diverse Turcoman elements tended also to push toward their frontiers in search of new pastures, and to join the Ghazis in raids across them, at a time when Byzantine defenses were weakening.

It was no part of the policy of the Seljuk sultans, bent on the southward conquest of a Moslem empire, to seek war with the Christian empire of Byzantium, whose neutrality secured their Syrian flank. They became involved in it nonetheless as an accomplished fact, largely owing to the concerted power of the warlike Ghazi and marauding Turcoman forces. This the Seljuk government must needs respect, and where possible turn to its own ends. The Seljuk sultan Tughrul thus diverted the holy warriors from the pillage of his Moslem provinces in successive campaigns against the Christian state of Armenia, a dissident border province of Byzantium. Here their success in battle was followed by raids of increasing extent and audacity, which penetrated from eastern into central Anatolia, and even as far as the coasts of the Aegean.

Against such incursions into his declining realm, the Byzantine Emperor Romanus IV Diogenes felt bound to retaliate. In an attempt to regain control of Armenia, he marched against the Turks with a motley army composed largely of foreign mercenaries. The result, in 1071, was the Emperor's defeat and capture by the Seljuk sultan Alp Arslan (the "Brave Lion") in the historic frontier battle of Manzikert. It was a battle forever to be remembered by the Greeks as "the dreadful day," a historic confrontation between two empires and two faiths, which opened the way for the Turks, once and for all, into Asia Minor.

The battle of Manzikert carried for the future momentous intimations of conquest farther afield. For the present, however, it involved no abrupt break of continuity in the situation of the conquered lands. For it was a victory sought and achieved by militant Moslem irregulars, rather than the regular forces of the Seljuk state. Its immediate effective result was the extension across eastern into central Asia Minor of the mixed borderland civilization of the Ghazis. The Turcoman nomads now moved into new lands in their wake, without frontier obstruction.

Theirs was a joint way of life and culture, common to conquerors and conquered, including Anatolians and Armenians, who did not see Turks wholly as foreigners. "It was really only the Byzantine varnish which vanished," Paul Wittek writes, "to be replaced later on by an Islamic one. The local substratum survived." Nor was the Seljuk state itself, with its eyes still on the Moslem world, in a serious hurry to drive home its conquest of a part of Byzantium. After releasing the imprisoned Emperor, its rulers were content with a formal occupation of the conquered districts under a Seljuk prince named Suleiman. Meanwhile, toward the end of the eleventh century, the First Crusade was launched into Asia Minor, thus creating a fluid frontier between Moslem and Christian.

It was not until the middle of the twelfth century that the Seljuks turned away from the old Moslem world to build up in Asia Minor, on the Moslem pattern and on stable foundations, an ordered principality with its own line of sultans, ruling central Anatolia from their capital in the city of Konya. Their dynasty became known to other Moslem powers as the Sultanate of Rum. They were in the Arabic language "Caesars of Rome," presuming to inherit this remnant of the "Roman" Empire. The Byzantine Christians themselves, after the battle of Myriokephalon, a century after Manzikert, continued to rule in western Anatolia behind an agreed frontier or "border zone," in peaceful relations with a consolidated Seljuk state. Thus the Seljuks of Rum, deriving prestige throughout Islam from their imperial origins in the Great Seljuks of Persia, developed into a strong and prosperous power, reaching its zenith in the first half of the thirteenth century.

But it was not to endure. For now there burst upon them a new and more explosive nomadic eruption—that of their kinsmen the Mongols. They poured over the Eurasian steppe, as the Turks themselves had done, sweeping northward into Russia, eastward into China, and westward across Asia to envelop the Moslem world. Theirs was an invasion launched early in the century by Genghiz Khan, and now pressed home by his successors. The Turkish nomads were driven before them until new hordes of Turcomans and warrior bands spilled over into Asia Minor to spread tension through the Seljuk state of Konya. On their heels in a ferocious onslaught came the Mongol armies. In 1243 they routed the hitherto invincible Seljuk army, reinforced though it was with Byzantine auxiliaries and normal mercenaries, at Köse Dagh, between Sivas and Erzinjan, and went on to occupy as much as they chose of the land and its cities. The entire course of the history of Asia Minor was changed in a day. The power of the Seljuks of Rum, as of the Great Seljuks of Persia, existed no longer. The sultans of Konya became vassals of a Mongol protectorate now governed by Hulagu. Mongol power itself, like that of other nomadic peoples over a settled society, proved ephemeral, lasting in Asia Minor for a mere generation. But the power that succeeded it was no longer that of the Seljuks.

The pattern of much of Asia Minor had reverted meanwhile to that of the old borderland civilization, independent of any central authority. The march-warriors were on the march once more, raiding and even capturing towns without hindrance across the Byzantine frontier zone. Soon they were reinforced not only by Turcoman tribes, as before, but also by bands of refugees from the former Seljuk state, and moreover by "holy men," sheikhs and dervishes of an unorthodox Moslem persuasion, who had fled from Turkestan and Persia into Asia Minor and who rekindled Turkish enthusiasm for war against the infidel.

Power now rested with these Ghazis. Taking advantage of a decline in the Byzantine defenses, driven as before not only by fanaticism but by the need for land and loot, little opposed even by their "brother enemies" the Akritai, now neglected by a divided and insecure Greek government, they poured almost unresisted into western Asia Minor, most of whose provinces by 1300 were virtually lost to Byzantium. Fighting for them among themselves, the tribal leaders became rulers of some ten settled Ghazi principalities. One of these, the principality of Osman, was destined to grow into a great world power, the Ottoman Empire. It filled the void left by the decline and fall of the Byzantine Empire and was to endure under his dynasty for more than six centuries.

PART

I

DAWN OF EMPIRE

((1))

LEGEND ENVELOPS THE EARLY HISTORY OF THE OTTOMAN DYNASTY. Traditionally its founder was a small tribal chieftain named Ertoghrul, who, as he migrated across Asia Minor with a band of some four hundred horsemen, came upon a battle between two groups of combatants unknown to him. Chivalrously he chose, after consultation with his men, to back the losing side, thus turning the scales and assuring their victory. They proved to be the troops of the Seljuk sultan Ala-ed-Din of Konya, fighting against a detachment of Mongols. Ala-ed-Din rewarded Ertoghrul with a territorial fief near Eskishehir, comprising lands for summer and winter residence at Sugut, to the west of the Anatolian plateau. This was later enlarged in return for support of the sultan's declining fortunes in another victorious battle—this time against the Greeks. Here was a legend designed to establish for the Ottoman line a legitimate connection with the reigning dynasty, later to be confirmed by the sultan's bestowal on Osman, the son of Ertoghrul, of the insignia of sovereignty in the form of a banner and drum.

Further such legends, characteristic of dynastic mythology in medieval and indeed biblical chronicles, concern significant dreams by Ertoghrul and his son Osman. It is said that Osman once passed the night in the house of a pious Moslem. Before Osman slept, his host put a book in his room. On enquiring its title he received the reply: "It is the Koran; the word of God given to the world through his prophet Mohammed." Osman, it seems, started to read the book and continued to do so, standing, throughout the night. He fell asleep toward morning, at the hour, so Moslems believe, most favourable to prophetic dreams; and indeed, as he slept, an angel appeared to him, saying the words: "Since thou has read my eternal word with so great respect, thy children and the children of thy children shall be honoured from generation to generation."

A subsequent dream concerned a girl, Malkatum, whom Osman sought to marry. She was the daughter of a Moslem kadi, or judge, in a nearby village, the sheikh Edebali, who for two years had refused his consent to the marriage. Then Osman, as he slept, received a further revelation. In this the moon rose from the breast of the sheikh, who lay by his side. When full it descended into his own breast. Then from his loins there sprang a tree, which as it grew came to cover the whole world with the shadow of its green and beautiful branches. Beneath it Osman saw four mountain ranges—the Caucasus, the Atlas, the Taurus, and the Balkans. From its roots there issued four rivers, the Tigris, the Euphrates, the Nile, and the Danube. The fields were rich with crops, the mountains thick with forests. In the valleys were cities adorned with domes, pyramids, obelisks, columns, and towers, all surmounted by the Crescent. Their balconies rang with the call to prayer, mingling with the song of nightingales and bright-coloured parrots, perched among interlaced, sweet-smelling branches.

Their leaves started to lengthen into sword blades. A wind arose, pointing them toward the city of Constantinople, which, "situated at the junction of two seas and of two continents, seemed like a diamond mounted between two sapphires and two emeralds, and appeared thus to form the precious stone of the ring of a vast dominion which embraced the entire world." Osman was about to put the ring on his finger when he awoke. He recounted the dream to Edebali, who interpreted it as a sign from God, and now gave his daughter to Osman in marriage, presaging the power and the glory of their posterity. The ceremony was performed, according to the strictest rites of the True Faith, by a holy dervish for whom Osman later built a convent, endowing it with rich villages and lands.

The first of these two legends suggests that Osman and his people—the Osmanlis—were not yet Moslems at the time of their settlement in the region of Eskishehir. The first wave of Turkish immigrants into Asia Minor from the eleventh century onward, as forerunners and followers of the Seljuk armies, consisted for the most part of converts to Islam through their previous association with the Moslem Arab world. But the second wave, in the thirteenth century, was composed mostly of pagans, and it was to this, so it seems, that the Ottomans belonged. Most of them came not as settlers but as refugees, driven westward by the invasion of the pagan Mongol hordes. Many of them remained in the eastern lands, to return home perhaps when the Mongols withdrew. But others, more warlike, pushed onward into the Seljuk lands.

Among these were the Ottomans, who thus came under the protection of Sultan Ala-ed-Din. Rather than enlist them as mercenaries in his own army, he preferred to grant them lands in the disturbed frontier districts, where they might keep order locally or fight for their newly won possessions against the Byzantine Greeks. This, it seems probable, was the stage at which the followers of Ertoghrul and Osman became converted to Islam. It was a conversion that inspired the Ottoman people, already well endowed with the nomadic virtues and the fighting qualities of the Turcoman march-warriors, with a new martial ardour to champion, as a community of Ghazis, the Moslem cause against that of the infidel Christian.

A people who saw themselves not simply as Turks—a name associated with the inhabitants of Turkestan in general—but Osmanlis, followers of Osman, they nevertheless possessed, in these early days, few qualities distinct from those of their Turkish neighbours. Theirs was simply one among the ten successor-states which survived from the Seljuk Empire and the Mongol protectorate—and still one of the smallest. The Ottomans owed their ultimate imperial destiny to an initial geographical accident: the fact of their strategic situation in the northwest corner of Asia Minor, right on the Asiatic frontiers of the Byzantine Empire at the time of its decline, moreover within easy reach of the sea and the lands of Balkan Europe beyond it.

The Ottomans proved unique among these warriors of the marches in that they were able to transform the fruits of their military conquest into an effective political organism. Osman was an administrator as much as a soldier, and as such had the cooperation of his father-in-law, Edebali, as *vezir,* or vizier. He was a wise, patient ruler, whom men revered and loved to serve, not as a warrior, least of all for any Islamic semidivine status, but for his calm, compelling personality as a leader of his own people. There was in Osman a natural superiority which he never sought to assert through domination, and which even his own equals and superiors in ability, whether in the field or in counsel, respected. Provoking in them no spirit of rivalry, but only of loyalty, he was a man (as H. A. Gibbons expresses it) "great enough to use masterful men." His followers came to serve and to work with him in harmony, conscientiously helping to lay for this small growing state in its social cohesion such foundations as to guarantee its endurance. Meanwhile they led their own armies and administered their own conquests as beys with a quasi-autonomous status, always coordinating their activities and submitting where required to the commands of their chieftain.

Fired with the true spirit of religious enthusiasm, Osman himself brought to his principality the simple faith and fresh zeal of the early Moslems, as inspired by his great forebear and namesake the caliph Osman. In their tradition he pursued justice above power and wealth. At the same time he ruled, as did his successors, on a basis of undivided, individual sovereignty. The early Ottomans were thus free from the dynastic rivalries of the other Seljuk principalities. Starting life afresh in a new environment, they had the patience and the will and the tolerance; they acquired the practical, constructive experience to adapt themselves to the social and economic conditions of the land in which they ruled.

The Osmanlis developed their own resources and drew upon those around them, intellectual and theological, productive and mercantile, in the more urban environment of these neighbouring states and, as time went on, upon others farther afield from the hinterland, seeking in this frontier region a refuge from internal disorders and the prospects of a new life and future. They drew above all on the administrative and other skills of the Greeks themselves, shrewdly studying their methods of government in this last Asiatic enclave of the dying Byzantine Empire. For the Ottomans, contrary to the image of Islam projected abroad since the earlier Arab conquests, dealt with their enemies in a spirit free from religious fanaticism. They were living among Greeks more than Turks. The chieftains of Osman's neighbouring villages and castles were Christians, with whom he remained often on amicable terms. Among his closest companions were the Greek families of Michaeloğli and Marcozoğli, the sons of Michael and Marcos, once enemies but later staunch friends and supporters of Osman. As a result of their association with him, they adopted the Moslem faith.

There was no general Islamization of Christians—least of all by compulsion—within Ottoman territory. But a number of Christians became Moslems from choice, in response to their own impulses and in pursuit of their own interests. With the gradual breakdown of the central administration in Constantinople, they felt themselves forgotten by their rulers, and in a realistic spirit, preferred the relative order and security of Osmanli rule, together with its greater freedom of opportunity for Moslems and their exemption from onerous taxes. Spiritually, with the decline in the authority of the Orthodox Church, these Asiatic Greeks responded to the stimulus of a new faith. Socially they did not differ profoundly from their frontier neighbours the Osmanlis in their background and habits of life. Whether converted or not, they adapted themselves easily to Ottoman ways. Intermarriage became common between Turks and Greeks, contributing to the birth and the growth of a new mixed society.

The Ottoman Turks, it soon became evident, were no longer mere nomads but settlers, creators, and builders too. As time went on they evolved, within their limits in this mountainous northwest corner of Asia Minor, their own frontier civilization, which was based on a form of popular culture. Compounded of elements Asiatic and European, Moslem and Christian, Turk and Turcoman, nomadic and sedentary, it was pragmatic in outlook and free from the more orthodox cultural and social constraints of the feudal Turkish principalities to the east. Theirs was the prototype of a society destined to inherit and transform Byzantium. Just so had the empire of the Seljuk Turks filled the vacuum left by the empire of the Arabs. Just so, indeed, had Byzantium itself succeeded Rome.

Osman himself was in no hurry to expand his inherited domain at the expense of his neighbours. Slow but assured, his plan was to watch and to wait, to live and to learn, to work his way only gradually into Byzantine territory. Three fortified imperial cities dominated these surviving lands of Byzantium in Asia. To the south lay Bursa, commanding the rich Bithynian plain from the slopes of Mount Olympus; in the center, at the head of a lake, Nicaea, the effective capital; to the north the port of Nicomedia, at the head of a long gulf commanding the sea route to Constantinople, and the overland route to the Black Sea. All were within a day's journey of Osman's capital. But at first he attacked none of them. In sixty years of sporadic village warfare, from the reign of Ertoghrul onward, the Ottomans advanced a mere sixty miles from the city of Eskishehir—the "old city"—to the "new city" of Yenishehir. Its capture obstructed communications between Nicaea and Bursa.

But Osman, aware of the strength of the city fortifications in this area so vital to Constantinople, and of his own relative weakness, still bided his time. Meanwhile his forces grew gradually in strength until Ertoghrul's band of four hundred warriors had grown by repute to four thousand. Sources of further recruitment were warriors in search of employment, from behind the static frontiers of neighbouring states; and indeed the Akritai, the Greek frontier warriors themselves, of whom a number were induced to change sides, driven to do so from neglect, confiscation of revenues, and oppression by Constantinople.

It was not until the first year of the fourteenth century, twelve years after his accession, that Osman came into direct conflict with the Byzantine imperial forces at Koyun Hisar (the Greek Baphaeon). Endeavouring to check an Ottoman raid into a fertile valley before Nicomedia, the Greeks were easily defeated by a swift and impetuous cavalry charge which broke their ranks. This defeat of an imperial army by an obscure Turcoman chief brought concern to Byzantium, where Osman's state was now seen as a factor to reckon with. It brought fame to him, as holy warriors from all parts of Anatolia flocked more than ever to his standard, proud to be known as Osmanlis. His principality was now well and truly established.

But he made no attempt to follow up his victory with an attack on Nicomedia itself, and his troops contented themselves with ravaging the lands around it. Seven years elapsed before he felt himself strong enough to attack the fortresses of Ak Hisar, commanding the descent of the River Sakarya (the Greek Sangarius) into the plain behind Nicomedia. This he captured, thus opening up for the Ottomans the road toward the sea. They appeared for the first time on the Bosporus, gradually occupied the harbours and fortresses of the Black Sea littoral on the peninsula to the east of it, and finally penetrated into the Sea of Marmara to capture the island of Kalolimini. Osman thus obstructed the sea route from Bursa and another from Nicomedia to

"Mount Olympus and Brusa." The town of Brusa, or Bursa, which was the first capital of the Ottoman state after it had begun to engulf western Anatolia, appears in the center background at the left, at the foot of Mt. Olympus.

Reproduced from Thomas Allom and Robert Walsh, *Constantinople and the Scenery of the Seven Churches of Asia Minor,* London and Paris, 1840, op. p. 28.

Constantinople, isolating the two cities from one another. Bursa was then invaded from the landward side, and eventually fell in 1326, just as Osman lay dying.

After a siege of seven years, in which the very suburbs fell into the hands of the enemy, its Greek garrison were so discouraged by the lack of support from Constantinople—torn as it now was by dynastic strife between rival emperors—that their commander, Evrenos, with other leading Greeks, surrendered the city and embraced the Moslem faith. Here, on the fertile slopes of Mount Olympus, the Ottomans created their first imperial capital, gradually transforming it, while enriching it with imperishable architecture, into a civilized center of art and learning. Following the later establishment of their dynasty in Europe it ceased to be the capital, but remained always the Holy City of their empire. Above all, with its schools of theology and of Islamic law and tradition, it developed into the prime source of education, thus the center of the ulema, the Moslem religious establishment. Complementing the free and often unorthodox warrior spirit of the Ghazis, the clergy of the ulema personified the traditional principles of Old Islam, and as such were to serve throughout the centuries as a predominant influence, whether guiding or restrictive, on the Ottoman state.

Here in Bursa Osman was now buried, in a tomb looking down over the sea toward Constantinople. With the tombs of his successors it was to become a center of Islamic pilgrimage. His epitaph was embodied in a prayer to be uttered through the centuries on the accession, girded with his double-edge sword, of every heir to the Ottoman throne: "May he be as good as Osman!" He was indeed a good man in the early Moslem tradition, enjoining his son, on his deathbed, to "cultivate justice and thereby embellish the earth. Rejoice my departed soul with a beautiful series of victories . . . propagate religion by thy arms. Promote the learned to honour, so the Divine Law shall be established."

Osman's historical role was that of the chieftain who gathered around him a people. His son Orkhan was to weld the people into a state; his grandson Murad I to expand the state into an empire. Their political achievement was worthily praised by an Ottoman poet of the nineteenth century with the words "We raised a world-subduing power from a tribe."

In building up their state and empire, the Ottomans owed much to the traditions and social institutions of the Ghazis, those fighters for the faith to whom they fervently adhered. These traditions had their roots in a communal life based on ethical principles, with corporations or brotherhoods subscribing to an Islamic canon of rules for virtuous conduct. Primarily religious in purpose, they embodied abstract conceptions, with a strong vein of unorthodox mysticism, which took concrete and practical form. In the towns they were adapted to embrace guilds of merchants and artisans. In the frontier marches and villages they became military fraternities, like the *akhis,* or brothers-in-arms, inspired by a militant and indeed almost fanatical enthusiasm for both religion and war. Chivalrous in spirit, they resembled popular orders of knighthood, imposing and accepting mutual obligations, gathering in places of reunion comparable to those of the mystical confraternities of Islam in earlier times.

The fourteenth-century traveller Ibn Battuta writes of these brotherhoods:

> Nowhere in the world are there to be found any to compare with them in solicitude for strangers, and in ardour to serve food to satisfy wants, to restrain the hands of the tyrannous, and to kill the agents of policy, and those ruffians who join with them. An *akhi,* in their idiom, is one whom the assembled members of his trade, together with others of the young unmarried men and those who have adopted the celibate life, choose to be their leader.

On the invitation of a cobbler in shabby clothes, with a felt bonnet on his head, Ibn Battuta visited a hospice which he, as a sheikh of the young *akhis,* and "about two hundred men of different trades" had built in order to entertain travellers and other guests, contributing for the common purpose all that they had earned during the day. It was

> a fine building, carpeted with beautiful Rumi rugs, and with a large number of lustres of Iraqi glass. . . . Standing in rows in the chamber were a number of young men wearing long cloaks and with boots on their feet. . . . On their heads were white bonnets of wool, with a piece of stuff about a cubit long attached to the peak of each bonnet. . . . When we had taken our places among them, they brought in a great banquet with fruits and sweetmeats, after which they began their singing and dancing. Everything about them filled us with admiration and we were greatly astonished at their generosity and innate nobility.

At Bursa, Ibn Battuta was received by Sultan Orkhan,

> who is the greatest of the Kings of the Turkmen Kings, and the richest in wealth, lands and military forces. Of fortresses he possesses nearly a hundred, and for most of his time he is continually engaged in making the rounds of them. . . . It is said that he has never stayed for a whole month in any town. He also fights with the infidels continually and keeps them under siege.

Orkhan was the younger of Osman's two sons, whom Osman named his successor on the strength of his military capacities. His elder son, Ala-ed-Din, was by contrast a man of scholarly pursuits, devoted to the law and religion. Legend relates that he refused an offer by his younger brother to share their inheritance, upon which Orkhan remarked: "Since, my brother, thou will not take the flocks and herds I offer thee, be the shepherd of my people. Be my Vezir." In this capacity he was occupied, until his death seven years later, with the administration of the state, the organization of the army, and the drafting of new legislation.

Orkhan, making his capital at Bursa, was glorified by the titles "Sultan, son of the Sultan of the Ghazis, Ghazi son of Ghazi, Marquis of the hero of the world." Here he struck, for the first time, an Ottoman silver coinage, replacing that of the Seljuks and inscribed "May God cause to endure the Empire of Orkhan, son of Osman." Orkhan's task was to complete the work of his father: to consolidate into a viable state the mixed population that Osman had gathered around him; to round off his conquests and extend his dominions; to weld all their inhabitants together and thus make of the state a new center of Ottoman power. Fairer in complexion, more civilized in manner, and more majestic in stature than his father, Orkhan was as simple in his tastes and as just in his disposition. Nor was he in character fanatical, deceitful, or cruel. Broader in vision than Osman and more vigorous in action, whether at war or in statecraft, he achieved these ends through inexhaustible energy, singleness of purpose, and above all a high capacity for both the intricacies of government and the skills of diplomacy.

First, the two cities of Nicaea and Nicomedia remained to be captured. Within their high defensive walls, they were fortresses hard to take by storm. Bursa had fallen through lack of assistance from Constantinople. When Orkhan turned his attention to Nicaea—capital of the Empire itself a century earlier, during the Latin occupation of Constantinople—the Emperor Andronicus III judged it his duty to go to its aid. But, wounded in battle with the Ottomans at Pelecanon (the present Manyas) in 1329, he hastily fled from the field back to Constantinople, abandoning the bulk of his army, whose survivors fled in his wake. The garrison of Nicaea thus surrendered. So did that of Nicomedia some eight years later.

All three cities fell largely for economic reasons. To thrive they depended on access to the surrounding countryside. When this fell into the hands of the Ottomans, not as mere raiders but as settlers, in a permanent occupation unchallenged from Constantinople, the abandoned citizens had little choice but to throw in their lot with the enemy. Nor did many take advantage of the agreed terms of surrender, to leave for Constantinople. They preferred to remain where they were, carrying on their trades and industries, playing their part in the new world now rising around them in place of the old. Thus by the end of Orkhan's reign, the population of his state had increased, so it was asserted, to some half-million souls—a far cry from Ertoghrul's legendary four hundred horsemen.

For all its toleration of Christians, this remained in essence a Moslem state, whose test of nationality lay in religion. For all their peaceful coexistence, a distinction still had to be preserved between Moslems and Christians. Basically this operated in terms of the land and its distribution. Moslems alone were obliged to perform military service, and were thus alone eligible for the tenure of land. This was distributed as a reward for service and provided a source of recruitment in the form of military fiefs, free of taxes. Christians were exempt from military service, hence benefitted from no such landed rights. Instead they paid a head tax for the army's support. In the country districts this made them subservient in status to the landholding Moslems. Thus they tended to live and work in the cities and towns, where such civil disabilities were counterbalanced by economic advantage. But through voluntary conversion to Islam, the Christian became automatically an Osmanli, with his origins soon forgotten, enjoying freedom from taxation, the right to hold land, opportunities for advancement, and a share in the benefits of the Moslem ruling elite. Hence, at this stage of Ottoman history in Asia, the growing number of converts to Islam.

Feudal though it was, this Ottoman system of land tenure through military fiefs differed essentially from the feudal system in Europe, in that the landholdings were small and above all seldom hereditary. For all land was the property of the state. Thus at this stage there was to arise in the Ottoman dominions no landed nobility, such as prevailed throughout Europe. The sultans retained absolute ownership of the soil they had conquered. Moreover, as they continued to conquer, more holdings became available as rewards for more soldiers. Within the framework of this system Orkhan now organized, with the initial advice of his brother, Ala-ed-Din, a regular standing army under the sovereign's command, a professional military force on a permanent war-footing, of a kind not to be emulated in Europe for a further two centuries.

The army of his father, Osman, had consisted only of Turcoman irregulars, volunteer cavalrymen, named *akinjis*. Recruited in the villages through cries summoning to arms on a certain date "whoever wanted to fight," they were expert horsemen, moving together "like a wall." Orkhan, recruiting them from among the holders of military fiefs, regularized this force as an advance guard of cavalry scouts, whose role was to open up the country before a projected attack. Thus faced with the greatest hazards, their loyalty was assured by the richest grants of land. They were supported by guides, named *chavush,* and by a regular paid corps of cavalry, the *sipahis.*

Orkhan recruited also an irregular infantry named *azabs,* an expendable force whose place was in the forefront of the battle, drawing the first fire of the enemy. Behind them the enemy, often to his initial surprise, came up against a more formidable second line of picked, disciplined troops. Drawn from the corps of salaried soldiers named *kapu-kulu ojaks,* they were a force well trained to fight together, under commanders they knew and respected. Unlike those mercenaries who prevailed at this period, they were united in devotion to their sovereign, sharing his cause and trusting him to safeguard their interests in terms of promotion and other rewards for their service. In principle they were continually "at the door of the Sultan's tent," submitting to his absolute authority, serving him in person whether directly or indirectly under a commander delegated to act in his name. The strength of these new regular Ottoman troops lay in their unity. It lay also in their perpetual readiness for battle.

The Ottomans were ever ready, never caught by surprise. Their army was equipped with a first-class intelligence service, well informed as to when and where the enemy was coming, also with an efficient service of guides to show their soldiers the way. A traveller, Bertrand de Broquière, wrote of these Ottoman troops:

> They can start suddenly, and a hundred Christian soldiers would make more noise than ten thousand Osmanlis. When the drum sounded they put themselves immediately in march, never breaking step, never stopping till the word is given. Lightly armed, in one night they travel as far as their Christian adversaries in three days.

Such were the military talents of a hardy, tenacious, and disciplined race, geared for centuries to the nomadic habits of speed and mobility; such, in terms also of organization and tactics, were the principles of a perfected instrument of warfare, destined through its invincibility to transform the Ottoman state into an empire. These were a people driven instinctively by an inherited impulse as nomads to move onward, over a deliberately planned westerly route, in search of pastures new. Since their conversion to Islam, this search was sanctified and further inspired by their religious duty as Ghazis, under the holy law, to seek out and fight the infidel in the Abode of War, or *Dar-el-Harb*: to raid and occupy his lands, seize his possessions, kill or carry into captivity his people, and subject their communities to Moslem rule. It was now propelled too by the social and economic need for expansion, through pressure of population, from the continuous flow into the frontier marches of other immigrants, whether fellow nomads, heterodox Moslems, or adventurers, from the central principalities of Anatolia. So from the steppes of Central Asia these Turks were now to venture across an unfamiliar and inhospitable element—the sea. By the middle of the fourteenth century their forces were ready to be launched into Europe.

((2))

THE ENTRY OF THE TURKS INTO EUROPE WAS NO SUDDEN IRRUPTION, like that of the Mongols across Asia. It was rather a process of gradual infiltration, a fateful corollary to the decline and fall of the Byzantine Empire. Inherent in this was the disunity, theological hence political, of the Christian powers—West against East, Catholic against Orthodox, Roman against Greek. This culminated at the beginning of the thirteenth century in a perfidious attack by the Latin knights of the Fourth Crusade, not against the Moslems of the Holy Land as first projected, but against their fellow Greek Christians in Constantinople. After capturing and plundering the city, in 1204, they established a Latin empire over much of the territory remaining to Byzantium in Europe. Thanks largely to disunity between its own Christian elements, it proved to be an ephemeral empire, lasting for little more than half a century, while the Greeks ruled over their surviving Asiatic territory from Nicaea. In 1261 they were able to reoccupy Constantinople.

But the blow to their empire proved ultimately fatal. Byzantium was to survive for a further two centuries, but only as a ghost of its former self. Its ancient glories as a world center of power and civilization had vanished. Never was it to regain its former strength and security. Its territory was greatly depleted. Bulgaria, Serbia, Macedonia had been successively lost. Constantinople was half ruined, deprived of its treasures, and largely depopulated. Its trade with the East had moved elsewhere. Such as remained of it in the West was in the hands of the Venetians and Genoese. Religious strife, with the papacy and the Latin powers, burned more fiercely than ever. Internally it was matched by administrative disintegration, social upheaval, and financial insolvency.

Nor, at this critical moment in Byzantine history, did a great dynasty of rulers arise to bind the surviving elements of the Empire together and give it new life. On the contrary, the reign of the first of the Palaeologue emperors, after the recapture of Constantinople, was followed—except indeed in the world of the arts—not by a renaissance but by a long period of imperial decadence. The aftermath of the unholy war between Christian and Christian was the internal disunity of an imperial house divided against itself, and a dynasty locked in an intermittent civil war, as son fought against father, grandson against grandfather, usurper against legitimate sovereign. This disunity played inevitably into the hands of the Turks, united as they were in the holy warfare of Islam. In its context they hardly had to invade Europe. They were invited into it.

Initially they had fulfilled here their traditional role of mercenaries, as they had done in the Arab Empire of the Abbasid Caliphate three centuries earlier. The first to do so came from a colony of Turcomans, who settled in the Dobruja, on the western Black Sea coast, after the accession as Emperor of the first Palaeologue, Michael VIII, who had taken refuge from the Latin occupation as an exile at the Seljuk court. These Turcomans came to the aid of a dethroned Seljuk sultan, Izz-ed-Din, who in turn had taken refuge at Constantinople. After a threatening demonstration against the Emperor, they secured the sultan's release from custody and withdrew with him to the Crimea. But his son and a detachment of his guard remained behind in Constantinople, turned Christian, and formed the nucleus of a corps of Turkish militia which soon grew in numbers, providing a welcome reinforcement to the imperial army.

At the beginning of the fourteenth century, the Byzantine Emperor Andronicus II similarly called to his aid a large force of Christian mercenaries from the Catalan Grand Company, under the command of a lawless soldier of fortune, Roger de Flor. When the Catalans made trouble in Constantinople, he deflected them across into Asia Minor. Here they fought successfully against the Turks, but took the spoils for themselves at the expense of the Greeks, with whom they finally came into open conflict, establishing a European headquarters at Gallipoli, and seeking to make of it a state of their own. When Roger de Flor was ill-advisedly murdered in the Emperor's palace, the Catalans turned savagely on the Greeks and called in their former enemies the Turks, from Asia Minor, to aid them against the Empire they had come to defend.

Thus it was the Catalans who were first responsible for introducing the Turks into Europe, to fight as an organized force against the Greeks. When the Catalans finally withdrew into Thessaly, they left behind them in Thrace and Macedonia a large force of Turks, who raided communications and spread general disorder. Their leader, Halil, reached an agreement to withdraw them in return for a safe-conduct across the Bosporus. But when the Greeks, in violation of this, tried to deprive the Turks of their booty, Halil summoned reinforcements from Asia, defeated and put to flight the young Emperor Michael IX, and with insolent mockery assumed the imperial headgear. The Emperor was finally able to dispose of these Turks only by calling in Serbian troops to his aid.

From now onward, throughout the fourteenth century, the islands and coasts of Byzantium in Europe were subjected to a succession of piratical raids by Turks from the various principalities of Asia Minor. Only rivalry among them prevented a concerted invasion, at a time when indeed there were as many Turks fighting for the Greeks as against them. Among them were Tatars, from north of the Black Sea, men of similar racial and traditional origins, who had swept in waves through southern Russia into the Crimea and as far west as Hungary. Meanwhile Turkish pirates from the principality of Aydin, in Asia Minor, harassed the islands of the Aegean, provoking a "crusade" by papal forces which captured the city of Smyrna.

The Ottomans themselves played no part in these hostilities, shrewdly calculating that they would only weaken their rival Turkish neighbours and kinsmen. Though they were virtually in occupation of the shores of the Bosporus, just opposite Constantinople, by 1330, they remained faithful to their patient, vigilant policy, and did not cross its waters into Europe until seven years later.

Then they did so on the invitation of the Grand Chancellor and usurper John Cantacuzene, an able and ambitious leader who had proclaimed himself Emperor against the legitimate child-Emperor John Palaeologue, and required Turkish support in the civil war which resulted. Now, in return for military aid, Cantacuzene offered his daughter Theodora in marriage to Orkhan, who had already received overtures on behalf of his rival. The offer was promptly accepted. In 1345 some six thousand Ottoman troops crossed into Europe. Here they enabled the usurping Emperor to wrest from John Palaeologue the coastal cities of the Black Sea, to ravage Thrace and threaten Adrianople (now Edirne), and to besiege Constantinople itself.

In the following year a marriage between the Byzantine princess and the Ottoman Sultan was celebrated on European shores with due pomp and ceremony. Orkhan, camped opposite at Scutari, sent a fleet of thirty Turkish vessels and an escort of cavalry to bear away his bride from a stately carpeted pavilion erected in the Emperor's camp at Selymbria. Here, as Gibbon recounts this "dishonour of the purple,"

> Theodora ascended a throne, which was surrounded with curtains of silk and gold; the troops were under arms; but the emperor alone was on horseback. At a signal the curtains were suddenly withdrawn, to disclose the bride, or the victim, encircled by kneeling eunuchs and hymenaeal torches; the sound of flutes and trumpets proclaimed the joyful event; and her pretended happiness was the theme of the nuptial song, which was chanted by such poets as the age could produce. Without the rites of the church, Theodora was delivered to her barbarous lord; but it had been stipulated that she should preserve her religion in the harem of Bursa; and her father celebrated her charity and devotion in this ambiguous situation.

In fact she was able to benefit her coreligionists through the purchase and liberation of numerous Christian slaves and prisoners.

This marital and military alliance with the Ottomans was followed, in 1347, by the entry of Cantacuzene into Constantinople, the marriage of another daughter, Helen, to the young John Palaeologue, and their recognition by both parties as joint emperors. Thus were the Ottoman Turks well entrenched with more than a mere foothold in Europe, not as enemies but as allies and indeed relatives of Byzantium, with a Sultan who was son-in-law of one Emperor, brother-in-law of the other—and also son-in-law of the neighbouring tsar of Bulgaria.

This did not deter Orkhan from entertaining rival overtures for a similar alliance from an enemy of Byzantium, Stephen Dushan, who had expanded his neighbouring state of Serbia into an "empire," arrogating to himself the title of "master of almost all the Roman Empire," and who was even acclaimed by the Venetians as "Emperor of Constantinople" itself. Failing nonetheless to obtain Venetian support for an attack on Constantinople, Stephen sought instead support from Orkhan, proposing a union of the Serbian and Ottoman armies for a joint campaign against the city. To seal the alliance, he offered his daughter in marriage to Orkhan's son. Orkhan sent envoys to Stephen to accept the proposal. But this plan was scotched by Cantacuzene, who intercepted the envoys, killing some, imprisoning others, and appropriating their gifts to the Serbian "emperor." Nor were negotiations reopened by either Stephen or Orkhan, whose respective aims were too closely identified to be easily reconciled. Ultimately Stephen, in 1355, attempted an attack on Constantinople on his own, with a force of eighty thousand men. But he died on the second day of the march, and his Serbian empire died with him.

Meanwhile, in 1350, Cantacuzene had called in another twenty thousand Ottoman cavalry to his aid, to save Salonika from Dushan by dislodging his forces from the coastal cities of Macedonia around it. Salonika was saved, though Turkish troops occupied none of these cities, being content, with the approval of their Sultan, to return to Asia Minor well laden with booty. Two years later Orkhan gave aid to the Genoese in a war against their traditional commercial rivals, the Venetians, and in the course of it against Cantacuzene himself. In 1352, when the Venetians, with the Bulgarians, declared openly for his rival John Palaeologue, Cantacuzene called once again for twenty thousand Ottoman troops, robbing the churches of Constantinople to pay for them, and promising to reward Orkhan with a fortress in the Thracian Chersonese. He thus relieved Adrianople, secured his position in Thrace and in most of Macedonia, and proclaimed his son Matthew co-Emperor.

In 1353 Suleiman Pasha, the son of Orkhan, crossed the Hellespont with an Ottoman force to take possession of the fortress promised to

Orkhan, named Tzympe, on the peninsula between Gallipoli and the Aegean Sea. Soon after his arrival an earthquake destroyed part of the walls of Gallipoli. Suleiman promptly took this fortress too. After restoring its walls he brought over from Asia the first colony of Ottoman settlers. Other such colonies were to follow in rapid succession, settling on the lands of the fugitive Christian lords under their own Moslem beys. These were the warrior companions of Orkhan, whom they regarded less as a master than as a unifying force and a rallying point among them as brothers-in-arms. Their large personal armies were to provide him with the sustaining foundations in Europe of the new Ottoman state. Meanwhile, apart from the peasants, the local Greeks in their various provinces took refuge in the citadels and towns, where they were left unmolested in return for voluntary submission.

Here was the start of an occupation which moved progressively westward, thus extending into Europe the open frontier society of the Ghazis, and imposing on the lands of Byzantium a new Ottoman pattern. In the wake of a swift advance force, ranging far and wide to block roads, destroy crops, and create general economic disruption, their main army established further settlements of Anatolian Turks along the main highways of its lines of march and down the four river valleys which led to the Danube. But it did not at first penetrate into the more mountainous regions adjoining them, where many of the native population took refuge. In this unsettled Balkan society there was relatively little resistance to the invaders, who were often in effect liberating an acquiescent people. The dervish brotherhoods founded hospices which were to serve as the nucleus of new Turkish villages. The Moslem beys, on the lands they controlled, established a new relationship with the Christian peasants which amounted to a form of social revolution. They drove out the hereditary land-owning class, whether Greek or Latin, which had hitherto oppressed and exploited its feudal peasantry. Instead they established, as overlords, a relaxed and indirect form of control, extracting from these peasants only limited taxation, and abolishing the former principle of unpaid labour. For under the Ottoman code they were not themselves landowners, but responsible intermediaries between peasantry and Sultan, who owned all land whether conquered or otherwise.

Thus at this time of social and political fragmentation in the Byzantine Empire, the Ottomans replaced decentralization with a strong system of central state control. As the occupation proceeded the local Christian lords, in lands bordering on captured Ottoman territory, came likewise to accept the sovereignty of the Sultan as vassals, paying him a small annual tribute as a token of submission to an Islamic state. The state adopted from the start a conciliatory policy toward Christians, thus to ensure that the peasantry would not join its feudal overlords in resistance to enemy occupation, and indeed to encourage peasant revolts against them. The Balkan peasant soon came to appreciate that conquest by the Moslem invader spelled for him liberation from Christian feudal power, whose manifold exactions and abuses had worsened with the increase of monastic lands. Ottomanization was now conferring upon him unforeseen benefits. Not the least of them was law and order. As a later French traveller was to write, "The country is safe, and there are no reports of brigands or highwaymen"—more than could be said, at that time, of other realms in Christendom.

At this early stage, meanwhile, the Ottomans controlled most of the Gallipoli peninsula and the European littoral of the Sea of Marmara, up to a point within a few miles of Constantinople. Cantacuzene, whose position had thus grown precarious, reproached Orkhan for breach of faith, and offered to buy back Tzympe for ten thousand ducats. Orkhan, aware that he could reoccupy it whenever he chose, handed it over in return for the ransom. But he firmly refused to cede Gallipoli, whose walls, so he insisted, had fallen to him not by force of his arms but by the will of his God. He declined to negotiate further. The Ottoman Turks, aided by divine intervention, had come to stay.

Cantacuzene found himself wholly discredited. Abroad, the Christian powers of the Balkans, Serbia and Bulgaria, refused his plea for support for the Empire. Such, retorted the tsar of Bulgaria, was the merited fruit of his unholy alliance with the Turks. Let the Byzantines weather the storm by themselves. "If the Turks come against us," he added, "we shall know how to defend ourselves." At home, the inhabitants of Constantinople rose against John Cantacuzene, barricaded him in his palace, and declared for John Palaeologue. Publicly scorned and accused of wishing to deliver the city to the Ottomans, he saw no choice but to abdicate, and retired to a monastery at Mistra, near Sparta. Here, under the name of Joasaph, he spent the remaining thirty years of his life, writing a distinguished history of his times.

Suleiman Pasha extended his conquests and colonial settlements inland, capturing Demotika and cutting off Constantinople from Adrianople by the occupation of Chorlu. This immigration met with little serious resistance from the local Greek inhabitants or from the forces of the Emperor John Palaeologue, who proved to be as much at the mercy of the Ottomans as John Cantacuzene had been. A worse humiliation indeed lay in store for him. When in 1357 his nephew Halil, the son of Orkhan and Theodora, was captured by pirates, the Sultan demanded of the Emperor that he go to Phocaea and rescue him. Thus while the Ottoman forces advanced in Thrace, the Emperor was besieging Phocaea. On his return to Constantinople, commanded by Orkhan to continue the siege in person, he set out once more, only to encounter his fleet, which had abandoned the siege and which he could not persuade to continue it. He begged Orkhan to excuse him from a task beyond his powers.

Orkhan, now the overlord of the Byzantine Emperor, remained inflexible in his demand. In 1359 John V went to him at Scutari, a vassal hoping to appease his suzerain. The Sultan dictated to the Emperor a treaty of peace by which he agreed to pay half his son's ransom and virtually accepted the *status quo* in Thrace. On rescuing Halil, the Emperor was to give him his ten-year-old daughter in marriage. The Emperor returned, at Orkhan's bidding, to Phocaea, paid over a large ransom, and brought Halil to Nicaea, where his betrothal to the Christian princess was celebrated with appropriate Moslem festivities. As John Cantacuzene had introduced the Ottomans into Europe as soldiers, so thus did his rival John Palaeologue accept their further presence as immigrants.

Orkhan died in 1359. His eldest son, Suleiman, had been killed in the previous year by a fall from his horse while hawking in the Gallipoli peninsula. His younger son succeeded him as Murad I. Orkhan, this second of the three Ottoman "founding fathers," had achieved his ends, less through the skills of a warrior than through the crafts of a diplomat. After building up his state into a "nation," he had entered Europe with a modern army behind him, not by the direct use of its force, but by its indirect use for bargaining purposes. Confronted with a weak, divided enemy, he had acted in no spirit of impetuosity but with an exemplary patience and an innate mastery of the wiles of manipulation and intrigue. Thus were the foundations of the Ottoman Empire established in Europe.

Now the time had come to extend its sphere of conquest, to launch the Ottoman army as an offensive force for the subjugation of the remains of the Byzantine Empire and of the Balkan Christian states within and beyond its frontiers. This was the task of the forty-year-old Murad I, a sultan destined to surpass his two predecessors both as a military leader and as a statesman, supreme in his time. Thanks initially to Murad, the West was now to fall to the East as the East had fallen to the West in the centuries of the Greeks and the Romans.

((3))

ORKHAN WAS THE PIONEER IN EUROPE OF THE OTTOMAN EMPIRE; Murad I was to be its first great Sultan. He reigned for a generation through the latter part of the fourteenth century. As a man of war, unflagging in his martial zeal and inspiring in his vigorous leadership, he extended Ottoman territories to the farthest limits of the Balkan peninsula, consolidating conquests which were to endure for five centuries. As a man of vision and political sagacity he constructed also, for the future, the framework of a grand, statesmanlike pattern of government. This in time drew together and brought new life to the composite remnants of Byzantium, filling a vacuum which no other power at this moment in history could fill. He heralded the dawn of a new Ottoman civilization, unique in the coalescence of its diversified elements of race, religion, and language.

Moreover, this age of Ottoman expansion into Eastern Europe coincided with an age of retraction in the West. No longer, with the final loss of Jerusalem in the mid-thirteenth century and the irruption of the Mongols into Asia Minor, could feudal Christendom thrust its frontiers eastward. The crusading impulse turned inward upon itself as Latin Christians disputed and fought with each other. The banking houses of Italy, which had opened up a profitable trade with the East and financed the Crusades, failed one by one. Financial and economic recession led to a general and prolonged social crisis. European society, inelastic and devitalized, reached a low ebb. Peasants' revolts against landlords, both feudal and monastic, workers' revolts against merchants, became rife.

The bubonic plague of the Black Death, introduced from the East, ravaged the populations of the Mediterranean and of all Western Europe. The discovery of new worlds was to turn the energies of its youth farther westward, across the Atlantic. Such meanwhile was the climacteric of the Middle Ages, a turning point which could only benefit in its dawning enlightenment the new Empire of the Ottoman Turks.

Murad's offensive in Europe, prepared before his accession and commanded by competent generals, was immediately launched, in 1360, and in its first stage swiftly completed. Within fifteen months the Ottomans were in effective control of Thrace, with its key fortresses and its rich plain spreading to the foot of the Balkan mountain range. At Chorlu the massacre of the garrison and the decapitation of its commandant were calculated to spread terror of the Turkish invaders throughout the Balkans. Adrianople opened its gates to them, soon to replace Bursa as the Ottoman imperial capital. Then the Ottomans moved westward, bypassing Constantinople. John Palaeologue, now a mere shadow of an emperor, signed a treaty which bound him to refrain from any attempt to regain his losses in Thrace, or from any support for the Serbians and Bulgarians in resisting the Ottoman advance; moreover to support the Ottomans against their own Turkish rivals in Asia Minor. A decade later he was to become no more than a vassal of Murad, recognizing him as his suzerain, and undertaking to do military service in the Ottoman army.

Meanwhile, as the Turks penetrated farther into Europe—into Bulgaria, Macedonia, Serbia, and soon into Hungary, a Latin Church stronghold—the Christian powers, under the auspices of Pope Urban V, made a series of vain attempts to unite with each other and with the Greeks in defense of Christendom. In 1363 a force of Serbs and, for the first time, Hungarians, without the aid of the Greeks, crossed the River Maritza in the direction of Adrianople, only to be pounced upon by the Turks—"caught even as wild beasts in their lair" (in the words of the Turkish historian Seadeddin) as they slept off the festive nocturnal celebrations of the unopposed crossing—then driven back into the river "as flames are driven before the wind," and thus all but exterminated.

Further such attempted "crusades" were bedevilled by the conflict between the Latin and Greek churches, a spirit reflected by Petrarch in a letter to Pope Urban: "The Osmanlis are merely enemies, but the schismatic Greeks are worse than enemies." The Emperor John Palaeologue could find allies only by promising the submission of the Greeks to the Roman Church. This he did on a secret visit to the Hungarians. On his way home he was detained in a fortress by the Bulgarians. This provoked the intervention of Amadeo of Savoy, who embarked on a further papal crusade in 1366. He captured Gallipoli from the Turks, but instead of staying to fight them sailed up into the Black Sea to fight the Bulgarian Christians. Releasing the Emperor, he insisted, as the Hungarians had done, on his submission to the Roman Church. Meeting this time with a refusal, Amadeo turned and fought the Greeks.

The Emperor submitted and in 1369 set out for Rome, where he abjured the errors of the Orthodox Church in return for promises of help against the Turks from the princes of Christendom. But no help came, and on his way home he was detained in Venice for debt. When his elder son, Andronicus, refused to provide money for his ransom, his younger son, Manuel, did so. But John's submission to Rome was totally inacceptable in Constantinople. Hence, on his release, his submission as vassal to Murad.

The Ottomans had everything to gain from this hatred of the Balkan Christians for the Latin Church, as from their mutual political hatreds, one people for another. It led to their official recognition of the Orthodox at the expense of the Catholic Church. It meant that each race, whether Greek or Slav, Serb or Bulgarian, was disposed to prefer Ottoman rule to that of its neighbours—and above all to that of the Hungarians. This spirit, coinciding with the demoralization caused in the Balkans by the Black Death, made easier the major task which, as his victories consolidated the Ottoman foothold, confronted Murad as a statesman. The Ottoman conquerors were relatively few in number. Now here confronting them in Europe were populations far in excess of any in the conquered lands of Asia, moreover far more various and complex in their racial, religious, and political character. How were they to be assimilated? Such was Murad's problem, which called for the exercise of far-ranging statecraft as one successful campaign followed another.

The Christian population of the Balkans, knowing little or nothing of Islam, was hardly amenable to assimilation through voluntary conversion, as the Asiatic Christians had been. Nor could there be any question of its elimination by the conqueror, if only for lack of sufficient Moslem colonists to replace it. Equally Murad, still waging his battles, lacked the spare military resources to keep it in subjection by police control. This ruled out a general policy of forcible conversion to Islam, which would in any case have served only to provoke and further to intensify any threat from the Christians. Thus Murad adopted a certain tolerance toward the indigenous Christians in the Balkan vassal states. Taking members of the military class into the Ottoman service, he employed as combatants thousands of native Christian troops, often still under the command of their own princes and overlords. In return they were guaranteed exemption from taxation and the usufruct of allotted state lands.

But the problem of assimilation was tackled largely by a policy based on enslavement, in various forms, such as the Turks themselves had experienced in the course of their own earlier history. The process of enslavement was applied to prisoners of war and the inhabitants of captured places. A law gave to the Ottoman soldier an absolute right to the possession of captives unless they consented to profess and practice Islam. He might keep them for domestic or agricultural employment; he might sell them in the open market, subject to the government's right to a fifth of the market value of the total captured. To the Greeks, slavery was a humiliation hard to bear. The Byzantine emperors had gone far toward the emancipation of slaves. The Turkish law thus precipitated a certain degree of conversion to Islam among Christians who preferred a change of religion to the loss of their freedom.

But the system remained elastic. Many Greeks had the opportunity to buy freedom without conversion. This would occur in a city fallen by assault, sometimes under the agreed terms of capitulation; and often the advancing armies of Murad preferred ransom money to the encumbrance of slaves. In the rural districts the threat of slavery was less. Refuge in the mountains was easy, and in the course of an advance there was little time for pursuit. Certain lands remained in the possession of their conquered proprietors, in return for a fixed tax. In other lands, captured from the enemy, the new Ottoman proprietors needed men to cultivate their domains, and among these many remained unconverted.

Women, on the other hand, whether war widows or the young daughters of Greeks, Serbs, and Bulgarians, were generally enslaved as wives and concubines for the conquerors, who had brought virtually no women of their own. The eventual result of this was the development of an Ottoman race vigorous and rich in the mixture of its blood. Eastern blood—Tatar, Mongol, Circassian, Georgian, Persian, and Arabian—which already flowed through Turkish veins was now mixed with the blood of the Balkan races and those of Europe beyond, to create, within a century, a civilization as cosmopolitan as that of the Greeks, Romans, and Byzantines.

Finally, in addition to this general system of serfdom, from which remission could be obtained through voluntary conversion or otherwise, Murad recruited into his army from among Christians a picked and disciplined infantry force to serve the Sultan in person. This was the corps of Janissaries, the Yeni Cheri or "New Troops." Introduced by Orkhan as a bodyguard, the Janissaries were now developed by Murad into a militia, designed primarily to maintain and defend his conquered Christian territories in Europe. Based on the practice of forcible conversion, the force was drafted from each conquered district on the principle that the privilege of exemption from military service, by payment of capitation tax, should be denied to Christian boys of a certain age. The Ottoman authorities would select from among them suitable recruits, who were taken from their families and brought up in the Moslem religion. Their function was to serve the Sultan; they depended personally upon him, and were paid by him on a scale higher than that of other troops. Handpicked for their virility, physique, and intelligence, inflexibly trained, strictly disciplined, and inured to all forms of hardship, they were, like monks, not permitted to marry, to own property, to perform other work. Their lives became dedicated to military service under the Sultan's direction.

In place of Christianity, they were brought up on the broad unorthodox Moslem precepts of the Bektashi order of dervishes, of which Orkhan had been a devout patron, building for them convents with monastic cells in Bursa. Their sheikh, Haji Bektash, blessed the new troops and gave them their standard, on which was emblazoned in scarlet the Crescent and the double-bladed sword of Osman. Drawing the sleeve of his coat over the head of the first soldier, he named the force and predicted its future: "Its visage shall be bright and shining, its arm strong, its sword keen, its arrow sharp-pointed. It shall be victorious in every battle and will never return except in triumph." Following this benediction, the white felt cap of the Janissaries—resembling the headgear of the march-warriors, the *akhis*—was given a tail, representing the sleeve of the dervish sheikh, and adorned with a wooden spoon in place of a pompom. The insignia of the force, symbolizing a standard of living higher than that of other troops, were the pot and the spoon; the titles of its officers were drawn from the camp kitchen—from First Maker of Soup to First Cook and First Carrier of Water—and the sacred object of the regiment was the stewpot, around which the Janissaries gathered, not merely to eat but to take counsel among themselves.

The peoples of Europe might well voice moral indignation at the inhumanity of these Turks from the East in thus imposing a blood tax on Christians, enslaving young captives, tearing them away from their parents, forcing upon them an alien religion and dictating the way of life they were henceforward to follow. Here allowance has to be made for the standards of a militant age, in which the fight against enemies was taken for granted as an ingredient of living. Christians themselves, in that century, were often as inhumane in their treatment of others, whether Christian or infidel. The Balkans moreover were a confused theater of war in which Christian soldiers continually fought for the Turks. At no time were the Moslem armies of Murad without infidel troops fighting wittingly under Christian commanders against other Christians. Such contingents greatly outnumbered the Janissaries, who, though they were vastly to increase their numbers as the centuries went by, still formed a relatively small minority in the Turkish armed forces. In the time of Murad they amounted to little more than a thousand men. Undoubtedly with time the threat of the draft lessened their numbers by inducing the peasantry, in a spirit of realistic self-interest, to embrace Islam rather than sacrifice sturdy sons needed for work on the land.

Once drafted, these youths received such benefits as a high degree of physical training and technical skill, an education geared to their capacities, a fair balance between barrack discipline and camp recreation, the promise of a lifelong career. There grew up among them an *esprit de corps* based on pride in their regiment, loyalty to their sovereign, and the kinship of a religious fraternity. The Janissaries thus

Karakullukchus, or wearers of black uniforms, here serving as Janissary foodbearers.

started with a fair share of advantages. As the Ottoman centuries wore on, they were to have more than their fair share of power.

This system of military slavery shocked the Christian world. But it was familiar enough to the Islamic world, and particularly to the Turks themselves. They had indeed benefitted from it in a servile capacity during the course of their earlier history. Under the rule of the Abbasid Caliphate, Turks had been captured, taken as tribute or purchased as slaves, from the non-Moslem steppes of Central Asia, brought up as Moslem converts, then trained in Baghdad as soldiers and administrators. "The supplying of slaves of this kind," notes Claude Cahen, "whose status was naturally far superior to that of domestic slaves belonging to private individuals, never seems to have been difficult or to have been resented by the Turkish populations themselves among whom it operated. Slavery did not arouse in everyone the sentiments it later evoked." Turks thus enslaved were often to rise through promotion to high military commands and administrative offices.

Under the successor state of the Samanids, their power proved in such capacities a strong factor in the preservation of the dynasty, which they ultimately overthrew, to replace it by a slave dynasty of their own. Similar dynasties established by Turks of slave origin ruled in Egypt, those of the Tulunids and later of the Mamluks, initially slaves of Saladin and the Ayyubid dynasty. They swept the latter aside to establish their own dynasty, likewise based on slavery, which was to continue under the Ottoman regime.

The Ottomans themselves were faced under Murad I with a challenge to which they now responded. Here, in the words of Arnold Toynbee, was

> the geographical transference of a native community from its native environment on the steppe, where it had been at grips with Physical Nature, to an alien environment in which it found itself free from the physical pressure of desiccation, but was confronted in exchange, with the novel problem of exercising dominion over alien communities of human beings.

Other nomad communities, confronted with the same problem, had attempted simply to "transform themselves from shepherds of sheep into shepherds of men."

Here they had generally failed. The dominion of the Avars over the Slavs had lasted for a mere fifty years; that of the Western Huns over the Hungarians for no longer than the life-span of Attila himself. The successive empires of the Mongols had all been of short duration. The fallacy of this nomad principle of government was that the "human cattle," remaining as cultivators of their own ground and thus still economically productive, would cooperate soon either to expel or to assimilate their "shepherds of men." For these proved, in this settled environment, to be mere unproductive parasites, as it were, "drones exploiting the worker-bees." Hence following the rapid rise, the equally rapid decline and fall of most nomad empires.

To this the Ottomans, now sedentary nomads, were to prove an exception unique in history. They evolved the practice of "the picking and training of human watch-dogs to keep the Padishah's human cattle in order and his human neighbours at bay." These human auxiliaries were Christian slaves. Sultan Murad, within the limits of the military dimension, had opened the way with his Janissaries to a ruling institution for the Ottoman Empire based on slavery, thus loyalty, to the Sultan, and soon widening into the civil field to comprise every branch of the public service. Henceforward the Christian subjects of the Empire were thus to be administered by men who were almost wholly of Christian origin. Here in short was the start of a long line of Moslem rulers, choosing to rule over their subjects, whether Moslem or Christian, through the agency of Christian rule.

Meanwhile the small, compact corps of Janissaries, a regular infantry force like the Roman Praetorian Guard, of which no equivalent existed in the Christian armies of the time, played an active part in the continuing campaign of Murad and his generals in the Balkans, and in the subsequent pacification and settlement of the conquered lands—men fighting, as Gibbon drily expresses it, "with the zeal of proselytes against their idolatrous countrymen."

The conquest of Thrace had opened up the road for the Ottoman armies into Bulgaria and thence into Macedonia. After a suitable interval for assimilation, Murad invaded Bulgaria. He profited from the fact that the country was divided, after the death of its tsar, between three rival brother princes. This division, between the eldest, Prince Sisman, and his two younger brothers, was so marked that for a generation the country was known as "the three Bulgarias." Further disruption occurred, to the advantage of Murad, through an invasion of western Bulgaria by the Hungarians, a "crusade" against Christians, blessed by the Pope, which resulted in the forcible conversion by Franciscan missionaries of some two hundred thousand Bulgarians from the Orthodox to the Latin rite. Their persecution was such that many welcomed the Moslem conquest as a restoration of their freedom of worship.

Over a period of three years, from 1366 onward, the Ottomans were able to take possession of all the Maritza Valley, and thus to annex most of southern Bulgaria. Sisman, following the example of John Palaeologue, became a vassal of Murad. His daughter joined the Sultan's harem, with the promise that she should not be converted to the Moslem religion. With the help of Ottoman troops he drove out the Hungarians but failed to obtain for himself, as he had hoped, his younger brother's portion of territory. In 1371, with Serbian help, he turned against the Ottomans as they launched a western advance, but was decisively defeated at Samakov, fleeing into the mountains and leaving open to the Turks the passes up into the great plain before Sofia.

Murad, however, was in no hurry to capture Sofia. Faithful, as befitted a man who was no mere raider but an empire-builder, to his principle of making haste slowly between swift, well-planned campaigns, he preferred first to secure his left flank, through occupation of the valleys of the Struma and the Vardar, against the Serbians. He thus gave orders for the invasion of Macedonia, up to the Vardar River.

Macedonia and Serbia were torn, even more than Bulgaria, by internal strife. The death of Stephen Dushan as he was starting to advance on Constantinople in 1355, and the succession of a son whom his people scorned as Nejaki, "the Weakling," had left his former "empire" in a state of anarchy and civil war. History was repeated when, in 1371, the Serbian army marched once more to the Maritza River. Here, as before, it was soundly defeated by the Ottomans, at Cernomen, and three of its princes drowned or killed.

So eastern Macedonia was now conquered, as swiftly as Thrace a decade earlier. Its cities of Drama and Serres were securely colonized by Ottomans and their churches converted into mosques. The cities and villages in and around the valley of the Struma acknowledged Ottoman sovereignty, while in the wilder districts Serbians ruled as Ottoman vassals. In 1372 the Ottoman armies reached and crossed the Vardar River. They Ottomanized the populations to the east of the valley, and to the north of it reduced to vassaldom Prince Lazar, who had been elected to rule as successor of the Serbian kings but was now acknowledged by no more than a few of his people. Such was the end of the Macedonian empire of Stephen Dushan.

After this successful campaign, Murad paused for a further decade of stabilization, judging it premature to embark on an invasion of Hungary, and turned his attention to operations in Anatolia. But he was obliged to return to Europe when his hated son, Cuntuz, entered into an unholy alliance with Andronicus, the Emperor John's elder son, who had been disgraced and supplanted by his brother Manuel, now his father's co-Emperor. Cuntuz and Andronicus proceeded to rebel against their respective fathers in Thrace. Besieged in Demotika, they were soon forced to surrender, and faced Murad's fierce vengeance. After the Greek rebels had been bound together and flung from the walls of the city to drown in the waters of the Maritza, Murad put out the eyes of his son, then had him beheaded. He ordered the fathers of the young Turks involved in the rebellion to follow his example by blinding and executing their own sons, and all did so but two, who were themselves executed instead. Murad insisted that the Emperor should likewise blind his own rebellious son and grandson, and this was done with boiling vinegar—but ineffectively, so that they recovered their eyesight. Their survival suited the interests of Murad, who had feared the rivalry of his own son but sought to keep alive that of Andronicus with his father the Emperor, and so to serve Ottoman ends in regard to Constantinople.

Soon afterward it was the turn of the Emperor's younger son, Manuel, to disgrace himself. As governor of Salonika he became implicated in a plot to overthrow Murad's authority in Serres. When it failed and the Ottomans besieged Salonika, he fled to Constantinople. Here his father, fearing Murad, refused to receive him. He was thus obliged to seek mercy from Murad in Bursa. The Sultan graciously pardoned Manuel, and thus restored him to the imperial throne with his father.

In due course Manuel's brother, Andronicus, escaped from the tower in which his father had imprisoned him. He besieged and entered Constantinople, in league with Genoese and Ottoman troops, and had himself crowned Emperor Andronicus IV—having first consigned to the same tower his father and brother Manuel. Three years later they escaped in their turn across the Bosporus, to appear jointly as suppliants before the Sultan. Murad, confident now in his game of manipulating both parties in the Byzantine dynastic struggle, insisted that Andronicus be pardoned and given the governorship of Salonika, together with other cities. But he restored John and Manuel to the imperial throne in return for a large annual tribute, the promise of a substantial contingent of Byzantine soldiers to serve in the Ottoman army, and the cession to the Ottomans of Philadelphia, the last remaining Byzantine city in Asia. When the Philadelphians objected, John and Manuel fought in the ranks of the Ottoman army to impose upon these fellow Christians the Moslem yoke. Such was the ultimate degradation to which a Byzantine emperor descended, that he might continue to rule by the grace and favour of a Turkish sultan.

Murad still needed three cities to assure his position in the Balkans: Sofia, to extend his sovereignty over northern Bulgaria to the Danube; Nish, as the key to Serbia; Monastir, to establish Ottoman rule in the territories west of the Vardar, hitherto entered only by raiders. Within six years of his return from campaigns in Asia, his generals achieved all these objectives. Monastir, with Prilep to the north of it, became a frontier fortress of the Ottoman Empire in 1380. Though the Ottoman troops did not yet attempt the conquest of the adjoining lands of Albania and Epirus, they entered them on the invitation of local princes seeking support against enemies of their own.

To proceed farther into Serbia it now became necessary to occupy the plain of Sofia. It lay in the heart of the Balkans, at the convergence of three ranges of mountains commanding the valleys of three key rivers, flowing respectively north and south to the Danube and the Mediterranean. Sofia itself, on the River Isker, which curved down into the Danube, fell without a struggle in 1385, its commandant betrayed outside the city—and subsequently strangled—by a young Turkish refugee who had become his trusted falconer. The way now lay open to the Serbian city of Nish, on the Morava. It fell after a struggle in the following year, and its ruler, Lazar, was obliged to render to the Ottomans the price of an increased tribute and a contingent for their army.

In Europe, Murad, as master of six key Balkan cities, now commanded four-fifths of the former Roman highway from Constantinople to Belgrade, and a section of that from Belgrade to Salonika. Virtually all but the last day's journey by road from the Bosporus to the Adriatic was now through Ottoman territory. Including the stretch across Asia Minor from Angora to the Bosporus, the total time for a journey from the eastern to the western boundaries of the Ottoman Empire was now forty-two days. At the time of Murad's accession, twenty-seven years earlier, there was a mere three days' journey between them.

As early as 1335 Murad had received confirmation of his status as heir to the Byzantine Empire from the coasts of the Adriatic, whence the republic of Ragusa made overtures for a commercial treaty. This was the first of many to be negotiated between the Ottoman Empire and other powers in the following centuries. In return for a substantial annual tribute, the Ragusans obtained the right to trade in the Empire and sail the high seas without Ottoman interference. The treaty was signed by Murad, who could not write, with a thumbprint. Such was the origin of the *tughra,* which, in calligraphic form, was to remain under each subsequent sultan the official signature-seal of the house of Osman.

Twenty years later, both Venice and Genoa signed treaties with the Byzantine emperor, undertaking to defend him against all enemies, but specifically excluding "Morat Bey and his Turks." The Genoese followed this up by a formal treaty of friendship with "the magnificent and powerful lord of lords, Moratibei." This did not however prevent them, a year later, from joining in an offensive alliance, "against that Turk, son of unrighteousness and evil, and enemy of the Holy Cross, Morat Bey and his sect, who are attempting so grievously to attack the Christian race."

Murad had been fighting a war on two alternate fronts, one in Europe and the other in Asia. An advance on the one regularly followed an advance on the other, to avoid the danger of fighting simultaneously on both. In Asia he required to extend and secure his dominion at the expense of the Turkish principalities of the interior. This was a task made easier as the expanding frontier principalities of the Ghazis grew in strength and prestige. After capturing Angora, in the center of Anatolia, in the second year of his reign, Murad had concentrated his forces largely in Europe. He had judged shrewdly that it was only with the resources in men and money of the Balkans and its assimilated Christian element behind him that he could be sure of the assimilation of Asia Minor; moreover, that meanwhile the threat from Christendom, before him, was greater than any from the Moslem elements in his rear. Now the prospect of any such crusade in the Balkans had receded. The southern Slavs were at odds with the Hungarians; there was anarchy in Serbia; Bulgaria lacked leaders; and Byzantium was torn by dynastic strife. Moreover Murad was now reinforced by the military contingents which the vassalage of the Christian princes compelled them to furnish to the Sultan. Hence, after his conquest of Macedonia, following that of Thrace and southern Bulgaria, Murad felt secure enough to switch his forces from Europe across into Asia.

In fact, he was able to achieve his preliminary objectives in Asia Minor without fighting. Much of the principality of Germiyan, neighbouring that of the Ottomans, with the important strategic city of Kutahya, was secured to him by the marriage in Bursa of his son Bayezid to the daughter of its emir, and the provision of a handsome territorial dowry. The ceremony was performed with a splendour alien to the traditions of Murad's simpler Ottoman forebears, but akin to the customs of the Byzantine court, which the Ottomans were coming to adopt. Next Murad acquired territory in Hamid, between Germiyan and the large state of Karamania, by purchase from its emir, who felt his security threatened by the Ottoman occupation of Kutahya. For the territory of Tekke, to the south of it, Murad had to fight. But he was content with the conquest of the uplands around its lake region, leaving to its emir the southern valleys and lowlands between the Taurus range and the Mediterranean Sea.

When the time came to tackle the larger and more formidable state of Karamania, with which he now had a common frontier, Murad mustered at Kutahya an army whose left wing, under the command of his son Bayezid, was composed of Greek, Serbian, and Bulgarian troops, provided under treaty by the Emperor John and their respective rulers. The battle was fought in 1387, in the great plain before Konya. It proved indecisive, both sides claiming victory. The city of Konya held out; Murad gained no territory, no booty, no promise of tribute or military aid, merely a reconciliation with the emir of Karamania in the form of a submissive kiss of the hand from him. Victorious against the Christians of the Balkans, Murad thus met his match in a powerful Moslem prince, and failed to extend farther his dominions in Asia.

Indirectly this battle involved him in another major campaign in the Balkans. To avoid antagonizing the Moslems of Asia Minor, Murad had ordered his troops to refrain from looting and violence. This order enraged his Serbian contingent, who regarded booty as soldiers' due, under the rules of war, in return for their services. Thus a number of them disobeyed it, and were put to death on the spot. The rest returned to Serbia, still seething with indignation at their treatment. This gave Lazar, the prince of Serbia, the opportunity to stimulate Serbian resistance to the Ottoman invasion which, after the capture of Nish, now threatened the rest of upper Serbia and Bosnia. He formed a Pan-Serbian alliance, with the support of the prince of Bosnia, a ruler whose power extended as far as the Adriatic coast. The response of the Ottomans was to cross the Vardar and invade Bosnia. Outnumbered, they were defeated, with the loss of four-fifths of their army, at Plochnik. At this break in the run of Ottoman victories, there was wild rejoicing among the Slavs of the Balkans. Serbians, Bosnians, Albanians, Bulgarians, Wallachians, and Hungarians from the frontier provinces all rallied around Lazar as never before, in a determination to drive the Turks out of Europe.

Murad remained for the present in Asia Minor, showing no undue haste in avenging his defeat at Plochnik. He preferred to wait, not only to recoup his losses but to see for how long his enemies, after this first emotional flush of confidence and hope, would remain united. In the light of past experience and of his own shrewd political judgment, he knew well that solidarity among these Slav races was often ephemeral.

Thus, before he turned once again on the Serbs, Murad launched in 1388 a campaign to complete the conquest of Bulgaria. Prince Sisman withdrew at an early stage to a fortress on the Danube, and sued for peace. After accepting Murad's terms, he changed his mind and decided on a last desperate resistance. But he had underrated the strength of the Ottomans, who soon defeated and captured him. As a result the Ottomans established their rule in northern and central Bulgaria right up to the Danube, taking possession of various fortresses strategically placed along its banks, to command the passes across the Balkan Mountains. Though Prince Sisman remained a vassal of the Sultan, he was hardly in a strong enough position to give aid to his fellow Slavs of the new grand alliance.

Having thus disposed of Bulgaria, Murad, now seventy years old, personally led a large army in a final campaign against the Serbians. He was joined by the forces of a Bulgarian and two Serbian renegades, with the prospect of aid from a third. The decisive battle for the fate of an independent Serbia was fought on the desolate mountainous "plain of the blackbirds" at Kossovo—a point where the frontiers of Serbia, Bosnia, Albania, and Herzegovina converged. The Ottoman army was inferior in numbers to that of the Serbians and their allies, but superior in confidence and morale. Murad was so sure of victory as to order, farsightedly, that no castles, cities, or villages of the region should be destroyed in the course of battle. Fighting as he was for the possession of a rich country, it was not in his interest to destroy its resources or unduly to alienate its people.

The Serbians, on the other hand, had premonitions of defeat, due largely to mutual distrust and intimations of treachery within their own ranks. In an oration on the eve of the battle Prince Lazar, always lacking in authority and now appearing to lack also in confidence, openly accused his own son-in-law, Milosh Obravitch, of treason. Murad himself expressed misgivings lest the wind, which was blowing from the enemy's side, should throw dust in the eyes of the Ottomans. Throughout the night, it is recorded, he prayed for heaven's protection and for the favour of dying for the true faith, the martyr's death which alone merited felicity.

Next morning the wind had dropped. The Ottoman army was drawn up for battle in its customary order: in the center was the Sultan, with his Janissaries and cavalry guard; on the right flank his elder son, Bayezid, commanding his European troops (since the battle was in Europe); on the left his younger son, Yakub, commanding his Asiatic troops. The Ottomans attacked with an advance guard of two thousand archers. The Serbians retaliated with a charge that broke through the left flank of the Ottomans. Bayezid, from the right flank, came to the rescue with a massive counterstroke, fighting valiantly and striking his enemies in person with a heavy iron mace. The issue remained in doubt, with the Ottomans still on the defensive, until another son-in-law of Lazar, Vuk Brankovitch—perhaps by treacherous prearrangement with Murad—withdrew from the battle with his twelve thousand men. His desertion so weakened the Serbians that they broke their ranks and fled.

Murad had been proved right in his estimate of Slav disunity in battle. But his evening prayer to the Almighty was all too literally granted. He lost his own life on the battlefield. The story of this dramatic tragedy has been related by different sources in a variety of conflicting ways. The likeliest version is that the deed was done, during or after the battle, by Milosh Obravitch. Stung by the allegations of treason from his father-in-law, Lazar, the evening before, he resolved to prove his loyalty. He pretended to desert to the Ottoman ranks, where he demanded, in view of his own high rank, an audience with Murad. When this was granted, Milosh knelt in pretended submission before the Sultan, then plunged a dagger into his breast—

"with two thrusts," it was later recounted, "which came out at his back." Failing to escape, he was slaughtered by the Ottoman soldiery. Murad lived long enough to order his reserves into battle, and thus to bring the Ottomans decisive victory. His last act before dying was to summon Lazar before him and condemn him to execution.

Such, at the moment of victory, in a historic battle from which the vanquished were not to recover, was the sudden end of this first great Sultan of the Ottoman Empire. Within a generation Murad I had raised the Ottoman state of his fathers into an empire destined to endure as a powerful force in the world. As a sultan he was to be outshone in the eyes of history by two mightier sovereigns, Mehmed the Conqueror and Suleiman the Lawgiver. His achievement matched theirs in that he laid, through his conquest and subsequent government of a wide sphere of territory, the imperial foundations on which both would be able to build and expand.

Murad was no mere warrior. Skilled he became in the arts of war, shrewd in strategy, ruthless—indeed cruel—in battle, confident in his generals, to whom he was always ready to delegate the power of command. But his strength lay as much in the arts of peace. He was a ruler of outstanding political wisdom. Once the battle was won, it became his concern that life in the conquered Christian territories should continue under Islam with as little disruption, social and economic, as possible. No established Ottoman traditions of government fitted exactly into the context of these European lands. New systems of administration must evolve, in pragmatic relation to the conditions of time and place and custom; and this was achieved under Murad—who trusted his administrators no less than his generals—on a competent and reasonably equitable basis.

In his estimate of the character of his subjects and enemies, whether Greek or Slav, Murad showed keen psychological discernment. Strictly Moslem as he was in his religious beliefs, he nonetheless handled the "infidel" Christians of his new empire with a tolerance striking in its contrast with the attitude of their own fellow Christians of the Latin persuasion. He countenanced no persecution of Christians and, apart from the Janissaries, enforced no conversions to Islam. The Orthodox Patriarch himself testified in a letter to the Pope in 1385 that the Sultan left to his Church complete liberty of action.

By such a process of assimilation did Murad I sow the seeds of a multiracial, multireligious, multilingual society which was to function effectively under the rule of his successors for centuries to come. It created over a wide area a Pax Ottomanica, which in due course would merit comparison with the Pax Romana of an earlier age. In its own essence the composite realm of the Ottoman Empire was indeed to become, through its eclectic policies, a true successor to the Empire of Rome. For it took over the Roman tradition of giving citizenship to foreigners, naturalizing them in its own fashion, and encouraging them to use their opportunities both to their own and to the Empire's advantage. It enabled the Sultan's Christian-born subjects, in common with the Moslem-born, to rise as first-class citizens to the highest offices of state. It was a like practice, in Professor Toynbee's view, "that had enabled the Romans first to build up an Empire and then to revive it again and again." In virtue of this he goes so far as to claim that the Ottomans "were able to build up an empire which was truly the fifth revival of the Roman Empire in the Near and Middle East"—and which was to survive as such into the first quarter of the twentieth century.

((4))

On Murad's assassination his elder son was instantly proclaimed his successor, as Bayezid I, here on the battlefield of Kossovo. In response to pressure from the state council, fearing conflict over the succession, his first act as Sultan, over his father's dead body, was to order the death, by strangulation with a bowstring, of his younger brother. This was Yakub, his fellow-commander in the battle, who had won distinction in the field and popularity with his troops. Bayezid thus initiated a practice of imperial fratricide which was to root itself all too permanently in the history of the Ottoman dynasty. It was based on the argument that assassination is preferable to sedition, as so often practiced by a sultan's brothers, and was conveniently excused for Bayezid by a text from the Koran: "So often, as they return to sedition, they shall be subverted therein; and if they depart not from you, and offer you peace and restrain their hands from warring against you, take them and kill them wheresoever ye find them."

In the ensuing century this inhuman tradition was to be given the force of law by an edict of his descendant Mehmed II, the Conqueror, who had earlier smothered an infant brother in his bath. Hitherto the Ottoman leaders had been flexible in regard to these laws of succession. From now onward, at the outset of each reign, they were to follow this inflexible practice, thus safeguarding in their own inhuman fashion the principles of their indivisible sovereignty—and thus indeed helping to ensure through the centuries the unbroken survival of their dynasty.

Bayezid, it was soon to become evident, possessed few of his father's more stable virtues. Hasty and impetuous by nature, he was unpredictable as a statesman, disturbing the more deliberate pattern of his earlier Osmanli forebears. On the other hand, he was a dashing and capable commander, with a true instinct for battle. For his swiftness in transporting his army across Europe and Asia, and from one continent to the other, he was named Yildirim, otherwise "Lightning," or "the Thunderbolt"—a name suitable, as Gibbon expresses it, to "the fiery energy of his soul and rapidity of his destructive march."

In Europe, having avenged his father's death by a massacre which wiped out most of the Serbian nobility on the field of Kossovo, he was quick to come to terms with the son of Prince Lazar, Stephen Bulco-

Sultan Bayezid I (1389–1402), nicknamed Yildirim or Thunderbolt, also earned the title of Gazi or warrior for the true faith, granted to those who enlarged the realm of Islam through fresh conquest of non-Islamic territory.

From an oil painting in the gallery of imperial portraits at the Topkapi Palace, Istanbul.

vitz, who had succeeded his father. Judging that the Serbians were no longer a threat to him, needing their troops—as Murad had done for his campaigns in Asia Minor—for the defense of the Danube Valley against coming threats from the more redoubtable Hungarians, Bayezid made an amicable alliance with Stephen which was to endure throughout his reign. Serbia was not incorporated in the Ottoman Empire, but remained an autonomous vassal state. Stephen, in return for the payment of an annual tribute secured by the revenue of the Serbian silver mines, was allowed all the privileges of his father; he gave his sister Despina in marriage to Bayezid; he undertook to command a contingent in the Ottoman army and to furnish Serbian troops whenever and wherever Bayezid required them—their earlier grievances now removed by an equitable share in the booty. Meanwhile colonies of Moslems were settled in parts of the conquered Serbian territories. Kossovo was thus forgiven—though never, in Serbian legend, forgotten.

Bayezid then turned his attention to Asia Minor. Here his impatient designs of conquest were to prove his eventual undoing, and to put the future of his whole empire in jeopardy. In the initial stages he met with success. He made a vassal of the emir of Aydin and defeated in battle those of Sarukhan and Mentese, thus establishing the Ottomans on the Aegean, where only other breeds of Turk had settled before them, and reaching for the first time the Mediterranean Sea. This prepared the way for their ultimate emergence as a naval power. Meanwhile, having failed to wrest Smyrna from the crusader Knights Hospitallers, they made their naval mark by devastating the island of Chios, raiding the coasts of Attica, and attempting a commercial blockade of other Aegean islands. But as sailors they were still no match for the fleets of the Italian mercantile cities Venice and Genoa.

Then, profiting by the aid of his Christian vassals, including Manuel Palaeologue, the future Byzantine Emperor—who came in person to serve the Sultan in the Ottoman camp—Bayezid invaded Karamania and besieged Konya, as his father had done before him. After two campaigns—with the violation by Karamanlis of a peace settlement in between, followed by a lightning switch of reinforcements from Europe—Karamania was defeated in the battle of Ak Tchai and occupied by the Ottomans. This move was followed by the occupation of Kayseri and Sivas, in the adjoining principality, and of the principality of Kastamuni in the north, which gave them access to a port on the Black Sea, Sinope. Bayezid could and did now boast that he was master of the greater part of Anatolia.

But this mastery was skin-deep. Often it did little more than scratch the surface of the lands he conquered. Murad, by a far-sighted policy of assimilation, had brought wide areas of Christian Europe under an Ottoman rule which their peoples accepted, not always unwillingly. Bayezid made no such attempt systematically to assimilate his lightning conquests in Asia. He had indeed brought wide areas of Anatolia under Ottoman occupation. But—with some exceptions—they were in no true sense under Ottoman rule. Their peoples, for the most part, sought a return from exile of their own former rulers. Bayezid, based habitually at his court in Europe, tackled none of the problems which these conquests involved. Between campaigns he preferred to relax in the sensual pleasures of a court notorious for a luxury that emulated that of Byzantium in its heyday, eating and drinking freely and indulging in various forms of debauchery among the women and boys of his harem. For all these excesses, he had a contrasting religious side to his nature, building himself a small chamber on the top of his mosque in Bursa, where he would for long periods retire into mystical seclusion and confer with the theologians of his Islamic establishment.

After his victories in Asia Minor, which he left in the hands of his governors, Bayezid soon returned to Europe. Here he was preoccupied with the challenge from Hungary, whose king, Sigismund, had become his principal enemy. Already, in a provocative spirit, Bayezid had initiated Ottoman raids into Hungary and beyond, where the Turks came to be seen as the terror of Central Europe. His raiders crossed the Danube and fought the first Ottoman battle on Hungarian soil, gaining an ally in the militant Wallachians, who sought freedom from Hungarian sovereignty. Sigismund, alive to the Ottoman threat, sent a message to Bayezid, complaining of his interference with Bulgaria, which was under Hungarian protection. Bayezid insolently refused to reply, only calling the attention of the king's ambassador to the weapons which hung in his tent.

Sigismund's response was to invade Bulgaria. He captured the fortress of Nicopolis on the Danube, but was obliged to abandon it when a large Ottoman force moved against him. Murad, on his defeat of Sisman, its ruler, had allowed Bulgaria to retain a degree of autonomy as a vassal state. But now Bayezid, mistrusting Sisman as an ally in the event of a further Hungarian invasion, sent an army against Bulgaria and, having executed Sisman, annexed the whole of it to the Ottoman Empire. Like Thrace and Macedonia, Bulgaria was henceforward an integral part of the Empire, helping, with Wallachia as a vassal state, to establish a strong buffer on the Danube against Hungary. By eliminating such local dynasties he had gone far toward the creation, in the Balkans, of a centralized imperial government. In the ensuing process of Ottomanization and, to a certain extent, conversion to Islam, Bulgaria lost not only its independence but its own autocephalous Orthodox Church, the living symbol of the Bulgarians as a people. Previously subjected in part to the Latin rite, it now fell under a domination by the priests of the Greek Orthodox Church, often harder to bear than that of its Moslem pashas.

Bayezid meanwhile was preparing to turn his forces against Constantinople. In 1391 the Emperor John V Palaeologue died. His successor, Manuel, as an obedient vassal of the Sultan, had been reduced to the ultimate humiliation—and indeed to near-starvation—as little more than a despised Groom of the Chamber at the court of his overlord. He now escaped to Constantinople, where he secured possession of the imperial throne. His late father had started to restore the walls of the city and to demolish churches in order to rebuild, as fortifications ornately disguised, the towers which flanked its Golden Gate. On hearing of this, Bayezid had ordered their demolition, threatening that otherwise Manuel, in reprisal, would be deprived of his sight. The last act of the Emperor John, before dying, was to obey the Sultan's command.

Manuel, on his succession, was now confronted with an ultimatum from Bayezid, demanding not only continued vassalage and an increased tribute, but the establishment of a kadi, or judge, in Constantinople, for its Moslem population. This demand was soon followed by the arrival before the walls of an Ottoman army, slaughtering or enslaving on its way such Greeks in southern Thrace as were still Christians. Thus the first Ottoman siege of Constantinople began.

The city was closely invested for seven months. Bayezid then raised the siege on stiffer terms than those initially demanded. The Emperor Manuel was forced to agree to the establishment within the walls of an Islamic tribunal, and the cession of a quarter in the city to Moslem settlers. Half of the port of Galata, on the opposite side of the Golden Horn, was ceded for occupation by a garrison of six thousand Ottoman troops. Besides an increased tribute, the Ottomans exacted a tithe on the vineyards and vegetable gardens outside the city walls. Henceforward, from the minarets of two mosques the Moslem call to prayer echoed through the city, which the Ottomans now called Istanbul, a corruption of the Greek words *is tin poli,* "to the city."

Bayezid continued to blockade the city on the landward side. Two years later it was attacked once more, at his instigation and with the aid of Ottoman troops, by young John Palaeologue, Manuel's nephew, who claimed with some justice to be the rightful heir to his throne. But the attack was repulsed. In 1395 Bayezid presumed to hold court as "heir to the Caesars" at Serres, where he summoned among his vassals the Emperor, his brother and nephew, and impulsively ordered the death of the entire Palaeologue family. The sentence was revoked, thanks to his Grand Vezir, Ali Pasha, who delayed its execution until the Sultan had changed his mind and agreed instead, as a compromise, to cut off the hands and put out the eyes of several Byzantine dignitaries. Thus Manuel II continued to reign, proving an able enough ruler.

Meanwhile, Bayezid's attention had been claimed by a new menace from King Sigismund of Hungary. Irked by the raids of the Ottomans and the threats from their fortresses on the Danube, he began to canvass support from the western Christian powers for a new crusade to "go against the Turks to their loss and destruction." Murad had always been careful, between campaigns, to avoid undue provocation of Christendom, the extent of whose power he appreciated. Bayezid was less circumspect in his policy toward Christians. Bombastic by nature, he had arrogantly declared to envoys from Italy at the outset of his reign that after conquering Hungary he would ride to Rome and would feed his horse with oats on the altar of St. Peter's. Since then, posing as the champion of Islam, he had continued openly to boast of his aggressive intentions against Christianity.

It was to counter such threats that Sigismund now endeavoured to mount his crusade. He met with little encouragement but words from a succession of popes. The Venetians too equivocated, mistrusting the power of the Hungarians more than that of the Ottomans; the Genoese merely vied with their Venetian rivals for commercial favours from Bayezid; while both Naples and Milan maintained amicable Ottoman contacts. Thus, to find volunteers for a campaign to "drive the Turks out of Europe," Sigismund was obliged to send his emissaries to France, to the court of the intermittently mad King Charles VI. The king's uncle, the Duke of Burgundy, proved ready, though for his own motives, to support the venture, promising Sigismund a force of chevaliers and mercenaries under the command of his young son, the Comte de Nevers.

Throughout feudal Europe there was a wide response to Sigismund's call, at this auspicious moment when the Hundred Years' War was over and there was otherwise peace in the Holy Roman Empire. There rallied to his standard not merely the French force but also knights from the nobility of England, Scotland, Flanders, Lombardy, Savoy, and all parts of Germany, together with adventurers from Poland, Bohemia, Italy, and Spain. For the last time in history, the finest flower of European chivalry gathered together for a crusade as much secular as religious in impulse, whose objective was to check Bayezid's lightning advance and eject the Turks, once and for all, from the Balkans. Thus an "international" army, composed with Sigismund's own force and the contingents of knights with their retinues and mercenary bands of some hundred thousand men, mustered at Buda in the early summer of 1396—the largest Christian force that had ever confronted the infidel. It had moreover the auxiliary support of a fleet in the Black Sea, off the mouth of the Danube, manned by the Knights Hospitallers, the Venetians and Genoese, which was later to sail up the river.

Sigismund had been expecting an invasion of Hungary across the Danube by Bayezid since the month of May. When it did not materialize, and his scouts could find no trace of the enemy, he favoured a defensive strategy, designed to lure the Turks into Hungary and attack them there. But the knights were spoiling for a great and glorious offensive. When the invasion still failed to materialize they believed, in their innocence of geography, that Bayezid (whom in any event they confused with Amurath, or Murad) was seeking recruits "in Cairo in Babylonia," rallying his forces at Alexandria and Damascus, receiving "under the command and prayers of the Khalif of Baghdad and Asia Minor" an army of "Saracens and miscreants," which included "people of Tartary, Persia, Media, Syria, Alexandria, and of many far-off countries of the miscreants (infidels)." If he did not come, then they would march, so they dreamed, through the Turkish dominions as far as the Persian Empire, "conquer Syria and the Holy Land and," in Froissart's words, "deliver Jerusalem from the hands of the Sultan and his enemies." Still Bayezid, occupied in fact with the siege of Constantinople, did not come.

The crusaders decided that meanwhile there was "no reason for them to stay idle; they should achieve some feats of arms, since that was the purpose of their being there." So they marched down the valley of the Danube, reaching Orsova, near the Iron Gates, and crossed the river in an operation that lasted eight days. The Hungarians spread without opposition into Serbia, moving up the valley of the Morava, where they found good wines "put into goatskins by the Turks, who are forbidden by law, on pain of death, to drink it; they sell it instead to the Christians." They captured Nish with "great slaughter of men, women and children. The Christians took no pity on anyone"—less indeed than the infidel Ottoman raiders themselves had done.

In Bulgaria the gates of Vidin, the first Danube fortress, were opened to them by its Christian commander, and the Turkish garrison was massacred. Proceeding down the river, they attacked the next fortress, Rahova. Here the large Turkish garrison, faced with the whole Christian army of Franks and Hungarians, surrendered, and the bulk of the population, including many Bulgarian Christians, was put to the sword. The Christian forces camped together before the key fortress of Nicopolis, where there was still no sign of an invading Turkish army. But their improvident troops from the West had brought no machines for siege warfare, while Sigismund had prepared only for a defensive campaign. Their equipment proving inadequate, they sat down before the walls, hoping to starve the city into surrender.

The Western knights, with no enemy to fight, treated the whole operation rather in the spirit of a picnic, enjoying the women and the wines and the luxuries they had brought from home, gambling and engaging in debauchery, ceasing in contemptuous fashion to believe that the Turk could ever be a dangerous foe to them. Those soldiers who dared to suggest otherwise had their ears cut off as a punishment for defeatism. Meanwhile there were quarrels between the different contingents, among whom the Wallachians and Transylvanians were not to be trusted.

For sixteen days there was still no sign of Bayezid. But now suddenly, with his habitual swiftness of movement, there he was before the city—where he had twice before been victorious—with an army reported to Sigismund to consist of anything up to two hundred thousand men. Sigismund knew his enemy and that the Ottoman army—well trained, strictly disciplined, and more mobile than that of the crusaders—was not to be trifled with. He insisted on the need for a carefully concerted plan of action. A preliminary reconnaissance was carried out by an experienced French knight, De Courcy, who came upon a detachment of the Turkish vanguard and defeated it in a mountain pass, charging with cries of "Our Lady for the Lord De Courcy!" This success merely aroused the jealousy of the other French knights, who accused him of vanity. Sigismund tried to urge on them the need to remain on the defensive, to allow the foot soldiers of the Hungarians and Wallachians to hold the first attack, while the cavalry and mercenaries of the knights formed a second line, whether for attack or defense. At this the French chevaliers were furious, insisting that the king of Hungary was trying to steal from them "the flower of the day and the honour" for himself. The first battle must be theirs.

The Comte d'Elu, with the support of others, refused to obey Sigismund and called to his standard-bearer: "Forward banner, in the name of God and Saint George, for they will see me today a good chevalier." So "beneath the banner of Our Lady" they charged without thought into battle, confident of defeating the despised infidel. "The Knights of France," records Froissart, "were sumptuously armed. . . . But I am told that when they advanced against the Turks, they were not more than seven hundred in number. Think of the folly, and the pity of it! If they had only waited for the King of Hungary, who had at least sixteen thousand men, they could have done great deeds; but pride was their downfall."

Charging uphill, they surprised and slaughtered Bayezid's outposts. After scattering his cavalry they dismounted and continued to charge on foot against his infantry, pulling up as they ran the line of stakes which protected its position, and maintaining an impetus which scattered these forces as well. The swords of the knights ran with blood. The day, they confidently believed, was theirs. Then, reaching the hilltop, they came up against the Sultan's main army of sixty thousand men, much strengthened by Serbian support, which was drawn up beyond the crest, fresh and ready for battle. According to his usual tactics, with which Sigismund was familiar, Bayezid had put his expendable untrained levies in the forefront of the battle, to exhaust the enemy's strength. Then "the horsemen of Bayezid and his hosts and chariots came against them in battle array, like the moon when she is new." The knights, being unhorsed and weighed down by their heavy armour, became helpless against attack. They were totally routed. Their horses galloped riderless back to camp. The finest flower of European chivalry lay dead on the field of Nicopolis or captive in the hands of the Turks.

The crusaders were still, by the standards of the time, essentially amateur soldiers, fighting in the past and in a romantic spirit. They had learned nothing of the professional art of war as it progressed through the centuries, none of the military skills of the Turks, with their superior discipline, training, briefing, and tactics, and above all the mobility of their light-armoured forces and archers on horseback. These were lessons which Sigismund, with his Hungarians, had begun to learn through experience. He advanced with his forces to follow up the crusaders, but knew that once his advice was disregarded, the day was lost. "If they had only believed me," he said, "we had forces in plenty to fight our enemies." As he had boasted before the battle, "If the sky fell on our army we should have enough lances to uphold it."

Presently he escaped, with the Grand Master of the Knights Hospitallers, to his ships in the Danube, while the survivors of his army, with those of the knights, fled before the Ottomans, some reaching the ships, but thousands of others enduring severe hardships as they trekked across the Carpathian Mountains. Next day Bayezid, inspecting the battlefield and assessing his casualties, ordered a general massacre of prisoners, sparing, in the hopes of a substantial ransom, only the Comte de Nevers, with his advisers and a number of richly clad chevaliers. They were forced to stand beside the Sultan, there to watch their kneeling companions at arms roped together and beheaded.

"The people that were killed that day," it is recorded, "were reckoned at ten thousand men." Thus did the last of the crusades end with a catastrophic defeat by the Moslems in the heart of Christian Europe. The Sultan, content with his victory, was not tempted to follow it up further. In a scornful farewell oration he challenged the knights to return and risk a further defeat at his hands. Meanwhile he led his army in an invasion of Greece, where he captured important strongholds in Thessaly and married another Christian bride, the daughter of Helen Cantacuzene. He left his generals to proceed with the invasion of the Morea, where Moslem colonies were settled with Turks from Anatolia. But Athens remained in the hands of the Christians.

Though the inheritance of Byzantium was now surely his, Bayezid did not at once attempt to clinch it by pressing to an assault his siege of Constantinople. He was deterred by his lack of naval power at this time when, following the defeat at Nicopolis, the two naval republics of Venice and Genoa were strongly opposed to him. After open conflict with the Genoese at Pera, he tried in 1399 to enter the city with a force of ten thousand men, but withdrew with the arrival of a small crusading force under the French marshal Boucicault, the only survivor of Nicopolis to accept the Sultan's challenge in the field. He came in two successive expeditions to aid the Genoese and Venetians, who sailed out to meet him, and fought the first recorded Ottoman naval engagement, defeating Bayezid's fleet in the Dardanelles and pursuing his galleys up the Asiatic coasts of the Bosporus. Before sailing away, he left a French garrison in the city and installed, as co-Emperor with Manuel, his hated usurping nephew, John.

Manuel himself travelled with him to Europe as a suppliant, the shadow of an emperor seeking further Christian aid. Received with appropriate imperial honours in Italy, France, and England, he nourished hopes, but returned empty-handed. There were to be no more crusades worthy of the name. Meanwhile the capital of his empire, blockaded for six years, was near to starvation. Inhabitants were letting themselves down over its walls with ropes and surrendering to the Ottomans. The imperial treasury was empty, and the surrender of the city itself was near. Everywhere—here, in the Morea, in Albania, in the Adriatic—Bayezid was ready for his *coup de grâce* against the Byzantine Empire.

At the eleventh hour, in the spring of 1402, he was foiled—by a formidable threat from the East. All campaigns were abandoned; all available troops in the Balkan peninsula, whether Moslem or Christian, were swiftly removed to Asia Minor. Constantinople and the relics of its empire were to have a last-minute respite. A new and world-shaking conqueror was marching westward, much as Genghiz Khan and his Mongol horde had erupted across the Eurasian steppes nearly two centuries earlier. This was a descendant of his line, Tamurlane, otherwise known as Timur the Tatar.

((5))

When iron first became known to the Tatars, and not even the strongest among them proved able to bend it as they could bend other metals, they assumed it must contain beneath its surface some especial unknown substance. So they gave it the name of *timur,* which meant something filled or stuffed. It became a custom to bestow the name on their great leaders, thus acknowledging in them something beyond ordinary physical strength. Among these Timur the Tatar ranked as the greatest of all Men of Iron, for he aspired to nothing less than the conquest of the world, contending that "as there was only one God in Heaven, so there should be only one ruler on Earth."

Born into a small Tatar tribe, of which he came in his youth to be chief, thus ruling over a region between Samarkand and the mountainous frontiers of Hindustan, he was endowed with high courage, fierce energy, a unique gift of leadership, and supreme military genius. Building up a mighty army, he rode at the head of it in a career of spectacular conquest, to become sovereign of three empires—Persia, Tartary (with Turkestan), and India. Within a generation Timur had extinguished nine dynasties to reign from Samarkand as lord, in the name of Islam, of a great part of Asia.

Timur's personal domination was absolute. He ruled without ministers. Muscular in build, with broad shoulders, a massive head, and a formidable high forehead, his skin was fair beneath the beard, with a vivid complexion, and from an early age his hair was white. He walked with a limp, whether due to an inborn paralysis, to an accident, or to a wound in battle, so it was said, from an arrow in the foot. He was thus Timur the Lame (Timurlenk)—and indeed at times his infirmity was such that, as in the advance of his army on Baghdad, he was unable to sit on a horse and was carried by his men in a litter.

Taciturn in his manner, devout in his religious beliefs, and strict in his conceptions of justice, he was a master of calculation and planning who spent hours of his time, often alone and at night, sitting at a great chessboard. He manipulated its figures to work out strategy in intricate campaigns "which, against any opponent, he invariably won." In his ever-victorious army, his horses were numbered in six figures. In their train followed herds not only of camels but of elephants, an animal which proved serviceable not only on the battlefield but as a motive power for the building of his fabled new capital of Samarkand. From here Timur, by the end of the fourteenth century, ruled over an empire which extended eastward to the Great Wall of China, northward into the steppes of Russia, southward to the River Ganges and the Persian Gulf, westward into Persia, Armenia, and the upper waters of the Euphrates and Tigris—and thus to the borders of Asia Minor. Beyond them spread the only other great Moslem empire, that of the Ottomans, whose conquests under Murad and Bayezid had coincided in time with his own. Now the two rival victorious emperors, Timur and Bayezid, Tatar and Ottoman, were to confront one another across this frontier, a region where (as Gibbon discerns their respective characters) "Timur was impatient of an equal, and Bajazet was ignorant of a superior."

Here was a crucial historic moment at which the interests of both, in their respective spheres, called for a tacit *modus vivendi.* Whether Timur at this time had designs on the territory of his Ottoman neighbours is doubtful. As a soldier he had a proper respect for the military power of the Turks. As an empire-builder, rounding off his dominions, he still had other fields to conquer; his road lay open southward into Syria, the Holy Land, Mesopotamia, Egypt. Similarly Bayezid needed above all to round off his own conquests in the Balkans with the capture of Constantinople, which would surely soon fall into his hands. Timur saw where their separate interests lay; Bayezid did not. On the one hand, puffed up with pride and delusions of invincibility, after a decade of victories without a single defeat, on the other hand perhaps led by false counsel to underrate the power of his adversary, Bayezid acted in such a fashion as gratuitously to goad Timur into action against him.

Bayezid, in occupying but at the same time failing to assimilate so large a part of Anatolia, had left behind him as refugees from its conquered principalities resentful princes who sought to regain their lands from the Ottomans and to rule once more over former subjects still loyal to them. A number of them lived in exile at Timur's court. Timur, however, did not seriously concern himself with their plight or with the Sultan's activities until after the Ottoman capture of Sivas. Had Bayezid then been prudent, he would have treated this fortified city as a defensive outpost. Instead, in 1399, he chose to use it as an offensive base for an advance farther east, under the command of his son Suleiman, toward the waters of the upper Euphrates. Here the Ottoman troops were soon trespassing on the territory of a Turcoman prince under Timur's protection, Kara Yussuf, who fell into their hands.

For the first time Timur's anger was roused against Bayezid, and he wrote to him (now back in Europe) requiring the return of his prisoner. Gibbon quotes a letter from the Persian historian Sheref-feddin: "What is the foundation of thy insolence and folly?" he demanded of the Sultan. "Thou hast fought some battles in the woods of Anatolia: contemptible trophies." Continuing as one champion of Islam to another, he nonetheless conceded: "Thou hast obtained some victories over the Christians of Europe; thy sword was blessed by the apostle of God; and thy obedience to the precept of the Koran, in waging war against the infidels, is the sole consideration that prevents us from destroying thy country, the frontier and bulwark of the Moslem world." In conclusion he urged him: "Be wise in time; reflect; repent; and avert the thunder of our vengeance, which is yet suspended over thy head. Thou art no more than a pismire [an ant]; why wilt thou seek to provoke the elephants? Alas! they will trample thee under their feet."

Bayezid chose to treat this and a subsequent message with contempt: "Thy armies are innumerable; be they so; but what are the arrows of the flying Tatar against the scimitars and battle-axes of my firm and invincible Janissaries? I will guard the princes who have implored my protection. Seek them in my tents." He concluded with an insult more intimate in character. "If I fly from thy arms, may my wives be thrice divorced from my bed; but if thou hast not courage to meet me in the field, mayest thou again receive thy wives after they have thrice endured the embraces of a stranger."

Timur's messages to Bayezid, whatever their content, had been in form diplomatic, following the usage as between equals of inscribing their two names side by side. Now Bayezid deliberately flouted all diplomacy, inscribing his own name in large letters of gold, with Timur's name below it in small letters of black. To so calculated a double affront, at once domestic and diplomatic, barring the door to negotiation, there could be but a single effective response.

Timur at once took the field against Sivas. Suleiman, who had only a small force of horsemen, sent an urgent appeal for reinforcements to his father, now in Thessaly, but received no reply. He thus boldly made a sortie, but finding his force greatly outnumbered, withdrew from the city. Timur nonetheless took eighteen days to undermine its fortifications and effect its capture, afterward burying some thousands of its more stubborn defenders, who were Armenian Christians, alive in the moats. Then, instead of advancing farther into Asia Minor, he marched away southward, capturing successively Aleppo, Damascus, and Baghdad, which he razed to the ground, making pyramids of the severed heads of its defenders. It was not until the autumn of 1401 that Timur returned to the frontiers of Asia Minor. Here he settled into winter quarters and debated in his mind whether or not to renew his attack against the Ottoman Empire.

Bayezid meanwhile had done curiously little to counter any such threat. The loss of Sivas had been the first serious blow to befall him, the humiliating result, after a run of easy victories against petty princes, both in Europe and Asia, of his first encounter with a truly redoubtable enemy. Meeting his match for the first time, Bayezid appeared as one paralyzed, stunned by defeat, slow to react to the crisis now facing him. Doubtless his physical and mental initiative was undermined by increasing debauchery. Timur, away for more than a year, after his capture of Sivas, on his Syrian and Mesopotamian campaign, left his forward Armenian headquarters wide open to just such an attack as had earned for Bayezid the name of "the Thunderbolt." But the thunder was stilled and the lightning flashed no longer. Bayezid, showing none of his habitual swiftness of decision or action, neither retaliated against Timur nor sought to placate him. Where now was that resolution, those military and diplomatic skills which had won him victory in Europe?

In the summer of 1402, Timur finally decided to march against Bayezid. He was sought now as an ally by the Genoese, and other powers of Christian Europe, against the Ottomans. Since his conquest of Syria he no longer felt impelled to maintain solidarity with the other forces of Islam. Thus he moved his victorious army westward to Sivas. Only now, nearly two years after the initial loss of the city, did Bayezid bestir himself to abandon the blockade of Constantinople and transfer the bulk of his own army across into Asia. From Bursa he marched, in the scorching midsummer heat over the sun-baked, dried-up plateau of Anatolia, to the fortress of Angora, in the heart of the country.

It was a hard, well-disciplined force, equal in courage and military skill to that of Timur and his Tatars from Central Asia. But it was not, as in the past, wholly united or indeed wholly contented. A quarter of its soldiers were themselves Tatars, hence of questionable loyalty. The troops as a whole were parched and exhausted by their long marches, and Bayezid allowed them no time to rest or recuperate. A further source of discontent in the ranks was his parsimony, his refusal to open his treasury and the consequent arrears in their pay.

The Sultan's generals meanwhile disagreed with his plan of campaign. Faced with an enemy greatly superior in numbers, they urged that, according to traditional Ottoman military tactics, Bayezid should remain at first on the defensive, thus in a position to choose his own ground. Instead of going out to take the offensive against Timur, he should withdraw for several days into the mountains, resting his troops and obliging Timur to seek him out in the scorching heat of the plateau. But Bayezid, with an obstinacy which clouded all judgment and self-control, was impatient for a head-on encounter. Thus his army moved eastward along the road to Sivas, taking up an advance position by a bend in the River Halys from which to give battle when Timur should arrive.

Several days passed and Bayezid's scouts found no trace of him. Finally the news came that Timur had evaded and encircled the Turkish forces and was marching against them from the rear. From Sivas, avoiding the rough hilly country to the west, he had moved southward down the river valley to Kayseri, harvesting ripe grain for his troops on the way; then northward to a point by the walls of Angora, with the Turks now to the east of him. Meanwhile Bayezid, as an act of bravado in the face of an enemy whose swiftness he compared to the crawling of a snail, scorned all precautions by sending his troops on a great hunt for game. The surrounding country was waterless, and they died by the thousand from thirst and fatigue.

Timur, meanwhile, reconnoitering around Angora, came upon Bayezid's former base camp, now deserted. Here, pillaging the baggage and occupying tents that the Turks had left behind, the Tatar army made its headquarters, first damming and diverting for its use the waters of a stream that flowed into Angora. Timur also ordered the destruction and pollution of a spring in the path of the Turks, now advancing from the east in pursuit of him. Here he prepared to give battle. Thus it was that Bayezid, with a tired and thirsty army behind him, found himself obliged to meet an enemy entrenched before his own city of Angora, in the very position where he himself should have stayed to confront him. Here battle was joined in the great plain stretching away from the walls of the city, a battlefield already familiar in history.

The left wing of Bayezid's army, composed of Anatolian troops known to be loyal, was commanded by his eldest son, Suleiman; the rear guard by his next most favoured son, Mehmed; the right wing, composed of Serbians and other loyal European contingents, by his brother-in-law, the Serbian Stephen Lazarevitch. Bayezid himself took up his position in the center, with his Janissaries around him. But in drawing up his order of battle, he had in his blindness made one last cardinal blunder. On the familiar tactical principle of using an inferior force to take the first shock of the enemy's attack, he placed his Anatolian Tatar cavalry in the front line. The battle had hardly begun when they deserted and went over, as might well have been foreseen of troops conscripted to fight their own kinsfolk, to Timur. The Sultan thus lost at a single stroke a quarter of his total force.

Bayezid could now only order an attack from the left. To cover it, Suleiman launched his Anatolian horsemen on a cavalry charge. They fought with courage against a hail of arrows and the naphtha flames of "Greek fire." But they failed to break the Tatar ranks and finally fell back in disorder, with a loss of some fifteen thousand men. Timur's army thenceforward took the offensive, his cavalry pursuing the Turks out of sight on his right, breaking up the Serbs on his left after a "lion-like" resistance which won Timur's personal praise, and finally converging on the center where the Sultan stood alone with his Janissaries and the rest of the Ottoman infantry.

Thus outmaneuvered, outgeneralled, and forced on to the defensive, Bayezid was driven back slowly, step by step, onto a small hilltop. Here hour after hour he continued to fight, with his bodyguard and the remnants of his fugitive forces, until nightfall. Now that all was lost, his old stubborn courage surged up within him. "The Thunderbolt," wrote the Turkish historian, "continued to wield a heavy battle-axe. As a starving wolf scatters a flock of sheep, he scattered the enemy. Each blow of his redoubtable axe struck in such a way that there was no need for a second blow." Thus, still fighting, he was found by Timur's main forces as they returned to the scene of battle from their encirclement and rout of the rest of the Ottoman forces. Taking to his horse, he made a last attempt to escape over the hill through the ranks of the Tatar archers. But he was overtaken, unhorsed, captured, and bound, then led as a prisoner into the tent of Timur, who was quietly playing chess with his son.

Bayezid comported himself with dignity in the presence of his conqueror, who at first accorded him the honours due to a sovereign, but later sought to degrade him as a captive. While on the march through Anatolia, Timur had him carried in a litter with bars, compared by some to a cage, thus openly subjecting him to the ridicule of the Tatar soldiery and of his former Asiatic subjects. Legends of Timur's treatment of Bayezid abound: that he was kept in chains by night; that he was made to serve as Timur's footstool; that in appropriating Bayezid's harem Timur humiliated his Serbian wife, Despina, by obliging her to serve naked at the table before her former lord and his conqueror. His sufferings broke Bayezid's spirit and finally his mind. Within eight months he was dead from an apoplectic seizure —or perhaps by his own hand.

Bayezid had fallen through exceeding his limitations. He had sought to go beyond the Ghazi traditions of his forebears in Asia Minor and Europe. He had embarked, prematurely and without adequate resources, on the pursuit of an empire in the Moslem East, seeking to follow those worldwide conquering traditions of High Islam so dear to the theologians of the Holy City of Bursa. He had thus collided to his ruin with the world empire of Timur, who, until provoked, desired only, beyond his western frontiers, peaceful coexistence with the Ghazi Ottoman state.

Timur was quick to overrun Asia Minor. His Tatar hordes speedily took Bursa, bore off its young women, stabled their horses in its mosques, pillaged the city and burned it, but failed to capture Bayezid's son Suleiman, who escaped as they galloped up to the gates and reached Europe in safety. Timur in person then launched his forces against Smyrna, the last Christian stronghold, capturing the city in a mere two weeks, driving the Knights Hospitallers down to their galleys and thus out to sea toward Rhodes, decapitating the few that had failed to get on board and piling up their skulls into the customary pyramid. Here was a demonstration against the infidel, in the Ghazi tradition, calculated to win the approval of the Moslem world.

From Angora his troops had pursued the survivors of the Ottoman army as they fled in their tens of thousands across the plateau and through the mountains, down toward the Dardanelles. Here the Genoese and the Venetians, who had willingly ferried them across into Asia, now as willingly ferried them back into Europe, to the fury of Timur at such an act of "bad faith." They preferred the enemy they knew to the enemy they knew not. Such was a measure of the extent to which the Ottomans within two generations had rooted themselves in the Balkans, winning the tacit acceptance of its Christian populations as heirs to Byzantium. In Anatolia, Timur played off one against the other the four sons of Bayezid, who remained in his hands now as vassals, encouraging in each the hope of acknowledgment as heir to the Ottoman throne. He invested Suleiman as a Tatar vassal with the Ottoman territories of Europe.

Now that the future destinies of the Ottoman Empire lay in his power, Timur graciously accepted overtures from the powers of Europe. But when the Byzantine Emperor offered to acknowledge his sovereignty and pay him the consequent tribute, Timur responded with an order to prepare a fleet to ferry his soldiers across the Straits into Europe. This prompted the panic assumption that he intended to besiege Constantinople. But Timur had no designs against Europe; nor indeed against Anatolia, where he favoured the Ghazi traditions and restored the dispossessed local princes to their lands. Here he regarded his campaign as little more than a glorified raid. As an empire-builder his ambitions lay eastward. Soon after Bayezid's death in 1403, he left Asia Minor for Samarkand, not to return. He prepared for the conquest of China, but died on the way there, within two years of Bayezid, from a fever accelerated by fatigue and (in Gibbon's words) "the indiscreet use of iced water." His Tatar hordes too departed, leaving chaos behind them.

This major defeat in Anatolia might well have spelled the final disintegration of the short-lived Ottoman Empire—much as that of the Seljuks in Asia Minor had disintegrated through the earlier Mongol invasion. It led indeed to a decade of disruption which came at times close to anarchy, as conflicting internal forces fought each other for power. There was a danger that in the process the central authority might fall to the provincial beys, as had occurred in other Moslem states. Four sons of Bayezid competed for the imperial throne—later joined by a pretender who claimed to be a fifth. The claims of each were supported by his own group of adherents from among local dynasties, concerned for their privileges, while the Byzantine Emperor incited the candidate likeliest to benefit his own interests, and the Christian vassal states of the Balkans acted to regain some of their lands.

The imperial territory became broadly divided into two, between Europe on the one hand, where the eldest son, Suleiman, ruled from Adrianople, and Anatolia on the other, where the youngest son, Mehmed, ruled from Bursa. Aware that no empire could survive such a partition, each fought to extend his rule at the expense of the other, waging a recurrent civil war in which two other sons, Issa and Musa, joined. After Musa had killed Suleiman he was in his own turn suppressed by Mehmed, whom the Emperor called to his aid across the Bosporus, and who thus emerged as the final victor.

In 1413 he was enthroned as Sultan Mehmed I. He had the backing of two powerful forces: the Anatolian beys, whom his father, Bayezid, had alienated, and whom Timur had reestablished; and the Janissaries, exerting their influence on internal affairs for the first but by no means the last time in Ottoman history, to hail him as "the most just and most virtuous of Ottoman princes." So, after an interregnum of disorder and subversive decentralization, the strongest elements won the day. The central authority was once more established and the Ottoman state reintegrated in the person of Mehmed I.

Thanks to his provident statesmanship, throughout a reign of only eight years, the Ottoman Empire was now restored to stable foundations, coming to life with renewed unity and vigour—to the disappointment of Christendom—at the moment when its extinction seemed imminent. As the Byzantine Empire pursued its inexorable course of decline, the dynasty of Osman, no longer divided against itself, stood purged and revived, proving its powers of recuperation and survival with the emergence of new rulers of caliber. Within a generation it was to father the greatest of Ottoman conquerors, Mehmed II.

PART

II

THE NEW BYZANTIUM

((6))

MEHMED THE CONQUERER, DESTINED ULTIMATELY TO CAPTURE Constantinople, was the grandson of Mehmed I and the son of Murad II. His father, Murad, was an enlightened ruler who over a period of thirty years won the affection and respect of the Ottoman people for his spirit of honour and justice, his sincerity and simplicity, his effective charitable concern for their welfare. He was essentially a man of peace. But he had wars and threats of wars thrust continually upon him. He sought peace for his country that it might become at last internally ordered and stabilized, following the decade of disintegration which his father had arrested. He sought it also for himself, craving leisure and tranquillity to enjoy the pleasures not merely of the senses but of the mind and the spirit. Seeking to realize this side of his nature, he twice renounced his throne in his young son's favour, but was each time obliged to return to it.

From the outset of his reign Murad's quest for peace was foiled by his enemies both in Europe and in Asia, provoking him to action and arousing in him inherent qualities of martial vigour and military skill. At the same time he was at pains to spare his own soldiery, whenever possible, and was fair with his enemies in the negotiation and observance of treaties.

First, with the aid of his Janissaries and the support of the ulema, he defeated an internal revolt by a pretender to the sultanate who had taken refuge with the Emperor in his father's reign. Then he embarked on a siege of Constantinople, using for the first time cannon to bombard its walls, and movable towers from which to assault them. But the Greeks defended the city with a heroism inspired by a miraculous vision of the Holy Virgin, and Murad was obliged by a diversion in Asia to raise the siege, which was not to be renewed until the accession of his own son in the next generation. Meanwhile, on Manuel's death, Murad signed a new treaty with his successor, John VIII, effectively reprieving Constantinople, but reducing the Empire to a further stage of subjection, with little territory left to it beyond the walls of the city.

He now moved his forces across into Anatolia, where another rebel, his own younger brother, named Mustafa, confronted him, and where all the subject princes had risen in revolt. Mustafa had the forces of

Sultan Mehmed II (1451–81), the Conqueror

Karamania behind him but was swiftly defeated and hanged. His rebellion was the work of the "Grand Karaman," a turbulent vassal presuming to rival the "Grand Turk" for power. Twice more was he to do so and twice more to be defeated, but each time to be granted a treaty by Murad in which Karamania retained its vassal status and was not incorporated in the Ottoman Empire. Meanwhile he had brought under his control the remaining principalities of western Anatolia.

In Europe now two powers, Hungary and Venice, rivalled the Ottomans for the reversion of the fragments of the Byzantine Empire—the Hungarians dreaming of a Pan-Slav empire which would incorporate Constantinople, the Venetians seeking to clinch their command of the seas. Murad was obliged to take action against them when the Emperor sold to the Republic of Venice the important port of Salonika, for long a bone of contention between Ottomans and Greeks. In 1430 he assaulted and in due course captured the city, which was annexed, with its surroundings, to the Ottoman Empire—a serious loss to the Venetians. He restrained his soldiers from massacre of its inhabitants, and in a peace treaty conceded to the Venetians the right to circulate freely and pursue their trade at sea throughout his dominions, retaining without interference those islands and castles in the Peloponnese where the standard of St. Mark then flew.

The spirit of Hungarian aggression in the Balkans reawakened with the death, in 1437, of King Sigismund, without a male heir and with consequent dynastic interruption. Concerned to secure command of the territory south of the Danube, hence to strengthen Ottoman control over Serbia, Murad in the following year captured the strong fortress of Semendria, which he had previously permitted the Serbians to erect on the Danube, and drove out the despot George Brankovitch, whose increasing power he mistrusted and who now sought the assistance and alliance of Hungary. Murad failed, after a siege of some months, to capture Belgrade. But as a result of Sigismund's death he was able to secure his hold over Wallachia, and now resumed Ottoman raids across the Danube into Hungary. Hungary meanwhile, beset by internal strife as she sought a ruler, chose to come under the crown of Poland, whose monarch, Ladislas III, thus now ruled over both countries. There emerged to support him a Hungarian national hero Hunyadi, a warrior leader who was to be a scourge of the Turks for the next twenty years.

Hunyadi, otherwise John Corvinus Huniades, whom the Turks nicknamed Yanko, was a man of Rumanian noble background and mysterious parentage who came to govern, on behalf of a grateful King Ladislas, a large territory in Transylvania, and eventually to govern Hungary itself. To the Hungarians and Serbs he became the romantic "White Knight," leading his cavalry charges in shining silver armour, whose heroic feats of arms offered a timely hope for Eastern Christendom, promising to liberate it once and for all from the infidel Turks and restore it to unity. Defending some two hundred miles of the southern Hungarian frontier, he won several signal victories against the Ottoman forces, inflicting severe casualties upon them and stimulating the zeal of the Christians as their churches became adorned with captured Ottoman flags and trophies. It is believed that Hunyadi may in fact have been the natural son of King Sigismund, conceived in the course of his homeward retreat from the battle of Nicopolis. Be that as it may, he now strove to repeat history with a new crusade designed, as that of Sigismund had been, to drive the Turks out of Europe.

Receiving, at this late stage in history, no support from the West, beyond the blessing of the papal legate Cardinal Julian and his presence with the armies in person, the crusade drew its forces only from Hungary and Poland, later joined by Wallachia, with some assistance from the Balkan peoples, the Serbs, Bulgarians, Bosnians, and Albanians. Their advance nonetheless met with success. Crossing the Danube in 1443, they captured Nish, at great loss to its Turkish garrison, restored the despot George Brankovitch to his Serbian domains, occupied Sofia, then boldly marched in wintry weather right across the snow-covered, icebound Balkan mountain range to reach the Thracian plain beneath.

Their road through the passes was often blocked by the Turks with fallen rocks, and at one point the flanks of the mountains were flooded all night long with water to make walls and paths of ice. This march of the crusaders was a military feat seldom paralleled in history. But finally, after a victory on Christmas Day, they were defeated by the elements, with consequent problems of supply, and by increased Turkish pressure, so that Hunyadi ordered a retreat to Buda. Here his troops, worn out by the cold and reduced almost to skeletons by hunger, eventually arrived, led by King Ladislas, on foot, singing Christian hymns and brandishing Ottoman banners, to receive a triumphant welcome from the Hungarian people and to give thanks in the cathedral for the help of Providence at a moment of extreme peril.

Murad, the man of peace, had forborne from pursuit of the crusading forces beyond the Danube. He negotiated a ten-year truce at Szeged, by which Serbia and Wallachia were effectively freed from dependence on the Ottoman Empire, while the Hungarians agreed not to cross the Danube or to press claims on Bulgaria. The treaty was sworn by Ladislas on the Gospel and by Murad on the Koran.

Within his imperial frontiers Murad, now that unity was restored to the Ottoman state, had taken constructive steps to achieve a strong centralized government. He increased the numbers and expanded the field of the corps of the Janissaries as its main instrument, now recruited not only from among youths captured in battle but from among the indigenous Christian population in the various provinces. Amounting to some seven thousand men, they were now supported as pillars of the state by the Sultan's own *sipahis,* or cavalrymen, and a corps of military administrators, all likewise of slave origin. Making good the damage done by Bayezid, here, within as without, were stable foundations upon which the dynasty of Murad II could confidently build for the future.

He thus for the first time planned to withdraw from the cares of state into the life of seclusion he craved in his Asiatic palace at Magnesia. In preparation for this Murad summoned his twelve-year-old son Mehmed to Adrianople, to serve as governor of the European provinces of the Empire under the supervision of his Grand Vezir, Halil Chandarli Pasha. This was a step which aroused the misgivings of Halil and his fellow vezirs, who held that the boy, alert and precocious as he was for his years, was not yet ripe for such responsibilities of government.

Mehmed II, born under auspices held to be ominous during a plague which carried off two of his father's brothers, had been afflicted with an unhappy childhood and upbringing. He was the third son of a father who preferred his two elder half-brothers, Ali and Ahmed, and did not envisage him as a likely successor to the throne. Their respective mothers moreover were women of some birth and standing, whereas the mother of Mehmed was a slave girl, of undetermined but probably Christian origin. He thus had blood in his veins that may have accounted for characteristics in him contrasting with those of his father and grandfather.

Brought up largely by his nurse, he was taken from Adrianople at the age of two, with his brother Ali, to Amasya, where their fourteen-year-old elder brother acted as governor. This was a mountainous province of northern Anatolia between the central plateau and the Black Sea coast. It was a place inhabited by old and influential Ottoman families, into one of which Murad's father had married, and a religious center both for the Islamic establishment and for itinerant dervishes, heretics from Persia. It was the birthplace of Murad himself, whose custom it became, in common with that of certain later sultans, to send his sons, under the supervision of trusted officials, to such Asiatic provinces far from the capital, thus ensuring their isolation from the bulk of the people and from possible movements of revolt nearer home. Here was a form of insurance against sedition more civilized than the practice of imperial fratricide introduced by his grandfather Bayezid and later to be given the force of law by his son Mehmed himself.

But Mehmed's elder brothers were to die prematurely. Ahmed died suddenly in Amasya, while still in his teens. Mehmed succeeded him as governor of the province at the age of six, while his surviving brother Ali was transferred as governor to Magnesia. Two years later they changed places of government, at Murad's direction, and some years afterward Ali himself died, strangled under unexplained circumstances in his bed at Amasya, to the evident grief of his father, whose favourite son he was said to have been.

Mehmed, now heir apparent at the age of eleven, was recalled by his father from Magnesia to Adrianople. Here Murad was at once shocked by his lack of education. The boy's teachers had found him a difficult pupil, reluctant to learn, and in particular unresponsive to religious instruction. His father therefore chose as his instructor in the Koran and religious beliefs an illustrious mullah named Ahmed Kourani. Kurdish in origin, he had studied Islamic law and Koranic theology in Cairo and now taught at the noted seminary at Bursa.

It is recorded that the Sultan gave the teacher a rod, authorizing him to chastise the prince if it proved necessary. The mullah waited on him with the rod in his hand and said: "Your father has sent me to instruct you, but also to keep you in order if you refuse to obey me." Mehmed laughed at his words. Thereupon the mullah launched upon him such a shower of blows that from then onward he treated his teacher with considerable respect, soon learning from him the whole of the Koran. Taught by a series of such enlightened scholars and advisers, Mehmed grew up well versed in the affairs of the mind.

To this at the court of Adrianople was now to be added instruction in the affairs of state from his father and, on his retirement into Asia, from the Grand Vezir Halil and his entourage. Mehmed, haughty and precocious for his years, soon showed in his relations with Halil an arrogant determination to have his own way. Not long after his father's departure, he caused concern at Adrianople by his apparent support for a heretical religious movement in the person of a Persian missionary, leader of a dervish sect which had preached, among other unorthodox views, of an affinity between Islam and Christianity. Mehmed responded to the exalted ideas of the preacher. He befriended him at his court and by this example furthered his quest for a receptive audience among the people of the city.

This aroused the alarm and indignation of the religious establishment, led by the Grand Mufti, and of the Grand Vezir Halil, who was a Moslem of the old school. Catching out the Persian in an utterance of heresies, they apprehended him. But he escaped and took refuge with Mehmed in the Sultan's palace. Mehmed, however, was

The famous portrait of Mehmed the Conqueror by Gentile Bellini.

obliged to relinquish his protégé to the Mufti, who denounced him from the pulpit of the mosque, and so excited the feelings of the crowd against him that they burned him at the stake—the Mufti singeing his own beard by approaching too close to stoke the flames. The heretic's followers were likewise exterminated. The incident showed on the part of Mehmed a predilection for the Persians and for heterodox views characteristic of his enquiring disposition, but fraught with disturbing implications for the future. A bad start to the young heir's relationship with the Ottoman religious and civil establishment, here was an affront to his pride which sowed in him the seeds of a bitter resentment, and for which he was not to forgive Halil. Driven in on himself as Mehmed had been from childhood, such crises hardened his aloof disposition.

This not long afterward was a factor which contributed to a revolt of the Janissaries. Loyal and respectful as they were to their accepted master, Murad, they resented now having to take orders from his inexperienced and overbearing young son. They demanded an increase of pay. When this was at first refused they rose against him, initiating a serious fire which spread through Adrianople, consuming the bazaar quarters, and which was followed by pillage and massacre. A prime objective of their hostility was Mehmed's private counsellor, the eunuch Chihab-ed-Din Pasha, who was obliged to take refuge in the palace. In appeasement the increase in their pay was eventually granted.

The episode, however, widening still further the breach between Halil and Mehmed, was symptomatic of a new source of conflict which had been growing since Murad's reorganization of the Janissary draft system, and its expansion of the principle of the recruitment of Christians to the discharge not merely of military but of civil responsibilities. This was to lead to the development of a ruling institution in which Christian renegades, of whom Chihab-ed-Din was one, came to rise to the highest offices of state. Increasingly often they rose at the expense of the former Moslem ruling families, as epitomized by Halil Chandarli, who found themselves gradually excluded from power. It may indeed have been Halil who encouraged this revolt of the Janissaries against Chihab, to assert his own power and teach the young Mehmed a lesson. Here was a conflict between old and new, traditional Moslem and renegade Christian, which now threatened to be a divisive internal force in the administration of the empire. This may well have influenced Murad in his decision to retire from the scene, leaving Halil to cope with a problem in which he preferred not to become personally involved.

But this first retirement was to last for a mere three months. The time for it was not yet ripe. Hunyadi's campaign had aroused enthusiasm abroad, together with promises of support for the Christian cause which included a naval force to protect the passage of the Straits. There was a revulsion against the treaty with Murad. The Byzantine Emperor, mobilizing forces for a campaign in the Morea, wrote to Ladislas begging that the "shield of Christendom" should stand firm. Ladislas, instead of ratifying the treaty, announced his resolve to proceed with the crusade to "hurl back the infidel sect of Mohammed overseas." In this he was largely influenced by Julian, the papal cardinal legate.

Taking advantage of the knowledge that Murad was now safely away in Asia, moreover held there through the control of the Hellespont by a Christian naval squadron, Julian absolved Ladislas from the perjury of a "rash and sacrilegious oath to the enemies of the Christ," on the specious implication that no promise to an infidel was valid. The treaty, signed on the Gospel, was abjured in the name of the Holy Trinity, the Virgin Mary, St. Etienne, and St. Ladislas, and the aims of the crusaders sanctified "to follow in the path of glory and salvation." Thus an array was launched against the Ottomans, without a Serbian contingent, since the despot Brankovitch, having got what he wanted in the treaty, disapproved of its abrogation and pretended to remain neutral, but with a substantial force from Wallachia to make up half its strength. All were buoyed up with hopes of victory by the absence of the Sultan and his army abroad.

But in November, 1444, Murad suddenly appeared before them at Varna. Eluding the naval watch, benefitting from favourable winds, bribing the treacherous Genoese to provide transport, he had crossed the Straits with the support of shore batteries to confront the Christians with a force which outnumbered them by three to one. In the ensuing battle the "palisade" of his Janissaries repulsed the main Christian attack and secured victory, with many losses on either side. Ladislas was unhorsed and put to death on the field, his head in its helmet raised upon a lance, while another lance beside it transfixed a copy of the broken treaty, to serve as a lesson in Christian perfidy for the Ottoman troops. Cardinal Julian, who had inspired it, took flight and was never seen again, alive or dead. Hunyadi escaped with Vlad Dracul, the Wallachian leader, who paid off an old score against him by holding him prisoner for a while in Wallachia. After the battle the head of King Ladislas was sent, preserved in honey, to Bursa, the original capital of the Ottoman Empire, where it was cleansed in the river, then fixed once more to a lance and borne through the streets.

Murad's victory had regained for him control of all the territory up to the Danube. He now felt able to retire in a more permanent sense. This time, at the end of 1444, he formally abdicated the throne in favour of Mehmed, who was now to rule not simply as governor in Europe, as before, but with full powers as Sultan. Murad took over as his personal domain, but under his son's jurisdiction, a territory in three districts of Anatolia, around Magnesia. He established himself in delectable surroundings, building a new palace with fine gardens overlooking a broad valley. Here in the company of poets, mystics, theologians, and men of letters, he sought to lead the ideal life of the religious fraternity, as his Ghazi ancestors had done, studying, writing, engaging in contemplation and in dervish devotions. He sought to inspire the development of the Turkish language as a medium of cultural expression, distinct from Persian and Arabic. He encouraged a new movement in Turkish historical studies, which became concerned, in a "romantic" fashion, with the exploits of the illustrious forebears of Osman and the origins of the ancestral Oghuz tribe. Foreign diplomatists, from whom he received occasional visits, remarked that he received them in no official reception rooms, but in his own private apartments.

But by the spring of 1446 he was back once more in Adrianople, summoned at the instance of Halil—whose relations with the young Mehmed had gone from bad to worse—and welcomed by the people of the city, responsive as always to Murad's simple and approachable ways. The occasion for this second return seems to have been an impolitic and impractical plan by his son for an attack on Constantinople, at a time when the Ottoman armies were engaged in operations both on the Greek and on the Albanian frontiers. This once again was a product of the conflict within the governing class, between Halil, who pursued peace, and a group of commanders who sought war, and who found an eager enough audience in the belligerent young heir to the throne. They failed, however, to override and break the power of Halil, who had the support of the Janissaries, and also of Murad himself, who was not again to abdicate. It was Mehmed who now retired to Magnesia, there to brood on his wrongs and contain his frustrated ambitions, while his father remained on the throne until his death five years later.

War claimed Murad's reluctant attention once more. Hungary, for the present, was quiescent. But trouble threatened through a revival of the power of the Byzantine despots on the Morea, which obliged Murad to march into Greece. Here he stormed with success the great fortified wall of the Hexamilion, which had been built to defend the Isthmus of Corinth, and sent his forces to ravage the country beyond it. He reduced the Greek despots to effective vassaldom and restored to power his Latin vassals, whom the Greeks had expelled.

Further conflict now arose in Albania, where a new champion of resistance to the Turk, comparable to Hunyadi in Hungary, had arisen. He was George Kastriota, son of an Albanian Christian vassal prince, who had been reared and educated as a hostage at the Sultan's court, been converted to Islam, and served in the Ottoman army. Here he received the name of Iskander Beg, or Lord Alexander, which caused him to be known as Skanderbeg. Proving to be a valiant and patriotic warrior, he deserted the Turks to fight for his own faith and country, leading his martial compatriots in a resistance which coincided with that of Hunyadi. In 1448 the two leaders joined forces in a further Hungarian offensive against the Turks, supported also by Serbia and Bosnia. Murad swiftly defeated them, on the historic battlefield of Kossovo, where sixty years earlier his forebear Murad I had met his death at the moment of victory against the Serbs and Hungarians. This defeat spelled the end of Serbian independence. The military power of Hungary was crippled for some time to come. Bosnia became a vassal state of the Ottomans. But in Albania Skanderbeg, from his impregnable fortress of Croia, held out by effective guerrilla warfare against all attempts at conquest, to the humiliation of Murad in his declining years, and under Mehmed for twenty years to come. Mehmed meanwhile at Magnesia had become attached to a slave girl, Gülbehar, presumed to be of Albanian or Greek Christian origin, who bore him a son, later to reign as Bayezid II. Murad considered her an unworthy bride for him dynastically, and later, when the young heir had reached the age of seventeen, arranged for him a more appropriate marriage, with due celebrations, to Sitt Hanum, the daughter of an important Turcoman prince. But Mehmed never cared for her; she bore him no children; and when he eventually moved his court to Constantinople she was left behind, neglected in the palace harem in Adrianople. Nor did any woman again play more than a marginal part in his otherwise essentially masculine way of life.

In his later years Murad grew more friendly toward his son, who paid visits to Adrianople and accompanied him on several campaigns. He received his baptism of fire in command of the Anatolian troops at the battle of Kossovo and fought with his father in the unsuccessful siege of Croia in Albania, in 1450. When Murad died of apoplexy in the following year, Mehmed was at Magnesia. On receiving the news, it is recounted, he immediately jumped on his Arab horse and rode northward to the Hellespont with the words "Whoever loves me, let him follow me!"

He stopped for two days at Gallipoli to await the arrival of his suite, then proceeded to Adrianople. There in the presence of a large assembly he mounted his throne. Observing that Halil and his father's closest friend and second vezir, Ishak Pasha, stood a trifle apart, as though nervous of their future, he bade them, through the chief eunuch, to take their accustomed places. He then confirmed

Halil in his post and appointed Ishak governor of Anatolia, with instructions to take his father's body to Bursa.

Murad's widow, daughter of a noble Ottoman family, then came to offer him condolences on his father's death and congratulations on his own accession. While she was doing so, her infant son, Ahmed, was smothered in his bath at his orders—a precautionary act of imperial fratricide by the Sultan who was son of a slave girl. The bereaved mother was sent to Anatolia as the enforced bride of the governor, Ishak Pasha.

Later, at Bursa, Mehmed was confronted once more with a revolt of the Janissaries. He suppressed it vigorously, expelling many from the corps, but took the precaution of raising the salaries of the rest, a shrewd enough act of expediency which nonetheless set an awkward precedent for sultans to come. At the same time he formed a number of new units from among the palace huntsmen and falconers, a strong force on which he was to draw for the appointment of aghas and for the service of his own household. Thus reorganized, the Janissaries developed into a more powerful nucleus of the Ottoman army than ever before. Soon Mehmed was ready to launch the great enterprise on which he had for long been determined—the siege of Constantinople.

((7))

THE CHRISTIAN POWERS HAD FORMED NO HIGH OPINION OF THE young Sultan, now Mehmed II. Judging him by the failures of his early career, they saw him still as an inexperienced youth, of little account, who was hardly likely to add to his father's conquests. But Mehmed was growing up into a personage of consequence. Short in build but strong and handsome, he had a dignified presence and a courteous but reserved disposition. Aquiline in features, with a penetrating gaze, he was cold and secretive in character. He thus inspired unease in those around him, but won their respect for an alert intelligence, an indomitable energy, and a relentless sense of purpose, the driving forces of a calculated ambition to achieve at any cost absolute power. It suited him at the start of his reign to give an impression of peaceful intentions.

"Peace was on his lips," writes Gibbon, "but war was in his heart." Receiving foreign envoys, he showed a willingness to confirm his father's treaty relations—with the Venetians and the Genoese, with Hunyadi, with Serbia, Wallachia, Ragusa, the Aegean islands, the Knights of Rhodes, even the monastic community of Mount Athos. The ambassadors of the Emperor Constantine met with an initial friendly reception from the Sultan, with an oath to respect Byzantine territory and a promise to pay for the maintenance in detention at Constantinople of his kinsman, the pretender Orkhan (who was Bayezid's grandson), with the revenues of certain Greek towns in the Struma Valley.

But subsequent envoys to his camp in Asia Minor were unwise enough to take up a truculent attitude, complaining that these moneys had not been paid, and even demanding an increase, with an implied threat to the Sultan of the use they could make of the pretender. At this the Grand Vezir, Halil, who knew his young master as they did not, gave them, as quoted by Gibbon, an outspoken warning:

> "Ye foolish and miserable Romans, we know your devices and ye are ignorant of your own danger! The scrupulous Amurath is no more; his throne is occupied by a young conqueror, whom no laws can bind and no obstacles can resist. . . . Why do ye seek to affright us by vain and indirect menaces? Release the fugitive Orkhan, crown him Sultan of Romania; call the Hungarians from beyond the Danube; arm against us

This W. H. Bartlett engraving is reproduced from J. C. H. Pardoe, *The Beauties of the Bosphorus,* London, 1839.

The castles of Europe (Rumeli Hisari on right) and Asia (Anadolu Hisari on left). Bayezid I built the latter; and a half century later, in the winter of 1451–52, Mehmed II built Rumeli Hisari in four and a half months and named it Boghaz Kesen, meaning "the cutter of the strait." The castles by design stand opposite each other at a point where, at 2,300 feet, the Bosporus is at its narrowest.

the nations of the West; and be assured that you will only provoke and precipitate your ruin."

The Sultan soothed the envoys with soft words. But the Emperor had given him a pretext for disregarding his former oath to respect imperial territory. Back at Adrianople, he ordered the expulsion of the Greeks from the Struma towns and the confiscation of their revenues. On his return to Asia Minor, having previously crossed the Bosporus at its narrowest point from a castle built on the Asiatic side by Sultan Bayezid at Anadolu Hisar, he gave orders for the building of a castle on the European side just opposite, in Byzantine territory. This would secure for him control of the Straits and provide him with a base for his projected siege of Constantinople.

The Emperor at once sent an embassy to protest this violation of the treaty between them, reminding Mehmed that Bayezid had asked the Emperor's permission before building his own castle. But the Sultan contemptuously refused to receive his ambassadors. When work on the fortress began, the Emperor sent further ambassadors, bringing gifts and supplies of food and drink, to request protection for the Greek villages on the Bosporus. Again the Sultan disregarded them. When a final embassy arrived, requesting an assurance that the building of the castle did not presage an attack on Constantinople, the Sultan imprisoned the ambassadors and cut off their heads. This was tantamount to a declaration of war. Fear reigned henceforward in Constantinople: "This is the end of the city," the people lamented, "the end of our race. These are the days of the Anti-Christ."

During the winter of 1451 the Sultan ordered the recruitment of a labour force of some five thousand masons and other workmen from all the provinces of his empire. Building materials were requisitioned from far and wide, and in the following spring churches and monasteries were demolished to clear the site and its surroundings and to provide the builders with masonry. The Sultan himself planned the walls of the fortress and arrived in the spring to supervise and expedite the work of construction. Within four and a half months it was finished and named Boghaz Kesen, meaning "the cutter of the Strait" or "of the Throat." The Greeks were to call it Rumeli Hisar, "the castle of Romeland"—in contrast with the opposing Anadolu Hisar, "the castle of Anatolia."

When it was completed the Sultan marched with his army to the walls of Constantinople itself, where he spent three days reconnoitering the fortifications. Then he returned for the winter to his court at Adrianople, garrisoning the castle with a force of five hundred men. He left orders that every vessel passing through the Straits, in either direction, should be obliged to lower its sails and anchor before the castle, to obtain authorization to continue its voyage and to pay for the right of passage. In the event of a refusal, the ship would be sunk by the castle's artillery, three immense cannons strategically placed on a tower near the water. Each was capable of discharging a stone cannonball six hundred pounds in weight.

These weapons were the handiwork of a Hungarian engineer named Urban, an expert metal-caster who specialized in the manufacture of artillery. He had first offered his services to the Emperor, who proved unable to give him the pay or the materials he needed. So he offered them instead to the Sultan, boasting of his capacity to make a cannon that could raze the walls not only of Byzantium but of Babylon itself. Mehmed, interested in every new development of military science, was determined to equip his forces with the most up-to-date armaments available. He was forever studying technical manuals on the construction of modern fortresses and siege machines, and consulting foreign experts on armaments whom he had drawn to his court. Thus he now immediately engaged Urban at a high salary and as a first test of his skill ordered him to make a cannon for the tower of the new fortress of Boghaz Kesen with sufficient range to command the Bosporus. Ready in three months, it rose to the test in spectacular fashion when a Venetian ship passed through the channel with a cargo of grain on the way to Constantinople and omitted to stop. She was immediately sunk by a direct hit from a cannonball.

Mehmed then ordered Urban to make for him, in a foundry at Adrianople, another cannon twice as large. When it was ready to be tested, a detachment of seven hundred men was appointed to service and transport it, equipped with fifteen pairs of oxen, which were only just able to move it. The monster weapon, measuring more than twenty-six feet in length and eight inches in diameter, was loaded with a twelve-hundredweight cannonball. The inhabitants were warned not to take fright from the noise of its firing. The fuse was then lit and the cannon was fired, from a point near the Sultan's new palace. The blast of the explosion was heard from some ten miles off, while the ball sped for a mile before burying itself in the earth to a depth of six feet.

Delighted with the success of these trials, the Sultan ordered the levelling of the road and the strengthening of its bridges, so that in the spring the cannon could be transported to a point outside the walls of Constantinople. Meanwhile other but smaller cannons were cast in the Sultan's foundries. He thus created a force of artillery, fired by gunpowder, such as the East had not yet seen, though it had been familiar in the West for a century past. Against it the stone walls of the capital, dating from the Middle Ages and earlier, would surely no longer furnish an adequate means of defense.

Throughout the winter of 1452 the Sultan was wholly occupied with preparations for his siege of the city. Sleepless, he would spend all night poring over drawings of its defenses, planning his lines of attack, the position to be occupied by his troops, the emplacements for his siege machines, his batteries, his mines. He would walk at midnight disguised as an ordinary soldier, with a pair of companions, through the streets of Adrianople, to sound out the spirit of his people and soldiery. If any man ventured to recognize and salute him, Mehmed, whose disregard of human life was proverbial, would instantly stab him to death. One night in the small hours he sent for Halil, the Grand Vezir, who, uneasy as to his position, took the precaution of taking with him a dish of gold coins. Asked what they were for, Halil replied that it was usual for the Sultan's servants to bring gifts when summoned unexpectedly by their master. Mehmed waved the dish aside, saying, "I want only one thing. Give me Constantinople." He then informed him that the siege would start as soon as possible. Dismissing him, he returned once more to his plans.

The army he was assembling in Thrace, from every province of his empire, amounted eventually to some hundred thousand men, including twenty thousand irregulars. Its hard core consisted of twelve thousand Janissaries. The Sultan saw in person to the army's equipment, employing armouries throughout his domains to make breastplates, shields and helmets, javelins, swords and arrows, while his engineers made catapults and battering rams. Against this force the Greeks in Constantinople, whose population was now reduced to less than fifty thousand, would only put up a force of some seven thousand defenders. This included about two thousand foreigners, principally Venetians and Genoese, who rallied to their aid "for the honour of God and Christendom," together with the crews of the ships in the Golden Horn. With these troops they had fourteen miles of walls to defend, moreover with light cannon alone.

They were encouraged only by the timely arrival, with seven hundred men, of a Genoese expert in the defense of walled cities, Giovanni Giustiniani, whom the Emperor appointed commander-in-chief and who at once set to work, with the unflagging aid of the population, to strengthen the walls, clear the moats, and improve the defenses in general. Meanwhile all arms were collected together for redistribution where most required. Short not only of men but of money, the Emperor set up a defense fund to which private persons, monasteries, and churches contributed, while silver plate was melted down in the churches to strike coinage.

The Sultan was fully aware that previous sieges of Constantinople had failed because the city was attacked from the landward side only. The Byzantines had always profited by command of the sea, and had thus been able to bring in supplies of water. The Turks, for their part, had been dependent on Christian ships to transport their troops from

Asia. Thus, as Mehmed clearly saw, it was vital to assemble not only a land but a naval force. To this, appreciating the importance of sea power, he gave his own especial attention. The resulting fleet, composed not only of old ships but of new, rapidly constructed in the Aegean shipyards, amounted to 125 vessels of differing sizes, together with various subsidiary craft.

When, in the spring of 1453, this armada, commanded by a Bulgarian admiral, sailed up from Gallipoli to cruise in the Sea of Marmara, the Greeks realized to their surprise and consternation that the Turks had acquired a fleet which outnumbered their own five times over. The Sultan, summoning his council of ministers to reveal his plans for war and obtain their sanction, was able to assure them that he now had command of the sea. Despite past achievements the Ottoman Empire, he insisted, would never be secure until it held Constantinople. Nor, for a number of reasons, was the city impregnable. For himself, he concluded, if he could not rule an empire which contained Constantinople, he would prefer not to rule an empire at all. The council gave him their unanimous support.

He had the support also of the prophets. The Prophet Mohammed himself, it was generally believed by the Sultan's army, would grant a special place in Paradise to the first soldier who should enter the city. Had he not prophesied: "They shall conquer Qostantiniya. Glory be to the prince and to the army that shall achieve it"? Often the Sultan had declared that he would be that prince, triumphing over the infidel in the name of Islam.

The Greeks, for their part, were discouraged throughout the long hard winter by such portents as earthquakes, torrential rains, floods, lightning, and shooting stars, seeming even more ominously to foreshadow the end of their empire and the coming of Anti-Christ. Before Christmas a solemn service was held in the great church of Hagia Sophia, at which the union between the Greek and Latin churches, previously agreed in Florence, was proclaimed. But the Greek congregation showed little inclination to accept it, and few Greeks thereafter would enter the church, where only the clergy supporting union were permitted to serve.

With the coming of spring, the Sultan started to march his great army through Thrace to the walls of the city, whither his heavy artillery had preceded him and where he arrived with his last detachment on April 2, 1453, Easter Monday. He established his headquarters on an eminence confronting the central point of the land walls, with his Janissaries camped around him, and the monster cannon with two smaller pieces in a nearby emplacement. The Emperor took up his position in front of the Sultan's, by the Gate of St. Romanus, with Genoese troops under Giustiniani on his flanks. To show that he had also Venetian Christian support, he paraded a thousand of his Venetian sailors, in their distinctive uniforms, along the walls, for all the Turks to see.

Diplomatic exchanges with the Greeks had come to nothing, and the Emperor wrote to the Sultan:

> As it is clear that you desire war more than peace, since I cannot satisfy you either by my protestations of sincerity, or by my readiness to swear allegiance, so let it be according to your desire. I turn now and look to God alone. Should it be his will that the city be yours, where is he who can oppose it? If he should inspire you with a desire for Peace, I shall be only too happy. However I release you from all your oaths and treaties with me, and, closing the gates of my capital, I will defend my people to the last drop of my blood. Reign in happiness with the All-Just, the Supreme God calls us both before his judgment seat.

So the gates of the city were closed and the bridges across the moat demolished. For the defense of the seawalls a chain of wooden floats was stretched, under Genoese supervision, across the entrance to the harbour of the Golden Horn, protecting the twenty-six ships inside it. Previously seven ships, six Cretan and one Venetian, had secretly sailed away to avoid the siege with seven hundred Italians on board them. But there were no other such deserters. Throughout Holy Week the people prayed in their churches for deliverance. When it was over, the Sultan, in conformity with Islamic law, sent in messengers with a flag of truce and a final offer of peace. In return for their voluntary surrender, he offered the inhabitants freedom of life and property under Ottoman protection. They refused to surrender. Thus on April 6 the bombardment began. A week later it was intensified, and it was to continue without a break for six weeks.

The Sultan had been counting on artillery rather than manpower to breach the walls of the city—not only cannon and mortars but catapults. His forces did not, however, make rapid progress. Though the walls were at many points destroyed by the great cannonballs and a number of towers demolished, no decisive breach was effected, while a four-hour assault by the Ottoman troops was a failure. The Greeks, under Giustiniani, were quick to repair the damage and to strengthen the weakened portions, even using for the purpose bales of wool and sheets of leather, but where the threat was greatest constructing a stockade from planks of wood and barrels of earth.

Nor was the attack more effective at sea, where the Sultan's ships twice failed to force the boom across the Golden Horn. Moreover, in the middle of April three Genoese galleys, laden with arms and supplies and accompanied by a Greek transport from Sicily, were able to sail through the Dardanelles, and appeared before the city. Informed of their arrival, the Sultan rode to give orders to his admiral in person. He must capture and sink the ships and if he failed to do so, must not return alive. Throughout the day a naval battle raged, in full view of the city's inhabitants. But the Christian ships, aided by superior armaments and seamanship, succeeded in eluding the Turks, and safely entered the shelter of the Golden Horn. The Sultan, watching the defeat of his ships from the shore of the Bosporus, grew so enraged that he rode his horse into the water, and for all his ignorance of seamanship started to shout curses and commands to the admiral and his crews, but without avail. After the battle he raged against the admiral, had him flogged, and threatened to impale him. Instead, he relieved him of his command and confiscated his personal possessions, which were distributed among the Janissaries.

Mehmed had recognized that Constantinople could not be captured by land attack alone; and now his sea attack had failed. To remedy this he formed the ingenious idea, probably put into his head by an Italian in his service, of transporting his ships overland, from the Bosporus to the Golden Horn, and so outflanking the boom across it. His engineers built a road for the purpose, up a valley, over a ridge two hundred feet above sea level, and then down another valley to the harbour. Along its whole length it was laid with a track of greased timbers, to carry metal-wheeled cradles. On these the ships were made fast, then lifted out of the water by pulleys, and drawn overland by teams of oxen.

Sails were hoisted, flags were flown, and the oarsmen waved their oars in the air, creating, for the astonished Christian sailors and watchmen, the illusion of a seaborne fleet moving down the hill toward their harbour. There, within the Greek naval defenses, some seventy Turkish ships soon lay afloat on the waters of the Golden Horn. An attempt by the Venetians and Genoese to launch light armed boats in among them, followed by two large galleys, failed through lack of surprise and the consequent fire of the Turkish shore batteries, which sank two ships. The Greeks thus lost control of the Golden Horn, where the Turks could now operate to their rear. They were able to encircle and control the Genoese in Pera; to build a pontoon bridge across the harbour, above the city, and so to strengthen their communications; to threaten the harbour walls and so to weaken the defense of both harbour and land walls.

No immediate land assault followed this Turkish naval victory, only a harassment of the enemy on both fronts. Within the city provisions had run low and a supply fleet from Venice failed to materialize. The morale of the defenders was strained. In the absence of help from the Christian West, there were those who tried to persuade the Emperor to leave the city and set up a resistance outside. But he refused with the words "It is impossible for me to go away: how could I leave the

The Wall of Theodosius was part of the fourteen miles of walls that figured in the Byzantine defense of Istanbul. This picture represents a much later time than that of the Ottoman conquest of the city in 1453. Note the minarets.

Reproduced from Allom and Walsh, *Constantinople*.

churches of our Lord, and His servants the clergy, and the throne, and my people in such a plight? . . . I pray you, my friends, in future do not say to me anything else but 'Nay, Sire, do not leave us.' Never will I leave you." He preferred to "follow the example of the Good Shepherd who lays down his life for his sheep."

But after nearly seven weeks of siege, with the most modern available armaments, no Turkish soldier had yet set foot in the city. An attempt to mine the walls and to bridge the moat resulted in failure. Operations in the Golden Horn were inconclusive. At this juncture the Grand Vezir, Halil, whose support for the siege had from the start been lukewarm, persuaded the Sultan, with the support of his older and in opposition to his younger colleagues, to make a final bid for peace with the Greeks. Through an emissary he proposed to the Emperor the choice between the payment of a heavy annual tribute or the abandonment of the city, with free evacuation for its citizens and all their possessions, and a kingdom in the Peloponnese for himself. The Emperor refused both. The Sultan retorted that no choice was now left for the Greeks but surrender, death by the sword, or conversion to Islam.

He announced plans for a final all-out assault on the walls, to take place on Tuesday, May 29. On the preceding Sunday he rode through the ranks of his army, accompanied by heralds who proclaimed that according to Islamic custom, the soldiers would be allowed three days in which to pillage the city, whose treasure would be fairly apportioned among them. The first to scale the walls would be rewarded with fiefs and high posts in the administration. Only the buildings and the walls would be reserved for the Sultan himself. The defenders within the city could hear shouts of joy from the troops outside and their cry: "There is no God but God, and Mohammed is His Prophet." Through the night the Turks worked to fill the moats and pile arms, to the music of pipes and trumpets, and to the light of flares and torches so bright at first as to suggest, from within the darkened city, that the Turkish camp was on fire. Guessing the true reason, the Greeks could only kneel and pray.

Throughout the next day there reigned without the walls a total and ominous silence, as the Turkish forces rested before the coming assault. Within them it was broken by the pealing of church bells and the sounding of gongs, as icons and sacred relics were carried through the streets and around the walls in procession and prayer. The Sultan, after a general tour of inspection, called his ministers and commanders to his tent. For centuries, he recalled to them, it had been a sacred duty of the faithful to capture the Christian capital, and the traditions promised success. Tomorrow he would send wave after wave of his men to the attack till from weariness and despair the defenders would yield. He exhorted his officers to display courage and maintain discipline.

The Emperor, addressing his own leaders, said that a man should always be ready to die for his faith, his country, his family, and his sovereign. Now they must be ready to die for all four. He spoke of the glories and traditions of the great imperial city, the perfidy of the infidel Sultan who sought to destroy the True Faith and install a false prophet in the seat of Christ. Let them prove worthy of their ancestors, the ancient heroes of Greece and Rome. Let them be brave and steadfast. With the help of God they would be victorious. Such, in Gibbon's words, was "the funeral oration of the Roman Empire."

In the small hours of the morning of May 29, 1453, the Sultan's offensive was launched, with a sudden pandemonium of sound: shrill battle cries amid the booming of cannon, the clashing of cymbals, the blasting of trumpets, the wailing of fifes from one end of the walls to the other. Instantly it discorded with the clang of church bells as the watchmen gave the alarm and the belfries spread it throughout the city, so that all should know that the battle had started. The fighting men ran to their posts, the women hurrying after them to carry stones and beams needed for the walls, while the old people and children crowded from their houses into the churches, to confess and communicate in a last intercession for their city's salvation. Until dawn the congregations watched and prayed.

Meanwhile the Sultan's attack on the walls came in three successive waves. First was the polyglot force of irregulars, the *bashi-bazouks,* spurred on with thongs and iron rods, lest they waver, by a line of military police. Pitted against troops better armed and trained than themselves, they nonetheless fought for nearly two hours, then were ordered by Mehmed to retire, having performed their function by initially wearying the enemy.

Next came a well-armed and well-disciplined assault by the Anatolian regimental troops. Once again the church bells gave the alarm, but this time their clangour was drowned by the thunder of the monster cannon and the rest of the heavy artillery as they pounded the walls, while the troops flung themselves at the stockade built under Giustiniani's direction from planks of wood and barrels of earth, to fill a gap in the walls made by an earlier bombardment. Clambering over one another to fix ladders against it and fight their way over the top, they were met by showers of stones from the defenders, and engaged in hand-to-hand fighting. Their numbers were too great for so narrow a front, and their losses were heavy. But an hour before dawn a ball from Urban's great cannon scored a direct hit on the stockade and demolished a large stretch of it. A band of three hundred Turks rushed wildly through the gap, crying that the city was theirs. But a detachment of Greeks, led by the Emperor in person, closed in on them, slaughtering many and forcing the rest back into the moat.

The Sultan, who had been urging on the assailants with an iron mace in his hand, alternately praising and threatening them, was indignant at this reverse. Nevertheless the time had come, according to plan, to launch into battle his Janissaries, who had been held in reserve for the main assault. Without delay they now advanced on the stockade at the double, spurred on by martial music and strictly keeping their ranks in face of a shower of missiles. Mehmed himself led them as far as the moat, then stood there as one wave of them followed another, shouting words of encouragement. After an hour of hand-to-hand fighting they had still made little headway The Christians, who had fought for four hours with hardly a respite, continued to fight with desperation.

Then two fatal misfortunes befell them. First, a small postern gate, the Kerkoporta, in the northern corner of the walls, was inadvertently left open after a sortie against the Turkish flank, and before it could be closed a band of Turks ran through it and began to climb up to the tower above. They could have been dealt with had it not been for a second disaster. Giustiniani was severely wounded at close range by a shot which pierced his breastplate. In great pain, he lost courage and begged to be taken from the battlefield. In vain did the Emperor plead with him: "Do not abandon me at this moment of danger. It is on you that the salvation of this city depends." The inner gate was opened, and his men carried him through the streets of the city to the Golden Horn, where he was placed on a Genoese ship. His Genoese troops saw him go, and many followed him, jumping to the conclusion that the battle was lost.

Demoralization and panic set in. Swift to take advantage of it, the Sultan cried, "The city is ours," and ordered a last charge of his Janissaries at the St. Romanus Gate. It was led by an Anatolian giant named Hassan, who fought his way, followed by others, to the top of the stockade. Forced to his knees, he was killed, together with half his comrades. But the remainder held the stockade and were soon joined by other Janissaries, who drove the Greeks from it, firing down upon them and slaughtering them below. Many Janissaries thus reached the inner wall and climbed up it without opposition. At the same time Turkish flags were seen flying from the tower above the postern gate, and the general cry went up: "The city is taken!"

The Emperor meanwhile had galloped to the postern gate. But here the confusion was now such that it was too late to close it, and the Turks poured through, with few Genoese left to resist them. Constantine galloped back to join in the main engagement at the St. Romanus Gate, where the Turks were now streaming through the breaches in the stockade. After a last attempt to rally the Greeks, the Emperor saw that the battle was lost. Exclaiming, "The city is taken and I am still alive," he dismounted from his horse, tore off his insignia, plunged headlong into the mêlée of the oncoming Janissaries, and was never seen again, alive or dead. "The prudent despair of Constantine," as Gibbon describes it, "cast away the purple; amidst the tumult he fell by an unknown hand, and his body was buried under a mountain of the slain."

After a disciplined march through the gates, the conquering army broke its ranks and the soldiery swarmed through the streets of the city in the orgy of slaughter and pillage to which custom entitled them, sacking churches, monasteries, and convents, plundering palaces and houses, carrying off not only their contents but their inhabitants. Greeks fled in their thousands toward the great church of Hagia Sophia:

> and in an hour [writes the historian Michael Ducas] the whole huge sanctuary was full of men and women . . . an immeasurable multitude. And shutting the gate, they stood there fervently hoping for deliverance by the angel. Then—fighting all about, killing, taking prisoners—the Turks came to the church, when the first hour of the day was not yet flown. And when they found the doors shut, they battered them with axes, without compunction.

While the priests continued to chant at the altar, most of the worshippers were tied together with vests and scarves, torn off the women, for ropes, and so herded through the streets to the bivouacs of the soldiers, who quarrelled fiercely for possession of the comelier girls and youths, and the nine richly clad senators.

Sultan Mehmed delayed his own triumphal entry into the city he had conquered until the late afternoon of that day. Then, escorted by his bodyguard of Janissaries and followed by his ministers, he rode slowly through the streets, straight to the church of Hagia Sophia. Dismounting on the threshold, he stooped down and, with oriental symbolism, picked up a handful of earth, which he poured over his head as an act of humility to his God. Entering the church, he walked toward the altar. On the way he noticed a Turkish soldier hacking at a piece of the marble pavement. The Sultan turned on him and asked why he thus destroyed the floor. "For the sake of the Faith," he replied. The Sultan then struck him with his sword, saying: "For you the treasures and the prisoners are enough. The buildings of the city fall to me." The Turk was dragged away by his feet and flung outside.

After he had released a few Greeks still crouching in corners, and let the priests go free, Mehmed gave orders that the church be turned into a mosque. A Moslem divine climbed into the pulpit and recited a prayer. The Sultan himself then mounted the steps of the altar and did obeisance to Allah, the One God, who had brought him victory. The streets were quiet as he emerged from the building. Order was restored; a single day's looting had been a sufficient reward for the soldiery. The Sultan rode across the square to the much-ruined imperial palace, where he recalled the lines of a Persian poet: "The spider weaves the curtains in the palace of the Caesars; the owl calls the watches in Afrasiab's towers."

((8))

THE FALL OF CONSTANTINOPLE STRUCK WESTERN CHRISTENDOM with a sense of doom. Lamentations arose from all those lands which had done so little to save it—the more so as an eleventh-hour effort to do so, with a papal armada of Venetian galleys, had failed to penetrate farther than the shores of the Aegean. Too late now, Christians awoke to the loss of this last bastion, behind which the West had for so long sheltered and squabbled in false security. Here surely was a calamity which threatened Western civilization itself. Such were the emotions engendered by the fall of the city. In impulse they were psychological. In effect Constantinople had been lost for a century past; nor at this eleventh hour could its fall have, in any event, been long delayed. But the shock of the actual event was nonetheless great to the people of the West for the fact that, preoccupied with their own local concerns, they had failed to foresee it, remaining blind to the military realities inherent in a garrison so immeasurably outnumbered and outgunned within medieval walls by a great modern army. The Ottoman occupation of the bulk of southeastern Europe had isolated the capital in a geographical, political, economic, military, and indeed all but a cultural sense, making of it no longer a bulwark but a mere outpost of the West, a Christian island, as it were, in the midst of an Islamic ocean.

The date of its fall, May 29, 1453, has been enshrined among the myths of history as the turning point between the Middle Ages and the modern age. This is true in a symbolic sense only. In the literal sense the Fall of Constantinople was but one among many transitional factors in a process of gradual change. The date was in fact that of the end of the Byzantine Empire and the death of its last effective emperor. Meanwhile a vacuum had been gradually filled in advance, over a period of 150 years, by the new Empire evolving through the Ghazi frontier warriors of the Ottoman tribal state. Destined to rule over as widespread a territory for a further 450 years, it commanded henceforward the focal point between the continents of Europe and Asia.

From the moment of his accession Mehmed II had seen himself as the heir to the classical Roman Empire and its Christian successor. Now his conquest of Constantinople confirmed him as such. Here was

Byzantium, to be reborn in a new idiom. In the course of his education and previous experience of government, Mehmed had matured into a young man of big imperial ideas and expansive horizons. Well-read in history, supremely confident in his capacity to achieve and to wield absolute power, he aspired to emulate and surpass, as a world conqueror, the achievement of Alexander the Great and the Caesars. As a Cretan historian, George Trapezountios, summoned later to his court was to assure him: "No one doubts that you are the Emperor of the Romans. Whoever is legally master of the capital of the Empire is the Emperor, and Constantinople is the capital of the Roman Empire." He was at once Kaisar-i-Rum, Roman Emperor in succession to Augustus and Constantine, and Padishah, in the Persian idiom Vice Regent of God.

In achieving this mastery, he inherited, in terms of his own Ottoman traditions of sovereignty, an old Islamic dream of worldwide dominion, defying the West to become "Sovereign of the Two Lands and the Two Seas"—Rumelia and Anatolia, the Mediterranean and the Black Sea. In capturing Constantinople he had succeeded where the earlier caliphs had failed. Revered as the greatest Moslem sovereign since the first four caliphs, he fulfilled a divine mission as the heir of a dynasty which he linked with those of a great Islamic past. Seeing himself as Khan, Ghazi, and Caesar in one, a universal sovereign personifying Turkish, Islamic, and Byzantine traditions, he must make of the city the center of one world and one empire.

His self-allotted task was not to destroy the Byzantine Empire, but to bring it to new life on a new Ottoman pattern, meanwhile rebuilding and restoring the imperial glories of a capital now to be named Istanbul. It was to reflect, in the words of Paul Wittek, "the true image of what was to be the fundamental feature of this state: the welding together of the indigenous cultural traditions of the old Byzantine orbit, and even already of occidental influences, with the traditions of Old Islam."

This was to be an empire under the rule, at once secular and religious, of Islam. But it was still to be a cosmopolitan empire, as Byzantium had been, embodying among its population all races and creeds, living together in order and harmony. No longer, with the fall of the last Emperor, were Church and State integrated, as a single authority. The Christian Church was now subordinated to the Islamic state and subjected to the payment of tribute. But in return for this its community was still to enjoy freedom of worship, and to retain its own observances and customs of life.

Such was the system devised and established throughout Moslem dominions to cover the status of religious minorities. They were *rayas,* literally "flocks," organized into *millets,* or nations, self-governing communities preserving their own laws and usages under a religious head responsible to the central power for the administration and good behaviour of his people. Precedents for this, in the form of the various Eastern Christian patriarchates, were familiar, both within the former empires of the Arab Caliphate and indeed of the Ottoman Empire itself, where the Orthodox Patriarch of Constantinople had for long been responsible for communities, whether in Asia or in Europe, living under Moslem rule. Now this was to apply to all Christian communities throughout the former Byzantine Empire. As a conquered people they were no longer to have the privilege of first-class citizenship or the ultimate sanction of political freedom. But within such limitations their opportunity to enjoy the benefits of peace and prosperity were to remain unimpaired and indeed, in the expanding commercial field, to become greatly enhanced. In these terms Mehmed now required that, side by side with the ulema, the Islamic authority, there should reside within the walls of Istanbul the Greek Orthodox Patriarch, the Armenian Patriarch, and the Jewish Chief Rabbi.

The Conqueror showed himself well enough disposed toward the Greeks in the city, who represented its largest, richest, and most cultured non-Moslem community. He saw clearly that they could be an asset to his empire, having an aptitude for industry, commerce, and seamanship which the Turks did not share. He had moreover a respect for Greek learning. In the course of his studies he had acquired a knowledge of Greek history. He may even have had Greek blood in his own veins, from his mother. He showed an especial respect and concern for his stepmother, Murad's half-Serbian, half-Greek widow, the Lady Mara—who had been considered, on her husband's death, as a possible bride for the Emperor Constantine.

He thus lost little time in providing the Greek Church with a new Patriarch. The last occupant of the patriarchal throne had fled to Italy in 1451, and was thus held to have abdicated. The Sultan's choice fell upon the monk Gennadius—otherwise George Scholarius, a scholar of considerable eminence. Gennadius had led the opposition to the union between the Greek and Roman churches, proposed as a last attempt to secure Western aid for the city, and was thus unlikely to intrigue with the Christians of the West. When he was summoned by the Sultan it was found that he had been removed from his monastic cell as a prisoner at the time of the Conquest and had been acquired as a slave by a rich Turk, who was impressed by his learning. Redeemed from his purchaser, he was brought before the Conqueror, who treated him with great respect, persuaded him to accept the patriarchal throne, and discussed with him the terms of the constitution to be granted to the Orthodox community. This provided them with such guarantees as to ensure them, at least in principle, freedom to manage their own affairs, both religious and to some extent secular, without interference and without fear of persecution.

His appointment as Patriarch was confirmed according to previous practice by the Holy Synod, on the Sultan's recommendation.

In January, 1454, Gennadius was enthroned as Greek Patriarch under the auspices of the Sultan, exercising the prerogative of the Byzantine emperors and carrying out much of their traditional ceremonial. The Sultan personally invested Gennadius with the insignia of his office—the robes, the pastoral staff, and a new silver gilt pectoral cross, to replace the old, which had vanished. He then blessed him with the words "Be Patriarch, with good fortune, and be assured of our friendship, keeping all the privileges that the Patriarchs before you enjoyed." He enjoyed complete authority over the *millet* of Rum, the East Roman (Byzantine) community, and was given the ceremonial rank of a pasha of three tails, with his own civil court and his own prison in the Greek quarter of the Phanar. The subsequent ceremony of his consecration and enthronement was performed, now that Hagia Sophia had been turned into a mosque, in the Church of the Holy Apostles, which Mehmed had specifically spared from destruction to serve as the patriarchal church. After receiving from the Sultan a generous gift of gold, the new Patriarch rode in procession through the city on a fine white horse, also the gift of the Sultan, then took up his residence in the precincts of the Holy Apostles.

This was one among a number of Christian churches which continued after the Conquest to be used for Christian worship, many of them in return for the submission to the Sultan of their respective parishes, while others were converted into mosques. Meanwhile, as a mosque, the church of Hagia Sophia retained its name in Islamic form as the great mosque of Aya Sofya, while the Cross which surmounted its dome was replaced by a Crescent, pointing toward Mecca—the traditional emblem of the Turks, familiar on their standards and dating from their earliest history, to which a star was to be added at a later period. From the outset the Conqueror treated Hagia Sophia, to which he added a minaret, with reverence, preserving its figural mosaics in defiance of the Islamic prohibition of all representation in art of the human form.

The new Patriarch was encouraged to look upon the Sultan as the benefactor and protector of the Greek Orthodox Church as against that of the Pope. His power and prestige became greater than any enjoyed by its forerunners in late Byzantine times, giving him almost the status of a "Greek Pope," and thoroughly vindicating such earlier popular cries as "Better Turks than Latins!" With Gennadius, Mehmed established a close relationship, engaging with him in amicable discussions on theological matters, and in his quest for knowledge displaying a marked interest in the Christian religion. At his request Gennadius wrote for him a statement of the Orthodox faith, which was translated into Turkish.

This gave rise in the West to pious hopes that the Sultan might emerge as a potential convert to Christianity. After the Fall of Constantinople a noted Italian Philhellene, Francesco Filfelfo, wrote to the Conqueror begging him for the release of his mother-in-law, the Italian widow of a Greek philosopher, who had been captured in the city, paying him fulsome compliments and expressing the fervent wish that he would join the Christian faith. Pope Nicholas V is said to have prayed for the conversion of the Sultan, after suitable instruction, following an alleged exchange of letters in which Mehmed, referring to himself as the successor and avenger of Hector, hinted at this possibility.

Later and more credibly Pope Pius II, alarmed lest the Sultan should become responsive to Orthodox doctrines, wrote to him expounding the superior wisdom and truth of Catholic doctrines and offering him baptism, so that he might become, under papal protection, the greatest of Christian princes. In Constantinople itself a Greek philosopher, George Amiroutzes, drew up a study for the Sultan, showing the common ground between Islam and Christianity, suggesting that they be combined in synthesis as one religion, or at least that each should recognize the other in sisterly fashion.

Such approaches were never likely to influence the Sultan, seeing himself as he did as an instrument of Allah and the heir to the caliphs, thus wedded spiritually and politically to Islam. Nonetheless he ensured the healthy survival of Orthodox Christian civilization. He remained always tolerant of Christians, and continued, as his father had done, to recruit converts from Christianity, showing a preference for them over Moslems of the old school, and in particular for those who shared his own broad-minded outlook.

Tolerant as he was in religious affairs, the Conqueror in political and personal situations could be as coolly and often cruelly ruthless as he invariably was on the battlefield. After the Conquest of the city he had released from captivity several of the Emperor's ministers, including the Megadux, Lucas Notaras—the minister reputed to have said, when frustrated over the negotiations for the union of the churches, that he would sooner see the Sultan's turban in Constantinople than a cardinal's hat. At first the Sultan treated him with respect, and even contemplated making him governor of the city—a course, however, against which he was warned by suspicious advisers. To test him, one evening at a banquet Mehmed, who was well flushed with wine, as was often his habit, and who was known to have ambivalent sexual tastes, sent a eunuch to the house of Notaras, demanding that he supply his good-looking fourteen-year-old son for the Sultan's pleasure. When he refused, the Sultan instantly ordered the decapitation of Notaras, together with that of his son and his son-in-law; and their three heads, so it is related, were placed on the banqueting table before him. Notaras had requested that the heads of the two boys be cut off first, lest the sight of his own execution impair their courage to die like Christians. Afterward other Greek notables were similarly executed, the Sultan coolly deciding that the chief officials of the former Empire were best out of the way.

Notaras meanwhile had hinted to the Sultan at complicity with the Greeks, on receipt of bribes, by his Grand Vezir, Halil Pasha, whom Mehmed had indeed long suspected of treachery, since his attempt to press upon him a compromise peace. Halil was at once arrested, deprived of his offices, then transferred to Adrianople. Here one day, it is said, the Sultan saw a fox tied up at the door of his palace, and ironically remarked to the animal, "Poor fool, why did you not ask Halil to give you your liberty?" Halil, hearing of this and fearing for his fate, at once declared his intention of making the pilgrimage to Mecca. Reassured by a message from the Sultan, he remained. But soon afterward he was beheaded. Mehmed thus paid off an old score which had rankled since his boyhood, ridding himself of a long-hated enemy.

Halil had been the fourth successive member of the Chandarli family to serve as Grand Vezir at the Sultan's court. Mehmed had dismissed the other ministers of the old Ottoman regime who had served under his father. Henceforward he had around him only advisers of the growing renegade ruling class, Christian converts to Islam whose careers depended directly on the Sultan's favour and on whom he could thus count to do his bidding. His new Grand Vezir was his general Zaganos Pasha, an Albanian in origin.

The Conqueror's most imperative task was the rebirth as a living city of Istanbul, whose destiny was to become the world's greatest capital. This involved in particular its repopulation. As the importance of the city, in its growing isolation, had declined, its population had dwindled to some thirty or forty thousand inhabitants. Large sections of it had been left uninhabited. Already far advanced in decay, it now presented as a result of the Conquest a scene of desolation and destruction, with its palaces and other great buildings in ruins. Now at once the debris was cleared from the streets, the walls repaired, and a new administration installed on the Ottoman model. All who had left the city, mostly Orthodox Christians, were immediately urged to return, with promises of protection for their property and religion, exemption from taxation, and often government aid for the rebuilding of their houses and shops. Prisoners captured by the Turkish forces were released, settled in the district of the Phanar, and exempted for a while from taxation. Provincial governors in both

Rumelia and Anatolia were ordered to send four thousand families to Istanbul, whether Christians or Moslems, to occupy the deserted houses. Some thirty thousand peasants, captured in successive campaigns, were brought to settle on the land in uninhabited villages around Istanbul, to provide the city with food.

On the orders of the Sultan, men of means, merchants, and artisans were selected from conquered cities and transferred to Istanbul to assist commercial and industrial development. These included immigrants from Salonika, with its large Jewish community, and Jews from Europe on a substantial scale. Within twenty-five years the Jews, with their own *millet,* were to become the third largest element in the capital after the Moslems and Christians. At a further stage in his conquests came five thousand families from Trebizond and its neighbourhood, besides others from Anatolia and from the Morea and the Aegean islands, all to be allotted their own respective quarters in the city, to which they would give the names of their places of origin, like Aksaray and Karamania. Besides noble families they included shopkeepers, with more artisans and masons to help in the increasing work of reconstruction. As time went on, Greeks began to immigrate of their own free will, eager to profit, like the Jews and Armenians, by the city's growing prosperity. Meanwhile across the Golden Horn, Pera, its fortifications demolished, was restored with its port of Galata to become as before a Turkish town, with Genoese and other Latin inhabitants.

"How curious," wrote a Turkish writer soon after the Conquest, "is this city of Istanbul; for one copper coin one can be rowed from Rumeli to Frankistan." Long before the end of the Conqueror's reign it was once more a flourishing city of workshops and bazaars, teeming with industrial activity, and with a mixed population three or four times larger than that at the time of the Conquest. Within a century it was to contain half a million inhabitants, of whom only a little over 50 percent were Turks.

Mehmed was especially active in the promotion of economic life, and for this purpose developed on a wide scale the traditional Islamic institution of the *imaret,* which was already familiar in the former capitals of Bursa and Adrianople and which now contributed to the growth of Istanbul, through its provision of markets and public services. It was in fact a combined religious, cultural, and commercial institution, a *vakf,* or charitable pious foundation, financed by the state or, if by individual endowment, confirmed and to a great extent controlled by the state. It embodied a complex of public buildings, grouped around a mosque, with on the one hand a *medresse* (a center of higher education), a hospital, and a hostel for travellers. On the other hand the proceeds of an inn, market, caravanserai,

Allom and Walsh, *Constantinople*.

The covered market of Istanbul, begun by Mehmed II soon after the conquest of the city, was greatly enlarged in the centuries that followed. This drawing by Allom offers a view of one of the main "avenues" with its stalls or shops on both sides of the street.

mills, bathhouses, dyehouses, warehouses, slaughterhouses, and soup kitchens supplemented the religious endowments and helped to finance them.

As part of the endowment of Aya Sofya, the first great mosque of Istanbul, Mehmed the Conqueror ordered the building of a *bedestan,* a large bazaar or covered market, with some hundred shops and storerooms, together with another thousand shops in the streets and markets around it. It was in effect a business and trade center, where merchants could securely store their goods and congregate to do business. When Mehmed built his own great mosque, there were eight *medresses* around it, where six hundred students studied each day, a children's school, a library, two hostels for travellers, a refectory, kitchens where the poor were given food, and a hospital, which employed for their free treatment an eye specialist, a surgeon, a pharmacist, and cooks to prepare food under the doctor's orders. Here was the free education and health service of a medieval Islamic welfare state.

Sultan Mehmed required the leading men of his empire to create *imarets* in other parts of the city, where they served as the center of new residential quarters. Similar complexes of buildings devoted to the public good came to mark the expanding caravan routes right across the country, as trade increased and Istanbul came to supplement and finally surpass Bursa and Adrianople as the Empire's great commercial center, commanding as it did the trade routes across the Black Sea, the Mediterranean, and the Asiatic continent.

Another traditional institution of Islamic economic life, which Mehmed encouraged and brought under closer state supervision, was that of the craft guilds, those professional organizations or unions to which much of the working population belonged. Originating perhaps in the corporations of the Greco-Roman world, they were familiar in medieval Europe and assumed a character of their own under Islam, where they developed also the character of religious and social fraternities. They had played an important part, under the leadership of the *akhis,* in the early Ottoman frontier society, when there was no strong centralized authority, and they afforded political protection to the craftsmen and workers. The guilds were organized according to trades. Each was represented by a leader, whom the master craftsmen elected to safeguard its autonomy and uphold its interests before the government, in terms of its own guild rules. Though the guilds were, at least in theory, independent of state control, they were responsible to the state by law for the execution of such commercial regulations as affected the measures, the costs of labour, the margin of profit, the quality of merchandise, the prevention of fraud and profiteering. Respecting the traditional structure of the guilds as a source of order and stability, the state did not intervene in their internal affairs but concerned itself only to protect the interests of the treasury and the general public.

This evolution of the guild system, together with the growth of urbanization and the increase of market facilities, reflected a new stage of economic evolution in the now full-fledged Ottoman Empire. It took the form of a major expansion of trade with the West which, through the last decades of the fifteenth century, became a cardinal element in its relations with the powers of Europe. Now that Byzantium was no more, and any real threat to the East from the crusaders belonged to past history, the Empire emerged of its own accord as a pivotal center of commerce, serving as the vital trading link between Asia and Europe, creating a broader field of economic exchange, which affected also social and cultural relations between the two opposite spheres. While Byzantium had been dominated economically by Venice, the Ottoman Empire, with its flourishing multi-ethnical society, traded with all powers alike on a basis of protective customs tariffs. Its merchants were in the course of time to penetrate from eastern through central and as far as northern Europe, establishing emporiums in key cities and developing their own credit system as they exchanged the agricultural products and manufactures of the East for the arms, minerals, and other raw materials of the West.

Having evolved from a series of settled nomadic communities into an Islamic empire with the basic structure of a traditional Eastern state, it was administered through time-honoured economic institutions and principles. Where it was the function of all classes of society and all sources of its wealth to preserve the power of the ruler, the populace was divided into two main classes. One of them represented the Sultan's authority—the administrators, the army, the men of religion; the other was composed of the *raya,* the cultivators of the soil and a section of the craftsmen, who alone were the producers and alone paid taxes. Their methods of production and margins of profit were strictly controlled by the state in the interests of social and political order, and it was ensured through a rigid process of logic that each man should remain in his own class.

But there was a third class now growing in importance—that of the merchants, who alone were free from such legal and social restrictions and who alone could become capitalists. They were the big businessmen—exclusive of the smaller tradesmen and craftsmen—who engaged to their profit in trade between regions and in the sale of goods imported from afar. The government's concern for commerce at this period of the fifteenth century was reflected in a passage from *An Ottoman Mirror for Princes* by Sinan Pasha:

> Look with favour on the merchants in the land; always care for them; let no one order them about, for through their trading the land becomes prosperous, and by their wares cheapness abounds in the world; through them the excellent fame of the Sultan is carried to surrounding lands, and by them the wealth within the land is increased.

Mehmed started to rebuild and refortify the walls of the city. He had determined to make of it architecturally as fine an imperial capital as ever it had been under Byzantium—a worthy image of the glories of that Ottoman Empire which had sprung from the Seljuk Sultanate of Rum. He lost little time in building his own mosque, to be known to his people as the Mosque of Fatih, "of the Conqueror." He employed a Greek architect and chose for the new building the site and the materials of the Church of the Holy Apostles, which was demolished, while the Greek Patriarch transferred his church to the Convent of the Pammakaristos, in the Greek quarter of the Phanar, on the Golden Horn. It was Mehmed's boast that his mosque, with its external precincts, surpassed that of Aya Sofya in its total dimensions. Crowning the opposite westerly crest of the ridge between the Sea of Marmara and the Golden Horn, it was the first of a new succession of great domed mosques which, as the centuries passed, were to give a new skyline to the city of Istanbul. Inspired initially by the Byzantine style of Hagia Sophia, they were to reflect in Islamic terms the grand imperial manner of a new race of architects, creating a Moslem metropolis to surpass that of the Christians.

Mehmed laid also the foundation stone of the Mosque of Eyub, a companion of the Prophet who had met his death before these walls, and whose tomb had been found in the course of the siege. Next, now that the palaces of the emperors were in ruins—moreover inadequate in scale to his own imperial standards—he built for himself a palace in the center of the ridge, an enlargement of the Monastery of the Pantocrator, into which he was to move from Adrianople, and which he made more accessible by a number of new, paved streets. To these, as to his other building works, he gave his close personal attention, mostly during the winter months between the annual campaigns which he was to wage throughout the remaining twenty-five years of his reign.

((9))

Sultan Mehmed's military task, with the conquered capital as a base securing his flank and his rear, was now to consolidate his empire and to extend and round off its frontiers. On the seaward side he had an enlarged fortified harbour, with an expanding naval force, while a new fortress was built on either side of the Dardanelles, between Sestos and Abydos, to command the Straits from the south as those of Rumeli and Anadolu Hisar commanded them from the north. The Sultan led his armies in person, dominating his generals, holding no councils of war, confiding no plans as to the destination of the well-disciplined armies which he mustered each year from both Europe and Asia. Questioned once by a general as to the objective of his next campaign, he replied that if a single hair of his beard knew his intentions, he would pluck it out and cast it into the fire.

He had inherited his father's enemies—Hunyadi in Hungary, the Despot George Brankovitch in Serbia, Skanderbeg in Albania, the Venetians in Greece and the Aegean. One after the other he moved systematically against them. In successive campaigns directly following the Conquest, in 1454 and 1455, his objective was Serbia, the buffer state for which Hungarians and Turks competed. Here he occupied the greater part of the principality, which his father, Murad, had revived after the battle of Varna, took possession of its valuable silver mines, and attached it more closely to the Ottoman Empire. But there still remained an obstacle to his main advance into Hungary —the city of Belgrade, on the Danube.

Determined on its capture, which his father had failed to achieve, Mehmed assembled in 1456 a well-armed force of some 150,000 men and a flotilla of light vessels, which sailed up the Danube to Vidin. The larger craft carried the heavy siege artillery, while the lighter guns were constructed in Serbia, largely by imported Western labour. Other weapons, munitions, and provisions were brought overland by well-organized trains of camels and other beasts of burden. To blockade the city from the Danube, Mehmed placed upstream of the fortress a chain of boats which served as a boom across the river. From the banks his heavy artillery faced its western land walls. Here early in June, as the corn was ripening, the Sultan's tent was pitched on a hilltop, with the forts of his Janissaries ranged in tiers

The second court of the Topkapi Palace, also known as the court of the Divan. Parts of it are believed to be remains of the original palace built by Mehmed II.

Melling, *Voyage pittoresque de Constantinople,* Paris, 1819.

around and beneath it. Overconfident, following his successful capture of Constantinople, Mehmed anticipated little trouble with that of Belgrade.

Early in July the Turkish cavalry ravaged the surrounding countryside, and the bombardment began, lasting a fortnight, severely damaging the walls, but causing few casualties. Then Hunyadi's river squadron appeared down the Danube, while his cavalry lined the banks to obstruct reinforcements and cut the Turkish line of retreat. The battle raged fiercely for five hours, while the Turks put up a desperate resistance and the waters of the Danube flowed with blood. Finally the Hungarians, with their lighter and more maneuverable craft, broke through the chain of clumsy Turkish vessels with their inexperienced navigators, dispersing them, sinking two galleys with their crews, and capturing four others with all their arms. The remaining ships of the Turkish flotilla, laden with dead and dying, contrived to escape, but were burned on the Sultan's orders to prevent then from falling into the hands of the enemy.

The Hungarian victory was decisive. Now Hunyadi and the fiery crusading monk Capistrano led their troops into the citadel to reinforce and encourage the beleaguered garrison. Breaches in the walls were hurriedly repaired and guns were reserviced. Mehmed, enraged by his defeat on the river and bent on taking the citadel, led his Janissaries in person by night in a major general assault on it. They finally forced their way into the lower part of the city, while groups of them scaled the walls to penetrate inside the citadel. Hunyadi cunningly withdrew his troops from the walls and ordered them to hide, while the Janissaries scattered through the empty streets in search of plunder. At a prearranged signal their shouts of victory were drowned by Hungarian war cries, and before they could reassemble they were surrounded in small groups and for the most part exterminated.

The survivors poured down from the fortress only to meet with an even grimmer surprise. During the previous night Hunyadi and Capistrano had heaped up piles of faggots with twigs steeped in sulphur. In the morning they were set alight and flung down on the enemy retreating below. Fire broke out from all directions. Countless Turks were trapped without means of escape and burned to death in the moats, which were soon blocked with piles of charred and mutilated corpses, while other fugitives were caught by the flames as they ran. The crusading bands in their ardour marched straight against the enemy's siege artillery. The Turks broke before them, abandoning their guns, and were driven back to their third line of defense, before the camp of the Sultan. Mehmed, roused to a fury, plunged into the battle, but after striking off the head of a crusader with his sword, he was wounded by an arrow in the thigh and obliged to withdraw from the field. His Janissaries disbanded in confusion. Enraged by such insubordination, the Sultan cursed their chief, Hassan Agha, who himself rushed into action and was killed before his master's eyes. After nightfall the Sultan sounded a retreat which developed into a rout, and a large haul of guns, ammunition, and supplies fell into the hands of the enemy.

The Christian victory aroused widespread rejoicing throughout Europe. But not long after the siege both Hunyadi and Capistrano lay dead from a plague which swept through the region of Belgrade. On Christmas Eve, a few months later, George Brankovitch died in the fullness of age. Serbia itself became divided between pro-Ottoman and pro-Hungarian factions, dynastic and religious disputes. Finally, after two successive campaigns, it was invaded by Mehmed and annexed to the Ottoman Empire, providing a serviceable base for northward expansion. It was to remain in Turkish hands for a further five centuries.

Throughout the year 1457 Mehmed, following the depletion of his armaments in the inglorious retreat from Belgrade, directed no military campaign. He chose instead to remain in his palace in Adrianople, newly built on an island in the Maritza River, while his palace in Istanbul was still under construction. Here his two young sons, Bayezid from Amasya and Mustafa from Magnesia, were circumcised with solemn ceremony and lively festivities, before an assembly of foreign ambassadors and men of religious, legal, and literary distinction, gathered from all parts of the Empire.

In the following year, 1458, Mehmed embarked on the first of his campaigns to subjugate Greece. Here much of the Byzantine ruling class had taken refuge in the two divided despotates of the Morea under the ineffectual rule of two survivors of the Palaeologue dynasty, Demetrius and Thomas. Brothers of the last Emperor, Constantine, they ruled respectively—at odds with one another—from Patras in the west and from Mistra in the east, with the obligation to pay tribute to the Sultan. This soon fell into arrears. Thus, crossing the Isthmus of Corinth, the Sultan and his army marched down the entire length of the western Morea, meeting with negligible resistance from a people who, under such shadowy rule, had as yet developed little national sentiment. He occupied and ravaged most of the western Morea, but postponed an assault on the key fortress of Corinth itself until his northward return march. Here he proposed to the inhabitants an honourable surrender, without conversion to Islam. On meeting with a refusal, he besieged the triple walls of the fortress, firing from his cannon marble balls hewn on the spot from among the ruins of the ancient classical city. After the first two walls had been pierced, the garrison surrendered, leaving the Janissaries in possession, and the two

Palaeologues agreed to a treaty which ceded much of the former despotate of Constantine. It left them still with some remnants of territory, but with the continued obligation to pay tribute.

The Sultan then paid a visit to Athens, which had been captured by the Turks from its Florentine duke two years earlier. To the Ottomans it was known as the "city of the wise," and Mehmed, their "wise and great Philhellene monarch," was duly impressed by its relics of classical antiquity. He especially admired the Acropolis. He treated the Athenians magnanimously, confirming their civil liberties and exemption from taxes, but delighted them especially, following the collapse of the Latin Church, by granting privileges to the Orthodox clergy.

Fratricidal strife between the two Palaeologue despots erupted again soon after the Sultan's departure, Demetrius supporting the Turks and their treaty and Thomas breaking it to call in papal forces. In 1460 Mehmed marched once more into Greece with his army. Demetrius at first fled from him, but eventually surrendered the city of Mistra and his despotate with the exception of Monemvasia, which held out against the Turks with the aid of the papal forces. Mehmed then set out to subdue the forces of the Despot Thomas. But he soon fled into exile in the West, abandoning his people to the Turks.

Thus they established their rule over the whole Greek peninsula but for a few coastal outposts, which could be supplied by sea and were thus to remain in Venetian hands. Henceforward Pax Ottomanica reigned there, replacing the feuds of the Franks, while the Greek people were treated with reasonable tolerance—unburdened with excessive taxation, exempted from the tribute of children, permitted freedom to trade and to elect their own local government. Western Christendom, on the other hand, preferred to see them as a people oppressed by the infidel and yearning for liberation at the hands of the Latins. As time went on it was humanist Greece which came to succeed Constantinople and the Holy Land as the goal of Europe's crusading zeal.

Mehmed II, in his aim to revive the Byzantine Empire under his rule, sought—so the Turkish historian records—to leave none "among the Byzantine Greeks who could be named King." He had disposed of the Palaeologues. Now came the turn of the Comnenes. It was time to eliminate the empire of Trebizond. Already the Grand Comnene, the Emperor John IV, had effectively renounced its independence by payment to the Sultan of a substantial annual tribute. On his death his younger brother, the Emperor David, chose to ally himself against the Sultan not only with his European enemies—Venice, Genoa, and the papacy—but with his declared enemy in Asia, the Turcoman prince Uzun Hassan, of the tribe of the White

Sheep. A Moslem with Christian blood in his veins, connected with the Comnenes by marriage, Uzun Hassan built up a powerful opposition to the Ottomans in eastern Anatolia, which rallied also the local Turkish princes of Sinope and Karamania and the Christian Georgian kings.

When David demanded of the Sultan a remission of his father's tribute, he did so through the ambassadors of Uzun Hassan in Istanbul, who were making other extravagant demands of him. The Sultan resolved that the time had come to break up this unholy alliance and finally to settle the affairs of Anatolia in the Ottoman interest. In 1461 he mounted a punitive expedition into Asia, by land and by sea. First capturing the port of Amastris, the last Genoese trading post on the Black Sea, he secured by negotiation the city of Sinope. Then he marched into the territory of Uzun Hassan, who, receiving no help from his Karamanian allies, retired eastward. His Syrian Christian mother, Princess Sara, came to the Sultan on his behalf laden with gifts, and agreed to a treaty of peace, by which Uzun Hassan undertook not to aid the Comnenes of Trebizond. But when she tried to persuade Mehmed to spare himself the dangers of attacking the city, he replied: "Mother, the sword of Islam is in my hand."

Marching with his troops, he made an arduous crossing of the Pontic mountain range, while his fleet besieged Trebizond from the sea—but with little effect. After an eighteen-day march the vanguard of the Ottoman army, under the command of Mahmud Pasha, the Sultan's Grand Vezir, appeared before the land walls. They had brought no siege artillery, and almost no cavalry, and moreover had a precarious supply line. But the Emperor David was no warrior. Deserted by his most powerful ally, he had no desire to perish amid the ruins of his city and empire, as his more heroic kinsman, the Emperor Constantine, had done. Preferring peace and survival, he was ready enough to heed overtures made to him by Mahmud through a Greek dignitary of equivocal loyalties, while the Sultan in his turn proved susceptible to the pacific pleas of the Princess Sara.

The upshot was a peace treaty without honour to the Greeks, by which the Ottoman army entered Trebizond unopposed. The last emperor, with his family and court officials, together with their gold and other precious personal possessions, were conveyed by the grace and favour of the Sultan in a special ship to Istanbul, while he rewarded Sara for her mediation with the gift of a pile of jewels. The people of the city were less generously treated. Males and females alike were enslaved and divided between the Sultan and his dignitaries, boys were enlisted into the corps of the Janissaries, and a large number of families were deprived of their property and deported to help populate Istanbul.

The days of the Comnenes were nonetheless numbered. Within

two years the Emperor David was secretly intriguing once more against the Ottomans with Uzun Hassan. He was incarcerated by the Sultan in his new Prison of the Seven Towers within the walls of Istanbul and there, a few months later, he and the rest of the Comnene family—his brother, his seven sons, and his nephew—were massacred. The Sultan moreover gave orders that their bodies be left unburied, to be devoured by scavenging dogs and birds of prey.

Mehmed, in the course of the Trebizond campaign, had incorporated into his empire most of the northern coastal region of Asia Minor, with three important Black Sea ports. In a later campaign, following the death in 1464 of Ibrahim Bey, the great prince of Karamania, and the disintegration of his dynasty among seven dissenting sons, he was to annex by conquest almost the whole of Karamania, a belligerent rival of the Ottomans for 150 years past. This was to lead to virtual Ottoman control of Cilicia and of the Asiatic coast of the Mediterranean.

Having thus secured for the time being his rear in the East, Mehmed turned his military attentions once more to the West. Here his objective was nothing less than direct, undivided Ottoman rule over the whole Balkan peninsula. To achieve this he now had to round off his territory at its various extremities, as already in the Greek peninsula, and consolidate it as a base for further conquest in western Europe. To the northeast beyond the Danube lay Wallachia, ruled by the earlier mentioned Vlad Dracul, otherwise Dracula, one of the monsters of history whose cruelties, far exceeding those familiar enough in that age of brutality, made of him also one of the devils of legend.

For all this, the Sultan was inclined to let Dracul alone as long as his tribute was paid and he left his Ottoman neighbours unmolested. But in 1461 he formed an alliance against the Turks with King Mathias Corvinus, who had succeeded Hunyadi as ruler of Hungary. Mehmed sent an envoy to lure Dracul to Istanbul, with his arrears of tribute and a contingent of Vlachs for the Ottoman army, and instructed the commander of his troops on the Danube to ambush and capture him on the way there. But the tables were turned by an encounter in which Dracul's bodyguard put the Turks to flight, and on his orders both envoy and commander were impaled, the highest pike being allotted to the highest in rank. Vlad Dracul then crossed the Danube into Bulgaria, at the head of an army with which he ravaged Ottoman territory and massacred much of its population.

At this the Sultan, determined on vengeance, led a large army into Wallachia. In the course of the campaign they came upon a "forest of corpses," in which there rotted the remains of some twenty thousand Bulgarians and Ottomans impaled on stakes and crucified—a grim example of the mass executions which Dracul liked to stage for his pleasure and for the edification of his neighbours. The Sultan's army, though harassed by bouts of unaccustomed mobile guerrilla warfare, finally overcame the enemy and drove Vlad Dracul into exile in Moldavia, while the Ottoman commander was able to place two thousand Vlach heads at the feet of his sovereign. Vlad was replaced as lord of Wallachia by his brother Radu, a hostage in Istanbul whose good looks had caught the Sultan's fancy, and who was thus singled out to serve as one of his most favoured pages. Under him Wallachia became a vassal state, but was not otherwise treated as a Turkish province.

Two years later, however, the Sultan's favourite was expelled from the country by the neighbouring prince, Stephen of Moldavia, a ruler of the caliber of Hunyadi, who with an effective peasant army twice defeated Turkish attempts to reinstate him. Stephen was eventually defeated by Mehmed in person with an army of Tatar forces, recruited in the Crimea after the capture of the Genoese colony there by his Black Sea fleet. They were unleashed on Moldavia from the north. Here, from the delta of the Danube, was a new potential Ottoman danger to Hunyadi's flank. But for the present Mehmed was obliged, by a Hungarian threat through Transylvania to his line of retreat, to withdraw from Moldavia and leave it unoccupied.

Meanwhile, in 1463, he had turned his attention northwestward to Bosnia, another tributary state which marched with Serbia, and which he required as a base for new aggressions farther west. Bosnia was in a vulnerable position, owing not only to dynastic but to religious dissensions. Once Orthodox, it had turned Roman Catholic, with the strong support of the Pope but to some extent only in appearance. Moreover it harboured a large sect of heretics, the Bogomils, whom the Pope tried to offset by the dispatch of Franciscan missions. But the heretics veered toward friendship with the Turks, who gave them protection in their own Ottoman provinces. Thus they were kept well-informed as to what was happening in Bosnia itself, and wooed the local peasantry with promises of freedom. Already, since 1461, King Stephen of Bosnia had been expecting invasion by the Sultan, whose "insatiable thirst for domination," so he warned the Pope, "knows no limits." Appealing for papal support, Stephen pointed out that the conquest of his kingdom would lead to the invasion of Hungary, and to that of Venice and other parts of Italy. Moreover, "He also speaks frequently of Rome, which he dreams of attaining."

The Pope's response was to send a legate who, for what this was worth, crowned Stephen in splendour, and pressed the king of Hungary to come to terms with him. But he would only do so on condition that Stephen withheld his tribute to the Ottomans. This infuriated the Sultan, who at once sent an army into Bosnia, receiving the surrender of the important fortress of Bobovats and, according to his custom, dividing its inhabitants into three groups—one to be left in the town, the second to be distributed among his pashas, and the third to be sent to increase the population of Istanbul. He then sent his Grand Vezir, Mahmud Pasha, with an advance guard to capture King Stephen and the fortress into which he had fled with his army. Stephen capitulated on the condition, to which Mahmud agreed in writing, that his life should be spared.

This promise displeased Mehmed, whose policy was to put to death the family of any reigning prince whom he conquered. He thus consulted a Persian holy man in his suite, who obligingly decreed that in terms of Islamic law no such reprieve of an infidel, promised by a subordinate, was binding on the Sultan. Thus the last king of Bosnia was beheaded by the holy man in person, in the Sultan's presence—or perhaps by the Sultan himself. Ottoman rule over Bosnia was thenceforward accepted at least by the Bogomils, who became converted in large numbers to Islam. The neighbouring mountainous territory of Herzegovina maintained for a while a precarious independence, to be finally incorporated in the Empire by the Conqueror's son Bayezid II.

Beyond it Albania continued robustly to survive, as the last bastion between the invading Turks and the Dalmatian coasts and islands of the Italians. Here Skanderbeg, that "champion of Christ," as he was named by the Pope, still fought and ruled with the encouragement of the Hungarians, Venetians, and other Italian states, as he had done since the time of Murad II more than twenty years earlier. In the course of time he had become an almost legendary hero to the Christian West. Albania owed much of its continued independence to the natural forces both of its geography and of its people, to the impregnability of its ranges of mountains, and to the fighting spirit of those hardy highland clansmen whom Skanderbeg had united and still held firmly under his leadership. The Turks might occupy its valleys but they would continually fail, as Mehmed's generals were to find at some cost, to storm and hold its peaks.

In 1466 the Sultan in person led a large force into Albania. After his advance guard had ravaged the surrounding country, he appeared with the bulk of his army to besiege the rockbound fortress of Croia. But the siege, thanks to the strength of the walls and the courage of the garrison, proceeded slowly, while Skanderbeg with his own mobile forces continually harassed the besieging Ottomans from the rear, causing them severe losses and often cutting off their supplies. The

Sultan finally marched off in a rage in the direction of Durazzo, leaving one of his pashas to continue the siege of the fortress, from which they were soon driven to retreat in a disorderly flight from the country.

Mehmed, after erecting a fortress under his own control within his frontiers, at Elbasan, returned to the attack in the following year, bent on the ultimate capture of Durazzo, from which refugees fled in their thousands to Italy. But Croia still held out, and he made little progress. Nor was he to succeed until after the death in 1467 of Skanderbeg, and the consequent disintegration of the clans he had united. On his death legend relates that the Sultan exclaimed, a shade prematurely: "At last Europe and Asia belong to me! Unhappy Christianity. It has lost both its sword and its buckler."

By now the Ottoman Empire was openly at war with the Republic of Venice, to which Skanderbeg had bequeathed his dominions. The war, whose origin was a dispute for mastery over the various naval bases still held by Venice, was to last sporadically for sixteen years.

Respite from it came only in the campaigning seasons when the Sultan was diverted to Asia. Here indeed pressure was intensified by an alliance of Venetian and other Italian papal and Christian powers, in diplomatic exchanges with Uzun Hassan and his tribe of the White Sheep. The West was pitting the East against the East in its endeavour to stem the advance of the Ottomans. To such overtures Uzun Hassan was ready enough to respond. He was aiming to follow in the footsteps of Timur with an invasion of central Anatolia, aided by Anatolians from Karamania and elsewhere whom Mehmed had dispossessed of their lands, thus driving them to seek Uzun Hassan's protection in Persia. For this he was assembling a formidable army at Erzinjan, while his allies captured and destroyed Tokat. They unsuccessfully attacked Amasya, where the Sultan's son Bayezid was governor, took Kayseri, ravaged the region of Angora, and penetrated as far west as Akshehir.

The time had come for Ottoman retaliation on a major scale. As between Timur and Bayezid, this confrontation was preceded by an exchange of threatening letters between the two rulers. In reply to an arrogant missive from Uzun Hassan, boasting of his conquests in Persia and declaring that he no longer feared any enemy, Mehmed wrote treating him loftily as a mere Persian khan. He rebuked him for his pride and warned him that his power could soon be engulfed in an abyss.

In the autumn of 1472, having duly consulted his astrologers—as was his habit before reaching any important decision—Mehmed crossed into Asia with a large army and marched to the east. Taking up his winter quarters in Amasya, he moved in the spring farther eastward to Erzinjan. Uzun Hassan, exclaiming at the great "tide" of the Sultan's army, took up a position with his right wing covered by the Upper Euphrates, and his rear by a range of mountains. Here at Terjan the youngest and most favoured of the Sultan's generals, Hass Murad Pasha—a descendant of the Palaeologues who had only lately risen to office as governor of Rumeli and here commanded a column of light cavalry—chose to launch with youthful ardour a heedless attack, which led him straight into an ambush prepared by the enemy. His force was encircled and largely annihilated, while Hass Murad himself was drowned in the waters of the Euphrates.

The Sultan, furious at this defeat for which he blamed his Grand Vezir, Mahmud Pasha, and discouraged at the death of his favourite, ordered a retreat. But first, so it is said, he had an opportune dream, which he related to his generals for the encouragement of their soldiery. In this he fought in hand-to-hand conflict with Uzun Hassan, first falling to his knees, then recovering his strength to deliver him such a blow on the chest that a piece of his heart fell to the ground. In reality, as Mehmed withdrew with his army through the mountains to the north of Erzinjan, that of Uzun Hassan suddenly appeared on the heights to its right. Battle was joined at Bashkent, and after an eight-hour struggle the chief of the White Sheep was routed and his armies put to flight, with losses which exceeded those of the enemy by ten to one. The entirc camp of Uzun Hassan with all its baggage fell into the hands of the Ottomans. The Sultan himself spent three days on the battlefield, supervising the execution of prisoners but, as befitted a patron of the arts and the sciences, sparing a group of savants and artisans, who were dispatched to Istanbul. When his army retreated westward it was accompanied by three thousand Turcoman prisoners, who were executed on the march at the rate of four hundred each day.

Uzun Hassan and his tribesmen of the White Sheep, spread as they were over so wide a territory, were not finally defeated—and indeed Venice renewed diplomatic relations with him immediately after the battle. He would surely rise again. But for the present, Sultan Mehmed did not expect further trouble from his direction—and in fact Uzun Hassan was to die in 1478.

Profiting by Skanderbeg's death, he turned again on Albania. His large army, commanded by a Bosnian eunuch named Suleiman Pasha, pitched camp before the fortress of Scutari, perched inland above the Adriatic on an isolated rock four hundred feet high, which the Sultan needed to secure his hinterland for trans-Adriatic operations. All along the coast cruised the Venetian fleet, reinforced by fishing boats across Lake Scutari, for the task of provisioning the city. The siege, with cannons cast on the spot, as was now the Sultan's practice, lasted for six weeks, when large stretches of the walls were reduced to dust. The long final assault cost the Ottomans thousands of casualties, including the deaths of some dozen generals, while countless soldiers had died from thirst and from the fever that prevailed in the marshes around. Finally Suleiman raised the siege, broke up his cannons, and bore off their metal on camelback. Among the inhabitants of Scutari there were wild scenes of joy, tempered by acute thirst and many deaths from drinking an excess of bad water. But none had the illusion that the battle for Albania was over; the Grand Turk would surely return. He did so three years later, once again besieging the "eagle's nest" of Croia. After an investment which dragged on for more than a year the fortress finally surrendered, driven to do so by a famine that reduced its inhabitants to living on the flesh of cats and dogs. Promised a safe-conduct from the city as an alternative to Ottoman occupation, the bulk of the inhabitants were nonetheless decapitated by the Sultan's orders.

Then he turned his full attention back to Scutari, the last remaining bastion of the West. Already from its citadel a common sight was that of columns of smoke, rising from Albanian villages destroyed by irregular bands of roving Turkish incendiaries. The town within the citadel itself was bombarded with blazing missiles, made from rags soaked in oil and tar, which did great damage. The old people and children were forced down into the cellars of their houses; the able-bodied were obliged to fight the flames from the rooftops, often removing roofs to prevent the fire from spreading. Two major assaults were launched by the Turks, but without appreciable success, and the Sultan, with the bulk of his army, decided to retreat, leaving a force to invest and blockade the fortress. Now almost isolated in occupied territory, it was soon to be reduced by starvation, the inhabitants living on bread and water, with no meat left for their sustenance—not even that of rats and mice.

Across on the Italian mainland there was fear and discouragement as the pressure of Ottoman raids on the Dalmatian coast intensified, raising fires which caused frequent alarms to be sounded from the campanile of St. Mark's in Venice. Raiders up the valleys from Bosnia, who had been devastating the mountainous provinces of Hungary, turned westward in 1477 with a cavalry force into Friuli, at the head of the Italian peninsula itself. They sacked towns and villages in the valleys of the Isonzo and the Tagliamento, and defeated the Venetians in battle in the plain between them to the north of Venice. They reached the banks of the Piave, where their campfires and burning villages were seen with dismay by Venetian senators from the campanile of St. Mark's. In the autumn the raiders withdrew, laden with booty and leaving behind them a sea of fire which consumed barns and villas, castles and palaces.

But in the following year the raids across the Isonzo were resumed on a larger scale, just as the harvest was ripening, by tens of thousands of Ottoman irregulars, spreading panic throughout the country. Mehmed's holy warriors were already crying in the name of Allah "Mehmed, Mehmed, Roma, Roma!" As far afield as the English court there was concern at the great peril to Christendom at this time, "when the Turk is at the gates of Italy and so powerful, as everyone knows."

The time had come for the Venetians to seek peace terms, and these were agreed with the Sultan in 1479, confirming Ottoman possession of Scutari, Croia, and the islands of Lemnos and Negropont, together with the Mani, the mountainous peninsula in the south of the Morea. Other places taken by Venice during the sixteen-year war were returned to the Ottomans, but with freedom to the Venetians to withdraw their garrisons, arms, and munitions without interference, while the Ottomans returned to them places occupied by their own forces in the Morea, Albania, and Dalmatia. A large annual tribute was imposed on the Venetians, in return for which freedom of trade was restored to them, with a consulate in Istanbul to protect the civil rights of their citizens. Mehmed had forced the strongest naval power in the Aegean and Mediterranean to come to terms with him. He had thus cleared the seas for an invasion of Italy by an Ottoman fleet, with an army under the command of Gedik Ahmed Pasha. A few months after the signature of the peace treaty he seized some of the Ionian islands as a naval base for a further attack on Italian shores.

This was launched in 1480 against Otranto, in the heel of the peninsula—chosen instead of Brindisi, the first planned objective, as lacking coastal defenses. The town was taken by surprise by a squadron of cavalry, with much fire and bloodshed. Eight hundred of its inhabitants were brutally put to death for refusing conversion to Islam, and were later canonized by the Pope. The surrounding countryside was sacked. Thrusts were made in the direction of Brindisi, Lecce, and Taranto, but repulsed by a vigorous force from Naples. The Sultan hoped to treat Otranto as an Ottoman bridgehead for the further conquest of Italy. But its inhabitants had fled and refused to be lured back to the city or to supply the occupying forces with provisions, so that the Turks withdrew the bulk of them, leaving only a small garrison supplied by sea from the Adriatic coast—probably with Venetian aid. It was rumoured that Mehmed was coming to Italy with an army in person, and the fear of a major Turkish invasion was such that the Pope considered fleeing to Avignon. Instead he mobilized help from such diverse sources as Genoa, Spain, and Portugal. But the

Sultan and his army failed to materialize. He had now switched his attention eastward to the island of Rhodes, and Ottoman forces were in due course withdrawn from Italian soil.

The island fortress of the Knights Hospitallers, otherwise Knights of St. John, the last of the crusaders, on Rhodes, was a key to the defense of Anatolia and to the Ottoman naval command of the eastern Mediterranean. The knights, under an indomitable grand master, Pierre d'Aubusson, had for some years been expecting an attack on the island, and had done their best to make the fortress impregnable, piling up enough supplies to last for three years, and contracting alliances with the Moslem rulers of Egypt and Tunisia. Underrating these defensive precautions, the Ottomans, under an admiral of the fleet, Mesih Pasha, a descendant of the Palaeologues, carried out during the winter of 1479 a cavalry reconnaissance in the northwest of the island, but were disappointed in their hope of a surprise attack on the fortress. Mesih's troops were driven out, and he returned to Psychos (Marmaris) on the mainland opposite, to await the arrival of a more substantial force in the spring. It duly arrived overland from the Hellespont, an army estimated at seventy thousand, followed by an armada of about fifty sailing ships which carried its heavier artillery.

After many weeks of bombardment against stout resistance, the main assault was launched in the last week in July—on the very day that, at the other end of the Mediterranean, the Ottomans landed at Otranto. Its imminence was conveyed to the enemy from dawn until dusk on the previous day with a continuous ear-splitting din of battle chants, with pipes and cymbals and drums, a martial custom of the Turks designed, though it deprived them of the weapon of surprise, to raise their own morale and to lower that of the enemy. To this the knights replied by blowing fanfares on their trumpets and ringing their church bells. A shower of messages was fired into the fortress, proclaiming that the pasha had hoisted the black flag and that the city would be sacked and its citizens slaughtered and sold into slavery. Then wave upon wave of irregulars—*bashi-bazouks*—poured headlong through the ruins of the ramparts and up into those of the Italian tower, where they planted the Ottoman standard. They were followed at the double by the unbroken ranks of the Janissaries.

Mesih Pasha, believing that the day was his, chose this moment to issue his troops the command that pillage was forbidden and the treasure of Rhodes was the Sultan's own. This was ultimately to break their combative spirit. Already the knights, fighting under the standards of the Holy Saviour, the Virgin, and St. John the Baptist, had rushed to block the way to the tower, grappling with the invaders chest to chest on the narrow rampart beneath it, slaughtering them until the walls and the fosses were piled with their corpses. Finally a detachment of knights forced its way into the tower itself, killed its occupants, and hurled their standard to the ground. At this the rest of the discouraged Ottoman soldiery broke and ran, hacking a way through their own advancing comrades, hotly pursued by the knights in full cry, and mowed down, in the words of an observer, "like swine."

The siege was raised. The Ottoman forces reembarked and reassembled at Marmaris for their march back to Istanbul. Here the grand admiral was deprived of his command and given a minor post in Gallipoli. The city of Rhodes was in ruins. But over them flew the white cross of St. John on its red field—the triumphant flag of the faith. It was to fly there for half a century longer. For now, after a generation of continuous campaigning, the days of the Conqueror were drawing to a close.

((10))

In aspiring to create a new world Islamic empire, Mehmed the Conqueror was concerned not only to consolidate and extend the territory of Byzantium, but to make of it internally a new state, with new institutions, administrative, legal, economic, and social. The quasi-independent open societies of the Ghazi frontier beys, which had joined in their diversity to lay its foundations, were now finally integrated within the social and political structure of a centralized imperial state.

This was in effect a military theocracy, as that of Byzantium had been, representing the principle of "government by God." Over it, through the medium of a highly organized bureaucracy, the Sultan was to exercise absolute power. Mehmed's task, as he saw it, was to eliminate or at least to transform and subject to his control every element which might threaten or compete with his personal authority. As one appointed by God, he, and he alone, would rule. It was to ensure for his dynasty the perpetuation of this divine sovereignty that he codified the practice of fratricide which already prevailed in his empire: "For the welfare of the state, the one of my sons to whom God grants the Sultanate may lawfully put his brothers to death. This has the approval of a majority of jurists."

His Grand Vezir, unlike some of those in previous reigns, was the steward of the Sultan, the dutiful instrument of royal commands. Though he had no power to decide on affairs of state, he exercised, within the limits of his duties, an authority wider than that of his predecessors. Until now the Sultan had always presided in person over meetings of the council of state—the Divan, as it was named—from the seat on which he sat, as his ancestors from nomadic times had done in their tents for centuries before him. But Mehmed in the course of his reign ceded the prerogative to his Grand Vezir, no longer frequenting the meetings of the Divan, but looking down on them, unseen, from a latticed bay above called "the Eye of the Sultan." This was to become a general precedent for his successors.

The change of system, so it is related, arose from an incident when a ragged Turcoman blundered into a meeting of the Divan and demanded in the gross dialect of his people, "Well, which of you is the happy Emperor?" The Sultan was incensed, and the Grand Vezir persuaded him that in future, to avoid such affronts to his sacred person, the affairs of the Divan should be left in the hands of the vezirs alone. So the Grand Vezir thus became in fact the head of government, holding the seal of state. He exercised, as the Sultan's lieutenant, wide temporal powers, discharged responsibility for every branch of the civil administration, supervised the appointment and the work of its officials.

The civil edifice over which the Grand Vezir thus presided in his master's name was founded on four "pillars of empire," deriving in martial terms from the four poles of the tents of the early Ottoman princes. The number four, as applied to the pillars, had a sacred significance, symbolizing also the four angels which, according to the Koran, supported the throne; the four companions of the Prophet who became the four caliphs; the four winds of heaven.

The first pillar was that of the Grand Vezir himself. Like other high dignitaries he bore the honourable title of Pasha, meaning literally "the Sultan's foot"—much as the officers of the crown among the ancient Persians were named after the king's eyes and hands. The Grand Vezir enjoyed the especial distinction of being authorized to display, as his pasha's insignia, five horse's tails, while the three vezirs under him were pashas of only three tails. This was an emblem deriving from the days of the nomad horsemen on the Turkish steppe. In their three branches of state these ministers, though autonomous in their own departments—concerned respectively with general, legal, and financial affairs—were directly answerable to the Sultan himself.

The second pillar covered those responsible for the administration of justice—the two *kadi-askers,* judges of the army, whose duty it was to nominate the other judges, one with jurisdiction over Anatolia and the other over Rumeli. The third pillar consisted of the *defterdars,* accountants or bookkeepers, the four treasurers of the exchequer responsible for financial and fiscal administration. Composing the fourth and final pillar were the *nishanjis,* chancellors and secretaries of state, who drew up the Sultan's edicts and placed upon them the imprint of his signature, the *tughra* or *nishan,* to carry his seal. Finally there were aghas, commanders or officers, divided into two classes—external, performing a military role, like the Agha of the Janissaries; and internal, attached exclusively to the court of the Sultan.

This system, as modified and supplemented by the Conqueror, was codified in the Kanun-name, derived from the Greek word *kanon* and the Arabic *kanun,* a "book of laws" and regulations drawn up at his command toward the end of his reign. It covered the hierarchy of the state, its customs and ceremonies, its duties and institutions, its revenues and the penalties it was entitled to impose.

The Kanun-name reflected not Moslem but Turkish state traditions. The Ottoman Empire, like other Moslem powers, was traditionally

A *nishanji*—a chancellor or secretary of state. Belonging to the fourth "pillar of Empire," he "drew up the Sultan's edicts and placed upon them the imprint of his signature, the *tughra* or *nishan,* to carry his seal."

governed by the overriding law of the Koran, the Sacred or Sheriat Law. But as the Empire grew in scope and complexity it became necessary to supplement the Koranic with a state law, extending its provisions and adapting them to changing temporal conditions. Murad I had initiated this change, which was carried a stage further by Murad II. The intervening century, with its multiplication of new administrative functions and problems, made necessary Mehmed II's new codification, which as the centuries passed was to be expanded and replaced in its turn by further such codes. These embodied the Sultan's own regulations and commands, which as Padishah, imperial sovereign, he had by Ottoman tradition the absolute right to promulgate without intervention by the Islamic legal establishment. But beyond the provisions of this state law, known as *urfi,* or supplemental, the Sultan still accepted the obligations and restraints of the Sheriat Law, based on the primary Islamic sources of Koran, the written word of God; the Sunna, or body of Moslem custom; and the pronouncements of the first four great caliphs. His imperial edicts, or Hatti-Sherifs, were regarded as subordinate to these, and any important political act of the Sultan would be sanctioned in advance by a *fetva* (legal opinion) of the Chief Mufti, the leading Islamic legal authority.

The Kanun-name covered also the customs and formalities of the Sultan's court, which in its rigid hierarchy, its pomp and luxury, and its elaborate ceremonial owed much to the Byzantine model—specifically to the "order of ceremonies" laid down in the tenth century by Constantine Porphyrogenitus. This applied in particular to the obeisances required of foreign ambassadors by the Sultan as by the Byzantine emperors. The traditional cry of salute to the Sultan resembled the salute to the Basileus, the title given to the Greek and Roman emperors, and the subjects of both served as slaves to their masters. Contemporary Byzantine chronicles did indeed still refer to the Sultan as Basileus—an Islamic Basileus.

As under Byzantium, such matters as court ceremony, costume, and etiquette were laid down in minute detail. Mehmed for his part decreed that the rank and duties of each court official must be recognizable by the colour of his dress. Vezirs, for example, wore green, chamberlains scarlet, while in the Islamic hierarchy muftis wore white, members of the ulema violet, mullahs sky blue. The colour of boots too had its importance, government employees wearing them green, palace employees light red. Besides the colour, the style of a costume had its own significance—the cut of its sleeves, the fur which trimmed it, above all the form of the turban and the shape of the wearer's beard. For in an Islamic society headgear had an especial symbolic importance. The turban was exclusively reserved for Moslems. But non-Moslems, whether Franks or Greeks, were expected to wear a bonnet of red, black, or yellow, while their shoes must be different in colour from those of the Moslems, the slippers and boots of the Greeks, Armenians, and Jews being respectively black, violet, and blue.

In one particular respect Mehmed II departed from the traditions of his Ottoman ancestors to follow directly the example of Byzantium. Previously sultans had been accessible to their subjects and mixed with them in relative informality. But with their conquests in Europe and through Byzantine influence, there developed an increasing concern for the sacredness of the person of the sovereign, together with a habit of seclusion appropriate to majesty, applied not only to his harem, which came to be well guarded by eunuchs, but to the Sultan himself. Already Mehmed had departed from the practice of his earlier forebears, who had taken meals freely with their subjects, and even from that of his father, Murad II, who had limited to ten the number of those who might be served with him at table. He ate his meals alone, issuing a decree which excluded all vezirs and other officers from the table: "It is not my will that anyone should be served with my Imperial Majesty, except those of royal blood."

In his first palace, built on the third hill, he could not achieve sufficient seclusion, since it was situated behind inadequate walls, in a quarter of the city too crowded to be compatible with the aloofness of majesty. This factor influenced his choice of the site for a new palace, the Grand Seraglio or Palace of the Cannon Gate. This he started to build in 1465 on the pivotal site of the former Byzantine Acropolis, the promontory commanding the confluence of the three seas—the Golden Horn, the Bosporus, and the Marmara—which was to become known as Seraglio Point. The plans for the palace, entrusted to Persian, Arab, and Greek architects, were so grandiose that its completion, so it was at first supposed, would take twenty-five years. But thanks to an extra high scale of wages, to the lavish *bakshish* he dispersed among the workers, and to the driving force of the Sultan's own personal supervision, it was completed within a quarter of that time. Within its high fortress walls with its three gates and two courtyards were innumerable buildings, designed mostly in the form of elegant kiosks, and on every side (records his contemporary Greek biographer Critoboulos) "vast and very beautiful gardens, in which grew every imaginable plant and fruit; water, fresh, clear and drinkable, flowed in abundance on every side; flocks of birds, both of the edible and the singing variety, chattered and warbled; herds of both domestic and wild animals browsed there." Here, during the winters between campaigns, the Sultan withdrew from the public eye, appearing in the streets of the city only on state occasions and heavily guarded.

In laying out this new Seraglio Mehmed was to establish the pattern

The Chief White Eunuch in the sixteenth century was the principal administrator of the Palace School and later became, in effect, the master of ceremonies at the Sultan's court.

A Mufti interpreted the law and belonged to the ulema or class of religious leaders.

of Ottoman court life for many centuries to come. The palace was divided into two main sections, an outer court devoted to the official services and offices of the Sultan, including the Divan, and an inner court containing his throne room and royal apartments, together with those of his eunuchs and pages. A century later it was to become the "House of Felicity," devoted to the apartments of his women and thus embodying the harem. This Mehmed himself preferred to house apart, in his former palace on the third hill, which, with its 370 eunuchs, thus remained the center of his private household.

To the Seraglio there were three successive gateways, the first, connecting it directly to the city, being the Imperial Gate, or *Bab-i-Humayun,* on which an inscription survives, commemorating its founder, "Sultan Mehmed . . . Shadow and Spirit of God amongst man, Monarch of this terrestrial orb, Lord of two continents and of two seas, and of the east and the west, and conqueror of the City of Constantinople." It was an early habit of the Turks to use palace gates for the dispensation of law and justice, and it may well be this gate, traditionally succeeding the lofty portal of the Sultan's tent with its four poles, which gave to the Turkish government the name of the Porte, or, as Europeans were to call it, the Sublime Porte.

The agha, or keeper of the gate, regulating communications between the Sultan's Seraglio and the outside world, was the Chief of the White Eunuchs, who controlled the official section of the court, with its personnel, and was in fact Master of Ceremonies. He was besides the Sultan's confidential agent. He had under him a hierarchy of other white eunuchs, who performed the various functions of court chamberlains. Parallel to him was the Chief of the Black Eunuchs, the agha in control of those who served the women's quarters, as eventually established within the Seraglio. The use of eunuchs, unknown to the earlier Ottoman sultans, was a custom introduced from the Byzantine Empire, which had in turn derived it from the Orient. Since castration was forbidden by Islam, the eunuchs were imported by the Ottomans from Christian countries, mostly at this time from the Caucasus through the agency of a trade which, like that of slaves in general, was largely in the hands of the Jews.

The Chief White Eunuch controlled the entire personnel of the Sultan's court, consisting of some 350 persons. All were former Christians, as indeed were all the civil and most of the military officials of the Ottoman state, from the Grand Vezir and his fellow vezirs down to provincial governors, fief holders, tax collectors, and executives of different grades. For all were members of the Sultan's "Slave Household," of which the Seraglio provided the prototype—personal slaves of their master, who remained so throughout life, regardless of any level of preferment and power to which they might attain. This was the product of a fusion of two institutions, military and civil. It derived initially from the *devshirme,* or law of draft, called by Europeans the "Law of Tribute Children," which had in the first place created the corps of the Janissaries and which subsequently developed in parallel terms under Murad II, as an instrument not merely of military power but of civil government. Murad had thus evolved a new and more vigorous ruling establishment to replace the old, and it was this that his son Mehmed inherited, enlarged, and improved.

Its strength and importance lay mainly in the fact that it was non-hereditary, precluding the further rise of a native-born aristocracy and nobility, such as the old had been, and thus safeguarding from political rivalry the absolute power of the sultanate. It was realistically argued that if Moslems were to become slaves of the Sultan they would abuse this privilege. Their relatives in the provinces would oppress the peasantry, refuse to pay taxes, rebel against the local authorities. "But if Christian children accept Islam they become zealous in the faith and enemies of their relatives." Thus as a foreign visitor to Istanbul, Baron Wenceslas Wradislaw, later expressed it: "Never . . . did I hear it said of any pasha, or observe either in Constantinople or in the whole land of Turkey, that any pasha was a national born Turk; on the contrary, kidnapped, or captured, or turned Turk."

The essential source of this system was the Palace School for the imperial pages within the walls of the Sultan's Seraglio. Its aim was the selection and promotion under a hereditary Sultan of this non-hereditary ruling class, with equality of opportunity, an elite recruited on the principle of merit alone. It was indeed to create for the Ottoman state a meritocracy unique in the aristocratic world of this age. Sultan Mehmed's ambition was to expand and develop the school, and the consequent need for more space may indeed have influenced his choice of Seraglio Point as a site for his new palace. Inspired by Mehmed's own high respect for education and the use of the intellect, and by his sense of the need for enlightened officials, both civil and military, as his empire expanded, it was to become under his direction a great school of state, highly organized and imaginatively planned.

The idea of such an instrument for the development of a ruling elite from among his Christian-born subjects was influenced at the start by a realization of the remarkable personal loyalty of his pages, and thus their potential value as a force to offset the Janissaries, with their rebellious inclinations. It aimed to create a type of Ottoman public servant who was at once warrior, statesman, and loyal Moslem and who should be also, in the words of a later, sixteenth-century Italian writer, "a man of letters and a gentleman of polished speech, profound courtesy and honest morals." Out of such promising material the Palace Schools were to produce from among their alumni

The *sarikche bashi* was the Sultan's Master of the Turban.

The *iskemliji* was the Sultan's footstool carrier.

four out of five Grand Vezirs from this time onward. Thriving for three and a half centuries on the general lines established by Mehmed, and on changed lines for a century and a half longer, they made a vital and permanent contribution to Ottoman history.

Under the administrative control of the Chief White Eunuch, through the Hall of the Imperial Treasury on the one hand and on the other of the Privy Commissariat, the school was composed, according to the age of the pupils, of two preparatory schools, then of two schools for vocational training. Within the limits of an early process of discrimination between pupils of intellectual and those of manual tendencies, they allowed in all for a fourteen-year period of instruction with a novitiate of seven or eight years. The majority of pages did not rise beyond this novitiate to become personal servants of the Sultan, but after their preparatory training were appointed to lesser military and government posts. Late in his reign Mehmed introduced a third vocational school, the Hall of the Royal Bedchamber, with some forty pages under four officers—the Swordbearer, the Master of the Horse, the Master of the Wardrobe, and the Master of the Turban. Each hall had a first officer, responsible for order and discipline, and a second officer, a steward, together with its own librarian, recorder, treasurer and imam, and three muezzins. Much attention was paid to the individual merits of pupils with a view to discerning ability, initiative, and capacity for leadership, and they were encouraged to study the subjects of their choice. Promotions within the Palace School, as subsequently in the offices of state, were strictly based on a system in which pages were "rewarded for the smallest service to their lord and punished for the smallest fault."

The purpose of the Palace School, after allowing for instruction in the Koran and the principles of Islamic theology and law, was essentially secular, with an emphasis on statecraft and military science rather than religion. It was thus without parallel in Islam. The teaching staff were in the first place drawn largely from the ulema, Moslem "priests" and professors of the Sacred Law. But to these Mehmed added scholars, scientists, and men of letters drawn from his court. Through them there was scope for education on the Greek and Latin model, so that this Ottoman state has even been compared with Plato's Republic. To this "Republic" Byzantine Greeks who had fled to Italy during the Conquest soon began to return.

In general, the curriculum of the Palace School, as inspired by Mehmed, combined instruction equally in the liberal arts, in physical exercise, and in manual and vocational training. The liberal arts covered the Turkish, Arabic, and Persian languages, with especial emphasis on Turkish, which with all its complexities had to be thoroughly and fluently mastered; on the Arabic alphabet, grammar, and syntax; on Persian literature, with its poetry and its preoccupation with chivalry and romance. Turkish history was also taught, and mathematics in terms of arithmetic and perhaps geometry. The pupils learned to practice those arts and crafts and sciences for which they were seen, by discriminating masters, to have an especial capacity. Among them was Turkish music, both martial and vocal. The chorus of the palace gave regular concerts for the Sultan, besides saluting him with song half an hour before dawn and an hour and a half after sunset, and with musical greetings on other occasions.

Physical training consisted of gymnastic exercises, which gave to the pages remarkable strength, health, and agility. They practiced all sports—archery, wrestling, swordsmanship, the throwing of javelins, and an early form of polo, with a ball attached to a cord. Horsemanship became increasingly important, as many of the pages were destined for cavalry service, and as befitted so fine an army they became skilled not only in riding but in other feats of arms.

Finally, all but the Janissaries practiced a chosen trade or craft, as taught in the various vocational schools. The sultans themselves did so. Mehmed II became an expert gardener, spending much of his leisure attending to his own palace gardens, where he liked to grow not only flowers and trees but vegetables. There is indeed a story that he once grew a giant cucumber of which he was especially proud but which vanished. In a fury of suspicion he cut open one of his gardeners—and found its remains in his stomach. Selim I and Suleiman I became skilled goldsmiths; Abdul Hamid II was to specialize in cabinetmaking with intricate inlay; while others of the imperial line worked at such crafts as embroidery, the making of bows, and the sharpening of knives and swords. Pages became trained in the mixing of drinks and the cooking of the Sultan's favourite dishes, the laundering of linen, the arrangement of the turban, haircutting, shaving, manicuring, and the various functions of the Turkish bath.

Outside the capital and its Sublime Porte, the administration of the Ottoman Empire was closely linked with the organization and development of the army, whose chiefs were the external or military aghas, as distinct from the internal Aghas of the court. They represented the Sultan's executive authority, as the kadis (judges), drawn from the ulema, represented his legal authority. The division of Ottoman territory into provinces, under tightening central control, was conditioned by military factors. It was divided into two halves, that of Anatolia and that of Rumeli, each controlled by a governor-general, or beylerbey—a pasha of two tails; each subdivided and directly administered through sanjaks, or districts, controlled by military governors, sanjak beys, of whom each received a standard, or *sanjak,* as a symbol of the Sultan's authority. The sanjak bey was a pasha of one tail, whose task it was to muster and lead in his domain the Sultan's forces, to command the police in the interests of public security, and to ensure the regular payment of taxes. In the time of the Conqueror there were twenty sanjaks in Asia and twenty-eight in Europe.

Each of these provinces was divided in turn into a quantity of fiefs, feudal domains large and small—*zeamet* and *timar*—as from the days of the early sultans. They were bestowed, with certain rights over their peasants, on the Turkish-born cavalrymen, the *sipahis*. Their squadrons formed the bulk of the military force of the Empire. They had to be ready at any moment to call their men to arms in specified numbers at the orders of the sanjak bey. In the event of his failure to do so, the *sipahi* was deprived of his fief. This was in any case not hereditary, as in the West. In the event of his death only a small portion of the fief would revert to his son, who would be obliged on his own military merits to earn the right to a larger domain.

The great bulk of the agricultural land in the imperial territories now belonged to the state and was thus controlled by the central government, unimpeded by rights of private property. Mehmed had converted into *timars* the large freehold estates of the Christian lords and the lands of the monasteries. Now he continued this process through the appropriation as "royal lands" of other properties, whether privately or collectively owned. Some of them were apportioned as fiefs among his *vezirs* and other officials, with similar limitations of the hereditary principle. But the bulk of them he allotted as fiefs for the purpose of increasing his cavalry.

The widespread and expanding *timar* system, born of the need to support a large imperial army on the basis of a medieval economy, became the mainspring of an administration geared in its financial, social, and agricultural policies to the military needs of the Empire. It was a system of "fragmented possession" under which the state, the *sipahi,* and the peasant divided rights and responsibilities with regard to the land. The state owned the land. The *sipahi* was authorized by the state to collect from the peasant certain specified revenues, in return for his military services and those of his own horsemen. The peasant—the *raya*—cultivated the land, enjoying its usufruct, in return for this tax and his labour, for the support of his family. It passed to his sons at his death. Here in general, soundly established, closely concerted, and strictly supervised under the rule of Sultan Mehmed, was a state feudal organization which linked to their mutual advantage his producing classes and fighting forces.

These *timar*-holding *sipahis* and their horsemen, armed with such conventional medieval weapons as the bow, sword, shield, lance, and mace, amounted by the end of Mehmed's reign to some forty thousand men. They formed the major part of the Ottoman army. They were distinct from the *sipahis* of the Porte, the Sultan's own palace troops. In case of war their forces were supplemented, as in Osman's time, by irregular cavalry, or *akinjis,* drawn from the mass of the population, who lived through the right to pillage the lands they occupied; also by an infantry militia, introduced by Orkhan, the *azabs*.

But the army's main strength still lay with the Janissaries, the infantry slave force, landless and Christian-born, whose numbers in the time of Mehmed rose to ten thousand men, with increased pay and improved modern firearms. They provided a nucleus of infantry unique at this time in the East, where cavalry predominated, and were matched in the West by no power with which the Turks came in conflict. In the capital they were the only regular force to be garrisoned, under their own Agha, in the imperial palace. In the field, where they would exclusively garrison newly conquered fortresses, with a responsibility which extended beyond their walls, the Janissaries were subject to the jurisdiction of no provincial authority, but took their orders directly from the Sultan, who personally appointed their commanders. Thus they served the central government as an effective counterweight to any such local opposition as might arise in the imperial territory. In this way they played their part as the loyal servants of a line of strong Ottoman sultans, bent since the time of Orkhan on curbing the growth of such an independent feudal nobility as existed in medieval Europe.

Throughout the Empire, with the elimination by Mehmed of the old ruling class and its replacement by ministers who were his own personal slaves, there were only dignities of grade, and these offered free opportunity for promotion. This was a flexible society in which a servant might surpass his master and the master his own superior, where an artisan might rise to the level of a Grand Vezir and a Grand Vezir fall back to the level of an artisan, all as an accepted personal hazard, without loss of caste. Such, based on imperial favours and rewards for merit, was the social and administrative organism of this Islamic empire, differing from any in the Christian West. In the general social pattern of the Ottoman Empire at this time, privilege of birth did not exist. All below the level of the absolute sovereign were equal in the eyes of the law and of their fellow Ottomans. Theirs was a meritocracy in which privilege had to be earned.

The revenues of the state came in the first place from the capitation tax, paid only by the conquered non-Moslems, the *rayas*. They formed the majority of the peasant population and much of the city population, especially in European Turkey. Moslem Turks themselves, and converts, were as in the past exempt from this tax but obliged to pay, only in the event of fighting in their regions, a tithe on their goods, which covered herds, cereals, rice crops, and beehives. When, in the course of fighting, a place by the edge of the sea, or at the entrance to a pass or a forest, acquired strategic importance, the inhabitants of the region, whether *rayas* or not, were exempt from taxation in return for corvées performed in the general interest or as an aid to the troops. Further tax sources included the tribute paid by such states as Wallachia, Moldavia, and the Republic of Ragusa.

But the bulk of the imperial revenue came from various state institutions and enterprises—customs, harbour dues, tolls, ferries, weighing dues, monopolies in such commodities as salt, soap, and candle wax. These, together with certain manufactures and natural resources, including mines for the working of silver, copper, and lead, were often let by the state to concessionaries. This was to their mutual advantage, but could involve social and financial abuses and an excessive exploitation of the means of production. Other means used by the Sultan to raise revenue, at a time when he needed large sums to maintain his armed forces (geared continuously to a war footing), included periodic devaluations of currency, by the minting of new coins and the purchase at a reduced rate of the old. This measure, amounting in effect to a tax on silver currency, caused discontent, especially when officials known as "silver seekers" were sent to the provinces to search premises and confiscate hidden coinage.

More constructively, however, Mehmed contrived in the long term to finance his campaigns by commercial and economic development and a consequent increase in state revenue. His predecessors, seeking to end the privileged political dominion of the Franks in the Levant, had abolished their immunity from customs dues, dating from the latter years of Byzantium, and imposed upon them a duty of 10 percent on the goods they handled. Mehmed now doubled this, and thus aroused loud laments from the Frankish merchants. But in fact their trade was to increase, through the development after the Conquest of a greater degree of political stability throughout the Sultan's dominions, and the opening up of secure communications between remote districts. Prosperity was thus increased through closer and more general economic integration. But internally other non-Moslems, notably Greeks, Armenians, and Jews, tended henceforward to replace the Italian merchants.

Not only Istanbul, with its rapid development, but other cities, like Bursa, Adrianople, and the port of Gallipoli, came to profit from this commercial growth. The cotton industry flourished in western Anatolia, the mohair industry in and around Angora, the silk industry in Istanbul and in Bursa, which was the export center for Western markets. Bursa in particular, the last stage on the road of the silk caravans from Persia, became the international entrepôt for merchandise, which included spices brought via Damascus from India and

Arabia. Such goods came either by the old overland trade routes across Anatolia, through Adana and Konya, or by sea from Egyptian and Syrian ports to Adalia and Alanya, whence iron ore and other goods were exported from Anatolia to Egypt. In this reverse direction, Bursa became also a center for the export of European woollens to the East.

Mehmed the Conqueror, bent on developing his country's resources to the full, devoted much of his formidable energy, with the advice of counsellors from the West, to such matters of trade and finance. From the start of his reign he had set himself besides to the reorganization of his administrative departments and in particular of his treasury, whose tax methods were reformed in an efficient and businesslike manner. In such practical matters he outdid his father. In intellectual respects he had his father to thank, after a delayed start, for a first-class education. He had grown up fluent in six languages—Turkish, Greek, Arabic, Latin, Persian, and Hebrew—and was well grounded by his numerous tutors in Islamic and Greek literature, in the study of philosophy and to a lesser extent of the sciences.

He developed a profound respect for Western as for Eastern culture. From the capture of Constantinople onward he drew to his court numbers of Italians, including Latin humanist scholars and specialists in other branches of learning. Admittedly his purpose in so doing was in part political—the need to provide himself with intelligence on the world which he aspired to conquer, the history and geography of the West and particularly of the Apennine peninsula, its systems of government, its religious beliefs, its internal rivalries and diplomatic intrigues, its armed forces and its military strategy. He relied on such counsellors too for advice on commercial and financial policy. With the aid of scholars he collected for his library in the Seraglio a number of classical manuscripts on which to base his studies, together with Greek works, translated for his benefit into Turkish, on the Christian religion.

Later in his reign, being always free from Islamic inhibitions on the portrayal of the human image, he extended his patronage to Western painting and sculpture, and a number of Italian artists visited his court. Chief among these was the Venetian Gentile Bellini, who came in 1479 in response to a request by the Sultan to the Doge to send him "a good painter." Bellini spent some fifteen months in Istanbul, where he was treated with especial favour. He painted portraits of the Sultan and of other personages at court. There is a tale that Bellini once showed him a picture of the beheading of John the Baptist. This the Sultan contemplated at length, then criticized, explaining from personal experience that the human neck after decapitation appears shorter and more contracted than the artist rendered it. Bellini decorated the internal apartments of the Seraglio with a number of murals and other paintings. All these works of the Renaissance were to be removed as "indecent" after Mehmed's death by his iconoclastic son Bayezid II, who sold them on the open market. Most vanished but for the portrait of the Sultan, which was bought by a Venetian merchant and centuries afterward found its way to the National Gallery in London. Besides asking for a good painter from Venice, Mehmed had asked also for a good sculptor in bronze. Some doubt exists as to who was sent in response to his request, though an undoubted visitor to the court of the Sultan was Costanzo of Ferrara, who made a medallion of the Sultan.

But Mehmed the Conqueror was himself no prince of the Renaissance. He was an imperial sovereign of the Middle Ages, steeped in those traditions of Islam through which he sought, as a holy warrior, to maintain a Pax Ottomanica throughout the former orthodox Christian Empire. Culturally his affinities lay rather with the East than with the West and particularly with Persia. He was drawn to Shi'ism, the heterodox Islam of Persia, with its dervish brotherhoods. But he was unable in practice to reconcile its heresies with the more rigid Sunnite principles of his own Orthodox Islamic state—for according to an Ottoman proverb, "He who reads Persian loses half his faith."

He read it nonetheless, and the especial favour which he showed to Persians, first in the intellectual, then often in the administrative field, was apt to arouse Turkish jealousy. The number of Persians living and writing in the Ottoman Empire under his patronage was greater than at any time before or since. Apart from jurists, most of them were poets, while the Ottoman poets took Persian verse as their model and transposed and reshaped it into Turkish—particularly the great epics of Firdausi and the lyrics of Hafiz. Mehmed himself wrote some eighty poems in the Turkish language, none of them of high quality, and was to become known as "the Rhyming Sultan." He encouraged literature by paying monthly pensions to poets and other masters of literary style. At the same time he did much to further the careers of his own former professors, men of intellectual and other capacities. He liked to converse at his court with an entourage of savants and theologians.

But in this environment the sciences made relatively slow progress. Mehmed himself was interested in astronomy, but mainly as a background to astrology. Never would he take an important step, especially in the military field, before consulting the favoured astrologers at his court. A date and even an hour must be fixed for it in view of the exact positions of the planets. Medical science was still largely undeveloped among the Turks, and the Sultan's own medical advisers were for the most part Jews from Italy. Prominent among these was Jacopo de Gaete, who as Yakub Pasha rose to be a vezir, who became over a period of thirty years a predominant influence at the Sultan's court, not only in medical but in financial affairs, and who accompanied him on all his campaigns. The Venetians, continually bent on the assassination of Mehmed, made over a period of some twenty years no fewer than fourteen attempts to have him poisoned, through their agents, and tried to enlist Jacopo's aid for this purpose—but without success.

Mehmed's health was not good. It first gave concern when he began to grow excessively stout in his early thirties, developing an acute arthritic condition which was hereditary and which at times made it painful for him to ride on horseback, as he had to do in the course of his campaigns. Overindulgent as he was in the pleasures of the flesh, both eating and—in this respect a bad Moslem—drinking to excess, he grew continually more corpulent. He suffered from acute attacks of gout and colic, and there were increasingly long spells when he could not move from his palace. In recent generations the average life-span of the Ottoman rulers had shortened. Over the past century and a half only one of them had lived beyond the age of fifty. In 1479, still in his late forties, Mehmed had a tumour on the leg which puzzled the physicians. By the end of the following year, when Bellini painted his portrait, he was clearly a very sick man.

In the spring of 1481 he crossed with his armies into Asia, and began to move in a southerly direction on a campaign whose destination was, according to his custom, kept secret. He might be planning to march in person once more against Rhodes. He might have designs on the domains of the Mamluk sultan of Egypt. But en route he was seized with violent colitis, aggravating the gout and the arthritis from which he still suffered. His private Persian physician gave him a remedy which was ineffective—and which his enemies declared was an overdose of opium, administered on the instructions of his son Bayezid. When Yakub Pasha finally reached his master's bedside he pronounced this dose to have been fatal: the Sultan's intestines were blocked. There was nothing more to be done. Mehmed the Conqueror died on May 4, 1481, at the hour of the afternoon prayer. He was forty-nine years old.

"The great eagle is dead." Thus did a messenger communicate the news to the Republic of Venice. The West could breathe again, freed from fear of the East—and to remain free from its threats for forty years to come. In fact Sultan Mehmed II in a generation of campaigning had not greatly extended his imperial frontiers. He had failed before Belgrade, before Rhodes, and before Otranto. He had nonetheless, as he claimed, become the master of two seas and two continents. As a conqueror he finally sealed the foundations of a great Islamic empire; as a statesman he had created within it the structure of a new and enduring Islamic state, worthy in its institutions, traditions, and policies to succeed the imperial civilizations of classical Rome and Christian Greece, and indeed serving as a zealous protector of Orthodox Christendom. For this cardinal achievement he must rank in historical perspective as an outstanding sovereign of the Middle Ages.

PART

III

ZENITH OF EMPIRE

((11))

The sixteenth century was to see the greatest of all Ottoman Sultans, Suleiman I, known to the world at large as Suleiman the Magnificent, and to his own subjects as Suleiman the Lawgiver. Great-grandson of Mehmed II, he was to expand and to raise the Ottoman Empire, further than the Conqueror himself had conceived it, to the zenith of its power and prestige. But meanwhile the spirit of fratricide inherent in the Ottoman dynasty was to erupt after Mehmed's death into a long period of strife between his two sons, Bayezid II and his younger brother, Prince Jem.

Sultan Bayezid, the antithesis of his father, was a peace-loving, contemplative scholar, mystical in his beliefs, austere in his habits, and tolerant in his outlook, who did not seek to make conquests and became known to contemporary writers as the "Law-Abiding." He was the first Ottoman Sultan to relinquish the practice of invariably leading his own armies in the field. Jem, on the other hand, twelve years younger, was a man of action and a figure of romance, vigorous and valiant, with a taste for the pleasures of life. He cultivated the arts, living among poets and himself becoming a poet of talent. "In his hand," wrote his biographer, "the Cup of Jamshid replaced the Seal of Solomon, and with him the voice of minstrelsy was heard for the drum of victory."

On the Conqueror's death, Jem at once took up arms and staked his claim to the throne, which his father had favoured. But the Ottoman succession was coming increasingly to depend on the power of the Janissaries, and they favoured Bayezid as more representative of the Ghazi tradition. With some official and popular backing, they strongly opposed the Conqueror's last Grand Vezir, Karamanli Mehmed Pasha, and his policies. Jem, who supported him, was governor of Karamania, with his capital in Konya, half as far from Istanbul as Amasya, where Bayezid was governor. But Bayezid, with opposition support, contrived to reach the capital first. Here he promised the requisite gifts and concessions to the Janissaries and thus assured his accession.

The Janissaries, anticipating his arrival, had meanwhile seized control of the capital. Here, in collusion with certain officials in the palace, they assassinated the Grand Vezir, bearing his head through the streets on a lance; then they intercepted and impaled the emissaries he was sending to Jem. In return, Bayezid undertook to abandon his father's unpopular practice of currency devaluation and to restore lands which he had alienated as fiefs to their private owners and pious foundations. In general, he was inclined to reverse his father's policies, and revert to those of his grandfather Murad II.

But Jem was a fighter and would not give in. Raising the standard of revolt against Bayezid, with the support of a force from Karamania and from among the Turcoman tribes of the Taurus, he captured Bursa, where he proclaimed himself Sultan. He minted his own coinage, caused the public prayer to be recited in his name, and reigned for eighteen days. He proposed to his brother that they should partition the Empire between them, Bayezid ruling over Europe and Jem over Asia. But Bayezid's troops marched against him under Gedik Ahmed Pasha, his father's leading commander and a hero of the Janissaries, who renounced for the purpose a renewal of his campaign from Albania against Italy.

He defeated Jem in two successive campaigns, each time failing to capture him, but driving him into exile. First he fled from Ottoman into Mamluk territory, through Aleppo and Damascus and Jerusalem to Cairo, where he was given the hospitality and protection of Kait Bey, the Mamluk sultan of Egypt. Thence he made the pilgrimage to the holy places of Mecca and Medina. Returning to Anatolia with the aid of his protector, he rallied Karamanian supporters around him once more, but was again defeated when his army deserted him before Angora; and he fled to Cilicia.

Bayezid, adopting a conciliatory tone, offered Jem the substantial revenues of the state of Karamania, which he had governed, if he would retire peacefully to Jerusalem. "The Empire," he insisted, "is a bride that cannot be shared between rivals." But Jem preferred now to seek the protection of the Knights of the Order of St. John of Jerusalem, the Knights Hospitallers, in Rhodes, where he was received with imperial honours by the grand master, D'Aubusson. Later a treaty was signed by which Bayezid paid the knights of the order an annual stipend of forty-five thousand gold pieces for as long as his brother remained in their custody.

Though Jem did not at first fully realize it, the concern of the knights for him was essentially political in motive. He was in fact a precious hostage in the hands of Christendom against Ottoman aggression. His hosts, first in France, then at the Vatican in Rome, were really his jailers and would-be exploiters, awaiting a propitious moment to let loose this "brother of the Turk" on their now formidable common enemy. He came to be used as a pawn in the diplomatic intrigues of the contending Christian princes. Finally he died in Naples, perhaps poisoned, as was widely and with evidence believed, by the Borgia Pope to spite the Frankish king, and with the connivance of his own brother, the Sultan—who could after all invoke the law of fratricide as a legitimate pretext for any such crime.

For all his peaceable inclinations, Bayezid, both before and after Jem's death, was inexorably involved in the maneuvers of European diplomacy. It became the practice of the European states to exploit against one another in Italy the threat of Ottoman support. The Ottoman Empire was now a factor to reckon with, not only on land but in the Mediterranean. Bayezid, determined to put an end to all crusading adventures, continued to build up the Ottoman fleet, as his father had initially done. Seeking in a massive shipbuilding program to achieve for it naval supremacy in the Mediterranean, he used it to effect in the renewal of the war against Venice, when his land and sea forces captured successively Lepanto, Modon, Coron, and Navarino, in Greece. Bayezid offered support to Milan and Naples, from whose monarch he hoped to secure the cession of Otranto. But he did not venture to cross the Adriatic. For Venice could count on naval support from the French, the Spaniards, and the Portuguese.

A peace treaty was signed in 1503 between the Sultan and the Venetians and these various allies which mainly confirmed the *status quo*. But the war had diminished the naval power of Venice, to the advantage of the Ottoman navy, which engaged thereafter in practical raids not merely on the eastern but on the western Mediterranean coasts. Here they were welcomed as "sea Ghazis" by the Moslems of Spain and North Africa. At the same time Bayezid encouraged on a large scale the commercial and economic expansion of his empire, trading profitably with the merchants of the Italian states, and furthering the immigration into his dominions of more Jews, when they were driven from Spain at the end of the fifteenth century.

In Asia, meanwhile, the Ottomans were having trouble with the Turcoman nomads, those turbulent tribesmen who had roamed the marches of Anatolia from earliest times, and who now, thanks to incitement from beyond the Syrian and Persian frontiers, were in repeated rebellion against the central authority. In six successive annual campaigns the Ottomans fought for supremacy over them against the forces of the Mamluk sultan in Syria, and pacification was finally achieved only at the cost of Ottoman border concessions to the Mamluks.

The grievances of the Turcomans arose from the establishment, as the Empire developed, of a centralized administration which sought to control and to tax them, curbing their previous tribal autonomy and protecting the settled agricultural peasantry against their destructive raids. Wearing red hats, hence known as Kizil Bash, or "redheads," they were religious heretics and as such encouraged, in the

THE EMPIRE
POLAND
UKRA
GALICIA
PODOLIA
Nemirov
Bug
Dniester
BESSARABIA
R. Pruth
MOLDAVIA
TRANSYLVANIA
JED
R. Danube
Vienna
STYRIA
Buda Pesth
HUNGARY
St. Gothard
Isonzo R.
R. Piave
Tisza R.
Szeged
Trieste
Venice
R. Drava
R. Sava
Fiume
R. Tagliamento
CROATIA
Karlowitz
Belgrade
RUMANIA
BOSNIA
Orsova
Bucharest
WALLACHIA
R. Danube
DOBRUJA
Silistria
DALMATIA
Sarajevo
SERBIA
Toulon
ITALY
HERZE-GOVINA
Morava R.
Nicopolis
Varna
NOVI BAZAR
Plevna
Ragusa
Tirnovo
MONTENEGRO
Kossovo
Sofia
BULGARIA
Cattaro
Kumanovo
Struma
Philippopolis
Scutari
Vardar
Rhodope Mts.
Adrianople
RUMELIA
Istanbul
ALBANIA
Monastir
THRACE
Tirana
Brindisi
Taranto
Otranto
MACEDONIA
Salonica
Thasos
Imbros
Gallipoli
OTTOMAN
Burs
KARASI
EPIRUS
Lemnos
Kutahy
GERM
Corfu
THESSALY
Parga
Lesbos
Bergama
SARUHAN
Messina
Preveso
Negroponte
Magnesia
Philadelph
Livadia
Chios
Izmir
Bizerta
Mesolonghi
Meander R.
Patras
Athens
Samos
AYDIN
Corinth
Tunis
MOREA
Milas
MENTESH
GREECE
Bodrum
Cos
Rhode
Malta
Cerigo
TUNISIA
Sfax
Candia
Gafsa
Crete
Jerba
MEDITERRANEAN SEA
Tripoli
Benghazi
TRIPOLI
CYRENAICA
EG
Boundary of Ottoman Empire
Vassal states

N E
Poltava
R. Don
R. Volga
Astrakhan
R. Dnieper
Taganrog
SEA OF AZOV
Kuban R.
Crimea
Eupatoria
Sebastopol
CASPIAN SEA
DAGHESTAN
MINGRELIA
GEORGIA
Tiflis
CK SEA
Batum
Kura R.
Sinope
Trebizond
TREBIZOND
KARABAGH
Erivan
Aras R.
Erzurum
ARMENIA
Erzinjan
AZERBAIJAN
Tabriz
KARA-KOYUNLU
L. Van
Angora
ERETNA
Bitlis
Tehran
AK-KOYUNLU
KURDISTAN
Halys R.
Kayseri
Malatya
KARAMAN
DULKADIR
Mardin
Urfa
Mosul
Konya
MESOPOTAMIA
Taurus Mts
Adana
Alexandretta
R. Tigris
LURISTAN
Ermenek
CILICIA
Antioch
Aleppo
Orontes R.
SYRIA
R. Euphrates
Baghdad
Nicosia
Cyprus
LEBANON
Beirut
Damascus
Basra
Acre
KUWAIT
PERSIAN GULF
Haifa
Jordan
Amman
Jaffa
Palestine
Jerusalem
EL HASA
Alexandria
Cairo
Suez
Sinai
P T
HEJAZ
RED SEA
R. Nile
0 100 200 300 400 miles
K.C.JORDAN

border regions of Persia, by the spiritual and political leadership of Ismail, a new ruler who proclaimed himself shah of Persia in 1502. Inheriting the ambitions of Uzun Hassan and the tribal affiliations of his White Sheep, Ismail followed his example by seeking alliance with Venice, and himself led incursions into Ottoman territory. Meanwhile the rebellious forces of the Kizil Bash penetrated in his name as far as the walls of Bursa, where Bayezid's Grand Vezir, Ali Pasha, was killed in battle. Ismail, claiming direct descent through Mohammed's son-in-law, Ali, from the Prophet, proclaimed Shi'ism, the branch of Islam which had supported the legitimacy of Ali's claims to the caliphate, and to which (with its mystical and intuitive qualities) the Persian people were particularly attached, to be the official religion of the realm—in contrast to Sunni Islam, which had supported the claims of the Umayyad family, and which, becoming the dominant faith of the Islamic community, has hence come to be known as "orthodox."

Ismail became known as the Great Sufi, while his heterodox beliefs won wide support throughout eastern and southern Anatolia. Bayezid himself, with his mystical inclinations, had shown some sympathy with the philosophical doctrines of Sufism. But he was bound to reject it when used as an instrument of political subversion by a foreign monarch within his own frontiers. The Ottoman armies thus opposed Ismail, though they did not bring him to battle. But his emergence to power was to create within the Ottoman dynasty a new conflict, now with religious implications. Of the Sultan's three surviving sons, all governors of provinces, the youngest, Selim, was the most vigorous and warlike, thus contrasting with his father but resembling his grandfather, the Conqueror. Bayezid's own favourite was his second son, Ahmed, whose talent was rather for administration.

Selim, knowing that Bayezid was in poor health and determined to ensure his claim to the succession, paid an impetuous visit to Istanbul, where he canvassed the support of the Janissaries, now resentful of Bayezid's military inaction and their consequent exclusion from the material fruits of conquest. But Bayezid was able for the present to thwart him and continued, with the support of his officials, to favour the cause of Ahmed. Selim fled to the Crimea, where his son, Suleiman—the great Sultan-to-be—was governor. Here he mobilized an army, marched around the north of the Black Sea, and seized Adrianople. Meanwhile, Ahmed in Anatolia had turned heretic, donning the red hat of the Kizil Bash and raising a force to take Bursa. He thus sacrificed the support of his father. Selim, clinching that of the Janissaries, now proceeded with a force of them to Istanbul, and here Bayezid agreed to abdicate in his favour. After yielding to him the imperial scepter, the deposed Sultan asked to be allowed to retire to his birthplace at Demotika. But he died en route—possibly poisoned on the orders of his son.

Thus began the reign of Selim I, Selim Yavuz, or "the Grim," as he came to be called. His first action on ascending the throne was to have his two brothers strangled with the bowstring. He extended the fratricidal principle to cover also the strangulation of his five orphan nephews, boys from the age of five upward, while he listened to their cries from an adjoining room. Having thus drastically secured his power at home, he turned his armed forces eastward into Asia, leaving Europe for the present alone.

Religious and indeed fanatical in impulse, the new Sultan was dedicated above all to the extermination from his empire of the heresy of Shi'ism. His main enemy was its exponent, the Persian shah Ismail. Before embarking on a holy war against him, Selim saw to the elimination of some forty thousand of Ismail's religious followers in Anatolia, an action comparable in Islamic terms to the contemporary Massacre of St. Bartholomew in Christian Europe. For its vindication of orthodoxy this won him the name of "the Just."

Proclaiming his planned campaign as that of a Ghazi against heretics, he addressed to the shah a series of provocative and truculent missives. Ismail refused to be provoked by him, proposing peaceful relations. When Selim and his forces advanced, he withdrew behind his frontiers, following a scorched-earth policy, but was finally forced to give battle in the valley of Chalderan, where Selim was victorious. He captured Tabriz, massacring his prisoners but dispatching to Istanbul some thousand of those craftsmen for whom the city was famous, there to ply their trade and enrich Ottoman architecture. In ensuing campaigns he occupied various other cities and territories, and finally annexed the high plateau of eastern Anatolia—providing the Ottoman Empire with a natural strategic rampart against all invasions from the east, and thus materially altering the balance of power in Asia.

As an economic weapon against Persia he banned the silk trade, source of the country's main exports to the West, which accounted for most of its revenue in silver and gold, and exiled to the Balkans the Persian silk merchants of Bursa. In a similar spirit of economic warfare, he later tried to stop the Mamluk trade in Circassian slaves from the Caucasus.

Having won his victory against Persia, Selim in 1516 turned his forces on the Mamluks. Hitherto they had relied on Ottoman support, on the one hand against the threat from Ismail, on the other in naval terms against new threats from the Portuguese in their rear, fruits of the African and Indian navigations of Vasco da Gama. To meet

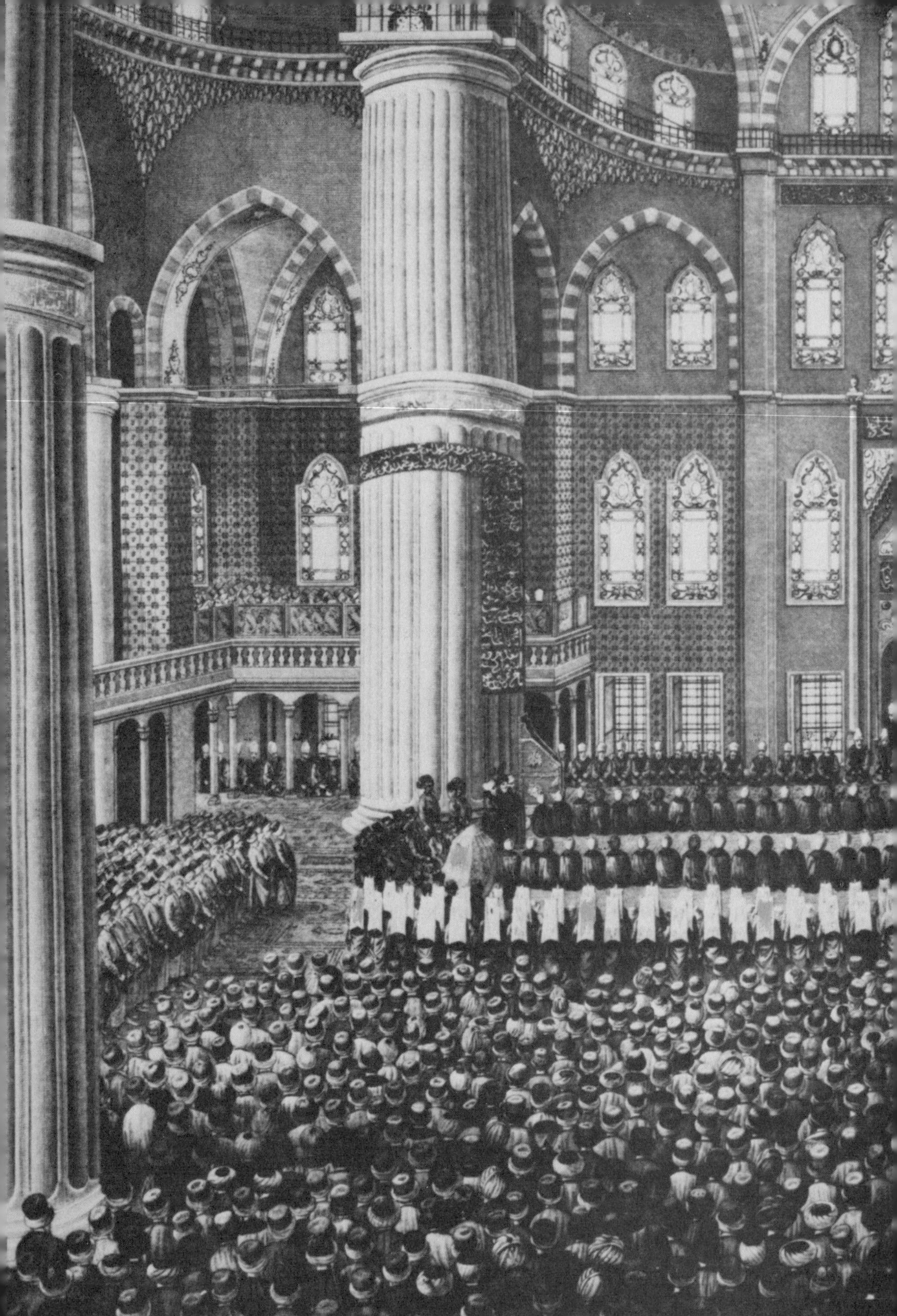

Ignatius Mouradger d'Ohsson, *Tableau général de l'empire Ottoman,* Paris, 1787, Vol. 1, plate 25.

Celebration of the feast of the birthday of the Prophet in the Sultanahmed (Blue) Mosque, and a good view of its interior architecture.

the Portuguese threat the Mamluks needed from the Ottomans timber and other materials for shipbuilding, together with gunpowder and arms.

But now that Selim's forces were encroaching on the frontier areas of Syria, the aged Mamluk sultan Al-Ghawri could no longer afford to remain neutral, and marched a force northward from Egypt. This provoked Selim to lead his army against Aleppo, routing the sultan before the city, leaving him dead from a stroke on the battlefield, then proceeding to capture Damascus, Beirut, and Gaza, in Palestine. Here he made a pilgrimage to the tombs of the prophets and the Rock of Abraham, at Jerusalem.

Ottoman governors were appointed in the various conquered cities. They treated the princes of the Lebanon only as nominal vassals, acted tolerantly toward Christians and Jews, and reduced tariffs and fees for pilgrims to Jerusalem, for Selim was more indulgent to Christians than to Moslem heretics.

On the frontiers of Egypt the Sultan paused. He now had in his hands the orthodox Abbasid caliph Al-Mutawakkil, who had accompanied the army of the defeated Mamluk sultan, and whom he treated with deference tempered by vigilance. He wrote to Al-Ghawri's successor in Cairo, Tuman Bey, declaring that the caliph and his judges had sworn him allegiance, hence that he was now the rightful sultan of all the Mamluk dominions. He was, however, prepared to leave the Mamluk in Cairo as governor, a vassal paying tribute to Istanbul.

When Tuman Bey refused to surrender and defiantly proclaimed himself Mamluk sultan, Selim with his army crossed the Sinai Desert. After a successful preliminary battle, he sent the caliph into Cairo with his army, promising to deal kindly with the people of Egypt, as distinct from their rulers, and thus hoping to calm their fears. The next day the Friday prayer was read in his name, signalizing the end of the Mamluk regime. After some days of fighting in Cairo itself and around it, Tuman Bey was defeated in a battle near the Pyramids, and hanged at the city gate which traditionally served as a scaffold.

Selim spent some six months in Cairo, planning the future of Egypt as a tributary state. In the autumn of 1517, leaving behind him a governor-general, he started to lead his army back to Istanbul. Meanwhile the caliph had been dispatched ahead of him to be kept at his court, and the office of the caliphate was now generally held to have passed to the Ottoman Sultans. Of more tangible significance was the transfer to Istanbul of the standard and cloak of the Prophet, relics whose possession symbolized the status of the sultans as protectors of the holy places of Mecca, Medina, and the pilgrim routes of the Hejaz, hence of Islam in general. Selim could thus now claim to be head of Islam, as the Mamluk sultans had claimed before him. As he was the most powerful sovereign in the Moslem world, all of its rulers were now in theory regarded as subject to his overriding authority.

Selim died painfully of cancer some two years later, in a village on the road to Adrianople, remarking a little beforehand that he had no journey left to make, save to the hereafter. A big man, fierce in aspect and violent in character, with fiery eyes and a choleric complexion, he had scant regard for human life. Stories of his impulsive brutalities abounded. One of his earliest public actions—so it was said—was to strike dead with his own sword a provincial governor who, following concessions the Sultan had made to the Janissaries, was rash enough to request an increase of revenue for himself. Selim was ready enough to order the execution on the spot, by the mutes who attended him, of any man who disagreed with or otherwise displeased him.

The lives and careers of his Grand Vezirs were thus inclined to be brief. Seven of them were beheaded by his orders, together with numerous other officials and generals. The phrase "Mayest thou be Selim's Vezir" came to be used in Turkish parlance as implying the curse "Strike you dead!" As a precautionary measure, vezirs developed the prudent habit of carrying their last testaments with them when summoned to the Sultan's presence. One of them ventured playfully to ask his master for some preliminary notice as to when he might expect his doom, so that he should have time to put his affairs in order. To this Selim replied with a robust laugh: "I have been thinking for some time of having thee killed, but I have at present no one fit to take thy place; otherwise I would willingly oblige thee."

Despite such hazards there was no shortage of applicants for the high offices. For the rewards were as great as the risks. Moreover, life at Selim's court and in his presence was eventful and stimulating, with undercurrents of reckless and full-blooded gaiety. His cruelties, all too characteristic as they were of the spirit of the time, were animated by a brutal gusto, contrasting with the cold calculation of those of his grandfather the Conqueror. For all this barbarism Selim was also paradoxically a man of notable culture, devoted to literature and with a talent for poetry. He wrote a book of odes in the Persian language, and liberally patronized learned men, taking with him on his campaigns bards and historians to record their events and recite the heroic exploits of the Ottomans.

He was above all a great warrior. Balancing by his imperial conquests in Islamic Asia those of his grandfather and his forebears in Christian Europe, he doubled in less than a decade the extent of the Ottoman Empire. By the time of his death it extended from the banks of the Danube to those of the Nile, from the coasts of the Adriatic to those of the Indian Ocean. Such now, extending far into two continents, was the imperial inheritance of his son Suleiman.

((12))

THE ACCESSION OF SULEIMAN TO THE OTTOMAN SULTANATE IN 1520 coincided with a turning point in the history of European civilization. The darkness of the late Middle Ages, with its dying feudal institutions, was giving place to the golden light of the Renaissance. Mature, civilized states were emerging to power, under youthful sovereigns of outstanding individual caliber. The sixteenth century was the age of Charles V and the Habsburg empire; of Francis I and the house of Valois in France; of Henry VIII and the Tudors in England. These three powerful monarchs were now matched by a "second Solomon," the twenty-six-year-old Sultan Suleiman.

In the West he was to become an integral element in the Christian balance of power. In the Islamic East great glories were predicted for him. The tenth Ottoman Sultan, reigning at the start of the tenth century of the Hegira, he was in Moslem eyes the living incarnation of the blessed number ten—the number of man's fingers and toes and ten senses, the ten parts of the Koran and its variants, the Ten Commandments of the Pentateuch, the ten disciples of the Prophet, the ten skies of the Islamic heavens and the ten guardian spirits presiding within them. Oriental tradition related that at the start of each century a great man arose, destined to "take it by the horns," to master it and become its embodiment; and here now he was, in the shape of Suleiman, the "Perfector of the Perfect Number," hence the Angel of Heaven.

Since the Fall of Constantinople and the subsequent conquests of Mehmed, the Western powers had been forced to take serious account of the advance of the Ottoman Turks. Seeing it as a permanent source of anxiety, they prepared to confront it in terms not only of military defense but of diplomatic action. The threat of an Ottoman intervention, the rumour of a secret Ottoman alliance, served as a useful weapon of diplomacy among the Italian states. There were people, at this period of religious ferment, who believed that a Turkish invasion would be the divine judgment on Europe's sins; there were places where the "Turk-bells" called the faithful each day to penitence and prayer. Crusader legends had foretold that the conquering Turks would advance as far as the holy city of Cologne, but that here their invasion would be repelled in a great victory by a Christian emperor

—not a Pope—and their forces driven back beyond Jerusalem itself. When Charles V became Holy Roman Emperor he was popularly acclaimed in this context as the champion of Christendom.

Charles's imperial dominion, thanks to a sequence of judicious marriages and opportune deaths, extended from the Baltic to the Mediterranean, from the Netherlands through Germany and Austria to Spain. It embodied also the kingdoms of Naples and Sicily and a foothold in Mexico and Peru. From his inherited Austrian lands beyond the Alps Charles confronted the neighbouring threat from the Ottoman Turks, now to be enhanced under Suleiman.

Aware as he increasingly became of this menace, his more immediate and direct enemy was Francis I of France, his defeated rival in the election for the mantle of Holy Roman Emperor, with whom he was at war soon after Suleiman's accession. It was Charles's ambition to unite Western Christendom in a Holy Roman Empire under Habsburg dominion. But France was an obstacle to such dreams of European conquest, dividing his German from his Spanish dominions, obstructing his designs in northern Italy, where the two rulers were engaged in continual frontier disputes, and presenting a threat to the sea communications on which his military security and commercial prosperity depended. Such was the conflict dividing the two main Christian powers, which made of the infidel not always a common foe but as often a potential and desirable ally.

So Francis was now to find. Having initially preached a grand papal crusade against the Turks, he soon started to canvass their support, for they shared this mutual enemy in the Habsburg empire. He did so secretly and with duplicity, forging on the basis of their respective political interests a "sacrilegious union of the Lily and the Crescent," which he sought at first to conceal from the Christian world but which was to endure, with interruptions and vicissitudes, for some three hundred years. Suleiman subsidized him on several occasions, sending him in 1533 a sum of one hundred thousand gold pieces to help him form a coalition against Charles V, with England and the German princes. Two years later Francis requested a subsidy of a million ducats. To the Venetian ambassador he admitted that he saw in the Ottoman Empire the only force guaranteeing the combined existence of the states of Europe against the Habsburg emperor.

When Charles taunted Francis with pro-Moslem sympathies, he would overtly promise to join a crusade, then explain away the promise through his envoy in Istanbul. Such explanations satisfied the astute Sultan, who well recognized the French need for an Ottoman alliance, and himself came to rely on it as a basic element in the fabric of his own foreign policy. Thus was Suleiman cast, in the Europe of the sixteenth century, in a balancing role which enhanced, in diplomatic as in military terms, the power and prestige of the Ottoman Empire.

As befitted a growing international power, the Ottomans developed an intelligence service which kept them continually well informed of events and trends in western Europe. Their chief informants were the Venetians, who despite their decline as a great power during the century remained always in touch with events, and who maintained a permanent diplomatic representative at the Sultan's court. Reciprocally, they reported to the West on the character and activities of Suleiman.

An early description of the new Sultan comes from a Venetian envoy, Bartholomeo Contarini, who wrote of him a few weeks after his accession:

> He is twenty-five years of age, tall, but wiry, and of a delicate complexion. His neck is a little too long, his face thin, and his nose aquiline. He has a shadow of a moustache and a small beard; nevertheless he has a pleasant mien, though his skin tends to pallor. He is said to be a wise Lord, fond of study, and all men hope for good from his rule.

Educated in the Palace School of Istanbul, he was throughout much of his youth familiar with the civilized ways and pursuits of the court, and came to be regarded by the people of Istanbul and Edirne (Adrianople) with respect and affection.

He became also well trained in administrative affairs as the young governor of three successive provinces. He was thus to grow into a statesman who combined vision with practical talents, a man of action who was also a man of culture and grace, worthy of the Renaissance into which he had been born. Finally he was a man of sincere religious convictions, which produced in him a spirit of kindness and tolerance and reflected no trace of his father's fanaticism. Above all he was imbued with a high conception of his duties as "Commander of the Faithful." Following the Ghazi traditions of his forebears, he was a holy warrior bound from the outset of his reign to prove his military power against that of the Christians. He sought by imperial conquest to achieve in the West what his father, Selim, had achieved in the East.

Westward, his expansionist horizons spread wider than those of their imperial progenitor, Mehmed the Conqueror. Immersing himself in the story of Alexander the Great, it became Suleiman's ambition to unite, as Iskander had sought to do, the lands and peoples of East and West. In pursuit of a comparable world empire, he would penetrate far beyond the present Ottoman fringe of eastern Europe, right into the imperial heart of central Europe itself.

Here he was resolved to confront, defeat, and occupy the territories of the Emperor Charles, threatening to overshadow him as "Lord of the Age." Suleiman's two preliminary fields of operation against him, respectively military and naval, were the kingdom of Hungary, the screen of the central Habsburg dominions, and the Mediterranean Sea, with its Christian islands and its coastlines of Spain and North Africa. His immediate objectives were those that Mehmed the Conqueror had failed to achieve—the city of Belgrade and the island of Rhodes.

In pursuit of the first, he was able to take advantage of the present weakness of Hungary as a link in the chain of the Habsburg defenses. In a brief victorious campaign he encircled Belgrade, then bombarded it with heavy cannon from an island in the Danube. "The Enemy," he recorded in his diary, "abandoned the defence of the town and set fire to it; they retired to the Citadel." Here the explosion of mines beneath the walls precipitated the surrender of the garrison, which had received no aid from the Hungarian government. Leaving Belgrade garrisoned by a force of Janissaries, Suleiman returned to a triumphal reception in Istanbul, confident that the Hungarian plains and the upper basin of the Danube now lay open to the Ottoman forces. Nevertheless, with his conflicting commitments, four more years were to elapse before the Sultan was able to resume his invasion.

His attention was now diverted from central Europe to the eastern Mediterranean. Here, astride his lines of sea communication between Istanbul and the new Ottoman territories of Egypt and Syria, lay that fortified outpost of Christendom, the island of Rhodes. Its Knights Hospitallers of the Order of St. John of Jerusalem, skilled, redoubtable seamen and warriors notorious to the Turks as "professional cutthroats and pirates," now continually threatened Ottoman trade with Alexandria; intercepted Turkish supply ships carrying timber and other such goods to Egypt and pilgrims en route to Mecca via Suez; interfered with the operations of the Sultan's own corsairs; and had supported a rebellion against the Ottoman authorities in Syria.

Thus Suleiman resolved on the capture of Rhodes. For the purpose he dispatched southward an armada of some four hundred ships while he himself led an army of a hundred thousand men overland through Asia Minor to a point on the coast confronting the island.

The knights had a new grand master, Villiers de l'Isle-Adam, a man of action, determination, and courage wholly dedicated in a militant spirit to the Christian faith. To an ultimatum from the Sultan embodying the customary peace offer prescribed by Koranic tradition to precede an attack, the grand master replied only by accelerating his plans for the defense of the fortress, whose walls had been strengthened since the previous siege by Mehmed the Conqueror.

The garrison had lately been reinforced by contingents from the various commanders of the order in Europe, making a force of at least seven hundred knights—the largest yet assembled in Rhodes. In addition the grand master contrived despite Venetian neutrality to procure five hundred archers from Crete, who disembarked in the guise of porters and deckhands from ships loaded with casks of Cretan wine and other welcome provisions.

But since this was a siege, the crucial arm was artillery. The Turks were renowned for their prowess in engineering, and their artillery was now held to rank with the best in the world. They excelled especially in the art of mounting and maintaining a continuous planned offensive against a fortified position. Moreover, at Rhodes it was Suleiman's intention to reinforce his bombardment with mines, to be exploded with gunpowder on a major scale. This rather than gunfire was to be his principal tactical weapon.

The Turks, when their fleet was assembled, disembarked engineers on the island who spent a month prospecting for suitable sites for their batteries. They were joined at the end of July, 1522, by the Sultan with his main force comprised of five army corps, which took up their prepared positions before the walls, forming a crescent around the five respective bastions of the knights of France and Germany; Auvergne, Castile, and Aragon; England; Provence; and Italy; and thus encircling the fortress southward, from sea to sea. On the following day a formidable bombardment began. This continued for a month against a counterbombardment, which soon disappointed any hopes by the Sultan of a speedy capture of the fortress by assault.

This, however, was in effect but a preliminary to the major operation of mining the fortress. It involved the digging by sappers of covered trenches in the stony soil, through which to move the batteries closer to the walls, then the placing of mines at chosen points beneath and within them. It was a gradual underground approach seldom attempted in siege warfare before this time. The most thankless and dangerous work of digging the trenches fell on that expendable portion of the Sultan's forces conscripted from among the predominantly Christian peasantry of such subject provinces as Bosnia, Bulgaria, and Wallachia.

It was not until the beginning of September that the necessary force could be moved close enough to the walls to burrow under them. Soon most of the enceinte had been undermined with tunnels, of which there were some fifty, running in different directions. But the knights had procured an Italian mine expert from the service of the Venetians named Martinengo, and he was burrowing too. He soon had his own subterranean warren of tunnels, crisscrossing those of the Turks and confronting them at various points, often with little more than the thickness of a plank between them. He had his network of listening posts furnished with mine detectors of his own invention—drums of parchment which signalled with their reverberations every blow of an enemy pick—and teams of Rhodians whom he had trained to operate them. He would then set off countermines and "ventilate" the detached mines by boring spiral vents to disperse their blast.

A series of attacks costly to the Turks culminated, at dawn on September 24, in a major general assault, heralded throughout the previous day by the detonation of a number of newly planted mines. Launched against four separate bastions under cover of a screen of black smoke from an artillery bombardment, it was led by the Janissaries, who planted banners at several points. But after six hours of fighting as fanatical as any in the history of Christian and Moslem warfare, the assailants were driven back with the loss of many thousands of men. The Sultan risked no more general attacks for a further two months, but confined himself to mining operations which penetrated ever deeper below the city and were followed, when successful, by less successful local assaults. The morale of the Turkish troops was low; furthermore, winter was approaching.

But the knights too were discouraged. Their casualties, though amounting to a mere tenth of those of the Turks, were heavy enough in relation to their strength. Munitions and other supplies were running low. Moreover, there were those among them who favoured surrender. Rationally they argued that Rhodes had been fortunate to survive for so long, after the Fall of Constantinople; that the Christian powers of Europe were never now likely to resolve their divided interests and unite for the island's salvation; that the Ottoman Empire, since its conquest of Egypt, was now the sole Islamic power in the eastern Mediterranean, with no others to play off against it; that its sea power was growing fast and its modern artillery so powerful as to be all but irresistible; that an honourable truce with the Ottomans would give the knights a new lease on life, fulfilling their mission in search of other worlds to conquer and convert to the faith. But De l'Isle-Adam was a romantic crusader of the old school of St. Louis, ready to sacrifice all in a resistance to the death, which would light the way for all Christendom to a triumphant final crusade against the infidel Turk.

After a renewed general assault, which failed, the Sultan on December 10 hoisted a white flag on the tower of a church outside the walls of the city, as an invitation to discuss surrender on honourable terms. But the grand master summoned a council: the knights in their turn hoisted a white flag, and a three-day truce was declared. Suleiman's proposals, as now transmitted to them, involved permission for the knights, and those among the inhabitants who chose, to depart unmolested with their portable possessions. Those who preferred to remain were granted undisturbed retention of their houses and property, complete religious liberty, and five years' exemption from tribute. After a heated debate a majority of the council agreed that "it would be a thing more agreeable to God to sue for peace and protect the lives of simple people, of women and children." The grand master still favoured resistance. But the garrison would endure no more and the citizens threatened open revolt.

Thus at Christmas, after a siege lasting 145 days, the capitulation of Rhodes was signed, the Sultan confirming his promise and now in addition promising ships, if required, for the inhabitants' departure. He promised also freedom of worship to those who remained, and freedom from taxes for five years to come. Hostages were exchanged, and a small body of well-disciplined Janissaries sent into the city. The Sultan scrupulously observed his terms, which were broken only, without his knowledge, by a detachment of fresh troops who got out of hand, broke into the streets, and committed a number of outrages before they could be called to order.

After a ceremonial Turkish entry into the city, the grand master made a formal submission to the Sultan, who treated him honourably. On January 1, 1523, De l'Isle-Adam left Rhodes for good, marching out of the city, flags flying, with his surviving knights and followers. Shipwrecked in a hurricane off Crete, they lost many of their remaining possessions but were enabled to continue their journey to Sicily and Rome. For five years they were homeless. Finally they were granted a home in Malta, where they were to fight the Turks once again. Meanwhile, their expedition from Rhodes was a blow to Christendom which for the present eliminated the last serious threat to Turkish naval power in the Aegean and the eastern Mediterranean.

((13))

HAVING THUS ASSERTED THE SUPREMACY OF HIS ARMS IN TWO successive campaigns, the young Sultan chose to rest on his laurels, allowing three summer seasons to elapse before embarking on a third. He occupied himself with improvements in the internal organization of his government: visited Adrianople for the first time since his accession and there relaxed in the pleasures of the chase; concerned himself with a crisis in Egypt, where a revolt by the Ottoman governor, Ahmed Pasha, renouncing his allegiance to the Sultan, had to be quelled by his forces. In command of them he sent his Grand Vezir, Ibrahim Pasha, to Cairo, to restore order and reorganize the administration of the province.

But on his return to Istanbul from Edirne the Sultan was confronted by a mutiny of the Janissaries. These belligerent, privileged infantrymen counted on annual campaigns to satisfy their lust not only for battle but for the traditional perquisites of loot. Thus they resented the Sultan's prolonged inaction. This was becoming, from one reign to another, a perennial problem. The Janissaries were growing perceptibly more powerful, and more aware of their power since they now formed as much as a quarter of the Sultan's standing army. In wartime they remained as a rule devoted and loyal servants to their master, though they might disobey his orders against plundering captured cities, and did on occasion limit his conquests by protesting against the continuation of unduly arduous campaigns. But in peacetime, restless from inaction, living no longer under strict discipline but in relative idleness, they were more and more apt to grow menacing and rapacious—particularly during the interval between the death of one Sultan and the accession of another, which they had come to treat as a period of license.

Now, in the spring of 1525, they broke out into a riot, plundering the customs, the Jewish quarter, and the houses of senior officials and others. A group of them forced their way into the presence of the Sultan, who is said to have killed three with his own hand but was obliged to withdraw when the rest threatened his life, drawing their bows at him. The mutiny was suppressed by the execution of their Agha and several officers suspected of complicity, while other officers were relieved of their commands. The soldiery, however, according to precedents which increasingly embarrassed the Ottoman treasury, were appeased by gifts of money; but also by the prospect of a campaign in the following year. Ibrahim Pasha was recalled from Egypt and made general-in-chief of the imperial forces, acting as second-in-command under the Sultan himself of a large army now mobilized for a second invasion of Hungary, to which the capture of Belgrade had opened the way up the Danube.

In Ibrahim Pasha there thus emerged fully into the limelight one of the most brilliant and powerful figures of Suleiman's reign. Ibrahim, now thirty-one years old, was by origin a Christian Greek, the son of a sailor from Parga, on the Ionian Sea, who was born in the same year—indeed, so he claimed, in the same week—as Suleiman himself. Captured as a child by Turkish corsairs, he was sold as a slave to a widow in Magnesia, who clothed him, gave him a good education, and had him trained to play a musical instrument. At some time in his youth he met and became the property of Suleiman, then heir to the throne and governor of Magnesia, who was won by his charm and impressed by his talents. He made him one of his personal pages, then his principal and most intimate favourite.

On Suleiman's accession to the throne the young man was appointed first to the post of Head Falconer, then to a sequence of offices in the imperial household. He came to enjoy with his master an unusual companionship, sleeping in the Sultan's apartments, taking his meals with him, sharing his recreations, exchanging notes with him through mutes when they were apart. Suleiman, withdrawn in his disposition, aloof in his demeanour, silent by nature and given to melancholy moods, needed just such a personal relationship to draw him out of himself and to respond with intelligence to his plans and ideas as a sovereign.

Under his auspices Ibrahim was married, with marked pomp and splendour, to a bride who was accepted as one of the Sultan's own sisters. His rise to power was indeed so rapid as to cause Ibrahim himself some alarm. All too aware of the vagaries of loyalty and fortune at the Ottoman court, he once went so far as to beg Suleiman, with lighthearted prescience, not to advance him so high that his fall would be his ruin. In reply Suleiman is said to have commended his modesty, and to have sworn that Ibrahim should not be put to death as long as he reigned, no matter what charges were made in the court. But, as a historian of the next century remarks in the light of events: "The condition of Kings, which is human and subject to change, and that of favourites, who are proud and unthankful, shall cause Suleiman to fail of his promise and Ibrahim to lose his faith and loyalty."

The revolt of the Janissaries may have hastened Suleiman's decision to march into Hungary. But he was influenced also by the defeat

Sultan Suleiman I—a miniature portrait.

and capture of Francis I by the Habsburg emperor at the battle of Pavia in 1525. Francis from his prison in Madrid sent a secret letter, concealed in the soles of an envoy's shoes, to Istanbul, begging the Sultan for deliverance by launching a general campaign against Charles, who would otherwise become "master of the world." The appeal fitted in with Suleiman's own plans at a time when Hungary, a country without patriotism and effectively without friends, was more than ever disordered and divided between the "Court party" of a weak King Louis II with his nobility, supporting the emperor but receiving little support from him and less from the West; the "national party" of John Zapolya, governor and effective ruler of Transylvania, with a group of lesser magnates; and an oppressed peasantry, who saw the Turks as deliverers. Suleiman was thus able to enter the country posing as the enemy of its king and the emperor and the friend both of magnates and peasants.

Since the fall of Belgrade, frontier clashes between Turks and Hungarians had continued intermittently, with varying fortunes. Now, on April 23, 1526, the Sultan, having previously ordered the building of two bridges across the Sava and the Drava, both tributaries of the Danube, started on his westward journey with an army of some hundred thousand men. Of these perhaps half were the hard core of disciplined regular troops, composed of infantry (Janissaries), cavalry (*sipahis*), whether paid soldiers or holders of fiefs, and artillery. The other half were irregulars, also infantry (*azabs*) and cavalry (*akinjis*)—unpaid, but living by the spoils of war. They were in general used either as an expendable force, whether placed in the front line at the start of an offensive, or let loose as raiders, to lay waste the invaded lands and terrorize their inhabitants. All—whether regular, feudal, or irregular, whether in camp, on the march, or in battle—were united beneath the eye and authority of the Sultan in person, the supreme commander and sovereign ruler, who stood forth visibly in the midst of his fighting subjects, always with the ministers of his government gathered around him.

The weather which the army now encountered was severe, with torrential rains and hailstorms recurring far into the summer. Streams were often impassable through floods, which swept away roads and bridges and tented encampments. Thus progress was slow, and it was almost three months before Suleiman's forces made contact with those of the enemy. Supporting them was a Danube flotilla of some hundreds of boats, which was held back by a strong current and found it hard to keep abreast of the land force.

Discipline, as usual, was strict. Successive entries in the Sultan's diary of this march in 1526 read: "May 10. A soldier is decapitated for trampling down the harvest, near the village of Kemal. . . . May 11. Two soldiers accused of stealing horses have their heads cut off."

Later: "June 5. Two *silihdars* [sword-bearers] are decapitated for pasturing their horses in unharvested fields." Throughout the march Suleiman relied with implicit confidence on Ibrahim, who, whenever difficulties arose, was sent ahead to prospect and prepare the way. Thus, on the army's arrival at Belgrade, it was found that bridges had already been thrown across the Sava. The enemy had retired to the north bank of the Danube, leaving a garrison on the south bank in the fortress of Peterwardein. Suleiman ordered Ibrahim to capture the town and its citadel, assuring him that "it would be but a bite to last him till breakfast at Vienna." He succeeded in doing so after a number of assaults, with the final aid of two mines to open a breach in the walls of the citadel. "The Grand Vezir," so the Sultan records, "has 500 soldiers of the garrison beheaded; 300 others are taken away into slavery."

Suleiman and his army then moved westward along the river to the strong strategic line of the River Drava, where they expected the Hungarians to make their first stand. But they were amazed to find its north bank undefended. Irresolute and slow to organize supplies, as one frontier fortress after another fell into the hands of the Turks, the Hungarians failed to resolve their mutual jealousies and agree on a coherent joint plan of campaign. The inhabitants of Essek, abandoned on the south bank, thus voluntarily submitted to the Sultan, who then ordered the construction of a pontoon bridge across the river. Experts—so the Turkish historian of the campaign, Kemal Pasha Zadeh, declares—estimated that this work would take at least three months. But "thanks to the skilful arrangements and the intelligent zeal of the Grand Vezir," it was completed within three days. Then, when the army had moved across it, the bridge was destroyed at the Sultan's command, so that "all other roads to safety being intercepted, his soldiers would stand firm and unshakeable on the field of battle, and that, with no idea of flight in their minds, the possibility of retreat should not show itself even in the mirror of an imagination struck with fear."

The Hungarians by now were mustering their forces on the plain of Mohacs, some thirty miles to the north. The young King Louis arrived with an army of a mere four thousand men. But a motley collection of reinforcements began to appear, until his total force, which included Poles, Germans, and Bohemians, amounted to some twenty-five thousand men. The emperor, when it came to providing troops for a war against the Turks, was largely at the mercy of a succession of Protestant Diets. They were to prove slow in granting them, even reluctant, since there were pacifist elements among them which saw the Pope, not the Sultan, as the principal enemy. At the same time they were quick to exploit, to their own religious ends, the secular conflict between Habsburg and Ottoman. Thus in 1521 the

Diet of Worms had refused to grant aid for the defense of Belgrade and now in 1526 the Diet of Speyer, after lengthy deliberations, voted it too late to reinforce the army at Mohacs.

On the field of battle the more astute among the Hungarian commanders counselled a strategic retreat in the direction of Buda, luring the Turks to follow them and thus lengthen their lines of communication, moreover benefitting in the process by reinforcements from the army of Zapolya, now only a few days distant, and from a Bohemian contingent already on the western frontier. But the majority of the Hungarians, overconfident and impatient, cherished dreams of instant martial glory. Led by the belligerent Magyar nobility, who were at once distrustful of the king and jealous of Zapolya, they clamoured for an immediate battle, taking the offensive on the spot. Their counsels prevailed, and it was fought on a marshy, six-mile plain to the west of the Danube, ground chosen to give scope to the Hungarian cavalry but giving it likewise to the superior and more numerous cavalry of the Turks. Learning of this reckless decision, a shrewd and witty prelate prophesied that "the Hungarian nation will have twenty thousand martyrs on the day of the battle, and it would be well to have them canonized by the Pope."

Impatient in tactics as in strategy, the Hungarians opened the battle with a needless head-on charge of their heavy-armed cavalry, led by King Louis himself and directed right at the center of the Turkish line. When this appeared to succeed it was quickly followed by a general advance of all the Hungarian forces. But the Turks, hoping thus to deceive their enemy and lead him on to destruction, had planned their defense in depth, placing its main line farther to the rear, with a hillside at the back of it. Thus presently the Hungarian cavalry, still galloping forward, came up against the hard core of the Janissaries grouped around the Sultan and his standard. There were furious hand-to-hand fights, and Suleiman himself was at one moment in danger, from arrows and lances that struck his cuirass. But the far superior Turkish artillery, carefully concentrated and skillfully handled as usual, decided the issue. It mowed the Hungarians down in their thousands and enabled the Turks to encircle and break the concentration of Hungarian troops in the center, slaughtering and scattering the enemy until survivors were fleeing in total disorder to north and to east. Thus within an hour and a half the battle was won.

The king of Hungary died on the battlefield while attempting to escape with a head wound. His body, identified by the jewels in the plume of his helmet, was found in a swamp, where, borne down by the weight of his armour, he had been smothered beneath his fallen horse. His kingdom died with him, since he had no heir; and the bulk of the Magyar nobles, together with eight of his bishops, died too. Suleiman is said to have expressed chivalrous grief at the king's death: "May Allah be merciful to him, and punish those who misled his inexperience: it was not my wish that he should thus be cut off, while he had scarcely tasted the sweets of life and royalty."

More expedient than chivalrous was the Sultan's order to take no prisoners. Before his scarlet imperial pavilion there soon towered a pyramid of a thousand heads of Hungarian noblemen. On August 31, 1526, the day following the battle, he wrote in his diary: "The Sultan, seated on a golden throne, receives the homage of the viziers and the beys; massacre of 2,000 prisoners; the rain falls in torrents." On September 2: "Rest at Mohacs, 20,000 Hungarian infantry and 4,000 of their cavalry are buried." Mohacs was then burned, and the countryside scorched by the *akinjis*. Not for nothing has "the Destruction of Mohacs," as the place is still named, been described as "the tomb of the Hungarian nation." To this day, when disaster overtakes him a Hungarian will say: "No matter, more was lost on Mohacs field."

Organized Hungarian resistance came to a virtual end with the battle of Mohacs, which sealed the position of Turkey as a predominant power in the heart of Europe for the next two centuries. John Zapolya and his troops, which might have affected the outcome of the battle, reached the Danube next day, but hastened to withdraw at the news of their countrymen's defeat. On September 10 the Sultan and his army entered Buda. On the way: "Sept. 4. Order to massacre all peasants in the camp. Women alone excepted: *Akinjis* forbidden to plunder." It was a prohibition which they were consistently to disregard and which the Sultan was not to enforce.

The city of Buda was burned to the ground, and only the royal palace, where Suleiman had taken up residence, survived. Here, in the company of Ibrahim, he made a collection of its treasures, which were transported by river to Belgrade and then to Istanbul. They included the great library, renowned throughout Europe, of Matthias Corvinus, together with three bronze statues from Italy, representing Hercules, Diana, and Apollo. The most treasured trophies, however, were two huge cannons which Mehmed the Conqueror had been obliged to abandon after his abortive siege of Belgrade, and which the Hungarians had since proudly exhibited as a proof of their valour.

The Sultan now engaged in the pleasures of hunting and falconry in the countryside, and of music and feasting in the palace, meanwhile reflecting on what he would do with this country which he had conquered with such unexpected ease. It was supposed that he would occupy and garrison Hungary, adding it to his empire, as he had Belgrade and Rhodes. But for the time being he preferred to rest content with his limited victory. His army, essentially a summer force, had suffered from the harsh, torrential weather of the Danube Valley.

Now winter was approaching and his available resources in manpower were inadequate to the task of controlling the country. Moreover, his presence was required in the capital to deal with disturbances in Anatolia, where revolts had to be suppressed in Cilicia and Karamania. The lines of communication between Buda and Istanbul were long. In the words of the historian Kemal Pasha Zadeh: "The time when this province should be annexed to the possession of Islam had not yet arrived. . . . The matter was therefore postponed to a more suitable occasion."

Thus Suleiman constructed a bridge of boats across the Danube to Pesth, and after burning the city led his troops homeward along the left bank of the river.

His evacuation left a political and dynastic vacuum in Hungary. Two rival claimants sought to fill it, contending for the crown of the dead King Louis. The first was the Archduke Ferdinand of Habsburg, brother of the Emperor Charles V and brother-in-law of the childless King Louis, to whose throne he had a legal claim. His rival claimant was John Zapolya, the ruling prince of Transylvania, who as a Hungarian could invoke a law excluding foreigners from the throne of his country and who, with his army still fresh and intact in the field, was already in effective control of the greater part of the kingdom. A Diet composed largely of Hungarian nobles elected Zapolya, and he entered Budapest to be crowned as king. This suited Suleiman, who could count on Zapolya to do his bidding, while Zapolya himself received material support from Francis I and his anti-Habsburg allies. But a few weeks later a rival Diet, supported by a pro-German faction of the nobility, chose Ferdinand, who had already been elected to the throne of Bohemia, as king of Hungary. This led to a civil war in which Ferdinand on his own account marched against Zapolya, defeated him, and drove him into exile in Poland. Ferdinand in his turn was crowned king of Hungary, occupied Buda, and began to envisage the establishment of a central European Habsburg state, composed of Austria, Bohemia, and Hungary.

Such plans, however, were to depend on the Turks, whose diplomacy was henceforward to influence the course of European history. From Poland, Zapolya sent an envoy to Istanbul, seeking a defensive and offensive alliance with the Sultan. He met at first with a haughty reception from Ibrahim and his fellow vezirs. But finally the Sultan agreed to give Zapolya the title of King, in effect granting him the lands that his armies had conquered and promising him protection against Ferdinand and all his enemies.

A treaty was concluded in which Zapolya undertook to pay an annual tribute to the Sultan, to place at his disposal every ten years a tenth part of the population of Hungary, of both sexes, and to grant in perpetuity free passage through his territory to the Ottoman forces. Thus did John Zapolya become a vassal of the Sultan, and his portion of Hungary a satellite kingdom under Ottoman protection.

Ferdinand now in his turn sent an embassy to Istanbul, in the hope of securing a truce. His envoys met with a hostile reception. The Sultan refused their extravagant demands and they were thrown into prison.

The Sultan now planned a third campaign up the Danube Valley, as protector of Zapolya against Ferdinand and in defiance of the Emperor Charles V himself. As a German folksong had foreboded of the Turks:

From Hungary he's soon away
In Austria by break of day,
Bavaria is just at hand,
From there he'll reach another land,
Soon to the Rhine perhaps he'll come.

On May 10, 1529, he left Istanbul with a larger army than before, again commanded by Ibrahim Pasha. The rains were more torrential than ever, and the expedition was to reach the neighbourhood of Vienna a month later than planned. Meanwhile, Zapolya had come to salute his overlord on the field of Mohacs with six thousand men. The Sultan received him with ceremony, crowning him with the sacred crown of St. Stephen. On the capture, after the siege, of Buda, he made his entry once more into the city to be enthroned as King John. On September 27, the Sultan, first letting loose the scourge of the *akinji,* arrived before the walls of Vienna. Already the citizens had seen the night sky reddened on the horizon by the flames of burning villages. Presently, as far as the eye could see around the walls of their city, the countryside was dotted with tens of thousands of white Moslem tents.

Ferdinand had found difficulty in raising adequate forces for Vienna's defense. The emperor, still fully occupied with his war in the West, consistently urged his brother to come to a temporary understanding with Zapolya, until his own forces should be free to participate in a major offensive against the Turks in the East. Instead, Ferdinand proceeded in person on a recruiting campaign through his various dominions. All promised contingents, and in Austria every tenth man was conscripted. But this was not enough. He also received support from the imperial princes of Germany. At first they were hesitant, but finally they voted a quota of troops for the Empire's defense.

Ferdinand addressed an appeal for help, in the common interest, to the Diet of Speyer, stressing Suleiman's boast that he would not lay down his arms before he had erected a monument to his victory on the bank of the Rhine. This made some impression, and finally, taking heed of a somewhat lukewarm appeal by Luther for a stand against the Turks, Protestants and Catholics joined in voting a quota of troops for the Empire's defense. It took some time to mobilize and, had Suleiman not been delayed for a month by the rains, might not have arrived in time to contribute to the city's salvation. As it was, reinforcements appeared only three days before the appearance of the Turks, raising the numbers of Vienna's garrison from twelve to some twenty thousand. They were, moreover, for the most part no mere feudal levies, but well-trained professional infantry, veterans of the emperor's campaigns in Italy, and they were commanded by a brave and experienced general with half a century of service behind him, Count Nicholas von Salm.

The defenses of Vienna had been hastily but resourcefully improvised. The defenders' task was to transform into an effective fortress a half-ruined city surrounded by medieval walls barely six feet thick, and a frail outer palisade well named the "city hedge." Houses too close to the walls were now razed to the ground. Later, to neutralize all possible advantage to the attackers, it was decided to sacrifice every building outside them within artillery range. This involved the burning of all the suburbs, eight hundred buildings in all, which included the city hospital, several churches and convents, and a castle on a hilltop which might have served the Turks as a stronghold. Within the city new entrenched earthen defenses were constructed and a new wall twenty feet high, with a new ditch. The bank of the Danube was similarly entrenched and palisaded. The countryside was scoured to lay in stocks of provisions. Fire precautions against incendiary missiles were organized, and inflammable roofs removed from the houses. Finally the city gates were bricked up, with the exception of one which was to serve as a sally port. Old men, women, children, and priests were evacuated from the city, that there might be fewer mouths to feed. But many on leaving fell into the hands of the *akinjis*. Meanwhile, Ferdinand himself was not in Vienna when the siege began but in Linz, still canvassing aid from the German princes.

Fortunately for the defenders, Suleiman had been obliged, by the rains, to leave behind him the bulk of his heavy siege artillery, so effective at Rhodes. He had only lighter cannon, which could make little impact on the strengthened walls, and thus he had to rely largely on mining. Nonetheless he underrated the task before him as he called upon the garrison to surrender, on agreed terms, declaring that he sought only to follow and find King Ferdinand. He boasted that, in the event of resistance, he would be breakfasting in Vienna within three days, on the Feast of St. Michael, and would so destroy the city that it might never have existed, sparing none of the population. But a fortnight passed, and the Viennese still held out. St. Michael's Day brought only unseasonable rains, from which the Turks in their light tents suffered. A released prisoner was sent with a message to the Sultan that his breakfast had grown cold and he must be content with such sustenance as the guns from the walls might provide.

The musketry of the Turks was so skilled and assiduous as to make it impossible for any defender to appear on these walls without the risk of being hit; their archers, concealed among the ruins of the suburbs, discharged an incessant hail of arrows with so deadly an aim that they penetrated the loopholes and embrasures in the walls, making it hazardous for the citizens to emerge into the streets. Arrows flew in all directions, and the Viennese kept as souvenirs some—presumably discharged by Turks of distinction—which were wrapped with costly fabrics and even set with pearls. Mines were exploded by the Turkish sappers, and despite active countermining from the cellars of the city, breaches were thus made in the walls. But the ensuing Turkish assaults were repulsed through the courage of the defenders, who celebrated their success with the sound of trumpets and martial music. Periodically they made sorties of their own, sometimes returning with prisoners and booty which on one occasion included eighty men and five camels.

Suleiman surveyed the operations from a carpeted tent, hung with fine tissues and furnished with bejewelled divans, whose numerous pinnacles, crowned with knobs of gold, soared high above the Turkish encampment. Here the Sultan interviewed Christian prisoners and sent them back into the city with threats and promises, laden with gifts of robes and Turkish ducats—but without any effect on the defenders, who, in the words of a popular song, were to the Sultan "not men but devils." Ibrahim Pasha, directing the siege, sought to encourage the attackers by distributing handfuls of gold in reward for an enemy's head or an important capture. But as their spirits flagged, they were driven on by blows with sticks and whips and sabers.

On the evening of October 12 a Divan was summoned in the Sultan's camp—a council of war to decide whether or not to continue the siege. Ibrahim, voicing the views of the majority, favoured withdrawal; morale was low, winter was approaching, supplies were running short, the Janissaries were grumbling, the enemy expected imminent reinforcements. After discussion it was decided to attempt a fourth and last major assault, with the offer to the troops of exceptional pecuniary rewards for success. On October 14 it was launched by the Janissaries and the pick of the Sultan's army. It met hour after hour with a ferocious resistance, the attackers failing to storm a breach in the walls 150 feet wide. Turkish losses were so heavy as to create widespread discouragement.

The Sultan's army was essentially a summer force, limited in its offensive scope by the fact that its feudal cavalry could not face a winter campaign lest their horses perish, hence were confined to a campaigning season of barely six months. Nor could the Sultan himself, and the ministers who accompanied him, conveniently remain absent from Istanbul for longer. Thus, now that it was already mid-October and the last assault had failed, Suleiman raised the siege and ordered a general retreat. The Turkish troops set fire to their camp, massacring or burning alive all their prisoners from the Austrian countryside, except those, of both sexes, young enough to qualify for the slave market. The army started on its long trek back to Istanbul, harassed by skirmishing enemy cavalry and by weather even worse than before. Silent through the siege, the bells of Vienna now pealed triumphantly amid salvos of gunfire, while St. Stephen's Cathedral resounded to the strains of a *Te Deum* of thanks for a great victory. Hans Sachs, the Meistersinger, composed his own ballad of thanksgiving, with the words "Except the Lord keep the city, the watchman waketh in vain."

The heart of Christian Europe was delivered from the Turk. Sultan Suleiman had suffered his first defeat, driven back from the walls of a great capital by a force which his own outnumbered by three to one. At Buda his vassal, Zapolya, came out to compliment him on his "successful campaign." It was as such that he endeavoured to present it to his subjects, celebrating his return with popular entertainments on the Feast of the Circumcision of his five sons, in a lavish and sumptuous style. He sought to save his face by pretending he had come not to take Vienna but to fight the Archduke Ferdinand, who had not dared to appear before him and who was clearly no king but—in the subsequent words of Ibrahim—"only a little fellow of Vienna, and worth small attention."

In the eyes of the world his face was saved by the arrival in Istanbul of a second embassy from Ferdinand, requesting a truce and offering to pay an annual "pension" to the Sultan—with another to the Grand Vezir—if they would recognize him as king of Hungary, relinquishing Buda and abandoning Zapolya. At this Ibrahim opened the window and pointed in pride to the celebrated Castle of the Seven Towers, where Suleiman's immense treasures were stored. Nor, he added, would any personal bribe induce him to betray his master. For all his haughtiness, his deliberately referring to the archduke simply as "Ferdinand" and his refusing to call Charles Emperor—a title he reserved for the Sultan alone—the atmosphere was friendlier than before. Nonetheless it was made clear to the envoys that they could have peace only on conditions to be laid down by the Sultan.

The Sultan still expressed his determination to cross swords with the Emperor Charles—to whom he chose to refer in tones of disparagement as "the King of Spain." Thus on April 26, 1532, he set forth once more up the Danube with his army and river fleet. Before reaching Belgrade he was met by further envoys from Ferdinand, who now offered peace on more conciliatory terms than before, increasing the amount of the proffered "pension" and ready even on certain conditions to recognize the claims of Zapolya. But the Sultan, receiving his envoys and addressing them in an audience of some splendour in which they were mortified to find themselves placed below the envoy of the king of France, made it clear to them that his enemy was not Ferdinand, but Charles: "The King of Spain," he challenged, "has for a long time declared his wish to go against the Turks; but I, by the grace of God, am proceeding with my army against him. If he is great in heart, let him await me in the field, and then, whatever God wills shall be. If, however, he does not wish to wait for me, let him send tribute to my Imperial Majesty."

This time the emperor, back in his own German dominions, temporarily at peace with France, fully awake to the gravity of the Turkish menace and his obligation to defend Europe against it, assembled an imperial force larger in scale and more formidable in strength than any which had opposed the Turk before. Inspired by a sense that this was a crucial turning point in the epic struggle between Christianity and Islam, soldiers thronged to the scene of war from all parts of his dominions. From beyond the Alps came contingents from Italy and Spain. Here was an army such as had never until now mustered in western Europe.

In order to muster it Charles had been obliged to come to terms with the Lutherans, who had hitherto frustrated all efforts for imperial defense by their reluctance to provide adequate funds, munitions, and supplies for the purpose. Now, in June, 1532, a truce was agreed at Nuremberg, in which the Catholic emperor, in return for such support, made important concessions to the Protestants and postponed indefinitely a final settlement of the religious question. Thus paradoxically the Ottoman Empire became in effect the "Ally of the Reformation." The alliance moreover was one which came directly to involve, in conquered Christian territories, Turkish support for Protestant as opposed to Catholic communities; it even involved some Turkish approval of the reformers' faith, not merely in political but in religious terms, taking account of its prohibition, common to Islam, of the worship of images.

Now Suleiman, instead of following the Danube Valley straight to Vienna as before, sent an irregular cavalry force ahead, to demonstrate his presence before the city and ravage its surroundings. He himself led his main army in a more southerly direction into open country, perhaps with the intention of enticing the enemy out of the city to give him battle on ground favourable to his regular cavalry. Some sixty miles to the south of the city he was held up before the small fortress of Güns, the last town in Hungary before the Austrian border. Here he met with an unexpected and heroic resistance from its meager garrison, which, under a Croatian nobleman named Nicholas Jurisitch, held out, delaying Suleiman's advance throughout most of the month of August.

The Turks brought their artillery to bear on the town from a wooden bulwark built opposite the most vulnerable point in the walls. They breached the defenses at a number of points. But twelve ensuing assaults were effectively resisted. Numerous Turkish mines were laid, most of which were detected and blown by the garrison. The Turkish trenches became swamped by continual rain. Demands for surrender were scornfully rejected. Finally Ibrahim devised a face-saving compromise. It was proclaimed to the defenders that the Sultan, in view of their bravery, had decided to spare them. The commander was honourably received by Ibrahim, and agreed to favourable terms for a surrender "on paper," handing over the keys of the town as a sign of nominal Turkish possession. Only a few token troops were then admitted within its walls, to man the breaches against massacre and pillage by the rest.

For the Turks, valuable time had been wasted and the weather was worsening. Suleiman nonetheless could still have marched on Vienna. Instead, perhaps in a last hope to lure his enemies out of the city into the open country, he let it be known that he was seeking not the city but the emperor himself, who he hoped would come forward with his army, to confront him on the field of battle. In fact, Charles was two hundred miles away up the Danube, at Ratisbon, with no intention of being drawn into any such major confrontation. So the Sultan, lacking heavy artillery and aware that the garrison of Vienna was stronger than that which had defeated him before, turned away southward from the city and began his homeward march, contenting himself with destructive raids on a wide scale, through the valleys and mountains of Styria, where he avoided the main fortresses to destroy villages, harry the peasantry, and lay waste large areas of the lower Austrian countryside.

Back in Istanbul two months later the Sultan wrote: "Five days of feasts and illuminations. . . . The Bazaars remain open all night, and Suleiman goes to visit them incognito"—doubtless seeking to discover whether or not his subjects saw this second campaign against Vienna as a defeat or as a victory. As in the case of the first, it was the official version, retailed for public consumption, that the Sultan had gone forth to give battle to his foe, the Christian emperor, who had not dared to face him but preferred to remain in hiding. To offset his own loss of prestige, Suleiman could at least claim that, by his enemy's choice, there had been no decisive trial of strength. Thus the main Ottoman army had returned to Istanbul intact to fight another day.

The time had come to treat for peace, for which the Habsburgs were as ready as the Ottomans. A settlement was agreed with Ferdinand, who in a formula dictated by Ibrahim addressed himself to the Sultan as a son to a father, and thus satisfied Ottoman pride and prestige. Suleiman for his part promised to treat him as a son, and granted him peace "not for seven years, for twenty-five years, for a hundred years, but for two centuries, three centuries, indeed for ever, if Ferdinand himself does not break it." Hungary was to be partitioned and its fortresses divided between the two sovereigns, Ferdinand and Zapolya.

Agreement in fact proved hard to achieve, Suleiman on the one hand playing off Zapolya—"my slave"—against Ferdinand, and insisting "Hungary is mine"; Ibrahim on the other hand favouring a settlement on the basis that each should have what he held. Finally, to Suleiman's discomfiture and behind his back, Ferdinand and Zapolya concluded an independent agreement, each reigning as king over his share of the country until Zapolya's death, when Ferdinand should reign over all. Meanwhile there was as yet no peace treaty between Sultan and emperor, who would not, at the first approach, reconcile their respective imperial pretensions in the matter of titles and dignities.

Thus it was that, at one of the turning points of history, Sultan Suleiman finally failed, before Vienna, to penetrate into the heart of Europe, much as the Moslems from Spain had failed eight hundred years earlier at the battle of Tours. His failure was due in part to the valiant resistance of well-trained, well-commanded European troops, experienced campaigners whose discipline and professional skill outclassed those of the feudal armies which had, until now, confronted the Ottomans in the Balkans and Hungary. In these he met his match.

But it was equally due to the facts of geography and climate, to the Sultan's overstretched lines of communication over seven hundred miles between the Bosporus and central Europe; to the irregular climatic hazards of the Danube Valley, with its continual rains and gales and floods. Both these factors hampered a campaigning season already unduly shortened, for an army which did not carry its own supplies, by the need of the mass of its cavalrymen to gather fodder for their horses—an impossibility through the winter and in a devastated countryside. Suleiman thus now recognized that there was a point in central Europe beyond which it was not profitable to press a campaign. Vienna, in the military context of the age, was in effect beyond the reach of a Sultan in Istanbul.

But Europe's fear of the Turkish peril had been reinforced, through hard experience, by a proper respect for Turkish arms. Here were no barbaric hordes from the steppes of Asia, but a highly organized modern army, such as the West, in this age, had not before encountered. Of its soldiers an Italian commentator observed:

> Their military discipline has such justice and severity as easily to surpass the ancient Greeks and Romans; the Turks surpass our soldiers for three reasons: they obey their commanders promptly; they never show the least concern for their lives in battle; they can live a long time without bread and wine, content with barley and water.

Countless other Europeans bore witness to their military virtues, their zeal for battle, their self-control, their single-hearted sense of purpose.

With this united force behind it, the Ottoman Empire was now more than ever a power in the affairs of the West. Suleiman had made of it a lasting political factor in what was later to be termed the Concert of Europe.

((14))

When Suleiman in his youth succeeded to the Ottoman throne, Cardinal Wolsey said of him to the Venetian ambassador at the court of King Henry VIII: "This Sultan Suleiman is twenty-five years old and has good judgment; it is to be feared he will act like his father." The Doge had written to his ambassador: "The Sultan is young, very powerful, and extremely hostile to the Christian race." The Grand Turk, "Signor Turco" to the Venetians, inspired the rulers of western Europe only with fear and mistrust as the "powerful and formidable enemy" of Christendom.

Except in such militant terms, little was at first reputed of Suleiman. But soon his campaigns in the field came to be matched more and more by the warfare of diplomacy. Hitherto foreign representatives at the Sultan's court had been confined mainly to those of Venice, who since her naval defeat by the Turks at the turn of the century and her consequent loss of supremacy in the Mediterranean had "learned to kiss the hand that she could not cut off." Venice thus cultivated close diplomatic relations with the Porte, which she came to treat as her leading diplomatic post, sending frequent missions to Istanbul and maintaining in residence a *bailo,* or minister, who was usually a man of top caliber. Their diplomats sent back frequent reports to the Doge and his government, and thus helped indirectly to keep Europe in general well-informed as to developments at the Sultan's court. King Francis I once said of them: "Nothing true comes from Constantinople, save by way of Venice."

But now foreign contacts, and thus the presence in the city of foreigners of consequence, increased with the arrival of new missions from other powers—from an early date the French themselves, the Hungarians, the Croatians, and above all the representatives, accompanied by ample suites, of King Ferdinand and the Emperor Charles V, with his widespread cosmopolitan dominions. Thanks to them and to a growing number of foreign travellers and writers, Western Christendom came to discover gradually more of the Grand Turk in person, his way of life, the institutions through which he ruled, the nature of his court with its elaborate ceremonial, the lives of his subjects with their outlandish but far from barbarous traditions and manners and customs. The image of Suleiman now increasingly pre-

A fanciful engraving of the Sultan's bath.

D'Ohsson, *Tableau général,* Vol. 3, plate 42.

sented to the West was, by comparison with those of his Ottoman forebears, that of a civilized monarch—in Eastern if not Western terms. He had, it was evident, raised to its peak an oriental civilization deriving from nomadic, tribal, and religious origins. Enriching it with new splendours, he was now aptly named by the West "the Magnificent."

Suleiman's daily life in his palace, from levee to couchee, followed a ritual comparable in its detailed precision to that of the French kings at Versailles. When the Sultan rose from his couch in the morning he would be clothed, by select members of his household, in a caftan, a robe which he would wear only once, with twenty gold ducats in one pocket and a thousand pieces of silver in the other—both robe and unspent cash becoming the perquisites of his chamberlain at the end of the day. His three daily meals were brought to him by a long train of pages, to be eaten alone from fine porcelain and silver dishes on a low silver table, with sweetened and perfumed water (seldom wine) to drink, and a doctor standing by his side as a precaution against possible poisoning.

He would retire to rest at night on three crimson velvet mattresses, one of down and two of cotton—lying in the summer between sheets of delicate tissue and in the winter wrapped in the softest fur of sable or black fox, with his head resting on two green-tasselled pillows. Above his couch was a golden canopy, and around it four high waxen tapers on silver stands, by which four armed guards stood throughout the night, extinguishing the candles on the side toward which the Sultan might turn, and keeping watch over him until he awoke. Each night, as a security measure, he would sleep in a different room of his choice, which his chamberlains would prepare meanwhile.

Much of his day would be occupied with formal audiences and consultations with officials. But when his Divan was not sitting he would occupy his leisure, perhaps reading *The Book of Alexander*, a legendary account by a Persian writer of the Great Conqueror's exploits; or studying religious and philosophical treatises; or listening to music or watching the antics of dwarfs or the contortions of wrestlers; or perhaps deriving amusement from the quips of court jesters. In the afternoon, after a siesta on two mattresses, one brocaded with silver and the other with gold, he would often cross with a chosen companion to the Asiatic side of the Bosporus, to relax in the gardens there. Alternatively the palace itself offered him, in the third court, relaxation and refreshment in a garden planted with palm trees and cypress and laurel, adorned with a glass-domed kiosk over whose roof in the hot weather there flowed cascades of glittering water.

His public entertainments lived up to his reputation for magnificence. When, seeking to detract attention from his first failure before Vienna, he celebrated the Feast of the Circumcision of his five sons in the summer of 1530, the festivities lasted for three whole weeks. The Hippodrome became a city of tents, gorgeous in their draperies, with a lofty pavilion in the center where the Sultan sat before his people on a throne with columns of lapis lazuli. Above him shone a canopy of gold, encrusted with jewels; beneath him, spread over all the ground, were soft precious carpets. Around were pitched tents of innumerable colours but, surpassing them all in brightness, the captured pavilions of princes defeated by Ottoman arms. Between the official ceremonies with their splendid processions and sumptuous banquets, the Hippodrome offered an infinite choice of entertainments for the people. There were games, tournaments, sham fights and displays of equitation; dances, concerts, shadow plays and stage reenactments of great sieges and battle scenes; circus shows with clowns, jugglers, acrobats galore, fireworks exploding, spluttering, cascading across the night sky—all on a scale never seen in the city before.

When the festivities were over, Suleiman proudly asked Ibrahim whose feast had been the finer, this for his sons, or the Grand Vezir's own wedding feast. Ibrahim disconcerted the Sultan by replying: "There never was a feast equal to my wedding"; then continued, "O my Padishah, my wedding was honoured by the presence of Suleiman, Lord of the Age, firm Rampart of Islam, Possessor of Mecca and Medina, Lord of Damascus and Egypt, Caliph of the Lofty Threshold, and Lord of the Residence of the Pleiades. But to your festival, who was there of equal rank who might come?"

Four Venetian envoys, sole representatives of the West, proved as always zealous in their observation and description of all that occurred at the feast. Suleiman himself was described at this time by one of them, Pietro Bragadino, the Venetian minister: "He is thirty-two years old, deadly pale, with an aquiline nose, and a long neck; of no apparent strength, but his hand is very strong, as I observed when I kissed it, and it is said to be able to bend a stiffer bow than anyone else. He is by nature melancholy, much addicted to women, liberal, proud, hasty, and yet sometimes very gentle."

But as time went on and the court of Suleiman grew in diplomatic importance, the Venetians were reinforced by the representatives of other powers, who recorded, for the benefit of the West, their own observations on Ottoman Turkey and its Sultan. Outstanding among them was Ogier Ghiselin de Busbecq, of Flemish noble origin, a notable scholar and a man of the world with an open-minded and civilized outlook who from 1554 onward was intermittently envoy in Istanbul for the Emperor Charles V. In a series of descriptive letters to a friend he was to give the West the benefit of a fresh, objective, and personal view of Suleiman, his court, and his people. From the start Busbecq, the man of the West, proved quick to appreciate the more civilized aspects of this unfamiliar world of the East. Soon after his arrival to take up his post, he was writing of the Sultan's hall of audience at Amasya:

> Now come with me and cast your eye over the immense crowd of turbaned heads, wrapped in countless folds of the whitest silk, and bright raiment of every kind and hue, and everywhere the brilliance of gold, silver, purple, silk and satin. . . . A more beautiful spectacle never was presented to my gaze. Yet amid all this luxury there was a great simplicity and economy. The dress of all has the same form, whatever the wearer's rank; and no edgings or useless trimmings are sewn on, as is the custom with us. . . . What struck me as particularly praiseworthy in that great multitude was the silence and good discipline. There were none of the cries and murmurs which usually proceed from a motley concourse and there was no crowding. Each man kept his appointed place in the quietest manner possible.

Busbecq was quick to discern the principles inherent in that society which was Suleiman's household, a society where a high degree of democratic equality prevailed beneath the rule of an absolute autocracy.

> In all that great assembly no single man owed his dignity to anything but his personal merits and bravery; no one is distinguished from the rest by his birth, and honour is paid to each man according to the nature of the duty and offices which he discharges. There is no struggle for precedence, every man having his place assigned to him by virtue of the function which he performs. The Sultan himself assigns to all their duties and offices, and in doing so pays no attention to wealth or the empty claims of rank, and takes no account of any influence or popularity which a candidate may possess: he only considers merit and scrutinises the character, natural ability and disposition of each. Thus each man is rewarded according to his deserts, and offices are filled by men capable of performing them.

The Sultan himself received Busbecq in audience, "seated on a rather low sofa, not more than a foot from the ground and spread with many coverlets and cushions embroidered with exquisite work. Near him were his bow and arrows. His expression . . . is anything but smiling, and has a sternness which, though sad, is full of majesty. On our arrival we were introduced into his presence by his Chamberlain. . . . After going through the pretence of kissing his hand, we were led to the wall facing him backwards, so as not to turn our backs or any part of them towards him."

Busbecq then stated the purpose of his mission, which was to persuade the Turks to check their raids into Hungary. This request and its accompanying arguments did not suit the policy of the Sultan, who "assumed an expression of disdain," replied only with a brief "Well, well," and caused the emperor's envoys to be dismissed forthwith to their lodging. Busbecq was not wholly surprised at the Sultan's cold attitude toward his petition. It was Suleiman's practice to draw, in his reception of foreign ambassadors, a clear distinction between those of a friendly country, like Venice or France, and those of a power regarded as hostile.

Busbecq's arrival at his court had coincided with that of a more favoured Persian envoy, bearing splendid gifts, whose request for peace had been granted on the spot. "No possible honour towards the Persian was omitted," wrote Busbecq, "that we might have no doubt about the genuineness of the peace which had been made with him. In all matters . . . the Turks are in the habit of going to extremes, whether in paying honour to their friends or in showing their contempt by humiliating their foes." When the Persian peace had been ratified, Busbecq could obtain only a truce for six months. Thus he preferred to go home to Vienna with a letter from Suleiman and perhaps to return with a reply. Introduced once again into the Sultan's presence,

> two ample embroidered robes reaching to my ankles were thrown about me, which were as much as I could carry. My attendants were also presented with silken robes of various colours and, clad in these, accompanied me. I thus proceeded in a stately procession, as though I were going to play the part of Agamemnon or some similar hero in a tragedy, and bade farewell to the Sultan after receiving his despatch wrapped up in cloth of gold.

He and his suite left without the official breakfast normally offered to departing ambassadors, for "this is only done when they are friendly, and our relations had not yet been placed on a footing of peace."

The style of Suleiman's diplomacy had evolved in close concert with Ibrahim Pasha, who remained his Grand Vezir until his fall from power in 1536. In this appointment the Sultan had broken new ground by selecting as his chief minister not, as his predecessors had generally done, some army judge or provincial governor from the official hierarchy, but a favourite from his own imperial household, of whose qualities he was thus able to judge from close personal experience. Here he set a significant precedent, for good or ill, for his successors in the sultanate. Ibrahim's status and influence among foreign rulers and their envoys—doubtless furthered initially by his Greek Christian origin—was such that both Francis and Ferdinand wrote letters to him in person, while invariably ambassadors proceeding to Constantinople were instructed to see him before anyone else.

Venetians, dubbing him "Ibrahim the Magnificent," were inclined to take at their face value the continued boasts by Ibrahim of his power to make the Sultan do what he wanted, his repeated bragging insistence that "It is I who govern." Together with his sarcasm and scorn, his browbeating, hectoring, taunting tactics, this bombast was simply a weapon in the stock-in-trade of his diplomatic armoury, designed to impress, deflate, and intimidate the ambassadors of rival powers. The art of handling them in this context of Ottoman victories and European overtures for peace called for a strong rather than a subtle approach. Nor, it seems, did Suleiman at any time object to the arrogant pretensions of his vezir. Ibrahim's haughtiness matched, in an outspoken fashion, the Sultan's own, expressed as befitting his Majesty in a reserved, aloof manner. Each of the two men, Suleiman and Ibrahim, formed a counterpart to the other. Suleiman's foreign policy, in terms of its general long-term direction, was consistently his own—that of extending his power into Europe at the expense of the Habsburgs and in alliance with France. Ibrahim complemented it mainly in terms of its tactical method and detail, of its more immediate exigencies, above all of his own understanding of Europe, to whose ideas, beyond his master's sphere, he was able to open his master's mind. At this important moment in Ottoman history, he thus contributed in a major sense to the initiation of diplomatic relations with the West, hence to the evolution of a new European relationship for the Ottoman Empire.

Ibrahim's final achievement was the negotiation, drafting, and signature, in 1535, of a treaty with his "good friend," Francis I. This permitted the French to carry on trade throughout the Ottoman Empire, by payment of the same dues to the Sultan as were paid by the Turks themselves. The Turks, for their part, were to enjoy reciprocal privileges in France. The treaty recognized as valid the jurisdiction within the Empire of French consular courts, with a Turkish obligation to carry out consular judgments, if necessary by force. It granted complete religious liberty to the French in the Ottoman Empire, with the right to keep guard over the holy places, and amounted in effect to a French protectorate over all Catholics in the Levant. It put an end to the commercial predominance of Venice in the Mediterranean, and obliged all Christian ships—with the exception of those of the Venetians—to fly the French flag as a guarantee of protection.

This treaty was momentous in that it marked the start of a system of privileges to foreign powers known as the Capitulations. Ably negotiated by the French and allowing for the exchange of permanent envoys between the two countries, it enabled France to become, and for long to remain, the predominant foreign influence at the Sublime Porte. The Franco-Turkish alliance may indeed, under the cover of commercial cooperation, have stabilized in the Sultan's favour the European balance of political and military power between king and emperor, whose axis was now shifting to the Mediterranean. But in granting to a foregin power a recognized status as such within the frontiers of the Empire, it created a precedent fraught with problems for the centuries to come. Meanwhile this was Ibrahim's last act of diplomacy. For his downfall was near.

"Magnificent" to the West, Sultan Suleiman, to his own Ottoman subjects, was "the Lawgiver." For not only was he a great military campaigner, a man of the sword, as his father and great-grandfather had been before him. He differed from them in the extent to which he was also a man of the pen. He was a great legislator, standing out in the eyes of his people as a high-minded sovereign and a magnanimous exponent of justice—which indeed he dispensed in person, on horseback, in the course of his campaigns. Always a devout Moslem, who grew stricter in his observances as the years went by, he became more than ever dedicated to the ideas and institutions of Islam. In this spirit he was to prove a wise, humane dispenser of laws.

The earlier Lawgiver of the Empire had been Mehmed the Conqueror. It was on the Conqueror's foundations that Suleiman the new Conqueror now expanded. In a land so conservative, already equipped with a comprehensive legal code and moreover involved over a process of time with regulations, written and unwritten—the established precedents of previous Sultans—he did not require to be a radical reformer or innovator. He sought, not to create a new legal structure, but to bring the old up-to-date, adapting the laws generally in line with the new conditions of new times and an immensely enlarged empire. He at once specified, codified, and simplified a confused system of custom and practice. This he did building still on the two main foundations of Ottoman government: the ruling institution, the secular and executive establishment; and the Moslem institution, the religious and legislative establishment. United beneath the apex of the Sultan's absolute rule, they represented, in terms of their several functions, a rough equivalent of the Western distinction between State and Church.

The ruling institution was comprised, together with the Sultan and his family, of the officials of his court, the executive officers of his government, the standing army, and the large body of young men who were being educated for service in one or another of the three. They were almost exclusively men or the sons of men born of Christian parents, and thus the Sultan's slaves. As described by the Venetian *bailo* Morosini, they "take great pride in being able to say 'I am a slave of the Grand Signor'; since they know that this is a lordship or a republic of slaves, where it is theirs to command." As Barbaro, another *bailo,* comments: "It is a fact truly worthy of much consideration that the riches, the forces, the government, and in short the whole state of the Ottoman Empire is founded upon and placed in the hands of persons all born in the faith of Christ."

Parallel to this structure of administration was the Moslem institution, composed only of men who had been born Moslem. Judges and jurists, theologians, priests, professors, they formed, as custodians and executors of the Sacred Law of Islam, the ulema, that class of learned men responsible for maintaining the whole structure of learning, religion, and law throughout the Empire.

The Sultan had no power to change or ignore the principles of the Sheriat, the Sacred Law, propounded by God and delegated through the Prophet, which thus acted as a limitation on his divine sovereign authority. Nor, as a good Moslem, had he any inclination to do so. But, if his own people were to remain also good Moslems in a world that was rapidly changing, he saw the need for changes in the law's application. For one thing the Ottoman Empire, whose conquered territories at the start of the century had been predominantly Christian, had since vastly extended its range through wide conquests in Asia, embracing such cities of the old Islamic Caliphate as Damascus, Baghdad, and Cairo, together with a protectorate over the holy cities of Mecca and Medina. Four-fifths of its total population—which by the end of his reign was estimated at fifteen million, from twenty different races under twenty-one different governments—were now inhabitants of Asia. Insofar as this accorded him the rights due to a Sultan-Caliph, Suleiman was at once Protector of Islam, Defender of its Faith, and defender, interpreter, executor of its holy law. The whole Moslem world looked to him as a leader in the holy war. In any event the Empire had come to acquire a more widely Moslem character, which called for a new legislative code within its overriding framework to supplement the previous code.

Suleiman charged a learned judge, Mullah Ibrahim of Aleppo, with its preparation, and the resulting code—fancifully named by him, for its oceanic scope, *Multeka-ul-uther,* "the Confluence of the Seas"—was to remain in effective force until the legal reforms of the nineteenth century. At the same time a new legal code, which amounted in effect to a new constitution, was drawn up for the administration of Egypt. In all his drafting of new legislation Suleiman was scrupulous to work in close concert with the jurists and theologians of the ulema, who advised him as to how far he could go without actually transgressing the original Sacred Law. They classified its provisions for him into different groups, specifying the different degrees of obligation to obey them, and did their best to assist him with elastic interpretations.

As distinct from the Sacred Law, canonical legislation (that of the *kanuns*) was the instrument of the Sultan's sovereign will alone. Here, conscientiously and with close attention to detail, he worked for the especial benefit of his Christian subjects, instructing his provincial governors, from the outset of his reign, to treat as their main objective the impartial dispensation of the law, as between Moslems and *rayas,* regardless of creed. Here there were legislative gaps which his two predecessors over the past forty years had neglected to fill. The task of filling them amounted in effect to a reform and adjustment of the state feudal system in terms of land tenure and taxation, as established through the legislation of Mehmed the Conqueror.

In the case of the larger fiefs, the *zeamets,* Suleiman sought to reform abuses by which hereditary transmission of lands theoretically, as under the earlier Sultans, granted only for life was becoming a general practice. So was the alienation by provincial governors and vezirs of fiefs, which had lapsed in default of male issue, to feudatories of their own choice. This led to abuses in the form of frequent and irresponsible changes in the ownership of land. This in turn infringed the prerogative of the Sultan, who in theory, as God's representative, was the owner of it all.

He reasserted this principle by a decree that governors in future might confer only *timars,* or small fiefs, while the transfer of *zeamets,* the large fiefs, must be referred for approval to the central government in Istanbul—otherwise to the Sultan himself. It was intended thus to bring the "country gentry" once more under control, and to thwart the accumulation of larger landed estates, while the Sultan ensured the regular and efficient service of the military force for which his lands were granted. At the same time there was, in the interests of impartial justice, a general purge of governors and officials found guilty of cruelties, exactions, injustices, corruption, and incompetence.

In the course of his reforms, Suleiman showed especial concern for the condition of the *rayas,* those Christian subjects who cultivated the lands of the *sipahis.* His *Kanune Raya,* or "Code of the Rayas," regulated the levy of their tithes and capitation tax, making them at once onerous and more productive, raising them from a position of serfdom or villeinage to a status approximating, in Ottoman terms, that of the European copyholder.

The lot of the *rayas* indeed, under the maligned "Turkish yoke," proved so superior to that of the serfs of Christendom under certain Christian masters that the inhabitants of neighbouring countries might often prefer, as described by a contemporary writer, to escape across the frontier: "I have seen multitudes of Hungarian rustics set fire to their cottages, and fly with their wives and children, their cattle and instruments of labour, to the Turkish territories, where they knew that, besides the payment of the tenths, they would be subject to no imposts or vexations." The same tendency was to prevail among the

Religious ceremony in the throne room.

D'Ohsson, *Tableau général,* Vol. 2, plate 43.

inhabitants of the Morea, who preferred Ottoman to Venetian rule.

New criminal and police legislation was likewise embodied in Suleiman's *kanuns,* covering offenses against morals, violence, and injuries, thefts and brigandage. Punishments became in general more lenient than before. A system of fines, prescribing a tariff for each offense, tended to replace corporal punishment. The penalties of death and mutilation were less frequent, though false witnesses, forgers, and passers of bad money were still liable to have the right hand severed at the wrist. Enlightened measures required slanderers and talebearers to make compensation for mischief caused; limited interest on loans to a maximum rate of 11 percent; enjoined kindness to beasts of burden.

Suleiman's taxation, beyond the traditional Islamic limits of taxes on land and on persons as authorized by the Sacred Law, was diverse and wide in its scope. In domestic affairs there was a tax both on bachelors and on entry into marriage. In the world of the court there were changes of ceremonial, minutely defined. In the commercial field Suleiman introduced a series of edicts designed to regulate markets and guilds, prices and wages, manufactures and the retail trade—here going so far as to prescribe in exact detail the manner in which foodstuffs should be prepared and sold.

Taxes were levied on various forms of produce, on animals, on mines, on the profits of trade, and in the form of export and import duties. Apart from taxation an appreciable source of revenue was the confiscation of the properties of high officials and other persons of wealth who had fallen into disgrace. The Sultan's campaigns more than paid for their initial outlay, adding to the Imperial Treasury the spoils of war from the conquered provinces and the tributes of Christian vassal states.

Financially the Ottoman Empire was increasingly prosperous. Suleiman's well-husbanded revenues, drawn in the main from the Sultan's own domains and from the taxes on the lands of his subjects, probably exceeded those of any contemporary Christian sovereign. They were, moreover, revenues which increased rapidly as his reign went on, calling for a proportionate expansion, to distinctly swollen proportions, of the bureaucracy required for their collection.

Suleiman's reforms, for all their liberal intentions and principles, were inevitably limited in their effect by the fact that he was legislating from above, with the advice only of a small circle of high officials and jurists. Remote in the capital from the bulk of his widely scattered subjects, out of close touch with them and lacking in personal experience of their needs and circumstances, he was not in a position either to consult them directly as to the likely effects of his legislation upon them, or to follow it through and ensure its just enforcement.

Hence inevitably decentralization, in its various forms, led in the provinces to extortions and venal abuses, to a degree of official corruption fraught with hazards for the future. But for the present, thanks to Suleiman's devotion to justice, fairness, and order as enforced by a strong central government, it did not yet bear heavily on the subjects of his empire, and his legislation tended in general to lighten their condition.

Throughout the country Suleiman strengthened his government, especially in terms of the Moslem institution. He confirmed and extended the powers and privileges of the head of the ulema, the Grand Mufti or Sheikh-ul-Islam, making him virtually the equal of the Grand Vezir and thus adjusting the balance between the powers of the legislative and the executive arms of the state. At the same time he reorganized and reinforced the rest of the ulema, which embraced in its hierarchy the other muftis, and the judges, to whom they served as jurisconsults, throughout the Empire. All were granted special privileges, notably immunity from taxation and from the confiscation of property. Their inheritance could thus descend from father to son, developing in the Empire a hereditary class drawn from the educational and legal professions—an "aristocracy of the brain," not of the land—whose privileges were nonetheless to create problems as time went on.

Suleiman developed the educational system of the ulema, whose schools continued to be financed by religious foundations and attached to mosques. They provided Moslem boys with an education which was largely free and moreover far in advance of any available at this time in Christian countries. Expanding the educational system developed by Mehmed the Conqueror, Suleiman was a generous founder of schools and colleges. In the course of his reign the number of primary schools, or *mektebs,* in the capital rose to fourteen. They gave children a course in reading, writing, and the fundamental principles of Islam, and when it was finished they were led through the streets in joyful processions, as on days of circumcision.

If they chose and had the capacity, they could proceed to one of the eight colleges (*medresses*) built in the precincts of the eight principal mosques and known as the "eight paradises of knowledge." These offered a course of ten studies, based on the liberal arts of the West—grammar, syntax, logic, metaphysics, philosophy, tropics, stylistics, geometry, astronomy, and astrology. There were also higher *medresses,* law schools of university status, most of whose graduates became imams (prayer leaders) or teachers. These academies, as before, formed part of the concourse of buildings surrounding and adjoining the courtyards of mosques. Their precincts still included also treasuries, banks, hospices for travellers, refectories, libraries,

The Suleimaniye Mosque as seen from the Golden Horn.
Choiseul-Gouffier, *Voyage pittoresque de la Grece,* Paris, 1819, plate 86.

bathhouses, fountains, and such other charitable amenities of the Ottoman "welfare state" as soup kitchens, hospitals, and madhouses.

Suleiman, in the grandeur of this Golden Age, was at once Sultan-Caliph of Islam and a Grand Signor in the traditions of the European Renaissance. Combining in his person the sacred majesty of the Eastern with the princely magnificence of the Western world, he sought to transform Istanbul into a capital worthy, in its architectural splendours, of the great cities of this blossoming sixteenth-century civilization. Hence, as his conquests and his revenues multiplied, the gradual evolution of that skyline of rounded domes and pointed minarets, whose unique silhouette still graces the Sea of Marmara four centuries after him. Here was the full flowering of that architectural tradition which Mehmed the Conqueror had first evolved from that of Byzantium, and which glorified in tangible form the religion of Islam and the spread of its civilization over a world where the religion of Christ had beforehand reigned supreme.

Providing a link between those two contrasting civilizations, it attained its peak with the work of a man who now ranks, in perspective, as one of history's great architects. This was Mirmar Sinan, the son of a Christian stonemason from Anatolia, who had been drafted as a Janissary in his youth and had served in campaigns with the Sultan as a military engineer, becoming adept in the construction of fortifications and arsenals, bridges and aqueducts. At the age of fifty he was brought into Suleiman's service to work with him closely as Royal Chief Architect, adapting his technical skills as a military engineer to the creation of fine religious buildings. He was to enrich the architectural heritage of the sixteenth century with many hundreds of mosques and tombs built in a sober and disciplined style, combining simplicity with grace and strength with lightness in a manner which is distinctively Ottoman Turkish. Outstanding among these was the Suleimaniye, Sultan Suleiman's own imperial mosque and mausoleum in which Sinan sought to surpass the Emperor Justinian's great church of Hagia Sophia (now the mosque of Aya Sofya). He studied its architectural features and adapted its ground plan to the needs of Islamic worship. Under his imperial patron, indeed, Sinan was to perfect in the city of Constantinople a style which was a true catalyst between East and West.

In the internal decoration of Ottoman buildings, whether religious or secular, designers of this period drew more from the East than from the West. Their walls were adorned with ceramic tiles in floral designs of bright colours, deriving from Persia in earlier centuries, but now manufactured in the workshops of Iznik (ancient Nicaea) and Istanbul by Persian craftsmen, brought from Tabriz for the purpose. The cultural influence of Persia still predominated in the literary field, as it had done since the time of Mehmed the Conqueror. It rose to a high level in the reign of Suleiman, who gave especial encouragement to poetry. Under his active patronage classic Ottoman poetry in the Persian tradition reached a standard higher than ever before. He instituted the high official post of Imperial Rhyming Chronicler, a kind of Ottoman poet laureate, whose duty was to versify current events after the manner of Firdausi and other such Persian chroniclers of historic occasions.

((15))

Sultan Suleiman was now to change the sphere of his operational strategy. Having stretched his resources to the limit before the walls of Vienna, he no longer contemplated landward expansion into central Europe. He remained content with a stable imperial dominion in southeastern Europe which now extended far to the north of the Danube to embrace much of Hungary, but stopped short of the frontiers of Austria. In his land operations he turned his back on Europe to pursue expansion in Asia, where he was to fight three long campaigns against Persia. His warfare against the Habsburgs, still seeking to confront the "King of Spain," continued as purposefully as before, but in a different element, that of the Mediterranean Sea, whose waters the Ottoman navy, rising to the height of its power on foundations laid earlier by Mehmed the Conqueror, was soon to command.

Hitherto the emperor had not ventured into the eastern Mediterranean, nor had the Sultan ventured to any extent into the western. But now he was to seek out the emperor in his home waters of Italy, Sicily, and Spain. Thanks to the great explorers and their recent voyages of discovery, the ocean, in the world of the sixteenth century, was coming to replace the steppe as the main medium of world communication. In commerce the Turks still adhered as far as possible to their traditional land routes, converging from far-flung Ottoman dominions on the impregnable harbour of Istanbul. But now that sea routes replaced or complemented them, the Turks must needs adapt themselves to the change. Thus the Ghazis of the Asiatic continent became the Ghazis of the Mediterranean Sea.

The time for this was propitious. The fall of the Fatimid Caliphate had been followed by the decline of its satellite Moslem dynasties. Thus the Barbary coast of North Africa had fallen into the hands of petty chieftains, beyond their control, using its harbours as bases for piracy. They met with active encouragement from the Moors, who had fled to North Africa following the fall to the Spanish Christians of the Moslem kingdom of Granada in 1492. These Moslems, in their thirst for revenge, inspired widespread anti-Christian hostility and prompted persistent piratical raids against the southern coasts of Spain. Against them the Spaniards, under Queen Isabella, were obliged to retaliate, carrying the war into North Africa and establishing their own control over a number of its ports. The Moors found effective leaders in a pair of seafaring brothers, Aruj and Khaireddin Barbarossa.

Stalwart, red-bearded sons of a potter, a Christian renegade retired from the Janissaries and married to the widow of a Greek priest, they were Turkish subjects from the island of Lesbos, a notorious center of Christian piracy, which commanded the entrance to the Dardanelles. Becoming at once corsairs and traders, they set up their headquarters on the island of Jerba, between Tunis and Tripoli, a serviceable springboard from which to raid the shipping lanes and the seacoasts of Christendom. Granted protection by the ruler of Tunis, Aruj subdued many of the local chieftains and liberated Algiers, with other ports, from the Spaniards. But on seeking to establish his forces inland at Tlemcen, he was defeated and lost his life at their hands—fighting, so it is chronicled, "to the very last gasp, like a lion."

After his death, in 1518, Khaireddin Barbarossa, proving to be the abler of the two corsair brothers, rose to be a great naval commander in the service of the Turks in the Mediterranean. First he reinforced his garrisons along the coast and made alliances with the Arab tribes of the interior; then he established contact with Sultan Selim, who had completed his conquest of Syria and Egypt, and whose right flank could, with advantage, be secured by the forces of fellow Ottomans along the North African coast. Barbarossa, it is recorded, sent a vessel to Istanbul with rich presents for the Sultan, who made him beylerbey of Africa, dispatching to Algiers the traditional insignia of the office—horse, scimitar, and banner of two horsetails—together with arms and a force of soldiers, with permission to levy others, with Janissary privileges.

It was not until 1533 that Selim's successor, Suleiman, until now preoccupied with his land campaigns in Europe, made direct contact with Barbarossa, whose exploits in conflict with the emperor's forces in the western Mediterranean had not escaped his attention. The Sultan was now alarmed at the fact that Christian naval forces had penetrated, in the previous year, from the western into the eastern Mediterranean. They were commanded by a skillful Genoese admiral, Andrea Doria, who had changed his allegiance from the French king to the Habsburg emperor. Passing through the Straits of Messina, Doria had entered Turkish home waters to capture Coron, on the southwestern promontory of Greece. He hoped thus to create a tactical diversion at the time when the Sultan was besieging Güns before Vienna. The Sultan sent a military and naval force which, despite superiority in numbers, failed to recapture Coron. Though the Christians were later to evacuate the port, Suleiman was concerned at this setback, realizing that, while he built up his land forces, his naval forces had been allowed to decline to a point at which they were no longer a match for those of the West. Drastic measures of reorganization were required, moreover without delay, since the Sultan was about to depart on a campaign against Persia, and needed in his absence to secure his naval defenses at home.

Thus the Sultan sent an envoy to Algiers, commanding Barbarossa to appear before him in Istanbul. Taking his time, as befitted his ruling status, Barbarossa in due course made a stately progress, with forty vessels of his Barbary fleet brightly caparisoned in full ceremonial rig, through the Dardanelles, around Seraglio Point, and into the harbour of the Golden Horn. He bore gifts on a regal scale for the Sultan, including camel loads of gold and jewels and precious fabrics, a menagerie of lions and other African beasts, and a large levy of young Christian women for the Sultan's harem, each bearing a gift of gold or silver. Hoary-bearded as he grew older, with fierce bushy eyebrows, but still burly and vigorous in build, Barbarossa paid homage to the Sultan at an audience in the Divan, accompanied by eighteen captains of galleys, well-seasoned sea dogs, who were invested with robes of honour and pecuniary stipends, while Barbarossa was appointed Kapudan Pasha, or admiral-in-chief. Commanded by the Sultan to "exercise their skill in constructing vessels," they proceeded to the imperial shipyards to supervise, accelerate, and improve on the works of construction in progress. Thanks to their efforts in the course of that winter, the naval power of the Sultan was soon to extend over all the Mediterranean waters and the greater part of the North African coastline.

Barbarossa was a convinced advocate of active Turkish collaboration with France in the Mediterranean. He saw in this alliance an effective counterweight to Spanish naval power. This suited also the designs of the Sultan, now that he had resolved to proceed against the Emperor Charles by sea rather than by land, and similarly those of King Francis himself, to whom it promised naval aid against the emperor's Italian states, directly here in the Mediterranean rather than indirectly in the remote Danube basin. This policy was to lead to the Turco-French Treaty of 1536, with its secret mutual defense clauses.

Meanwhile, in the summer of 1534, shortly before the Sultan's departure for Persia, Barbarossa sailed forth with his reconditioned fleet, through the Dardanelles and out into the Mediterranean. The fleets of this age, which his typified, were composed primarily of large galleys, the "battleships" of the time, propelled by oarsmen who were predominantly slaves, captured in battle or otherwise; lean galleons, or "destroyers," smaller and swifter and propelled by freemen, of a more professional stamp; galleons, the "ships of the line," propelled entirely by sail; besides galleasses, propelled partly by sail and partly by oarsmen.

Barbarossa proceeded westward to ravage the coasts and ports of Italy, around the Straits of Messina and northward in the domains of the kingdom of Naples. But his more urgent objective was Tunis, whose kingdom, now weakened by bloodthirsty rifts in the local Hafsid dynasty, he had promised to the Sultan. He had begun to envisage an Ottoman dominion, under his own effective rule, which would stretch with a chain of harbours along the whole coast of North Africa from the Straits of Gibraltar to Tripoli. On the pretext of restoring to power a fugitive prince of the dynasty, he landed his Janissaries at La Goletta, the neck of the channel which led into the lake harbour of Tunis. Here as a pirate of little account he and his brother, Aruj, had in the past been permitted to shelter their galleys. Barbarossa was ready to mount an attack. But the repute of his name and power was now such that the ruler, Muley Hassan, fled from the city, the claimant to his throne was discarded, and Tunisia was annexed to the Ottoman Empire. It gave the Turks a strategic foothold, commanding from the south the narrow channel which links the eastern with the western Mediterranean basin, within easy raiding distance by galley of Malta, where the former Knights of Rhodes (the Knights of St. John) were now based, and of Sicily, an island which had been conquered from here, first by Carthage and later by the Saracens, and which would now surely be the next Ottoman objective in the Mediterranean.

The Emperor Charles awoke at once to the danger, which threatened to make Sicily untenable. At first he tried to meet it by means of intrigue. He sent a Genoese envoy familiar with North Africa as a spy to Tunis, instructing him to organize a revolt against the Turks with the support of the dethroned ruler, Muley Hassan. If that failed he was either to induce Barbarossa through bribery to abandon the Sultan for the emperor, or to arrange for his assassination. But Barbarossa discovered the plot, and it was the Genoese spy who was put to death.

Thus the emperor, obliged to take action, assembled a formidable fleet, drawn from Spanish and Italian ports, of four hundred sail under the command of Andrea Doria, together with a force of imperial troops composed of Spaniards, Germans, and Italians. In the summer of 1535 they disembarked near the ruins of Carthage. Before reaching Tunis itself, they had to capture the twin towers of the fortress of La Goletta which guarded the "throat of the torrent," leading to the city through its otherwise landlocked harbour. They besieged it for twenty-four days, with great losses, against fierce Turkish resistance. It was well defended, under an able Jewish corsair commander from Smyrna, by artillery transferred from the ships in the lake harbour. But it finally fell, largely through a breach in the walls by the guns from a ship of the Knights of St. John—an eight-decked galleon of unusual size which was probably the best-armed fighting vessel then in existence.

The way to Tunis thus lay open to the imperial forces, which, on entering the lake, captured the bulk of Barbarossa's fleet. Barbarossa, however, as an insurance against possible defeat, had sent a squadron of his largest and best-armed galleys as a reserve force to Bône, between Tunis and Algiers. He now prepared to meet the emperor's land army which was advancing in extreme heat along the lakeside. After failing to bar its access to the wells en route, Barbarossa withdrew to the walls of Tunis, where he prepared to give battle next day with his own army of Turks and Berbers.

But within the city meanwhile some thousands of Christian captives, aided by renegades and led by a Knight of St. John, broke loose at the approach of their coreligionists, captured the arsenal, and thus arming themselves, turned upon the Turks, for whom the Berbers refused to fight. The emperor entered the city against only slight opposition and after three days of massacre, plunder, and rape by his Christian soldiery—deeds as hideous as any in the annals of Moslem barbarities—reinstated Muley Hassan on the throne as his vassal, with a Spanish garrison to hold La Goletta. Charles was acclaimed as a conqueror throughout Christendom, and created a new order of crusading chivalry, the Cross of Tunis, with the motto "Barbaria." Hans Sachs, the Meistersinger of Nuremberg, celebrated the victory with a pageant, portraying the mock siege of a model fortress manned by Turkish puppets, whose red-bearded captain was consumed amid cheers by the flames.

But no such fate was to befall Barbarossa. As soon as he saw that the city was lost and given over to pillage, he fled in the confusion with some thousands of Turks to Bône, where, thanks to his foresight, his reserve fleet awaited him. Nor, with his army fully engaged in destruction, did the emperor pursue him; while Andrea Doria, who had previously failed despite the emperor's orders to take the precaution of occupying Bône, was now too late to catch him. For Barbarossa wasted no time. Consummate in his mastery of strategy and tactics, he instantly sailed out of Bône with his galleys and troops, not in retreat, not to defend Algiers as his enemies might have anticipated, but after reinforcing his fleet there to retaliate directly, against the emperor's own territory in the Balearic Islands.

Here he achieved complete surprise. His squadron appeared suddenly with Spanish and Italian flags flying from its mastheads, and so received an initial welcome as though it were part of the returning armada of the victorious emperor. Then, after capturing a large Portuguese merchantman, it entered the harbour of Mago (now Mahòn) in Minorca. Turning defeat into victory, its troops sacked the town, captured and enslaved thousands of Christians, destroyed the harbour defenses, and carried off Spanish treasures and stores to Algiers. The capture of Tunis—quite apart from presenting internal political problems—availed the emperor little as long as Barbarossa remained at large on the seas, to fight many another day in that element of which he was now the acknowledged master.

In 1536 Barbarossa was once again in Istanbul, "rubbing his face against the royal stirrup" (as the payment of respects to his master was literally phrased). The Sultan, lately returned from his reconquest of Baghdad, instructed him to build a new fleet of two hundred vessels for a major expedition against Italy. The shipyards and arsenals of the city became once more alive with activity. Andrea Doria had provoked Suleiman by a raid on his sea-lanes from Messina, in which he captured ten Turkish merchantmen; then he had sailed eastward across the Ionian Sea to defeat a Turkish naval squadron off the island of Paxos. This justified Barbarossa's advice to the Sultan that, having established his naval power in the western and central Mediterranean basin, he should now establish it on a firmer base nearer home, in the eastern basin.

In 1537 Barbarossa sailed his new fleet out of the Golden Horn for an attack on the southeast coast of Italy, to be followed by a sweep up the Adriatic. This was planned as a combined operation, to be supported by a large Turkish land force under the Sultan's command, which would cross from Albania and march northward through Italy. The plan counted on the intervention in the north of King Francis I, with the aid of Turkish galleys, whose presence throughout the winter in the harbour of Marseilles had overtly proclaimed Franco-Turkish collaboration. Barbarossa landed at Otranto and "laid waste the coast of Apulia like a pestilence," so intimidating Andrea Doria by the size of his new armada that he did not again venture to intervene from Messina. But the land campaign failed to materialize, partly because Francis, with his habitual duplicity, preferred to negotiate a truce with the emperor.

Thus the Sultan, now in Albania, decided to switch his forces against Venice. The Venetian islands in the Ionian Sea had long been a source of contention between the two powers; moreover lately, jealous of the commercial favour now shown by the Turks to the French, the Venetians had committed acts of overt hostility against Turkish shipping. Off Corfu they captured a vessel carrying the governor of Gallipoli and murdered all on board but a youth who escaped, afloat on a plank, to report the outrage to the Grand Vezir. Suleiman at once ordered the siege of Corfu. His army was landed by a bridge of boats from the Albanian coast, and villages were plundered, but the fortress resisted stoutly and with the approach of winter the siege was abandoned.

In a spirit of ruthless revenge for this defeat, Barbarossa and his crews ranged down the Ionian and up into the Aegean Sea, sacking and despoiling the Venetian islands which had for so long contributed to the republic's prosperity, enslaving their inhabitants, seizing their vessels, and obliging them, under the threat of more raids, to pay to the Porte an extortionate annual tribute. He then returned in triumph to Istanbul, laden, according to the Turkish historian Haji Khalifeh, with "cloth, money, a thousand girls, and fifteen hundred boys—plunder amounting in all to the value of four hundred thousand pieces of gold: such at least was the calculation of his wealth." Next day, paying his respects and bearing gifts to the Sultan, "the Pasha dressed two hundred boys in scarlet, bearing in their hands flasks and goblets of gold and silver. Behind them followed thirty others, each carrying on his shoulders a purse of gold; after these came two hundred men, each carrying a purse of money; and lastly two hundred infidels wearing collars, each bearing a roll of cloth on his back." He received handsome rewards in return, "for never at any period had any Kapudan done such signal service." By a Spanish historian he was described as "the creator of the Turkish navy, its admiral and its soul."

He now represented a threat to Christendom which for once the Christian powers, the papacy and the emperor in league with Venice, united to meet. Each sent naval contingents which, under the chief command of Andrea Doria, amounted in all to some two hundred vessels, together with sixty thousand men and a large armoury of artillery. This fleet, which considerably outnumbered that of Barbarossa, included fifty large, square-sailed galleons, of a modern type already dominant in the New World, but still unfamiliar in the Mediterranean. Doria was confident that their massive firepower should easily overcome the smaller galleys of the corsairs and break Turkish sea power once and for all.

While the Christian vessels assembled off the island of Corfu, Barbarossa, off the Greek mainland, was able to take up a strategic position to the south, sailing through the fortified channel of Prevesa, around the historic point of Actium and into the comfortable shelter of the almost landlocked Gulf of Arta. He followed exactly the course taken fifteen hundred years earlier by Octavian, the future Augustus Caesar, in preparation for his defeat of Anthony, with Cleopatra, in the battle of Actium. In this strong position he lay in wait for Doria and his mixed armada, which in due course anchored off Prevesa, at the mouth of the gulf.

Barbarossa had no intention of emerging from his own secure anchorage. Nor could Doria enter the gulf beyond the point of Actium, where the full fire of the Turkish galleys awaited him. His only chance of coming to grips with his enemy was to land troops and cannon, to capture the fortress of Prevesa and block the mouth of the harbour. He could thus trap the Turkish fleet within its waters, and bombard it from the heights onshore. Some such landing operation was indeed

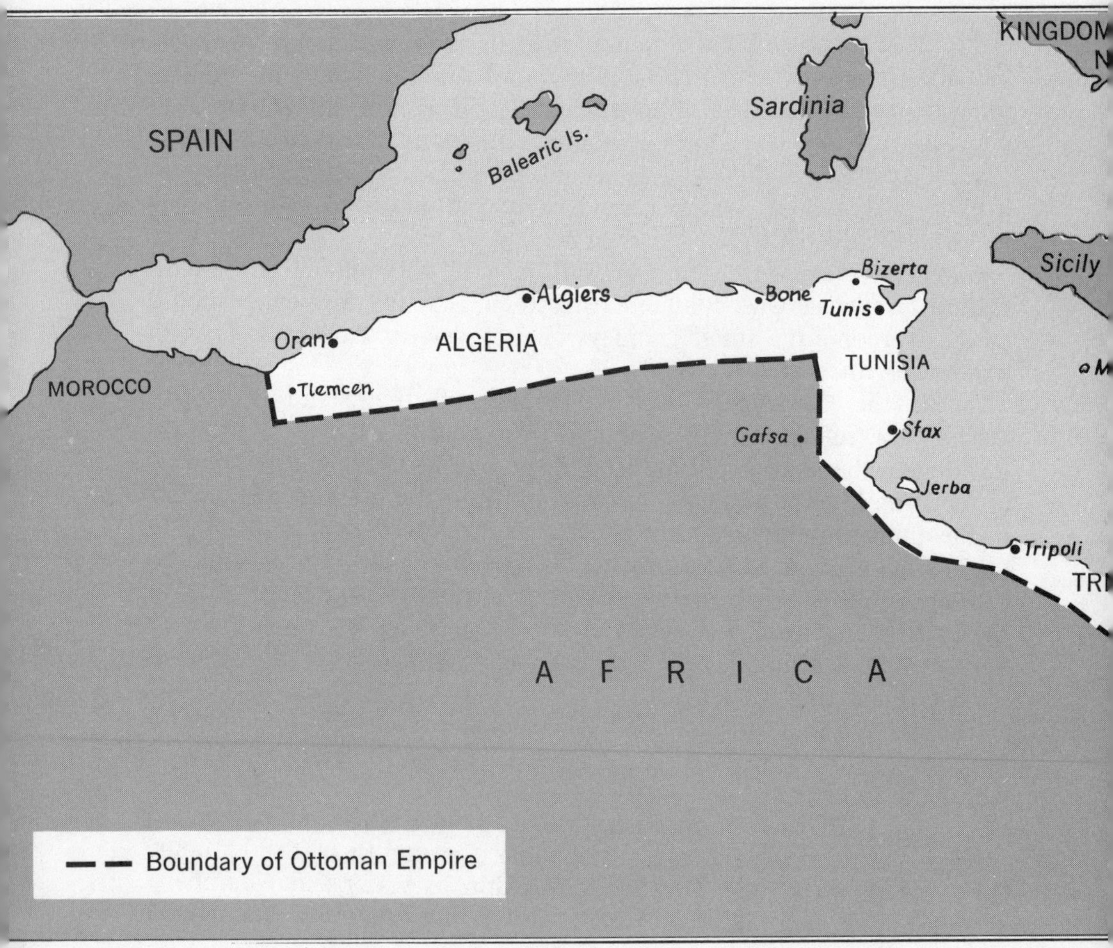
KINGDOM
N
Sardinia
SPAIN
Balearic Is.
Sicily
Bizerta
Algiers
Bone
Tunis
Oran
ALGERIA
TUNISIA
MOROCCO
Tlemcen
Gafsa
Sfax
Jerba
Tripoli
TR
A F R I C A
Boundary of Ottoman Empire

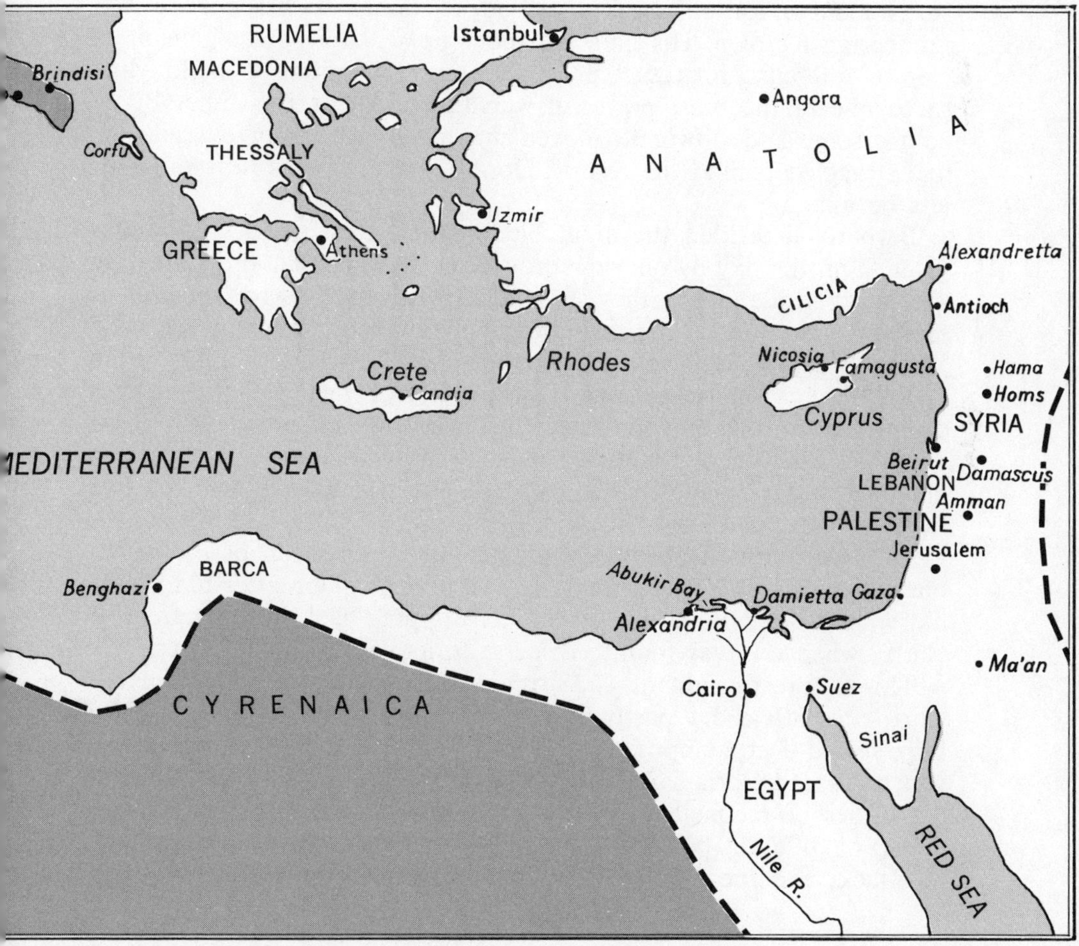
RUMELIA
Istanbul
MACEDONIA
Brindisi
Angora
Corfu
THESSALY
ANATOLIA
Izmir
GREECE
Athens
Alexandretta
CILICIA
Antioch
Crete
Rhodes
Nicosia
Famagusta
Hama
Candia
Homs
Cyprus
SYRIA
EDITERRANEAN SEA
Beirut
LEBANON
Damascus
Amman
PALESTINE
Jerusalem
BARCA
Abukir Bay
Benghazi
Damietta
Gaza
Alexandria
Ma'an
Cairo
Suez
CYRENAICA
Sinai
EGYPT
Nile R.
RED SEA

discussed, but rejected by Doria for fear that at this late season of the year—the month of September—a gale was likely to blow up, forcing the withdrawal of the fleet and the abandonment of the troops to the mercies of Barbarossa's Janissaries on land.

Thus, what with Doria trying to lure Barbarossa out to sea, and Barbarossa trying to lure Doria into the gulf, no major encounter between them took place. All that each did was to send a token squadron of galleys to the mouth of the channel, where an inconclusive naval skirmish occurred. Then Andrea Doria and his fleet moved away southward from Prevesa, as though in retreat, hoping that at last Barbarossa would emerge in pursuit of him. When he duly did go, he found the Christian ships scattered in a long line down the coast.

Now was the time for Doria, with his greatly superior forces and firepower, to regroup his fleet and move northward, benefitting from a fair wind, to confront the Turk. But he failed unaccountably to do so. Nor did Barbarossa seek an all-out encounter with a fleet so outnumbering his own. His galleys caught up with the great galleon of Venice, a floating fortress which was reputed, like that of the knights, to be one of the most powerful warships afloat at this time. Being cumbersome and slower in movement, moreover driven by sail, she had straggled behind the rest of Doria's fleet and was now more or less becalmed.

Barbarossa tackled the giant circumspectly, in a series of rushes throughout the day by one squadron of galleys after another. Meeting with a broadside of fire, they suffered damage and loss but themselves scored a direct hit on the mainmast, which crashed into the sea. The Venetian commander called for galleys from Doria to combat those of the Turks. But none came. Doria preferred to lie at anchor at a distance or to tack and maneuver up and down offshore. Barbarossa continued his worrying tactics, persisting in his attacks on the galleon, pursuing stragglers down the coast, capturing two galleys and five sailing vessels, and losing no ships of his own. Finally, late in the day, Doria ordered his fleet northward, not in the direction of the Turks but out to sea, perhaps hoping, in vain, to draw them after him. Next morning at dawn the armada was seen slipping back in full retreat to Corfu, whence it was soon to disperse to its various home ports.

This failure to fight in 1538 amounted to a major defeat for the Christians. It was due partly to the problems of handling an unusually large mixed fleet, composed of both oar and sail, galleys and galleons, which Andrea Doria failed to master. It was due also to the political difficulties of reconciling with each other the commanders and interests of different powers—especially the Venetians, who were keen to attack, and the Spaniards, who were anxious above all to avoid loss. For the Emperor Charles, whose interests lay in the western Mediterranean, had little to gain from a war in its eastern waters. Before the campaign he had endeavoured to bribe Barbarossa away from the Sultan's service but without success—as he was to do once again when the campaign was over. Once more Christendom had failed, despite initial appearances, to unite or at least to remain united. The result, as in previous land campaigns, was a victory for the united Turks and the consequent conversion of the Mediterranean into an Ottoman lake. Thanks to the achievements of Barbarossa, "the King of the Sea," it was so to remain for a further generation.

Venice now withdrew from the imperial alliance, and with the backing of French diplomacy made a separate peace with the Turks. Nothing could now prevent the Ottoman armada from shifting naval operations from the eastern into the western basin of the Mediterranean. Their fleet sailed in triumph through the Sicilian channel and as far as the Pillars of Hercules, mounting a fierce raid on Gibraltar from its corsair stronghold at Algiers. In the autumn of 1541, taking advantage of the absence of Barbarossa in Istanbul, the Emperor Charles V with his Christian allies made an unseasonable and ill-fated attempt, with a large armada and army, to capture Algiers. Thanks to a hurricane this ended in total disaster, thus inflicting on the emperor the humiliation of his first major personal defeat.

The seas were thus cleared for full naval cooperation between Charles's enemies of the "impious" Franco-Turkish alliance, which his Algerian expedition had sought to disrupt. In 1543 the Sultan sent Barbarossa westward once more, in command of a fleet of a hundred galleys, with a French envoy on board. Once more he ravaged the coasts of Naples and Sicily, sacking Reggio di Calabria, where he captured the governor's eighteen-year-old wife and as a price for being permitted to marry her released both her parents. Panic reigned in Rome, whose streets were patrolled at night by officers with torches, preventing the flight of the terror-struck citizens. The Turkish fleet thus reached the coasts of the French Riviera. Landing at Marseilles, Barbarossa was received by the young Bourbon Duke of Enghien. He was granted as his naval headquarters the port of Toulon, from which a portion of the inhabitants was evacuated, and which the French were presently describing as a second Constantinople, full of "San-Jacobeis" (otherwise sanjak beys).

The port indeed presented a curious spectacle, humiliating to the French Catholics, with turbanned Moslems pacing the decks and Christian slaves—Italians, Germans, and even some Frenchmen—chained to the benches of the galleys. To replenish their crews, following deaths from an epidemic of fever, the Turks took to raiding French villages, carrying off peasants to serve in the galleys, while

Christian captives were openly sold in the market. Meanwhile, as in a Moslem city, the muezzins freely chanted their own call to prayer and their imams recited the Koran.

Francis I, having asked for Turkish support, soon grew disturbed at the overt nature and extent of it, and its unpopularity with his subjects. Equivocal as ever, he was reluctant to commit himself to a major naval offensive with his ally against the emperor, for which in any case his naval resources were insufficient. Instead, to the annoyance of Barbarossa, who sought adventures on a wider and more ambitious scale, he settled for a limited objective—an attack on the port of Nice, a gateway into Italy, which was held by the emperor's ally, the Duke of Savoy.

Though the castle of Nice held out under a redoubtable Knight of St. John, the city was soon captured, as the Turkish artillery opened a large breach in the walls, and its governor formally surrendered. Then it was sacked and burned to the ground, a breach of the terms of capitulation for which the French blamed the Turks and the Turks blamed the French. In the spring of 1554 Francis I rid himself of his embarrassing ally through bribery, making substantial payments to the Turkish forces and presenting precious gifts to the admiral himself. For he was about once more to come to terms with Charles V. Barbarossa and his fleet sailed away to Istanbul.

This was his final campaign. Two years afterward he died of a fever in the fullness of age in his palace in Istanbul, and all Islam lamented, "The Chief of the Sea is dead!"

((16))

SULEIMAN WAS PERENNIALLY WAGING WAR ON TWO FRONTS. DIVERTing his land forces into Asia, while his sea forces built up their command of the Mediterranean, he waged in person between 1534 and 1533 three successive campaigns against Persia. Persia was Turkey's traditional hereditary enemy, not only in national but in religious terms, since the Turks were orthodox Sunnites and the Persians heterodox Shi'ites. But since the victory at Chalderan by Suleiman's father, Sultan Selim, against Shah Ismail, relations between the two countries had been relatively quiescent, though no peace between them had been signed and the Sultan continued to strike threatening attitudes. When Shah Ismail died, his ten-year-old son and successor, Tahmasp, was similarly threatened with invasion. But ten years elapsed before the threat was carried out. Meanwhile Tahmasp, taking advantage of the absence of the Turks, suborned into his service the governor of Bitlis, in the Turkish frontier region, while the governor of Baghdad, who had promised allegiance to Suleiman, was murdered and replaced by an adherent of the shah. As a prelude to retaliation Suleiman ordered the execution of a number of Persian prisoners still held at Gallipoli. Then he sent the Grand Vezir Ibrahim ahead of him to prepare the ground for an Asiatic campaign.

Ibrahim—whose last campaign this was fated to be—succeeded in securing the surrender to the Turkish side of several Persian frontier fortresses. Then, in the summer of 1534, he entered Tabriz, from which the shah had withdrawn rather than fight a pitched battle in defense of the city as his father had so imprudently done. After four months on the march through arid and mountainous country, the Sultan joined his Grand Vezir before Tabriz, and in October their joint forces moved laboriously southward to Baghdad, contending with extreme winter conditions in the mountainous lands.

Finally, at the end of November, 1534, Suleiman made his proud entry into the Holy City of Baghdad, liberating it, as Commander of the Faithful, from the Shi'ite rule of Persia. Its heretical inhabitants were treated with exemplary tolerance, as Ibrahim had treated those of Tabriz—and as the Christian Emperor Charles V had notably failed to treat the Moslems of Tunis. Suleiman, impressing his orthodox followers, contrived to unearth the remains of the great Sunnite imam Abu Hanifa, a renowned jurist and theologian in the time of the Prophet, which the heterodox Persians were said to have destroyed, but which were identified by their emission of an odour of musk. A new tomb was at once built for the holy man, which has since remained a resort of pilgrimage. Thus here, on the capture of Baghdad from the Moslem heretic, was a miraculous discovery held to be comparable in the eyes of God to that of the remains of Eyub, the companion of the Prophet, on the capture from the Christian infidel of Constantinople.

In the spring of 1535 Suleiman left Baghdad, by an easier route than before, for Tabriz, where he remained for some months, asserting Ottoman power and prestige but sacking the city before his departure. For he was aware that at so remote a distance from his capital he could not hope to control it. Indeed on his long journey home his rear guard was continually and effectively harassed by the Persian forces, and it was January, 1536, before he reached and triumphantly entered Istanbul.

This first campaign in Persia was to mark the downfall of Ibrahim, who had served the Sultan for thirteen years as Grand Vezir, and who was now commanding his armies in the field. Inevitably, in the course of these years, Ibrahim had made enemies among those who resented his rapid rise to power, his undue position of influence, his consequent phenomenal wealth. There were those too who resented his Christian predilections and disregard for Moslem susceptibilities. In Persia he seems to have overreached his powers. After capturing Tabriz from the Persians before Suleiman's arrival, he chose to adopt the title of sultan, adding it to that of Serasker, or commander-in-chief, and liking to be addressed as Sultan Ibrahim. In these parts this was a usual enough style, generally applied to minor Kurdish chieftains. But the Ottoman Sultan himself was hardly likely to see it as such, were Ibrahim's adoption of it to be interpreted to him as an act of disloyalty. As it was, Ibrahim was accompanied on the campaign by a personal enemy of long standing, Iskender Chelebi, the *defterdar* or Chief Treasurer, who objected to his use of the title and tried to persuade him to drop it.

The result was a quarrel between the two men, which became a war to the death. It ended in the disgrace of Iskender on charges of intrigues against the Sultan and misuse of public moneys, and his execution on the scaffold. Before it Iskender called for pen and paper, and in writing accused Ibrahim himself of conspiracy against his master. Since these were his dying words, hence to a Moslem sacred testimony, the Sultan became persuaded of Ibrahim's guilt. His conviction was reinforced, so the Turkish chronicles relate, by a dream in which the dead man appeared with a celestial halo before the

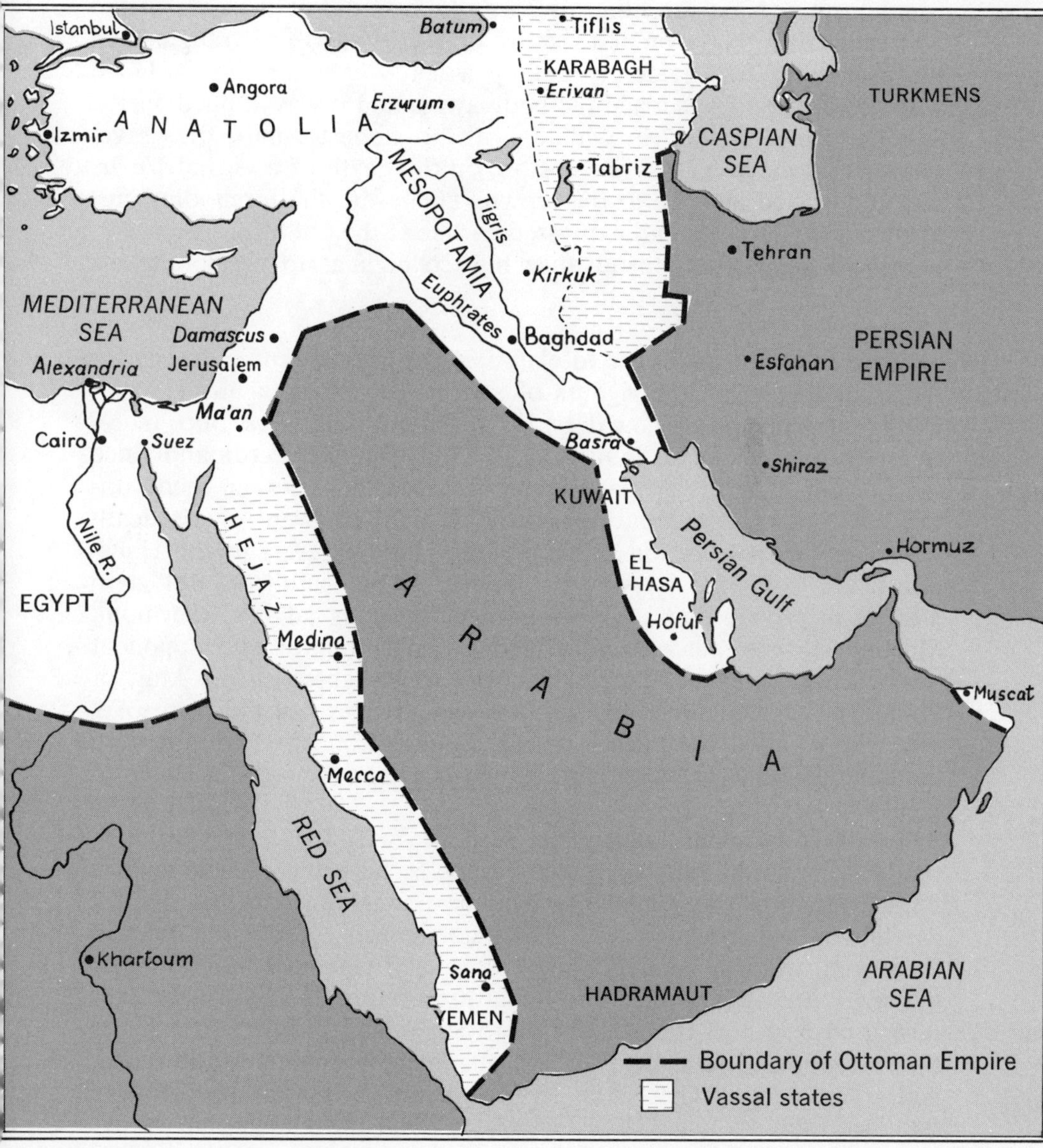
Istanbul
Angora
ANATOLIA
Izmir
Erzurum
Batum
Tiflis
KARABAGH
Erivan
TURKMENS
CASPIAN SEA
Tabriz
MESOPOTAMIA
Tigris
Euphrates
Tehran
Kirkuk
MEDITERRANEAN SEA
Damascus
Baghdad
PERSIAN EMPIRE
Esfahan
Alexandria
Jerusalem
Ma'an
Cairo
Suez
Basra
Shiraz
KUWAIT
HEJAZ
Nile R.
Persian Gulf
Hormuz
EL HASA
EGYPT
Hofuf
Medina
ARABIA
Muscat
Mecca
RED SEA
Khartoum
Sana
YEMEN
HADRAMAUT
ARABIAN SEA
Boundary of Ottoman Empire
Vassal states

Sultan and attempted to strangle him. Undoubtedly it was influenced also, in his own harem, by Suleiman's new and ambitious favourite, a concubine of Russian-Ukrainian origin who became known as Roxelana. She was jealous of Ibrahim's intimacy with the Sultan and of his powers, which she herself aspired to exercise.

In any event Suleiman decided to act swiftly and secretly. One evening after his return in the spring of 1536, Ibrahim Pasha was summoned to dine with the Sultan in his apartment in the Grand Seraglio, and to sleep the night there afterward, according to his usual custom. Next morning his corpse was found at the gate of the Seraglio, with marks on it to show that he had been strangled. In the process he had evidently put up a fierce fight for life. A horse with black trappings carried the body away, and it was at once buried in a dervish monastery in Galata, with no stone to mark the grave. His vast property, as was the custom on the death of a Grand Vezir, was confiscated and fell to the crown. Thus were the forebodings realized which Ibrahim had expressed earlier at the outset of his career, begging Suleiman not to advance him so high as to precipitate his ruin.

More than a decade was to elapse before the Sultan ventured, for the second time, on the rigours of another campaign against Persia. For events in Hungary now drew his attention to the West once more. In 1540 John Zapolya, joint king of Hungary with Ferdinand since their recent secret treaty partitioning its territories between them, unexpectedly died. The treaty provided that in the event of his death without issue, his portion of the country should revert to the Habsburgs. At that time he was unmarried, hence childless. But soon afterward, probably at the instigation of a crafty adviser, the monk Martinuzzi, who was a fervent Hungarian nationalist and opponent of the Habsburgs, he married Isabella, a daughter of the king of Poland. On his deathbed at Buda he received news of the birth of a son, who at his dying behest, with the added injunction to appeal to the Sultan for aid, was proclaimed king of Hungary, with the name of Stephen.

To this Ferdinand's immediate response was to march with such funds as he could raise and such troops as he could muster against Buda, which as king of all Hungary he now claimed as his rightful capital. But his forces proved inadequate for a siege of the city, and he retired, leaving a garrison in Pesth—and retaining several other towns. At this, Martinuzzi and his group of anti-Habsburg adherents turned on behalf of the infant king to Suleiman, who, in his anger at the surreptitious treaty and the devious maneuvers which followed it, had commented: "These two Kings are unworthy to wear crowns; they are faithless men." The Sultan received the Hungarian envoys with favour. They requested his support for King Stephen. Suleiman granted recognition in principle in return for the payment of an annual tribute. But he wished first to be sure that Isabella had really borne a child, and sent to her a high official to verify its existence. She received the Turk with the infant in her arms. Then she gracefully uncovered her breast and gave milk to the child in his presence. He fell on his knees and kissed the feet of the newly born child, as the son of King John.

In the course of that winter the Sultan prepared for yet another campaign against Hungary. In the summer of 1541 he entered Buda, which Ferdinand's troops had again attacked but of which Martinuzzi, donning a cuirass over his priestly robes, had led an energetic and successful defense. Here, after crossing the Danube to occupy Pesth and thus routing his enemy's fugitive soldiers, the Sultan received Martinuzzi, with his nationalist supporters. Then, pretending that Moslem law prevented him from receiving Isabella in person, he sent for the child, which was brought to his tent in a golden cradle, attended by three nurses and the queen's principal counsellors. After looking closely at the baby, Suleiman instructed his son Bayezid to take him in his arms and kiss him. Then he was sent back to his mother.

Later she was assured that her son, who was now to be given the names of his forebears, John Sigismund, should rule at the appropriate age over Hungary. But for the present she was bidden to retire with him to Lippa, in Transylvania. In theory the young king was to have tributary status as a vassal of the Sultan. But in practice there was soon every sign of a permanent Ottoman occupation of the country. Buda and its surrounding territory were transformed into a Turkish province under a pasha with an all-Turkish administration, whose churches began to be converted into mosques.

This disturbed the Austrians, who had fears once again for the safety of Vienna. Ferdinand sent envoys with peace overtures to the Sultan's camp. Their gifts included a large and elaborate clock which told not only the hours but the days and the months of the calendar and the movements of the sun, moon, and planets and was thus calculated to appeal to Suleiman's astronomical interests in the cosmos and the movements of the heavenly bodies. Nonetheless it did not persuade him to heed the excessive demands of the envoys, whose master still aspired to be king of all Hungary. After enquiring of his vezir, "What do they say? What do they want?" he interrupted their opening speech with the command "If they have nothing more to say, let them go." The vezir in his turn rebuked them: "Do you believe that the Padishah is out of his mind, that he should relinquish what he has won for the third time with his sword?"

Ferdinand took the field yet again in an attempt to recapture Pesth.

But his siege proved abortive and his forces dispersed. Then Suleiman, in the spring of 1543, marched once more into Hungary. Capturing Gran after a brief siege and turning its cathedral into a mosque, he assigned it to the Turkish pashalik of Buda and fortified it as his northwestern outpost against Europe. His armies then proceeded, in a series of sieges and engagements in the field, to conquer from the Austrians a number of important strongholds and to bring under Ottoman rule an area of territory so wide that he was able to divide it into twelve sanjaks. Thus the bulk of Hungary—knit together by an ordered system of Turkish government at once military, civil, and financial—was effectively incorporated in the Ottoman Empire. It was so to remain for a century and a half to come.

Such was the climax of Suleiman's victories on the Danube. In the interests of all the contending parties the time had now come to negotiate peace. The emperor himself desired it, to free his hands in his dealings with the Protestants. Thus for once the Habsburg brothers, Charles and Ferdinand, were united in their efforts to come to terms, on land if not at sea, with the Sultan. After an armistice agreed with the pasha of Buda, they sent a series of joint embassies to Istanbul. Three years passed before they finally bore fruit in 1547, in the five-year truce of Adrianople which was based on the *status quo*. Under its terms Suleiman retained all his conquests, but for a small part of Hungary which Ferdinand still held and on which he now agreed to pay a tribute to the Porte. Not only the emperor, who appended his signature at Augsburg, but the king of France, the Republic of Venice, and Pope Paul III—though he was on bad terms with the emperor on account of his attitude to the Protestants—were parties to the agreement.

It was timely for Suleiman, who was now ready, in the spring of 1548, for his second campaign in Persia. This, however, proved inconclusive, but for the capture of the city of Van, which remained in Turkish hands.

After it, with the accustomed swing of the pendulum between East and West, Suleiman became involved once more with events in Hungary. The truce of Adrianople had failed to run its agreed course of five years. Ferdinand did not for long remain content with his share of what was in effect a tripartite Hungary. For the Turkish pashalik of Buda separated his lands from Transylvania. Here the widowed Queen Isabella was preparing her young son at Lippa for the inheritance of this small but prosperous state. But within it the predominant influence was that of the ambitious monk Martinuzzi. Of this Isabella had complained to Suleiman, who demanded that the monk be relieved of his power and delivered in bonds to the Porte.

Now scheming against the Sultan in Ferdinand's interests—and his own—Martinuzzi secretly persuaded Isabella, in 1551, to relinquish

Transylvania to Ferdinand in return for certain lands elsewhere, thus making it a part of the Austrian dominions. For this he was rewarded with a cardinal's hat. But the Sultan, on hearing the news, immediately flung the Austrian envoy into the Black Tower of the fortress of Anadolu Hisar, a notorious prison on the Bosporus, where he was to languish for two years, finally emerging more dead than alive. Then on his orders a trusted commander and future Grand Vezir, Mehmed Sokollu, marched late in the season into Transylvania, where he captured Lippa and withdrew, leaving a garrison behind him.

Though Martinuzzi joined with Ferdinand to besiege and recover Lippa, he sought in secret to placate the Turks, treating with undue leniency the hard-pressed Turkish garrison in the hope of pardon and suitable rewards from the Sultan. Warned of his treachery, Ferdinand authorized his generals to put Martinuzzi to death. This they did, suborning his secretary to stab him as he sat at his desk, then entering with a troop of armed Spaniards and Italians who fired at him as he cried, "Jesus Mary!" They left sixty-three wounds in his body.

In 1552 Turkish troops invaded the country again. They captured a number of fortresses, greatly increasing the area of Hungary under Turkish control; they defeated an army which Ferdinand had put into the field, capturing half of it and taking their prisoners to Buda, where they were sold for low prices in an overstocked market. But in the autumn the Turks were checked by a heroic defense at Erlau, to the northeast of Buda, and after a long siege were forced to retreat.

Negotiating an armistice, the Sultan then embarked in 1553 on his third and last Persian campaign. Profiting by Suleiman's preoccupation with Hungary, the shah—possibly at the instigation of the emperor—had taken the initiative against the Turks. His son, acting as commander-in-chief of the Persian forces, captured Erzurum, whose pasha was decoyed into an ambush and soundly defeated. The Persians achieved further successes, causing jubilant reports to spread through Europe that they had seized the passes of the Taurus and threatened all Syria. Now the Sultan was ready to retaliate.

After a winter spent in Aleppo, Suleiman and his army advanced in the spring, recapturing Erzurum, then crossing the Upper Euphrates near Kars to lay waste Persian territory by incendiary methods more savage than anything attempted in previous campaigns. Engagements with the enemy resulted now in Persian, now in Turkish successes. The superiority of the Sultan's army was eventually proved by the fact that the Persians could neither face his forces in the open field nor regain from them the lands they had conquered. The Turks, on the other hand, could not retain indefinitely these distant conquests against an enemy whom they could not ignore, but with whom they could not come to grips. The result was a stalemate, from which neither side benefitted. Finally, with the arrival of a Persian envoy in Erzurum in the autumn of 1554, a truce was signed, to be confirmed in the following year by a treaty of peace.

Such were Suleiman's Asiatic campaigns. On balance they had not been unprofitable. Abandoning under the treaty all claims to Tabriz and its region, he admitted failure to make permanent inroads into the heart of Persia itself—as indeed already into the heart of central Europe. But he had extended his empire in the East to embrace, on a secure basis, Baghdad, lower Mesopotamia, the mouths of the Euphrates and Tigris, and a foothold on the Persian Gulf—a notable extension to a domain which now stretched from the Indian to the Atlantic Ocean.

The first of these three campaigns had been tainted by the subsequent execution of Suleiman's favourite, Ibrahim. The start of the third provoked a deed more heinous—and certainly more fateful—than many in the annals of the Ottoman dynasty.

Through the two intervening decades Suleiman had fallen more than ever under the spell of his Slav favourite, who had become generally known to Europeans as La Rossa, or Roxelana. Originally a captive from Galicia, the daughter of a Ukrainian priest, she was named by the Turks Khurren, or "the Laughing One," from her joyous smile and her merry disposition, and she had replaced in the Sultan's affections his previous favourite, Gülbehar, or "the Rose of Spring." In his counsels she came to replace Ibrahim, whose fate she may well have precipitated. Slight but graceful in figure, she seduced more by her gaiety than by her beauty. She soothed by charm of manner and stimulated by liveliness of mind. Quick in her understanding and subtle in her ways, Roxelana cleverly learned to read Suleiman's thoughts and to guide them in the directions that suited her ambition for power. First she disposed of her predecessor, Gülbehar, who had become the "first lady" of the harem after Suleiman's mother, the Sultana Valide, and who now withdrew into partial exile for a portion of the year in Magnesia.

Then, after bearing the Sultan a child, Roxelana contrived to become in terms of Moslem law his acknowledged legal wife, with a marriage portion, as no concubine of an Ottoman Sultan had been for two centuries past. When, in about 1541, the interior of the Old Palace, which had housed the Sultan's harem, was gutted by a serious fire, she created a new precedent by moving into the Grand Seraglio itself, where the Sultan resided and carried on the business of government. Here she took her possessions and a large retinue, which included a hundred ladies-in-waiting, together with her own personal dressmaker and her purveyor, who had thirty slaves of his own. No

Sultan Suleiman I (1520–66), whose reign brought the Ottoman Empire to its zenith. This full-length portrait shows the Suleimaniye Mosque in the background.

Reproduced from the English edition of Pieter Coeck van Aelst, *The Turks in MDLIII,* privately printed in London and Edinburgh in 1873, p. 54.

woman had been permitted by tradition to sleep in the Grand Seraglio before. But Roxelana remained there for the rest of her life, and in time a new harem was built here, within its own secluded courtyards, to take the place of the old.

Finally, seven years after the execution of Ibrahim, Roxelana gained a supreme hold over the Sultan by achieving the appointment as Grand Vezir of Rustem Pasha, who had married her daughter by the Sultan, Mihrimah, and was thus Suleiman's son-in-law, as Ibrahim had been Suleiman's brother-in-law. Somber and industrious, he was an administrator of outstanding ability, especially in matters of finance. As the Sultan increasingly relinquished the reins of government to Rustem, so did Roxelana approach the zenith of her power.

Suleiman, for all the tolerance of his disposition, the fairness of his principles, and the warmth of his attachments, had within him an ugly reserve of coldness, a latent cruelty born of addiction to absolute power and a congenital suspicion of any who might seek to rival him. On this Roxelana knew well how to trade. She had borne him three surviving sons, Selim, Bayezid, and Jehangir, for the eldest of whom she was determined to secure the succession to the throne. But Suleiman saw as his successor his firstborn son, Mustafa, whose mother was Gülbehar. He was a handsome young man of remarkable promise, "marvellously well-educated and prudent and of the age to reign," who had been groomed by his father for government in a number of responsible posts, and was now governor of Amasya, on the road to Persia. Generous in spirit and courageous in battle, he had won the devotion of the Janissaries, who saw in him a worthy successor to his father.

At the outset of the third Persian campaign Suleiman, now entering his sixtieth year, was at first reluctant to head his armies in person and delegated the supreme command to Rustem Pasha. But soon reports came back through a messenger from Rustem that the Janissaries had grown restive and were calling, in view of Suleiman's age, for Mustafa to lead them. They were saying, he reported, that the Sultan had grown too old to march in person against the enemy, and that only the Grand Vezir now opposed the elevation of Mustafa in his place. He declared that Mustafa was listening favourably to such rumours of sedition and begged the Sultan, for the sake of his throne's salvation, to come immediately to take over the command of the army in person. Here was Roxelana's chance. It was easy for her to play on the suspicious side of the Sultan's nature, to stir in him a latent jealousy of Mustafa's ambitions, to sow in his mind the idea that his son had designs on the sultanate comparable to those which had driven his father, Selim, to depose his own father, Bayezid II.

In deciding whether or not to march, Suleiman was delayed by doubts and moral scruples as to the action he should take against his son. Finally, putting forward his case in impersonal and theoretical terms, he sought an impartial verdict from the Mufti, the Sheikh of Islam. He told him, records Busbecq,

> that there was at Constantinople a merchant of good position who, when about to leave home for some time, placed over his property and household a slave to whom he had shown the greatest favour, and entrusted his wife and children to his loyalty. No sooner was the Master gone than this slave began to embezzle his Master's property, and plot against the lives of his wife and children; nay more, had attempted to compass his Master's destruction. The question which he (the Sultan) asked the Mufti to answer was this: "What sentence could be lawfully pronounced against the slave?" The Mufti answered that in his judgment he deserved to be tortured to death.

Thus Suleiman's religious conscience was salved. Marching eastward he reached his headquarters in the field at Eregli in the month of September and summoned Mustafa from Amasya. His friends, aware of the fate that might lie in store for him, urged him not to obey. But Mustafa replied that if he must lose his life he could not do better than give it back to the source from which it came. "Mustafa," writes Busbecq, "was confronted by a difficult choice: if he entered the presence of his angry and offended father, he ran an undoubted risk; if he refused, he clearly admitted that he had contemplated an act of treason. He chose the braver and more dangerous course." He proceeded to his father's camp.

Here his arrival created much excitement. Boldly he had his tents pitched beside his father's. After receiving the homage of the vezirs, he rode on a richly caparisoned charger, escorted by the vezirs and acclaimed by Janissaries crowding around him, to the Sultan's tent, where he expected to be received in audience. Within

> Everything appeared peaceful; there were no soldiers, no body-servants or attendants. However, several mutes (a class of servant highly valued by the Turks), strong, sturdy men, were there—his destined murderers. As soon as he entered the inner tent, they made a determined attack upon him and did their best to throw a noose around him. Being a man of powerful build, he defended himself stoutly and fought not only for his life but for the throne; for there was no doubt that, if he could escape and throw himself among the Janissaries, they would be so moved with indignation and with pity for their favourite, that they would not only protect him but also proclaim him as Sultan. Suleiman, fearing this, and being only separated by the linen tent-hangings from the scene . . . thrust his head out of the part of the tent in which he was and directed fierce and threatening glances upon the mutes, and by menacing gestures sternly rebuked their hesitation. Thereupon the mutes in their alarm, redoubling their efforts, hurled the unhappy Mustafa to the ground and, throwing the bowstring round his neck, strangled him.

His body was exposed on a rug before the tent for all the army to see. Mourning and lamentation were general; consternation and rage seized the Janissaries. But with their chosen leader lying dead, they were powerless to act.

To appease them the Sultan deprived Rustem—doubtless not wholly against his will—of his command and other dignities, and sent him back to Istanbul. But within two years, on the execution of his successor, Ahmed Pasha, he was back in power as Grand Vezir—doubtless on Roxelana's insistence.

Within three years Roxelana herself was dead, grievously mourned by the Sultan. She was buried in the tomb he had built for her beside his great new mosque of the Suleimaniye. But she had achieved her nefarious ends. She had ensured the succession to the sultanate of one or the other of her two elder sons: Selim, the eldest and her favourite, who was an incompetent drunkard; and Bayezid, the younger, an infinitely worthier successor, moreover the favourite of the Janissaries, who resembled his father and had inherited his more upright qualities. The youngest son, Jehangir, a hunchback, robust neither in mind nor in body but a warmhearted admirer of Mustafa, had fallen ill and died, grief-stricken and fearful of his own ultimate fate, soon after his half-brother's murder.

The two surviving brothers hated each other, and to separate them Suleiman gave each a command in a different part of the Empire. But within a few years civil war broke out between them, each backed by his own local military forces. Selim, with the aid of his father's forces, defeated Bayezid at Konya in 1559, driving him, with his four sons and a small but effective military force, to take refuge at the court of the Shah Tahmasp of Persia. Here he was at first received with the royal honours and presents due to an Ottoman prince. These Bayezid reciprocated in kind, presenting the shah with further gifts which included fifty Turcoman horses, richly harnessed, and astonishing the Persians with a show of the equestrian skill of his cavaliers. A tortuous diplomatic exchange of dispatches followed between the envoys of the Sultan, demanding the extradition or alternatively the execution of his son, and the shah, who resisted both in terms of the laws of Moslem hospitality. At first he hoped to exploit his hostage in order to bargain for the restoration of the Mesopotamian lands that the Sultan had conquered in his first campaign. But the hope was vain. Bayezid languished in captivity.

In the end the shah was obliged to bow before the supremacy of Ottoman military force, and to agree to a compromise. Under this the prince was to be executed on Persian soil, but by the Sultan's men. Thus, in return for a large sum of gold, the shah handed over Bayezid to an official executioner from Istanbul. When the prince asked to be allowed to see and embrace his four sons before death, he was told to "attend to the business in hand." Then the bowstring was put around his neck, and he was strangled.

So, afterward, were his four sons. A fifth son, only three years old, met with the same fate at Bursa by Suleiman's orders, at the hands of a trusted eunuch detailed for the purpose.

So the succession to Suleiman's throne lay open, without obstacle, to the debauched Selim—and to the consequent decline of the Ottoman Empire.

((17))

SULEIMAN'S CONQUESTS ON LAND IN THE EAST HAD EXTENDED HIS sphere of expansion at sea beyond the waters of the Mediterranean. During the summer of 1538, while Barbarossa and his fleet from the Golden Horn were fighting against the forces of Charles V in the Mediterranean, a second naval front was opened, with the emergence from Suez into the Red Sea of another Ottoman fleet. Its commander was Suleiman the Eunuch, the pasha of Egypt. Its destination was the Indian Ocean, in whose waters the Portuguese had now established a threatening degree of supremacy. Their plan was to divert the trade of the East from the old channels of the Red Sea and the Persian Gulf to the new route around the Cape of Good Hope.

This was a matter of concern for the Sultan, as it had been for his father, and he was now moved to take action in response to an appeal from a fellow Moslem ruler, Bahadur Shah of Gujarat, on the Malabar Coast to the north of Bombay. Bahadur had been driven into the arms of the Portuguese under pressure from the forces of the Mogul emperor, Humayun, who had invaded his lands together with those of the sultan of Delhi. He had allowed them to build a fortress on the island of Diu, from which he now sought to eject them.

Suleiman listened as one Moslem to another with sympathy. As Commander of the Faithful he had a duty, as he saw it, to support the Crescent whenever it came into conflict with the Cross. Thus his Christian enemies must be driven from the Indian Ocean. More specifically, the Portuguese awakened his hostility by their obstruction of Ottoman trade. They had occupied the island of Hormuz, commanding the entrance of the Persian Gulf, and aspired similarly to capture Aden, commanding that of the Red Sea. Furthermore, they had sent a naval contingent to the aid of the Christian emperor in his capture of Tunis. It thus suited the Sultan's purposes to launch against them an Asiatic expedition which he had already contemplated some years before.

Suleiman Pasha the Eunuch, who commanded it, was a man of advanced age and of so corpulent a build that he could with difficulty rise to his feet even with the aid of four men. But his fleet consisted of some seventy ships, well armed and well equipped, and carried a substantial land force with a nucleus of Janissaries. He now sailed down the Red Sea, whose Arab coasts, held by unruly sheikhs, had been ravaged before by a corsair in the course of the Sultan's pacification of Egypt. On reaching Aden, the admiral hanged its sheikh from the yardarm of his flagship, sacked his city, and made of his territory a Turkish sanjak. Thus the entrance to the Red Sea was now securely in the hands of the Turks. As their Indian Moslem ally, Bahadur, had meanwhile died, Suleiman Pasha dispatched as a gift to the Sultan in Istanbul the rich treasure of gold and silver which he had left for safekeeping in the holy city of Mecca.

Then, instead of seeking out the Portuguese fleet for a naval engagement in the Indian Ocean, as the Sultan had ordered and in which with his superior gunpower might have won him success, the pasha, preferring to take advantage of a favourable following wind, sailed right across the ocean to the western Indian coast. Here he landed troops on the island of Diu and, armed with a number of huge cannon which had been dragged across the Isthmus of Suez, laid siege to its Portuguese fortress. The soldiers of the garrison, with the aid of their womenfolk, resisted with courage. In Gujarat the successor of Bahadur was inclined, following the fate of the sheikh of Aden, to look upon the Turks as a more serious threat than the Portuguese. He thus declined to go on board Suleiman's flagship, and failed to furnish him with promised supplies.

A report then reached the Turks that the Portuguese were mustering a large fleet at Goa for the relief of Diu. At this Suleiman prudently retired, sailing back across the ocean and into the Red Sea. Here he slew the ruler of Yemen as he had slain that of Aden, and placed his territory under an Ottoman governor. Finally, hoping despite the Indian defeat to confirm his status as a holy warrior in the eyes of the Sultan, he made the pilgrimage to Mecca before proceeding via Cairo to Istanbul. Here he was indeed rewarded for his devotion with a place in the Divan among the Sultan's vezirs. But the Turks did not again seek to extend their authority so far eastward as the coast of India.

The Sultan, however, continued to challenge the Portuguese in the Indian Ocean. Here, though he commanded the Red Sea, he was hampered in the Persian Gulf, from which they denied him egress through their command of the Strait of Hormuz. This effectively neutralized for naval purposes his possession of Baghdad and the port of Basra, on the delta of the Euphrates and Tigris. In 1551 he sent the admiral in command of his naval forces in Egypt, Piri Reis, with a fleet of thirty ships down the Red Sea and around the Arabian peninsula to eject the Portuguese from Hormuz. Piri Reis was a notable mariner born at Gallipoli, a port whose children (in the words of a Turkish historian) "grow up in water like alligators. Their cradles are the boats. They are rocked to sleep with the lullaby of the sea and of the ships day and night." Profiting from a youth spent in piratical excursions, he became a geographer of distinction, writing well-informed nautical works—one on conditions of navigation in the Aegean and the Mediterranean seas—and made one of the earliest maps of the world, which incorporated a part of America. Now he captured Muscat on the Gulf of Oman, which faced the hostile strait, and laid waste the land around Hormuz. But he was unable to capture the fortress which protected its harbour. Instead he sailed northwestward up the Persian Gulf, laden with treasures of which he had fleeced the local inhabitants, then up the estuary to Basra, where he anchored his ships. The Portuguese pursued him, hoping to bottle his fleet up in their harbour.

At this advance of "the vile infidels," Piri Reis basely fled with three richly laden galleys, evading the Portuguese to escape through the narrows, and abandoning his fleet to the enemy. Arriving back in Egypt, with the loss of one galley, he was immediately imprisoned by the Ottoman authorities, and on receipt of an order from the Sultan was beheaded in Cairo. His treasures, including large porcelain urns filled with gold, were dispatched to the Sultan in Istanbul.

Piri's successor, the corsair Murad Bey, was now instructed by Suleiman to break through the Strait of Hormuz from Basra and to bring the remnants of his fleet back to Egypt. After he had failed, the task was entrusted to an experienced seaman named Sidi Ali Reis, whose forebears had been governors of the naval arsenal in Istanbul. He too, under the pen name of Katibi Rumi, was a distinguished writer, not only on mathematics, navigation, and astronomy but on theology, and in addition a poet of some repute. After refitting fifteen ships in Basra, he sailed forth to meet the Portuguese fleet, which outnumbered his own. In the course of two engagements off Hormuz, fiercer, so he afterward wrote, than any fight between Barbarossa and Andrea Doria in the Mediterranean, he lost a third of his ships, but broke through with the rest into the Indian Ocean.

Here a hurricane fell upon him, by comparison with which "a storm in the Mediterranean is as insignificant as a grain of sand; day could not be distinguished from night, and the waves rose like huge mountains." He finally drifted to the coast of Gujarat. Here, now defenseless against the Portuguese, he surrendered to the local sultan, in whose service a number of his followers enlisted. He himself with a group of companions set forth into the interior, where he embarked on a long journey home through India, Uzbekistan, Transoxiana, and Persia, writing an account, half in verse, half in prose, of his travels, and rewarded by the Sultan with a raise in his salary, together with substantial arrears for himself and his companions. He was also to write a useful work on the seas of India, based on his own experience and on Arabic and Persian sources.

But those seas were not again to be sailed by Sultan Suleiman. His naval operations in this sphere had served a purpose by maintaining Turkish hold over the Red Sea, and by holding down a permanent Portuguese force at the entrance to the Persian Gulf. But he had overextended his resources and could no longer sustain a war on two such divergent naval fronts. Just so had the Emperor Charles V, though he retained Oran as Suleiman retained Aden, failed, through conflicting commitments, to hold his position in the western Mediterranean basin.

One more brief campaign was to be forced upon Suleiman east of Suez. This centered on the isolated mountain kingdom of Abyssinia. Since the Ottoman conquest of Egypt its Christian rulers had sought Portuguese aid against the threat from the Turks. This took the form of increasing Ottoman support for the Moslem chiefs around the Red Sea coast and its hinterland, who waged intermittent warfare against the Christians and finally wrested from them the whole of eastern Abyssinia. To this, in 1540, the Portuguese responded with the dispatch of an armed force to the country under the command of a son of Vasco da Gama. Its arrival coincided with the accession to the Abyssinian throne of an energetic young ruler (or *negus*) named Claudius, known otherwise as Gradeus. He at once took the offensive, and in concert with the Portuguese kept the Turks on the alert over a period of fifteen years. Rallying tribesmen to his side who had hitherto supported them, the Sultan finally took vigorous action in a campaign for the conquest of Nubia designed to threaten Abyssinia from the north. In 1557 he captured the Red Sea port of Massawa, which had been the base for all Portuguese operations inland, and Claudius was left to fight in isolation and was killed in battle two years later. Abyssinian resistance then dwindled to nothing; and this mountainous Christian land, though it was to retain its independence, no longer represented a threat to its Moslem neighbours.

Back in the Mediterranean, following the death of Barbarossa, the mantle of the corsairs had fallen on his protégé, Dragut (otherwise Torghut). An Anatolian with an Egyptian education, he had served the Mamluks as a gunner, becoming an expert in artillery warfare before taking to the sea in search of adventure and fortune.

His gallant exploits attracted the attention of Suleiman, who appointed him commander of the Sultan's galleys. Henceforward the corsair thus operated officially under the flag of the Sultan in the Ottoman fleet, commanded by its chief admiral. The enemy against whom they moved, in 1551, was the Order of the Knights of St. John of Jerusalem, ejected from Rhodes but now established in the island of Malta. He first captured Tripoli from the knights, to become appointed its official governor.

When in 1558 the Emperor Charles V died, his son and successor, Philip II, assembled at Messina a large Christian fleet for the recapture of Tripoli, first occupying and fortifying with his land forces the island of Jerba, which had been an early stronghold of Barbarossa. But here he was surprised by the timely descent of a large Ottoman fleet from the Golden Horn. This spread panic among the Christians, driving them back to their ships, of which many were sunk while the remainder fled homeward to Italy. The garrison of the fortress was then starved into submission, largely owing to the ingenuity of Dragut, who located and captured all its wells. The scale of the defeat was a disaster for Christendom greater than any in these waters since the failure of the Emperor Charles to capture Algiers. The Turkish corsairs followed it up by establishing control over most of the North African coast with the exception of Oran, which remained in the hands of the Spaniards. Having done so they ventured out into the Atlantic, through the Straits of Gibraltar, to reach the Canaries and seek the Spanish argosies from the New World, with their cargoes of treasure.

As a result of this the way was now open to the final outstanding Christian stronghold, the island fortress of Malta. The strategic base of the knights, south of Sicily, it commanded the narrows between east and west, and thus formed the main barrier to the Sultan's complete control of the Mediterranean. As Suleiman well realized, the time had come, in Dragut's words, to "smoke out this nest of vipers." The Sultan's daughter Mihrimah, the child of Roxelana and the widow of Rustem, who consoled and influenced him in his advancing years, urged the campaign upon him as a sacred duty against the infidel. Her voice was echoed by an uproar in the Seraglio, following the capture by the knights of a large merchant ship en route from Venice to Istanbul. The property of the Chief of the Black Eunuchs, it carried a valuable cargo of luxury goods, in which the principal ladies of the harem owned shares.

Suleiman, now seventy years old, did not propose to lead an expedition against Malta in person, as he had done in his youth against Rhodes. He divided the command in two, his young admiral-in-chief, Piale Pasha, leading the naval force and his old general, Mustafa Pasha, the land force. Together they fought under the Sultan's personal standard, the familiar disk with a golden ball and crescent, surmounted by horse's tails. Aware of the discrepancy between them, Suleiman, urging their cooperation, enjoined Piale to regard Mustafa as a respected father and Mustafa to regard Piale as a beloved son.

His Grand Vezir, Ali Pasha, as he escorted the two commanders on board, remarked jovially: "Here we have two good-humoured gentlemen, always ready to relish coffee and opium, embarking on a pleasure-trip to the islands. I wager that their ships are amply laden with Arabian beans and extract of henbane." But in terms of Mediterranean warfare the Sultan had an especial respect for the skill and experience of Dragut, also for that of a rising corsair, Uluj Ali, at present with him in Tripoli. He now employed them as consultants to the expedition, instructing both commanders to confide in them and to attempt nothing without their advice and approval.

Their enemy, the grand master of the knights, Jean de la Valette, was a hard, fanatical warrior for the Christian faith. Born in the same year as Suleiman, he had fought against him at the siege of Rhodes, and had since devoted to his order a lifetime of service. La Valette combined in himself the skill of a hardened campaigner with the dedication of a religious leader. When the siege was clearly imminent he delivered to his knights a final exhortation: "To-day our Faith is at stake and whether the Gospel must yield to the Koran. God is asking for the lives which we pledged to Him at our profession. Happy are those who may sacrifice their lives."

The fortress city of Malta on its Grand Harbour, the Marsa, was flanked by rocky hilltops and defended from spits of rock. These projected into the water from its southerly flank, with smaller harbours between. The strongest points were those in the center, the adjoining promontories of Il Burgo and Senglea, defended respectively by the forts of St. Angelo and St. Michael. In expectation of a major Turkish attack, of which a brief raid by Dragut had provided a foretaste, these defenses had lately been supplemented by the construction of a new fort, that of St. Elmo. Situated opposite, at the extremity of the harbour's northerly flank, it was designed to protect the entrance both to the Grand Harbour itself and to a parallel inlet, the Middle Harbour, or Marsa Muscet, to the north of it.

The enemy's great force appeared on the Maltese horizon through a dawn haze on May 18, 1565. From the outset, in the absence of the Sultan himself as supreme commander, its operations were hampered by discord between its military and naval arm—between Mustafa "the father" and Piale "the son." The general wanted first to occupy Gozo and the north of the island, with its central capital at Mdina, and thus to secure his rear. He would then bypass St. Elmo to strike directly at the two strongpoints of the harbour, Il Burgo and Senglea. The admiral protested that, before any such land operations were launched, a safe anchorage must be found for his fleet. None was available for this purpose but the Middle Harbour, the Marsa Muscet. To secure this it would be necessary first to capture the fort of St. Elmo. Bowing to these naval demands Mustafa thus landed his troops and began to besiege it. Dragut arrived with his own fleet two weeks later than promised. But within a day of his arrival, he had doubled with new and reinforced batteries the fire against Fort St. Elmo and it was progressively to increase, from different points of the compass, as the siege went on.

The knights, numbered only in hundreds, fought to the death for the fort against successive waves of assault by an enemy numbered in thousands. Its fate began to look ominous with the fall to the Turks of its ravelin, or outwork, whose capture was followed by the storming of the fort itself in the first of a series of murderous encounters. As the Janissaries, wave upon wave of them advancing to the exhortations of fanatical dervishes, crowded forward onto the bridge across the ditch, firing fusillades through the grille of the portcullis, scaling the walls of the fort with their ladders, they were literally set alight in their loose flowing robes as the Christians rained down among them the flame of "Greek fire."

Their heavy losses were nonetheless offset by the capture of the ravelin, which the Turks hastened to make impregnable, dominating not only the walls, which they were soon pounding into rubble, but the interior of the fort itself. It now seemed to them that the fall of St. Elmo could only be a matter of days. In fact it was to hold out for a little over a month, for the Turks, fanatical and ready themselves to die as holy warriors for the cause of Islam, had underrated a like spirit of fanaticism in these Christian knights, holy warriors too and as ready to die in obedience to their vows of chivalry and in the service of Jesus Christ. As their grand master had ordained, they would fight with him to the last man and to the last stone of their city. The bombardment became so heavy as to rock St. Elmo "like a ship in a storm," but thanks largely to the skillful and continuous artillery fire of the knights, one assault after another was repulsed, with heavy losses to the Turks.

Then Dragut, rightly assessing the cause of his failure, worked with Mustafa to set up additional siege works. As he supervised them, standing all too prominently in the line of Christian fire, a cannonball from St. Angelo crashed to the spot, throwing up jagged splinters of rock. One of these struck him in the head and he fell, apparently dead. Fearing that the news of a mortal wound to their leader would undermine the morale of his men, Mustafa threw a cloak over Dragut and had him carried to his headquarters. In fact he lived, in constant delirium, for just long enough to hear the news, on the Eve of St. John, that St. Elmo, after one last murderous fight to the death, had fallen at last. At this—so it is recorded—"he manifested his joy by several signs and, raising his eyes to heaven as if in thankfulness for its mercies, immediately expired."

Only nine Knights of St. John were found still alive in the fortress.

The Turks had lost many thousands of their own men. Counting the cost, Mustafa looked from its ruined ramparts to those, still intact, of the fort of St. Angelo, looming formidably from the opposite shore of the Grand Harbour. With an invocation to his God he exclaimed: "If this small son cost so much, what shall we have to pay for the father?"

Thus Mustafa, with the precedent of the surrender of Rhodes in his mind, now offered terms to the knights. The grand master's contemptuous reply was to offer him the ditch beneath the fortifications of Il Burgo, making the condition that he fill it with the bodies of his Janissaries. Enraged at the insult, Mustafa, like Mehmed the Conqueror at Istanbul, transported a fleet of eighty galleys overland from the Middle to the Grand Harbour. There, in concert with his army from the landward side, he prepared at once to invest the two strongholds of Il Burgo and Senglea, with their respective forts of St. Angelo and St. Michael.

As a seaward defense, the creek between the two fortified promontories had been closed by the knights with a boom. The Turks sent in sappers with axes to break it. Plunging into the water, they were met, in a series of hand-to-hand swimming combats, by naked Maltese, armed literally to the teeth, with daggers and knives in their mouths, who as sons of the sea in their own native element grappled fiercely with the invaders and preserved the boom intact.

The Turks then launched a series of assaults aimed successively at the various fortified points of the Grand Harbour of Malta, which were to continue with little interruption for nearly two months. They fought with shrewd tactics and unrelenting persistence, but still with indecisive effect, and still with losses far out of proportion to those of the Christians. The knights in mortal combat were as tenacious as ever. Their garrison, though its morale remained high, was nonetheless hard pressed. But so if to a lesser extent were the besiegers, whose supply ships had been intercepted by Christian corsairs; who were thus running short of food and ammunition; and who, lacking any such medical services as those of the Knights Hospitallers, suffered seriously from fever and dysentery, with fears of an outbreak of plague. Their morale was beginning to decline, the fire within them to wane. Above all it was now the month of September, with bad weather threatening, and this prospect gave rise to a new source of conflict between the military and the naval commander.

Mustafa Pasha was prepared to spend the winter in the island if necessary, hoping to starve out the Christian garrisons and occupy the old capital, Mdina, as a base for his troops. But Piale Pasha, arguing as before that the fleet mattered more than the army, insisted that he would not risk his ships in these remote Maltese waters without an adequate anchorage and moreover without maintenance facilities, beyond the middle of September. Nor was there now a Dragut to resolve the differences of the Turkish commanders.

They were resolved unexpectedly by the arrival, to the joy of the knights, of a Christian fleet from Sicily, with a force of some ten thousand men under Don Garcia de Toledo, successor to Andrea Doria as imperial commander in the Mediterranean. It sailed past the fort of St. Angelo and fired a three-gun salute. Piale Pasha, who had made no previous attempt to intercept it, was now eager to be gone and made no move to attack it. The Christian army thus landed without interference in the north of the island. Mustafa at once raised the siege and gave orders for the evacuation of Malta. His camp was struck, his guns were dismantled and carried down to the ships, his troops were embarked.

Then he became aware that the relief force was smaller than he had been led (through a sly move of deception by the grand master) to believe. He immediately landed his troops once again to engage it. But they were already demoralized, with little heart for more fighting on Maltese soil. Assailed by a force of the dreaded, well-trained Spanish infantry, they broke and ran. After fierce bouts of hand-to-hand fighting onshore, they were reembarked with some casualties on the ships, which had moved northward to await them in the shelter of the Bay of St. Paul.

Soon the Turkish armada was sailing away eastward on its thousand-mile journey to the Bosporus. Hardly more than a quarter of its total force had survived. Apprehensive as to their reception by the Sultan, the two Turkish commanders took the precaution of sending dispatches by fast galley ahead of them, to break the news and give his temper time to cool. On reaching home waters, they received orders that the fleet must on no account enter the harbour of Istanbul until after dark. Suleiman had indeed been enraged at the news of this second major defeat at the hands of the Christians. He had found means of saving face after the retreat from Vienna. But in Malta there was no concealing the hard fact that he had suffered a major reverse. Here was the beginning of the end of the Sultan's attempt to establish Ottoman dominance over the entire Mediterranean.

On this failure Suleiman remarked bitterly: "Only with me do my armies triumph!" This was no idle boast. Malta had indeed been lost, in his old age, through the want of so strong and united a command as had won him the island of Rhodes, in his youth, from the same implacable Christian enemy. Only the Sultan himself, wielding unchallenged personal authority over his forces, could achieve such an end. Only thus had Suleiman, with his added powers of judgment in counsel, decision in leadership, and resolution in action, achieved it through forty-five years of almost unbroken Ottoman victories. But Suleiman was now nearing the end of his span.

Lonely in his personal life since the death of Roxelana, the Sultan had withdrawn within himself, growing more than ever silent, more melancholy in aspect, more remote from human contacts. Even success and applause failed to move him. When on a more auspicious occasion Piale Pasha had returned with the fleet to Istanbul after his historic victories at Jerba and Tripoli, which sealed Islamic domination over the central Mediterranean, Busbecq records that "those who saw Suleiman's face in this hour of triumph failed to detect in it the slightest trace of undue elation. . . . The expression of his countenance was unchanged, his stern features had lost nothing of their habitual gloom . . . all the applause and triumphs of that day wrung from him no sign of satisfaction." Long since Busbecq had noted the pallor of the Sultan's complexion—due perhaps to "some lurking malady"—and the fact that when ambassadors were leaving he would conceal it "under a coat of rouge, his notion being that foreign powers will fear him more if they think that he is strong and well."

> His Majesty during many months of the year was very feeble of body, so that he lacked little of dying, being dropsical, with swollen legs, appetite gone, and face swelled and of a very bad colour. In the month of March last, he had four or five fainting fits, and he had had one since, in which his attendants doubted whether he was alive or dead, and hardly expected that he would recover from them. According to the common opinion his death must occur soon.

As he aged, he grew increasingly superstitious. "He used," writes Busbecq, "to enjoy listening to a choir of boys who sang and played to him; but this has been brought to an end by the intervention of some sibyl (that is to say some old woman famous for her profession of sanctity), who declared that penalties awaited him in a future life if he did not give up this entertainment." The instruments were thus broken up and committed to the flames. In response to similar ascetic scruples he took to eating off earthenware instead of silver plate, moreover banned the importation into the city of all wine—whose consumption had been forbidden by the Prophet. "When the non-Moslem communities objected, arguing that so drastic a change of diet would cause disease and even death among them, the Divan relented to the extent of permitting them to have a weekly supply put ashore for them at the Sea Gate."

But the Sultan's naval humiliation at Malta could hardly be appeased by such gestures of self-mortification. Suleiman, after a lifetime of war, could only salve his wounded pride, regardless of age and ill health, by one final triumphant campaign to vindicate the invincibility of Ottoman arms. At first he had sworn to reattempt in person the conquest of Malta in the following spring. Instead he now resolved to return to his natural campaigning element, the land. He would proceed once more against Hungary and Austria, where Ferdinand's Habsburg successor, Maximilian II, not only neglected to pay his tribute but had made incursions, at the expense of the Turks, into Hungary. Here, furthermore, the Sultan still burned to avenge the earlier repulse of his own forces before Sziget and Erlau.

Thus on May 1, 1566, Suleiman set out for the last time from Istanbul, at the head of the largest force he had ever commanded, on the thirteenth campaign he had led in person—and the seventh into Hungary. His imperial tent was destroyed beyond Belgrade in the all too familiar floods of the Danube basin, and he was obliged to move into that of his Grand Vezir. He could no longer sit on a horse (except at an occasional parade) but travelled instead in a curtained litter. At Semlin he received ceremoniously the young John Sigismund Zapolya, whose ultimate claims to the Hungarian throne he had acknowledged when he was a baby in arms. As a loyal vassal Sigismund now bent the knee three times before his master, each time to be invited to rise, and on kissing the Sultan's hand to be greeted as his dearly beloved son. Proffering assistance as an ally, Suleiman showed himself ready enough to accommodate the young Sigismund over such modest territorial demands as he put before him.

From Semlin the Sultan turned toward the fortress of Sziget, bent on revenge against its Croatian commander, Count Nicholas Zrinyi. A bitter enemy of the Turks since the days of the siege of Vienna, Zrinyi had just attacked the camp of a sanjak bey and favourite of the Sultan, killing him together with his son, carrying off as booty all his possessions and a large sum of money.

The march to Sziget, thanks to the misplaced zeal of a quartermaster, was completed against orders in one day instead of two, thus exhausting the Sultan in his poor state of health, and so angering him that he gave orders for the man's decapitation. But the Grand Vezir, Mehmed Sokollu, interceded to save him. The enemy, he shrewdly argued, would be cowed at this proof that the Sultan, despite the weight of his years, could still double the length of a day's march as in the full vigour of his youth. Instead, wrathful and impatient for blood as he was, Suleiman ordered the execution of his governor of Buda for incompetence in the field.

The fortress of Sziget was then invested, against stubborn and costly resistance by Zrinyi, who had erected a cross in the center of it. After the loss of the town itself he retired to its citadel, with a garrison which hoisted a black flag and proclaimed its resolve to fight to the last man. Impressed by such heroism, but nonetheless frustrated at the delay in capturing so insignificant a fortress, Suleiman offered generous terms for surrender, seeking to lure Zrinyi into the Ottoman service as effective ruler of Croatia. But they were rejected with contempt. Turkish sappers then worked for two weeks under Suleiman's orders to run an immense mine under the principal bastion, in preparation for a final assault. On September 5 the mine was fired with devastating effect, shattering the walls, creating a huge conflagration within them, and making the citadel untenable.

But Suleiman was not to see his last victory. He died that night in his tent, perhaps from apoplexy, perhaps from a heart attack resulting from his extreme exertions. A few hours earlier he had remarked to his Grand Vezir: "The great drum of conquest is not yet to be heard." Sokollu now concealed the news of the Sultan's death, letting it be supposed that he was confined to his tent by an attack of gout, which prevented him from appearing in public. In the interests of secrecy he is even said to have had Suleiman's doctor strangled. So the battle carried on to its victorious end. The Turkish batteries continued their bombardment for four more days, until the citadel was destroyed but for a single tower and its garrison killed but for six hundred survivors, led by Zrinyi splendidly garbed and bejewelled as though for a feast, who prepared them for Christian martyrdom in a spirit of glorious self-sacrifice. When the Janissaries broke in upon him he fired a large mortar, with a shower of ammunition which felled them in hundreds; then, saber in hand, he and his companions fought heroically until Zrinyi himself fell and hardly one of the six hundred survived. His last act was to lay a fuse beneath a magazine in the tower, which exploded, killing some three thousand Turks.

The Grand Vezir Sokollu was above all things intent on ensuring the peaceful succession of Selim, to whom he had sent the news of his father's death by swift messenger to Kutahya, in Anatolia. He kept his secret for several weeks more. The business of government continued as though the Sultan still lived. Orders emerged from his tent as though under his signature. Appointments to vacant offices were made, promotions and rewards distributed in customary style. A Divan was summoned and the traditional letters of victory sent to the governors of the imperial provinces in the Sultan's name. After the fall of Sziget the campaign continued as though still under his command, the army gradually withdrawing toward the Turkish frontier and launching on the way a minor siege which he had ostensibly ordered. Suleiman's entrails had been buried and his body embalmed. It was now carried homeward in his covered litter, flanked, as on his outward journey, by guards and attended by the respect due to a living Sultan.

Only when Sokollu received the news that Prince Selim had reached Istanbul for his official enthronement did he divulge to the soldiers on the march that their Sultan was dead. They had halted for the night on the outskirts of a forest not far from Belgrade. The Grand Vezir summoned the readers of the Koran to gather around the Sultan's litter, where they called upon the name of God and read the service prescribed for the dead. The army was awakened by the call of the muezzins, chanting solemnly around the imperial tent. Recognizing the familiar announcement of death, the soldiers swarmed together in groups and uttered cries of lament. Before daybreak the Grand Vezir moved among them, telling them that their Padishah, the soldier's friend, was now at rest in the bosom of the One God, reminding them of the great deeds he had done for Islam, and enjoining them to show respect for his memory not by lamentations but by loyal obedience to his son, the glorious Sultan Selim who now reigned in his stead. Calmed by his words—and at the prospect of donatives from the new Sultan—the troops resumed their march in military order, escorting the mortal remains of their great ruler and commander to Belgrade, the scene of his first victory. Thence the body was conveyed to Istanbul, where it was entombed, as he had planned, in the precincts of his great mosque of the Suleimaniye.

Thus did Suleiman die as he had essentially lived—in his tent, among his troops on the field of battle. This earned martyrdom, for the holy warrior, in Moslem eyes. Hence the final elegiac lines of Baqi, the great lyric poet of the time:

At length is struck the parting-drum and thou hast journeyed hence;
Lo, thy first halting-place is mid the Paradised plain
Praise be to God, for he in either world has blessed thee,
And writ before thine honoured name both Martyr and Ghazi

It was a fitting end, in the fullness of age and at the moment of victory, for a campaigning Sultan who reigned over a great military empire. Suleiman the Conqueror, the man of action, had expanded and secured it; Suleiman the Legislator, the man of order and justice and wisdom, had perfected it, through the strength of his institutions and the humanity of his policies, into an enlightened structure of government; Suleiman the Statesman had won for it the commanding status of a world power. The tenth and perhaps greatest of the Ottoman sultans, he had raised their empire to a peak of unsurpassed power and prestige.

But the very greatness of his achievement carried within it seeds of ultimate degeneration. For lesser men were now to follow him—not conquerors, not legislators, not statesmen; and the peak of the Ottoman Empire became all too abruptly a watershed, the top of a slope which led inexorably but nonetheless gradually downward to the depths of decline and an ultimate fall.

PART

IV

SEEDS OF DECLINE

((18))

SULEIMAN, THE GRAND TURK, WAS A PRINCE OF THE RENAISSANCE, outdoing in the magnificence of his court and of his style of living many of those in this Golden Age of Western Christian civilization. He outdid them too not only in his high personal character but in his wise judgment of the character of others. Breaking free, in his appointments to high office, of the conventional graduated hierarchy of the Ottoman imperial service, he appointed instead men of his own personal choice, in whom he reposed absolute confidence as stewards of the sovereign's will. It may well be, as a Turkish historian of this period accuses, that he condoned in these favourites the accumulation of large fortunes and the adoption of an extravagant style of life, often rooted in corruption. But this after all was but part of the pattern of this age, the wages of that imperial splendour which suffused Suleiman's reign with the glow of majesty in the eyes of Western civilization.

Two at least of his Grand Vezirs, Christian in origin, who spanned two-thirds of his reign, contributed positively for all their personal failings to the greatness of his empire—Ibrahim Pasha, the Greek, an outstanding diplomat and military commander; Rustem Pasha, the Bulgarian, who as an economist skillfully handled the Ottoman treasury, with all its complexities, through a time of expansion in which the Empire more than doubled its revenues. Surviving him was a third and last, Sokollu Pasha, a Slav from Bosnia who in boyhood had served as an acolyte in a Serbian church, and who was to uphold for a crucial period the power and prestige of his late master. The inherent strength of Suleiman's despotic regime largely offset any such excesses and weaknesses; their implications for the future could not easily, at this stage, be foreseen. Only in the hands of a weak Sultan would they be liable to weaken the Ottoman state.

But ironically this was the very situation that Suleiman himself in two calamitous actions precipitated. Where his judgment—to say nothing of his humanity—conspicuously failed was in his manipulation of the succession to the Ottoman throne by the shameful executions firstly of his eldest son, Mustafa, then of his youngest son, Bayezid. Both were endowed with such inherited qualities as to make either of them worthy to carry on the line of the first ten Ottoman

Sultans, hence to ensure the continuance of their empire as a respected power in the world of its time. By these blind and pitiless deeds, crimes of filicide worse than his dynasty's traditional fratricide, Suleiman ensured the succession of a ruler of exceptionally low caliber, the degenerate Selim. Here was the first of a new line of twenty-five Ottoman Sultans who as the centuries passed were to preside over the slow decline, with admitted periods of respite, of the Ottoman Empire.

Suleiman's passions, fanned by Roxelana, had overridden his judgment, his wisdom, his sense of statesmanship, to destroy at his death much that he had worked for in his life in the evolution of Ottoman greatness. He had trusted in the infallibility of the blood of Osman. But now it was to betray him—so sorely that history has even been tempted to speculate as to whether Selim was in truth the offspring of his father or of an illicit paramour of his Slav mother.

Selim II cut a dismally poor figure as Sultan. Short and obese, with a flushed complexion, he was aptly named "the Sot"—Selim the Drunk—from his chronic addiction to wine. Indolent and dissolute in character, he was a nonentity, absorbed in himself and his pleasures, who had inherited no trace of his father's abilities or of his mother's scheming but forceful nature, and who won little respect from either his ministers or his subjects at large. He had no stomach either for the hazards of war or for the affairs of state, shunning the sword and the tent to idle his time away in the Seraglio. Here, with cronies and flatterers around him, he lived without purpose for the day, giving little or no thought to the morrow.

Selim's sole talent was for poetry, which he wrote elegantly, in the Turkish language, but in emulation of Hafiz the Persian. Quoting the Prophet, who had condemned wine as 'the mother of all the vices," Hafiz found it to be on the contrary "sweeter to us than the kiss of a young girl." Echoing his sentiments, Selim ended a lovesick poem with the couplet

O dear one, give Selim thy wine-hued liplet
Then by thine absence turn my tears to wine, love . . .

To salve consciences in view of the Prophet's prohibition, the Grand Mufti had delivered himself of a casuistical judgment, which condoned the drinking of wine if the Sultan himself chose to drink it. This, following Selim's abolition in the first edict of his reign of restrictions on its sale and consumption, became a matter of popular jest, inspiring the query, "Where shall we go for our wine today? To the mufti or the kadi?"

Selim's lack of all interest in the business of government proved nonetheless a benefit to the country. For it left effective power in the hands of Sokollu, whom the new Sultan regarded with proper respect,

Sultan Selim II (1566–74), known to posterity as the Sot—the immediate successor to the illustrious Suleiman.

and who had indeed married his daughter. He accepted thoroughly the judgment of Suleiman in his choice of Grand Vezirs whom he trusted and to whom he was thus ready to delegate authority. He set indeed a precedent for the pattern of the centuries to come when from time to time a strong vezir, often Christian in origin, would emerge to counterbalance a weak Sultan, and help guide the state through its periods of crisis. Now under Sokollu's auspices there was no break in the continuity of policy. The momentum of Suleiman's reign was maintained in an interregnum which arrested the turn of the tide for a further twelve years.

Sokollu was a man of vigour and capacity, with high ambitions and expansive ideas. First, having concluded Suleiman's campaign in Hungary, he made in 1568 an honourable peace with the Habsburg emperor, planned to last for eight years and involving in effect the maintenance of the territorial *status quo*. Next, Sokollu turned the Ottoman armies for the first time in a new direction—that of Russia. Throughout the sixteenth century the Grand Duchy of Muscovy had been developing into a united and vigorous power. At first the Russians were not seen by the Turks as a danger, and from 1492 they were allowed to trade freely in Ottoman territory. Then Ivan the Terrible emerged on the scene. In 1547 he assumed the title of Tsar, aspiring to expand the Grand Duchy into an empire. His grandfather and predecessor Ivan III had married Sophia, a niece of the last Emperor of Byzantium. He thus claimed for Moscow the inheritance of the East Roman Empire, with the Byzantine double-headed eagle as his insignia of sovereignty.

Ivan's expansion southward, at the expense of the Tatar khans, led to his capture of Astrakhan, on the Caspian Sea. With a raid on Azov and the Crimean coast he encroached directly on the Ottoman sphere, the vassal state of the Tatar khan of the Crimea. Sokollu was aroused to the need for intervention. This need had its religious as well as its political aspect—that of preserving the prestige of the Sultan as caliph and thus protector of the holy places of Medina and Mecca. For the Moslems of Turkestan were being denied access to his empire, whether as pilgrims or traders, already through the closing of the Persian frontiers against them, and now through the refusal of transit facilities to Moslems and other obstructions in the newly conquered Muscovite territory. Their rulers were thus pleading with the Porte for the reconquest of Astrakhan, hence the reopening of the traditional pilgrimage road.

In this connection, confident in the resources and capacity of the Empire, Sokollu had now been nurturing for some time a grandiose project designed at once to halt Russian expansion to the south and promote Turkish expansion to the east. He planned to cut a canal between the Don, running into the Sea of Azov from the northwest, and the Volga, running into the Caspian Sea from the northeast, at a point where the two rivers were a mere thirty miles apart. This would link the two seas, the Black Sea, already an Ottoman lake, with the Caspian. By means of a Caspian fleet it would facilitate the entry of the Turks into Persia, encircling the country, bypassing the long, hard overland route, opening a new gateway to the Caucasus and the roads into Central Asia through Tabriz. This would involve the revival of a historic intercontinental highway, the Central Asian–Astrakhan–Crimean road, and thus offered prospects of commercial and strategic advantage which it was vital for Islam to deny to the Muscovites. Such a canal as his Grand Vezir now conceived had been planned eighteen centuries earlier by Seleucus Nicator, a general and successor monarch of Alexander the Great.

Sokollu now pursued the project with zeal. In 1568 he sent a large force across the Black Sea to Azov, which the Ottomans controlled, with a larger force destined to capture Astrakhan. Troops were conveyed by a fleet up the Don to the point from which the canal was to be dug with the aid of a local force of Tatars. Preliminary work on it was thus started. But under the technical conditions of the sixteenth century it ran into difficulties after a third of the canal had been finished. So a part of the fleet was hauled overland to the Volga, where it sailed downstream to besiege Astrakhan. The siege failed through the initial want of cannon, an increasingly harsh winter, and a general collapse in the morale of the Turkish troops, who now suffered cruelly as they trekked in retreat across the steppes, back to the Crimea.

The ambitious and independent-minded khan of the Crimea, Devlet Ghirai, anxious to discourage further such incursions by the Sultan into his domain, was at pains to dwell, for the benefit of the Ottoman soldiery, on the hardships that threatened good Moslems in these northern parts. He stressed the shortness of the nights—a mere five hours in summer—hence the lack of sleep which would afflict them, called to prayer as they would be two hours after sunset and again at break of day. The Ottomans abandoned the enterprise, and on their return journey much of their force was lost in a violent storm in the Black Sea. The north, so the survivors concluded, was not for Moslems. In fact, Devlet Ghirai, who had strong dynastic pretensions, was plotting a direct offensive on his own against Moscow at a time when the internal situation of Ivan the Terrible was critical; and indeed, with no more than a raiding force of his Tatar cavalry, he got so far as to burn the suburbs of the city. Meanwhile, no more was heard of the imaginative Don–Volga project of Sokollu, Sultan Selim making clear to him: "The costs and losses will be totalled and you will have to make them good."

Soon afterward the tsar sent an ambassador to the Porte, and a peace agreement was reached. The Sultan retained his sovereignty over the Khanate of the Crimea and tacitly renounced his claims to Astrakhan. Muscovites and Tatars were left to fight out their differences between themselves, and the rule of the tsars was extended eastward, as far as Siberia. Such, ending in a peace which was to last for almost a century, was the preliminary encounter between the two mighty empires of Turkey and Russia.

Sokollu, with his eyes still on trade with the East, now contemplated a second grand technical enterprise in the form of a canal across the Isthmus of Suez, designed to link the Mediterranean with the Red Sea and the Indian Ocean beyond. But he was forestalled by a major revolt in the province of the Yemen which called for immediate subjugation, and this was successfully achieved.

Sokollu had meanwhile turned his attention westward to Tunis, where Uluj Ali, the chief admiral and governor of Algiers, reoccupied the town, driving out the native prince whom Charles V had installed there, but leaving the Spanish garrison in control of the citadel. Sokollu, wedded in his main objectives to the traditional Ottoman policy, still saw Spain as the main enemy of the Empire, and sought, preferably with the aid of the French, to launch a new major campaign against the Spaniards in the Mediterranean. He now had a timely opportunity to do so, renewing the role of the Turks as the champions of Islam against Christian oppression by responding to a revolt of the Moors of Granada against Philip II of Spain. The Moors, needing more support than their brethren in North Africa could provide, sent a deputation to Istanbul to seek the Sultan's intervention. Here they had a sympathetic reception from their fellow Moslems.

But now for the first time the Sultan showed disconcerting signs of a will of his own. He sought instead to proceed against the Venetians, with whom the Empire was at peace. For they possessed the island of Cyprus, and this was a territory not only rich in cotton and sugar but above all renowned for the high quality of its wine. So Selim was reminded by an influential favourite, a Portuguese Jewish financier named Joseph Nasi—until recently "Don Miguez"—who was notoriously hostile to Venice. With the support of another royal favourite, Lala Mustafa, Nasi incited Selim to an invasion of Cyprus, whose rewards would be not only its fine wines but in equal abundance the gold ducats of Venice. Selim agreed, and on a convivial wine-bibbing occasion went so far as to embrace Nasi and to promise him that in the event of success he would be crowned king of Cyprus. Meanwhile, on the dispossession of the present incumbent, he was made Duke of Naxos, Paros, Andros, and ten other islands of the Cyclades, whose substantial revenues, together with the profits on the sale of their wines, he was to enjoy, subject only to a moderate scale of taxation.

Sokollu was thus, for the first and last time, overruled by Selim. The Sultan dispatched an envoy to Venice, reciting a series of grievances against the republic and demanding either their redress or the cession of the island. The Venetian senate responded doubly in the negative, and in 1570 the force which Sokollu had hoped to send to the aid of the Moors was sent instead against Cyprus.

The Venetians had for some time neglected this far eastern outpost of their Mediterranean dominions, and its population had greatly declined. The bulk of it was composed of Greek Orthodox peasants who were enslaved and oppressed by the Frankish ruling class, and it was estimated that there were some fifty thousand serfs who would be ready to join the Turks. Sultan Selim in a firman, or decree, now instructed his neighbouring sanjak bey to do his utmost to win the hearts of the masses, adding a solemn promise that in the event of the island's capture the population would not be molested and their property would be respected. Such was a formula, here strictly observed, which had for long preceded acts of Turkish expansion.

When the Ottoman forces landed in 1570 with Lala Mustafa, Sokollu's rival and Selim's favourite, in command of the army, and Piale Pasha in command of the fleet, the Venetians became concerned at the prospect of a Greek uprising, of which signs were observed in one district. To forestall it they surprised and put four hundred Greeks to the sword. On arrival the Ottomans gave especially favourable treatment to the people of this district, and exempted them from taxes for a specified period. In the subsequent hostilities the Greek peasants proved reluctant to fight against their Latin masters, preferring to assist the Ottomans with food supplies and with information on the state of affairs on the island. Many of those who took refuge in the mountains were induced easily enough to return and make obeisance to the conqueror.

The Ottoman forces had landed from southern Turkey without opposition. Their main task was to subdue the two Venetian fortresses of Nicosia and Famagusta. After awaiting reinforcements from North Africa and Anatolia, they advanced on Nicosia with a force estimated at some fifty thousand men. The Venetians, prepared for an eventual Turkish invasion, had called in advance upon expert military engineers to modernize their fortifications. But the defense of Nicosia was incompetently commanded and it surrendered to the Turks within six weeks. The remnants of its garrison were slaughtered, and the ensuing sack of the city, which was said to contain as many churches as days in the year, was compared by the Franks to that of Constantinople. The cathedral was converted into a mosque. The youth and beauty of both sexes were put up for sale into slavery. They were loaded aboard a galleon which however before sailing for Istanbul was blown up in the interest of chastity by a devout Christian lady who put a flame to its magazine.

Only the fortress of Famagusta now remained, and this was invested in the following spring. Heroically defended, it held out for three months. The Venetian garrison was fired by the eloquence of its governor, Marc Antonio Bragadino. Lala Mustafa, to encourage the besiegers, promised that their opponents were the same men as at Nicosia, unwarlike and untried. He was nonetheless impressed by the Venetian resistance, and a dispatch to Istanbul reported that Famagusta was defended not by men but by giants. After labouring to build forts and to sink trenches deep enough to contain cavalry, the Turks made a series of assaults through a breach blown by a mine in the walls, but met with stubborn, courageous resistance. The enemy filled the ditch before the ravelin with firewood, faggots, and other inflammable substances, setting them on fire, keeping a blaze going for days, and tormenting the Turks further by the stench of a certain wood, grown in the island, which when set alight gave out a poisonous odour. The defenders were reduced to a diet of horses, donkeys, dogs, "and suchlike nauseous food." When, after a siege of three months, only seven barrels of powder remained to them, Bragadino, having fought to the last, could now do little else but seek surrender on honourable terms.

These Mustafa was disposed to grant, on the basis that, in return for the surrender of the fortress, all lives should be spared, and the garrison transported with their arms in Turkish ships to Crete, while the inhabitants of the city should be granted a safe-conduct to proceed wherever they chose. When Bragadino rode to the Ottoman camp with three of his commanders and a military escort to deliver up the keys of the city, Mustafa at first treated him with courtesy, and they conferred amicably together. Then trouble arose, first over an accusation that Bragadino had massacred Turkish prisoners, then over a demand by Mustafa for a hostage for the safe return of his ships.

When Bragadino refused this as contrary to the terms of the armistice, Mustafa, notoriously subject to bouts of frenzy which amounted to madness, flew into a rage and in a torment of abuse denounced the whole of it as invalid. Bragadino was bound in chains, then forced to stretch out his neck while Mustafa, so it is asserted, cut off his right ear and his nose. After languishing for a fortnight in prison he was bound to the pillory in the main square of Famagusta, where, refusing conversion to Islam, he was flayed alive. His body was dismembered and displayed for all to see. Then on Mustafa's orders his skin was cured, stuffed with straw, and carried through the city on the back of a cow.

Venice was to cede the island to the Sultan two years later in a peace treaty which allowed for compensation sufficient to cover the cost of its conquest. Its subsequent administration was enlightened enough, following the standard Ottoman practice at this time in conquered territories. The former privileges of the Greek Orthodox Church were revived at the expense of the Latin Catholics, and its property restored to it. The Latin system of serfdom was abolished. The land which had formerly belonged to the Venetian nobility was transferred to the Ottoman state. The local inhabitants were assisted by the development of economic and financial resources. Large numbers of immigrants were brought from central Anatolia, with their cattle and farming implements, to settle in the empty lands.

The conquest of Cyprus was now to provoke retribution on a formidable scale. The invasion of the island had led to the formation, under the active inspiration of Pope Pius V, of a "perpetual" Holy League, which sought yet again in a crusading spirit to unite the Christian powers. Thanks to the familiar mutual suspicions and conflicts of interest between the Christian states, the League took more than a year to materialize. Venice feared that it might increase, at the expense of Italy, the power of Spain. Nor did Spain desire to benefit Venice, which might moreover at any moment switch her allegiance back to the Sultan. France in her turn mistrusted aggrandizement by Spain, her hereditary enemy, and was inclined as before rather to turn to her secret ally, the Sultan. Hence she played no part in the Holy League, but on the contrary sought to prevent it.

It was sealed as a triple alliance against the Turks between the papacy, Spain, and Venice in the summer of 1571, while the Turks were still besieging Famagusta. Its combined fleets included also contingents from other Italian states and from the Knights of Malta. The effectiveness of so composite an armada depended largely on the choice of a supreme commander. This at length fell upon Don John of Austria, natural son of the Emperor Charles V and half-brother of King Philip II. Don John, who had won his spurs as a commander against the Moors of Granada, was a young man of vigorous personality and fiery enthusiasm, endowed with a natural talent for leadership. For once the Christians had found a leader who could rouse to unity and put heart into the discordant elements composing the forces of such a latter-day "crusade"—the thirteenth to be fought against the Ottoman Turks.

His naval force, slightly smaller than that of the Turks, consisted of some two hundred galleys, but enjoyed the advantage of six galleasses from Venice—vessels larger and more heavily armed than any hitherto seen in the Mediterranean. Don John carried on board some thirty thousand fighting troops. The Turkish fleet, with a similar fighting force, was commanded by Muhsinzade Ali Pasha, who had under his orders the earlier-mentioned Uluj Ali—known to the West as Ochiale—and two other corsair commanders, together with fifteen beys of maritime sanjaks, each entitled to hoist on the poops of his galleys his own banner as a "prince of the sea."

The armada of the Holy League gathered at Messina in September, 1571, and sailed forth to seek the infidel in his waters of the eastern Mediterranean. Forming a forest of masts, decked with pennants and flags, its galleys were blessed by the papal nuncio from the end of the mole as they swept out into the Straits in the wake of the flagship. Arriving at Corfu, from which the Turks had withdrawn after an ineffective siege, Don John received the first reports of the fate of Famagusta and its desecrations. The crusaders were thus fired by an added determination to come to grips with the Turk.

The Turkish fleet meanwhile had retired southward from Corfu toward Patras, and was anchored within the Gulf of Lepanto. When the Christian fleet, passing through the strait between Cephalonia and Ithaca, was first sighted off the mouth of the gulf, the Turkish admiral called a council of war on board his flagship, the *Sultana*. Opinions were divided, as indeed also in the Christian fleet—some clamouring for action, others counselling caution. Uluj Ali in a combative spirit scorned as dishonourable those of his colleagues who preferred to remain shut up in Lepanto, "looking after the women and children." But as a seasoned, realistic corsair he agreed with Pertau Pasha, the commander of the land forces on board, who favoured a pause before taking the offensive, to allow time for the completion of their equipment and training.

Ali Pasha, the chief admiral, was more valorous than cautious, and in any case bound by the orders of the Sultan, combative since the fall of Famagusta, to capture the Christian fleet and escort it back to the Golden Horn. He therefore ordered an immediate attack. Exhorting his soldiery to battle, Pertau Pasha reminded them of the infinite number of Christian cities they had conquered, assuring them of their present superiority in men and galleys, and disparaging the enemy now before them.

So the Turkish fleet sailed out from its safe harbour within the Gulf of Lepanto to confront that of the Christians in the open waters beyond its mouth.

Here the Crescent was to meet the Cross in the last great naval battle between galley fleets in the history of Europe. Symbolizing the Cross was the papal banner of Don John, which represented the figure of the crucified Christ; symbolizing the Crescent, a sacred standard from Mecca embroidered with verses from the Koran. At sunrise on

Sunday, October 7, 1571, which was to be a bright, sunny day, Don John ordered the celebration of Mass throughout his fleet. Then across the horizon the Turks appeared.

Drawn up in battle formation, the fleets confronted one another, that of the Turks forming a wide crescent into which that of the Christians projected. Each was divided into three squadrons, with that of the admirals in the center of the line. In advance of the center the two high admirals, commanders-in-chief, thus faced one another directly, each in his flagship. Don John's was flanked by those of the papal and the Venetian squadrons, while Ali Pasha, rising to the challenge of the three, flanked his own with those of Pertau Pasha and his treasurer. Uluj Ali commanded his left wing, facing the Genoese squadron. The bey of Alexandria, Mehmed Chuluk, generally known as Scirocco, commanded his right, facing the Venetian squadron. Ali Pasha, seeing that the Christian fleet was stronger than he had anticipated, took the precaution of straightening out his crescent formation. At intervals some thousand yards in advance of the Christian line, Don John had placed his formidable galleasses, firm as redoubts.

For a while the two fleets lay motionless, surveying and assessing each other. Then the Ottomans as a formal challenge fired the first cannon shot with a charge of gunpowder. The Christians responded with a heavy cannonball, which hurtled through the Ottoman rigging. The Turks rowed forward, shouting amid the clangour of drums and fifes. The two fleets came to grips and the engagement was soon general, from one side of the line to the other. Broadsides of fire from the galleasses at once confused the advance of the Turks, who began to scatter, then pertinaciously re-formed and resumed their traditional tactics of ramming and boarding. Gradually the battle developed into three separate actions. On the right of their line the Turks, under Scirocco, tried to outflank the ships of their enemy by moving inshore. But the Venetians, with their well-disciplined crews and better-built galleys, turned the tables by driving them aground on the coast, pursuing and slaughtering their fugitive crews inland, and destroying the whole squadron. Their own commander, Barbarigo, was killed, struck in the eye by an arrow which pierced his brain. But so was Scirocco himself, falling wounded into the sea to be dragged out and beheaded by the enemy.

The main battle developed in the center, where the flagships of the two commanders-in-chief, *La Real* and the *Sultana,* made head on for one another, prow to prow. They collided with such violence that the beak of the *Sultana* became embedded in the rigging of *La Real,* locking the two ships together to make a central battlefield, with the Venetian and papal flagships on either hand. Here fighting raged desperately for two hours, between the well-matched arquebusiers of the Christians and the Janissaries, armed with arquebuses and bows, while reinforcements clambered aboard, when required, from supporting galleys and galleons. Gradually the fight went in favour of the Christians, whose artillery was superior, while the Turkish ships had been provided with inadequate defenses against boarding parties. Don John, after his men had twice been repulsed by the Janissaries, led a boarding party onto the *Sultana* in person, which was gallantly resisted by Ali Pasha at the head of his defenders. In the resulting struggle the pasha was hit in the forehead by a bullet and fell forward, dead on the gangway. His head was struck off and presented to Don John, who is said to have shown displeasure, since he had respected his enemy, but who nonetheless now exhibited the head on a pike on his flagship.

The Ottoman flagship was boarded and captured, and a desperate attempt to recapture it failed. The Turkish center was broken. In the Turkish galleys the Christian galley slaves broke free of their chains and seized weapons to turn on their captors. After more than three hours of fierce, heroic fighting, the battle of Lepanto was effectively won by the Christians. The bulk of the Ottoman fleet, amounting to some 230 galleys, was sunk or captured. The Christians lost no more than fifteen galleys and half as many men as the Turks, but many of them from the flower of the Spanish and Italian nobility. Among the Spaniards who fought was Cervantes, who in the attack on the flagship of Scirocco suffered a wound, permanently maiming his left hand. This, so he afterward wrote of himself: "Although it looks ugly, he holds it for lovely, because he received it on the most memorable and lofty occasion which past centuries have beheld—nor do those to come hope to see the like."

Nonetheless the Turks, on the left of their line, lived to fight another day. Here Uluj Ali the corsair had been maneuvering, as a skillful tactician, first to turn the right flank of his enemy—Gian Andrea Doria, nephew of an illustrious naval uncle—who moved southward to avoid him; then, as the main battle developed northward, to take advantage of a consequent gap in the Christian line by rowing through it and taking Don John in the rear. Here he was at first checked by the galleys of the Knights of St. John, upon whom his Algerians fell with murderous alacrity, then turning on a relief force of Sicilian galleys, to capture and hoist their banner on the Maltese flagship. The fighting was ferocious, until Doria hurried northward to join a stronger Christian reserve force. At this the shrewd corsair, realizing that the main battle was lost, fled in the dusk with some forty galleys which, to the general discredit of Doria, survived to mitigate the Turkish defeat. But it was a Christian victory nonetheless, to be remembered (so Cervantes wrote in *Don Quixote*) as "that day so fortunate to

Christendom when all nations were undeceived of their error in believing that the Turks were invincible."

Europe rejoiced over the news of the victory with rapture. Pope Pius V had by divine communication received it at the exact moment of Ali Pasha's death, and had duly knelt to give thanks for this event before a crucifix. Now, seated on the papal throne, he received the messenger of the victor with appropriate words from the Gospel: "There was a man sent from God, whose name was John."

Venice, the first to receive the news, was seized by a delirium of joy and relief when a galley appeared from the lagoon before the crowds on the Piazza of San Marco with salvos of gunfire, trailing captured Turkish banners astern in the water, and flaunting a crew on its poop clad in Turkish costume, stripped from the victims of battle. Spain was swept by a tide of rejoicing at so proud a conclusion, under Spanish auspices, of this late crusade against the infidel Turk. King Charles IX of France ordered a *Te Deum* and other celebrations for the defeat of his ally the Turk. Even in faraway England the victory was marked with bonfires, sermons, and a great peal of bells from St. Martin-in-the-Fields for the "overthrow of the Turk," while the boy king James VI, of Scotland, contributed for the occasion some thousand lines of doggerel verse. For centuries to come the heroic "Fight of Lepanto" was to live as a legend throughout Europe, a triumph depicted by painters, sung by poets and versifiers, folk singers and balladmongers to the eternal glorification of Don John and the destroyers of the Turkish invader.

While Europe thus rejoiced at its victory, the Ottoman capital was overwhelmed with dismay at its first major defeat. Such at least was the initial reaction of the Turks to the loss of their fleet and the humiliation of their army at Lepanto. Sultan Selim spent three days in fasting and prayer, begging his God to have pity on his people. Then, in response to popular disturbances, he ordered a massacre of all Spaniards and Venetians in his dominions. No such order was carried out, thanks to Mehmed Sokollu, who steered his master in a more constructive direction.

Toward the end of the year Uluj Ali sailed proudly into the Golden Horn with a fleet of some eighty vessels, half consisting of the squadron with which he had escaped from the battle, the other half gathered from among the Turkish galleys lying in various ports of the eastern Mediterranean. At the instance of Sokollu he was elevated to the rank of chief admiral (Kapudan Pasha) in place of Muhsinzade Ali, who had fallen in the battle; and his name was felicitously changed by the Sultan from Uluj to Kilij, meaning "the Sword." Then, in cooperation with the veteran Piale Pasha and with the support of Selim, who personally contributed funds and ceded a portion of his garden in the Seraglio for conversion into a dockyard, he worked through the winter, constructing a new fleet to replace the old.

Thus by the spring of 1572, hardly more than six months after the battle of Lepanto, a new Ottoman fleet, consisting in all of some 250 sail and incorporating eight large modern galleasses, was ready to vindicate Turkish arms at sea, a shipbuilding achievement which no Christian state at this time could have equalled. The fleet's appearance off Cyprus in 1572 took the Christian allies aback and discouraged them from attempting the island's recovery. It then proceeded to sail into Greek waters, showing the Turkish flag in a display of revived sea power, going so far as to threaten the island of Crete, but avoiding at this stage any direct confrontation with its enemies. The Christians, for their part, though their fleet was still larger than that of the Turks, failed to bring Kilij Ali to battle and eject him from the coasts of the Ionian Sea.

This situation precipitated the peace treaty in which Venice formally ceded Cyprus, the more ready to do so since a strong peace party was urging the resumption of trade with the Ottoman territories. When the Venetian minister in Istanbul first sounded the Grand Vezir as to the prospects of a settlement, Sokollu replied: "There is a wide difference between your loss and ours. In capturing Cyprus from you we have cut off one of your arms; in defeating our fleet you have merely shaved off our beard; the lopped arm will not grow again, but the shorn beard will grow stronger than before."

The negotiation of the peace treaty received active support from an ambassador sent to the Porte by King Charles IX of France, who, in common with the Venetians, feared the aggrandizement of Spain at her expense in the Levant, and sought the breakup of the Holy League. The Christians, indeed, for all their boasts of divinely concerted plans to follow up their great naval advantage, were already engaging in petty disputes as they dispersed to their various ports. The common cause was soon so subordinated to their own respective rivalries and conflicting commitments as to reduce their great victory of Lepanto to virtual sterility. Nonetheless it remained a victory in the moral and psychological sense. In the eyes of Europe the Ottoman spell had indeed been broken. The Turk, who had held Europe in thrall since his capture of Constantinople more than a century earlier, was for the first time seen not to be invincible. A legend was exploded, and the Christians breathed more freely.

In terms of Turkish prestige, here was a turning point. But in terms of power the Empire of Suleiman still rode high. Its material resources unsurpassed, its practical skills unimpaired, it rose resilient from defeat. Thanks to the leadership of Sokollu and regardless of the nullity of Selim it stood, in the present as in the past and for some twenty years to come, united in fact as in spirit, vigorous in action, decisive in policy, and realistic in its application—still a cohesive Islamic power which might well furnish an example to its enemies in Christendom.

The Empire's main enemy was still Spain. The present bone of contention between them was Tunis, which the Ottomans had recaptured in the course of the Cyprus campaign, only to lose it again in the year after Lepanto to a Spanish squadron under the command of Don John. In the following year Kilij Ali returned to the assault with a fleet as large as that which had fought at Lepanto. Once and for all he captured the city, together with the fortress of La Goletta, which had for long been held by Spain. Within a mere three years of the Ottoman defeat at Lepanto the corsair admiral was leading a victorious fleet into the Golden Horn.

Tunis became, with Algiers and Tripoli, an Ottoman province, helping to maintain through the ensuing centuries a degree of Turkish authority over these unruly piratical states of the Barbary Coast. Turkish influence was to be extended, in 1578, to Morocco. Here the sherif of Fez called for the aid of the Turks against the Portuguese, who had landed a large force in support of a pretender. This was granted with alacrity, for fear of Spanish cooperation with Portugal, and a great battle was won against the Portuguese at Alcazarquivir, in which their king, Sebastian, was killed, together with the pretender and a quarter of their army. Thus started the decline of Portugal, of which King Philip speedily took advantage by its armed occupation.

Not long after this recapture of Tunis, Selim the Sot suddenly died, as the accidental result of a last solitary debauch. Superstitious by nature, he had seen portents of his approaching end in the appearance of a comet, a destructive earthquake in Constantinople, floods which threatened the holy places of Mecca, but above all a serious fire in the kitchens of his Seraglio, which destroyed also its wine cellars. This seemed to confirm his premonitions, since the death of his grandfather had been preceded by a fire in the Seraglio of Adrianople. Disconsolate, he paid a visit to a Turkish bath that he had lately built and whose walls were not yet dry. To deaden his fears he drank, at a single draft, a whole bottle of Cyprus wine. Then, tottering unsteadily, he slipped and fell to the floor, cracking his skull on its marble flags and thus precipitating a fatal fever. Such was the not inappropriate end of Turkey's least distinguished Sultan.

Selim's reign had been unproductive, but his death was untimely. Mehmed Sokollu ensured the peaceful succession of his son Murad III. But Murad was to curtail Sokollu's effective power and so hamper the completion of his statesmanlike task, that of conserving the Empire of Suleiman and bringing to it a further stable lease of life. Though Sokollu survived still as Grand Vezir for four years more, he no longer enjoyed the full authority which Selim had allowed him, but was continually at the mercy of the capricious intrigues of his new master's slave favourites and the women of his harem, who sought maliciously to influence the Sultan against him.

On the night of his arrival in Istanbul, seasick after a long crossing from his seat of government at Magnesia, Murad had ordered his five brothers to be strangled. Next morning he received his officers of state. The first words of the new Sultan were awaited in an anxious silence, inspired by the oriental superstition that they would furnish an omen for his reign to come. The words, since a night's sleep had relieved his seasickness and restored his appetite, were "I am hungry; bring me something to eat." This seemed to presage a famine, which sure enough occurred in the following year. Murad did not share the favourite vice of his father, and one of his first decrees was against the consumption of wine. This was provoked by a group of Janissaries who, outside a tavern, raised their glasses to drink his health. When they rebelled against the decree, with threats and insults against the Grand Vezir, it was rescinded, and they were again permitted to drink wine, but with the provision that they should refrain from violence.

Murad had vices of his own, notably avarice and lust. He loved, to the point of obsession, both women and gold. Until the death of Suleiman the state treasure had been kept in the Castle of the Seven Towers, one of which contained gold, another silver, the third gold and silver plate and jewels, the fourth valuable relics of antiquity, the fifth further such objects from Persia and Egypt, while the sixth was an arsenal and the seventh contained the state archives. Selim II had removed what remained of the treasure after his costly wars to his private treasury, and the Seven Towers became mainly a prison. But Murad III went further. He built a special vault with triple locks for the treasure, and slept over it throughout his reign. It was opened only four times each year to receive fresh loads of wealth, which was generally estimated in millions of ducats.

Murad surrounded himself with innumerable courtiers, among whom he led a life of indolent self-indulgence, dealing himself with affairs of state only to gratify their ambitions. Four women—likened ironically to the four pillars of the Empire—ruled his life. One was his mother, the Sultana Valide, who presided over the harem. A second—though her influence soon waned—was his sister, the wife of Sokollu. Another was a Venetian beauty named Safiye. She had been captured by a Turkish corsair en route for Corfu, where her father, of the noble Baffo family, was governor, and she became the mother of his eldest son, Mehmed. In his infatuation he long remained faithful to her. Disturbed at Safiye's ascendancy, his mother did her best to direct his desires into more promiscuous channels, and he plunged into a life of license, requiring the services of two or three concubines in a single night. This doubled the price of girls from the slave market of Istanbul, and enabled him to sire more than a hundred children.

From among these ladies a Hungarian took his fancy and for a while wielded some influence. But the fourth woman in his life and in his counsels was one Janfeda, who, on his mother's death and by her dying request, was to become the "grand mistress" of the harem. Since she did not herself share his bed her main role was to procure for him others to do so. Individually and collectively they presumed to advise him on matters of state. But it was the Venetian, Sultana Safiye Baffo, who continued to exercise the predominant influence, particularly in foreign affairs. In face of strong provocation from Venetian shipping, she dissuaded the Sultan from attacking her native Republic of St. Mark; and indeed Venice obtained from the Porte the renewal of capitulations and other commercial advantages. Her influence was to prevail equally as Sultana Valide over her son, Mehmed III, in the next generation.

Since gold was as precious to Murad as women, venality at his court soon reached the point at which every official appointment in the state was obtainable only through influence and purchase, with a tariff fixed in advance. The depths of corruption were reached when the Sultan himself became accessible to bribes on a substantial scale, as his share of the sums paid by petitioners to his courtiers and ministers. This practice was introduced to Murad by a powerful favourite named Shemsi Pasha, who was known as the "Falconer of Petitions." Shemsi claimed descent from the Seljuk princes, and thus looked upon their supplanters, the Ottomans, as enemies. On one occasion (so his biographer records) he emerged from the Sultan's presence in a state of some elation, declaiming: "At last I have avenged my dynasty on that of the House of Ottoman. As it caused our ruin I have now prepared its own." Asked how he had done this, the favourite replied: "By persuading the Sultan to share in the sale of his own favours. It is true that I offered him a tempting bait. Forty thousand ducats is no small sum. From this day the Sultan himself will set the example of corruption, and corruption will destroy the Empire."

Shemsi, like Lala Mustafa Pasha, was a bitter enemy of Sokollu. When the Grand Vezir complained to him of the corrupt influence of the palace in the affairs of state, he was informed that he had only to obey the palace, which could do no wrong. Sokollu's end came four years after Murad's accession. He was still in power through the initial stages of a campaign which won new—if not permanent—acquisitions for the Empire, as he had won for it Cyprus, Tunis, and the Yemen. The campaign was waged against Persia, following the death of the old Shah Tahmasp (poisoned, it was said, by his wife) and consequent murderous internal upheavals.

Taking advantage of this situation, in 1578, an Ottoman invasion was launched without warning from the Crimea, under Mustafa Pasha in command of an army stiffened by Tatar auxiliaries. It achieved the defeat of two Persian armies in rapid succession, and the resulting conquest of the greater part of Georgia, a Christian kingdom which was allied to the Persians. The Turks entered Tiflis, where they converted the churches into mosques. They invested submissive Georgian chiefs with sanjaks, occupied most of the adjacent provinces, and established an Ottoman provincial administration divided among four beylerbeys.

They penetrated into Daghestan and thus to the shores of the Caspian, as Sokollu had sought to do early in Selim's reign through his unsuccessful attempt to cut a canal between the Don and the Volga. The bey of Azov, who had led the vanguard of the invasion across the steppes to the north of the Black Sea, was rewarded with the high-sounding title of Kapudan Pasha, or Chief Admiral, of the Caspian. But the Persians began to resist more effectively, and the war was to drag on for a further twelve years. After this Persia signed a peace treaty confirming the cession of Georgia, Azerbaijan, Shirvan, Tabriz, and other provinces. Meanwhile the Ottomans had established against Persia a base at Kars, with strong fortifications, which was to serve as a bulwark of the Empire in the East for some centuries to come.

But the occupied provinces were hard to hold. Most of the population were Shi'ites by religion, and thus remained loyal to the Persian regime. The unaccustomed Ottoman administration, with its own systems of taxation and land tenure, was resented, and the nomad tribesmen preferred the relatively indirect rule of the shah to the direct centralized rule of the Sultan. Above all the Turks, as in previous Persian campaigns, were hampered by remoteness from their bases and consequent problems of transport and supply. For these reasons Sokollu, though he had confidently favoured a water link, for military purposes, was generally opposed to this overland campaign as falling beyond the Empire's resources; and so indeed in the long run, through recurrent campaigns over the next fifty years, it was fatally to prove.

Meanwhile Sokollu's enemies at court were working inexorably against him. First they conspired to disgrace his friends and protégés, finding easy pretexts for their execution. Finally Sokollu himself was approached in the council chamber of his palace by an apparent suppliant dressed as a dervish who plunged a dagger into his heart, striking him dead. The murderer, a Bosnian like Sokollu himself, admitted nothing under torture, and the crime was attributed to a private grievance concerning the diminution of a fief. Only the evening before, it was related, an equerry had been reading to the Grand Vezir an account of the stabbing of Sultan Murad I at the battle of Kossovo. At this Sokollu cried out: "May God grant me a similar death!" And so it was. "With Mehmed Sokollu," as a Venetian ambassador put it, "Turkish virtue sank into the grave." His was certainly the assassination which set the seal on a long period of Ottoman decadence.

((19))

THE LONG PERIOD OF DECLINE WHICH THUS BEFELL THE EMPIRE so soon was directly evident in the weakening of the Sultan's authority, through lack of his serious concern with the affairs of state; also of his machinery of government, through neglect and dispersal of its responsibilities and disregard of its institutional principles. In a state which had hitherto depended on the absolute personal power of its sovereign, capably exercised, and his effective control of its administration through his own capable Slave Household, this led quickly to disintegration, confusion, and widespread disorder. In part this derived from the fact that the Empire had, if only for the present, exhausted both its field and its capacity for territorial conquest in Europe, which from the outset had served as its chief motive force. Centuries of war had inspired in the Ottomans unity of purpose; had provided wealth for them in the form not only of spoils but of territories for landed settlement. Now there remained few such outlets, few such rewards. In default of an enemy to plunder, men plundered one another; in default of land, they flocked to the cities or spread disorder through the countryside.

The flaw in Suleiman's land reforms now became evident. It arose from the fact that, with the best motives but not, as time passed, with the best effects, his distribution of the principal fiefs was centralized in the capital, not decentralized as before in the hands of the provincial authorities. All too often it thus came to depend less on the justice of claims to them than on palace intrigues and the corrupt distribution of favours. It led to the development of larger landed estates, which was the opposite of Suleiman's intention, and in the process to the growth of the hereditary principle. This accompanied the gradual ending of the period of continuous Turkish conquest with its profits to landholders, and thus to their increasing exactions from the peasantry and their avidity for more lands for themselves.

Furthermore the fief-holding *sipahis,* hitherto the mainstay of the Ottoman state as they lived on the revenues of their land and on the labour of their peasantry, were now ceasing to serve their former purpose as a military arm. Moulded by the old Ottoman traditions, and accustomed to a short campaigning season, they were unadaptable to more modern warfare, with its general need for foot soldiers, trained to use firearms, and for specialist corps, skilled in other techniques. In Europe they had proved unable to stand up to the professional German fusiliers, with their heavier weapons. Thus they became a dwindling or at least a changing class—and indeed a growing element of insubordination and disruption. Often now the *sipahis* would refuse to embark on campaigns which offered hardship and danger without, as in the past, compensating material rewards. Otherwise they might choose to abandon the battlefield when it suited them to do so, as they were to do at the battle of Mezo-Keresztes, in Hungary, in 1596. Following this thirty thousand *sipahis* were dismissed from their holdings—a clear indication that the system had by now outlived its purpose.

For any breach of duty, unless prepared to make payments in lieu of service they were liable to be deprived of their fiefs, thus swelling the numbers of the landless malcontents. Their lands would be appropriated by others, sometimes within the law, sometimes through bribery of the judges concerned in awarding the claims to them. Thus there grew up a new class of landlords who were often officials, courtiers, and servants of the palace and indeed often from outside it, moreover as a rule absentees, living in the cities. By such corrupt means it became possible for a single person to accumulate any number of fiefs, and thus build up a big landed property. When the *sipahis* were able to retain their fiefs, they now often contrived to make them hereditary, passing them on to their sons, who fulfilled no obligation to perform military service and might well abandon the rigours of the saddle to pursue, like the purchasers of fiefs, lives of urban leisure. Thus there grew up, at the expense of the peasantry, a system of absentee hereditary land tenure, often irresponsible, and both in principle and in practice wholly contrary to the state system conscientiously established by previous Sultans. This helped to create an ever-widening gap between the lives and interests of the peasants and those of the urban population.

In the capital itself the entire character of government service, in terms of appointments to office, similarly underwent a radical change. Hitherto the Sultan's household, which administered the country, had been recruited exclusively from among enslaved Christians, hence generally from among peasants, reared in the villages, who had retained peasant affinities and an understanding of rural affairs. But this system began to loosen in the last phase of Suleiman's reign, and by the end of the sixteenth century appointments to the Sultan's Slave Household were open to his Moslem subjects, freemen who had been reared in the towns; they entered it often through family influence or purchase of office, and were now permitted to bequeath their posts to their sons. Thus in government too the hereditary system, with its inevitable nepotism, was generally established, and it became possible for an ambitious young Moslem with good connections, sufficient financial resources, a competitive spirit, and an astute political sense to climb upward to his profit from one lucrative and privileged post to another. To reach the top still called nonetheless for high qualities of energy and intelligence, as it had done in the past. But the Empire no longer enjoyed government by an exclusive elite, trained and chosen by its sovereign on the basic principles of merit and quality.

Inherent besides in these various elements of Ottoman decline lay certain fundamental factors of social and economic disruption. The first of these was an increase of population exceeding any increase in the area of cultivated land. The second was an increase in prices, following the influx of Spanish-American bullion from the New World. This led to the depreciation of the Ottoman silver currency and to a high degree of inflation—common at this time to a large area of Mediterranean Europe.

Because of the consequent economic crisis the Ottoman government (following the example of Persia) was driven in 1584 to manipulate its currency on a substantial scale. Gold coinage was devalued by 50 percent, while aspers, the standard silver coinage—which was the normal medium of the soldiers' pay—were melted down and reissued as thinner coins with more copper, becoming (in the words of a contemporary Turkish historian) "as light as the leaves of the almond tree and as worthless as drops of dew." Depreciation continued to a point at which the Spanish ambassador in Venice could declare to Philip II: "The empire is so poor and so exhausted that the only coins now circulating are aspers made entirely of iron." With continuing crises over the turn of the century it became indeed so weak economically as to be, if not bankrupt, often unable to pay its armed forces, and in the prevailing discontent the diminishing authority of the central power failed to control demonstrations, revolts, and disturbances.

Meanwhile, the population of the Empire had doubled in the course of the sixteenth century, and with the limitation of expansion into Europe—in which population pressure had played its part—there was a shortage of land where the surplus could be settled. Land hunger was driving young villagers from home to seek a livelihood elsewhere. Nor was the Ottoman state and its traditional medieval guild system geared to the development of economic resources other than the

THE CITY OF
of the
owers
Tower of Bellisarius
Wath Tower
Fanarikiosc
Port of Calcedon
THE BOSPHOR

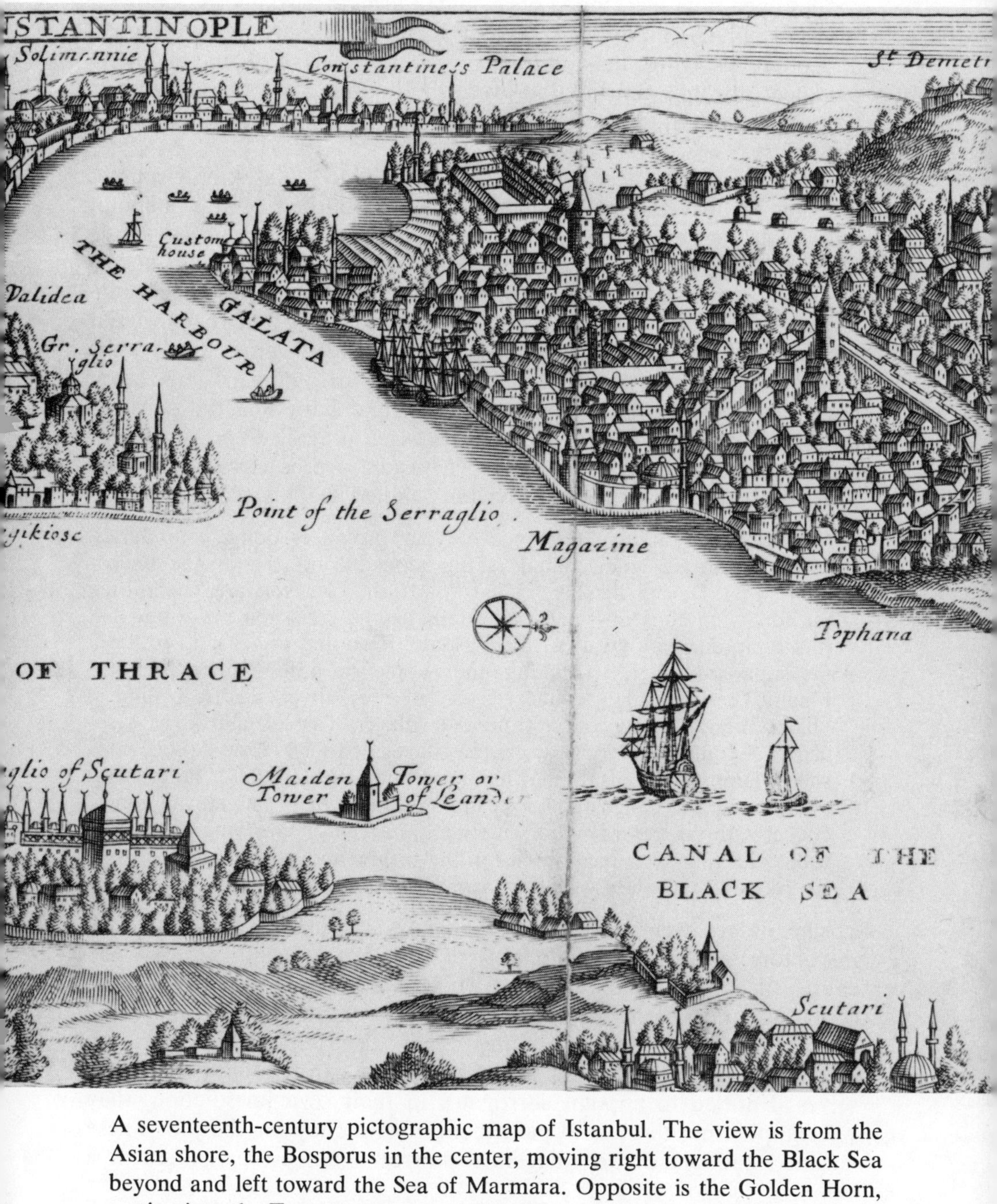

A seventeenth-century pictographic map of Istanbul. The view is from the Asian shore, the Bosporus in the center, moving right toward the Black Sea beyond and left toward the Sea of Marmara. Opposite is the Golden Horn, cutting into the European sector of the city.

From Guillaume Joseph Grelot, *A Late Voyage to Constantinople,* London, 1683, p. 57.

products of the land. Only with the conquest of Cyprus did an opportunity arise for further settlement on any scale. Other such outlets were now blocked. Anatolia in particular thus swarmed with landless, rootless peasants, seeking service under arms as irregulars, or other forms of official employment, and in default of it causing disturbances and often resorting to banditry. Aggravating this problem of unemployment, through devaluation, were the doubling of prices, adulteration and counterfeiting of coinage, speculation, high rates of interest, and usury.

The treasury, to meet a deficit, became obliged to seek new sources of revenue through increased taxation. The burden of this fell ultimately on the peasants, officially through the imposition of increasing levies by both the central and provincial governments. But in unofficial fact it was a burden grossly augmented by abuses and unauthorized practices. For the effects of inflation were felt in particular by classes living on fixed incomes, now halved in value, thus by the officials themselves, whether military, civil, or judicial. This drove them to bribery and corruption, fleecing and harassing the peasants through illegal extortions. Such practices as prevailed at the turn of the sixteenth century were listed in a justice decree circulated to his provincial officials in 1609 by Sultan Ahmed I. This read:

> You are not making the rounds of your provinces doing your duties. Instead you are going round taking money from the people unlawfully. . . . During these so-called "patrols" . . . you are committing the following abuses: if somebody falls from a tree, you make out that it is a murder, you go to a village, settle down and in order to rout out the supposed killer, you harass the people by putting them in irons. Finally, besides taking hundreds of gold or silver pieces, calling it "blood-money," you collect from the villagers free of charge, as a so-called "requisition," horses, mules, slaves, barley, straw, wood, hay, sheep, lambs, chickens, butter, honey and other foodstuffs. You lease out your incomes to collectors at excessive rates. On their part they go out to collect with far too many horsemen, and instead of satisfying themselves with collecting your incomes according to law and as it is prescribed in the record, they try to get about as much money as they please.

The judges were as corrupt as the other officials. Appointed as inspectors to hear the complaints of the villagers and establish the causes of confusion, they were all too liable to interpret the decrees of the Sultan to their own advantage and to extract bribes from those charged with offenses. In making up tax registers, they were overstating the number of those liable for tax, to extort money for themselves. Entitled to appoint surrogates in their own jurisdiction, they were appointing those who paid them most money for the job. These various exactions drove villagers to borrow from usurers, often at a rate as high as 50 percent, for the payment of their taxes and debts, working for them for nothing and becoming in effect their slaves.

To replace the dwindling feudal *sipahis,* the government was obliged to increase the strength of its regular forces. This applied both to the Janissaries and to the other paid troops of the Sultan's household, who included such "men of the Sultan" as the regular *sipahis* of the Porte. Here new sources of recruitment were needed. That of Christian-born captives, whether through wars or purchase, was no longer sufficient for the purpose. It was necessary for the first time to enlist into the armed forces on a large scale Moslem subjects, previously debarred from their ranks as from those of the civil administration. They were recruited not only into the Janissaries but into the other arms of the standing forces, the *kapi-kulus.* This meant a dilution of these troops, the introduction of new mixed elements causing a change in their exclusive character, which was profoundly to affect not only their discipline but that spirit of team solidarity which was the root of their *esprit de corps.*

Already the Janissaries, during their more frequent spells of idleness in barracks, were permitted to work as artisans, supplementing their pay with the sale of manufactured goods. Engaging thus for the first time in commerce, they became merged with the civilian artisan population of Istanbul and other garrison cities, becoming in effect townsmen and losing much of their discipline and zeal for war. This, combined with the fact that since Suleiman's reign they were permitted to marry, led inevitably to the growth of the hereditary principle among them as among the administrative and landed classes, and from this it was but a short step to the admission of their sons into the corps. At first, since it was a slave corps, this had been done through a process of legal evasion, since it was not lawful to enslave a born Moslem. But under Selim II a certain quota was officially established for their admission. Finally, under Murad IV the traditional recruitment only of Christian slaves, both to the Janissaries and to the rest of the Sultan's household, was altogether abolished, thus legally recognizing a process which was already an accomplished fact.

From the last decade of the sixteenth century onward they became, as their masters the Sultans grew weaker, progressively more turbulent and exacting in their demands. In 1589 they gave serious trouble to Murad III, protesting against the new debased coinage in which they were to be paid. For the first time in history they stormed their way into the Seraglio, where the Divan was in session, and demanded the heads of the ministers held to be responsible for its debasement.

Rather than face the insurgent troops in person, the Sultan bowed the knee to their superior force by sanctioning the two executions. Twice more during the next three years they drove home their advantage, demanding and securing the deposition of two successive Grand Vezirs. In 1593 it was the Sultan's guard of regular cavalry, the *sipahis* of the Porte, who revolted. This time, turning against them, the Janissaries themselves reestablished order, the authorities shrewdly exploiting—as again in the future—the rivalry between the two forces. Further such revolts by the Sultan's troops disturbed various provinces of the Empire. On the vassal state of Moldavia the Janissaries were audacious enough to impose, in response to bribery, a governor of their own choice—who was, however, soon deposed for nonpayment of tribute, and later robbed and murdered by the Janissaries themselves in Istanbul.

From 1596 onward more serious troubles arose in Anatolia, which was for a while thrown into complete anarchy by irregular rebel elements, known as the Jelalis. The household troops were now stationed in Anatolia in considerable strength. A counterpart to them was an increased number of *sekhans,* the irregular infantry and cavalry who were now armed with muskets to become, under the governors, the main provincial army. But in peacetime, receiving no pay, moreover jealous of the privileges of the Sultan's regular imperial troops, they became a source of chronic disorder—bands of landless, rootless peasants who roamed the countryside as bandits and freebooters.

The Jelalis drew their strength from these irregulars, the unemployed *sekhans;* from Turcoman, Kurdish, and other Asiatic tribesmen; and not least from the dispossessed feudal *sipahis.* A large force of them with other irregulars, all deserters from the army in Europe, were vindictively punished by their commander and driven to flee as *firaris* (runaways) into Anatolia, whence most of them originated. Added strength came to the Jelalis from those irregulars sent by the provincial authorities to suppress them, who often preferred to join the ranks of the rebels. Initially, in an attempt to control these forces, the government, intent on its campaign in Hungary, appointed two successive press-gang leaders to conscript troops against them. But having done so, they in turn rebelled with these troops, extorting money and supplies from the population to support them.

The more capable of these two commanders, Kara-Yaziji, gathered around him a rebellious force of Jelalis amounting to some tens of thousands, which was drawn from a wide range of the discontented elements in Anatolia. Formed into large groups, they forced towns to pay tribute and came thus to dominate a number of provinces in central Anatolia. Driven by government forces into southeastern Anatolia, they resisted strongly from the fortress of Urfa. After Kara-

Yaziji's death, the revolt spread throughout Anatolia under his brother, Deli Hassan, or Hassan the Mad, who arrogated to himself the title of shah, and who boasted after defeating the governors of several provinces, "I have overthrown in those countries the Ottoman power, and the domination undivided now belongs to me."

In an exodus which became known as the Great Flight, peasants on the run from his men scattered everywhere in confused masses, abandoning their villages to seek refuge in fortresses, while the wealthier Anatolians fled to Istanbul, Rumeli, and as far afield as the Crimea. Finally Deli Hassan was induced by the central government to lay down his arms, and as a condition was made governor of Bosnia. This enabled him to use his wild troops in Europe. In a new invasion of half-naked, long-haired Asiatic "barbarians," they ravaged Rumeli, slaughtering Moslems and Christians alike, but in 1603 were finally annihilated on the banks of the Danube by a force of Hungarians.

In Anatolia the revolts continued, as a series of governments sought in vain to reassert their authority. Much of it became a devastated area, with the soil left uncultivated, thus a land wasted by outbreaks of famine. The consequent abandonment of land by the peasants led to its appropriation by military leaders and others. They established large private estates which they ran rather as ranches for the rearing of livestock, and thus further radically changed the traditional agrarian pattern of land use throughout Anatolia.

These revolts of the Jelalis impeded all efforts by the Ottoman government to form an imperial army for the renewal of the war against Persia. In 1603 Shah Abbas, who had been restoring the strength of the Persian armies, took advantage of the situation to launch an offensive. In this he swiftly recaptured Tabriz, his father's former capital, Erivan, and the Ottoman fortress of Kars. Within five years he had reoccupied the various provinces lost to the Turks by his predecessor, and reduced to virtual ruin the precarious structure of Ottoman rule in the Caucasus, which had in any event proved tenuous. Resisting counteroffensives, he was able in 1612 to impose a peace settlement in which the Turks ceded most of the territory they had gained through the peace treaty of 1590.

By now another insignificant Sultan, the fourth since the death of Suleiman, had ascended the throne. He was Ahmed I, the fourteen-year-old grandson of Murad III and the son of Mehmed III. Murad had been forewarned of death through the dream of a favourite, followed by a cramp in his stomach. Conveyed to a kiosk on the Bosporus, he lay watching the ships as they sailed past the window. His musicians played a melancholy air to which he murmured the words "Come and keep watch by me tonight, O Death." Two Egyptian galleys fired a salute, shattering the glass of the dome of the kiosk, scattering fragments around the Sultan and reducing him to tears. "Another time," he lamented, "the salvos of the whole fleet would not have broken that glass, and now it is shivered. . . . This kiosk is the kiosk of my life." Conveyed back to his palace, he died on the following day.

The first action of his son, who succeeded him as Mehmed III, was to have his nineteen brothers strangled by mutes—the largest fratricidal sacrifice in Ottoman history. Then he accorded them a solemn state funeral, burying them with honours beside their father, in coffins decked with turbans and plumes. Meanwhile six pregnant slaves, their favourites from the harem, had been sewn up in sacks and thrown into the Bosporus, lest they give birth to claimants to the throne. Later Mehmed put to death his own chosen son, Mahmud, a young man of spirit who had begged to be given command of the armies fighting the rebels in Anatolia, and this had inflamed his father's jealous suspicions. His mother and his favourite companions were thrown into prison and later suffered the same fate. When Mehmed himself died not long afterward, an inscription was placed on his tomb: "Almighty Allah hath said everything perisheth except merely a judgment, and they return to thee."

Mehmed III was the last heir to the throne to serve as a provincial governor, and thus to acquire experience of public affairs in the course of his father's lifetime. Henceforward, for fear of revolts, all princes of the blood were confined permanently to the Seraglio, cut off from the world in a building to be known as the Cage, and thus benefitting from no such experience. Mehmed, content enough now to remain there, fell under the domination of his mother, the Venetian favourite of his father, the Sultana Valide Baffo. His ministers were anxious that, following the example of his ancestors, he should command his armies in person in the war against Hungary which dragged on perennially, with varying fortunes. His presence, it was urged, could revive their martial zeal after the loss of Gran and other Ottoman towns. But the Sultana obstructed this plan, fearing to let the Sultan out of Istanbul, hence beyond the sphere of her influence. She preferred instead to provide him with distractions in the form of well-chosen concubines.

Weakling as he was, Mehmed nonetheless had his moments of resolution, and finally, taking account of an ominous earthquake and of the demands of the Janissaries, who in anticipation of gratuities now refused to march without their Sultan, he yielded to the exhortations of his ministers. In the summer of 1596 he had taken the field with appropriate pomp at the head of his armies in Europe, blessed and encouraged for the first time by the unfurling before them of the Prophet's own sacred standard, which had been brought from Damascus for just such an emergency.

The Ottoman forces besieged and captured Erlau, then confronted the enemy in battle on the plain of Mezo-Keresztes. The battle was long, with vicissitudes (including the mass desertions of *sipahis*) which easily discouraged the Sultan. After an early reverse he urged, from his seat on the back of a camel, a general retreat—or at least his own retreat. But after a council of war he grasped the Prophet's standard, donned his sacred mantle, and agreed to remain with his troops. The tide turned. The Christians broke their ranks to plunder the enemy's camp. At this moment the Turkish cavalry charged and they fled before it in total disorder.

It was a Christian defeat in which more than thirty thousand Germans and Hungarians were killed and considerable booty was captured, including some hundred cannons of fine workmanship. It was a decisive Turkish victory which at a perilous moment indubitably saved for the Ottoman Empire Bulgaria, Macedonia, half of Hungary, and, with the exception of Transylvania, most of the territories north of the Danube which still remained in its hands. These it was to retain for some centuries. Meanwhile, Sultan Mehmed, who had at least served as a spectator of his victory, returned with relief and in triumph to an ovation in Istanbul. Here he relaxed as before amid the pleasures of the harem, leaving the direction of affairs to his Venetian mother. At the end of October, 1603, he is said to have met a dervish who prophesied that within fifty-five days a calamity would befall him. Obsessed by superstition, he died just fifty-five days later.

The adolescent Ahmed, who succeeded him, refrained from fratricide if only because his surviving brother, Mustafa, was a lunatic—and Moslems had a sacred respect for the mad. Ahmed was, in the words of a Turkish poet, "the first among all the sons of Osman who possessed Empire before having carried the standard." He was, however, soon circumcised—the first Ottoman Sultan to undergo the operation on his throne. Soon afterward he contracted smallpox, thus causing the curtailment of the usual festivities of Bairam.

Recovering, Ahmed showed in his boyhood certain sparks of hotheadedness and even of vigour. When his Grand Vezir refused to set forth on a Hungarian campaign without an extra large grant from the treasury, the Sultan sent him a message: "If you value your life you will march at once." When the Janissaries and *sipahis* of the Porte complained of arrears in their pay and flung stones at their officers, the boy Sultan robed himself in scarlet—as the caliph Harun-al-Rashid had done on days of execution—summoned their senior officials before him, and arraigned them imperiously. They had been told that the wages of these troops were on the way. "Why do you not believe this? Why do you allow yourselves to insult my Sublime Porte? Hand over the guilty ones." After an astonished silence, one of the aghas replied that those responsible were not the Sultan's own slaves but strangers recruited into the force for garrison purposes, on Ahmed's orders. They were named and immediately executed. Their chiefs, ordered to remove the bodies, were severely admonished: "Next time you overstep the bounds of obedience, I shall have you all executed, without distinction."

But Ahmed, as he matured, belied this robust early promise. Presiding over his Divan in May, 1606, in connection with an imminent campaign against Persia for which the army was already assembled at Scutari, the Sultan proposed its postponement. There was an astonished silence. Then the Grand Mufti argued that the horsetail standards of the Empire had already been planted on the Asiatic shore, for all the world to see. It was impossible now to strike camp and retreat without dishonour. The Sultan suggested a limited campaign, by a part of the army under Ferhad Pasha. The Mufti enquired whether, if the public treasury were empty as the Sultan declared, he could himself provide funds for this purpose, as Sultan Suleiman had done from his privy purse for his own last campaign. To this Ahmed replied merely that times had changed, and what was necessary then was now no longer convenient. The Divan was dismissed. Thus Ferhad Pasha, known as Ferhad the Foolhardy, set forth into Asia with a force but without adequate funds for pay or supplies. His march was soon interrupted by a mutiny among his Janissaries, who were then routed by the first rebel bands to cross their path.

Otherwise Ahmed, in the course of his reign, did little on his own initiative. Capricious and deficient in judgment, he lacked the faculty of choosing good advisers, and was forever changing his Grand Vezirs, largely at the behest of the harem. Its inmates, pursuing their selfish interests, established increasing authority over him, particularly the Chief of the Black Eunuchs, who kept a court of his own as ostentatious as that of his master. As an Italian contemporary remarked, "One knows not in truth who is the sovereign." The harem, moreover, now spread its corrupting influence everywhere, with the growing custom of marriages between the ladies of the Sultan's family and his officials and favourites. Under cover of this relationship at court they were able to engage to the fullest extent in the various extortions and malpractices now ravaging the lands and demoralizing the public services of the Empire.

Ahmed I died in 1617, at the age of twenty-seven. The last of fourteen generations of Ottoman Sultans through which the Empire had been transmitted from father to son, he was succeeded by his imbecile brother, Mustafa I, who was brought in a daze from his dungeon in the Seraglio. Here he had languished for fourteen years, by some (according to the English envoy Sir Thomas Roe) esteemed a holy man, since he had "visions and angelic superstitions, in plain terms between a madman and a fool." One of his diversions in captivity was to throw gold pieces instead of crumbs of bread to the fishes in the Bosporus. But the Divan put a stop to this habit at the instance of the Chief of the Black Eunuchs, who suggested that it would be better to save the gold for the prescribed donative to the Janissaries when he should come to the throne.

Ahmed, seeking to preserve the direct succession when he started to sire sons of his own, had twice contemplated his execution (so Richard Knolles informs us). The first time he was deterred during the previous night by "apparitions and fearful dreams." The second time, enraged at the sight of his brother walking with his guard in the garden of the Seraglio, he took his bow and arrow and raised an arm to shoot at him. But being suddenly stricken with a great pain in his arm and shoulder, he desisted, concluding that the Prophet did not wish Mustafa to die. Thus, stultified by his long imprisonment, Mustafa now ascended the throne. At once it became apparent that he was unfit to rule. He was soon dethroned, led back to his place of confinement, and succeeded as Sultan by his nephew, Ahmed's fourteen-year-old son, Osman.

His deposition was prompted by the Janissaries, who now virtually dominated the capital and who, with the advent of a new sovereign, benefitted from two substantial donatives in the course of a mere three months. The adolescent Osman cherished dreams of martial glory in emulation of his ancestor Suleiman the Lawgiver. He was proficient in the use of arms, and was reputed to show off his skill with the bow by setting up prisoners of war or even his own pages as human targets before him. Though relative peace now reigned on both foreign fronts, he soon insisted, against the advice of his ministers, on launching a war against Poland. A pretext for this could be found in recurrent frontier disputes over slave and cattle thefts between the Sultan's vassals, the Crimean Tatars, and the Cossacks of the Ukraine, who were held to be subjects of the Poles.

Encouraged by a preliminary Ottoman victory, he assembled in 1621 an army which was declared to be larger than any since Suleiman's time; and, donning a suit of mail that had belonged to his ancestor, he led it via Adrianople across the Danube to the banks of the Dneister. It was a hard march, hampered by premature wintry weather, mutinous mercenaries, and other vicissitudes. The Sultan's construction of a bridge across the river was followed by a series of unsuccessful assaults beyond it on the fortified strongpoint of Choczim, which was well equipped for defense. His troops were disgruntled and (as Knolles expresses it) "would rather die running, or pillaging, or eating, than in the face of the enemy"; while the Sultan himself, though ready enough to risk his own person in battle, could not, unlike "his ancestors in like enterprises," induce them to fight. He was thus obliged to retire with heavy losses, and to treat for peace with the Poles. He then returned to Istanbul, claiming a victory. But as reported to London: "The Grand Signor entered this city the first of January, clothed like a common soldier, without great train, and less pomp. His losses in this war have been exceedingly great, especially of horses."

The young Osman had alienated the Janissaries, not only by a failure in battle for which they, in fact, were largely to blame, but by an intrinsic fault, that of avarice, of which they were quick to accuse him. Whether owing to this or to the chronic depletion of the Imperial Treasury, payments to them and the scale of their perquisites fell below the level that they had come to expect. They complained, for example, that the reward payable for the head of an enemy severed in battle was now no more than a single ducat—and for this a man was expected to risk his own head.

They resented also, in common with many of the Sultan's subjects, his habit of prowling through the streets of the city, often by night and in disguise, with a few palace officials, "prying into houses and taverns, like a petty officer," to detect infringements of his laws against the consumption of wine and tobacco, ordering arrests and inflicting punishments on offenders. In the course of these visitations his chief gardener was reputed to have flung into the Bosporus Janissaries and *sipahis* caught in the wineshops, and to have consigned drunken soldiers to the galleys as slaves.

The Janissaries had indeed begun to present a serious threat to the Empire. For centuries the strong arm of the Ottoman forces in their imperial conquests, they were now in their greed and indiscipline deteriorating as a warlike force abroad and developing into a subversive force at home. On the battlefield they were gaining the reputation among the modern foreign armies for ineptitude and even cowardice under arms. The Janissaries, so their enemies now observed, were still swift of foot and sharp of eye, but only to discern the moment at which the *sipahis* began to waver and then to flee as fast as they could. In the capital, as one inadequate Sultan followed another, each at the mercy of his corrupt Seraglio, they came to be a dominant power and a focus of sedition.

The eighteen-year-old Sultan Osman, stung to indignation by the stigma of becoming "subject to his own slaves," and prompted by advisers known for their advocacy of reform, devised an elaborate scheme to counter this threat to his sovereignty. The moving spirit of it, brought from the Asiatic frontiers of his empire, was "a man of great wit" named Dilawar Pasha, "the Courageous." As governor of the large province of Diyarbekir, he was widely respected for his power in these militant regions. Thus it was decided that he should recruit, from among their hardy inhabitants and with the cooperation of their provincial governors, a large Asiatic army to serve the Sultan as a new militia. Designed to act as a counterpoise to the household troops of Istanbul, it would be composed of some forty thousand men, including a large force of Kurds and other warlike tribesmen, together with well-disciplined mercenary units from Egypt and Syria. When it was mustered, the Sultan would proceed to Asia and thence march it back to the capital, where his objective would be the suppression of the Janissaries and *sipahis.*

As a cover for this operation it was announced in the spring of 1622 that the Sultan was about to depart with his personal retinue on a pilgrimage to Mecca. In fact he intended to proceed to Damascus, in Syria, where an alternative pretext was the suppression of a rebellion of the Druzes. But unfortunately Osman, in his youth and inexperience, lacked the circumspection required for so ambitious a venture, which depended for its success on strict secrecy. His ministers, moreover, were divided in their views on the plan, while the Grand Mufti explicitly opposed it and sought to prevent the Sultan's departure "for Mecca." Furthermore, the Janissaries and *sipahis* were quick to suspect its ulterior motives when orders were given to transport the imperial tents across to Asia; and indeed he was preparing to carry away all of his jewels and his treasure and "whatsoever could be converted to bullion."

At this they determined to rise in revolt. They massed together in the Hippodrome. Thence "by the mouth of the multitude" they sent a demand to the Sultan for the surrender of the offending ministers. On his refusal they broke into the palaces of the Grand Vezir and another minister, and plundered them. The Sultan deferred to them by promising to abandon his journey to Asia. Nonetheless, they now broke into the Seraglio itself, which in default of any precaution by Osman to muster within it a force loyal to him was largely defended by his gardeners. Here, as their excitement grew, they revealed the unprecedented intention of attacking the sacred person of the Sultan himself.

As the insurgents gathered in the courtyard a voice cried, "We want Mustafa as Sultan!" Instantly the rest echoed the cry, and swarmed through all the apartments of the palace in search of him. Barred by the gates of the harem, they tore off a portion of its roof and, descending by curtain cords, found the mad Mustafa in a vault, where he had spent the past three days without food or drink, in the company of two Negro slaves. After bringing him water, they seized him, terror-stricken as to his possible fate, and carried him off, to be enthroned once more as Sultan. Soon afterward the Grand Vezir and the Chief of the Black Eunuchs emerged through the doors of the harem to confront the rebels—who tore them to pieces. Mustafa's mother, the Sultana Valide, took charge of him, seeking to soothe him with words of encouragement—"Come, my Lion"—then forming in his name a new government.

Meanwhile, the troops were still searching for Osman, who had fled from his apartments in the palace. He was found in his hiding place, a pitiful figure wearing only an undergarment and a skullcap, by a *sipahi* who contemptuously removed his own turban to put on his head, then made him ride on a broken-down nag amid the insults of a derisive crowd to the Janissaries' barracks. On the way they came upon the corpse of his former Grand Vezir and favourite, Hussein, whom the rebels had beheaded. At the sight of it lying in the middle of the road, Osman lamented: "He is innocent. If I had followed his advice, this misfortune would never have befallen me." In the barracks, near to tears, he made an appeal to his captors. "What are you proposing to do with me? You will bring about the ruin of the Empire and your own, you Janissaries." Then, removing his turban, he turned piteously to their leaders and implored them: "Forgive me if I have offended you without knowing it. Yesterday I was Padishah. Today I am stripped bare. Let me be an example to you. You also may suffer the vicissitudes of fate in this world." In the presence of the new Grand Vezir and the Sultana Valide he pleaded, when faced with the threat of the bowstring, to be allowed to address his "servitors," the troops, outside.

The window was opened and the unhappy youth made a final oration. "My aghas of the *sipahis,* and you, the elders of the Janissaries, who are my fathers, with a young man's imprudence I have lent an ear to bad advice. Why do you humiliate me in this way? Do you want me no longer?"

At this there was a unanimous cry. "We want neither your rule nor your blood." Osman was then conducted, through a large crowd of people, to the dreaded prison of the Seven Towers. Later, having fallen asleep from exhaustion, he was rudely awakened in his cell by Daud Pasha, with three henchmen, who at once set upon him. Being young and strong he put up a good fight. But at length (as recorded by Sir Thomas Roe) "a strong knave struck him on the head with a battle-axe and the rest leaping upon him, strangled him without much ado." One of his ears was then cut off and dispatched to the implacable Sultana Valide, who had authorized the execution.

His burial took place the same evening. Though fratricide was a commonplace, this was the first act of regicide to taint the annals of the Ottoman Empire. Its victim was, in Roe's words, "the first Emperor that ever they laid hands on; a fatal sign, I think, of their declination."

((20))

FOLLOWING THE MURDER OF OSMAN THERE WAS A REPENTANT REaction among Janissaries and *sipahis*. "Now, they mourned for their dead King as freshly as they raged unreasonably." Carried away by mob hysteria and confronted by all too little opposition, they had run berserk, going beyond their initial intentions and against their ultimate interests to land themselves, under an idiot Sultan, in a state of confusion worse confounded. As the mind of Mustafa became slowly aware of the truth, he expressed grief at Osman's death, issuing an order that his murderers should be punished. But later in his imbecility he would forget that Osman was dead, running in search of him throughout the Seraglio, knocking on doors and crying out to his nephew to relieve him from the burden of sovereignty. Incapable of governing, Sultan Mustafa was nonetheless to remain on the throne for fifteen months.

Anarchy became such as to inspire the prediction of Sir Thomas Roe: "I can say no more than that the disease works internally that must ruin this Empire; we daily expect more changes, and effusion of blood; the wisest men refuse to sit at the helm, and fools will soon run themselves and others upon the rocks. If any able hand were ready to take the advantage, there is not so easy a prey in the world." The Empire, he wrote again, "has become like an old body, crazed through many vices, which remain when the youth and strength is decayed." Nonetheless, two and a half Ottoman centuries were to pass before this "old body" was diagnosed by the world as "the sick man of Europe."

Now the effective instrument of government was a woman, the Sultana Valide, with the soldiery, themselves divided, as the power behind her son's throne. Official posts became the fruits of intrigue with one or another of their two factions, allotted by caprice or through purchase. Ministers became prodigal in their promotions and bribes to the party in the ascendant, and increases in pay to both Janissaries and *sipahis*. Grand Vezirs followed one another in rapid succession after Daud Pasha had been deposed by the troops on the belated grounds that he had ordered Osman's execution.

He was succeeded by Mere Hussein Pasha, an Albanian, a "tyrant hated of all men," who had started his career as a cook and had lately

Janissary officers—a picture that should dispel any lingering doubt about the Ottoman penchant for striking costumes and headgear.

Reproduced from William Alexander, *The Dress and Manners of the Turks*, London, Murray, 1815.

A Janissary guard of the Sultan, while encamped.

earned notoriety as an extortionate governor of Egypt. In two periods of office he played off Janissaries against *sipahis,* granting them extra privileges and rations at the public expense, and finally opening the Sultan's stores to the Janissaries with the injunction "Take from wherever you like your meat, your candles and all that you need. Good heavens, the Padishah is rich enough!" The *sipahis* in their turn then rebelled and demanded that he melt down for them all the silver and gold vessels in the Seraglio. Throughout Istanbul there was incessant pillage, assassination, and incendiarism, as in a city taken by siege.

When Janissaries and *sipahis* together momentarily turned against Hussein, the Sultana, fully veiled but nonetheless in contravention of the laws of the Koran, appeared publicly before them to ask which of these candidates they would now prefer as Grand Vezir. When they disagreed, the post was conferred on one whose wife was the Sultan's nurse. When they demanded his deposition in turn on the grounds that he had appointed a donkey driver and a trumpeter as muezzins for Aya Sofya and the Sultan's mosque, he was duly replaced by another, the third Grand Vezir within four months to be deposed by the tyrannical whims of the soldiery. This was a signal for the return to power of Hussein, "who consumed the public treasure so fast and exacted money from private men so violently, to maintain his faction with the Janissaries, that even the receivers were afraid and weary, and the wisest foresaw their own ruin in the general consumption."

Events moved to a crisis following the outbreak in Asia, not long after Osman's execution, of a revolt by the governor of Erzurum, Abaza Mehmed Pasha, whose ostensible object was to avenge his death. A sworn enemy of the Janissaries, he had been an undoubted confederate of the Sultan in his plan for an Asiatic army to crush them. With his own large force of irregulars and with the support of other rebel forces of the country, he soon controlled most of central and eastern Anatolia. This territory he was to dominate, with continuous slaughter of the Sultan's troops, for five years to come. After an attempted revolt by the ulema in Istanbul the civil and military elements took counsel and secured the appointment of a new Grand Vezir, Ali Pasha, a man of reputed honesty. Then they called upon the mad Mustafa to renounce the throne, which "he did, they say, with much joy." Osman's younger brother, Murad, "the true heir," was then chosen as Sultan, proving acceptable to both Janissaries and *sipahis*. They even agreed, in view of the treasury's total exhaustion, to forgo the donative due to them on his accession.

Thus in 1623 Sultan Murad IV made his first solemn entry into Istanbul, another fourteen-year-old boy, still untried, but "fat and of a lively countenance and good stature." For the moment at least all seemed serene and quiet. Saving itself from the brink of an abyss, the

Ottoman Empire breathed once more. Resilient in spirit, it cherished hopes of a new lease on life and power under a new Sultan strong enough to exert his sovereign will.

What the Ottoman state needed and merited at this juncture was a tyrant, to counter the tyranny of its armed forces and the venality of their civil confederates; a sovereign to confound violence, as ruthless as they, to enforce a respect for the rule of law which they had reduced to contempt. Such was Murad IV as he matured, to become—in his own brief spell of power—an Ottoman Nero. In the words of Evliya Chelebi, the alert Ottoman writer and traveller who was favoured at court and who came to revere him, "Murad was the most bloody of the Ottoman Sultans."

The young Sultan, having been properly girded in the Mosque of Eyub, proceeded to the Seraglio, where he prayed that his services as sovereign be acceptable to God and his people. Then, adhering to tradition, he proceeded to the Imperial Treasury. Here, as recorded by Evliya,

> there were no golden vessels to be seen, and besides a quantity of lumber, there were found only six purses of money (30,000 piastres), a bag of coral, and a chest of china-ware. On seeing this Sultan Murad filled the empty Treasury with his tears and having made two prostrations in prayer, he said, *"Insh'allah,* please God, I will replenish this treasury with the property of those who have spoiled it, and establish fifty treasuries in addition."

Funds had indeed fallen so law that the vezirs had been driven—with little success—to approach certain foreign ambassadors for loans, on the precedent that in the past they had been obliged to pay tribute. Murad, however, contrived to find 3,040 purses from his own private treasury, which was distributed to the Janissaries within a month of his accession—regardless of the fact that they had previously agreed to forgo it.

Nearly a decade, however, was to pass before Murad was old enough to take over in person the reins of authority. His Greek-born mother Kösem (the Sultana Valide) held them throughout his minority with energy and ability. But for all her forceful intentions she could do little to check the indiscipline of the soldiery or the corruption of officialdom. Abroad, while Asia Minor remained torn by civil war and rebellion, the Persians recaptured Baghdad and the province of Erivan; the tribes of the Lebanon rebelled; the governors of Egypt and other provinces wavered in their allegiance; the Barbary states asserted independence; the Tatars of the Crimea revolted, capturing so many Ottoman prisoners that their market price fell to that of a drink of *boza,* or fermented millet; while the marauding Cossacks raided the coasts of the Black Sea, penetrated into the Bosporus, and threatened the outskirts of the capital itself. A certain semblance of traditional authority survived nonetheless to serve as an example to the boy Murad as he grew to adolescence, keenly assimilating knowledge and observing the march of events with an acute eye to the future of his state.

Murad grew into a vigorous young man, with a frowning, ferocious expression. Never was there a modern prince, recounts Evliya, "so athletic, so well-made, so despotic, so much feared by his enemies, or so dignified." Legends of his physical exploits abounded. He was so strong a bowman that he could shoot an arrow further than a bullet from a gun, causing it to penetrate a sheet of metal four inches thick; so skilled a spearman that he could with ease pierce a shield made from ten camel hides. He could fling a javelin prodigious distances, and once thus killed a raven, perched in a minaret a mile off. As a horseman, displaying his dexterity in the saddle each day in the Hippodrome, he could easily leap at full gallop from one horse to another. Boastful of his muscular strength, he was a redoubtable wrestler, "like the Prophet Mohammed himself." Evliya declares that he once saw the Sultan pick up his two stalwart sword-bearers, lift them over his head, and fling them one to the right and the other to the left. Once, playfully, he fastened on Evliya himself as his victim: "He seized me as an eagle, by my belt, raised me over his head, and whirled me about as children do a top." Finally Murad released him with a laugh and rewarded him with forty-eight pieces of gold.

Soon, however, such acrobatic pranks were to take a murderous turn. For events, in the all-too-familiar form of a mutiny of the household troops, precipitated Murad's assumption of effective power as Sultan. In 1632 the *sipahis* of the Porte massed together in the Hippodrome for three successive days while the shops closed their doors and terror reigned, both in the city and in the Palace itself.

The rebels were calling for the heads of no fewer than seventeen specified officials and favourites of the Sultan, including the Grand Vezir, Hafiz Pasha, and the Mufti. Hafiz was a brother-in-law of Murad, to whom he was especially attached, and who on the recent campaign had regaled the Sultan with dispatches in verse. Couched in an imagery derived from the game of chess, they had inspired verses from the Sultan in reply. Now, breaking into the first courtyard of the Seraglio, the rebels hurled stones at Hafiz and unhorsed him as he rode to a meeting of the Divan. Rescued meanwhile by his followers and delivering up his seals of office to the Sultan, he escaped at his command, taking a boat from the water gate of the palace for Scutari.

The mutineers then broke into the second courtyard, swarmed up to the hall of the Divan, and insisted that the Sultan hold a meeting of it before them. He emerged to face his troops on foot and inquired their wishes. Pressing furiously around him, they demanded the delivery of the seventeen traitors, that they might tear them to pieces. Otherwise, they threatened, there would be serious trouble. Seeing amid the hubbub that they were prepared to lay hands on him, Murad replied with dignity: "You are incapable of hearing me. Why have you called me here?" Guarded by his pages, he then withdrew, pursued by the soldiers to the gates of the inner courtyard with a menacing clamour.

The new vezir, Rejeb Pasha, then urged the young Sultan that the revolt of the troops could only be stilled if he would grant their demands—"Better the head of the Grand Vezir than that of the Sultan." Reluctantly Murad accepted defeat, and sent for his friend Hafiz, whom he met at the water gate. Mounting his throne he harangued a delegation of *sipahis* and Janissaries, imploring them in vain not to profane the honour of the caliphate with their bloodthirsty deeds. Hafiz now appeared before the Sultan and said: "Grand Padishah, let a thousand slaves like Hafiz perish for the safety of your throne. I beg of you only one thing: do not strike me yourself. Deliver me up to these madmen, so that I may die a martyr and my innocent blood fall on their heads." Hafiz then bent to kiss the earth, uttered a prayer, and advanced with a resolute step toward his executioners. He resisted them, striking the first assailant to the ground with a blow to his head, while the others sprang upon him with their daggers and felled him, riddling him with seventeen wounds. A Janissary then knelt on his chest and struck off his head. The pages of the Seraglio covered the corpse with a shroud of green silk for his burial.

The Sultan, moved to tears by the heroic performance of his friend, slowly returned to his palace, pausing before its gates to declare to the mob: "If God wills, you will suffer a terrible vengeance, you infamous assassins who neither fear God nor are shamed before the Prophet." Making light of his words, the rebels secured the deposition of the Mufti, and continued publicly to discuss that of Murad himself. But their ranks were divided not only once again as in the past between Janissaries and *sipahis,* but also between the extremists and a small force of moderates, shocked at the prevailing brigandage, who gradually rallied with their swords to the side of the Sultan.

Murad, burning with humiliation, thirsting for vengeance, fearing for himself the fate of Sultan Osman, resolved henceforward on a policy of either "kill or be killed." Aware now that the treacherous power behind the revolt was Rejeb Pasha, successor of Hafiz as Grand Vezir, who had counselled his surrender, the Sultan decided to act. One morning as Rejeb returned to his house from a meeting of the Divan, he was met by a chamberlain, who recalled him to the palace. Here, expecting to be received by the Sultan, he was shown into a room filled only with Black Eunuchs, precursors of doom, who motioned him to an adjoining chamber. Hobbling slowly and painfully from an attack of the gout, he entered, to be commanded by the Sultan: "Come here, lame rebel." Disregarding his protestations of innocence, the Sultan continued: "Ask for the waters of ablution, you infidel!" Before Rejeb had time to obey, the Sultan imperiously ordered the Eunuchs: "Cut off the head of the traitor, without further delay." The deed was done, and the corpse of Rejeb was instantly flung out from the gate of the palace. The spectacle spread consternation among a band of rebel troops outside, who had accompanied their master but now dispersed in alarm. Thus were the tables effectively turned.

With the last breath of Rejeb the reign of Murad IV, now emancipated from the yoke of his *vezirs* and the tutelage of his mother, began in earnest. The civil arm had been quelled. Next he must crush the tyranny of his military forces. For this purpose the Sultan convoked a public Divan in a kiosk on the edge of the Bosporus. Seated upon his throne, flanked by a detachment of his loyal guards and attended by the Mufti, the leading judges, his chief officials, and the two military commanders who had taken his side against the rebels, he summoned a deputation from the *sipahis,* then spoke to the Janissaries who were drawn up before him. Addressing them in the words of the Koran as faithful servants, blindly obedient to their Lord, he enjoined them to cease protecting the rebels in the corps of the *sipahis*. In reply they shouted out protestations of loyalty: "We are the slaves of the Padishah: we do not protect rebels; his enemies are our enemies." In these terms they swore an oath of loyalty, on copies of the Koran distributed from hand to hand.

The Sultan then turned to address the elders of the *sipahis,* who had arrived as deputies before the Divan:

> You others, the Sipahis, you are a singular troop, and it is hard to make you understand justice. There are forty thousand of you, and you all want offices, though the number of places available is no more than five hundred, in the whole of the Empire. Your demands have overturned the Kingdom, your exactions have emptied it. The lure of office has increased the numbers of malcontents among you, who, refusing to listen to the words of the elders and wise men of the troops, like yourselves, spend their time oppressing the people, devouring the pious foundations, and giving you a disastrously bad name for tyranny and rebellion.

At this the elders of the *sipahis* insisted that they were personally loyal to the Sultan but that it was beyond their power to control all their own ranks. The Sultan replied that they should hand over the leading rebels to him and swear an oath of loyalty, as the Janissaries had done. The *sipahis* obeyed. Finally the Sultan summoned the judges before him. "You are accused," he said to their elders, "of selling your judgments for money and ruining the subjects of the Empire." To this they replied that not one of them would thus oppress the people. But they were unable to ensure free and independent justice because of the violence of the *sipahis* in their own collection of taxes. A judge from Rumeli declared that, for having opposed these exactions, his tribunal had been assailed and his house pillaged. At this an Arab judge from Asia rose to his feet, drew his sword, and declared with flashing eyes: "My Padishah, the only remedy against all these abuses is the scimitar." Such was the accepted verdict, now confirmed on oath. A decree was signed by all, binding the signatories to suppress abuse and restore public order.

Deeds now followed words. Murad's own reign of terror brought military anarchy to an end. His trusted henchmen and well-trained spies scoured the city of Istanbul on his orders, tracking down the known traitors and ringleaders of the revolt, executing them on the spot with sword or bowstring, flinging their corpses into the Bosporus to be washed up on shore before the populace. Bloodshed similarly swept through the provinces. The troops, deprived of their leaders and confederates, were cowed and silent.

Murad, now more feared for his strong arm than any Sultan before him, would ride in among them in person, by day or by night, in disguise or otherwise, breaking up illegal assemblies, striking down with his own hand offenders against the edicts of his police. Later, to deprive the public of its centers of reunion and possible trouble, he closed all cafés and wineshops in the cities of the Empire—on no temporary basis but for the rest of his reign—and made the smoking of tobacco illegal. Offenders caught at night smoking a pipe, drinking coffee, or flushed with wine might instantly be hanged or impaled, and their bodies thrown out into the street as a warning to the rest.

As time went on Murad became carried away by the thirst for blood. At first his executions were justified by unquestionable guilt; then they grew more sweeping, but still depended on suspicion of guilt, however ill founded; eventually he was killing, heedless of any suspicion, for the sake of killing, from wanton caprice or impulsive ill humour. Steeped in the corruption of bloodshed, he had grown devoid of respect for human life. His approach created everywhere a frozen, terrified silence, in which all, like his dumb servants, acted as mutes, speaking not in words but in flickers of the eyelids, mouthings of the lips, clickings of the teeth.

His cruelties became legendary. Disturbed by the boisterous merriment of a party of women dancing in a meadow by the water, he had

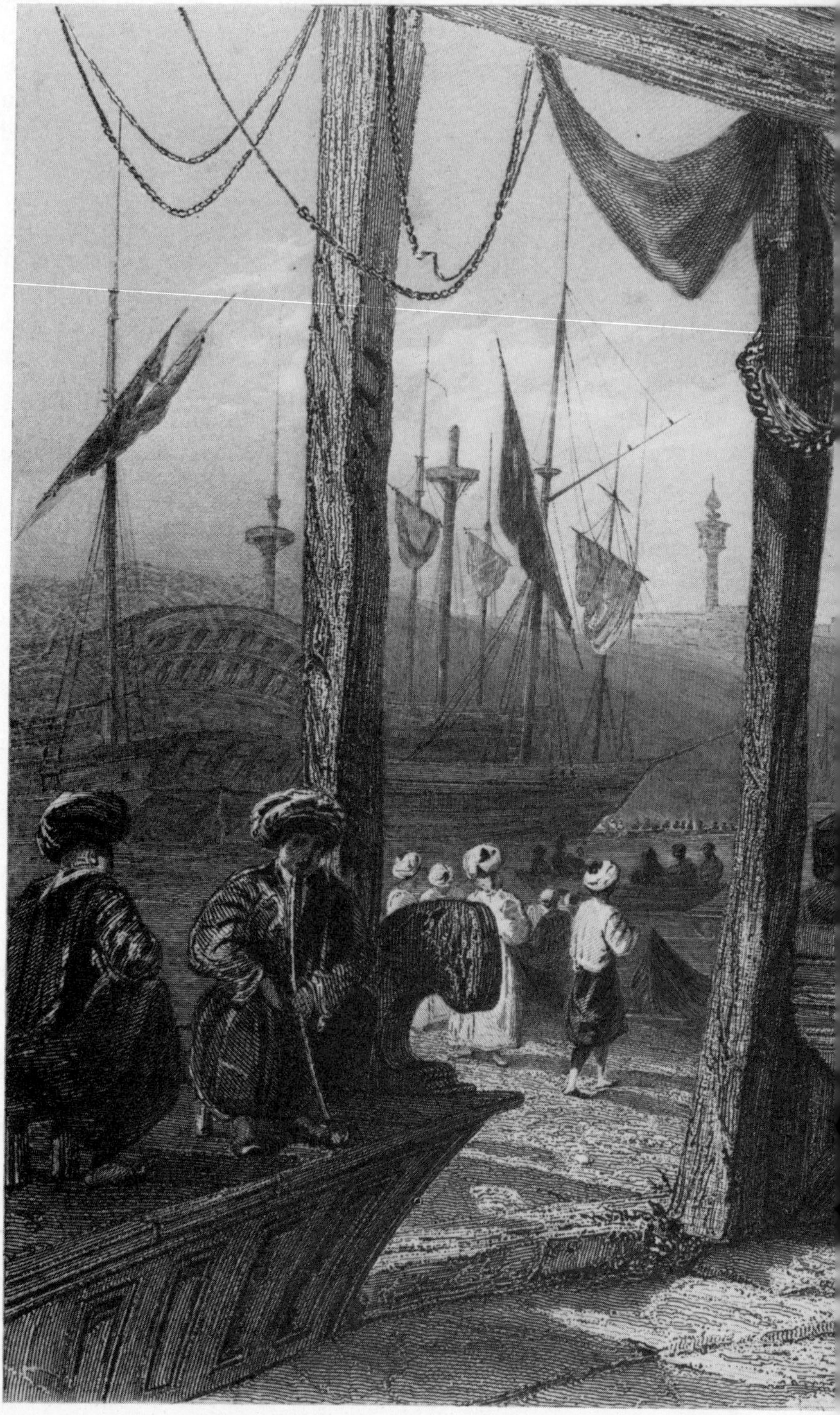

A coffee kiosk in the port of Galata. The Suleimaniye Mosque can be seen in the distance, the fire tower to its left and the aqueduct at far right.
A W. H. Bartlett engraving from Pardoe, *The Beauties*.

The interior of a public café in Tophane (Arsenal) Square, Istanbul, located at the juncture of the Bosporus and the Golden Horn. Note the coffeepots at left, the pipe rack at right, and the water pipe beside the first seated patron on left.

Melling, *Voyage pittoresque.*

them all seized and drowned. He murdered one of his doctors by forcing him to swallow an overdose of his own opium. He impaled a courier for informing him mistakenly that the Sultana had given birth to a son, whereas in fact it was a daughter. He beheaded his chief musician for singing a Persian air, and so honouring the enemies of his Empire. When a favoured dervish taunted him as a "master butcher," he laughed at the jest. "Vengeance," he would say, "never grows decrepit, though she may grow grey." In five years it is said that twenty-five thousand men perished at his orders, many of these by his own hand.

Nonetheless Murad's tyrannies rescued his empire from anarchy. No longer did petty local tyrants hold sway. He punished not merely the people but those in authority over them. His iron rule restored order. Under it discipline returned to the barracks and justice to the courts. He reorganized and strengthened the army, whether regular or irregular, and had plans for reforming it. He introduced reforms at court. He increased the imperial revenues, which were now honestly raised and administered. He deprived the *sipahis* of their privileges in the administration of the pious foundations and other government offices. He reformed abuses in the feudal landholdings and legislated for proper protection of the peasantry.

Above all Murad's merciless exercise of military power vindicated the aims of the Ottoman Empire in Asia. His first venture across the Bosporus was brief. Proceeding to Bursa, he found the roads in bad repair and at once hanged the judge of Nicomedia. This had roused a furore among the ulema in Istanbul. He hurried home, where he ordered the execution of the Grand Mufti—the first to meet with such a fate at the hands of a Sultan. In Asia Minor the rebellion had been finally crushed after five years, but its leader, Abaza, had been spared by the Sultan, who shared his hatred of the Janissaries. After a period of office as governor of Bosnia he was now summoned to Istanbul, to serve as their agha. He filled the post in ruthless style. But he fell out of favour through intrigues by his enemies which turned Murad against him and led to his execution.

Finally, in the spring of 1635, the Sultan set forth on his first Asiatic campaign. It started as a ruthless visitation of his Asiatic dominions, a bloody, inquisitorial march in which every halt saw a butchery of incompetents or suspects among his provincial officials, thronging in apprehension to kiss their Sultan's stirrup. After a solemn entry into Erzurum, between ranks of his Janissaries and *sipahis,* the Sultan proceeded to recapture Erivan from the Persians. His discipline was strict, but in the spirit of his forebears the troops were well provided for, his generalship won respect, and he shared all their hardships in person. He urged on his generals to deeds of valour and encouraged his troops with purses of gold and silver. "Weary not, my wolves," he would cry to them, "the time has come to spread your wings, my falcons."

After Erivan had fallen he dispatched officials to prepare for his first victorious entry into Istanbul. He gave them also discreet orders to strangle two of his brothers. This was an act which he had not found politic to perform on his accession, but for which the moment of victory now seemed propitious. The fraternal cries of fear, so he hoped, would be drowned by the popular cries of triumph; the torches of the two funeral processions would pale before the festive brilliance of the city's illumination.

Again, in the early summer of 1638 Sultan Murad planted his imperial standard of seven horsetails on the heights of Scutari, and set forth on his second and last campaign. Its objective was the recovery of the city of Baghdad, whose fortifications were reached, precisely according to plan, in a hundred and ten days' marches, with fixed periods for halts in between. There was a tradition that Baghdad, first annexed by Suleiman, could only be captured by a sovereign in person. The city was well commanded and strongly defended by trained musketeers, and it was only after a forty-day siege that—on the anniversary of Suleiman's conquest of Rhodes—it fell to the superior leadership of their Sultan. He set a resolute example to his men, donning a Janissary's uniform to work with his own hands in the trenches and point the cannon in person. When in the course of a sortie a Persian giant challenged the boldest Turk to single combat, it was the Sultan (so legend recounts) who accepted the challenge, rending his adversary from skull to chin with a single stroke of the sword. The capture of the city was followed, on the Sultan's orders, by a general massacre of both troops and civilians.

The Sultan then returned home to make a second triumphal entry into Istanbul. This time he flaunted a suit of Persian armour with a leopard skin over his shoulders, and was accompanied at the imperial stirrups by twenty-two Persian chieftains in chains. Soon afterward a peace was signed with Persia on similar terms to that granted by Suleiman a century earlier—the last such peace to be made by a victorious Ottoman sovereign who, in the Ghazi tradition, had led his armies in person. Baghdad was retained, but Erivan was restored to the Persians—who had indeed in the interval recaptured it. Murad, after his return from Baghdad, though hampered by attacks of gout and sciatica, saw to the suppression of a spirit of revolt in Albania, busied himself with attempts to revive Ottoman naval power, and was believed to be contemplating a war against Venice. In the long run he was planning fundamental military reforms, involving a smaller but regularly paid and fully professional army.

But early in 1640 he died, after a fortnight's illness, at the age of twenty-eight. His end was hastened by debauches with drinking com-

Sultan Murad IV (1623–40).

panions (of whom several were favoured Persians)—in ironic contrast with the prohibitions he imposed on his subjects. He was troubled also by the implications of an eclipse of the sun.

In his final fever, as though determined in a spirit of dynastic suicide to be the last of his line, he gave orders for the execution of his only surviving brother, Ibrahim, now sole heir in male descent of the house of Osman. His life was saved through the intervention of the Sultana Valide. The Sultan was assured that his orders had been obeyed and that his brother was dead. An infernal smile crept over his features, but he still demanded to see the corpse, and tried to rise from his bed for the purpose. His attendants held him back, and he died, amid suitable prayers for the dying, in the presence of the imam, who had been awaiting his end.

After this fruitful spell of tyranny and regeneration the Ottoman Empire relapsed once more into disorder and decline. In the person of Sultan Ibrahim the dynasty plumbed depths of human inadequacy lower than ever before. Reared exclusively in the Seraglio, in virtual imprisonment and often in fear, Ibrahim was a weakling who had inherited his father's vice of cruelty but none of his virtues. An irresponsible voluptuary, fitful in temper, unscrupulous in character, and avaricious in spirit, he was ruled by his harem and by frivolous moods and desires.

The baths of the city were scoured at his orders to find beauties for his pleasure. The shops of the jewellers and of the European merchants were pillaged to gratify his whims and tastes of the moment. Favoured ladies were authorized to take what they pleased from the bazaars, without payment, and for the benefit of those who disliked shopping by daylight shopkeepers were ordered to keep their premises open all night. One especial concubine told the Sultan that she wished to see his beard decked with jewels, and he appeared thus in public—to the concern of many Turks who interpreted this as an ominous tradition derived from the Pharaohs. For the use of another such favourite a chariot was built at great cost, all encrusted with precious stones.

The Sultan himself developed a craze for scents, especially amber, and another for furs, imposing on his subjects an amber tax and a fur tax, for their collection in kind or their cash equivalent. In this he was inspired by an old woman who told stories to the ladies of the harem at night, recounting the legend of a prince of antiquity who not only dressed himself entirely in sables but covered his sofas, carpeted his floors, and lined his walls with fur. The Sultan instantly resolved to emulate the prince in his own Seraglio. Dreaming all night of sables, he commanded the Divan next morning to organize the collection of their skins from all provinces of the Empire. Similar demands were made of the ulema and the civil and military officials of the capital. A furious colonel of the Janissaries, returning from the wars, declared angrily to the tax official that he know nothing of such things as amber or sables, that he had brought back with him only gunpowder and lead; nor had he any money to pay for such trifles.

At first Ibrahim had a Grand Vezir, Kara Mustafa, the conqueror of Baghdad, who dealt with him frankly, trying to repair his deficiencies and curb his excesses, to set his finances in order and counter the corrupt influences of the harem, which was trafficking as before, with the Sultan's participation, in the sale of state offices and dignities. Kara Mustafa fell through his failure to obey an order from a female official of the harem for five hundred carts of firewood for the use of its ladies. When he omitted to do so he was instantly ordered by the Sultan to dismiss the Divan, then in session, to appear before him and explain his omission. Promising that the loads would be sent, Kara Mustafa exploded: "My Padishah, was it necessary to make me, as your representative, suspend a sitting of the Divan and thus neglect affairs of importance for the sake of five hundred carts of faggots, whose value is no more than fifteen hundred *aspers*? Why do you interrogate me about faggots and not about the condition of your subjects, the state of the frontier and of the treasury?"

Warned afterward by the Mufti to take care what he said, since nothing that pleased the Sultan could be of trifling importance, Kara Mustafa replied: "Surely it is a service to him that I should tell him the truth? Must I flatter him? I would rather die free than live as a slave." For this, but above all for an unsuccessful intrigue against a rival official in favour with the Sultan, he was indeed to die, not meekly submitting, as most did, but drawing his sword for a fight to the death with his stranglers. His successor as Grand Vezir was Sultanzade Pasha, a flatterer so obsequious as to prompt his master's question: "How is it that you always so approve my actions, good or evil?" To this he received and accepted the reassuring reply: "Thou art Caliph. Thou art God's shadow upon earth. Every idea which your spirit entertains is a revelation from heaven. Your orders, even when they appear unreasonable, have an innate reasonableness which your slave always reveres though he may not always understand it."

Sultan Ibrahim's irrelevant frivolities did not endear him to his armed forces, who were fighting campaigns under capable commanders in the name of the Empire. The first of these was aimed at the recovery of Azov, whose inland sea commanded the Crimea and the northern coast of the Black Sea, and which had fallen into the hands of the Cossacks, nominal vassals of the tsar of Muscovy. The first Turkish siege of it, with the aid of an army of Crimean Tatars, was repulsed with severe losses to the Janissaries. A second siege followed it, this time with an army of as many as a hundred thousand

Tatars to support the regular Turkish forces, and the Cossacks were driven out, leaving the city in total ruin, to be rebuilt and equipped with a Turkish garrison.

The tsar refused support to his Cossacks, appearing to disown their vassaldom and seeking by means of an embassy to Ibrahim to restore the initial friendship between Russia and Persia. Nonetheless frontier warfare between Cossacks and Tatars continued, each power requiring the other to keep his unruly vassals in check, but Turks meeting Russians in battle several times during the reign of Ibrahim. The khan of the Crimea was more hostile to the Russians than the Sultan, reporting to the Porte: "If we give them breathing time they ravage the coasts of Anatolia with their squadrons. I have more than once represented to the Divan that there were two neglected strongpoints in this neighbourhood, which it would be prudent for us to occupy. Now the Russians have made themselves masters of them."

The second Turkish campaign was waged against Crete, hence against the Republic of Venice, to which the island belonged. The occasion for it was the capture by corsairs from Malta of a splendidly equipped Turkish galleon, travelling in convoy with a valuable cargo to Egypt and carrying pilgrims to Mecca. It was the property of the Chief of the Black Eunuchs, who was killed in the course of a fierce fight to resist its capture. On board was an important lady of the harem, finely dressed and decked with jewels, with a baby son who was assumed to be a child of the Sultan (but who was in fact more probably a foster-brother of his son, the future Mehmed IV).

At the news of this capture the Sultan exploded with fury. His immediate reaction was to order a massacre of all Christians in his empire. Relenting, he imprisoned in their houses all the Christian ambassadors and ordered the closing of the offices of the Frankish merchants. When it was pointed out to him that the Order of Malta was composed almost entirely of Frenchmen, he contemplated action against France. Instead, his Grand Vezir proposed an attack on Crete, under the guise of an attack on Malta, using the pretext that the Maltese galleys had been harboured there on the way home from their raid, and conveniently disregarding the fact that the Porte was at peace with Venice. The island was the last Greek possession of the Venetians, and in Turkish hands could form an effective barrier across the southern Aegean.

Thus in 1645 a Turkish fleet, achieving surprise, besieged and captured Canea, at the western end of the island. The next year they followed up this initial success with the capture of Retimo. Then they settled down to besiege the capital, Candia. Here was a siege which was to last for twenty years—twice as long as the siege of Troy—against an effective campaign of naval blockade by the Venetians in uneasy but effective alliance with the Knights of Malta. It was a campaign into which the child initially captured by the Maltese on the Turkish galley—whether the son of Ibrahim or otherwise—was introduced at a certain stage as a possible Ottoman pretender. Now a Catholic priest named Père Osman, he aspired without success to rally all Ottoman subjects, whether Moslem or Christian, to the cause of a new eastern state, blending the concepts of the Byzantine and the Ottoman empires.

Meanwhile, as the conflict with Venice dragged on, resentment mounted at home against the Sultan, voiced not only by the leaders of the Janissaries and *sipahis* but also by the Mufti and the body of the ulema. The moment for a change in the sultanate was ripe. For Ibrahim was no longer the last of his line, as at his accession, but had sons of his own. The insurgents secured the dismissal of the Grand Vezir, who went into hiding, and imposed in his place a candidate of their own. They surrounded the palace, and when the Sultan sent a high official to bid them disperse, a veteran Agha of the Janissaries replied to him with a recital of the Empire's sorry plight.

He made three demands of the Sultan: first the suppression of the sale of offices; secondly the removal of the favourite Sultanas; thirdly the death of the dismissed Grand Vezir. Next day the Vezir was unearthed from his hiding place and killed. When the Sultan refused a demand to appear before his troops, a deputation from the army and the ulema approached his mother, the Sultana Valide, who had been removed from the Seraglio through the intrigues of the favourites and was now threatened with exile. She received the delegates arrayed in a black veil and turban and attended by two Black Eunuchs. They disclosed to her their resolve to depose the Sultan and to enthrone in his place her seven-year-old grandson, Mehmed. The Mufti, they informed her, had issued a *fetva* legalizing this action.

The Sultana had alienated Ibrahim through endeavouring, without success, to persuade him to mend his ways. She now pleaded for him, insisting that he was a victim of bad ministers, begging that he should be allowed to retain his sovereignty but placed under the guardianship of the ulema and the new Grand Vezir. The grand judge of Anatolia sought to convince her that the trouble had gone too far, and that the time had come to end it. The Sultan, as she herself had discovered, would no longer heed sensible advice. Traffic in places and ranks had spread beyond all bounds; the Padishah, absorbed in the gratification of his passions, was straying ever farther from the path of the law; the call to prayer from the minarets of Aya Sofya was drowned by the clangour of fifes and flutes and cymbals from the palace; the markets were being plundered and the innocent put to death, while the Sultan's favourite slaves ruled the Ottoman world.

The Sultana then asked how it was possible to put a child of seven on the throne. The judge replied that, according to the verdict of the jurists as now embodied in the *fetva,* a madman should not reign whatever his age; far rather a child who was endowed with reason. Under such a child "a wise Vezir can restore order. But an adult sovereign, without reason, ruins his empire through murder, shame, and corruption." Finally the Sultana replied: "So be it. I shall fetch my grandson, Mehmed, and place the turban on his head." Her words were acclaimed with enthusiasm. A throne was placed before the Gate of Felicity, and the young prince, escorted by the Aghas of the court, mounted it to receive homage from the leading dignitaries of the Empire. They were admitted only a few at a time, for fear that a crowd would cause the child alarm.

The *vezirs* and the ulema then waited upon Ibrahim. "My Padishah," the grand judge of Rumeli informed him, "according to the decision of the ulemas and the principal dignitaries, you must retire from the throne."

Ibrahim cried: "Traitors! Am I not your Padishah? What does this mean?"

Boldly the Mufti replied: "You are no longer Padishah, since you trample on justice and holiness and have ruined the world. You have wasted your years in play and debauchery; you have squandered the treasures of the Empire on vanities; corruption and cruelty have governed the world in your place." Asking again after an excited discussion why he must descend from the throne, Ibrahim received the reply "Because you have made yourself unworthy of it by leaving the path which your ancestors trod."

After a further flood of reproaches for this act of "treachery," Ibrahim resigned himself to his lot with the words "It was written on my forehead; it is the command of God." Offering no further opposition, he allowed himself to be led off into prison in the Seraglio.

His ultimate fate, still in doubt, was settled by the revolt of a section of the *sipahis,* loudly championing his cause. In alarm the Grand Vezir and the rest sought a *fetva* from the Mufti to sanction his execution. His reply was a laconic "Yes," based on a principle of Islamic law: "If there are two Caliphs, kill one of them." The Mufti and the Grand Vezir repaired to Ibrahim's chamber with two executioners, while the judges and the Aghas watched from the window. They found Ibrahim reading the Koran. Recognizing the chief executioner, who had so often served him, he exclaimed: "Is there no one among those who have eaten my bread who will take pity on me and protect me? These cruel men have come to kill me. Mercy! Mercy!" When the executioners laid hands on him, he broke out into blasphemies and curses, invoking the vengeance of heaven against the Turkish people for its infidelity to its sovereigns.

Such, in the year 1648, was the second act of regicide in Ottoman history. For the second time it had placed a child upon the throne. In this crisis, as the pattern of events unfolded, lay a vindication of the Ottoman balance of internal power. The counterbalancing pillars of the state proved at this critical moment strong enough to counteract and to survive the shortcomings of its personal rulers, and thus to uphold its basic structure. The Moslem institution, embodying the voice of the ulema, had acted with decisive legal authority in the name of religion by deposing a decadent Sultan. The ruling institution now acted as decisively in the social and political interests of the state.

In good time it evolved and maintained new powers through the first of a "dynasty" of exceptional Grand Vezirs, all from a single family, the Köprülüs, who were to guide the boy Sultan to maturity and throughout his adult reign. Thanks to the statesmanship of this family the absolute despotism of the Sultans was to be effectively modified by enlightened ministerial government.

So did its two basic institutional elements, religious and secular, successively restore to the Ottoman state a degree of internal stability. This happened, moreover, at a fortunate period when the Empire was not menaced externally from Europe. Throughout the latter half of the seventeenth century the process of Ottoman decline was thus checked, and the Empire was enabled to reemerge into a period of comparative power and prosperity.

((21))

Close on a century had now passed since the death of Suleiman, the last great Ottoman Sultan. At home this had been a time of troubles. In Europe it was no longer a time of Ottoman conquests; but equally it was for the Empire a time of reprieve from any threats of reconquest. This was due to the fact that Europe was divided, both in religion and in politics, first by the Counter-Reformation, then by the Thirty Years' War. In the course of this conflict there were, on the contrary, moves from Europe to seek support from the Turks, whether naval or military; but support they now lacked both the will and the resources to supply. For their empire this was a period of adjustment to a new level of relations with the Christian powers. The first sure sign of this had been the signature, in 1606, on neutral ground by the Hungarian frontier, of the Treaty of Zsitvatörök, between the Ottoman and Habsburg empires.

Previously such treaties, as befitted a "superpower" which pretended to world supremacy, had been granted—if not imposed—by the Sultan only for such limited periods as suited him and not ostensibly on his own initiative, but as an act of grace and favour to a suppliant enemy, who was moreover obliged to send envoys to Istanbul for their negotiation. Previous treaties with the Christian emperor had embodied the formula "Graciously accorded by the Sultan, ever victorious, to the infidel King of Vienna, ever vanquished." Now for the first time a treaty was signed between the two powers as between equals. "The Emperor and the Sultan," it specified, "shall treat on a footing of equality." The Sultan, who had previously chosen in a contemptuous spirit to refer to the Habsburg emperor merely as "the King of Spain" (if not of Vienna), now condescended, following the normal diplomatic usage of the powers of Europe, to recognize him as an equal and acknowledge his title of Kaiser. There was to be no more vassalage. The annual tribute that Austria had hitherto paid to the Sultan was now suppressed, giving place to a single lump sum, which would subsequently be replaced by a triennial exchange of voluntary gifts through ambassadors, their value to be predetermined by either side.

The treaty, unlike previous truces limited to brief periods, was to last by mutual agreement for twenty years—and in fact lasted for fifty. Territorially the Turks were on balance slightly the losers. But they retained the frontier fortresses of Erlau, Gran, and Kanischa. Territories in Hungary under Ottoman rule were also retained and two new provinces formed. But claims to the tributary portions of the old Hungary were renounced, while the province of Transylvania, whose ruling prince was a party to the treaty, was granted a wide degree of emancipation. The treaty nonetheless, to the humiliation of the Ottoman armies, marked the beginning of a new diplomatic relationship between East and West. It was a submission by the Turks to the general principles and courtesies of international law, based on the acceptance of limits to Ottoman conquest and the overt acknowledgment of Habsburg power.

Hitherto the diplomatic relations of the Porte with Christian Europe had been geared to the exigencies of war. With regard to alliances it had otherwise maintained a policy of isolation, to which France, the consistent enemy of the Habsburgs, was for long the sole exception. But now, with the dawn of a period of relative peace, the Porte was breaking out of its isolation and growing receptive to such approaches from the West as might offer commercial and kindred advantages. This was to amount in effect to an extension of the traditional system of *millets,* those racial or religious communities among the Sultan's subjects which paid certain tolls in return for a semi-autonomous status. This was now to embrace also the subjects of foreign powers, principally merchants. Under their respective ambassadors and consuls, they were granted extraterritorial privileges to be embodied in charters—otherwise "Capitulations." Professor Toynbee has written: "The Osmanlis regarded the western commercial colonies as their nomadic ancestors on the steppes had regarded the alien inhabitants of the oases, from whom they used to purchase the few articles of necessity or luxury which they wanted and could not produce for themselves." Throughout the seventeenth century and afterward these were radically to alter the pattern and character of the Empire's foreign relations.

The enjoyment of capitulatory benefits by France dated as far back as the treaty signed with Suleiman in 1535. This was the stronger through being on a bilateral, not a unilateral, basis, thus not revocable, as others, at the Sultan's will, but mutually binding on both parties. Thanks to it the French had maintained for close on half a century an unrivalled foreign influence at the Porte.

During the reign of Murad III, in 1579, King Henry III of France thought it advisable to strengthen this relationship, and sent to Istanbul an ambassador of higher standing than the previous French agents.

He was the Baron de Germigny, who won the confidence of the Divan and secured a renewal of the Turco-French alliance, confirming its commercial Capitulations and with them the precedence of the French above other ambassadors. It confirmed also the privileges of French protection over the holy places of Jerusalem and Sinai and the Christians of the Ottoman Empire in general, excepting the Venetians but specifying "the Genoese, the English, the Portuguese, the Spaniards, the Catalans, Sicilians and Ragusans, and entirely all those who have walked under the name and banner of France, from old time until the present day."

Germigny, however, well recognized "the disposition in which the Grand Signor and his pashas were to collect and receive from all parts indifferently the friendship and alliances they were able to find." Quite apart from political implications, all overtures from foreign agents were coming, in this age of corruption, to be exploited as a rich source of revenue by vezirs, palace and army officials, and the various favourites of the Sultan in his harem and elsewhere. The Sultan indeed, within a mere two years of the renewal of the French Capitulations, was laying down the principle that "the Sublime Porte was open to all who came thither to seek protection."

The specific occasion for this was a demand from England by Queen Elizabeth that her ships should sail under their own flag, instead of as hitherto under the French flag, and that her subjects should be granted freedom of navigation and commerce within the Empire. English merchants had been slow to extend their trade into the Mediterranean. In the early part of the sixteenth century they had penetrated, in contact with the Venetians, into its eastern waters. But the growth of Turkish sea power with its belligerent corsair fleets discouraged further such commercial ventures, and the English trade with the Levant dwindled away. Instead, with the development by the Portuguese of the Cape route, the English merchants turned to the Netherlands, where the port of Antwerp was coming to supersede that of Venice as a depot for Eastern merchandise. This source of supply was interrupted in the latter half of the sixteenth century by the revolt in the Netherlands, while the conquest of Portugal by Queen Elizabeth's archenemy Philip of Spain threatened to transfer the precious Portuguese trade with the East into Spanish hands.

Politically, moreover, as hostility to Spain intensified, it became clear that cooperation with the Turks as allies might prove a useful counterpoise to Spanish power in the Mediterranean. Queen Elizabeth, unlike the French king Francis I, was not one to smile on an alliance with the infidel. But when she herself, as she was to do, described Sultan Murad as "the unconquered and most puissant defender of the true faith against the idolaters," she specified "those who

A European-Ottoman diplomatic exchange.

falsely profess the name of Christ" and in particular "that arch-idolater, the King of Spain." Thus in fact it was not merely commercial but political motives which underlay her present opening of negotiations with the Turks and the dispatch of an English ambassador to Istanbul.

The first steps in this direction were made by two London merchant princes, Sir Edward Osborne and his colleague, Richard Staper, who among their manifold commercial interests discerned the interest in a revival of trade with the Levant. In 1575 they sent two agents to Istanbul. One of them after a stay of eighteen months secured from the Sultan a safe-conduct for Osborne's factor, William Harborne, allowing him free access to the Sultan's dominions. Thus in the summer of 1578 Harborne, destined to become England's first ambassador, set out for Istanbul, travelling by sea to Hamburg, thence overland through Poland.

At the Sublime Porte, proving to be a man of some diplomatic skill and finesse, Harborne soon won despite active French opposition a promise of freedom to trade in Turkey, which was confirmed through an exchange of letters between Sultan Murad and Queen Elizabeth, and formalized in 1580 in a treaty based on those Capitulations already enjoyed by the French. Sultan Murad's preliminary letter to the English sovereign addressed her in fulsome terms as the "most renowned Elizabeth, most sacred Queen, and noble prince of the most mighty worshippers of Jesus . . . lady and heir of the perpetual happiness and glory of the noble Realm of England." An imperial commandment, he informed her, had been sent out to ensure that such persons "as shall resort hither by sea from the Realm of England . . . may lawfully come to our imperial dominions, and surely return home again, and that no man shall dare to molest or trouble them." The English were in fact to enjoy the same liberties as "our familiars and confederates, the French, Venetians, Polonians, and the King of Germany, with divers other neighbours about us," free to "use and trade all kinds of merchandise as any other Christians, without let or disturbance of any."

In the final agreement it was specified that if ever imprisoned, the English should immediately be released; they were not to pay poll tax but only "our lawful toll and custom"; they should have the right to appoint consuls, who were to decide disputes within their nation; any enslaved Englishman could be released on repayment of his purchase price; Turkish sailors were to help English ships during storms or when shipwrecked, and the crews were to be allowed to buy food supplies without hindrance. These, with similar specific items, were generous concessions enough, provided they were strictly recognized and enforced by Turkish authorities. This still remained to be seen. Harborne returned to England to report progress to the queen's ministers and to his own mercantile masters.

This agreement with the English aroused the immediate wrath of the French. It contravened their own quasi-monopolist agreement by which all ships permitted to trade in Turkish waters, including those of the English, did so under the French flag. After Harborne's departure Germigny, the French ambassador, worked hard with the Sultan and his ministers to achieve revocation of their capitulatory grant to him, but in fact achieved only a provisional suspension. The Turks at this time needed especially to obtain arms and munitions from the West, of which their war with Persia had created a shortage. Approached in this sense, Germigny gave a negative answer, on the grounds that the Civil War had created a similar shortage in France. England, on the other hand, was in a position to supply the Turks with such raw materials for weapons as iron, steel, tin, and brass; these in fact included fragments of broken Catholic images, an ingredient which might well appeal to the iconoclastic Moslem. Moreover, the Sultan saw in Queen Elizabeth a potential ally against Spain.

Back in England, Harborne found valuable support for his venture from Queen Elizabeth's chief minister, Lord Burghley; also from Sir Francis Walsingham, his representative in foreign affairs, who though he foresaw opposition, through diplomacy and possibly by force, from France and Venice favoured the trade as a means of promoting the English mercantile marine and so benefitting the navy. The result was official blessing for an application to the Turks by Osborne and his group, following up Harborne's initial foothold, for a charter of incorporation—a normal method of commercial organization in these times—granting them a monopoly of English trade within the Turkish dominions. Despite French machinations, this was granted by the Porte in September, 1581, for a seven-year period, and was to be renewed at subsequent intervals. Thus the Levant Company—the "Company of Turkey Merchants"—came into being.

The Turkish hesitation in ratifying the initial agreement had been due in part to Harborne's lack of official status. This was now to be remedied in negotiations between the queen and the company. Queen Elizabeth in person had paid the expenses of his first journey to Istanbul. She was now ready enough to appoint him her ambassador to the Sultan. But it was beyond the resources of the English government at this time to establish and maintain at the Porte a permanent diplomatic mission, with an embassy and several consulates equipped to supervise the English mercantile community; above all, an ambassador with the necessary power and prestige to ensure their protection and that of their goods by the Turkish authorities. It was therefore argued that the expenses of the mission should be borne by the company, and eventually this solution was agreed. Thus in November, 1582, William Harborne was honoured with the rank of the first English ambassador at the Sultan's court. His task was a dual one: that of a royal representative, with diplomatic duties, on the one hand; and on the other that of a commercial agent, with duties to the company which financed him.

Harborne thus returned to Istanbul, this time by sea in a "tall ship called the *Susan of London,*" to be piloted into the harbour by galleys. The ambassador landed amid salvos of gunfire, with the sounding of trumpets and drums and other signs of rejoicing, to be received by a squadron of cavalry. It chanced to be Good Friday, and the Christians of the city were at divine service, "singing melodies suitable to the Passion of the Cross." The rival Venetian ambassador reported of him that "even the Turks in contempt" call him "a Lutheran," and refused to attend "a sumptuous feast of meats" which he gave that evening. After distributing quantities of appropriate gifts among the various pashas, Harborne was received, bearing further gifts and a letter from Queen Elizabeth, by Uluj Ali in his galley. But he was not to receive much support from the old corsair. Nor later was Francis Drake himself, who got little in return for a present of "many vases of silver."

Harborne and his men were then entertained in the Sultan's palace at a banquet of 150 dishes. To drink there was "rose water and sugar and spices brewed together." Finally Harborne, treading on cloth of gold with a retinue bearing his gifts, was received in audience by the Sultan himself, wearing cloth of silver. Among the gifts were "three fair mastiffs in coats of red cloth, three spaniels, two bloodhounds, one common hunting hound, two greyhounds, two little dogs in coats of silk." The finest gift of all, valued at "five hundred pounds sterling," was a jewelled and highly decorated silver clock with a castle on top of it.

Germigny, denigrating Harborne as "a mere stipendiary of the merchants," made a vigorous protest at this official welcome, threatening the dissolution of the Franco-Turkish alliance if English ships were entitled to sail under their own flag. Morosini, the Venetian ambassador, sought by bribery to persuade the Grand Vezir that the admission of the English to the Turkish trade would have an adverse effect on Turkish customs revenue. "The French and Venetians," reported Harborne, "have to the uttermost opposed themselves, but their malice contraried." The Grand Vezir firmly told Germigny that "there was no occasion for such a row," and repeated that the Porte was open to all who desired peace.

Harborne rose admirably to the challenge of his position. He had a calm pertinacity, contrasting with Germigny's excitable temperament, and was soon able not only to renew the suspended Capitulations but to improve on them, in terms of customs dues, at the expense of his rivals. As a patriot he was always ready to boast of his country's greatness. To the Grand Vezir, when his rivals disparaged him as a mere merchant, he insisted that "he was a great noble, greater than any other here," and that in any case "they had no right to consider his private position but only the magnificence of the Queen, his mistress."

England held in practice an advantage over France, in that her Capitulations were confined to commercial privileges, whereas those of the French covered also protection of all Christians and their churches. There came a moment when the Sultan, in a mood of religious zeal inspired by the Mufti, turned against the Christians and threatened to convert all the churches in Istanbul into mosques. Protests by Germigny and donations by the Orthodox Greeks forestalled this threat, but three churches in Galata were nonetheless closed, only to be reopened after a judicious distribution of gifts. But when Germigny was succeeded by Savary de Lancosme, the new ambassador provoked a dispute in the principal church by usurping the place of honour reserved for the imperial ambassador. Thus it was again closed by the orders of the Grand Vezir, who refused to reopen it until "M. de Lancosme ceased to play the fool." England gained much of the influence lost in such ways by France, and when Harborne was warned of Lancosme's anti-English intrigues, he was able calmly and confidently to remark: "I do not think he will be quite strong enough to turn me out."

But for both European powers the present benefits proved to be rather economic than political. It soon became clear that the Ottoman Empire, for all its surviving naval power, was now reluctant to engage in belligerent action, whether in the political interests of France or of England. At a time when King Philip in his Atlantic ports was clearly building up a large Spanish armada for his invasion of England, the Porte remained politely but obstinately deaf to appeals from Harborne for naval support, if only in the form of a diversionary Turkish attack on the Spanish Mediterranean coasts. He left Istanbul for England at the end of his mission, prudently avoiding the Straits of Gibraltar to travel overland, shortly before the armada sailed. After it had done so, it was generally supposed at the Porte that England was lost, and the news of the Spanish defeat in 1588 was greeted with some incredulity. Later it was to become credible enough, with the arrival in Mediterranean waters of armed English privateers comparable to the Barbary corsairs, raiding indiscriminately, under the pretext of trade, the merchant convoys of the Mediterranean powers. Unable to control them, the English ambassador called upon London to do so.

France too sought to secure Turkish support for the Huguenot Henry of Navarre, who had assumed the throne as King Henry IV, against his internal Catholic enemies, the Guises, whom Philip of Spain supported. The Sultan wrote both to Queen Elizabeth and to King Henry, encouraging them to expect Turkish cooperation against the Spaniards.

The Turkish fleet, it was hoped, would thus act with the cooperation of both England and France, for once united in a Protestant cause against the threat from "idolatrous" Spain. Harborne's successor, Edward Barton, reported on this plan to the Queen's ministers. But whether from the Sultan's parsimony or from a real lack of funds in his treasury, no such Turkish armada materialized.

On the accession of Sultan Mehmed III in 1595, Queen Elizabeth, continuing to court Ottoman support against her Catholic enemies, sent him a shipload of presents. They included woollen goods, which disquieted the Venetians as a possible threat to their own trade, and bales of other cloth which they maliciously declared to have become mildewed on the voyage. But the *pièce de résistance* was a self-playing organ, unique in the ingenuity and complexity of its design. It was conveyed to Istanbul by its designer and builder, Thomas Dallam, a man well respected for his skill at his craft. The Sultan marvelled at its play and its other gyrations, including a bush full of artificial blackbirds and thrushes, which sang and shook their wings at the end of the music.

Mehmed was impressed especially by the well-armed English naval vessel, the *Hector,* which had brought Dallam and his organ, prompting a comment by his entourage that they had "not seen him so delight in any Christian prince's strength and defence." In the Golden Horn, freely open to crowds of visitors, the *Hector* aroused much curiosity. The Venetian ambassador feared that this display would "do a damage to Christendom and will open the eyes of the Turks to things they do not know." But there was no cause for alarm; no such lessons were learned, and the Porte grew, as Sir Thomas Roe later expressed it, "decayed in gallies." By the end of the sixteenth century, after the death of Uluj Ali, the Ottoman navy could offer neither a threat to an enemy nor support to an ally. Its recovery after Lepanto was little exploited. Its arsenal became gradually paralyzed. The sea power of the Turkish Empire had had its day, killed, as has been said, "not by its war but by its peace with Spain."

Anglo-French relations at the Porte deteriorated once more following the recall by Henry IV of Lancosme, a supporter of the Catholic cause, and the appointment in his place of an altogether more formidable ambassador, Savary de Brèves. He was to contribute much to the extension of French influence at the Porte both commercially and politically, and wherever convenient at the expense of his sovereign's allies, the English. Barton's successor, Henry Lello, was to echo such complaints: "The French Ambassador with his great bribes, receiving now the Pope's pay, spares nothing to hinder all my designs." Feeling between the two communities ran so high that one winter the Venetian ambassador reported: "Yesterday evening, as the result of a snowballing match, a violent quarrel arose between the households of the French and English Ambassadors. Several were badly wounded, and had not night fallen, worse would have happened, for the Ambassadors themselves began to take part."

Anglo-French conflict arose at first over Mehmed III's continuing war in Hungary (before the Treaty of Zsitvatörök). This was fanned by De Brèves in the interests of his master, Henry IV, who cherished ambitions to become Holy Roman Emperor, remarking: "The [Catholic] League made me King, who knows but the Turk may make me Emperor?" To this, with the present weakness of Austria, the defeat of Hungary would conveniently pave the way. Queen Elizabeth on the other hand sought peace in so unproductive a land campaign. Between French and English the principal bone of contention was in the economic field, where De Brèves consistently worked to prevent the renewal of the English Capitulations.

This came to involve the Dutch, the United Provinces of the Low Countries, now independent from Spain. Dutch merchants had entered into competition with those of England and France to trade in Turkish waters. The English, who had established a strong link with the Dutch through support for their struggle for independence, insisted that they do so under the protection of the English flag. But the French, claiming that the Dutch were still Spanish subjects, worked hard to bring them under the protection of the French flag. In 1601 the Grand Vezir, finally renewing the English Capitulations with wide new concessions, commanded the Dutch to sail under Queen Elizabeth's banner.

In 1612 the United Provinces were accorded a capitulatory treaty of their own, similar to those granted to England and France but limited to trade. They made free use of it to introduce tobacco into Turkey in the face of vigorous but vain opposition by the Mufti. The Ottoman Turks took to it with such relish that within half a century the pipe was seen almost as their national emblem. Coffee had already been introduced under Suleiman. Thus with opium and wine the Turks could now enjoy the "four cushions of the sofa of pleasure" and "the four elements of the world of enjoyment." So the poets described them. But to the strict Moslem legists they remained "the four pillars of the tent of debauchery" and "the four ministers of the Devil."

Such following the end of the age of Suleiman was the start of a period both of English influence and of Anglo-French rivalry throughout the Ottoman Empire.

((22))

REGENERATION HAD NOT IMMEDIATELY FOLLOWED THE EXECUTION of Sultan Ibrahim and the accession in 1648 of his son, the boy Sultan Mehmed IV. Throughout the first eight years of his reign sedition continued at home in a partisan spirit among the Janissaries and *sipahis,* playing off against one another the two Sultanas Valide: Mehmed's mother, Turhan, and his once powerful grandmother, Kösem, who in due course was murdered at the instance of her rival. This was accompanied by reverses and new threats from abroad. The continuing Ottoman campaign against Crete made it clearer than ever that the Turks no longer had command of the sea. From the middle of the seventeenth century this passed into the hands of the Venetians, while Maltese and Tuscan privateers ranged the Mediterranean without hindrance, and the Barbary corsairs were shaking themselves free of Ottoman control. The Turks could no longer defend their own sea routes or even their own coasts.

After the initial Turkish landing at Canea, in Crete, the Venetians established a blockade of the Straits, the Aegean coast, and the ports of the Morea. Events came to a head with a major battle off the Dardanelles in which the Venetians defeated and destroyed an Ottoman fleet conveying supplies and reinforcements to Crete for the long siege of Candia; then proceeded to capture the islands of Tenedos and Lemnos, which commanded the Straits. This was seen by the Turks as a naval defeat comparable to that of Lepanto. It led to an intensification of the Venetian blockade of the Straits and the denial of supplies to the capital, where food prices soared, discontent became rife, and there was general panic at the possibility of an attack on the city itself.

It was only now, to meet this crisis, that the Sultana Turhan, mother of the Sultan, summoned in secret the one strong man in his service with the standing and capacity to serve and regenerate the Ottoman state. This was Köprülü Mehmed, to whom she now offered the post of Grand Vezir. An Albanian of humble origin, whose forebears had settled in the town of Köprü (meaning "the bridge") in northern Anatolia, Mehmed was a scullion who had risen to be a cook in the Sultan's household and thereafter the honoured holder of official posts and successively governor of various provinces. He was by now seventy-one years old, with no lack of younger enemies ready to proclaim that he was in his dotage. Köprülü would only accept the post of Grand Vezir under certain explicit conditions: that all his measures be ratified without question; that he have an entirely free hand in his appointments to all offices, regardless of rank; that no vezir or official or favourite compete with his authority; that all reports to the court pass through his hands; that he enjoy the exclusive confidence of the Sultan, who would reject all calumnies against him. In short he insisted on such a degree of absolute power as none but a Sultan had held hitherto. The Sultana, invoking the name of the All-Highest, swore on behalf of her son that all these conditions would be fulfilled. Köprülü obtained from the Mufti a *fetva* which sanctioned in advance all his actions. The Sultan, honouring his mother's promises, received him in person and nominated him Grand Vezir. He was the eleventh so far to be nominated in a reign of eight years. His appointment stimulated a growing process of recruitment and conversion to Islam of Balkan Christian mountain tribesmen, both in Albania, his native province, and Bulgaria, which was to infuse the army and the administration with new sources of energy and loyalty.

Sultan Mehmed, heeding the counsel of reforming elements, left the government of his empire implicitly in Köprülü's hands and later in those of his son, Ahmed, who succeeded him. He did not himself aspire to govern, but gave each of them in turn implicit and consistent support against all intrigues and rivals for power. Thus for the next twenty years and—after an unhappy interregnum—for a similar spell at the end of the seventeenth century, the Ottoman state, hitherto alien in its structure to the hereditary principle outside the imperial dynasty itself, tasted strong ministerial rule under this dynastic family with its outstanding intelligence and governing capacity. From this significant turning point in the seventeenth century, the effective center of government of the Empire was no longer the Sultan's palace itself, but the palace of the Grand Vezir at its gate—Bab-i Ali, which had given its name to the Sublime Porte.

Köprülü Mehmed was a man of experience, with a shrewd knowledge of the government machine and its defects. Vigorous in action, he was a man of deeds rather than words, a dictator of inflexible willpower who started his "reign" with a purge of key officials and the appointment of others. Bent on the elimination at any cost of disorder, corruption, and incompetence, vigilant in his detection and ruthless in his punishment of all who thus endangered the security and wellbeing of the Empire, he is said to have executed, in the course of five years in office, some thirty-five thousand offenders—among whom the chief executioner claimed to have strangled in person four thousand persons of note.

Köprülü did this in no passionate spirit, least of all with the indiscriminate cruelty of his predecessor Murad IV. His strong arm, falling with shrewd calculation upon officials, soldiers, judges, men of religion alike, was combined with a cool head, discerning just where the danger might lie to his authority and that of the state. This he exercised to the full, acting within the existing machinery of government, strictly enforcing its laws, making of it a single effective instrument of the sovereign will. His determination was to revive the Ottoman Empire while some life was still left in it, to restore to it not only internal stability but external prestige and power.

For above all it became Köprülü's resolve to renew discipline and pride within the army, deflecting it from troublesome dissensions at home to campaigns abroad in renewal of the Ottoman conquering tradition. Swiftly clearing the Dardanelles of the Venetians and recapturing the islands of Tenedos and Lemnos, he restored confidence by reinvigorating the Ottoman fleet, constructing two permanent fortresses to guard the entrance to the Straits, reasserting a degree of Turkish power in the ports and islands of the Aegean and thus reopening lines of communication for reinforcements to Crete. Though the Ottoman navy was not again to recover command of the Mediterranean, the situation was eased meanwhile for the war against Venice, and the siege of Candia resumed without further interruption.

Elsewhere Mehmed suppressed a rising by another rebel named Abaza in Asia Minor, causing his head, with that of thirty other rebels, to be dispatched to the capital for public display. Beyond the Black Sea he strengthened Ottoman defenses against the Cossacks by the erection of fortresses on the Don and the Dnieper. He led a successful expedition into Transylvania, forming a new province from which to strengthen Ottoman control, and opening the way for a major campaign against Hungary and Austria which was in fact to be launched by his successor.

Köprülü Mehmed died in the fullness of age in 1661, after a "reign" of five years. He was succeeded as Grand Vezir, at his master's previous request, by his twenty-six-year-old son, Ahmed, who as Köprülü II was to rule the Empire in a statesmanlike spirit for another fifteen years. On his deathbed Köprülü Mehmed bequeathed four principles of conduct to Sultan Mehmed IV, now twenty years old: never to heed the advice of a woman; never to let a subject grow too rich; always to keep the public treasury well filled; always to be on horseback, keeping the armies in constant action.

Sultan Mehmed was indeed to spend much of his life on horseback—but in pursuit rather of the pleasures of the chase than the rigours of war. Given scant education as a boy, he developed an early taste for games of all kinds and was to become known as "the Mighty

Hunter." "Never," wrote the historian Paul Rycaut, "was a Prince so great a Nimrod . . . never was he at quiet, but continually in the field on horseback." His sporting "campaigns," in the region of Adrianople and elsewhere in the Balkans, imposed rigours of their own on his subjects. On one major occasion they called for the mobilization from fifteen different districts of some thirty or forty thousand peasants, "appointed to beat the woods for three or four days . . . enclosing all the game and wild beasts within that circuit, which on the day of the hunt the Grand Signor kills and destroys with dogs, guns, or any other way, with abundance of noise and confusion." Levies were imposed on the country districts for the subsistence of these "troops," who endured many hardships and not infrequent casualties, obliged in the dead of winter to pass long, unaccustomed nights in the woods, so that "many of them paid for the Emperor's pastime with their own lives."

Not always did the Sultan's own attendants take kindly to their master's exertions on horseback, growing often nostalgic for the easy life of the Seraglio and "beginning to believe the amorous humours of the Father more supportable than the wandering vagaries and restless spirit of the Son." When, one winter day, they hinted to the Sultan that it was time to return home to Adrianople, he ironically agreed and, obliging them to follow him, rode back there in twenty continuous hours without once putting his foot to the ground. For his hunts Sultan Mehmed caused pedigree hounds and falcons to be brought from abroad, often from Russia. His hunting exploits were immortalized in poetry, like the military exploits of his more illustrious forebears. He would write accounts of them with his own hand, while exact and detailed records were kept of every beast he killed.

Mehmed could seldom be induced to take part in the successive military campaigns up the Danube which Köprülü Ahmed now started to wage on a major scale. While the Grand Vezir fought, the Sultan hunted. On the first of these, in the summer of 1663, he marched with his armies as far as Adrianople, but there handed over the sacred standard of the Prophet to Köprülü and left them, to engage in the chase. The force that Ahmed had led to Belgrade was the largest and most imposing assembled since Suleiman's time. It waged a campaign remarkable for the support given to the Turks by their Christian vassals in Wallachia and Rumania and by the Hungarian peasantry, to whom they appeared in the guise of liberators from Habsburg tyranny.

Crossing the Danube, his troops soon overran Hungary and Transylvania. On reaching the Drava he demanded payment of tribute, as in Suleiman's reign. When it was refused he proceeded to Buda, then marched northwestward to besiege and capture the important stronghold of Neuhäusel. Here, taking the Austrians by surprise, was a Turkish victory more notable than any in Europe since the battle of Mezo-Keresztes almost seventy years earlier. It was a success which, though it amounted in effect to little more than a spectacular, plunderous raid, encouraged in the mind of Köprülü Ahmed "ambitious thoughts of possessing Vienna itself and outvying the acts of Suleiman the Magnificent."

After wintering in Belgrade, Köprülü renewed his westward march in the following year, preceded by hordes of Tatar irregulars, who laid waste the land and spread fear, like the *akinjis* of Suleiman. Determined now to capture all fortresses on the road to Vienna, he approached, after a few further successes, the key point of Körmend on the River Raab, close to the frontier between Hungary and Austria. Conscious of this threat, the Austrians at Vasvar made overtures for a peaceful settlement, which was in principle agreed. Before it could be ratified, Ahmed moved onward with the intention of crossing the Raab. But here, in the neighbourhood of the Convent of St. Gothard, he was to meet with a resolute and well-planned resistance at the hands of an imperial force weaker in numbers but stronger in arms and more proficient in tactics and techniques than his own. It inflicted upon him a swift and humiliating defeat.

Confidently dispatching half his force across the Raab, Köprülü Ahmed had stayed behind with the other half, intending to cross in the morning. A rainstorm and consequent floods during the night prevented him from doing so. Nonetheless he was so confident as to announce in a dispatch to the Sultan the successful passage of the river, thus prompting premature celebrations of victory in Istanbul. But the advance force, after an initial success, met with defeat, largely at the hands of the Austrian cavalry, which broke the ranks of the Turks and drove them back into the river by the thousand, leaving "the Glory of the Day to the Christians."

Here at St. Gothard in 1664 was a fateful turn of the tide in the conflict between the Ottoman and Habsburg empires, the first great defeat in a pitched battle of the infidel Turks by the Christian forces of Europe. It broke that spell of Turkish victories which had started at Mohacs in 1526, and had persisted at Mezo-Keresztes seventy years later. It first brought home to the Turks the extent of the new military experience, in terms of organization, training, equipment, tactics, and authoritative leadership, which the armies of Europe had gained as a result of the Thirty Years' War. The Ottomans, for all Köprülü's initial success and subsequent optimism conceived in a sixteenth-century spirit, had failed to keep pace with the developments of seventeenth-century warfare. Their armies, compared to those of the West, were becoming, in their adherence to traditional methods, outmoded. For the Turks this was a revelation fraught with discomfort for the future.

At St. Gothard the Austrians had been stiffened for once by a contingent of auxiliaries from France, a country now more advanced than any in Europe in its military techniques. This was sent by Louis XIV in support of a papal Holy League. For the French, though still in principle adhering to the policy of a Turkish alliance, had been close to diplomatic rupture with the Porte since the accession of the first Köprülü, Mehmed. Their ambassador had underrated and slighted him, so that their Capitulations were now in abeyance. At first the French auxiliaries aroused the scorn of Köprülü Ahmed as he watched them advancing with their shaven chins and cheeks and powdered wigs, and he exclaimed: "Who are these young girls?" But they rushed upon the Turks and cut them down, echoing the infidel cries of "Allah!" with their own cries of *"Allons! Allons! Tue! Tue!"* They spread carnage among the Janissaries, who long remembered the cry, repeating it in their own military exercises and talking of the French leader, the Duc de la Feuillade, as "Fouladi"—the Man of Steel.

The losses of the Austrians nonetheless had been heavy, and within ten days of the battle they were ready to confirm the preliminary peace settlement with the Grand Vezir. The result was the Treaty of Vasvar, which in effect renewed the Treaty of Zsitvatörök, and in view of the Austrian victory remained surprisingly favourable to the Ottomans. They retained several of their principal conquests, including Neuhäusel; they achieved the recognition, subject to the payment of tribute, of their vassal prince, Apafy, in Transylvania, which was to be evacuated by both Turks and Austrians. There was to be no eastward extension of the power of the Habsburgs, who were effectively confined to the western and northern parts of the country. Köprülü had at this late date increased the territory of the Sultan. He had won through the arts of diplomacy what he had lost through the acts of war. He returned in triumph to a popular ovation in Istanbul.

Köprülü Ahmed's next undertaking was to complete the conquest, against defenses known to be weaker, of the island of Crete, thus concluding a series of campaigns which had lasted, as a continual drain on the Empire, for twenty-five years. In 1666 he proceeded with large reinforcements to the island, where he remained for three years, free to absent himself from the capital thanks to the services of a Cretan slave girl who now dominated Sultan Mehmed as his favourite and most influential Sultana, who zealously supported Köprülü's cause and thus confirmed his authority in the eyes of her master. So this third stage of the siege of Candia was pressed with little respite throughout summer and winter—"the most impregnable fortress in the world," as Rycaut described it, "strengthened with as much art and industry as the human wit of this age was capable to invent." The art was that of the engineer, with his mines and his countermines, his trenches and traverses, and here the Turks, pioneers of it in the siege of Rhodes, still excelled. Skillfully and inexorably they undermined and burrowed beneath Candia.

At each phase in the campaign the Turks were now able to get naval forces through to the island. The Venetians, for their part, had the aid, in the name of yet another crusade, not only of papal, other Italian and Habsburg imperial forces, but of the French, who had secretly aided them from the start. The "young girls" of St. Gothard, reputed to be the finest flower of French chivalry, sailed with their commander, the Duc de la Feuillade, under the Maltese flag for Candia. Here in a spirit of romantic heroism and in disregard of the orders of the Venetian commander, Morosini, they insisted on making a sally from the fortress, led by monks carrying a crucifix, and killed a quantity of Turks before being overpowered and forced to retreat. In the following year a more substantial French force sailed to Candia under the command of the Duc de Noailles, this time flying the papal flag. Noailles insisted upon an all-French sortie, refusing the aid of Morosini's Venetian troops. When this failed, the French fleet joined the Venetian in a naval bombardment designed to draw the Turks from their trenches before the city. This in its turn failed, partly owing to the explosion of a French ship in the course of it; and the French, now in serious conflict with the Venetians, sailed away home with their army.

Four days later Morosini surrendered the city of Candia, acknowledging that it was no longer tenable. Its siege had lasted longer than the siege of Troy. Köprülü Ahmed granted honourable terms, which were loyally observed. The depleted Venetian garrison were allowed to take with them a portion of their artillery, while the Cretans were left free to seek homes elsewhere. Venice kept ports in the island, which otherwise became Turkish territory, forming a natural barrier across the southern Aegean, making the eastern Mediterranean a Turkish lake. Its Greek Christian inhabitants welcomed the Turks as liberators from the oppressions of Latin Catholic rule; moreover, as time went on they became, to a substantial extent, converts to Islam.

Köprülü Mehmed had bequeathed to his son Ahmed the termination of these two imperial wars, together with a military organization which sought, if not with entire success, to match that of Suleiman. But in fact Ahmed was more than a mere warrior. He had also high qualities as a statesman. As such he has been compared by Turkish historians with Sokollu, Suleiman's last Grand Vezir, who enlarged the Empire and arrested its decay through the period which followed his death. Ahmed's semiliterate father had given him a good education with a training in the law, which he supplemented, as previous Sultans themselves had done, with experience of public affairs, serving as the governor of two successive provinces. He had his father's strength without his cruelty. He relaxed the severity of the Köprülü regime as soon as he felt secure enough to do so, and established an administration which was at once humane, just, and relatively free from corruption. He himself was devoid of cupidity and so immune to bribery that the presentation of a gift, so it was said, predisposed him against rather than in favour of its donor.

A strict Moslem, he was nonetheless free from fanaticism, tolerating the beliefs of others, protecting Christians and Jews from injustice, and abolishing restrictions on the building of churches. Here he was unlike his father, who had banished unorthodox sheikhs and dervishes and hanged the Greek Patriarch for alleged incitement to a Christian revolt. Lucid in judgment, with a direct, incisive mind which saw straight to the root of a problem, Köprülü Ahmed was a man of few words and many good intentions, combining a dignified presence with a polite, modest demeanour, regarded by his people as honourable and true to his word, and for all his qualities winning their respect and affection.

Ahmed's main task in the civil field was to carry to fruition the various reforms which his father had prompted. He introduced measures to assure observance of the laws of Islam and the *kanuns* of the Sultans. He reduced the numbers of the household troops, which had become at once a financial burden and a source of disturbance to the state. He reduced burdens borne by the central treasury, and gave protection to the peasantry by a revised system of taxation and public order. Finally, for all his preoccupation with political and military matters, he found time for the patronage of men of letters, poets and historians, who sought to immortalize his victories and other exploits.

Köprülü Ahmed now sought conquests new. In 1672 he looked beyond the Black Sea toward a front destined in the future to become a major theater of war for the Turks—that of Russia and Poland. He looked in particular toward the Ukraine, which was disputed between the two powers, hence offered a promising field for Turkish intervention. Recently the Russians and Poles had sought to divide between them the territories of the independent and vigorous Cossacks, both in the Ukraine and farther south, around the mouths of the Bug and the Dnieper, which ran into the Black Sea, and to control them as the Russian Tsar controlled those of the Don, farther east. The Cossacks of the Polish Ukraine rebelled robustly against their masters, provoking armed intervention against them by a Polish army under John Sobieski.

The Cossack leader then appealed for aid to the Sultan and offered him suzerainty over his territory. He was honourably received in Istanbul and duly invested by Sultan Mehmed with a banner with two horsetails, as Ottoman sanjak bey of the province of the Ukraine, while the khan of the Crimea in his turn was ordered to give his support to the Cossacks. This action aroused vociferous protests, both from the king of Poland and the Tsar of Russia, who threatened to unite for a war against the Sultan of Turkey. At this the Sublime Porte in its turn haughtily protested, while the Grand Vezir in person wrote in his own hand to the Polish envoy:

> The Cossacks, a free people, submitted to the Poles. But, being unable to endure any longer the cruelty, injustice, oppression and exactions which weighed upon them, they have . . . sought the protection of the Khan of the Crimea, and are now with his support, under the Turkish banner. . . . If the inhabitants of a country, to obtain their freedom, beg for the support of a powerful Sultan, is it prudent to pursue them while under such patronage?

When the king of Poland disregarded this missive, the Sultan in 1672 marched a substantial Turkish army through Moldavia to the banks of the Dniester, where it was joined by the forces of the Tatars. This time the Sultan himself took part in the campaign, accompanying, if not exactly leading, his forces.

Crossing the river, the Turks were soon successful with the capture of two important fortresses. In a humiliating peace settlement at Buczacs the king of Poland ceded the Ukrainian province of Podolia, between the Dnieper and the Dniester, to the Turks, and his portion of the Ukraine to the Cossacks; moreover, he agreed to pay tribute to the Porte. This treaty was repudiated by Sobieski, who fought three more campaigns against the Turks with varying fortunes. But in 1676 he met with final defeat at their hands, conceding in a new treaty at Zurawno more than had initially been promised to them. Ottoman power was thus established for a while to the northwest of the Black Sea, with the opportunity to put pressure on the Poles and to hamper the Ukrainian designs of the Russians.

Such was the achievement of Köprülü Ahmed, with his skilled use of the Empire's new resources. But it was to be short-lived. This was his last campaign. Within a few days of the end of it he was dead at the age of forty-two, from a dropsical condition induced by excessive consumption of wine and brandy—the sole vice of an otherwise exemplary ruler.

((23))

It was generally hoped and anticipated that Köprülü Ahmed —who had only an infant son—would be succeeded as Grand Vezir by his brother, Mustafa Zade. This would have prolonged the family rule of the Köprülüs, which through the past two decades had so revived the declining Empire within and without. But there was now to be a lamentable break in the succession. Sultan Mehmed, in an unfortunate moment of self-assertion, chose to exercise that imperial prerogative which he had held hitherto in abeyance. He appointed to the office of Grand Vezir Ahmed's brother-in-law, who had lately become also his own son-in-law, Kara Mustafa. This created an "interregnum" of thirteen years which was to do irreparable harm to his empire.

"Black Mustafa"—as he was named from his swarthy aspect—was a man inflated with pride and presumptuous ambitions. The ostentation of his way of life, revelling in pompous display, was notorious. His harem was reputed to house fifteen hundred concubines and as many female slaves, with seven hundred Black Eunuchs to attend them. He endeared himself to the Sultan through his array of innumerable horses, hounds, and falcons. As Grand Vezir his cupidity involved him in countless extortions and acts of corruption, selling offices of all kinds without scruple, bargaining with foreign envoys for capitulations, and fixing a price, to his own advantage, for audiences with the Sultan.

Above all Black Mustafa, in his *folie de grandeur,* nourished dreams of world fame as an imperial conqueror. Fanatically anti-Christian, he is said to have repeated the threat of Bayezid I that he would one day stable his horses in St. Peter's at Rome, and that after capturing Vienna he would march to the Rhine to fight Louis XIV. He saw himself reigning as nominal viceroy but actual sovereign of a great European dominion. But as a general he proved to be of remarkably inferior caliber, squandering through his mistakes in the field much of what the Köprülüs, with their military competence and strengthened resources, had gained for the Empire.

Within five years the Ottomans under his leadership had lost their share of the Ukraine, won by Köprülü, to the Russians. This followed two unsuccessful campaigns with heavy losses both in men and artillery, in a harsh alien climate and terrain, against an enemy whom the Turks came increasingly to fear. In 1681 a treaty of peace was signed with the Russians, by which the Turks renounced all claim to the Ukraine and withdrew their troops from the area, with the stipulation that neither side should erect fortresses between the Bug and the Dniester. Thus a fateful bridgehead was lost by the declining Ottoman to the expanding Russian Empire, in a theater of war which was to become progressively more vital in the centuries to come.

This did not greatly concern Kara Mustafa, whose ambitions for conquest lay elsewhere, in the heart of central Europe. His determination was to capture Vienna, as the great Suleiman before him had failed to do. His opportunity arose through a revolt in Hungary, largely inspired by Protestant malcontents against Habsburg Catholic oppression. Its leader, Count Emmerich Tekeli, after inflicting a defeat on the emperor's forces, then rejecting an unacceptable truce, appealed to the Sultan for aid. This he promised, recognizing Tekeli as King of Western Hungary under Ottoman suzerainty. With this backing Tekeli resumed his hostilities. He appealed also for aid to the French. For Louis XIV, seeking to counterbalance the power of the Habsburgs, had already given support against them to Apafy, as prince of Transylvania. Now he gave subsidies to Tekeli, while his envoy at Istanbul promised the Sultan benevolent neutrality, thus encouraging an Ottoman attack against Austria.

When the Austrian envoy to the Porte sought a renewal of Köprülü's Treaty of Vasvar with the emperor, the Grand Vezir rejected his proposals and delivered to him instead what amounted to an ultimatum. This demanded as a condition of peace the surrender of the important fortress of Györ, together with a refund of the expenses he had incurred in preparing for war. To this the Austrian envoy replied: "A castle may be taken by force of arms but not by force of words." Thus war between the Ottoman and the Habsburg empires became once more inevitable. In the autumn of the year 1682 the horsetails of the Sultan's insignia were hoisted before the Seraglio in Istanbul, proclaiming his imminent departure from the city. He left for Adrianople, where by the spring of 1683 a substantial army had been assembled. It included a large force of engineers and artillerymen, with maintenance units, and a host of Crimean Tatar and other irregular horsemen; it was swelled by the usual artisans, tradesmen, and camp followers who, with their pack animals—mules, buffaloes, and camels—always made an Ottoman army look larger than in fact it was.

Such was the last great Moslem force to set forth, in the name of the faith and in the old Ottoman tradition, against Christian Europe. To confront it the Emperor Leopold mustered under a skilled general, Duke Charles of Lorraine, an army inferior in numbers but fortified by the promise of subsidies from the Pope, together with armed support not only from the German princes but also, in breach of his recent treaty with the Porte, from King John Sobieski of Poland. This confounded the schemes of King Louis XIV, who had sought to prevent such an alliance, nourishing designs of his own on the Holy Roman Empire at Leopold's expense. Hence, as before, he was not ill-disposed to a Turco-Austrian confrontation.

Thus in the spring of 1683 the Ottoman army marched forward, headed by the Sultan, who on reaching Belgrade transferred its command, with the standard of the Prophet, to Kara Mustafa. At Essek the Grand Vezir was joined by the dissident Hungarian forces of Tekeli, marching under a contrasting Christian standard with the inscription in Latin "For God and Country," and bearing the name of KRUCZES, or "men of the Cross." Here, in the eyes of the Grand Vezir, was a repetition of history, recalling the encounter as allies of Sultan Suleiman and John Zapolya. Kara Mustafa had not yet openly declared his intention of besieging Vienna itself. Between Buda and the Austrian frontier there lay a stretch of imperial Hungary, screening the approach to the capital at points where the Danube was joined by its several tributaries. It was supposed that before advancing on Vienna itself, he would reduce these enemy garrisons, of which the most important were Györ and Körmend.

Before Raab, the Grand Vezir held a council of war with his commanders, who included the khan of the Crimea. At this, so it is said, he was strongly advised by Ibrahim, the veteran pasha of Buda, to pursue such precautionary tactics. In support of his argument the pasha recounted the fable of a king who placed a pile of gold in the center of a carpet, then offered it to any man who could take it without treading on the carpet. The winner was one who rolled up the carpet from the edge, until he reached and was able to grab the prize. Just so, Ibrahim insisted, should Kara Mustafa pursue the prize of Vienna, first "rolling up" this hostile frontier region by securing control of its fortresses, and postponing any attack on the city itself until the autumn or the following spring. Then it would surely fall to him of its own accord.

The Grand Vezir answered him: "You are an old man of eighty—your mind is defective." The khan of the Crimea, Selim Ghirai, voiced the same view as the pasha, thus incurring henceforward the enmity of the Grand Vezir. This course had other supporters. But Kara Mustafa revealed his determination to march directly on Vienna itself. For after its capture "all the Christians would obey the Ottomans." He ordered his engineers to construct pontoon bridges across the Raab. He crossed it with his army and at once marched westward. Ibrahim Pasha remained behind to take care of the stores. A small force was left, as a feint to contain Györ. The Tatar irregulars were

Rhine R.
Elbe R.
Vistula R.
Dnieper R.
Warsaw
Kiev
UKRAINE
POLAND
Frankfurt
THE EMPIRE
Prague
GALICIA
Brno
PODOLIA
Bug
Munich
Linz
R. Danube
Vienna
Györ
Vasvar
Gran
Erlau
Keresztes
TRANSYLVANIA
R. Pruth
Dniester
BESSARABIA
MOLDAVIA
STYRIA
Buda
Pesth
Körmend
St. Gothard
HUNGARY
Grosswardein
Isonzo R.
R. Piave
Tisza R.
Szeged
Mohacs
R. Drava
Venice
Trieste
R. Sava
Fiume
Temesvar
Peterwardein
Karlowitz
Slankamen
R. Tagliamento
CROATIA
Belgrade
Semlin
BOSNIA
RUMANIA
Hirsova
Orsova
Bucharest
DOBRUJA
Semendria
WALLACHIA
R. Danube
Silistria
Sarajevo
SERBIA
Vidin
Rahova
Rustchuk
Toulon
DALMATIA
HERZE-GOVINA
Morava R.
Nicopolis
Plevna
Varna
NOVI BAZAR
Nish
Corsica
ITALY
Ragusa
MONTENEGRO
Kossovo
Tirnovo
Sofia
BULGARIA
Cattaro
Kumanovo
Philippopolis
Kirk Kilissa
Scutari
Struma
Maritza
Adrianople
Croia
ALBANIA
Vardar
Rhodope Mts.
RUMELIA
Istanbul
Tirana
Monastir
Drama
THRACE
Mudanya
Sardinia
Brindisi
Taranto
Otranto
MACEDONIA
Salonica
Thasos
Lecce
Athos
Imbros
Gallipoli
KARASI
EPIRUS
Janina
Lemnos
Corfu
THESSALY
Parga
Lesbos
Prevesa
Negroponte
Messina
Lepanto
Livadia
Chios
Izmir
Mesolonghi
Bône
Bizerta
Patras
Athens
Samos
La Goletta
Sicily
Corinth
MOREA
Milas
Tunis
GREECE
Bodrum
Cos
Navarino
Modon
Coron
Monemvasia
Cerigo
TUNISIA
Malta
Candia
Sfax
Gafsa
MEDITERRANEAN SEA
Crete
Jerba
Boundary of Ottoman Empire
Vassal states
Tripoli

let loose with the forces of Tekeli to ravage the lands before and around him—to set the "Turk-bells" ringing once more the alarm through central Europe.

Kara Mustafa thus appeared with the bulk of his army before the walls of Vienna on July 13. When his batteries were in position the customary message, demanding surrender and conversion to Islam, or evacuation with a safe-conduct to the citizens, was conveyed to the walls by a Turkish officer and handed over to a soldier for transmission to Count Stahremberg, the governor of the city. It evoked no reply. The emperor himself with his court had withdrawn westward to Passau, and his commander-in-chief, Charles of Lorraine, with some two-thirds of the small Austrian army, to Linz, up the Danube. The remaining third was left within the walls to reinforce the garrison, which nonetheless amounted only to some twelve thousand.

The Ottoman camp, pitched to the west of the city in the form of a crescent moon, was in itself a city of canvas, with twenty-five thousand tents and fifty thousand baggage carts. In the center of it reigned Black Mustafa, directing the conduct of the siege and the business of government from a concourse of tents rivalling in splendour the memorable pavilions of Suleiman. For the repulse of the Turkish armies and the salvation of his capital the Emperor Leopold relied largely on his allies in Europe—the Electors of Bavaria and Saxony, and above all King John Sobieski of Poland. But he had called for their help only when the threat to Vienna itself became imminent, and it was slow to materialize. On the other hand Kara Mustafa was slow to forestall it, as he might well have done, by storming the walls with his superior forces in a swift all-out assault. Here it seems that he was influenced by avarice. If the city fell by assault, the booty within it would fall to his plundering soldiers. If it capitulated, the booty would be all his own, as the representative of the Sultan.

When the siege began it was soon evident that the defenders were superior in artillery, with more and better guns than the besiegers. Kara Mustafa had no heavy artillery, thus repeating the omission of Suleiman, who could not transport it this far. He used only guns of light and medium caliber, effective enough against adversaries in the field but inadequate against strong fortress walls. Moreover, much of their ammunition, manufactured at Buda, was poor, and shells failed to explode. Treating artillery as an auxiliary, the Turks chose to rely rather on mining, at which they had excelled in sieges elsewhere, notably at Candia.

Kara Mustafa first encircled the greater part of the city and the surrounding countryside, sealing it off from the forces of the enemy over a long stretch of the Danube. Then he started, with the aid of Christian captive labour, to build a network of trenches, approaching the walls and their bastions to mine them at various points. But the stonework was solid and the defenders were courageous, not content to remain static but making vigorous sorties, moreover always quick to repair any damages to their defenses. Often the Turks with their sabers were ineffective in assaults against the Germans with their halberds, scythes, and battle-axes. But their mines made breaches in the walls. On September 4, following a major explosion, they drove Stahremberg's men from the ravelin, then poured through a wide breach into the Burg, calling upon Allah as they waved their standards and brandished their weapons. After a two-hour fight with heavy losses on both sides, they were driven back. Nonetheless the situation of the defenders was critical.

But at this moment came news that at last the reinforcing army of the Poles was at hand. The advance of King John Sobieski, starting from Warsaw and delaying at Cracow, had been as slow as Mustafa's attack. En route he met with little resistance. Soon he was crossing the Danube by a bridge of boats, to link up with the main Austrian army of the Duke of Lorraine and with the contingents from Bavaria and Saxony. After a council of war they marched for three days—again without interference—up difficult forest paths to the heights of the Kahlenberg, commanding Vienna, which they found to their surprise to be unoccupied. From here Sobieski looked down on the besieged city, whose standing walls, surrounded by a maze of mining trenches, were intermittently broken by piles of rubble; and on his enemy's camp, still spread openly around it without entrenchment or concentration of his forces. At this he commented with confidence: "This man is badly encamped. He knows nothing of war, we shall certainly defeat him."

Kara Mustafa, intent on the siege, had indeed failed to plan in advance for the defense of his besiegers against such a relief force. The Ottoman camp was unfortified, and largely unprotected either by observation posts on the ridges or cavalry patrols on the plain. Moreover, even now, when Mustafa knew that the arrival of the relieving army was imminent, he made no immediate move to transfer any part of his forces to meet its attack. He neglected to prevent either the Austrian or the Polish troops from crossing the Danube, an operation which called for the dispatch of a well-armed force under his own command, but which he left to the Tatar khan of the Crimea on the spot, blaming him afterward as a scapegoat for his failure to oppose them. Similarly he made no attempt either to check the enemy's advance up the steep rocky flanks of the Kahlenberg, or to forestall him by guarding its heights. Only when the crest and the slopes of it burst into flame, with the enemy's rockets and bonfires, did he realize that it was too late to do so. All he could do now was to march a force to the lower slopes of the range and await Sobieski's headlong, downhill onslaught.

Before dawn on September 12 it came, the disciplined Christians descending in exact order of battle and precedence, but seeming to the Turks like "a flood of black pitch coming down the mountain consuming everything it touched." Kara Mustafa believed that a force of cavalry would be adequate to repulse it. Only when the khan of the Crimea urged the use of the Janissaries did he detach a contingent of them for the purpose, leaving their main force still in the trenches before the city. Nor was there now time to bring up adequate artillery.

The ensuing battle, with the Turkish forces thus caught between the two fires of a well-armed garrison and a well-led relief force, lasted throughout that day. At first it took the form of a confused series of encounters amid the rocks and the ravines of the hillside. Then down in the plain, following a fierce engagement between the Turkish and the Polish cavalry, with that of the Germans, Sobieski led his best troops directly against the Turkish center and into the camp, where the Grand Vezir's tent was conspicuous. At the sight of the Christian conqueror in person the Tatar khan exclaimed: "By Allah! The King is really among us," and with his men galloped off in flight. The great mass of the Ottoman army broke and fled in confusion, leaving ten thousand dead on the battlefield.

The Janissaries in their trenches before the city, who had risked no assault yet would not retreat, were cut to pieces between its defenders in front of them and the victorious Poles in their rear. In the general panic the whole of the Ottoman camp was abandoned with all its artillery, a hundred thousand oxen, and such spoils as jewelled weapons and girdles, rich carpets and tissues and furs, which became the perquisites of Sobieski and his army. But to their disappointment they found little coin or bullion, since the Turks had grabbed it to carry off with them, just in time. Curiosities among the booty included a newly beheaded female ostrich; a parrot which obstinately evaded capture; an aviary of other birds in gilded cages; and above all large supplies of coffee, which led to the establishment of Vienna's first coffeehouse.

The Grand Vezir fled in haste with the rest, rescuing only the standard of the Prophet and a substantial sum of money, leaving his sumptuous tent to the Polish king, who dispatched to his queen as a token of victory a golden stirrup from Mustafa's charger. Boasting in an accompanying letter of his capture of the infidel's camp with all its riches, he related in detail the precious fruits of his own personal plunder, then concluded: "We are driving before us a host of camels, mules and Turkish prisoners." Count Stahremberg came to the Ottoman tent to pay his respects to Sobieski as Vienna's deliverer. Before the tent was a great banner of cloth of gold, between gilded staves, bearing the horsetails of the Sultan, and next day this was borne through the city in triumph, while the Christian commanders rode in a victory procession behind it.

Suleiman the Magnificent, close on a century and a half earlier, had failed in his siege of Vienna, largely through problems of transport and shortage of supplies. But he had withdrawn from its walls with his army intact. Black Mustafa, on the other hand, had fought and lost a pitched battle in the field against an enemy inferior in numbers; and his army, insofar as it survived, was reduced to a fugitive rabble. His was the defeat which in the eyes of Europe broke the prestige of the Ottoman Turks once and for all as a conquering nation.

After the fall of the city the Christian armies, under Sobieski and Lorraine, were quick to pursue the fugitive Turks. Kara Mustafa in his flight paused at Raab, to reassemble the remnants of his forces and redistribute his commands. In a rage he accused his enemy, and the opponent of his tactics, Ibrahim Pasha, the governor of Buda, of deliberate disloyalty in fleeing first from the field with his troops and thus precipitating the flight of the rest. He then ordered his execution, together with that of other high-ranking officers selected as scapegoats.

The routed army struggled on toward Buda, continually harassed by the Austrian militia from the various fortresses left in enemy hands, while its Tatar irregulars ravaged the Hungarian lands throughout the retreat, as they had done in the advance. In a rear-guard action at Parkany, the pursuing Poles, first checked and caught in an ambush, were impetuously attacked by the Turks, but in a murderous encounter drove them back to the banks of the Danube. As they crowded onto a bridge of boats it collapsed from the weight of their fugitives, of whom seven thousand were either drowned or slaughtered. This led to the siege and surrender of Gran, which became a rampart no longer of the imperial Turks, as its initial capture by Suleiman had made it, but of the imperial Austrians and Germans. The Turkish forces then withdrew to Belgrade, whence the Sultan had previously withdrawn to Adrianople. From here he now sent his Grand Chamberlain with orders to return with the head of the Grand Vezir. So Kara Mustafa was executed in his turn, as he had executed so many others. Such was the fate of the vain, covetous, flamboyant minister whose military ineptitude had brought upon the Ottoman Empire its greatest defeat. Such was the end of the fateful year of the last siege of Vienna. Sixteen more years, nonetheless, were to pass before the end of the war it had launched.

Christendom greeted the news of the relief of the imperial city with rapture. Here at long last must be the death knell of Moslem aggression, silencing forever the alarm of the Turk-bells in Europe. Scriptural prophecies were recalled, foretelling the end of the Ottoman Empire in 1691. Surely this had indeed come to pass. The Pope, who had prayed for a Christian victory, celebrated it with a service of thanksgiving, then urged yet another—the fourteenth—crusade to clinch it, as the allied commanders resolved to press home their advantage. His long-cherished plans for a Holy League now sprang into life with its formation at Linz in the spring of 1684, comprising the three Christian powers of Austria, Poland, and Venice—with the hope of additional cooperation from Persia. Each power would strike in the region which most concerned its interests—Austria into Hungary and the mid-Danube basin in the direction of the Balkan passes; Poland southward to the Black Sea coast and along it; Venice in Dalmatia, Greece, and the islands. A medal was struck commemorating the harmony and concord of the three "heroes" of the League, the Emperor Leopold, Sobieski King of Poland, and the Doge of Venice. In fact, as always in the past, the political interests of the three soon conflicted over their mutual frontiers and spheres of interest. But for some five years the League seemed effective enough as a military instrument.

Initiating its planned campaign in 1684, the Republic of Venice, for the first time in its history, declared open war against the Sultan. The Venetians under Morosini fitted out a fleet, with the aid of Malta and Tuscany, which captured Prevesa and the offshore island of Santa Maura; then landed with some local corsair support in Dalmatia, and launched land forces into Albania and Bosnia. In the following year Morosini accomplished the conquest of the Morea, deriving support, despite firm Turkish action, from the obstreperous inhabitants of the Mani, and winning for himself the epithet of "Peloponnesiaco."

A year later his land forces, composed largely of German contingents under a Swedish commander, advanced northward to Corinth, then besieged and captured Athens. In the course of the Venetian bombardment the Parthenon, carefully preserved for two thousand years past, was hit by a shell. This blew up a powder magazine concealed there by the Turks and destroyed a large part of the temple, thus bequeathing to posterity a ruin. Afterward the Venetians evacuated Athens for fear of reprisals from the Turkish garrison still at Thebes, but removed the lion of the Piraeus which now adorns, with a lioness from Delos, the Arsenal of Venice.

The second of the three "heroic" Christian allies, the Poles, failed in Podolia before Kamieniec, which remained a Turkish fortress. But Sobieski had more ambitious designs, farther afield, in Moldavia and Transylvania, which he aspired to control; and here he soon came into conflict with the interests of his ally the emperor, who was quick to assert rival claims in the area. He thus failed to obtain imperial support for a campaign in Moldavia in 1686, which he fought with inconclusive results.

Meanwhile, in 1684 the Austrian forces had occupied much of Croatia, which was soon to become an Austrian province. At the same time, advancing from Gran, the Austrians recaptured Neuhäusel against a fierce resistance from the Ottoman garrison. A year later they renewed their siege of Buda, which the Turks, who were fighting a series of determined rear-guard actions, made three attempts to relieve. But it fell to the imperial troops, with the slaughter of its commanders and garrison. Thus in 1686, after a century and a half of Turkish rule, having survived six separate sieges, the city of Buda, to the delight of all Europe, passed finally into Hungarian hands.

A year later, in a counteroffensive, the new Grand Vezir, Suleiman, led a large Ottoman army toward the Drava. Here he encountered the forces of Charles of Lorraine on the historic field of Mohacs, where those of Sultan Suleiman had won their first crucial battle for Hungary. Now history was reversed with a disastrous defeat, in which the Grand Vezir's army was routed with the loss of some twenty thousand men. The bulk of Hungary was thus now secured for the Emperor Leopold, who crowned as its king his eldest son, Joseph, later in his turn to become emperor. For the effective defense of the recaptured territories it now remained only to recover Belgrade, which would serve as their bulwark. This was achieved within a year by Prince Ludwig of Bavaria, after only a brief resistance. Its recapture was followed by that of other key fortresses in the Danube basin, pushing the campaign of imperial reconquest eastward into Bulgaria as far as Nicopolis, and into Serbia as far southward as Nish.

Meanwhile, the defeat at Mohacs had provoked mutiny in the Ottoman army and an insurrection in the capital, which led to the deposition—but not to the execution—of Mehmed IV. He retired into exile, where he was forbidden to indulge in his one favourite pastime of hunting. The elder of his two brothers was brought out from the Cage to succeed him as Suleiman II. Proving, despite his seclusion, to be a ruler more responsible than his brother, moreover seriously concerned to quell the continuing and mounting disorders, he convened an extraordinary council of the Divan at Adrianople. Accepting the advice of his counsellors, he appointed as Grand Vezir the third of the Köprülüs, Mustafa Zade, who had been passed over in favour of Kara Mustafa on the death of his brother, Ahmed, thirteen years earlier. Accepting office on the same absolute terms as his father and brother, he summoned to a Divan the chief imperial dignitaries and warned them severely of the acute perils confronting the Empire: "If we go on in this way," he predicted, "another campaign will see the enemy encamped before the gates of Istanbul."

Animated by the spirit and well trained in the methods of his "dynasty," Köprülü III, as he thus became, set vigorously to work, replenishing the treasury, reforming the administration, reviving and strengthening the army for a campaign to recover lost ground. Consistently invoking the name and the laws of the Prophet, he inspired the Turks for a spell against the Habsburgs. As it happened the emperor at this moment, in 1688, became diverted by events further afield. These sprang from the English Revolution and the emergence of William of Orange. With his Grand Alliance, involving the powers of the League of Augsburg, he was soon at war against Louis XIV, requiring the aid of the emperor in a second front, to which he sent contingents under his two commanders, Charles of Lorraine and Ludwig of Bavaria. This gave the Ottomans a breathing space. When the French ambassador urged Köprülü that the Porte should refuse recognition to William of Orange, he rejected such a course, reasonably insisting that it was not for the Ottomans, who had so often dethroned their sovereigns, to contest the right of the English to dethrone theirs. He was, however, only too willing to oblige the ambassador in his second request, to make war against the emperor.

In 1690, bearing the Prophet's sacred standard, he did so. After a series of preparatory operations in which the Tatars were involved, Köprülü unleashed Tekeli once more into Transylvania, where he created a well-timed diversion. Then at the head of his main army he advanced into Serbia, recaptured Nish with other fortresses and a large stretch of lost territory, and laid siege to Belgrade, which capitulated once more with unexpected abruptness, largely owing to the explosion under fire of a large powder magazine within the fortress. Judging that it was by now too late in the season for large-scale campaigning, he sent a small force into Transylvania to reinforce Tekeli in his drive against the Austrians. Köprülü Mustafa Zade then left a strong garrison in Belgrade and returned to Istanbul, where the Sultan staged for his Grand Vezir a triumphal reception.

Throughout the winter Köprülü organized an even larger army, which in the summer of 1691 marched from Belgrade up the Danube. A short distance upstream, at Slankamen, it encountered the army of the experienced Prince Ludwig, descending from Peterwardein. The Grand Vezir consulted his own generals as to whether to take the offensive or remain on the defensive, waiting for the enemy to attack. They advised delay in the expectation of Tatar reinforcements. But Köprülü, whose military judgment was less sure than his administrative skill, decided on an attack. Reproaching the bearded veteran commander who opposed it as more of a phantom than a man, he cried, "Let the cannon advance!"

From the start the fierce battle went badly for the Turks despite the fact that their boats had won the advantage on the river. Their successive impetuous charges were met by the deadly, sustained, disciplined fire of an enemy superior in musketry. When defeat appeared imminent Köprülü himself, hoping in the last resort to save the day, led a desperate charge. Calling upon Allah, he cleared his way with a drawn sword, flanked by his guards, through the ranks of the Austrians. The heroic gesture was in vain. Their ranks stood firm. He was hit in the forehead and killed by a bullet. His guards saw him fall, lost courage, and fled. His commanders, who might for a while have concealed the news of his death from the troops, broke into lamentations and allowed it to spread, thus undermining morale and creating a general panic. The army fled in total disorder, abandoning its camp to the enemy, with the usual haul of artillery.

The Austrians, if at substantial cost, had gained a decisive victory. For the Ottomans, the death in battle after a mere two years in power of their last shining hope, Köprülü the Virtuous, was a crucial disaster. Hungary was lost to them. So, with the accompanying defeat and expulsion of Tekeli, was Transylvania. Sultan Suleiman II had died soon after the start of the campaign after a reign of four years. His brother was brought from the Cage to succeed him as Ahmed II, reigning for four years more under a burden of shame and despair which was to hasten his end.

Only the operations in the Aegean now provided the Turks with a grain of consolation. The Venetians had found the Morea hard to hold in the continuing presence of the Turkish pasha at Thebes, and had failed in their attempts either to recover a base in Crete or to capture an Aegean island. But in 1693 Morosini, now of a great age, became Doge and commander of all the armed forces of Venice. He resolved on the capture of Chios, an island off Smyrna which was almost as important a base for the Turks as the Dardanelles. Having planned the operation, he died before its execution. The Venetian fleet, however, captured Chios with the aid of papal and Maltese squadrons, greatly to the distress of the already grieved and now ailing Sultan Ahmed. But the Venetian garrison held it only until the following year, when a Turkish fleet drove off a reinforcing Venetian squadron and recaptured the island. This opportune victory was hailed with celebrations in Istanbul, though the Sultan did not live to hear the good news of it. He had died meanwhile of the dropsical condition that had afflicted both his brothers, to be succeeded by his nephew, Mustafa II.

Credit for this Ottoman naval recovery was due to a new chief admiral, a Barbary corsair named Hassan and nicknamed Mezzomorto, since in his youth he had reappeared unexpectedly in Algiers, having been left for dead during an engagement with the Venetians. By active if otherwise indecisive operations against them he now brought a spell of new life and hope to Turkish naval power in the eastern Mediterranean.

On the other hand, this was counterbalanced in the Black Sea by new defeats at the hands of the new enemy, Russia. Hitherto, thanks to the Crimean Tatars, the Turks had enjoyed some success in this region against both Poles, whom they defeated in 1688, and Russians, who failed in two successive campaigns in the Crimea, instigated by Sobieski, to make headway against the Tatars. But there had now come to power an adversary more formidable, Peter the Great. In 1695 he renewed the Russian war in the Crimea on a new strategic basis. His objective was now Azov, at the mouth of the Don. First he captured four Turkish forts on the lower Dnieper. In the following year he captured Azov itself, with the aid not only of a shallow-draft flotilla but of a seagoing fleet which he had built up far from the river and placed in the hands of experienced commanders and crews. He then set up a naval station nearby at Taganrog. Here he carried out a major shipbuilding program, assembling technicians, engineers, and shipwrights from among Austrian, Dutch, Italian, and English experts, recruiting not only Slav but foreign seamen, and launching a squadron of vessels on the lines of the ships of the Barbary corsairs. His fleet was still confined to the Sea of Azov, barred from the Black Sea by the Turkish fortress on the Straits of Kertch. But the possession and control of this outlet were now his determined objectives. He was establishing for the first time a degree of Russian naval power fraught with menace for the Ottoman Empire.

Meanwhile, in the central theater of war, the new Sultan Mustafa II was proving to be a young man of spirit and energy, no mere hunter like his father, Mehmed IV, but a warrior burning with ardour to revive in his own person the martial traditions of his great Ottoman forebears. Three days after Sultan Ahmed's death, he issued a remarkable and outspoken document, a Hatti-Sherif, or imperial writ, which denounced the ways of his recent predecessors and proposed that he should lead his armies in person against the Habsburg emperor. He declared himself resolved to fight them in person.

Upon this the Grand Vezir, the other vezirs, his ulema, the lieutenants and the aghas of his armies were ordered to assemble and seriously to consider whether he should personally open hostilities against the emperor or remain in Adrianople. After deliberating for three days, the Divan decided against the assumption of the command by the Sultan—who was in any case inexperienced in military matters—on the grounds both of danger to his person and expense to the state.

To this Mustafa's reply was a brief declaration: "I persist in marching." He did so in 1696, to the enthusiasm of troops for so long unused to being led in the field by their own revered Sultan. He led an army from Belgrade to capture several small fortresses and to repulse the siege of Temesvar, by the Duke of Saxony. Since the season was late, he proceeded no farther but returned to Istanbul. Here he received an appropriate welcome from the officials who had discouraged his enterprise, and proceeded in triumph to the Seraglio to the accompaniment of music and gunfire, with the prisoners—three hundred of them, all announced to the public as generals—and various trophies which his army had captured.

In the following year, full of hope for another successful campaign, he again marched with an army to Belgrade. But this time he was confronted by the emperor's new and brilliant commander, Prince Eugen of Savoy. Moreover, his own commanders, in repeated councils of war, were deeply divided in their opinions as to the line of advance to pursue—whether westward into Slavonia or northward into Hungary—and the Sultan was indecisive and irresolute. Finally it was decided to march northward up the valley of the Tisza and to cross it at Zenta.

But Prince Eugen, learning from a prisoner of war, under the threat of death, of the Sultan's decision, made a series of resolute forced marches to forestall his crossing. He arrived at Zenta with a large army when the Turks, who had erected a temporary bridge, were halfway across the river. The Sultan with his cavalry and most of his artillery were already on the left bank, the rest of the artillery with his infantry still entrenched on the right bank. Had the Turks, with their infantry and artillery support, attacked Prince Eugen's army at once, when it was still incomplete and not yet ready for battle, they might have driven him back. As it was, discord still reigned among their officers; the Sultan remained on the left bank; and the infantry made no move from their trenches, enabling Eugen to complete his preparations for an attack. Though only two hours were left to him before sunset, and though a courier had arrived from Vienna with orders not to risk a battle, he was a man always ready to take chances, and in a spirit of bold decision disregarded the order.

Drawing up his forces in the form of a half-moon before the semicircle of the enemy trenches, he launched a concerted attack from left, right, and center against the whole Turkish line. The result was, as Eugen described it, "a frightful blood-bath" and a swift defeat for the Turks. Their troops fell into confusion, their commanders remained disunited, a body of Janissaries mutinied and turned on their officers to slaughter them. More than twenty thousand Turks perished, including the Grand Vezir, four other vezirs, a large number of pashas, and thirty Aghas of the Janissaries. Another ten thousand men were drowned while attempting to cross the river, and hardly more than a thousand succeeded in doing so. Eugen's men, so he reported to the Emperor, "could stand on the dead bodies as though on an island." All was over by nightfall.

The Sultan, from the opposite bank of the river, watched the destruction of his army in helpless dismay, then retreated with his cavalry to Temesvar and so to Belgrade and Istanbul. Prince Eugen was prevented, by problems of supply and the onset of bad weather, from following up his victory. But he had captured, quite apart from money and arms, nine thousand wagons, sixty thousand camels, fifteen hundred head of cattle, seven hundred horses—and the Great Seal of the Grand Vezir, the symbol of the Sultan's authority, which had never before fallen into enemy hands. The discouraged young Sultan Mustafa was never again to appear in the field in command of an army. His gallant attempt, without military experience or the inherited skills of his forebears, to pit himself against the seasoned commanders of a revived western Europe, and thus to emerge as the final famed saviour of his country, had pathetically failed.

He fell back once again on the Köprülü family to restore Ottoman fortunes, and nominated as Grand Vezir Köprülü Hussein, a son of the elder brother of Mehmed and cousin of Ahmed. As the fourth of his line he did his best to restore the administrative and economic situation at home. But in Europe there was now little left to be done. Since the siege of Vienna the Habsburg imperial forces had won nine major victories and captured nine major fortresses. If Hussein still prepared in a precautionary spirit for war, he was, as a former governor of Belgrade, familiar enough with the superiority of the imperial armies to advocate peace; and peace was at last imminent.

The moment had arrived when an end to the long war suited not only the defeated Turks—who had sought it at intervals from the start as they fought their courageous rear-guard action—but their victorious European enemies. Venice was exhausted. Poland, with the death of Sobieski in 1696, was fading out of the picture. The Emperor Leopold was preoccupied with European commitments, notably now the impending War of the Spanish Succession. He was moreover inclined, in a realistic spirit, to appraise and consolidate the conquests of Ottoman territory with which the war had enriched his empire, rather than pursue ambitious dreams of wider conquest through a march to the Bosporus. Only Peter the Great, for the first time starting on that career of Russian aggression which was henceforward to plague the Ottoman Empire, sought to prolong the war. He paid a visit to Vienna to put pressure on the emperor for an alliance to do so. But he was too late in the day. For meanwhile, overtures for peace had been initiated by two powers not directly involved in the war—England and Holland.

English relations with the Porte had hitherto been concerned mainly with matters of commerce—in particular with the protection of English vessels against attacks by the Barbary corsairs, and at the time of the Cretan war against their attempted conscription by the Turks into service against Venice. During the Civil War at home, English prestige at the Porte had been lowered by the presence of rival ambassadors from both sides. But now, with the accession of William III, the situation had changed. Already, with Holland, he had pressed for peace with the Turks in the interests of his war against Louis XIV. This was now at an end. But it was still in the interests of Britain and Holland, both politically and commercially, to prevent France from emerging as the successor to the mercantile empire of Venice. This Louis XIV's representative at the Porte was seeking to achieve, by inducing the Sultan to expel all Venetians from his dominions. Moreover, the war of the Holy League had seriously damaged the English Levant trade, through a decline in the demand at the Sultan's court for luxury goods from England.

Thus the English ambassador, Lord Paget, and his Dutch colleague, Jacob Colyer, now offered to act as mediators for a peace treaty between the Porte and the Christian powers on the basis of *uti possidetis.* This meant that each should keep the territory it now held, and thus in principle the treaty would ratify all European conquests of Turkish territory. Köprülü Hussein summoned a council of state, and a few days later the Sultan put before Paget, for transmission to the king of England, counterproposals involving specific modifications and especially the restoration to Turkey of Transylvania. The Anglo-Dutch mediation was nonetheless accepted.

Thus a peace conference was held in the last months of 1698 at Karlowitz, in Croatia, on the right bank of the Danube. It took place in a hall especially designed to neutralize differences of precedence between victors and vanquished, with four equally placed entrances for the four powers. To these Russia was added at the request of the emperor.

Peter the Great, with his naval designs on the Straits of Kertch, leading into the Black Sea, was not satisfied with a settlement that allowed him only Azov and the adjoining districts already in his possession, and would sign no more than a truce for two years. Effectively isolated at the conference, he became embittered against the Habsburgs for "taking no more notice of him than a dog," and leaving him to "come off with empty pockets." The other powers, after long and often acrimonious negotiations, agreed to treaties of twenty-five years and upward, involving only minor modifications of the principle of *uti possidetis.* The Habsburg empire retained Slavonia, Transylvania, a large section of Hungary without Temesvar, and a stretch of territory east of the Tisza, leaving the Turks with about one-third of their previous Hungarian possessions and thus becoming now finally established at the gates of the Balkans. Poland regained Podolia, Kamieniec, and the western Ukraine, with a stretch of territory east of the Tisza, but withdrew from Moldavia. Venice retained the Morea, the island of Santa Maura, and most of her conquests in Dalmatia and Albania, but relinquished conquered territories north of the Isthmus of Corinth. The Turks refused to give up Tekeli, the

Hungarian rebel now a refugee in Istanbul, to the Austrians, but removed him to Asia Minor, at a safe distance from the imperial frontiers, where his wife, with her confiscated dowry returned to her, was permitted by the emperor to join him. The Treaty of Karlowitz was signed on January 26, 1699, at an hour selected by the Turks for astrological reasons. Its signature was announced by the firing of cannon which echoed, for once peacefully, from the Danube fortresses of Peterwardein and Belgrade.

Such, as the seventeenth century drew to its close, was the end of an era in the history of the Ottoman Empire. No longer was it to be accounted an aggressive, expanding power, as the Christian powers had known and feared it for more than three centuries past. Once and for all, though it remained strong in Asia, its period of retraction in Europe had started, to continue with a series of defeats marked by a series of progressively more unfavourable treaties. Definitely there would be no return to the great days of the conquerors. By the European statesmen the inferiority of the Ottoman Empire to Europe and increasing dependence upon it was henceforward accepted as a political fact.

Once and for all the power of the West, with its rising nation-states, had outstripped the power of the East. The gap between them was to widen from now onward, not only in military standards, but in the pattern of economic and social development which underlay and conditioned them. Internally the Ottoman Empire was, in modern terms, backward; its evolution, in the face of its continuing decline, remained obstinately slow and indeed at periods deliberately static. Internationally its future status was thus to be a matter of concern, no longer in military but increasingly in diplomatic terms. No more a danger in itself, the Ottoman Empire could become so, through its very weakness, as the instrument of another power bent on aggression. Such now, at the dawn of the eighteenth century, was imperial Russia.

PART

V

RUSSIAN RIVALRY

((24))

Peter the Great was an absolute monarch, comparable to Mehmed, the conqueror of Byzantium, two and a half centuries earlier. As emperor of the "third Rome," presuming to be not only the "Sovereign and Autocrat of all Russia" but "the new Tsar Constantine for the new city of Constantinople," he aspired, under the insignia of the double-headed eagle, to reconquer it from the Ottoman Turks. Supreme ruler, as the Sultan had been, of a military state, divinely instituted and geared to imperial conquest, Peter was well launched on an aggressive policy of widespread expansion in Europe and Asia, which successive tsars were to pursue through the centuries to come. Imperial Russia threatened to be an enemy more formidable than any the Ottomans had yet encountered. For she was a united, nationalistic power such as the rest of Christian Europe, with its disparate religious, political, and national interests, had never succeeded in becoming; a power endowed with immense territorial and human resources; a power moreover enjoying, through identity of faith, a strong potential hold over the European subjects of her infidel enemy.

Above all, Peter the Great was a man of the present, while the Ottomans had remained men of the past. The earlier Sultans had triumphed in unity through the adoption and adaptation of institutions and instruments, essentially of the East, at a time of its superiority to the West. They derived experience first from the pagan nomadic way of life on the Asiatic steppes, then from that of the settled civilizations of medieval Islam. They improved upon these to create, through the centralized organization of manpower and resources, an enlightened, well-ordered state with a well-disciplined professional army. Medieval Europe, still geared, with its city-states and feudal principalities, to the fragmentations of an outmoded and ill-disciplined society, had proved unable effectively to resist this.

But now, with the process of evolution and the passage of time, the tide had turned. The West had become stronger than the East. Moreover, poised between the two and ready to strike, was this new imperial conqueror, a leader of vision, resolution, and energy, the Tsar Peter I of Russia. Determined to achieve victory for a people still primitive, over the Ottomans now in decline, he opted at home for a policy of Westernization. His first lesson was learned when as a boy he witnessed and endured a savage *coup d'état* by the Muscovite equivalent of the Janissaries, the *streltsy*. When they mutinied six years later, in 1698, he destroyed the entire force, quite as savagely. They were, as he saw them, "in truth nothing but begetters of evil, and not soldiers." Their removal opened the way to a major reorganization, modernization, and expansion of the Russian army, through a new establishment of guard regiments. Trained by modern European methods, they were militarily up-to-date and efficient, moreover politically in sympathy with the aims of their Tsar.

Through twenty-five years of active warfare—a spell more or less equal to that of Mehmed the Conqueror—he exploited vigorously the material resources and military skills of his country, with the ambition of building up a Russian world empire. Against this all that the Ottomans could do was to bolster up an empire in decline. Their military development had failed to keep pace with that of the West. Pioneers of the art of war in their time, early developers of heavy artillery, invincible in open country as a cavalry horde, inviolable within the palisades of their infantry, the Janissaries, the Turks of the great age had been dedicated fighters, well trained, well disciplined, led and inspired by cool-headed and competent commanders as their enemies of that period too often were not.

But now the forces of the West were outclassing them with the development of highly mobile field artillery and the limitation of light cavalry in favour of infantry. Decisively they had embarked at high cost on the training, arming, and administration of large professional armies, with well-equipped infantry regiments, capable of countering all cavalry assaults. Such, depending on a large-scale organization for the transport and supply of munitions, weapons, uniforms, foodstuffs, and other materials, was the developing war machine, based on up-to-date military techniques, which the Ottomans, still wedded to earlier military practices, were unable and indeed often, in their adamant conservatism, unwilling to match. Thus the Ottoman armies of the eighteenth—as of the seventeenth—century were hampered by the use of second-rate and unstandardized matériel; their commissariat and supply system remained, by the standards of the new age, haphazard and unprofessional; their general organization had grown casual; their financial administration was totally inadequate. No longer could a campaigning army, on its present large and complex scale, be financed as in the past solely by plunder, and fed from the produce of the surrounding countryside. Modern warfare called for the support of a revised, well-planned, and well-administered economy.

Christian Europe over the past two centuries had emerged from the Middle Ages fortified, through a Reformation and a Renaissance, by economic forces and institutions which, seen in terms of trade and technology, were the foundations of a new Western civilization. The Ottoman Empire, two centuries behindhand, had yet so to emerge. Within the structure of an inflated bureaucracy it languished still in the toils of an economic decline, commercial, industrial, and rural, from which it lacked both the resources and the will to evolve. It was hampered from doing so at once by a lack of financial and mercantile experience and by an obstinate belief in its own superior forces and institutions.

An aspect of this, strictly relevant to its military predicament, was the large, skilled artisan force on which the Ottoman armed forces depended. This was a product of that corporative system of trade guilds which had served a positive social purpose in the past, safeguarding the artisan's moral level and his standards of craftsmanship. Economically, however, now that industry needed a new and more flexible spirit of invention and enterprise, the restrictive nature of the guilds militated against any such progress. They remained obstinate in their resistance to all innovation, in their adherence to outdated techniques, in the rigidity of their accustomed rules and hours of work. Furthermore, taxation and such fiscal restrictions, often irresponsibly imposed, stifled incentive and intensified a native inertia, so hampering progress and prosperity as to make Ottoman industry incapable of competing with European imports. The Janissaries made common cause with the guilds, suspecting and rejecting any hint of that military reform at their expense which was so sorely needed and which their enemy Peter the Great was achieving.

This attitude aggravated a problem which was in essence economic. Inherently the Ottoman Empire, with its development of a money economy based largely on the spread of commercial agriculture, was at no great economic disadvantage compared with the powers of Europe. Where the disadvantage arose was in the fact that its financial operations lay in the hands of its minorities, the bankers and merchants of its Greek, Jewish, and Armenian communities. Its rulers, in their own inexperience and contempt for the infidel, were thus constantly incapable of establishing, indeed of comprehending, the need for a coherent economic system based on close cooperation between the institutions of the governing and of the financial and commercial classes. Such a system, founded on a mutual alliance between the forces of government and capital, men and money, now flourished in the societies of Europe. It still barely existed in the Ottoman state, or indeed in other Moslem states at this time, where the arts of government and commerce remained obstinately separate and aloof from one another. Thus the Ottoman state economy, excluding itself from the concerted planning of long-term, large-scale financial projects, remained at its lowest level, shrinking under European pressure with the changing pattern of trade and the competitive demand, at the expense of native handicraft industries, for European factory-made textiles and other manufactured products.

Basically the inability to combat such problems was due to an attitude of mind rooted in Islam. It was due to a persistent illusion, blind to present evidence, as to the immutable superiority of Islamic civilization and a reluctance to recognize the full implications of an Ottoman power now declining before the new civilization of the advancing West. It was due likewise to fatalism. The Moslem system of education created a spirit of rigid adherence to tradition, based on the belief that God's will would be done, regardless of any human intervention which might presume to divert the course of events. It was thus not only the Janissaries and the guilds but the ulema itself which, in a reactionary spirit, opposed radical changes, to perpetuate its vested interests in the existing military and economic order. By the start of the eighteenth century, whether or not as a sign that God had transferred his allegiance from Islam to Christianity, this had begun to crumble into obsolescence around them. In the Ottoman Empire the rot had set in—just at the time when the sap of the new Russian Empire was rising.

But the old fabric was not yet wholly rotten. Apart from the survival of Islam as a positive spiritual force for the Empire, the very rigidity of its state institutions gave it, for all their misuse and corruption, a certain obstinate faculty of survival, with sporadic powers of recovery. Rigor mortis remained some way ahead. There was life in the old Turk yet. The Sultan no longer governed. But among those who governed for him there still existed enough adequate governing material at various levels to keep the traditional machine of state running. This included a new type of elite—men of the pen rather than men of the sword. Effendis rather than pashas or beys, they were of a different class from the bureaucrats of the past in that most of them were not Christian converts of the old Palace School but Moslems of the second and third generation. But they were nonetheless inclined to employ Greeks and other Christians in subordinate capacities.

A lull between storms, both in domestic and in foreign affairs, followed the signature of the Treaty of Karlowitz. At home Köprülü Hussein, a cultivated, public-spirited Grand Vezir—justly known as Köprülü the Wise, as his predecessors had been respectively Köprülü the Cruel, the Politic, and the Virtuous—took full advantage of this to press forward with a policy of internal reform, notably of an administrative nature, which as one of a discerning few he so clearly saw to be necessary. He embarked upon reforms in the

Empire's finances, in its laws, in its centers of education. In the armed forces he revised the muster rolls of the Janissaries, with an eye to better order and discipline among them, providing for the improved equipment of both army and navy, erecting new barracks for them, and putting the imperial defenses in order. As Mehmed the Conqueror and other great Sultans had done in the past, he built, whether at his own cost or that of the state, such works of public utility as canals, bridges, aqueducts, mosques, schools, and markets. Above all he concerned himself zealously with the welfare of the Christian communities, which was now often deplorable. The inhabitants of Serbia and the Hungarian frontier province of Temesvar were given a year's exemption from capitation tax; throughout Rumeli he remitted a large percentage of contributions due in arrears from the *rayas;* in Syria he granted freedom of pasturage for flocks.

Such measures to ensure the loyalty of the peasants, who were predominantly Christians, were all the more timely because of the fact that Peter the Great, in his designs on the Ottoman Empire, was seeking at its expense not only territorial expansion but internal disruption. He aspired to gain a hold over its Christian minorities. It had long been the pretension of the Russian Church, thinking in temporal as in spiritual terms, to serve as the Orthodox Defender of the Christian Faith, recruiting under its sway those peoples in other countries who subscribed to its creed. Greeks in particular, many of them Slav in race and all of them in religion mistrusting the Latins, began to see the Russians as potential liberators and welcomed Russian agents among them. Peter the Great was now pursuing this long-term aim through propaganda, with promises of financial support and covert incitement to Ottoman Christians to throw off the yoke of the infidel. He was served in the various Christian provinces by influential agents in the ecclesiastical establishment itself. Notable among these was Dositheus, the patriarch of Jerusalem.

But in the Balkans the prelates were at this time more inclined to seek Russian protection against the Catholic Austrians, who sought to convert them from the Orthodox to their own faith, rather than against the Moslem Turks, who did not seek to make converts. They pleaded with Moscow for salvation "from the Papists and Jesuits who rage against the Orthodox more than against the Turks and Jews." In fact Peter the Great, though ready enough in his own good time to emerge as Orthodox Christian champion against the infidel, was too wary a sovereign to be hurried into any such role, intent as he now was on his immediate strategic objective of establishing Russia as a power on the Black Sea.

The Ottoman Empire itself, with a policy of peace now prevailing in the Divan, had easier relations than before with the Christian West. They were cemented, six months after the Treaty of Karlowitz, by its ratification, with lavish and appropriate ceremonies before the Sultan in Istanbul. This generated a friendly atmosphere, and was accompanied by the exchange of ambassadors between the Porte and its former European enemies, on more permanent terms than before. From the start of the eighteenth century Ottoman diplomats, who had hitherto made only brief and sporadic sojourns in their several foreign capitals, thus began to acquire in certain countries a new familiarity with the civilization and culture of the West, together with a closer understanding of its methods of government and political attitudes.

The new Ottoman envoy to the Austrian empire was one Ibrahim Pasha, a general of distinction who had fought at the siege of Vienna with Kara Mustafa. He now made his entry into Vienna with an impressive load of jewelled gifts for the emperor including a satin-lined tent, like those of the Sultan, whose poles were crowned with knobs of gold, while the emperor presented the Sultan with a whole treasury of silver, an artificial fountain, and other refined Viennese artefacts. In Istanbul the Austrian ambassador, at the banquet given for him before his audience with the Sultan, had the signal honour of being served with fried fish from the Bosporus—a delicacy denied to envoys of lower status, who included the representative from Poland.

Not long afterward there arrived a new ambassador from England, Sir Robert Sutton, replacing Lord Paget, who with the Dutch representative had promoted and acted as mediator for the Treaty of Karlowitz. For these services to peace by his country Sutton was warmly welcomed by the Sultan. His feelings toward Russia on the other hand were far from friendly. Peter the Great had refused to sign the Treaty of Karlowitz, agreeing only to a two-year truce, which now called for renewal. The Russian envoy, charged with this mission, caused surprise and alarm by arriving in Istanbul on board a warship in full battle array, built in the Tsar's new shipyards, which fired a salute from all its forty guns and later repeated the cannonade, in celebration of some Russian festival, as though firing a signal for the arrival of the rest of the Russian fleet.

In this atmosphere the negotiations, which lasted through the first six months of 1700, were tense and at times explosive. Finally the Ottomans accepted a treaty. Under its terms the Russians agreed to demolish—but not, as the Turks had demanded, to cede—their four fortresses on the Dnieper, conquered in the previous campaign and since forming an obstacle both to the land communications and to the grazing grounds of the Crimean Tatars in the lands of the steppe. They were granted also a limited extension of territory around Azov itself. A compromise frontier between the two empires was delineated in the form of an unoccupied zone of desert and steppe between

The Chief Black Eunuch was the master or manager of the harem.

Azov and the Perekop Isthmus, sealing off the Crimean peninsula. The Crimean Tatars were to cease their incursions into Russian territory, but were to be allowed equal rights with the Russians in the fisheries and saltworks around the delta of the river, and inland on both its banks for the pursuits of hunting, fishing, beekeeping, and woodcutting. The khan of the Crimea to his rage was no longer to receive the annual tribute from the Tsar, which had been his proudest boast.

Meanwhile, Russia secured the right to maintain a permanent ambassador at the Porte on the same basis of diplomatic representation as the other Christian powers, and the post was filled by Count Tolstoi. But none of this prevented the Russians from continuing to build up their naval strength, with the erection of new fortresses, on the Sea of Azov. This enraged the Crimean khan, who sought in vain a renewal of the war. The Russians repeated at the Porte their demands for freedom of navigation in the Black Sea and the cession of Kertch. These were adamantly rejected. The Turks, alarmed as they were by the growth of the Russian fleet in the Sea of Azov, were determined that the Black Sea should be preserved, "as a pure and immaculate virgin," and played with the idea of damming the Strait. Instead, having already refortified Kertch, they proceeded to build on the opposite side, near Taganrog, a new fortress named Yenikale, designed by a renegade from Modena and completed in 1703. This commanded the northern entrance to the Strait, with batteries at water level capable of destroying any vessel which tried to force a passage.

At home Köprülü Hussein, the reforming Grand Vezir, met with opposition from reactionary elements, notably the Mufti and the Chief of the Black Eunuchs. Their intrigues drove him, already worn out and in failing health, to resign his office, which he had held for a mere five years. Permitted to retire to the place of his choice, a farm on the Sea of Marmara, and to retain his fortune and possessions, he handsomely presented the Sultan on departure with sixty of his best horses and all his jewels. Only three months later he died of an illness which had proved to be incurable.

Thus in 1703 the Empire, with changing Grand Vezirs, relapsed once more into disorder, with an insurrection by Janissaries and other troops demanding arrears of pay. This lasted for six weeks and came close to civil war. Sultan Mustafa, in Adrianople, prevaricated when they required his presence in Istanbul. This large army of rebels, together with students, marched, with the sacred standard of the Prophet and the approval of the Mufti, on Adrianople. Here a rival army, supposedly loyal to the Sultan, had been assembled to crush the rebellion. But its Janissaries, weakly led, joined the rebels and together they forced the abdication of Mustafa II. The unhappy creature had shown little or no will to resist. His spirit had been broken by the calamitous failure of his youthful ambitions to command his own armies in the field, and he had since relapsed into a state of dispirited indolence.

((25))

SUCH TROUBLES SUBSIDED WITH THE ACCESSION TO THE SULTANATE of Mustafa's brother, Ahmed III. He was to reign for a generation, a man of the world given to the more civilized pleasures of peace. On behalf of Louis XIV, now in the midst of his War of the Spanish Succession, the French ambassador De Ferriol was urging upon the Porte the advantages of a French alliance, and pressing for its military support with a campaign against the Habsburgs in Hungary. But Sultan Ahmed refused to become involved in a war to assist infidels who were simply fighting each other. Still less was he disposed to do so when the war went badly for the French.

On the Russian front there was an interval of peace for the Porte, which Peter the Great himself required. Alternating in his orbits of imperial expansion between the two outlets to his vast Russian landmass, the Black Sea in the south and the Baltic in the north, he had now been diverted northward against Sweden, a hostile power of long standing whose king, Charles XII, was now aspiring at Russian expense to extend his own empire. Soon after his settlement with the Sultan in 1700, the Tsar embarked in alliance with Denmark and Poland on a Great Northern War, the "War for the Baltic," against Sweden. Here for the Turks was a breathing space. Russo-Turkish negotiations led in 1705 to a further provisional agreement on the delineation of frontiers in the Crimean zone. But the Turks were taking no chances. They continued to strengthen their northern defenses and to keep a keen eye on Russian movements, sending a fleet of galleys for the purpose each year to cruise in the Black Sea.

Meanwhile, Russian power emerged stronger than ever with the Tsar's dramatic defeat of the Swedish king in the crucial battle of Poltava in 1709. King Charles sought asylum with the Ottomans, with whom he had omitted hitherto to establish diplomatic relations, but whose Sultan, Ahmed III, nonetheless received him hospitably. The Sultan rejected Russian demands for his extradition, but made it clear that he had no intention of breaking his peace with the Tsar to restore the king of Sweden to power. The Russians nonetheless violated Ottoman territory by a raid into Moldavia, where their agents had been stirring up trouble, and where their troops now captured a detachment of Swedes. The Turks at once took the precaution of providing a small force for the king's protection at Bender, on the Dniester. There was indignation at the Porte, where a war party pressed for an attack on the Russians. Finally the Sultan was persuaded to declare war against them. He mobilized his Janissaries, imprisoned Peter's ambassador Tolstoi in the Seven Towers, and prepared to march an army across the Danube to the River Pruth, in Moldavia.

The timing of this offensive did not suit the Tsar, who was still busy in the north securing himself in the Baltic and not yet fully prepared, as was his ultimate intention, to switch his forces to the Black Sea. But after a delay which he prolonged by attempts at mediation, he led them in person on a campaign to the banks of the Pruth. Lured into crossing the river by the prospect of attracting Christian support, the Tsar found himself short of supplies in a drought-stricken land and with little or no help from the cautious Christians, who were unsure of his power to win. Nor this time was he to do so. Through faulty intelligence, he had failed to forestall the rapid advance over the Danube or to foresee the strength of a large army of Tatars and Turks, well armed with artillery and greatly outnumbering his own, which now occupied the heights above the Pruth. From here it proceeded to blockade him, with the riverbanks at his rear and an impassable morass on his flank. Thus his army faced total defeat or surrender. It was a crisis which brought upon Peter an epileptic attack. He shut himself up in his tent, confessing that he had never been "in such desperation," that he feared capture by the Turks, and that in the last resort he would accept any terms "except slavery," the loss of any conquest but his "darling paradise" of St. Petersburg.

At this critical moment the Tsar's strong-minded peasant wife, Catherine, who had insisted on accompanying the campaign, came to the rescue. Her firm words and soothing caresses roused his courage and restored him to reason. He accepted her suggestion, inspired by a group of his officers, that he send proposals for a truce to the Ottoman Grand Vezir Baltaji. Catherine, producing her own jewelry and collecting some thousands of gold roubles from his officers, sent this hoard to his camp as a customary but more than usually handsome gift, designed as an inducement to discuss terms of surrender. Thus an agreement was reached.

Its terms as accepted by Peter involved the surrender of Azov and its surrounding district; the dismantling of Taganrog and the Dnieper fortresses; the withdrawal of the Russian army from Poland, hence from interference with the Cossacks; and a safe-conduct for King Charles through Russian territory back to his dominions in Sweden. Here was an end to Peter's dreams for his conquest of the Black Sea. "The Lord God," as he expressed it, "drove me out of this place, like Adam out of paradise." Here was an end too to his dreams for a southern fleet, whose unfinished ships now rotted on the stocks, while their timbers were dispatched to the shipyards of St. Petersburg.

But for the Tsar the terms, signed by a Grand Vezir who was in spirit no warrior, on behalf of an empire here bent on defense, not on conquest, were better than Peter was entitled to expect. They involved for him no loss of territory beyond the immediate Ottoman sphere of interest. Indeed they enraged the frustrated conqueror, Charles XII, as he saw the retreat of the Tsar and his rear guard, drums beating and flags flying, without interference. He begged in vain for a force to pursue the Russians and received equally indignant support from the khan of the Crimea, who considered that the defeated Tsar should now, as before, pay him tribute.

But more pacific policies prevailed, largely through the influence of the British ambassador, Sir Robert Sutton, who from the start had reported that the Turks, despite the efforts of the Swedish king and the Crimean khan, "seem universally well-pleased with the peace in the manner it was concluded." By his mediation and that of the Dutch ambassador, following further Turkish threats of war, its terms were reenacted when at Adrianople the Turkish territory of Azov was enlarged and the Russians were finally debarred from access to the Black Sea. These terms were effectively executed in two new treaties, successively in 1712 and 1713. Thus on balance the peace treaty of the Pruth, cheaply won but overgenerous as it was, served the present purpose of the Ottomans, with their limited and in essence defensive objectives in Russia.

As for the king of Sweden, he proved obstreperous and hard to get rid of, but finally, realizing at last that the Porte would not take up his cause, he accepted from the Sultan an escort to his frontier, then rode northward through Europe to the shores of the Baltic.

Thanks to Peter the Great's defeat on the Pruth, a quarter of a century was to pass without further disturbance by Russia of its peace with the Ottoman Empire. But the Empire was not content to rest on the laurels it had gained at the Tsar's expense. Its forces were still mobilized, moreover now commanded by a belligerent Grand Vezir, Damad Ali, who resolved to launch them against an older enemy, Venice. The Venetian republic was falling into a state of decline worse than that of the Ottoman Empire, and appeared to lack allies.

Taking advantage of this, Damad Ali, known to the Greeks as Coumourgi, the "dauntless Vezir" of the Byronic muse, embarked on a bid to regain the Morea, avenging its loss to the aged Venetian general Morosini, now dead, which had been confirmed by the Treaty of Karlowitz. In 1715, invoking a suitable pretext—and not forgetting to consult astrological omens—he marched a large army, supported by a naval force, through Thessaly, and after a siege of three weeks captured Corinth.

In fact, as previously in Cyprus and Crete, the Greeks were inclined to welcome the Turks as liberators from the Latin tyranny of their Venetian masters, to whom they gave no assistance. Thus the Ottoman army proceeded, in the Morea, to recapture all the Venetian fortresses, including Modon, Coron, and Navarino. The campaign was over in a few months, in the course of which the Venetians prudently avoided the risk of a pitched battle. By the end of 1714 the republic had lost the whole of the Morea and the islands of the Archipelago. Following this up, it was the Ottoman intention, having meanwhile captured the two remaining Christian ports in Crete, to complete the expulsion of the Venetians from Greek territory by an attack on Corfu and the Ionian islands.

But Damad Ali's historic victory was to be counterbalanced on another front by an equally spectacular defeat. For he had miscalculated the reaction of the Habsburg emperor, Charles VI. He had failed to allow for his possible intervention on behalf of the Venetians, despite his equivocal response to an Ottoman request for Austrian neutrality and furthermore an imperial offer of mediation for peace. Thus when Venice invoked the emperor's support on the grounds of Ottoman violation of the Treaty of Karlowitz, Charles responded by signing a general defensive alliance with the republic. Here he was influenced by the shrewd and redoubtable Prince Eugen of Savoy, who was disturbed by the rapid success of the Turks and who saw clearly its potential danger, not only from the Ionian islands to the emperor's Italian dominions but, if they chose to resume a policy of aggression in eastern Europe, to his German dominions as well.

At the Porte there were disagreements as to whether this alliance should be treated as a *casus belli*. The peace party in the Divan wisely opposed another war with the empire. But after heated debates it was finally overruled by the militant Grand Vezir, who won some support from the ulema, and finally an injunction from the Mufti in favour of war.

Thus yet again, in 1716, a substantial Ottoman army marched to Belgrade. There history repeated itself, as at the earlier encounter between Sultan Mustafa II and Prince Eugen, when the Ottoman generals disagreed over tactics. Should they march northward to Temesvar or westward to Peterwardein? On this course Damad Ali, overruling his opponents (and this time disregarding the astrological omens), now decided. He crossed the Sava and marched along the south bank of the Danube to besiege Peterwardein.

The Austrian commanders themselves disagreed at first over their tactics, greatly outnumbered as they were by the Ottoman forces and inclined to be overawed by the reputation of Damad Ali since his triumphs in Greece. Some of them shrank from the risk of an open battle and counselled a policy of attrition, to wear down the Turks. But this was contrary to the temperament of the dashing Prince Eugen. Moreover, he knew his Turks, the antiquated nature of their weapons, their proficiency in headlong assault, but their limitations when confronted with unforeseen tactics, and their tendency to break in retreat. Thus in the summer of 1716 he decided to take the offensive. A preliminary encounter took place near the village of Karlowitz itself, where the treaty had been signed, and where the Ottomans in breach of it now attacked and defeated the Austrian vanguard.

So Damad Ali marched upon Peterwardein, where Prince Eugen's forces were drawn up ready to confront him. The Janissaries gained an initial success, breaking the center of the Austrian infantry. But Eugen reinforced it for a counteroffensive and attacked the Janissaries with another infantry force from the flank. They broke, and a charge of the heavy imperial cavalry—an arm still unfamiliar to the Turks—routed their *sipahis,* who broke too and retreated in panic. The Grand Vezir strove with angry reproaches and strokes with his saber to check them, then galloped forward with a group of officers into the heart of the melee (just as Köprülü Mehmed had done nearby at Slankamen more than twenty years earlier) in a desperate hope to save the day. Like Mehmed he was hit in the forehead by a bullet and mortally wounded, to be carried on horseback to Karlowitz, where his death precipitated the final breakup of the Ottoman forces.

Following up his victory, Prince Eugen besieged and captured the fortress of Temesvar, the last surviving bulwark of Islam in Hungary, which had been in Ottoman hands since the reign of Suleiman the Magnificent. He treated its garrison well, assisting its Moslem inhabitants to depart without interference as a prelude to a planned repopulation and colonization of the province by Germans and Austrians. When this materialized, Temesvar was to become known as "Little Vienna."

Its capture was a prelude to Eugen's siege of Belgrade in the following year. Here the Ottomans, marching to the rescue of their garrison, once again put an army in the field twice as large as his own. Though the position of the Austrians was critical, they were saved by delays, hesitations, and incompetent tactics on the part of the Turks. Overconfident that the fortress was bound to fall into Turkish hands, they were slow to launch an attack against the besiegers. At this the hard-pressed Prince Eugen resolved, despite the heavy odds against him, to strike out in a daring retaliation. So he stormed the Ottoman lines, achieving surprise and at once creating panic. Right in the center his infantry, flanked by cavalry, advanced, with colours flying and drums beating, against a fierce bombardment from the principal Ottoman battery. Holding their fire until they were close to it, they lowered their bayonets and charged, with an impact on the Janissaries so devastating as to break up their whole line in disorder.

So the bold generalship of Prince Eugen abruptly turned the scale, and Belgrade fell to the Austrians—again, as at Peterwardein, with immense losses in men and arms to the routed Ottoman forces. Prince Eugen himself was wounded in the battle, which the emperor declared to be "the greatest victory of all time." It was a victory which entered into Austrian folklore with a song, to be sung thereafter by generations of imperial armies as they marched into battle.

Meanwhile the time had come for peace. Once more, as at Karlowitz, England and Holland came forward in the role of mediators on the basis of *uti possidetis*—"what we have we hold." At Passarowitz, a small town in Serbia, a treaty was signed in 1718. By this the Ottoman Empire finally yielded to that of the Habsburgs all that remained to it of Hungary, if not to the entire satisfaction of all its inhabitants; also the greater part of Serbia, including Belgrade and Semendria; a large part of Wallachia; and an important part of Bosnia. This gave to the Emperor Charles VI a dominant position in eastern Europe, such as his predecessors in the great days of the fighting Turks had been unable to achieve.

Only Venice, in a separate treaty, fared badly at the hands of the Ottomans, yielding the whole of the Morea, retaining only Corfu, the Ionian islands, and a few ports in Dalmatia and Albania, but ceding to the Sultan an area of territory which gave him access to that of his ally, Ragusa. Here, thanks to the Ottoman Empire and in spite of its weakness, was the final death knell of the Venetian republic as an effective political force. This at least was a compensation to the Turks. But the price of it had to be paid in eastern Europe, with a further downward stage in the Empire's own decline. The Treaty of Karlowitz had shown that the Turks need no longer be accounted a serious threat to the West. The Treaty of Passarowitz established them finally on the defensive, unlikely to contemplate, on their own initiative, further aggression at Europe's expense.

((26))

Sultan Ahmed III, the man of peace, was now free to enjoy it for the last twelve years of his reign—years which were to initiate a serious trend toward Westernization and reform. Born outside the Seraglio, in the course of a campaign in the field, as the offspring of his father's most loved favourite, he had evaded the confinement of the Cage, and though attracted by women had remained since his youth relatively immune from the powers and intrigues of the harem. A tolerant ruler, he was a man of sophistication, a man of the world and of culture, discerning in his response to the civilized tastes both of the West and the East. Taking pleasure in music, literature, and the arts, he gathered around him a school of court poets of especial distinction, and endowed his Seraglio with a new library which became filled with valuable manuscripts.

Ahmed's personal talents were largely aesthetic, and for these he found an outlet in the design and creation of innumerable buildings. No man of the city, but one relishing the refreshments of nature—the shade of trees, the scent of flowers, the singing of birds, the rippling of water—he broke out from the confines of his Grand Seraglio to create for his court and his pashas a new fashion of summertime living, in palatial resorts on its various seashores. One of these was by the Sweet Waters of Europe, at the head of the Golden Horn, where he diverted the course of two streams to make marble-lined canals, artificial lakes, cascades and fountains, and thus to water a profusion of gardens.

In the center he built for himself the summer palace of Sa'adabad, basing it on the seventeenth-century French château of Marly, whose plans his ambassador had brought him from Paris. There sprang up around it other palaces, pavilions, kiosks, villas by the hundred. These were generally built, no longer as in the past from stone and carved marble, but—and more economically—from timber and moulded plaster. This gave a free rein to fantasies of style with an eye to French decorative fashion, which came to be matched in Paris itself by a vogue for *turquerie*. Similar "cities of pleasure" soon adorned the Sweet Waters of Asia, and select stretches of the Asiatic shores of the Bosporus. Built by a variety of architects brought both from Europe and from Asia, these residences—as observed by the French ambassador Louis Sauveur de Villeneuve—reflected styles so diverse as to suggest sometimes Versailles and sometimes Isfahan. They resembled in effect improvised stage settings for a continuous round of lavish and picturesque entertainments. The Turkish court, in its search for diversion and change, seemed perpetually bent on some new excursion:

> Sometimes it appeared floating upon the waves of the Bosporus or the Golden Horn, on elegant *caïques* covered with tents of silk; sometimes proceeding in a long cavalcade towards one of the haunts designed for its pleasures. . . . the beauty of the horses and the luxury of their equipment gave to these processions a special attraction; they advanced in harness of gold or of silver, their foreheads plumed, their coverings resplendent with precious stones.

Catering for Sultan Ahmed's pleasure in the splendours of court life, with its brilliant fêtes and pageants, was a son-in-law, Damad Ibrahim Pasha, who shared his love of the *beaux arts,* and who served as his Grand Vezir through the last twelve years of his reign—contrasting with the first fifteen years, in which the Sultan had successively as many as thirteen Grand Vezirs. Ibrahim was himself a lover of luxury and display. Devising spectacles which lasted far into the night, he engaged special experts who could invent for him new means of festive illumination for the city of Istanbul. Thus from the heights of Pera at night the newly arrived French ambassador looked across to a city whose buildings and gardens and even its waters sparkled and glowed with flame, "the domes of its mosques surrounded by innumerable crowns of light, while between their minarets, thanks to an invisible apparatus, the verses from the Koran were inscribed across the sky in letters of fire." On especial occasions Istanbul was illuminated for three successive days and nights. For one celebration, on the marriage of three of the Sultan's daughters and two of his nieces, and the circumcision of four of his sons, the Grand Vezir ordered rejoicing throughout the Empire. He recruited from its provinces as many as two thousand musicians, fifteen hundred mimics, wrestlers, jugglers, and acrobats, and as many cooks. The Sultan put the inspector of the imperial kitchens in charge of the ceremonies, ordering him to fabricate four nuptial palms, fertility symbols of gigantic size, for the young princes, and smaller ones for the rest, while the cooks created miracles of confectionery, including a garden some five yards long and four yards wide, made entirely of sugar, to symbolize the sweetness of marriage.

The Seraglio during the winter was regaled with *helva fêtes,* social gatherings in which philosophical symposia, together with poetry recitals, dancing, Chinese shadow plays, and prayers were accompanied by the distribution of sweets, otherwise helva. But when the winter was over there was now introduced for the Sultan's delectation a spring fête which developed largely into a festival of tulips. Ahmed had a great love for flowers—for the rose, the carnation (which his moustache was said to resemble), the lilac, the jasmine. But it was eventually the tulip that captured his fancy above all the rest. Its name in Turkish was *lale,* held to have a sacred significance from its resemblance to "Allah," and the reign of Ahmed III became known to posterity as *Lale Devri,* or the Reign of the Tulip.

The tulip was a wild flower of the Asiatic steppes which had strewn the path of the Turks throughout their centuries of westward migration. It was Busbecq, the Austrian imperial ambassador of the sixteenth century, who as a keen botanist first introduced the tulip to the West, taking tulip bulbs back to Flanders on his journey home. Its European name was derived from the nickname the Turks gave it: *tulbend,* or "turban" in the Persian language. Not long afterward the tulip was imported by European merchants and propagated in large quantities in Holland, where in time some twelve hundred varieties of it were known. This gave rise in the seventeenth century to a craze of tulipomania among the Ottoman elite, in the course of which fortunes were made and lost from rare tulip bulbs, and the tulip became known as "the gold of Europe."

It was Mehmed IV, the father of Ahmed, who first reintroduced the tulip into Turkey, making a tulip parterre, which comprised several varieties, in the gardens of the Seraglio. But it was Ahmed himself who first imported tulips in large quantities, not only from Holland but from Persia. Their cultivation in his gardens was carefully planned, with only a single variety to each bed.

Ahmed III's fête of spring, the Tulip Fête, in the gardens of the Grand Seraglio came for a while to outshine in importance the established religious feasts of Islam. It was held always in the month of April on two successive evenings, preferably by the light of a full moon. The Sultan covered over like a conservatory a part of his gardens where the parterres of tulips were planted. Here ranged on shelves were countless vases of the flowers, carefully chosen and placed for their harmonizing colours and shapes, interspersed with minute lamps of coloured glass and glass globes filled with liquids of different colours, so as to shine as it were with their own light. On the branches of the trees, combining aviary with conservatory, were cages of canaries and rare singing birds. The Sultan sat throned in the center beneath an imperial pavilion, receiving homage. On the second evening the entertainment was for the ladies of the harem, whom he received alone, entertaining them with music and poetry and song and the dancing of his slaves, while turtles wandered through the gardens with candles on their backs, to light up the tulips. Sometimes there was a treasure hunt—as for Easter eggs in Europe—with coloured bonbons and trinkets concealed amid the flowers, and the concubines fluttering hither and thither, "tiptoeing through the tulips," as it were, in search of them. Ibrahim Pasha himself admired above all a variety named "Blue Pearl," offering handsome rewards to anyone who could acclimatize it, and covering it with white veils to protect it from the sun in hot weather.

Not only did the tulip become a prominent feature in the tiles and other decorative arts of the Ottomans; with its accompanying cult of the spring it became a source of inspiration to the Ottoman poets at a time when they were shedding Persian influences to evolve a new muse of their own. The leading poet of the reign of Ahmed III, with its gaiety and luxury and *douceur de vivre* in these elegant surroundings, was Nedim, "the Boon Companion," a poet of pleasure with a lighthearted philosophy: "Let us all laugh and play, let us enjoy the world's delights."

The tulip was to survive as an image in Turkish poetry right up to the republican era of the twentieth century. "Victory," wrote a contemporary poet, Yahya Kemal, "is a shattering beauty with a rose face and tulip kisses."

For the Tulip Age was more than a mere passing fashion. In its essentials it marked the birth of a modern era in the Ottoman Empire. Here was the dawn of a new worldliness, a new enlightenment, reflecting a spirit of rational inquiry and liberal reform. It looked for inspiration to the West, in its own new phase of scientific progress, economic wealth, and military power, to provide a secular counterpoise to the traditional religious values of the Islamic East. In Western civilization lay the pattern of that social and cultural reform which was increasingly seen to be necessary, if only still by a relatively small element among the Ottoman elite. Thus the tulip became a symbol, that of a dawning Turkish renaissance under the influence of Western civilization.

In 1720 the Turkish government sent a special envoy named Chelebi Mehmed to the court of Louis XV. His official task—in which he did not at this juncture succeed—was to seek an alliance with France. But he had been instructed besides by the Grand Vezir to "visit the fortresses, factories, and the works of French civilization generally and report on those which might be applicable." The result was an account of his visit which served as a manual for future changes in Turkey.

Mehmed, accompanied by his son Said, was one of the first Turks to learn the French language. He wrote of Paris as one discovering a new world and fascinated by its novelties—its technical and medical arts, its zoological and botanical gardens, its operas and theaters, and above all the sophistication of its social habits. He looked with astonishment and admiration upon those of the women who "enjoy higher status than men and are free to go anywhere they wish." He showed especial interest in the Paris Observatory, and in the zodiacal tables of Uluj Bey, the fifteenth-century astronomer prince of Samarkand. He met Saint-Simon, who wrote of his grand manner and his taste and his charm with the ladies, approving also of his intention to establish a printing press back in Constantinople.

This innovation, which had for long been opposed by the forces of reaction, and which was fraught with significance for the future of the Ottoman Empire, was largely the work of his son Said, who in France had become interested in the art of printing and its cultural value. In 1727 he established the press, the first in any Moslem country, in conjunction with Ibrahim Müteferrika, a renegade from the Hungarian nobility, who as a cultural intermediary saw the printing press as a means to the end of bringing home to the Ottoman Turks those new ideas and methods that the West had to teach them.

He presented a memorandum to Ibrahim Pasha, for the eye of the Sultan, which was subsequently printed. In this he asked the question, "Why do Christian nations, which were so weak in the past compared with Moslem nations, begin to dominate so many lands in modern times and even defeat the once victorious Ottoman armies?" Giving the answers, he urged that the Moslems should awaken from the slumber of heedlessness. "Let them be informed of the conditions of their enemies. Let them act with foresight and become intimately acquainted with new European methods, organization, strategy, tactics and warfare." Let them widen their military and political horizons by the study of geography, also of the science of navigation by naval charts, such as had led the Christians to the discovery of a New World and to the conquest of Moslem lands. Let them learn a lesson in particular from their neighbours, the Russians, whose Tsar had "sought and brought experts skilled in these sciences from other countries and reformed his armies by heeding their counsels, recommendations and assistance."

The Turks, he concluded, were always known to excel all other peoples in their acceptance of law and order. If they were to learn the new military sciences and techniques "no enemy can ever withstand this state." He applied to the Sheikh-ul-Islam for an authorization to print books, and this was granted, prohibiting the printing of the Koran and other sacred texts, but permitting that of such secular works as dictionaries and books on the sciences.

But the peaceful reign of Sultan Ahmed III was now nearing its end. As often after a long period of relative peace, the Janissaries grew restless at their inaction, resenting the extravagances and frivolity of the court with its "Frankish manners" and the apparent indifference of the government to their own interests. Reports were received in the autumn of 1730 of an encroachment on Ottoman territory across the frontiers of Persia where a new and aggressive ruler, Nadir Khan, was seizing power. These provided the pretext for a mutiny led by an Albanian Janissary which was supported by elements of the civilian population and thus swelled into an insurrection. It was aimed largely at Ibrahim, the Grand Vezir, who at the start underrated its force, while the chief admiral, on the day of the outbreak, was quietly transplanting tulips in his garden on the Asiatic shores of the Bosporus.

The Sultan lost his courage, and yielded to the demands of the Janissaries. He delivered up to them the Grand Vezir, the chief admiral, and another senior official, who were strangled. He then abdicated on the condition that his life be spared, together with that of his children. He made obeisance to his nephew, Mahmud I, who was brought from the Cage—where his uncle, regardless of his own freedom from it, had confined him—to be enthroned in his place as Sultan. Then Ahmed himself retired to the Cage, where he was to spend the last few years of his life in confinement.

His reign nonetheless had initiated a new trend of Ottoman reform, which was to grow henceforward. Ibrahim Müteferrika's memorandum on the need for military reform, now printed, was put before the new Sultan Mahmud I. This victim of the Cage was to prove an ineffective ruler. But throughout his reign, Ibrahim Müteferrika and his press propagated the new ideas and discoveries of European science. With the aid of a committee of twenty-five translators, he published a flow of works revealing to his adopted compatriots the mysteries of such objects of study as geography and cartography, in which he himself specialized; physics and astronomy, including a translation of Aristotle with information for the first time on the telescope and microscope, on magnetism and the compass, on the theories of Galileo; on mathematics in its various branches, with discussion of the ideas of Descartes; and finally on medicine. Ibrahim Müteferrika died in 1745, his printing press ceased to operate, and a number of translations remained in manuscript. Circumstances prevented the resumption of printing in Turkey till 1783. The delay arrested that progress which had given to the Tulip Age some of the character of a Turkish renaissance.

((27))

DIPLOMACY, RATHER THAN WAR, WAS HENCEFORWARD THE ESSENTIAL weapon of the Ottoman Empire in its relations with Europe. The proud days when the Crescent could dream of vanquishing the Cross by a combination of religious impulse and military valour were no more. They had ended at Peterwardein, with the defeat of Damad Ali, the last of the holy warriors, by Prince Eugen, the skilled, scientific commander of a modern age of secular warfare. Once and for all the Ottomans were to recognize in practical terms that their role in European affairs was now defensive and dependent upon allies, the Crescent relying upon the Cross, hence upon the organization at the Porte of a permanent system of diplomacy in line with those of the powers of Europe.

Until the Treaty of Karlowitz the diplomacy of the Ottoman Turks, as that of an Asiatic Moslem power irrupting into Christian Europe, had been unilateral, without reciprocity. Regardless of any law of nations, they were a law unto themselves, "the only nation on earth," reflecting a degree of contempt for the Christian states as inferiors by receiving their resident diplomatic missions but sending them none in return. This practice, though it isolated the Turks from the European system at the significant time of the emergence of its states into nations, worked well enough throughout the centuries of their expansion at Europe's expense. But it left them inconveniently isolated now that European contacts became for them a matter of integral need. For Karlowitz, and still more Passarowitz, treaties, both signed according to international law and the usages of Western diplomacy, had sealed the status of the Ottoman Empire in relation to the West as a retracting, no longer an expanding power. Henceforward the Porte was compelled to negotiate from weakness rather than strength. For a while longer it continued to do so on a nonreciprocal basis, without permanent missions abroad—and indeed at home with little consistent machinery for the handling of foreign affairs.

From this the immediate sufferers were the foreign missions themselves. Labouring and intriguing to carry out their instructions and pressing on behalf of their governments policies which might indeed coincide with Ottoman interests, they led a life of continual frustration. Already separated from home by the interminable time lags and hazards of communication, they would find themselves equally isolated here with their diplomatic rivals, in the foreign quarter of Pera, from the government to which they were accredited. Permitted access only at rare intervals to the center of affairs in Stambul, across the Golden Horn, they found themselves obstructed by the petty rigidities of Ottoman protocol; the shifts of power within a government where in an atmosphere of continual intrigue one Grand Vezir was perpetually succeeding another; the delays, deviations, and evasions inherent in the process of negotiation.

Above all, foreign diplomats had to contend with the problem of language. For none knew Turkish, and few Turks—since power had passed from a ruling institution of renegade Christians to one of predominantly Moslem-born officials—knew a European language. The foreign envoy thus depended upon his own dragoman—his interpreter and intelligence agent—who was usually a Greek or a Levantine of Latin origin. Acting as his intermediary with the officials of the Porte, the dragoman was in a position, by selective or slanted interpretation, to influence talks as he chose; to further his own interests through calculated leakages to his fellow dragomen and other confederates.

But in 1669 this system was rationalized and improved by the creation, for Christian subjects alone whether Greeks or Armenians, of the high office of Dragoman of the Porte. Drawn as a rule from the Greek mercantile community, the Phanariots, his rank amounted in fact to that of a minister of foreign affairs. Around him other responsible official posts were allotted henceforward to Christians, mostly of the Greek Orthodox faith. For the Greeks, through their trade, were familiar with the languages of the West, of which the Moslem Turkish elite were in general ignorant, and would send their sons to such Western universities as Padua. In particular they were to serve often as ambassadors or as governors of autonomous Christian provinces. Thus, with the lapsing of the Sultan's Slave Household did the Ottomans continue, without either conscription or enforced conversion, to draw on the abilities of their Christian subjects. The work of the Dragoman of the Porte as relations with Europe developed became increasingly arduous. It took the form of regular contacts with foreign envoys, for discussion of their business, his services as interpreter at audiences with the Sultan and interviews with the Grand Vezir; correspondence with foreign governments, which he and his staff had to translate from the Turkish; a perusal of foreign news sheets and similar sources to familiarize his government with European affairs.

Nonetheless foreign envoys were still subject, whether deliberately or otherwise, to diplomatic frustrations. Such, early in the eighteenth century, was the experience of the Marquis de Villeneuve, instructed as ambassador by Louis XV to strengthen the position at the Porte of France, which during the past century had lost much of its influence to England. Following the traditional lines of Franco-Turkish friendship, initiated by Francis I, he was to seek from the Porte by means of good personal relations a more positive policy in favour of France, now that the disparity between Ottoman weakness and Muscovite strength threatened the balance of power in Europe.

Villeneuve arrived in the Golden Horn in an imposing convoy dressed to display the naval might of France. But it was festival time on the shores of the Bosporus, when pleasure reigned to the exclusion of political business, and the presentation of his credentials was long delayed. Eventually he was received in a formal ten-minute audience with the Sultan. A few days later the Grand Vezir welcomed him with a long exchange of civilities. Obliged, though a nonsmoker, to smoke a pipe with him "twenty feet long," the ambassador eventually tried to broach the two issues of the Capitulations and the protection of Christian minorities. At this the Grand Vezir blandly inquired whether the gardens of Versailles were as beautiful and well kept as ever. He then spoke at length of their counterpart, which he had created by the Sweet Waters of Europe. Some days later the Dragoman of the Porte appeared at the French embassy, asking in the name of his masters for a supply of plants and bulbs from France. A further eight months were to pass before Villeneuve, fretting impatiently, was received by the Grand Vezir again.

For the Porte, in the present phase of its defensive policy, favoured the Austrian imperial resident at the expense of the French ambassador. The Turks, after their humiliating defeat at Belgrade, sought to avoid further conflict through appeasement of the emperor with sundry concessions. Having obtained at Passarowitz trading privileges, embodied in an Imperial Ostend Company, he could now emerge as a serious competitor for the Levant trade; and certain sects among the Latin Christians, disappointed in the French, turned toward him for aid. But this situation abruptly changed in 1730, with the deposition of Ahmed III and the execution of his Grand Vezir. Thanks to his disappearance and the resulting new regime, Villeneuve was at last able to report favourably on the prospects of Ottoman support for French policy.

Within a few months he had obtained, through a new chief admiral, the remission of duties on French merchandise. Then a new Francophil Grand Vezir, Topal Osman, restored to France her privileged religious status. The missionaries, who under his predecessor had been reduced to the status of consular chaplains, became free once more to practice their ministry in all Christian provinces; the immunities of the fathers of the holy places were expressly confirmed and the Turkish authorities excluded from their churches; permission was given to the Christians to restore churches which had been burned by the Moslems (on the grounds that the sound of their bells by night kept the angels awake in their mosques) and to erect new ones. The "Emperor of France" was thus seen once more as the all-powerful protector of his faith.

Ambassador Villeneuve, resuming the role of his earlier predecessors, now saw himself as free to act as French adviser to the Porte in its foreign relations. In a belligerent spirit his friend the Grand Vezir fell in with his views, making no secret of his belief in the need for Ottoman action, at the appropriate moment, against the Austrian emperor on one flank and the Tsarina Anna (who had lately succeeded Peter the Great) on the other.

But as he fell from power, to be succeeded by a succession of Grand Vezirs, with less Francophil policies, this "appropriate moment" was a long time in coming. For meanwhile, in 1733, the emperor and Tsarina became involved as allies in a war for the spoils of the Polish Succession with France backing a rival candidate. Austria and Russia pressed for Ottoman neutrality, which was readily enough granted; France pressed for Ottoman intervention, in the form of an advance against the southern Russian flank, from the Crimea through the Ukraine into Poland. But the Turkish price for this was an implacable demand for nothing less than a formal offensive and defensive alliance, affirmed with guarantees between the Sultan and the king of France. Amounting to an overt alliance between Christian and infidel, the proposal went far beyond the tacit statement of friendship and mutual interest such as had governed Franco-Turkish relations since the days of Francis I and must govern them still. At Versailles it was vehemently and obstinately rejected by Cardinal Fleury, the power behind Louis XV, owing to its provocative nature and implied risk of conflict with the Christian powers of Europe, especially England and Holland. This outright rejection led to a protracted spell of negotiations between the Porte and Versailles which lasted for some eighteen months, proving the Turks now to be as tenacious in diplomacy as once in war.

Then in 1734 the Russians, banking on the Porte's neutrality, moved a large army northward from the Ukraine, and proceeded to besiege and capture their main objective of Danzig and, with their own satellite monarch in Warsaw, thereby came to control much of Poland. This left them free to move back from the Baltic to the Black Sea coast, there to avenge Peter the Great's defeat by the Turks on the Pruth.

Thus, using as a pretext the violation of Russian territory by the army of the Tatar khan, the Sultan's vassal, a Russian force marched without a declaration of war upon Azov, which it captured. At the same time the main Russian army invaded the Crimea through the Perekop Isthmus, whose defense lines and fortress they captured against a stubborn Tatar resistance. Then they proceeded to lay waste, with devastation and massacre, much of the Crimean peninsula, into which neither Peter the Great nor any previous Russian army had ventured. But its desolate and largely waterless steppes finally defeated them, and their forces, prostrated by exhaustion, hunger, and disease, were obliged to withdraw before winter approached. The initial Russian success was thus balanced by a failure whose immediate effect was to give the Turks a sense of false security.

The Porte nonetheless prepared for war, mobilizing an Ottoman army to march to the mouth of the Danube. In fact, Turkish resistance to the Russians was crucial, if the loss of Azov were not this time to be followed by a Russian irruption into the Black Sea and the siege of the three other fortresses which guarded the mouths of its rivers. Here the Tsarina was claiming freedom of navigation for her warships and commercial vessels. This would make of it a Russian lake, opening the way to Istanbul, thence through the Straits into the eastern Mediterranean, where the Levant trade offered rich prizes at the expense of the Western powers. Now too the Emperor Charles VI sought a share of the spoils, and with a view to joint armed intervention, a secret treaty was agreed between Austria and Russia.

But the Turks remained obstinately reluctant to confront their enemies in battle. They preferred to bid for mediation by one of the Christian powers, whose respective envoys, the imperial resident and the English and Dutch representatives, competed for the role of mediator. In the summer of 1736 the Grand Vezir—another new occupant of the post, with whom Villeneuve had hitherto achieved little contact—prepared with his army to move into camp at Bender, in Bessarabia, near the mouth of the Danube. Here in fact he was expecting not war but negotiations for peace. Nor were the emperor's forces, depleted and disorganized by the War of the Polish Succession, yet ready for any new war against Turkey. Thus he gained time through the offer of his services, jointly with those of Russia, as mediator with the Porte.

A congress was held in the summer of 1737 at Nemirov, in the Polish Ukraine. Here, with their respective armies ready to march, Austria and Russia barely troubled to conceal their real designs on the Ottoman Empire. Negotiating sword in hand, the Russians demanded not only freedom of navigation in the Black Sea but access for their fleets through the Bosporus into the Mediterranean; the extension of the Russian frontier to the Dniester; the cession of the Kuban and of other Tatar lands to the north of the Black Sea; the recognition of Moldavia and Wallachia as independent principalities under the suzerainty of Russia. The Austrians demanded the cession of what amounted to the whole of Bosnia and Serbia. Their respective troops meanwhile were already marching into the territories demanded, the Austrians recapturing in Serbia the fortress of Nish. Their joint proposals were in effect an ultimatum, as to an enemy already defeated. Now the Turks had no choice but to reject the terms, disband the conference, and take up arms for the defense of the Ottoman Empire.

Its only hope of salvation now lay with France. To Villeneuve's impatience, the government of Louis XV had at first proved hesitant in its approach to the crisis, favouring the cession by the Porte of Azov. Assuming that the Russians would be content with this, they saw it as a preferable alternative to war. But Russia's threatened presence in the Mediterranean through the Black Sea at last awakened Versailles to the need for a complete reappraisal of policy. Face to face with the prospect of the joint dismemberment of the Ottoman Empire by Russia and Austria, Cardinal Fleury acknowledged the imperative necessity to maintain its integrity, whatever the cost. Quite apart from the importance of the Levant as a commercial sphere for France, the Ottoman Empire itself, however inert and decrepit, must be preserved as an element essential to the equilibrium of Europe. Hence, from Versailles, a new and positive diplomatic offensive designed, through agents in Vienna, to split the Austro-Russian alliance, and through moves on the spot to stiffen the Turks and convince them that it was better to fight than to yield to dishonourable conditions of peace.

When the Grand Vezir realized that he had been thoroughly deceived by both Austria and Russia, he at once proved responsive to the overtures of the French, and a letter was dispatched to Versailles officially requesting the mediation of the king of France. This was in principle granted. Meanwhile, the Turks bestirred themselves for a war on two fronts. Under yet another new Grand Vezir their army marched westward in the direction of the Austrian frontier. The moment was propitious, for a year earlier Prince Eugen of Savoy had died, and the imperial armies, already much reduced in strength and fighting spirit, were left at the mercy of incompetent generals. The Austrians moreover were consistently on bad terms with their distant "allies," the Russians, with whom they lacked any concerted plan of campaign. In the west, among the mountains of Bosnia they met with a fanatical resistance from the feudal forces of their belligerent chieftains, Christian Slavs turned Moslem; in the east the Ottoman forces recaptured Nish, thus opening the way up the valley of the Morava to Belgrade. The Russian armies were more successful than their Austrian allies, capturing the fortresses of Ochakov and Kinburn at the mouth of the Bug, but failing, in the fierce heat of the steppes, to proceed farther in their intended advance to the Danube.

The success of the Turkish armed forces was due to a French renegade and soldier of fortune, the Comte de Bonneval, who had served the Austrian emperor and now entered the service of the Sultan. He had established for him a bombardier corps, trained on European lines, and had otherwise worked methodically to reorganize, modernize, and improve the training of the Ottoman armed forces in general.

Their victories surprised and impressed Europe, enabling Villeneuve to envisage mediation for the Porte from a position of strength. But among the Turkish troops themselves they so rekindled passions against the infidel that they could not be restrained from a second seasonal campaign. This time the Austrians were content with a defensive strategy in Belgrade, while the Turks took the fortresses of Semendria and Orsova on the Danube, before Belgrade. The Russians, continuing their operations in the hinterland of the Black Sea, were repulsed on the Dniester and obliged to retire because of disease and supply problems, evacuating the newly captured fortresses of Ochakov and Kinburn.

This, Villeneuve decided, was the moment to mediate. Furnished now with credentials, including a letter from King Louis XV to his "dear and perfect friend the Ottoman Emperor," he chose in the interests of French prestige to present this to the Sultan in his Seraglio with a show of some pomp. Accompanied by a large and imposing suite, he was received in audience with respectful solemnity. He was gratified besides to sense around him an atmosphere of overt friendliness to France, such as the Porte had not before shown. Presents poured into the French embassy, where the Sultan's band played continuously in a forecourt, while the ambassador was escorted wherever he went by a guard of honour of Janissaries.

Soon afterward he left with his own large official convoy to join the Grand Vezir at Adrianople. Here he learned that the Grand Vezir and his army had moved on to Nish. By the time he reached there they had moved on to Belgrade. Instructed by the Grand Vezir to remain at Nish meanwhile, he now received news of a major battle at Krotzka, downstream from Belgrade. In this the Austrians, aiming to recapture Orsova but greatly underrating the strength of the Ottoman forces opposed to them, were caught after an inept tactical move at the mouth of a defile, driven back with great losses, and forced to retreat on Belgrade. The Turks were so elated by this victory that Villeneuve grew anxious. He was well aware that the fortress of Belgrade, since its capture by Prince Eugen, had been modernized by German engineers to become by repute one of the strongest in Europe. He now feared lest the Turks, carried away by the euphoria of success, should forestall mediation by storming it and thus risking a major defeat. When finally he was summoned to the Grand Vezir's camp, the Turks had indeed begun, without due preparation, to bombard the city.

Fortunately Austrian morale was now faltering, and of this Villeneuve was quick to take advantage. The emperor sent an emissary, General von Neipperg, to Belgrade from Vienna with full powers to negotiate a separate peace with the Porte, regardless of Russia. Arriving in the Ottoman camp, he proved, as the negotiations proceeded, ready to cede tracts of territory in the name of the emperor. But when it came to Belgrade itself he would cede the city only if its fortifications were razed to the ground. The Grand Vezir haughtily rejected such terms, insisting that he could agree to no negotiation until the keys of Belgrade, as it stood, were in his hands. Yet, though he felt the need to satisfy his belligerent soldiery, he wanted peace.

Villeneuve, well aware of this and quick to profit by the evident Austrian impatience for a settlement, came decisively to the rescue with an acceptable compromise solution. The Austrians would be required to demolish the fortifications which they themselves had erected. But they would leave intact the original Turkish walls. Under the terms of the subsequent peace, which the emperor, despite some reluctance, was obliged to ratify since it was formally guaranteed by France, the Ottoman Empire regained all it had lost in Serbia, Bosnia, and Wallachia through the Treaty of Passarowitz. The Danube, the Sava, and the mountainous province of Temesvar became once more the frontiers between the two empires.

This separate surrender on the Austrian front came at an unfortunate moment for Turkey's other enemy. For on the Russian front it coincided exactly with a major victory over the Turks which might otherwise have transformed the whole course of their joint campaign. The Russian commander, Marshal Münnich, abandoning his abortive operations across the steppes of the Black Sea, had followed a new line of advance into Ottoman territory. Moving northward to violate that of Poland, he crossed in succession the Dniester and the Pruth into Moldavia. Here he captured by assault the key fortress of Choczim. He set up his own puppet prince, who rallied the Christians to his arms as a liberator from Moslem oppression. Jassy opened its gates to him, and Russian advance guards were soon reconnoitering on the north bank of the Danube itself. Then he turned into Bessarabia, to reduce Bender as a base for southward operations, for a Russian drive into the heart of European Turkey, right along the road to Istanbul. But now, thanks to the Austrian lapse into defeatism, there stood, released and ready to move against the Russian flank on the Danube, an Ottoman army some two hundred thousand strong and in the full flush of victory. As Marshal Münnich wryly remarked: "Let the Turks give thanks to Mohammed, to Villeneuve, and to Neipperg!"

The Russians were left with no choice but to sign at Belgrade their own treaty with the Porte, a second triumph for French mediation. The Turks renounced Azov, on condition that its fortress be razed to the ground and its surrounding territory reduced to a neutral strip of desert between the two empires.

The Porte reserved the right to build a fortress on the lower Don, below Azov, denying access to either sea by the Russians. No Russian vessel, whether warship or merchantman, would be permitted to enter the Black Sea; nor in future might naval shipyards be maintained on its coasts, where Russia retained only a strip of territory between the Bug and the Dnieper. All Russian conquests in the Crimea, Moldavia, and Bessarabia were restored to the Turks, but the Russians were granted a slight increase of territory in the region of the Ukraine. On the diplomatic advice of the French mediator, the Porte did not insist on the renewal of the clause in the Treaty of the Pruth, forbidding the Russians to become involved in the internal affairs of Poland.

This Treaty of Belgrade, as the culmination of a brief war, spelled humiliation to the Habsburgs, frustration to the Russians, relief to the Ottoman Empire. At this time of declining power, when in a defensive spirit it sought only peace, the Empire was now to enjoy a respite from conflict with its new and most formidable enemy, Russia, for a generation to come. In face of its old hereditary enemy, Austria, it had at once regained its pride and closed the breaches in its system of security, laid open by the last humiliating defeat. Though the victory of the Turks in the field was due largely to the faults of the Austrian commanders, the Ottoman soldiery had shown itself still capable of the old fighting spirit, if not of the new military skills, while the strategy of the Ottoman commanders, faced with a war on two fronts, had proved to be shrewd.

Nonetheless honour was primarily due, for both victory and peace, to diplomacy, and outstandingly to the skill and intelligence and foresight of France. It was the French who at the moment of crisis induced the reluctant Turk to fight; who at the moment of victory induced him to treat for peace; and who in negotiation confounded each of his enemies at the expense of the other. Here effectively at work was the new pattern of the age in the foreign relations of the Ottoman Empire. No longer was this to be based on the deliberate, independent assertion of Ottoman power. For here was an era in which the Turk, who had once aspired to be master of Christian Europe, had ceased to be fully master of his own dominions. For the survival of his imperial power against that of an imperial rival, he now depended on alliance with the powers of Christian Europe itself.

Among these France, through her mediation, now rose above the rest to an unchallengeable position of influence and prestige at the Porte. In 1740 a formal treaty of friendship and commerce, in twenty-four articles, renewed her Capitulations on more favourable and permanent terms than before, thus sealing the preponderance of French trade in the eastern Mediterranean. At the same time, at French instigation, the Porte fortified itself against the threat from Russia by signing with Sweden first a similar treaty of friendship and commerce, then a solemn offensive and defensive alliance, such as it had previously sought with France itself—the first treaty of its kind ever contracted by the Ottoman Empire with a Christian power. Finally the confirmation, on specified terms, of French protective rights over the Latin Christians guaranteed the influence of France throughout a significant part of the Empire. It was to France in her eighteenth-century heyday that the Ottoman Turks in their turn now looked for inspiration and support, in the evolving world of Western power and civilization.

((28))

Peace now reigned for a generation through the European dominions of the Ottoman Empire. The powers of Europe themselves were throughout much of this period at war. Following the death in 1740 of the Habsburg emperor Charles VI, there were spoils to be grabbed through the dismemberment of those Austrian dominions inherited, under the Pragmatic Sanction, by his daughter Maria Theresa. This led first to the War of the Austrian Succession, then to the Seven Years' War and the rise to power in Europe of the Prussian king Frederick the Great.

France, having assumed the role of peacemaker and protector of the Ottoman Empire, was still ready enough, in pursuit of her own if not always of Ottoman interests, to involve the Turks not merely as a passive but as an active balancing force in her European conflicts. At this moment, having designs upon Austria in concert with Prussia and the German princes, the French put pressure on the Turks to invade Hungary, promising them its kingdom as a reward for such a diversionary move. But Sultan Mahmud I, the successor of Ahmed, was not to be drawn. He firmly insisted on Turkish neutrality, publishing a manifesto in which he sought to dissuade the other powers from war and presumed to offer them his own mediation, that of an infidel between Christians, for peace. It was a gesture which provoked from them little more than a smile.

The French fell back upon the renegade Bonneval, lately awarded a pension, with the promise of return to France, hoping that his influence might decide the Porte in favour of war. But the Sultan and his ministers remained adamant. A persistent renewal of French efforts during the next decade to draw the Porte into an alliance with Prussia and Sweden met only with a persistent refusal. The Porte was indeed so determined on insurance against war at any cost as to contract, in response to the overtures of Maria Theresa and the mediation of England, a treaty of "perpetual" peace with Austria and Russia.

Through these decades the Ottoman Turks, blind to such perils as might loom over the future, succumbed with relief to that fatalistic inertia which suited their temperament. Only a tiny minority of the elite, realistically aware of the Empire's present weakness, with its crying need for rearmament and reorganization, saw this respite as a chance to set the Ottoman house in order for the next major encounter with Russia which must invariably follow.

Otherwise, throughout the ruling establishment a complacent improvidence reigned. Pervading it at all levels was an apparent blindness to shortcomings, or at least an obstinate reluctance to face their existence. This spirit had roots in the traditional habit of belief in the infallibility of Ottoman institutions and, heedless of experience, in the inferiority of those of the infidel. Turning to self-interest, it spread downward and outward from the ever-changing succession of Grand Vezirs to permeate the official hierarchy and, through ever-widening fields of corruption, to pollute the government machine as a whole. It descended to the Janissaries, the hard core of the armed forces. Granted by Sultan Mehmed the privilege of exemption from import duties, they no longer relied on war but extended the commercial scope of their sideline pursuits to develop, like the rest of the community, a vested interest in peace. From its interruption, there was altogether too much to be lost.

Sultan Mahmud died in 1754, to be succeeded by his brother, Osman III, a victim of the Cage so deformed as to be almost a hunchback. He was to reign as Sultan, carrying on his brother's pacific policy, for a mere three years. From the final year, and through the first year of the reign of Mustafa III, who succeeded him, the Empire was effectively ruled by Raghib Pasha, a Grand Vezir comparable in caliber to the Köprülüs. A man of strict honesty and enlightened ideas, schooled in European science and an admirer of the work of Isaac Newton, he sought the ideal of Westernization, but at this stage, in the interests of order, saw in it the need to pursue reforms without endangering "the harmony of the existing institutions."

Abroad he pursued the Porte's policy of peace in terms of a search for equilibrium. Seeking a counterpoise to the power of Austria and Russia, he signed in 1761 a treaty with Prussia, which he hoped—had events not overtaken him—to contract into an offensive and defensive alliance. For Prussia was a power with no territorial designs on the Ottoman Empire. Fully alive to the Russian menace, thus to the need for reform in the Ottoman army, Raghib reorganized its arsenal, created a foundry for cannon, formed a corps of bridge builders, and started to construct new warships. He established schools of mathematics, naval training, engineering, and artillery; he imposed routine exercises on Janissaries, sappers, *sipahis,* and the feudal cavalry of Anatolia. He reorganized the administration, sought to restore order to the Empire's finances, suppressed brigandage in Anatolia, and assured much-needed supplies of grain to the holy cities of Medina and Mecca. Turning to public works and utilities, he revived an old project of digging a canal between the Black Sea and the Mediterranean, which would bypass the Bosporus, cutting across Asia Minor to the head of the Gulf of Iznik and thence to the Sea of Marmara. By such various means the Grand Vezir sought to guide the energies and control the restless spirit of the new Sultan Mustafa III, who at first proved content to entrust him with the direction of affairs.

But Mustafa III was no man of peace. He was energetic, industrious, eager to lead his people and to benefit his country's interests, and there shone in him a spark of that conquering spirit, lacking in his predecessors, which had fired his early Ottoman forebears. However, it was not often tempered by their coolness of judgment. From his accession Mustafa resolved to govern as befitted the Sultan he was, dropping a hint of martial designs to the Janissaries over the inaugural cup of sherbet which tradition prescribed. "Comrades," he assured them, "I hope next spring to drink it with you under the walls of Bender."

It was indeed his intention that the Porte should play a more belligerent part in the affairs of Europe. But it was not until the death of Raghib, in 1763, that he began effectively to rule in person. This move coincided with the abrupt rise to power of a new militant enemy, at once able and unscrupulous, the Empress Catherine the Great. The "Semiramis of the North," brought to the throne by a military coup at the expense of Peter III, her debauched and ineffectual husband, it was Catherine's implacable ambition to reign as Tsarina on the shores of the Bosporus, through the dismemberment of the Ottoman Empire.

First, however, the death of its king, Augustus III, called once again for the dismemberment of Poland. Seeking a confederate in a former enemy, Frederick the Great of Prussia, she changed sides to contract with him in 1764 an unholy alliance against Polish independence. It led to the occupation and partition of Poland by Russian and Prussian forces, with the connivance of Austria, and the imposition upon it as king of a former lover of Catherine's, who in the event was to prove its last.

Mustafa III was quick to voice his indignation at this fraudulent act of aggression by Russia, protesting at the so-called election of Catherine's puppet prince with the boast, "I will find some means of humbling those infidels." But his Divan was still opposed to war; nor were the forces of the Empire prepared for it. The Porte at first did no more than protest passively, content, despite pleas from the suffering Poles, to be deluded by reassurances from Russian and Prussian envoys. It suited Catherine to keep the Porte quiet until she had finally disposed of Poland, and Russian gold, so she found, could buy influential votes in the Divan.

But she made little secret of her ultimate intention to dispose similarly of the Ottoman Empire, and this soon enough became evident. In insidious preparation, internal dissensions were fomented by Russian agents in various parts of the Empire—in Montenegro, Albania, Moldavia, and Wallachia; in Georgia; in the region of the Crimea. Here in "New Serbia," between the Bug and the frontier of the Ukraine, the Russians fortified a frontier zone pronounced neutral under the Treaty of Belgrade, thus cutting communications, in the event of war, between Turks and Tatars. Their final act of provocation was the pursuit of fugitive Poles into the Ottoman vassal territory of the Tatar khan at Balta, near the frontier of Bessarabia, which they besieged and burned to the ground, with a slaughter of Poles and Turks alike. Here was a flagrant breach of the treaty which goaded the Sultan into fury. The Divan reversed its policy and opted for the immediate declaration of war. Only the Grand Vezir, Muhsinzade Pasha, opposed its decision—not in principle, but on the grounds that the armed forces and frontier defenses of the Empire were still unprepared, that no military operations could start until the following spring, and that such a gratuitous warning would give Russia a predominant advantage.

But the impatient Sultan saw that his chance had come at last. He dismissed the Grand Vezir, and all too hastily, through his successor Hamza Pasha, served an ultimatum on the Russian envoy, Obreskov, demanding that the Tsarina withdraw her forces from Poland. When Obreskov refused, in default of instructions from St. Petersburg, to sign the ultimatum, he was imprisoned in the Seven Towers, and war was declared against Russia. France, as "an ancient and faithful ally," had for some time been pressing upon the Divan the need for such action. Her current ambassador at the Porte, De Vergennes, had been instructed by Choiseul, at Versailles, to enlighten the Turkish ministers as to the dangers of Russian action in Poland and elsewhere. In vain De Vergennes had warned Versailles of the extent of Ottoman unreadiness. But now all illusions were dispelled. When Baron de Tott, sent by Versailles as an emissary and adviser on military matters, was authorized by the Sultan to carry out an inventory of arms and munitions, he was amazed and appalled at the deficiencies of the arsenal at Istanbul.

It seemed to him that the traditional practice of war was forgotten. Fortifications, army maneuvers, training and discipline—all were deplorable. Incompetence paralyzed the armed forces. Ignorance reigned in official circles, even as to the most elementary aspects of geography. Indiscipline was rife in the field of battle. Large units of the soldiery refused to fight; thieving from the Commissariat led to a famine in rations; fief-holding cavalry leased their military duties to all types of adventurers; the Janissaries would often strike their officers and, though infantrymen, insisted on riding into battle unless the officers too consented to march on foot. The Ottoman army was degenerating into a barbarous rabble.

The ships of the navy, which the Grand Vezir Raghib had labored to reform and recoup, suffered from defective construction, outdated design, and rotten material. As De Tott was to report, "high-decked vessels, the lower tier guns of which were laid under water by the least gale of wind, presented the enemy with much wood, and little fire." The heights of the decks were geared to those of the turbans which the sailors immutably wore. De Tott wrote of other numerous "defects of this armament, which was to be commanded by men too ignorant to perceive it had any imperfections." The chief admiral had the right to dispose of the command of each ship to the highest bidder, and gave his captains the same right to put up commissions for auction.

Sultan Mustafa's impetuosity in thus plunging into war before he was prepared for it gave the Empress Catherine the time to mobilize against him five separate armies. From west to east they were based respectively on the line of the Dniester, covering Moldavia, in the Ukraine; before the Perekop Isthmus, which led into the Crimea; in the territory between the Don and the Caucasus; and in the region of Tiflis, covering Georgia and eastern Anatolia. From the Ottoman front only the khan of the Crimea, Krim Ghirai, launched an offensive in the cruel winter of January, 1769. He was accompanied by Baron de Tott, clothed at his behest like a Tatar, and supplied with ten Circassian horses. When his own more delicate white Arab steed fell, dying of the cold, it was speedily finished off and transformed into smoked horseflesh to be consumed as a special delicacy, together with caviar. The khan's large army of seasoned Tatar cavalry swept across the Dniester and the Bug into the icebound steppes of New Serbia, devastating tracts of southern Russia in a large-scale predatory raid, and returning laden with prisoners by the thousand. But he died soon after his return, and his successor, chosen by the Porte, failed altogether to rise to his stature.

The same applied to the new Ottoman Grand Vezir and commander-in-chief, Mehmed Emin, whose appointment revealed the Sultan's ineptitude in the selection of leaders. By admission a man of the pen, not of the sword, thus devoid of all military experience, he summoned a council of his generals on reaching the Danube in the spring of 1769, and amazed them by pleading for their advice as to how the campaign should be planned. The resulting disagreement led to the crossing of the Danube into Moldavia, with no definite plan of operations. There followed an inevitable series of setbacks, due in part to lack of provisions and to a plague of gnats and mosquitoes in the surrounding marshes. This led to a Turkish retreat, to the Russian capture of Choczim and advance into Moldavia and Wallachia, finally

The Castle of the Seven Towers in Istanbul. Sultan Suleiman stored his vast treasures here, and in later centuries it was used as a prison for important Ottoman political and military leaders who had fallen into disfavor or for European diplomats of countries at war with the Ottoman Empire.

Melling, *Voyage pittoresque.*

to the recall and execution by the Sultan of his Grand Vezir. Such was the first of a sequence of Ottoman reverses between the Dniester and the Danube.

Toward the end of that year the Empress Catherine embarked on a project dear to her imagination—an invasion of Greece, aimed at the liberation of its Christian people from the yoke of the infidel Turk. Such a triumph would surely excite the acclaim of the whole Western world. For some time past the Russian Orthodox Church, through its agents in Greece, had been assiduous in its spread of propaganda through crosses, gospels, and images of Catherine, who had promised arms to the Greeks in support of a revolt. The Turks, in their innocence of geography, shrugged off the reported threat with an incredulous query: How ever could the Russians convey a fleet from the Baltic to the Mediterranean?

The fleet was assembled at Kronstadt and adjoining ports, under the official command of two Russian admirals unused to the sea, but under the effective command of an experienced English admiral, John Elphinston. The Russian navy was still backward. Its ships lacked stability; it had yet to find an adequate cannon founder; its crews were supplemented by novices—peasants torn from the plow, convalescents from the hospitals. To Admiral Elphinston's comment on the deficiencies of his fellow commanders, Catherine replied: "The ignorance of the Russians is due to youth, that of the Turks to decrepitude." When her ships anchored in British ports they received a warm welcome. They were supplied by the orders of the Admiralty with equipment and rations, and staffed with efficient pilots and other officers, so that no Russian vessel was without its English naval complement. For England at this time favoured the expansion of Russia as opposed to that of her enemy France; nor did she yet support the policy of upholding the integrity of the Ottoman Empire. The government thus indicated that any attempt by France or Spain to obstruct the entrance of the Russian fleet into the Mediterranean would be treated as a hostile act.

The Russian expeditionary force was commanded by Count Orloff, the brother of Catherine's favourite, who dreamed of a throne for himself from which to reign over Greece. The force appeared off the coast of the Morea early in 1770, encouraged through Venetian agents by secret agreements with Greek tribal leaders to count upon a massive uprising by the Christian population. Its troops, under the Russian flag, landed in the Mani, whose restive inhabitants were eager enough to rise against their Turkish oppressors. But there was no joint plan of campaign, and the Russians failed to establish systematic control over these wild mountain brigands bent only on the indiscriminate slaughter of Turks.

The governor of the Morea, the former Grand Vezir Muhsinzade Pasha, reacted with vigour. He called in as reinforcements bands of Albanians, and defeated both Greek insurgents and foreign invaders, driving the Russian troops back to their ships and slaughtering the Christian rebels onshore. The Russians thus evacuated the peninsula while—on the anniversary of the Conquest of Constantinople—Muhsinzade Pasha signalized his victory with the title of Fatiji Mora, "Conqueror of the Morea."

But the Russian force remained in the Mediterranean. It proved more successful at sea than in land operations. It defeated an Ottoman fleet in the straits of Chios, driving it to take refuge in the narrow inlet of Cheshme. Here it was blockaded, then burned through the introduction of two unsuspected fire ships—one piloted by an English lieutenant. Thanks to this "ingenious ambuscade," as recorded by Baron de Tott, the harbour, "encumbered with ships, powder and artillery, soon became a volcano, which engulfed the whole naval force of the Turks."

Here was the worst disaster that had befallen an Ottoman fleet since the battle of Lepanto. It was celebrated by Catherine with the erection of an *arc de triomphe* at Tsarsko-selo, and the striking of a medal for each combatant with the inscription "I was there." It might have had decisive long-term effects had the advice of the English admiral been heeded. He urged that the fleet should sail at once for the Dardanelles, whose defenses were poor, thence force its way into the Sea of Marmara to bombard and reduce Istanbul. But Orloff, his Russian superior—soon to be honoured by Catherine with the name of Cheshmeski—was hesitant. Cruising indecisively around the mouth of the Straits, he gave time for the Turks, with the expert aid of Baron de Tott and a team of Frankish engineers, to erect four heavy batteries, two on the European and two on the Asiatic side, so placed as to rake with their crossfire any vessel which attempted to pass.

Thus Elphinston instead closed the Straits from the waters of Tenedos, while Orloff besieged the fortress of Lemnos. After sixty days the Turkish garrison was on the point of surrender when Hassan of Algiers, an admiral of the Sultan in the heroic corsair tradition, undertook from Istanbul to raise the siege. He demanded only a force of four thousand volunteers, armed with pistols and sabers, from among the fanatical rabble of the streets of Istanbul. Landing unobserved on the eastern side of the island, they surprised the besiegers, cut them down in their trenches, and drove the rest of the Russian force in a panic to abandon the siege and reembark in their ships. Hassan was thus honoured with promotion to chief admiral.

Orloff's naval force remained for some time in the Mediterranean, where it harassed Turkish shipping, impeded communications between the capital and its Asiatic possessions, and in the now familiar Russian

Boundary of Ottoman Empire
Vassal states
RUSSIA
UKRAINE
Poltava
R. Don
R. Volga
Astrakhan
R. Dnieper
Nemirov
PODOLIA
Bug
Taganrog
Azov
Dniester
R. Pruth
BESSARABIA
MOLDAVIA
Jassy
JEDISAN
Bender
SEA OF AZOV
Kuban R.
Perekop
Oczakov
Kertch
Crimea
Eupatoria
Sebastopol
RUMANIA
Hirsova
DOBRUJA
Bucharest
R. Danube
Silistria
BLACK SEA
MINGRELIA
GEORGIA
Tiflis
Rustchuk
Nicopolis
Varna
Tirnovo
Mesembria
Batum
Kura R.
Ardahan
Sinope
Trebizond
TREBIZOND
Kars
Erivan
BULGARIA
Samsun
Aras R.
Bayezid
Philippopolis
Maritza
Kirk Kilissa
Adrianople
Kastamonu
Niksar
Bayburt
Erzurum
ARMENIA
Merzifon
Amasya
Erzinian
Manzikert
Istanbul
Chorum
Tokat
KARA-KOYUNLU
Ahlat
L. Van
Drama
THRACE
Nicomedia
Sivas
Mush
Mudanya
Iznik
Thasos
OTTOMANS
Sakarya R.
Angora
ERETNA
Bitlis
Imbros
Gallipoli
Bursa
Athos
Eskishehir
Halys R.
AK-KOYUNLU
KURDISTAN
KARASI
ANATOLIA
Kayseri
Lemnos
Kutahya
Malatya
Diyarbekir
GERMIAN
Aksaray
Lesbos
Bergama
Afyonkarahisar
DULKADIR
Mardin
Magnesia
SARUHAN
Myriokephalon
KARAMAN
Nigde
Urfa
Mosul
Philadelphia
Akshehir
Eregli
Marash
Chios
Izmir
Meander R.
Yenishehir
Konya
Şis
MESOPOTAMIA
Athens
Samos
AYDIN
Isparta
Taurus Mts
Adana
Alexandretta
R. Tigris
Denizli
HAMID
Milas
MENTESHE
Antalya
Ermenek
Antioch
Aleppo
Bodrum
Cos
CILICIA
Silifke
Orontes R.
TEKKE
Alanya
SYRIA
R. Euphrates
Hama
Rhodes
Nicosia
Homs
Famagusta
Candia
LEBANON
Cyprus
Crete
Beirut
Damascus
MEDITERRANEAN SEA
Acre
Haifa

fashion intervened in the internal affairs both of Egypt and Syria. Hence he supported with troops and munitions an insurrection against the Porte by the Mamluk chief Ali Bey, in confederation with the sheikh of Acre. Ali occupied a large part of Syria at the expense of the pasha of Damascus, but was ultimately defeated through treachery nearer home in a battle in which four hundred Russian troops perished. The rebellious pasha's head, together with four Russian officers as prisoners, was then dispatched to the Sultan in Istanbul.

Meanwhile, in the main theater of operations, along and across the Russo-Turkish frontiers, the fortunes of war, in successive annual campaigns, moved relentlessly against the Ottoman forces. In 1770 the Russians overran successively Moldavia and Wallachia, driving the Turks back in panic across the Danube. Soon all Turkish fortresses north of the river, traditional bulwarks of the Empire, were in Russian hands. Serious resistance was offered only by the Tatar population of Bender. After two months' siege, followed by furious street fighting, only one-third of them remained alive. The fortresses on the Dniester, like those on the Danube, thus fell to the Russians.

In 1771 came the turn of the Crimea itself, which was invaded from both flanks by Russian armies, through the Perekop Isthmus and across the Strait of Kertch. Its territory was entirely overrun, amid scenes of utter disorder, intensified by internal conflict between Tatar and Turk. The Turkish governor was taken prisoner; the khan had fled ignominiously without an attempt at defense, thus depriving the Tatars of their last source of authority. His two sons were promised independence for the peninsula under Russian protection, and with a delegation of others proceeded to St. Petersburg, there to swear an oath of allegiance to the Empress Catherine. Most of the northern coast of the Black Sea—apart from the fortresses of Oczakov and Kinburn—was thus lost to the Ottoman Empire. At the same time, in the region of the Caucasus, the Russians drove the Turks from Mingrelia and Georgia.

Austria and Prussia now grew concerned at the continued conquests of their powerful Russian neighbour, and offered the Tsarina their mediation for peace with the Porte. But Catherine replied that she would negotiate only with the Sultan himself, without the intervention of outside powers. There followed a tangled process of diplomatic maneuver between the powers and Turkey, involving also the spoils of a planned partition of Poland. The Porte envisaged successively alliances with Austria and with France, in return for support against Russia. Finally, at the end of the campaign of 1771, Russia and the Porte agreed to an armistice, which led, first at Fokschani and then at Bucharest, to the discussion of peace terms.

The negotiations broke down, largely because the Mufti and the whole body of the ulema opposed the cession of the Crimea, as a Moslem state under the Sultan-Caliph's authority, to the protection of a Christian power. Though Sultan Mustafa, with his Grand Vezir and principal ministers, favoured the terms proposed, he was obliged to reject them for fear of an insurrection by the ulema in Istanbul. Thus the war, after a breathing space of more than a year, was resumed. Taking advantage of this respite, the Sultan reinstated Muhsinzade Pasha, the liberator of the Morea, as Grand Vezir.

Reorganizing and reinforcing the army, he inspired it with a last new lease on life, and in 1773 embarked on a campaign now confined to the south bank of the Danube and that region of Bulgaria which extended from the two fortresses of Silistria and Hustchuk to the shores of the Black Sea. First the Turks withstood a Russian siege of Silistria, fighting for it street by street and enforcing a withdrawal. For this a Russian force took revenge by massacring the civilian inhabitants of the undefended town of Bazarjik. Surprised as they did so by the appearance of a detachment of Turks, they withdrew precipitately, abandoning by their campfires pots filled with half-cooked meat. Meanwhile, another Russian force advanced upon Varna, but was effectively repulsed by the Turks with the aid of a unit of marines from a Turkish naval squadron, then cruising off the Black Sea coast.

Encouraged by this run of unexpected success, the Turks resumed the offensive in 1774 from their headquarters at Shumla, which commanded the valley of the Danube from the foothills of the Balkan range. This time they marched downstream toward the mouth of the river, with the aim of driving the enemy from the fortress of Hirsova. But the Russians attacked first, completely defeating the large Turkish army, capturing their camp with all it contained, and leaving the Turks with a force quite inadequate to defend Shumla. Its communications with Istanbul were threatened as the encircling Russians moved south in the direction of the Balkan gorges.

This was the end. The Grand Vezir sent an officer to the Russian camp requesting an armistice. Instead, he was invited to send plenipotentiaries to treat for peace. With the assent of the Porte, negotiations were opened and terms settled in the Treaty of Küchük Kainarji. Agreement was reached within seven hours, largely on the basis of the terms rejected two years before. The signature was delayed for four days by the Russians, to coincide with the anniversary of the Treaty of the Pruth, and thus wipe out the bitter memory of that Russian defeat.

Humiliating as the new treaty was to the Ottoman Empire, its terms were less drastic than they might have been. For the Tsarina herself was now ready for peace, owing to the costliness of Russia's victories and to internal troubles both at home and in Poland. Russia neither retained control of the Crimea nor restored it to the Turks, but recognized the political independence of its Tatars, there and in Bessarabia, up to the frontiers of Poland. It was to be ruled by a native prince, who should be elected and reign without either Russian or Turkish interference. In religious affairs the Tatars would remain subject to the Ottoman Sultan-Caliph—the first international acknowledgment of the Sultan's rights over Moslems beyond his frontiers.

On the other hand, the retention by Russia of the two key fortresses of Kertch and Yenikale and the cities of Azov and Kinburn gave her a strong foothold in and adjoining the Crimea, hence the means of taking it over whenever she chose. Above all it gave her that access for her fleets to the Black Sea which she had coveted since the days of Peter the Great, almost a century earlier. No longer was it to remain exclusively a "pure and immaculate" Ottoman lake. Under the treaty Russia was to enjoy rights of navigation in its waters. This was held to apply reciprocally to both powers in such waters as washed their respective shores, and involved Russian consular representation in those parts of the Empire which affected her interests.

In the Mediterranean the Russian fleet was to be withdrawn from the Greek Archipelago. In Asia, Georgia and Mingrelia were restored to the Porte. So in Europe were the Rumanian provinces of Wallachia and Moldavia. But here there was a significant reservation. Not only was there to be a guarantee of fair government and freedom of worship for the Christian population, but the Russians were to have the right of intervention on their behalf through the Russian ministers accredited to the Porte. This implied rights of protection, whose later extension by the Russians to cover the Christian subjects of the Empire in general opened the way to ominous future conflicts. Meanwhile, Russian subjects were to have free access as pilgrims, without capitation tax and under the protection of Ottoman laws, to the holy places of Palestine.

The Treaty of Küchük Kainarji did not yet aspire to dismember the Ottoman Empire, from without, in the territorial sense. But it was the starting point of a serious new policy of dismemberment from within. On religious grounds it furthered seeds of that internal disruption at which the Russians in the future were to show themselves masters. Meanwhile, in effect facilitating this policy, the Sultan undertook to permit once more the residence of a permanent Russian minister at the Porte, and to accord the Russian sovereign the status and title of Padishah.

Mustafa had proved himself a ruler of goodwill and constructive intentions, who had within him the germ of a reforming spirit. He had encouraged in this context the activities of Baron de Tott, who at his instigation founded and directed a mathematical school. This initiated officers of the navy and army—among others—into the forgotten mysteries of trigonometry.

Sultan Mustafa III did not survive to see the defeat of his brave aspirations and its sorrowful aftermath. Still believing in his stars—and in his destiny as Cihangir, or "World Conqueror," the pen name under which he wrote poetry—he had determined in 1773 to proceed in person to the Danube front, there to take over the command from his generals. But his ministers restrained him; the ulema opposed his departure, largely because of the bad state of his health; and indeed he died from an illness, after some weeks of pain, at the turn of the year. Honourable in his resolve to breathe new life into the Ottoman Empire and to defend it against Russian aggression, he lacked not only the political judgment and stability of character but the material and human resources to achieve its regeneration—not the first of the line of latter-day Sultans to be thus thwarted in his emulation of stronger and more illustrious forebears.

His brother emerged—after forty-three years in the Cage—to succeed him in the sultanate as Abdul Hamid I. On his accession he found a treasury so depleted that he would not pay to the Janissaries the donative customary at the start of each reign. He was a courteous but ineffectual monarch, good enough in intentions but deficient in character, who nonetheless became so rejuvenated as to produce twenty-two children. Most of these died prematurely. One who survived and was to reign eventually with notable distinction as Mahmud II may have had French blood in his veins as the supposed offspring of Aimée Dubucq de Rivery, cousin of the future Empress Josephine and a much-favoured inmate of his father's harem.

The Sultan's ministers had ruled over an empire, exhausted by war, which for some thirteen years was to be relieved by a spell of relative peace. But it was a precarious respite, more apparent than real. For the Empress Catherine it was no more than a temporary interval in which to tackle internal problems before the resumption of her provocative "grand project" for the dismemberment of the Ottoman Empire.

As her Habsburg confederate, the Emperor Joseph, discovered: "That woman has a singular will of her own which nothing stops." In 1778, when a second grandson was born to her, he was christened imperially Constantine. As an Englishman at her court, Mr. Eton, revealed: "Greek women were given to him for nurses, and he sucked in with his milk the Greek language, in which he afterwards was perfected by learned Greek teachers; in short his whole education was such as to fit him for the throne of Constantinople, and nobody then doubted the Empress's design." It was planned that he should reign in confederation with the Austrian emperor but independently of St. Petersburg, over the partitioned European domains of Byzantium, as sovereign of a Christian empire comprising Wallachia, Moldavia, and the ancient republic of Athens, and Sparta in Greece. Catherine intensified her propaganda throughout Greece, urging its Christian inhabitants to join her in taking up arms against the infidel.

Thus encouraged, the mountain tribes of Epirus rose in an active insurrection. As the young Prince Constantine approached adolescence, a deputation of Greeks travelled to St. Petersburg to present the Tsarina with a petition. As citizens of "a nation whose genius is not extinguished," they insisted, "We have never asked for your treasure; we do not ask for it now; we only ask for powder and shot, which we cannot purchase, and to be led to battle." When the assistance was promised they pressed her to give them her grandson for a sovereign of their own, and were permitted to wait upon him in his private apartment as Basileus. When they had paid him homage as the Emperor of the Greeks, the young Constantine in Greek replied to them: "Go, and let everything be done according to your wishes."

Meanwhile, Catherine was busy with the manipulation to her own ends of the Crimea, since the Treaty of Kainarji an independent state. When the Tatars elected as their khan a member of the princely family, Devlet Ghirai, the Russians, not finding him sufficiently servile, stirred up disaffection against him, marched an army into the Crimea on the pretext of restoring order, and deposed him in favour of their own rival khan. A former hostage at St. Petersburg, he was described by Tatars and Turks alike as a weak puppet, subject to Russian dictation. But the Turks, in their unreadiness for war, decided to yield over the Crimea. In 1779 at the instigation of the French they signed a convention with Russia, renewing the Treaty of Kainarji, acquiescing in the choice of the new khan, and granting him the necessary recognition in Moslem terms.

When the Tatars revolted against him as a creature of the Russians, whose insolent manners and profligate ways he assumed, he sent a delegation to St. Petersburg, begging the Empress for protection. Once again a Russian army was sent to the Crimea, and the rebels were mercilessly slaughtered or expelled. The Empress and Prince Potemkin, her commander-in-chief, counsellor, and principal favourite, now judged that the time was ripe to take over the Crimea directly. The luckless khan was induced, by a combination of threats and bribes, to relinquish his crown to the Empress, who in 1783 proclaimed the annexation of the Crimea, together with that of the Kuban and adjacent territories, by Russia. The khan, thus callously sacrificed, was imprisoned for a while in barbaric conditions, then pushed across the frontier into Turkey, where he was forthwith decapitated.

The Western world was cynically assured that Russia had performed in the Crimea a great act of liberation, rescuing its Tatar population both from the miseries of civil strife and from the dangers of foreign war, to which their situation, on the frontiers between Russia and Turkey, exposed them. "It was," she proclaimed, "the love of good order and tranquillity that had brought the Russians into the Crimea." When the more noble of the Tatars preferred to fight to the death for their country's independence, General Paul Potemkin, the prince's cousin, put them to the sword in a massacre which was said to have accounted for thirty thousand Tatars, while tens of thousands more fled into exile, together with a large population of Armenian Christians, dying from cold and starvation as they swarmed across the steppes to the east of the Sea of Azov. For all this the general was rewarded with the dignity of Chief Admiral of the Black Sea and governor of the new Russian province of Tauris—as the Crimea and its surrounding territories became—while Prince Potemkin himself rose to new heights of glory with the title of "the Taurian."

A few years later the Empress Catherine, now strengthening her ties with the Austrian empire, made a triumphant progress with the victorious Potemkin and a spectacular entourage through this new southern dominion, where the process of development and colonization was starting. They were joined by the Emperor Joseph at the new fortress of Kherson, on the Dnieper, where an *arc de triomphe* bore the inscription "The Road to Byzantium," and where he paid respectful court to the Empress. He was shown the new port of Sebastopol, with Russian warships at anchor, thence traversed the steppes in their company and discussed in detail their plotted dismemberment of the Ottoman Empire, jesting as they did so on what was to become of "those poor devils the Turks."

Their arrogant progress, advertised to the world and coinciding with instigations to revolt in other parts of the Ottoman Empire, served the deliberate purpose of provoking the Turks to declare war and so brand themselves as aggressors in the eyes of the intelligentsia of western Europe, where Russia now enjoyed fame and prestige. French men of letters in particular saw Catherine as an enlightened despot, promising much for civilization. To Voltaire her war against Mustafa III had been a war between reason and fanaticism, civilization and backwardness. To the Comte de Volney the Turks were the "barbarians of the Bosporus," that "ignorant and degenerate nation whose invasion by Russia was to be encouraged as giving new life to Persia."

So the Porte declared war in 1787, and in the following year the Emperor Joseph—who had breached his peace with them by a sly attempt to surprise the fortress of Belgrade—supported the Empress with his own declaration of war against the Ottoman Empire. There followed, as before, a sequence of campaigns on both fronts, each more unfortunate than the last for the Turkish forces. At sea they now had a redoubtable commander in the veteran Algerian corsair Hassan, who as a ruthless chief admiral had regenerated the Ottoman fleet, and who had since restored the Sultan's authority in the rebellious provinces of Syria; in the Morea, where the Albanians, first introduced to combat the Russian intervention, had remained as lawless bandits; and lately against a rebellion of the Mamluks in Egypt.

From Cairo he was now recalled to command the Ottoman military and naval forces in the region of the Black Sea, operating from Ochakov to recover the fortress of Kinburn, and so to regain control of the mouths of the Bug and the Dnieper. But here he was confronted by Suvarow, a Russian general of genius, supreme among the commanders of his age. At once a shrewd planner and a rousing leader, he combined an acute grasp of military science with a human insight into the nature and capacities of the men he commanded. He mixed with the Russian peasant soldiery in a rough brotherly fashion, sharing their dangers and discomforts, arousing their pride and their patriotism, inspiring in them a fighting spirit and a dedication to duty. He now awaited the landing of Hassan's force, then, with a relatively small force of his own, swiftly attacked and annihilated it. Finally, opening fire from a battery placed by the mouth of the estuary to cover the entry into the harbour of a flotilla of gunboats from upriver, he destroyed almost the whole of Hassan's fleet, thus earning for Kinburn the name of "Suvarow's Glory."

In the winter of the following year, in support of Potemkin, he invested and captured the outstanding bulwark of Oczakov, sinking further Ottoman vessels at the mouth of the Dniester, and advancing on the fortress, against heavy fire, across the frozen waters of the harbour. The Russian troops, avenging themselves for their own casualties and their sufferings in a long cruel march across the Tatar steppes, moreover enraged at the Turkish massacre of the inhabitants of a neighbouring Russian village, now slaughtered all but a few women and children among the city's inhabitants. Thus by the end of 1788 the Turks had virtually lost the war on their eastern front.

On the Austrian front they had won a respite through the incompetence of the emperor, who chose to command his own forces. After a large Ottoman army had crossed the Danube to defeat an Austrian force, Joseph assembled his own large army to march against it. But unsure of victory, he took fright, and instead retreated by night in the direction of Temesvar. Confusion and panic reigned in the darkness when the Austrians mistook a force of their own, late in retreating, for the Turks in pursuit. Forming themselves into defensive groups, they started to fire blindly in every direction. Only the light of daybreak revealed that they had been firing on their own Austrian comrades, who now lay in thousands, dead or dying around them. Of this catastrophic blunder the Turks took full advantage, swiftly attacking their enemy to capture much of his artillery, then pursuing him in retreat through an unhealthy tract of country where, quite apart from casualties in battle, the emperor lost tens of thousands of his men through disease and pestilence. Never again—to the misfortune of the Turks—did he venture to command his own army in the field.

In 1789 the command of the Austrian imperial forces was entrusted to Marshal Loudon, a vigorous, experienced veteran with Scottish blood in his veins. He had risen from the ranks to achieve distinction in the Seven Years' War, and it was reputed of him that he "made war like a gentleman." He infused new life into the Austrian army, and launched a successful invasion of Bosnia and Serbia, which led to the occupation of much of their territory. Another force, under the Prince of Coburg, linked up in Moldavia with the Russian army of Potemkin, which now occupied the area between the Dnieper and the delta of the Danube.

Earlier in the year Sultan Abdul Hamid had died, to be succeeded by his nephew as Selim III. Selim was a young man of energy and vision, bent on the salvation and reform of his country. He at once decreed a mass recruitment to his forces of all Moslems between the ages of sixteen and sixty. Then he summoned the veteran Hassan from his command of the fleet on the Black Sea to serve as Grand Vezir and commander-in-chief of the army beyond the Danube. Though more experienced on sea than on land, he had under him an army judged large enough to overwhelm that of Coburg, on the Moldavian frontier.

But Hassan was no match for the great Suvarow, who after a day-and-night march with his Russian troops across wild mountain territory appeared dramatically upon the scene, to the salvation of the Austrians. Suvarow's consistent injunction to his troops was "Forward and Strike!" Without delay, boldly forestalling Hassan's attack, he led them, two hours before daybreak, in a mass assault on the Ottoman camp, capturing its stores, munitions, and siege artillery, and routing the Turks in a succession of ferocious bayonet charges. Here was a sharp taste for them of the dreaded Russian "cold steel." He was no great believer in musketry; it was Suvarow's maxim in battle, "Push hard with the bayonet: the ball will lose its way—the bayonet never . . . the ball is a fool, the bayonet never."

Another, larger army, dispatched by Selim, was likewise defeated by Suvarow, on the River Rivnik, earning for him from the Empress the victorious triumphant surname of Rivnikski. These two defeats created panic in Istanbul, which the Sultan discreditably sought to appease by the execution of the old warrior Hassan, who had so staunchly served his country. Meanwhile Loudon, after a siege of three weeks, had captured the city of Belgrade and neighbouring fortress of Semendria. But in 1790 the Emperor Joseph died, to be succeeded by his brother Leopold, who had been opposed to his alliance with Russia against Turkey, and now withdrew from it. He signed a treaty of peace with the Turks at Sistova, restoring conquests and reverting in principle to the prewar *status quo*. The dismemberment of Turkey was in Leopold's eyes not a policy which would benefit his own empire.

Disconcerted but undismayed by this Austrian defection, the Russians went ahead in 1790 with their offensive, to drive the Turks from the coastal district of Bessarabia and Bulgaria. An obstacle to this was the fortress of Ismail, on the estuary of the Danube.

Suvarow fired its besiegers with ardour and, rather than face a long winter siege, at once gave them orders to assault the strongly garrisoned fortress, adding the cynical jest: "My brothers, no quarter; provisions are scarce." The assault was launched at night. After heavy Russian losses the walls were forced: within them the carnage was unprecedented as the Turks, soldiers and civilians alike, fought from street to street and from house to house, with an energy fortified by despair. Finally, at noonday, the Turks and Tatars of the garrison rallied in the marketplace, where all perished in a two-hour fight to the death. Fresh Russian troops then poured into the ruined city for three days of pillage and indiscriminate massacre. Even Suvarow himself retired to his tent, reduced to crocodile tears at the horror of the spectacle. Then he drafted a triumphant dispatch, partly in doggerel verse, to his Empress.

Nothing could now arrest the defeat of the Ottoman Empire. The time for mediation had arrived once more; and this time there was a significant new shift in the alignment of the powers of Europe. Throughout the eighteenth century the foreign policy of England, relatively indifferent to the fortunes of the Ottoman Empire, had favoured Russia, largely as a counterpoise to her principal enemy, France. It had been the constant view of Lord Chatham, as Prime Minister, that intervention on behalf of the Turks was not in the interests of England. She had remained indifferent when Catherine annexed the Crimea. Charles James Fox, as foreign minister, voiced the Whig policy that alliance with the northern powers "ever has been and ever will be the system of every enlightened Englishman"—and those powers included Russia, with whom moreover England traded with profit. But now, with France in the throes of revolution, the pattern of power in Europe was changing and the danger from Russia becoming more evident.

England's pro-Russian policy was thus reversed by the younger

Pitt, with the formation in 1790 of a triple alliance between England, Prussia, and Holland for the preservation of the Ottoman Empire. Hence the withdrawal from the war of the Emperor Joseph and the signature of the Treaty of Sistova between Austria and Turkey. Now Prussia and England worked hard to achieve a treaty between Russia and Turkey on the similar basis of restoring all conquests. But when mediation was offered to Catherine in 1790, she reacted indignantly, rebuking the allies for so arbitrary an attempt to dictate to an independent sovereign. To the king of Prussia she haughtily declared: "The Empress makes war and makes peace when she pleases." She was bent above all on the retention of Oczakov and of the lands between the Dniester and the Bug. But the allies, seeing in the sheltered estuary a potential naval base from which Russia could threaten Constantinople directly, insisted on its restoration, in return for which Britain would seek from the Turks a formal renunciation of their claims to the Crimea itself.

Meanwhile, they prepared to back up their mediation by force of arms. England would send a fleet of thirty-five ships into the Baltic and a smaller one into the Black Sea; Prussia would march an army into Livonia—neither power seeking territorial gains but only greater security for the Porte. When Pitt sought a parliamentary grant for this purpose, he argued that the Ottoman Empire weighed heavily in the scales of Europe, and that Russian aggrandizement at Turkish expense would endanger Prussia and the rest of Europe. He was strongly opposed in the House of Commons both by Fox and Burke. Russia, declared Fox, was the natural ally of England. What had English interests to gain by opposing her acquisition of a fortress on the Dniester and "a strip of barren land along the northern shore of the Black Sea"? To Burke "the Turks were an essentially Asiatic people who completely isolated themselves from European affairs" and had no part to play in the balance of power.

In the course of the debates the opposition, reviling the Turks as barbarians, praised the Empress by comparison as the most magnanimous of sovereigns. One speaker went so far as to declare that her conquest of Constantinople and the expulsion of the Turks from Europe could only be a benefit to mankind. The government sought to dispel such delusions, exposing the ruthlessness of the Empress in her treatment of weak nations, and urging that if her aggression were left unchecked it would lead to the predominance of Russian naval power, not only in the Black Sea but through the Bosporus and into the Mediterranean. Though Pitt's motion was carried by a reduced majority, the pressure against him both of parliamentary and public opinion was such that he wisely abandoned his policy of war, which was not in fact to be revived until the outbreak of the Crimean War, two generations later. Nonetheless, he was able to establish in men's minds the doctrine of preserving the balance of power in Europe, whose essential principle was to prevent the Russian Empire from growing and the Ottoman Empire from shrinking.

After the Turks, with their ill-trained soldiery, had suffered a further series of defeats and losses on both fronts, the Porte was ready to treat for peace. So indeed now was Catherine herself, bent on a final partition to establish her control over Poland. In negotiations at Jassy in 1791, she relinquished all conquests west of the Dniester, which had become the frontier of the Russian Empire. But she achieved her main objective with the retention of Oczakov and the territory between the Dnieper and the Bug. Potemkin was thus denied a long-cherished dream of reigning over a Christian kingdom north of the Danube composed of Moldavia, Wallachia, and Bessarabia—and in fact he died a few days afterward. There was, for the present, no further talk of a Greek empire under Constantine, and Greece itself was abandoned once more to the mercies of its Turkish masters. But Catherine could now dominate the Black Sea and the sea-lanes to Constantinople with a fleet far outnumbering that of the Turks. Moreover, on the landward side she could march against them with a formidable army from Poland. Such was the "great design" which she was on the eve of launching when in 1796, suddenly and unexpectedly, she died of a stroke, thus granting further respite to the Ottoman Empire.

Meanwhile, the historical pattern was changed, with profound implications not only for West but for East, through that momentous upheaval, the French Revolution.

PART VI

THE AGE OF REFORM

((29))

THE YOUNG SELIM III HAD SUCCEEDED TO THE SULTANATE IN 1789, the year of the French Revolution. When the Turco-Russian War was over, he emerged as an active, wholehearted reformer bent on carrying to fruition, in concrete and practical terms, those tentative ideas for reform which had been broached during the Tulip Age and after it, half a century earlier. The French Revolution itself gave those ideas a major incentive. Generally regarded at first as an internal affair, concerning Europe alone, it soon came to be seen by a discerning minority as the start of a new movement of ideas, with lessons for the East as for the West. For unlike the advances of the Renaissance in Christian Europe, it was a social upheaval divorced from Christianity, nonreligious and even anti-Christian in character. It was a movement of secularism, and as such had lessons from the West to teach the world of Islam, while not necessarily conflicting with its own religious beliefs and traditions.

Selim came to the throne of the Ottoman Empire at a period in its decline when it was still nonetheless in possession of the bulk of its territory (having lost only Hungary and Transylvania, the Crimea and Azov). But it had for long remained stagnant and had now started to crumble through internal disintegration. The central authority of the Sultan over his own dominions was continually defied by strong local pashas, abusing their powers of life and death and taxation, and by insubordinate officials in general. Furthermore, many provinces were inflamed by revolt or the threat of it—from the Wahhabites, all-powerful in the deserts of Arabia; the Druzes in the hills of Syria and Palestine; the Suliot tribesmen in Epirus and northern Greece; the Mamluk beys, contemptuous of the Porte, in Egypt; the stirrings of a spirit of independence among various Christian subjects.

Throughout the Empire there existed other sources of disorder as disruptive as any in feudal Christian Europe: through the growth of that system of heredity from which the Empire of Suleiman had still been kept mercifully free; through the multiplication of hereditary fief holders, petty local princes known as *derebeys,* or "lords of the valleys," who seized power and lands, spurning their sovereign and oppressing their dependents. Among the peasantry and the people as a whole there was widespread poverty and misery, while the financial problems of the central government were acute and hard to solve. To combat the situation it was Selim's objective, at least at the center, to introduce reforms on the Western model, as far as possible within the framework of traditional Ottoman institutions. It remained to be seen how far the institutions themselves were the obstacles to change, requiring modernization.

Selim's schemes for reform, as initiated after the conclusion of peace with Russia, were to become collectively known as the *Nizam-i-Jedid,* or "The New Order." The name was derived from the New Order in France which had followed the Revolution, and of which Louis XVI had written to the Sultan, arousing his interest. In preparing his plans Selim broke unaccustomed ground with his use of the principle of consultation.

In 1791, while the returning army was still on the Danube, he sent out instructions to twenty-two dignitaries, civil, military, and religious, including two Christian officials, to submit projects to him—"memorials" like the French *cahiers* of 1789—which were then freely discussed in a number of councils and committees, formed as never before for purposes of affairs of state. The scope of his New Order, as planned over the next two years, spread wider than anything hitherto attempted. It was to cover not merely military but civil reform; it envisaged a comprehensive plan to be devised by deliberation and universal consent; it afforded a high priority to economic recuperation.

The main stress, however, was still on the need for military reform. The Sultan had sent two special envoys to seek direct information on conditions in Europe in the military field, as in those of government, society, and political ideas. In 1792 he received a detailed report on the military systems of the European states and especially of the Austrian empire. But it was mainly on the French that he relied for the training and instruction of his new armed forces. He sent lists to Paris of those posts, for officers and technicians, which he required to fill—and indeed for one of these an early applicant was the young Napoleon Bonaparte.

Their advice was sought on such matters as artillery—a subject in which Selim was so interested as to have written a treatise on it before his accession—on arms equipment, on the improvement of gun foundries and arsenals. The earlier school of engineering was greatly expanded. New military and naval schools were established for instruction in gunnery, fortification, navigation, and ancillary sciences. The instructors were largely French officers, who with the Sultan's aid and encouragement built up for their benefit a large library of European books. These were mostly in French, including Diderot's rationalist *Encyclopédie,* while the French language was made compulsory for all the students. This process was expanded in 1795,

Sultan Selim III (1789–1807), known to the Turks as "Lord of the World" and "The Inspired," introduced major reforms, which aroused opposition among conservatives and in the end deprived him of his throne and of his life. This portrait, the original of which is an oil painting in Istanbul, shows him in closeup with his monogram or signature.

through the revival of the former French printing press in Istanbul, now under a director of the Imprimerie Nationale, with a staff of French printers from Paris. There thus arose among the new generation an enlightened few, growing familiar through their tutors and through this literature with the principles of Western culture and civilization.

Such influence was continuously reinforced, partly in a missionary spirit but largely to secure for France at this critical time the political support of the Ottoman Empire, by the rest of the French community in Istanbul and elsewhere. An influential section of them backed the Revolution, angering the Austrian and Prussian diplomats by wearing revolutionary emblems and holding revolutionary meetings. In 1793 the inauguration of the French republican flag was celebrated in a public ceremony by a salute of two French ships off Seraglio Point, flying also the Ottoman flag with those of the American Republic and of "a few other powers that had not sullied their arms in the impious league of Tyrants." A "tree of liberty" was then solemnly planted in Turkish soil. As a result of French efforts there developed a change in the society of Istanbul, where the former exclusiveness between Moslem and Frank gave place to a new intimacy between Turkish-speaking Frenchmen and French-speaking Turks. In the course of this, views on contemporary needs and ideas were exchanged, and some of the French revolutionary enthusiasm spread to a small but influential body of Turks, looking to the West for advice and inspiration.

For some time the Christian elements in the Empire, especially the Greek and Armenian elite of Istanbul, had themselves been on close terms with the West, holding influential positions in government circles and in especial relation to the Ottoman economy. Opening up of education, under Selim's reforms, enabled them increasingly to translate Western books, to teach Western languages, and to act as interpreters, in Turkish, for Western teachers. But their reaction to the French Revolution itself was inclined to be negative, if not indeed hostile, as in the attitude of the wealthier Greeks, who had too much to lose by a change in the existing regime. They were later to respond when the French began to busy themselves with the national aspirations of the Greeks and other Christian minorities. But now their main inclination was to cushion the Turks against the impact of undue direct connection with the West, both in trade and diplomacy.

Here in fact the Porte was to have its own new official window on the West. Among the various reports submitted to Sultan Selim was one which advised "sending men to Europe to study and observe European methods." This led in 1793 to the establishment of permanent diplomatic embassies on a reciprocal basis in five of the leading European capitals, of which the first was London, at the court of George III.

The ambassadors were instructed to study the institutions of the countries to which they were accredited. They were accompanied not only by the usual Greek dragomen but by young Turkish secretaries, whose duty it was to master the language and study the ways of European society—especially in France.

Politically this innovation may in fact have achieved little, at this time when the workings of European diplomacy were dislocated by the effects of the French Revolution and the subsequent Napoleonic Wars. Nor was it yet coordinated with the establishment of an official foreign ministry as a source of foreign policy in Turkey itself. But at least it added to the small body of young Turks who, like those now entering the armed forces, had acquired some experience and appreciation of the secular trends of the West, and who often rose to positions at the Porte in which their new knowledge could benefit the Empire. With the reciprocal infiltration of more foreign residents into Istanbul, this led during the reign of Selim to closer understanding of the European manner of life.

Meanwhile the New Order, acting on its various reports and memorials, had started to tackle problems of social and economic reform. In the field of provincial administration it produced regulations to curtail the powers of the pashas, limiting a governor's term of office to three years and making his reappointment conditional on the degree of satisfaction he gave to his people. Other regulations concerned provincial taxation. They sought to abolish tax farming, with a decree that government revenues should be collected by the Imperial Treasury. In the central government itself the power of the Grand Vezir was restrained by an obligation to consult the Divan on all important matters. Attempts were made at land reform, covering the *timars* and other benefices. Those which fell vacant on the death of their holders must no longer be sold or farmed, a practice which had contributed to the growth of the lawless, hereditary *derebeys*. These lands were now to revert to the sovereign, and their revenues likewise to be collected by the Imperial Treasury.

Economic measures for the rehabilitation of the country were seriously discussed. There were attempts to reform the currency, which had again been debased, with consequent inflation and devaluation, under the economic pressure of the war against Russia, and to restore its real value. There was to be government control of the grain trade. In recognition of the fact that the country's financial well-being depended on a favourable trade balance, it was proposed to create an Ottoman merchant marine, financed by Turks and bringing Turkish commerce into the hands of the Moslems, at the expense of Christian subjects. Foreign loans were considered as a remedy for the financial crisis. But these were opposed on the grounds that it was degrading for a Moslem government to borrow from a Christian country, and there was no Moslem country able to lend.

It was planned to prohibit the export of precious metals and stones and to encourage the exploitation of mines; there was even a move toward state industrial enterprise through attempts to found powder and paper mills. Few of these measures materialized in terms of tangible economic reform. But concerted as they were from among a number of fresh minds, freely expressing opinions, they broke the surface of new ground with a dawning awareness of the need for a more modern national economy.

But the essence of Selim's New Order lay still in the military dimension. Effective reform, it was realized, depended on an effective government, and this in turn was held to depend on an effective modern army. From the fighting material now produced in the military schools it was proposed to form a new corps of regular infantry, trained and equipped on Western lines. This experiment was financed by a special treasury set up for the purpose under a minister of the Divan, with revenues from fiefs, forfeited or otherwise falling into the hands of the crown, and from new taxes on spirits, tobacco, coffee, and other commodities.

It was indeed to this force that the term New Order, originally applied to the reformed system as a whole, came more specifically to apply. Here was a measure of large-scale military reform, and it provoked among Turks conflicting reactions. There were the conservatives, who aspired to revive the military glories of the Empire by reversion to the old Ottoman military methods. There were the men of compromise, who favoured the introduction of Frankish methods on the equivocal grounds that this meant, in effect, a return to the Ottoman past. Finally there were the radicals, who believed the old army to be incapable of reform, and urged the Sultan to create a new one, based wholly on a European pattern.

It was this course that Sultan Selim now pursued. He knew that a disciplined, loyal armed force was essential; on the one hand for the preservation of order within the Empire and for the enforcement of his internal reforms, on the other hand for the preservation of its integrity against the threats from without. Here he was especially responsive to the example of Peter the Great, who with a new army, trained on the Western model, had defeated his enemies both at home and abroad.

During the late Russian war the Grand Vezir, Yussuf Pasha, had captured a prisoner named Omar Agha, a Turk by origin but in the Russian service, with whom he liked to converse on the military systems of the two countries. As an experiment he permitted the formation of a small corps, composed chiefly of renegades, to be armed and drilled on the European plan. When the war was over, Omar took it with him and established it in a village not far from Istanbul. Sultan Selim, wishing to see "how the infidels fought battles," went to one of its parades. He was at once impressed by the superiority of its fire to that of his own Turkish troops. He realized more than ever the general superiority of his Christian enemies both in arms and in discipline. The corps was kept in being, recruited from among other renegades but including only a few impoverished Moslem Turks, who consented with reluctance to learn the exercises and use the weapons of the *giaour*. When the Divan, at the command of the Sultan, considered the introduction of such methods among the Janissaries, the immediate result was a mutiny, and he did not persist with his plans.

In 1796 there arrived in Istanbul, as ambassador from the French Republic, the distinguished General Aubert-Dubayet. He obtained the complete restitution of the French embassy, with all its former rights and privileges, and the reestablishment of Catholic churches. He brought with him as gifts to the Sultan several pieces of modern artillery, with munitions, to serve the Turks as models, together with a number of French engineers and artillerymen, to instruct those of the Turks and to assist in the management of their arsenals and foundries. Their efforts produced notable improvements in the construction, equipment, and performance of Turkish guns. He brought also drill sergeants from French infantry and cavalry regiments, to give lessons to the Janissaries and *sipahis*. A squadron of horse was armed and trained on the European model. But the Janissaries remained implacable in their refusal to adopt the arms or learn the maneuvers of Frankish infantry, and the only role left for the French ambassador's drill sergeants was to improve the discipline of Omar Agha's small corps, now called the Topijis. When the ambassador died and many of his officers left Turkey, the chief admiral, Hussein, took some of them into his service, and induced more Moslems to join the corps, whose strength nonetheless amounted to a mere six hundred men.

When all was said and done, it was still no more than a small minority of Turks that responded to the progressive ideas of the French Revolution and supported the Sultan's New Order. To the reactionary majority in government circles, the Revolution was but an internal affair of the barbarous Christian West, thus of no concern to them—except indirectly. Characteristic of their attitude was the comment, in his journal, of the Sultan's own privy secretary, Ahmed Effendi, in January, 1792: "May God cause the upheaval in France to spread like syphilis to the enemies of the Empire, hurl them into prolonged conflict with one another and thus accomplish results beneficial to the

Empire, amen." For his own part, Selim hoped to keep clear of this conflict, since involvement in war could only harm his reform policy at home.

Nonetheless war became inevitable. With Napoleon now rising to power in France, Selim's pacific hopes could hardly be realized. The scale of Bonaparte's imperial ambitions was such that the Ottoman Empire could not long escape their impact, whether directly or otherwise. In 1797 peace was signed, in the Treaty of Campo Formio, between France and the Austrian empire, involving the dissolution and dismemberment of the Venetian Republic. The French share was the Ionian islands and the adjoining mainland cities, giving France a common frontier for Liberty and Equality with the Ottoman Empire, and the opportunity, if she chose, to foment rebellion in Greece and the Balkans. Napoleon was now free to switch his forces against other rivals. But he resolved, in the words of the Directory of the revolutionary government, on "the reestablishment of French power in the East," as this was "one of the necessities of the struggle with England."

But Napoleon, unlike the Tsar Alexander of Russia, did not at this stage seek to precipitate the collapse of the Ottoman Empire as such. Already, through his eyes, it was crumbling of its own accord. As he declared to the Directory, "We shall see its fall in our time." Meanwhile, with an eye on this ultimate advantage, he sought to strengthen within its borders the interests, commercial and religious, of France but at the same time to detach from it one of its dissident provinces, Egypt. Here he was influenced by the ideas of Talleyrand on the advantage of acquiring new colonies, naming Egypt as one; also by the petitions of French merchants in Cairo, who sought to make Egypt an *entrepôt* for French trade with the East, at the expense of British supremacy in India.

Thus Napoleon assembled at Toulon a large fleet and army, whose destination and purpose aroused speculation. At first it was said to be the left wing of the army designed for the invasion of England. Not until after it had sailed eastward, in April, 1798, was it seen to be designed for the invasion of Egypt. Napoleon's "orders," from the Directory, which he had doubtless drafted in person, were "to clear the English from all their oriental possessions which he will be able to reach, and notably to destroy all their stations in the Red Sea; to cut through the Isthmus of Suez and to take the necessary measures to assume the free and exclusive possession of that sea to the French Republic." He was to investigate the prospect of a canal, linking it with the Mediterranean. Cherishing ambitions to follow in the conquering footsteps of Alexander the Great, his ultimate objective was to supplant the rising British Empire in India.

After seizing and annexing Malta from the remnants of the Knights of St. John, Napoleon and his army landed against little opposition on the beaches of Alexandria. He then marched his army toward Cairo. Thus was Egypt awakened from a long sleep by the first Christian force to penetrate into the heartland of Islam since the time of the Crusades. Napoleon was zealous in his protestations of respect for Islam. With exhortations to his troops—"Forty centuries are watching you"—he defeated the Mamluks at the battle of the Pyramids in the summer of 1798. He took possession of Cairo in the role of a "liberator" from usurping tyrants. The Mamluks, not the Turks, were his true enemies. So, in repeated assurances of respect for the Franco-Turkish alliance, he was careful to proclaim. Indeed, in common with Talleyrand, he cherished a false illusion that the Porte, whose authority in Egypt, under the arbitrary lordship of the Mamluks, had become little more than a nominal symbol, might acquiesce in their suppression through French opposition. But this was not to be. Imperial interests and pride called for the assertion of Ottoman sovereignty over a province which indeed had been temporarily reduced to effective obedience as recently as 1787.

Thus, after an initial hesitation, the Porte, in alliance with Russia and England, declared war against France. The French ambassador was conveyed to the Seven Towers, and a quantity of French subjects were locked in other prisons, while the English fleet ensured the arrest, by the Moslem authorities, of French merchants in the harbours of the Levant. Meanwhile, a Russian fleet sailed from the Black Sea into the Bosporus, where it was honourably welcomed and visited by the Sultan in person. It sailed onward to link up with a Turkish naval squadron and to proceed through the Mediterranean. The Russian standard flew for the first and last time side by side with the Crescent, as the joint Austrian-infidel fleet wrested the Ionian islands from the French, established over them a Russo-Turkish protectorate, and as incongruously cooperated in aiding the Pope against the allies of Napoleon on the Italian coasts.

Napoleon's second false illusion concerned the power of his own large fleet. Confident in its size, he overrated its caliber and tactical competence. The smaller but superior English fleet of Lord Nelson, in pursuit of him from Naples, had failed to intercept it—and thus probably to prevent the Alexandrian landings—only through the mischance of a dense night haze, which destroyed visibility between Crete and the African mainland. Now he came upon the French fleet anchored in Aboukir Bay, and annihilated it but for two ships which escaped but were soon afterward captured. Napoleon's army was thus stranded in Egypt without means of getting home.

Instead, in 1799 he led it, reinforced by sailors from the sunken fleet and recruits from among the Mamluks, overland into Syria. He hoped to rally to his standard the various dissident Arab provinces of the Ottoman Empire, boastfully declaring that his troops would be on the Euphrates by midsummer and ready in the autumn to march on the Indies. So after capturing Gaza and Jaffa he advanced, in the steps of the crusaders, on the key fortress of St. Jean d'Acre. Its powerful governor, the notorious Ahmed Djezzar ("the Butcher") Pasha, who was normally, with his private army of Albanians and Bosnians, a threat to the Sultan himself, now took command of his Syrian forces against the infidel.

Napoleon's siege of Acre lasted for two months, hampered once again by the English command of the sea. The squadron of the English admiral Sir Sidney Smith intercepted a French flotilla, bringing him much-needed heavy artillery. He landed gunners and marines from his own ships, and finally brought in Turkish reinforcements by sea. These included a contingent of Selim's new troops, well armed with musket and bayonet. Though Napoleon defeated a large relieving army from Damascus, he failed to overcome the garrison of Acre. "In that miserable fort," he conceded, "lay the fate of the East." He was forced to retreat with heavy losses through the desert back to Egypt.

Here he encountered a second Ottoman army, escorted from Rhodes by Sir Sidney Smith's squadron, which he swiftly defeated in a land battle at Aboukir, charging the Turks with the bayonet and driving them into the sea, where the waters of the bay bobbed with their turbans as they drowned by the thousand. Napoleon thus reestablished his prestige with the Mamluks. But, thanks largely to British naval power, his short-lived dream of an empire in the East had forever been shattered. Handing over his army to the command of General Kléber, he forsook it, sailing secretly with his staff back to France. Here, contriving triumphantly to pose as a conquerer, he turned his attention to alternative imperial dreams in the West, overthrowing the Directory meanwhile by a *coup d'état* and establishing himself as first consul.

Two years later an Anglo-Turkish expedition under General Sir Ralph Abercromby landed in Egypt, to force the surrender of the demoralized French army and transport it back to France. This led to the signature, in 1802, of the Treaty of Amiens, with terms agreed separately between England and France and, to the advantage of both, between France and the Porte. The Sultan's sovereignty over Egypt and his other dominions was recognized, and for a while the rule of pashas from the Porte replaced that of the Mamluks. The British forces withdrew from Egypt.

But Napoleon's escapade had aroused Britain to a new forward policy in the Red Sea and beyond. A treaty was signed with the local sultan of Aden as a prelude to its later annexation. Britain made clear that if India could be invaded from Egypt, then Egypt could equally be invaded from India. Similar precautions were taken in the coastlands of other Ottoman dominions. In the Persian Gulf the East India Company excluded the French from Oman, established its residency in Baghdad on a permanent basis, and took over the functions of the British consul in Basra as "Political Agent in Turkish Arabia." Napoleon's failure had inspired and sealed British success.

Under the short-lived Treaty of Amiens, France relinquished her claims on the Ionian islands and the adjoining mainland, which remained meanwhile under Russo-Turkish protection, with Russia in the islands and Turkey in the mainland towns and strongholds. A number of them had already been appropriated by the formidable Ali Pasha of Janina, an astute, ruthless Albanian with a large brigand force of his own. An awkward servant of the Porte, he had eliminated most of his neighbouring tribesmen—including the Christian rebel Suliots—to reign with a high degree of autonomy over the hinterland of Epirus and lower Albania.

At peace once more with France, with Turkish pride doubly vindicated, the Porte liberated its French prisoners and restored French property. The French Capitulations were renewed in their previous form, with added rights of trade and navigation in the Black Sea, and a brisk revival of French mercantile activity created concern among both Russians and British. After a lapse of three years French prestige prevailed once more in Istanbul—raised paradoxically by the swift success of Napoleon's army and the apparent tolerance of his rule in Egypt. The alliance flourished as before. A new French ambassador worked at the Porte to seal his country's regained influence. A new Ottoman ambassador to Paris could not easily disguise his interest in all things French.

The Sultan, while he thus had a brief respite from the foreigner, was confronted with serious internal disorders in Serbia. These were due to a tyrannical regime now established by the Janissaries, who had usurped the powers of the central authority in the region of Belgrade, much as the Mamluks had done in Egypt. They murdered its official governor, reduced his successor to insignificance, and partitioned the country among four of their chiefs. They grabbed for themselves the lands of the *sipahis,* the Turkish feudal cavalry; they fleeced and oppressed the *rayas,* the Christian peasantry, who made a plea to the Sultan for protection through a deputation to Istanbul of their own local mayors. "Art thou still our tsar?" they begged. "Then come and free us from these evildoers, and if thou wilt not save us, at least tell us, that we may decide whether to flee to the mountains and forests, or seek in the rivers a termination of our miserable existence."

Seeking to reestablish his authority, the Sultan lacked a sufficient force with which to crush his own Janissaries. After threatening them and thus only provoking a massacre of Christians he gave support, in cooperation with the dispossessed local *sipahis,* the loyal army of the pasha of Bosnia, and a few Moslem and Turkish recruits, to an insurrection against Janissary rule by the Serbians themselves. This peasants' revolt provided the unusual spectacle of a Christian minority rebelling not against but on behalf of its Moslem sovereign. The Janissaries had the support of the mutinous pasha of Vidin and of the more fanatical Moslem elements in the towns. They were nonetheless wholly defeated and their tyranny mercilessly broken, with the proud exhibition by the Christians of the four bleeding heads of their chiefs in the Serbian camp. All Serbia was now in the hands of the Serbians themselves, with the exception of Belgrade and a few other fortresses still garrisoned by the Sultan's troops.

Having achieved his objective, the Sultan now required the Christian *rayas* to lay down their arms and return to their flocks and herds. But their victory had aroused in the Serbians a nationalist temper which was not to be quelled. Given military training and a baptism of fire by the army on the occupation of Serbia by the Austrian emperor some twenty years earlier, they had by now developed a proud fighting spirit. This had been observed with surprise by the Turkish commissioners, sent to reoccupy the country when peace was signed. Hitherto accustomed to regard the Serbians as "a weaponless and submissive herd," one of them had exclaimed with some concern to an Austrian officer: "Neighbours, what have you made of our *rayas*?"—and the Serbian regiments had been immediately disbanded.

Having now proved their mettle in the Sultan's own interest, they considered themselves entitled to a degree of autonomy. They rallied around an elected chief, Kara George—or "Black George"—the son of a peasant who had risen to be a trader in swine. Scorning marks of rank and dressed always as a herdsman, he had taken to the mountains to wage a fierce guerrilla campaign against the Janissaries. Inspired by him, the Serbians petitioned for support from the Russians as fellow Christians of the Greek Church. The Tsar, then allied with the Turks, advised them to present their claims at the Porte and promised them support there. Thus they sent a deputation to the Sultan, with a claim not only for the remission of arrears of tribute but for the cession to them of Belgrade and its neighbouring fortresses.

Such presumptuous demands from the despised Christians infuriated the good Moslems of the Divan, and were rejected by the Sultan, who ordered the imprisonment of the delegates. He then sent three successive armies to suppress his former Serbian allies. But each was defeated, without foreign aid, by the redoubtable Kara George, who finally expelled the Turkish garrisons from Belgrade and other fortresses, to secure promises of protection from Russia. He thus made history by achieving for the Serbs a spell of effective independence from Ottoman rule, the first Balkan Christian community to do so by its own efforts in this century of dawning nationalist consciousness.

In Istanbul this was a moment of high diplomatic activity. In 1805 Russia and England were in strong competition with France for Turkish support in the war now launched in coalition against her. Despite the Treaty of Amiens, Napoleon still looked toward the East. He sent to the Levant a mission under François Sebastiani, a man of the world who had once been a priest and could now boast of accomplishments as both soldier and diplomat. Ostensibly he sought to reestablish French commercial interests. But in fact he contemplated a possible French campaign in the eastern Mediterranean.

Now, after Napoleon's proclamation as Emperor of the French, Sebastiani became ambassador extraordinary at the Porte, where he intensified pressure for Turkish military intervention against Russia. His hand was strengthened by French victories against Austria. These culminated in the Treaty of Pressburg, in 1805, and the acquisition of territories in Croatia and Dalmatia which brought the dominions of France into direct contact with those of the Ottoman Empire. They would enable Napoleon to establish a frontier force, ready either to support or to invade Turkey as the occasion demanded. Encouraged by this success of French arms, Sultan Selim, in an imperial edict, recognized Napoleon as emperor, accorded to him the title of Padishah, and sent him an ambassador extraordinary, "to signalize in an eminent manner [his] feelings of confidence, attachment and admiration." To this Napoleon replied, through his own ambassador: "Everything that shall happen, whether fortunate or unfortunate, for the Ottomans will be fortunate or unfortunate for France." The Sultan's recognition of the emperor was strongly opposed by both the British and the Russian ambassadors.

Similar demands for Turkish support, in the form of a full offensive and defensive alliance, had come from Russia. The Tsar went so far as to demand that the Sultan should recognize him as the protector of all Christians of the Orthodox faith in the Ottoman Empire, with the right of intervention on their behalf by the Russian ambassador. This so stung Moslem pride that Selim, prompted by Sebastiani's advice, retaliated with the deposition of the Phanariot hospodars of the Danubian principalities of Wallachia and Moldavia. Both were known to be tsarist agents, and were believed also to have fomented the troubles in Serbia through Kara George. The Russians protested angrily at this breach of treaty engagements; their protests were echoed by those of the British ambassador; and it was hinted at the Porte that the military arm of the one and the naval arm of the other were about to "receive a new impulse."

The Sultan, still anxious for peace, was prepared to temporize. But a Russian army, without a previous declaration of war, marched into Moldavia and Wallachia, which it speedily overran, entering Bucharest and preparing to cross the Danube. The Porte, repelling force with force, declared war against Russia and refused to be cowed into submission by the threats of the British ambassador, who demanded a renewal of its alliances with Britain and Russia and the dismissal of the ambassador of France.

Thus in 1807 the British fleet in its turn intervened, sailing through the Dardanelles into the Sea of Marmara under Admiral Duckworth. He presented an ultimatum to the Porte, demanding the surrender of the Ottoman fleet and in default threatening to burn it and to bombard Istanbul, as he was in a position to do through immediate action. The Turks shrewdly gained for themselves a breathing space by drawing the British minister and his admiral into negotiations and continuing to spin them out for ten days. This allowed them time, with the aid of Sebastiani, who had pitched his tent in the gardens of the Seraglio, to mount artillery on the batteries and generally to strengthen the city's fortifications. The Sultan moved his own fleet out of range, while Sebastiani's military engineers repaired the defenses of the Dardanelles.

Admiral Duckworth had lost his chance. He reached the reluctant conclusion that a bombardment would now expose his own fleet to too great a hazard. Thus he weighed anchor and sailed back through the Dardanelles. Here, thanks to Sebastiani's rapid work on the batteries, his ships had to face bombardment from huge ancient cannon, firing balls of stone which weighed hundreds of pounds. He lost two ships and was fortunate not to lose more. Meanwhile, Selim brought in a force of some five hundred French artillerymen to defend the Straits and thus openly to seal his French alliance.

Admiral Duckworth's misconceived naval adventure was directly followed by another, as abortive, which was conducted from Malta against Egypt. Inspired by the British government's fear of a renewed French invasion, its aim was to establish a bridgehead by the occupation of Alexandria, which indeed soon surrendered, and of Rosetta, at the mouth of the Nile, where the small British force was repulsed by Turkish troops. It had been hoped to obtain the support of the Mamluks against a new power which had now arisen, to restore a semblance of order to the country. It was that of Mehmed Ali, an Albanian from Macedonia, born in the same year as Napoleon, who had fought against him at Aboukir, who had returned to make himself master of Cairo with the aid of the Sultan's Albanian mercenaries, and who was now recognized by the Porte as pasha of Egypt.

Mehmed Ali isolated the British force in Alexandria, and was astute enough to negotiate its withdrawal on conciliatory terms. These enabled him in due course to benefit himself, and his fertile province, as general purveyor of supplies to the British naval and military forces in the Mediterranean. Such was the first appearance on the scene of that formidable ruler who was to establish in Egypt his own autonomous dynasty, effectively free from the Sultan's control.

The war against Russia on the Danube front moved slowly. Neither Turks nor Russians, with their eyes on Napoleon, put forth their full strength. Sultan Selim chose to profit by the absence at the front of his main force of Janissaries to continue at home with the reforms of his military New Order. The Topijis, his French-trained corps of artillery, had been placed on a footing superior to that of the Janissaries. The original small corps of Omar Agha, which had distinguished itself at Acre, had since repressed bands of brigands in Bulgaria and Rumelia and defeated Janissaries led against it by dissident provincial governors. The Sultan had increased its numbers by two regiments, armed and accoutered and trained on the French model.

In 1805, short of troops to put into the field against Russia, the Sultan took the bold step of decreeing a general levy for the new corps, to replace the normal system of voluntary recruitment. This was required not only from the population in general but from among the Janissaries themselves, whose youngest and best soldiers were to be transferred to its ranks. Though they had been crushed at Belgrade —thanks to the *rayas*—they were still truculent in other provinces, and at Adrianople they resisted the Sultan's decree with force. The official who tried to enforce it was set upon and strangled. A force of new troops from Anatolia commanded by the pasha of Karamania, who supported the Sultan's reforms, was attacked by a large force of Janissaries in the Danubian theater of war, and entirely defeated.

This encounter aroused protests from the Janissaries in Istanbul, which were actively supported by the reactionaries in the Divan and among the ulema. Rather than face a revolt and the possible extension of civil war to the capital at this time of war with Russia, the Sultan was obliged to suspend the reforms, disbanding the Anatolian force, dismissing some of his reformist advisers, and entrusting the office of Grand Vezir to the Agha of the Janissaries.

But in the early summer of 1807, not long after the departure of the English naval force, an order was given to the Yamaks, the auxiliary levies now employed as a garrison for the Bosporus batteries, to adopt new uniforms and equipment designed in the European style. At this they mutinied and marched to the Hippodrome in Istanbul, where some hundreds of Janissaries joined them, overturning their camp kettles in traditional style to indicate that they would no longer accept food from the Sultan. Here, in confederation with the *kaimakam* subgovernor Musa Pasha, an official notorious for his intriguing and

A Topiji or Topchu—one of the Sultan's French-trained artillerymen.

treacherous disposition, and with the compliance of the Chief Mufti, lately appointed, they set up a tribunal to judge counsellors and ministers of the Sultan who supported reform and aroused the Istanbul mob against them. They were rounded up and many of them killed, whether in their own houses or in the Hippodrome, and the heads of seventeen reformers were proudly flaunted before those who had inspired the revolt.

Unfortunately for Sultan Selim his loyal ally, the previous Mufti, had died earlier in the year, and the bulk of the ulema had always opposed his reforms. Now forced to submit, he decreed the abolition of his New Order. But he was too late to save his throne. In reply to a deputation of Janissary officers the Chief Mufti declared that since the Sultan's government had "introduced among Moslems the manners of infidels and shown an intention to suppress the Janissaries, the true defenders of the law and the prophets," the Sultan should be deposed, in the interests of the Moslem religion and the house of Osman. His deposition was proclaimed in a *fetva,* the forces of the New Order were disbanded, and the chief mutineer invested with the command of the Bosporus fortresses. Selim meanwhile had repaired to the Cage, where he made obeisance to his young cousin Mustafa as Sultan, counselling him not to be led into great changes, and wishing him a happier reign than his own. He then tried to drink poison, but Mustafa dashed the cup from his lips, swearing that his life would be spared. Thus Selim withdrew with resigned dignity to his prison apartments, from which a new Sultan emerged to ascend the throne as Mustafa IV.

He was to reign only for a few months. Selim still had his friends and supporters, notably Mustafa Bayrakdar, or "Standard-bearer," the independent pasha of Rustchuk on the Danube. A convert to the reform program, he owed his career to Selim and now resolved on a *coup d'état* to restore him. The signature at that moment of a truce with the Russians released his large army, composed mainly of Bosnians and Albanians, together with that of the loyal Grand Vezir at Adrianople, enabling them to march beneath the standard of the Prophet to Istanbul.

His aim here was to overawe the Janissaries, occupy the palace, dethrone Mustafa, and reinstate Selim. Demanding to see "the true Sultan Selim," but denied admission by the palace guards, he broke in with his troops. But the brief delay had been fatal. Reacting to his demand, Sultan Mustafa had ordered the immediate strangulation of Selim and of his brother Mahmud, whose deaths would leave him the last survivor of the house of Osman.

The executioners slaughtered Selim against a gallant resistance, and with the cry "Behold the Sultan ye seek" his body was cast before the Bayrakdar as he entered the gate of the inner courtyard. With the Albanians he then dragged Mustafa down from his throne, demanding "What dost thou there? Yield that place to a worthier." The murderers meanwhile failed to find Mahmud, who had been hidden by a faithful slave in the furnace of a bath. Here the victorious Albanians discovered him, and before nightfall it was proclaimed, with a salvo of fire from the Seraglio, that Mustafa IV was deposed and Mahmud II enthroned as Sultan of the Ottoman Empire.

Mustafa Bayrakdar became his vigorous Grand Vezir. After executing the assassins, the favourites of Mustafa, and the chief of the Yamak rebels, he resumed with determination the measures of reform which Selim had initiated. He reestablished the troops of the New Order, with European methods of training, under the old name of the Seymens. He revived and supplemented the various reform edicts, and for the first time convened, from all parts of the Empire, a consultative assembly of high officials. It sat in the imperial palace, where in a rousing inaugural address he announced a specific reform program. This involved a widespread reorganization of the corps of Janissaries, aimed at the elimination of long-standing abuses. At the same time he confirmed the privileges and rights of the powerful *ayans* and *derebeys.*

After a lively debate an agreement was reached between those provincial vassals—from whom he himself sprang—and the central government. Their pact represented, in legal and political terms, a significant landmark in the definition of the respective responsibilities of the estates of the realm. As a threatened erosion of his powers, Sultan Mahmud reached it only with reluctance. The Janissaries and the ulema at first feigned assent, and Bayrakdar, counting on the support of the Seymens and other local forces, unwisely sent home his Albanian and Bosnian armies.

Seizing their opportunity, the Janissaries then rose once again in rebellion. They attacked the Bayrakdar in his palace, setting fire to it and blowing up a tower to which he had fled, and thus burned him to death. The forces of reaction had finally triumphed. The old disordered system, with all its abuses, seemed to be reestablished as strongly as ever before.

The reform movement of Selim III thus fell into abeyance for some time to come. Alone hitherto among Sultans of the Ottoman line, he had dedicated himself wholly and with steadfast conviction to the radical reform of his empire. What Suleiman the Lawgiver had achieved for it 250 years earlier, in terms of the East and the traditions of Islam, Selim sought to achieve in terms of the West and the new spirit of secularization. He failed, dying in bitter disillusionment, owing in part to certain failings of character which belied his intentions. Enlightened, altruistic, and sincere though he was in his ambition to start the Ottoman Empire on the road toward European civilization, there lay within him a certain blindness to the true psychology of the bulk of his own people, whose welfare he sought, but whom he could not aspire to lead in battle, as his great predecessors had done, and whose loyalty and trust he thus failed to kindle. On the contrary, through indiscretion and excess of zeal in his cultivation of the West and its ideas, he enabled the antireformers within his own ranks to rekindle in them deep-rooted reactionary prejudices and harden their resistance to all innovation.

But in essence Selim's failure was due to the hard fact that he was attempting an impossible task. He was powerless, at this stage in Ottoman history, to change at a single stroke a traditional system of government which had built itself up over the centuries and was still, for all its weaknesses, intact and tenacious. If Selim, as a radical Sultan, hoped to succeed with a policy of reform in his empire, he would have had to reorganize the basic structure of its existing institutions, in effect to create a new state, with new machinery for applying decisions and the strength to enforce them. This would have implied above all a restriction, at the dictation of an all-powerful and respected Sultan, of the authority of the Sheikh-ul-Islam and his ulema, of the forces of Islam itself. Selim was not such a sovereign, nor in the context of his time was such a task yet attainable. All he could do, as a ruler ahead of his time, was to attempt innovations within the traditional structure, and these he failed to achieve.

Selim's reform policy, which he thus lacked the power to enforce, reflected the views of a minority of his elite only one degree larger than that of the earlier reforming Age of the Tulip. The large and all-powerful conservative majority consisted of the army, an inflated and increasingly corrupt bureaucracy, and the ulema, who as the traditional voice of Islam had been beneficiaries of Suleiman's own reforms. They still held the internal balance of power in which he had confirmed and reinforced them.

But they had since deteriorated in quality, exploiting and indeed abusing this power in their own wordly interests, selling offices, privileges, and favour, engaging in usury, in tax farming, in the appropriation of estates, in irregular control of the pious foundations. At the lower levels many maintained themselves in a similarly parasitic position, as also did the Janissaries, engaged as they now were in a number of commercial activities. Each of these groups, in which too many had too much to lose by a change, made common cause to support at any cost the traditional *status quo,* and the influence and wealth which it brought them.

They formed a monolithic establishment all the stronger because it was free from divisive class interests. In a country where industry was still in its infancy and commerce largely conceded to the foreigner, there was no such element of social and economic disruption as had provoked the French Revolution and was elsewhere in Europe to nourish the revolutionary spirit in the course of the century to come. The reformist minority, with no such pressure group behind them, were thus all the more isolated and at the mercy of the conservative elements, should they seek either to dominate the ruler or to force his deposition.

Such, thanks to his Francophil policies, was the fate of Selim III. Though his reforms were repealed, he had nonetheless given impetus to a movement of new and enlightened ideas from the West. After his time this was destined to penetrate the fortress of Islam, gradually widening its horizons throughout the nineteenth century from a tentative stream into an enveloping flood. The French Revolution was eventually to nourish, in this unfamiliar soil, the principles of Liberty, under Islam primarily a legal conception but in time to develop a political meaning; Equality, which from the start had little relevance in a society with a strong charitable tradition, rooted in Islam and without unacceptable extremes of wealth and social privilege; and Fraternity, which was to take the form of Nationality throughout the Ottoman Empire, with its Christian minorities, and in the Islamic world as a whole.

Meanwhile, paradoxically, the moral lapse from the principles of Islam, which nonetheless continued to survive as a dominant social and political force, proved in the short term more cohesive than disruptive in its effects on the latter-day Ottoman regime. There was, after all, a certain negative strength in stagnation. As a sophisticated Ottoman diplomat later jested: "Our state is the strongest state. For you are trying to cause its collapse from the outside, and we from the inside, but still it does not collapse."

((30))

Mahmud II, at this time the only surviving male heir to the dynasty of Osman, was to reign for a generation and in the course of it to prove himself a resolute reforming Sultan. Within the context of his own more turbulent century, he ranks as worthy successor to Mehmed the Conqueror and Suleiman the Lawgiver. In his role of internal reformer, Mahmud liked to see himself as the Peter the Great of the Ottoman Empire. Though his mother may possibly have been French, he knew no European language, while his conventional Islamic education gave him no direct access to Western ideas. But he was strongly influenced in his early youth by Selim III, his cousin and confidant, especially during the brief interval between Selim's deposition and that of his brother, Mustafa, when both shared the Cage. Nonetheless, if he inherited Selim's mantle he well realized that, with the military and religious establishments now invincibly united against change, he must bide his time in patience. Nearly two decades, in fact, were to pass before he could reestablish for the sultanate sufficient authority to proceed with the reforming policy which he saw as essential to the Empire's survival.

Meanwhile, his energies were occupied by the Ottoman conflict with Russia. Napoleon, foreseeing the imminent ruin of their empire, abandoned his Ottoman allies by contracting over their heads an alliance with the Tsar Alexander of Russia. Signed in 1807, this was aimed, against the Tsar's English ally, at a division of Europe between Russia and France. Demanding a cessation of hostilities between Turkey and Russia, the two all-powerful imperial potentates hatched secret plans for the dismemberment between them of the Ottoman Empire. Its territories were to be confined mainly to Asia, allowing to Russia most of eastern Balkan Europe, with compensation for Austria in the West. France would have Albania, Greece, Crete, and other islands of the Archipelago, with prospects of further expansion eastward. If the Porte refused French mediation, France would make common cause with Russia, to free Europe "from the yoke and vexations of the Turks." Thus the Porte, under the auspices of France, signed an armistice with Russia, which was to last for two years, with no agreement on peace terms, and to end with a renewal of Turco-Russian hostilities.

Sultan Mahmud II (1808–39) as a boy. The original oil painting is in Istanbul.

Meanwhile, upon the murder of Mustafa IV and the accession of the childless Mahmud II, the Tsar Alexander began to see prospects of failure in the line of the Ottoman dynastic succession and its consequent easy reversion to Russia. He thus sought to expedite the Empire's partition. But now he presumed to demand Constantinople itself, and the Dardanelles, which in the secret treaty had been allotted to neither contracting party. To such a concession Napoleon, as his ambassador at St. Petersburg tried forcibly to convince Alexander, could in no circumstances consent. Nor was he impressed by the Tsar's pretension that Constantinople, as a provincial city at the extremity of his empire, was no more than a door to his own house to which he required to hold the key.

The French ambassador proposed that the city and the shores of the Straits should remain a free territory. But the Russian negotiator demanded Constantinople, as the metropolis of the Greek Orthodox Church, hence naturally and historically of the Empire of the East. The Frenchman insisted that if it were indeed ceded, France should have the Dardanelles and their coasts, as the classic crusader route into Syria. But the Russians rejected any access by France to free passage between the Black Sea and the Mediterranean.

Deadlock thus halted Napoleon's chimerical dream of a Franco-Russian duumvirate, dividing and ruling the Ottoman Empire. To evade the issue he changed course, advocating delay for fear of the risk that the richest of its spoils, in the shape of Egypt, might fall to England. Instead, at Erfurt in 1808, he reviewed his alliance with Russia against the Porte, recognizing, as a *quid pro quo* for her rupture with Britain, her possession of Wallachia and Moldavia, which her armies in fact still provisionally occupied. To this he awaited the English reaction.

Alarmed at this confirmation of Russian dominion over the Danubian principalities, the Austrian empire now mediated to secure, as a counterweight to the Franco-Russian alliance, a reconciliation between Britain and Turkey. Despite menaces from France, this was achieved in 1809, through the Treaty of the Dardanelles. Thus war broke out once again between Turkey and Russia. The Russians, marching against ill-organized and diminished Turkish forces, crossed the Danube from Wallachia to capture fortresses on its right bank, including Silistria, but were resisted by the army of the Grand Vezir from his fortified camp at Shumla. They hence failed to cross the formidable Balkan range, and it was only after further resistance by a Bosnian army that they were able to capture Rustchuk.

By 1811, as their alliance with Napoleon broke up and they awaited his invasion from the West, the Russians switched to the defensive on the Danube front. They now needed peace with the Porte, and in the summer of 1812, only a few weeks before the march of Napoleon's

Grand Army on Moscow, a treaty was signed at Bucharest. By this the Pruth became the recognized frontier between the Russian and Ottoman empires. The Tsar restored the rest of Moldavia and all Wallachia to the Sultan, but retained Bessarabia, with its access to the mouth of the Danube. Too late in the day Napoleon had sought in his own interests to regain Turkish friendship, urging the Sultan to advance in full strength against the Russians on the Danube front, promising in return the security of Moldavia and Wallachia and the restoration of the Crimea to the Ottoman Empire. But the Turks had resolved, under pressure from Britain, on peace with Russia, mistrusting Napoleon the more from now learning in full of his earlier plans for their empire's dismemberment.

The chief sufferers from the Treaty of Bucharest were the Serbs, to whom Russia had afforded protection. They were indeed granted an amnesty for their rebels, and in vague terms the management of their internal affairs. But this was effectively neutralized by the restoration of Belgrade and other fortresses to the Sultan, for occupation by Turkish garrisons, and the demolition of fortresses built meanwhile by the Serbs themselves. In the following year, after the fall of Napoleon, the Turks made a vassal state of Serbia once more.

The Empire which Napoleon and Alexander had planned prematurely to dismember was to outlive them both for a century longer. But in Mahmud's time it continued to shrink in extent, retaining despite decay its internal organs while losing through disruption its outlying limbs. Of these the first to be amputated was Greece. The Greek nationalist movement dated back to the beginning of the nineteenth century. From the start it took the indeterminate form of a cultural revival. Here was a Greek renaissance in the classical tradition, drawing in its ideas from the liberal philosophers of the French Revolution and from the general diffusion of knowledge among the Greeks, as among enlightened Turks, since the time of Selim III. This took the form of improved education, endowed by wealthy Greeks through schools which revived the study of Greek history, and through the dissemination of books published abroad in the Greek language.

Within it lay the seeds of an ultimate liberation and rebirth of the Greek national spirit. Expatriates in the West played a part in it. So, within the Empire itself, did the Phanariot Greeks in the service of the Porte; also the affluent Greek commercial communities of Istanbul, Salonika, Smyrna, and the various islands of the Greek Archipelago. Several of these in effect governed themselves, notably Chios, where the Turks kept the enlightened government system of the former Genoese chartered company under local officials and soldiers; and also the three "nautical islands" of Hydra, Spetsai, and Psara, seafaring communities whose sailors had a share in their ships and cargoes, and which were to serve as the "nurseries" of a future Greek fleet. Thus in the coastal parts of the country there were many Greeks who maintained close and continuous contact with the West.

Throughout mainland Greece a less elastic spirit prevailed. The Ottoman administration maintained an oppressive control over the people, geared not to their welfare or security but to the collection of taxes, often to the profit of the corrupt pashas imposing them. But the direct exactions of Turkish officials were in a sense the least of their burdens. As burdensome was control by the Greek official classes themselves, whether landowners who had embraced Islam for the sake of retaining their property and power, or local dignitaries of the administration—elders and headmen, primates and *koja-bashis* (headmen) of the villages and towns. Their task it was, as agents of the Turkish officials, to assess the taxes due from their respective communities, and as tax farmers they adopted the methods of their Ottoman masters. Enjoying and abusing a privileged position in the maintenance of local law and order, they were often harsh in their oppression of their own fellow Christians.

As oppressive in its own way was the Christian priesthood, narrow and conservative in its outlook, which as part of the civil establishment enjoyed the Sultan's protection and wielded a wide authority over the Greek population. Hence there prevailed—among clerics, landowners, and local officials—Greek vested interests, which had too much to lose by supporting any transition from a Greek cultural renaissance to a Greek political revolution in terms of national independence. The idea of a Greek nation, as distinct from a Greek religion and language, was thus slow to materialize in concrete terms.

When in the course of time it did so, encouraging the use of military force to attain national ends, its active roots among the Greek population were twofold. First there were the *klephts,* wild lawless bands which had long ranged the mountains to evade Turkish authority, living by banditry and violence. Their traditional profession of brigandage now rose in Greek esteem beyond that of mere rapacity to become acknowledged as an honourable and legitimate weapon against Ottoman tyranny. It thus developed into a patriotic focus of revolt in the Greek nationalist cause. The *klephts* operated in separate mountainous areas of the mainland—in the Morea, Epirus, and Rumeli, besides Crete and other islands—led by powerful hereditary chiefs who were to become political leaders of the revolution to come. The Turks had armed a Christian gendarmerie, the *armatoli,* against them, which often in fact came to take their side.

They had counterparts at sea among the vigorous privateers of the islands and coastlands, who lived by piracy as the landsmen lived by banditry. The spirit of adventure in both drew example and experience from the British operations, both naval and military, which led to the capture of the Ionian islands from Napoleon in 1814. The planting of the British flag in these islands helped to stimulate a fever for liberty, firing a revolt throughout the mainland of Greece.

But if this were to succeed it must be systematically planned and coordinated. Here an integral part was played by the Greek merchant community, with its widespread contacts both in Greece and abroad. Its instrument of organization was the *Philike Hetaeria,* or "Society of Friends," originally a product of the unsuccessful Greek rising against the Turks, with the aid of the Russians, in 1770. Its founder toward the end of the century was the Greek national poet Rhigas Pheraios, who gave to the revolution its *Marseillaise*. By birth a Vlach, hence a native of Rumania, he dreamed, in terms more poetic than realistic, not merely of a liberated Greece but of a multinational Balkan federation of autonomous Christian states, like a miniature Byzantine Empire, whose official language and church would be Greek and for which, so he imagined, Serbs, Bulgarians, Albanians, and Rumanians would readily draw the sword in Christian unity for the cause of Greek freedom. Into this indeed Kara George and the leaders of the first Christian rebellion against the Sultan were in fact to be initiated. The execution of Rhigas by the Turks led to the decline of his *Hetaeria*. Now however, in 1814, it was revived, not in Greece but in Russia, by three Greek merchants of Odessa. In Athens itself it took shape under cover of a Greek literary society, so as to spread its ideas among educated Greeks without arousing Turkish suspicions.

The society's activities were overbold nonetheless, and became generally known as it spread its branches and agents throughout European Turkey and the cities of Asia Minor. It grew into a conspiratorial Freemasonry, with its own elaborate hierarchy, secret signs, mysterious rituals, and a solemn oath of allegiance. Its plots and intrigues stirred elements of sedition among the Balkan communities. Among its members were Russian officers, while its adherents were assured by Russian consular agents of the Tsar's secret patronage, with hints of his readiness to furnish military support in the event of a rising. On this the Greeks were only too ready to rely.

The presidency of the *Hetaeria* was offered at first to Count John Capodistria, a Corfiote of commanding influence and prestige in the service of the Tsar at St. Petersburg, who had signed on his behalf the agreement for the British protectorate over the Ionian islands. When Capodistria refused the offer, its leadership was conferred on Alexander Ypsilantis, a Phanariot Greek whose family had been hospodars of Moldavia and Wallachia, moreover an aide-de-camp to the Tsar who had served with honour and distinction in the Russian army. In 1820 the society appointed him "General Commissioner of the Supreme Authority."

Deciding to launch his revolt in the north, Ypsilantis, more adventurously than wisely, led a mixed force across the Pruth—now the boundary between the Russian and Turkish empires—into Moldavia and Wallachia. Loud in his affirmations and lofty in his sentiments, he nonetheless lacked experience of men and affairs. He was counting on a spirit of unity between Rumanian and Greek Christians which did not exist. Though welcomed by the hospodar of Moldavia, he found little or no support for the Hellenic cause in Wallachia, where a local rebel enlightened him: "Greece belongs to the Greeks, Romania to the Romans." The Tsar disowned him and expelled him from his army. The Oecumenical Patriarch excommunicated him at the Sultan's behest. The Turks sent an army to Bucharest, which wiped out his "sacred battalion," and Ypsilantis himself fled into Austrian territory, where the emperor imprisoned him. Such, ironically, was the end of the rule of the Phanariot Greeks in the Danube principalities, and the birth of Rumanian independence, with the rule of hospodars to be selected from among the ranks of the Rumanian princes.

Greek independence was nonetheless born, simultaneously, through a coordinated series of revolts over a wide area of the country. These were initiated through the *Hetaeria* with the dispatch to Greece of Phanariot and other leaders, including the brother of Ypsilantis, Dimitri, who was to command in the Peloponnese, and by others who went there of their own accord, linking up with rebel leaders on the spot. The revolt started with a proclamation from the Metropolitan of Patras on March 25, 1821.

It was well timed. For Sultan Mahmud, whose Divan seemed unaware of any such immediate Greek danger, had chosen this moment to embark on the final subjugation in Epirus of his nominal vassal Ali Pasha, the rebellious "Lion of Janina." Ali, with the aid of his Albanian army, had so built up his power and expanded his dominion as to rank in effect as an independent potentate—and he had been recognized as such by Napoleon. In 1819 he had taken triumphant possession of the important Adriatic port of Parga. In the following year Ismail, a fellow Albanian and personal enemy of Ali, fled from him for protection to Istanbul, where the Sultan made him one of his chamberlains. Ali sent after him two hired assassins, who were arrested in an attempt to shoot him. This gave Sultan Mahmud a long-sought opportunity to crush his enemy once and for all. He officially declared Ali a rebel and an outlaw, conferred his pashalik on Ismail, his intended victim, and launched under his command an immediate war against him. As Ali, the lion now at bay, held out stubbornly for close on two years, the Sultan called upon his seasoned and ruthless commander in the Morea, Kirshid Pasha, with his troops, to finish off the campaign. They finally defeated and destroyed the old rebel, who had taken refuge in his lake-island fortress. His head, with the heads of his three sons and grandson, was dispatched to the Sultan in Istanbul.

As a result the Morean fortresses had been left relatively undefended, and the Greek rebels were able to surprise and overwhelm most of their garrisons. Synchronization at sea, by the Greek privateers with their deadly, maneuverable fireships, won them control of key ports around the coastline. This limited Turkish supply and reinforcement to overland communications through mountainous, guerrilla-held territory. Among the islands the rebels held Spetsai—where a rich Greek widow blockaded the Gulf of Nauplia in person and at her own expense—then Psara, and eventually Hydra, thanks to a ship's captain who roused the people against their own Greek primates.

Throughout the peninsula the popular song of the revolt, "Not a Turk Shall Remain in the Morea," inspired indiscriminate and murderous action against all Moslems. The rebellion spread across the Gulf of Corinth, where the infidel townsmen of Livadia were similarly massacred. Peasants surmounted an improvised wall to capture Athens, then an insignificant provincial town of ten thousand inhabitants, which was the Sultan's own personal property. But its Acropolis, refortified since its siege by the Venetians, held out for over a year longer. In the west, Mesolonghi rose in vigorous rebellion. In the north revolt flared among the "folds of Pelion" and on the triple Macedonian peninsulas of Chalcidice, where the monks of Mount Athos readily armed for a cause at once religious and national. In Crete, an island with a predominant Moslem population, a detachment of Janissaries, fanatical Cretan Moslems of Greek origin, committed atrocities against Christians, going so far as to slaughter the Metropolitan of Candia and five bishops at the altar of his cathedral. This provoked in retaliation a rising of the warlike Sphakians from the mountains, who for a while, with the aid of a Greek fleet, were able to blockade the port of Canea.

Sultan Mahmud was not a man to accept defiance of his rule with impunity. When his armies had recovered from the first shock of surprise at the revolt, he retaliated savagely in kind against the Greeks for this massacre of Turks throughout the Morea. In Istanbul he executed the Greek Dragoman of the Porte and other prominent Phanariots. In revenge for the Greek atrocities in Tripolitza he hanged the Greek Patriarch—a native of the Morea—from the gate of his palace on Easter Sunday, exhibiting the body for three days, then permitting it to be dragged away by despised Jews and flung into the sea. When before Chios a fireship of the rebel Greek fleet destroyed the Turkish flagship, with admiral and crew, the Turks took their revenge with the destruction of the whole prosperous island, selling into slavery or driving into exile a population of some hundred thousand Christians. They generally succeeded in crushing the revolt north of the Gulf of Corinth, but failed to make headway in a major invasion of the Morea.

But the Greeks, rather than consolidate their military advantages, involved themselves too hastily in the political problems of local constitutional government. In each region of their occupation they convened an assembly—a senate in Messenia, a "central government" in the Peloponnese, and further elected institutions of government in eastern and western Rumeli. These bodies represented contestants for power with rival interests and ambitions—the primates, the landowners, the leaders of the Church, the Phanariots, the island merchants, and the *klephts,* who remained a law unto themselves. Unity among them was a vain aspiration, since they did not yet feel themselves to be Greeks in a national sense.

A first attempt to combine their interests in a central government of Greece was made after the fall of Tripoli, with the convocation by Dimitri Ypsilantis of a National Assembly near Epidaurus; then the proclamation, on New Year's Day, 1822, of a constitution, complete with a legislature and an executive conceived on republican principles. It was drafted largely by Alexander Mavrokordatos, the able Phanariot leader of the rebel assembly at Mesolonghi in the west, who was named as its president. Ypsilantis meanwhile faded into the background. But for a people only now emerging from centuries of oriental despotism, moreover tied by traditional loyalties to their own rival communal groups, such an experiment in the liberal constitutional arts of the West proved sadly premature.

Later in 1822 Nauplia, the leading port of the eastern Peloponnese and its natural capital, fell to the Greek rebels in the person of the *klepht* leader Kolokotrones. He refused to countenance a meeting of the national assembly at Nauplia, and when it met elsewhere and sought to curtail his governing powers, his reply was to kidnap four members of the government. Its remnants withdrew to a remote promontory under the protection of Hydra and Spetsai, electing the wealthy Hydriot Koundouriotis, of Albanian descent, as their president, but leaving Kolokotrones as the effective master of the Morea. It had all too soon become evident that no Greek would accept the sovereignty of another Greek. Hence the solution must eventually be found in a sovereign prince from the West.

From an early stage the Greeks had counted overoptimistically on Western support. In the military sense they were soon disappointed. For after the defeat of Napoleon the Western powers, together with Russia, sought a period of peace. As an antirevolutionary "league of sovereigns" they were to maintain a semblance of pacific unity for a decade to come. Thus neither Britain nor Austria nor, to its relief,

Russia (for all her implied promises) was prepared to fight for the cause of Greek nationalism. On the outbreak of the revolt the powers joined in denouncing it, and in 1822 at an allied conference at Verona refused to receive the Greek delegates, as being revolutionaries.

But among their subjects there was arising a new and romantic spirit of Philhellenism, which saw the Greeks not merely as oppressed Christians but as the brave descendants of the heroes of the classical age. Enthusiasm for Hellas was fired in them by travellers on the Grand Tour, collectors of antiquities, classical scholars, intellectuals, men of letters, and poets. They opened the eyes of the cultural world to this birthplace of civilization, still inhabited (whatever the more skeptical scholars might say) by the Greeks of old, and awakened in it visions of its renewal.

In the business world the Hellenic message was spread by the Greek merchant communities through the capitals of western Europe and Russia. In concrete terms, their efforts led to the formation of Philhellenic committees to collect funds for the revolution. Rich expatriates, especially in Russia, came forward with substantial contributions, while adventurous young men, not only from Europe but from America, volunteered, often in defiance of their own governments, to fight for the Greek cause. As William Cobbett cynically commented, the Greek revolution was "a war got up by poets and stock-jobbers for the benefit of Russia."

Outstanding among the poets—for the benefit of the Greeks themselves—was Lord Byron, who had first visited Greece in 1809 and soon immortalized it in verse. He translated the revolutionary war song of Rhigas and became close friends in Italy with Mavrokordatos. In 1823 he arrived in Cephalonia, where he remained for five months, en route for Greece. "Trust not for freedom to the Franks," he had warned the Greeks when they sought military aid. Now he came to them as the bearer of financial aid, in the form of a six-figure loan from the Greek committee in London.

Disunity among the rebels now amounted to civil strife. When Byron arrived on the Greek mainland at Mesolonghi in 1824, he found Greek fighting Greek in a new Peloponnesian War. It was waged between the supporters of Kolokotrones and those of Koundouriotis, with their rival government assemblies respectively inland and on the coasts and islands. This hardly surprised or disillusioned Lord Byron. Romantic in his espousal of the Greek cause, he was realistic in his estimate of the Greek nature. What he saw here around him was a people freed only in part from a demoralizing tyranny, and now at odds with one another as to the best means of replacing it, moreover overinclined to pursue liberal theory at the expense of workable practice.

It became Byron's immediate task to compose these disputes, and here he was momentarily to succeed. For according to his instructions the expenditure of his funds could be entrusted only to Koundouriotis. Thus Kolokotrones for sake of his share surrendered Nauplia. But inevitably, after a few months, civil war erupted once more. Kolokotrones turned against Koundouriotis, but was captured and imprisoned on Hydra. Mavrokordatos retired in some disgust from the scene. The English loan, raised for defense against the Turks, was thus dissipated in internal strife between Greek and Greek. Lord Byron, its provider, was spared this outcome of his efforts; he had died of malarial fever in the swamps of Mesolonghi. But he died a martyr to the Greek cause, and an eternal hero among Greeks. His death kept alive and intensified the flames of Philhellenism in Europe, thus helping to ensure that a Greek nation would one day be recognized and upheld by the civilized world.

In this first phase of the War of Independence the Greeks had, for all their internal disputes, proved on balance successful. Their success was indeed such that in 1825 the Sultan, realizing the inadequacy of his own forces to defeat them single-handed, moreover failing to recruit reinforcements from his Asiatic provinces, summoned to his aid his powerful vassal Mehmed Ali, the Albanian-born pasha of Egypt. His army, since the time of Napoleon, had been trained and armed on Western lines. It had already served Sultan Mahmud by crushing a rebellion in Arabia. Now he called upon Mehmed Ali for its support in crushing the rebellious Greeks. He promised in return to make him pasha of Crete and the Peloponnese—while Mehmed Ali himself cherished designs farther afield, on the pashalik of Syria.

Mehmed's son, Ibrahim Pasha, was thus dispatched from Alexandria in command of a naval force which was the strongest yet launched by a non-European power in the Mediterranean. It proceeded via Crete to the fortified port of Modon, on the westernmost point of the Morea. Here Ibrahim established his headquarters, thus initiating the second phase of the Greek War of Independence. For three years his disciplined forces were to dominate the Peloponnese, spreading fear and devastation as they reconquered for the Turks the positions which they had lost to the Greeks, and thus reestablished Turkish control over most of the country. This startled the Greeks into a degree of unity. Kolokotrones was released and reestablished as commander-in-chief of the Morea, where he suffered two successive defeats at the hands of Ibrahim.

Next, in 1826, Ibrahim switched his forces to continental Greece, to reinforce the Turkish commander, Reshid Pasha, in his siege of Mesolonghi. Here his naval force turned the scale, preventing a Greek relief fleet from entering the harbour, and provoking the Greek garrison, with much of the civilian population, to a final desperate resistance which nonetheless failed.

The fall of Mesolonghi led to the fall of the government of Koundouriotis, and a further period of internal strife between the two rival assemblies and presidents. Previously, however, he had officially invited two able British officers, Sir Richard Church, an Irishman, and Lord Cochrane, a Scot, to command respectively the Greek army and navy. As a condition for their service, they insisted on the reconciliation of the two rival factions. Thus a new session of the National Assembly, with a new constitution, elected Capodistria, a man of autocratic spirit, to serve as its president. Meanwhile, Reshid Pasha embarked on a long siege of Athens, whose Acropolis, following an abortive attempt by Lord Cochrane to relieve it, fell to the Turks in June, 1827. This, completing the subjugation of continental Greece, seemed to signal the end of the War of Independence.

But it was not the end. For the time had come at last, after six years of bloodshed, for the powers of Europe to intervene. Among them the Russians had proved the most active in their pressure against the Turks. The Austrians, as fellow imperialists under Metternich's rule, favoured the suppression of the rebels. The British and the French feared the consequences of a new Russo-Turkish war. On the other hand, France, since 1824, had a liberal sovereign in the person of Charles X. French and British naval forces in the Mediterranean saw in those of the Greeks an insurance against piracy.

Right-wing Toryism in England had given place to a more liberal policy with the fall of Lord Castlereagh and the succession to his office of the liberal-minded George Canning, whose Philhellenic kinsman, Stratford Canning, was now appointed ambassador to the Porte. English consciences had been outraged by tales of the atrocities of Ibrahim Pasha, who was reputed to be enslaving the Greeks with a view to the repopulation of the Peloponnese with Egyptians. Public opinion was stirred above all by the heroic sacrifice, in so noble a cause, of Lord Byron.

The first task of the powers was to determine the future boundaries and status of Greece. Here a preliminary decision was reached in the spring of 1826, with the signature at St. Petersburg of a protocol between Britain and Russia, designed to arrest bloodshed and to effect the reconciliation of Turks and Greeks. They agreed to the general principle of obtaining for the Greeks not independence but, in return for payment of an annual tribute to the Sultan, the autonomous right of managing their own internal affairs.

In the autumn of that year the Greeks appealed for the extension of this protocol to include France. On the initiative of Canning—who died shortly afterward—a treaty to this effect was signed in London in July, 1827, a month after the fall of Athens. On this basis the three powers offered mediation to the Porte. If this was refused, they asserted the right to establish international relations with the Greeks, involving the exchange of consuls and the recognition of the rebel provinces as an independent state. This was accepted by the Greeks but rejected, in uncompromising terms, by the Sultan. Obstinately blind to realities, he denounced it as a flagrant violation by the foreigner of his full and legitimate sovereign rights. These he refused, on any terms, to renounce or to modify.

The treaty provided for an armistice, to be enforced by a combined fleet, "without however taking any part in the hostilities." The Russians sent a fleet to the Mediterranean, where the admirals of the three powers conferred, perplexed both by the ambiguity of their instructions and by the difficulty of establishing contact with Ibrahim, who, on the grounds of continued Greek aggression, was refusing to accept the armistice without the Sultan's orders. Finally, following a blockade, the admirals sailed into the bay of Navarino and insisted with a show of force—but with an agreement among themselves not to fire unless the Turks fired first—that Ibrahim should accept the armistice and sail back to Alexandria.

Unhappily an Egyptian ship fired on an open boat carrying the delegates. The French flagship at once retaliated with rifle fire, and a major naval engagement inevitably followed. In this Ibrahim's fleet was all but annihilated. It was the worst naval disaster to befall the Ottoman Empire since the battle of Lepanto. The Russians and the French were content. For Metternich it was a "fearful catastrophe." For the Duke of Wellington, soon to be Prime Minister, it was an "untoward event," for which the Duke of Clarence (soon to be King William IV) nonetheless rewarded the British admiral, Edward Codrington, with a knighthood of the Order of the Bath—later acceding to his removal, under another pretext, from his naval command. The Greeks were triumphant. Here surely at long last was freedom.

Capodistria, the new president of the National Assembly, had since his election been touring the European capitals to canvass support. Early in 1828 he arrived at Nauplia to take up his duties and to re-establish peace. First he sent forces to ensure Greek recovery from Ibrahim of those territories which he intended to claim for the new state. In this he achieved partial success. Then he ensured his own personal power through the appointment of a new governing body, the Panhellenion, under his effective control. He made promises to convene in due course a new National Assembly, in terms of the new constitution, and meanwhile "reigned" through a secretariat which served as his cabinet.

The English secured an undertaking from Mehmed Ali to withdraw Ibrahim's forces. Those that still remained were finally expelled by a French force, after they had razed to the ground the capital city of the Morea, Tripolitza. Then, delaying a final settlement, a new war broke out between Russia and Turkey.

The Russians had for some years past exerted diplomatic pressure on the Turks. In 1826 they imposed upon the Porte the humiliating Convention of Ackerman, which confirmed the provisions of the Treaty of Bucharest and extended them, to Russian advantage, through the cession of certain Turkish fortresses in Asia. It conferred full privileges on the Moldavians and Wallachians, and new political rights on the Serbs. Now that the Turks had lost their fleet at Navarino, leaving Russia with naval supremacy in the Black Sea, the militant Tsar Nicholas I sought not conciliation but armed confrontation with the "old arch enemy of Muscovy." When it became clear that he was planning an invasion of Turkey for the spring of 1828, the Sultan preempted him with a declaration of war against Russia in the winter of 1827.

The Tsar Nicholas led his army in person across the Pruth in the following spring. After occupying the Principalities, it crossed the Danube before June, then besieged a series of fortresses to open its way up to the Balkan range and beyond, in the direction of the Sultan's capital. The Turks, more redoubtable behind walls than in open country, resisted them with much of their former defiance. Varna fell after a stout defense, thanks partly to the treacherous defection to the enemy of a Turkish commander with some thousands of troops, but largely to the Russian command of the Black Sea. Silistria held out; so did Shumla, the key to the mountain passes.

The Russians had lost heavily, and in the following year sent a more substantial force under a commander, Marshal Diebitsch, who was armed (in the words of Baron Moltke) "with the reputation of invincible success." He was to earn the name of Sabalskanski, "the crosser of the Balkan." While a small force besieged Silistria, this time with ultimate success, his main army fought a major battle on the field of Kulewtska, before Shumla. In this a large force of Turks was defeated and put to flight, with the loss of all its artillery, by a smaller force of Russians.

Diebitsch then took the bold decision to cross the Balkan range without first subduing the fortress of Shumla, which, with its garrison and the survivors of Kulewtska, still held out. While Reshid Pasha, the Turkish commander, prepared for its defense, Diebitsch left a small force to contain it, then led the bulk of his troops for nine days of forced marches up the deep gorges and across the formidable mountain passes of the range. Surprisingly he was able to perform this feat almost without opposition, since Reshid, showing total lack of foresight, had withdrawn the detachments defending them to help meet the expected attack upon Shumla.

Having thus penetrated the hitherto well-nigh impenetrable barrier, the Russian army opened up a supply route to the Russian fleet in the Black Sea at Burgas. Then, disposing of a few pockets of Turkish resistance and taking care to protect the Christian peasants—who gave them a warm welcome—the Russians appeared in the plains before the walls of Adrianople, the capital of Turkey in Europe. Its garrison surrendered without firing a shot, dazed at the sudden appearance of such an army across a mountain barrier which had never before been crossed. In fact, in the course of so cruel a passage, the Russian army had been reduced to a fraction of its former strength through the ravages of dysentery, pestilence, and general exhaustion; nor had it any prospect of reinforcement or safe retreat. The Turks, had they not so overestimated its numbers, might now have sought with success to destroy it. Fully aware of this danger and putting on a bold show of strength, Diebitsch prepared, with the Black Sea fleet covering his flank, to march on Istanbul and the Bosporus. He at once moved his forces a hundred miles forward.

Dismay and panic swept through the capital, releasing latent forces of disorder and revolt. The Sultan at first kept his head, confident in the strength of his garrison and calling upon Turks to volunteer for its reinforcement in the city's defense. He unfurled the sacred banner of the Prophet and declared his intention of taking command of his forces in person. Preparing to do so, he appeared, ill-advisedly, not on horseback like the defenders of old, but in a carriage, an "unheard-of and indecorous innovation" which dampened public enthusiasm. The chief ministers of the Divan urged him to sue for peace. So did the British and French ambassadors, equally ignorant of the true extent of the Russian weakness. In response to these pressures, the Sultan, who was far from pusillanimous by nature, gave way. He fell for the Russian bluff, saving Diebitsch from inevitable disaster, and in the autumn of 1829 sent a delegation to his camp to negotiate the Treaty of Adrianople.

Thus reprieved, the Russian marshal agreed to terms which seemed deceptively moderate. Russia, in the name of the Tsar, forswore territorial aggrandizement and renounced most of her conquests achieved in the course of the war. But she obtained a part of Moldavia and a mouth of the Danube at Sulina, which was to give her effective control of the river. With the demolition of certain fortresses, the river ceased to be the first line of defense of the Ottoman Empire. Moldavia and Wallachia, though nominally restored to the sovereignty of the Sultan, were effectively freed from it by grants of autonomy. They won the right to raise their own armies and to appoint hospodars for life, without Turkish interference in their affairs and with the removal of most of their Moslem population. The virtual independence of Serbia, apart from the fortresses of Belgrade and Orsova, was likewise confirmed. In Asia, where another outstanding general, Paskievitch, had won equally notable victories, Kars, Erzurum, and Bayezid were restored to the Turks. But the Russians retained other fortresses and permanently annexed Georgia, together with various parts of the Caucasus.

When it came to Greece, from which Turkish forces had now been withdrawn, the Sultan was obliged to accept the terms, which he had previously rejected, of the Treaty of London, together with any settlement proposed by the three powers. This meant the acceptance of a Greek state, no longer subject to his sovereignty but entirely independent. After much wrangling with the Greeks as to frontiers, the new Greece was established in 1830 as a kingdom-to-be. It embraced much of the Greek mainland and many of the islands, with the exclusion of Crete, and left the Sultan with Thessaly and Albania as his frontier provinces.

The new state was to be governed by a hereditary monarch, with the title of Sovereign Prince of Greece, selected from outside the reigning families of Great Britain, France, and Russia. The first choice of the powers fell on the able Prince Leopold of Saxe-Coburg, son-in-law of King George IV. Forcefully discouraged by Capodistria, who aspired to reign, with one eye on Russian interests, as life president in person, he withdrew his acceptance—to show his caliber later as king of the Belgians. Only after Capodistria's fall from power and assassination in 1831, at the hands of proud Maniot enemies resentful of his dictatorial spirit, was the crown of Greece conferred on Prince Otho, son of the Philhellenic King Ludwig of Bavaria. Duly recognized by the Sultan, he was to reign as the first king of the Hellenes for a generation to come.

These major losses, over less than a decade, were an irreparable misfortune for the Ottoman Empire. They were due in part to the Sultan's ill-judged rejection abroad, at a crucial moment, of the opportunity to achieve honourable terms with the three European powers. This cost him in turn the loss of his navy, the loss of Greece, and the effective loss of other widespread Ottoman territories. With tragic irony this befell him just as he had embarked at home, with combined vigour and success, on a policy of far-reaching reform which was radically to change the political structure and social conceptions of the Ottoman state.

((31))

MAHMUD THE REFORMER HAD FOUND IT POLITIC TO WAIT PATIENTLY for a full seventeen years before venturing to put into practice his radical program of change. For this amounted to nothing less than the transformation of Turkey from a medieval empire, based on the principles of Islam, into a modern constitutional state, based equally on the secular principles of the West. What he planned was a break with the past in the form of new institutions and more flexible concepts of government such as Europe was at this time evolving.

But like the reforms of the past—those of Mehmed the Conqueror and Suleiman the Lawgiver—this could only be realized by inflexible means. In Mahmud's eyes it was imperative to restore to the Sultan that supreme power by which the Padishah's will, whether in his capital or in the imperial provinces, ceased to be challenged as the sole and absolute source of authority. Over the years Sultan Mahmud II reasserted this mastery. Deprived, through execution or exile, of such counsellors as had aided Selim III, Mahmud achieved this virtually on his own, through his outstanding personal qualities of resolution, persistence, and foresight; through his wide-ranging vision and the concentrated powers of a mind both realistic in its grasp of hard problems and systematic in its plans for their solution; above all through his strength of character and unwavering energy in the subjection of such enemies, within the state, as had halted the reform plans of his predecessor.

First, to assure the power of his own centralized government, he had to eliminate such provincial autonomy as sought to restrict it. In an empire shrinking in any case through foreign encroachment, he had to check at least the forces of internal disruption, restoring a positive degree of cohesion to the smaller whole which remained. By slow and patient stages he rid himself of his own rebellious pashas. Then he set himself to overcome the divisive pretensions and curtail the abused privileges of the lords of the valleys and other disloyal provincial notables. In pursuit of centralization, thus of the elimination of all intermediate sources of authority between government and people, he set to work to suppress all local powers deriving from inheritance, tradition, custom, or popular consent. He thus restored large areas of Anatolia and Rumelia to the control of his central sovereign authority.

The royal harem of the Topkapi Palace. This is a fanciful engraving by Melling, but he had had ample opportunity to learn about the harem in his role as architect to the favorite sister of Selim III, as indeed also about many other aspects of Ottoman life at the turn of the nineteenth century. Note the two women embracing in the colonnade at the right.

Reproduced from N. M. Penzer, *The Harem*, London, 1936.

A culmination of these operations had been his ruthless suppression of Ali Pasha in Janina.

The way thus now lay open for the elimination of the most powerful enemy within the Ottoman state, the corps of the Janissaries. Once its redoubtable champions, they were now the chief source of the rot at its core. No campaign of reform could proceed until the Janissaries were liquidated, once and for all. Sultan Mahmud chose his moment for this decisive stroke in the summer of 1826, just after the Greek fortress of Mesolonghi had fallen to the forces of Ibrahim Pasha. It was well enough chosen. For this modern army of his vassal Mehmed Ali was in itself an object lesson, galling to the Sultan had he not learned it long since, of the Empire's own need for a modern army—of which this might indeed serve as a prototype. His vassal, after liquidating the Mamluks in Egypt, had been ahead of any sultan in proving that a European standard of discipline and training could be achieved as effectively by Moslem as by Christian troops, and had in general pursued a policy of reform which won him respect and support in the West.

For his coup against the Janissaries the Sultan had prepared his own troops in advance, foreseeing fierce conflict in the streets and thus concentrating on the enlargement and improvement of his force of artillery, which alone could ensure their destruction. He entrusted its command to officers picked for their loyalty, under a general so ruthless as to earn in the ensuing slaughter the name of "Black Hell." Ready to reinforce him at the appropriate moment was a substantial force of Asiatic troops, beyond the Bosporus. Now Sultan Mahmud, having gradually raised to the high offices of state men of caliber who favoured his interests, proclaimed in a *fetva,* formally signed by them all, the foundation of a new corps, to be trained and equipped on European lines.

Though this was conceived on the basis of Selim III's New Order, the Sultan judiciously presented it not as the product of a reform policy but as a revival of the old military order of Suleiman, designed to restore the Ottoman Empire to that heyday of its prime. Mahmud specified that the corps should be instructed not by Christians and foreigners but by modern-trained Moslem officers. He thus achieved the support of the Chief Mufti and the ulema in council, a much-needed arm for the holy war against the infidel. The corps of the Janissaries was to be retained, but each of its battalions, stationed in the capital, was to provide 150 men for the new corps, to be instructed in new military exercises.

As the Sultan had anticipated, the Janissaries refused to accept this provision. Once more they overturned their camp kettles in the traditional gesture of revolt. Once more, as in the mutiny of 1807, they swarmed into the Hippodrome, bent on massacre, then advanced on the Sultan's palace, crying for the heads of his chief ministers, and thus repeating the all-too-familiar pattern. But this time the Sultan was prepared for them. His troops and artillery were ready for action; the bulk of his people were rallying to the support of the throne. Mahmud unfurled in person the sacred standard of the Prophet, and called upon all believers to gather around it. As the mob of Janissaries pressed through the narrow streets toward the Seraglio, the guns opened fire from its walls, cutting swathes through their columns as they fell helpless against an unrelenting blast of grapeshot. This drove them back into the Hippodrome, whence, after a defiant resistance, they retired within the walls of their barracks, to barricade themselves against an expected assault.

But no assault came. Mahmud was not so to risk his troops. Instead, his heavy artillery thundered shells into the barracks, setting them on fire and soon laying them in ruins, while four thousand of the mutineers perished. Such, within little more than half an hour, was the extermination by modern arms of the nucleus of a military force five centuries old, successively the terror of Europe and of the declining Ottoman Sultans themselves. It was completed with unremitting severity, by the slaughter throughout the provinces of thousands more. On the same day the Sultan abolished, by proclamation, the corps of the Janissaries; their name was proscribed and their standards destroyed. A month later the brotherhood of the Bektashi dervishes, who had for centuries aided and abetted them, was outlawed, with the destruction of its convents, the public execution of its principal leaders, and the exile of its other adherents. Such was the "Auspicious Incident," as reformers were to name it, which finally released Sultan Mahmud from all armed opposition within his own frontiers. He now proclaimed the formation of a new Turkish army to be named "The Victorious Mohammedan Soldiery."

After long years of patient determination, culminating in a single hour of ruthless action, a strong, wise Sultan had reestablished the autocracy of his earlier Ottoman forebears. But he had thus revived the past only to create a new future. Mahmud II pursued no despotic end, but rather a despotic means to an end which was in its essence progressive. After his *coup d'état* came a period of enlightened development, in which the Sultan specified his plans for a more elastic and liberal society. He initiated himself and laid down for his successors the main lines of a widespread reform program, which was intended, as time went by, to raise a new Turkey in closer affinity with Western civilization. Realistically, if regretfully, accepting the loss of old Ottoman territories, he was to create for the smaller Empire now left to him a radical structure of government, so designed as to give it new growth and arrest its decline.

The Sultan's dominions, both in Europe and in Asia, should become as it were an Ottoman commonwealth, strong and united enough to withstand further threats from without, yet flexible enough within to secure the interests and the allegiance of a diversity of peoples and religions. The essence of his internal policy, ensuring the Empire's further survival through the nineteenth and into the twentieth century, lay in the establishment of new principles of secular sovereignty, aimed at a gradual separation between the institutions of state and religion.

When he had rid himself of the Janissaries, Mahmud's most urgent objective was military. He went ahead rapidly with the formation of his new army. In place of the Agha of the Janissaries, he established the office of Serasker, thus reviving a title given to army commanders in the past. The Serasker was now to combine the duties of commander-in-chief and Minister of War, with especial responsibility for the new force. He also inherited from the Agha the responsibility for public security, covering police duties in Istanbul. The maintenance and expansion of the police system became one of his principal duties. For the army a code of regulations provided for a basic force of twelve thousand men, to be stationed in the capital, while further troops were recruited for the provinces. All were to serve for a period of twelve years.

To complete his military reforms, with his new army established as an effective and dependable force, Mahmud needed a respite from war for a decade. Of this need the Russians, discerning in him a stern ruler with a power and energy denied for so long to his predecessors, were all too aware. It was largely in the hope of nipping his military reforms in the bud, and of defeating the army before it had grown into a seasoned force, that the Tsar had provoked the recent disastrous war, to the Sultan's discomfiture in the Treaty of Adrianople.

Now that it was signed, Mahmud devoted himself actively to the training and arming of the new force, all the more because he had reason to fear an ultimate reckoning with Mehmed Ali, the pasha of Egypt, whose own modernized forces furnished him with so salutary an example. It was indeed to his vassal that Mahmud in 1826 sent his first request for aid in the form of twelve expert instructors. When it was refused he looked toward Europe. But France was compromised in Turkish eyes by her sympathy with the Greek insurgents—and later by her support for Mehmed Ali. Britain too was suspect for her Philhellenic sympathies, and in 1834 the Sultan rejected an offer from Lord Palmerston of a team of officers to train his forces. But later, while some Turkish cadets went to Woolwich, three British officers were sent to Istanbul to advise on the army's reorganization. They were followed in 1838 by a naval mission. But they achieved little, owing partly to their own resentment at the slighting attitude of the Turks toward them.

Finally it was the Prussians who served the Sultan's purpose, in the person of the young Lieutenant Helmuth von Moltke, who greatly impressed him, and whom he engaged as adviser on the Empire's defenses and the army's training and organization. An exchange of cadets and officers took place between Turkey and both Prussia and Austria. Here was the start of a Germanic tradition in the Turkish armed forces, which was to prevail—not always altogether happily—into the twentieth century. But Moltke himself was not greatly impressed by Mahmud II, finding him inferior to Peter the Great, and affronted by the evident disrespect of the Turkish officers for foreign military advisers. "The Colonels," he wrote, "gave us precedence, the officers were still tolerably polite, but the ordinary men would not present arms to us, and the women and children from time to time followed us with curses. The soldier obeyed but did not salute." Among Turks of all classes contempt for the *giaour* died hard. Meanwhile, the department of the Serasker, or commander-in-chief, grew into a powerful Ministry of War, maintaining a strong central control over the armed forces of the Ottoman Empire and retaining it right into the next century.

Next Mahmud had to reduce the power of the ulema, guardians of the religious establishment as the Janissaries, lately their confederates, had been guardians of the military establishment. Here was the second potential source of opposition to the Sultan's supreme authority. Reigning supreme with the Janissaries, the ulema had destroyed Selim III and his plans for a New Order. This other pillar of the traditional state must be eroded if he were to erect a new structure of government. For Mahmud's basic reform policy was to separate the religious from the secular authority. At present two dignitaries stood supreme above all other holders of office, whether temporal or spiritual. They represented the sovereign's dual powers as Sultan and caliph. One was the Grand Vezir, whose functions were executive, covering the fields of administration and justice; the other was the Sheikh-ul-Islam, otherwise the Grand Mufti, whose functions were consultative and interpretative. Both were powerful offices, whose entrenched occupants through the period of decline had recurrently threatened, for better or for worse, the supreme power and prestige of the sultanate. What Mahmud now projected was the dilution of their powers through a system of government vested not in autocratic individuals but in consultative groups, each with its own responsibilities.

First, the office of the Sheikh-ul-Islam was removed from the realm of temporal government, to preside only over the realm of religion. But within this realm, ceasing to remain merely consultative and interpretative, the Grand Mufti acquired new judicial powers, taking over from the Grand Vezir's office his former religious jurisdiction. This he now exercised over all the Sultan's Moslem subjects. Meanwhile a new civil jurisdiction was to evolve separately, in the secular realm.

Until now the Grand Mufti had given his counsel and issued his rulings (often with political implications) from his own residence. Now he was to preside over a government department, installed in offices in the former residence of the Agha of the Janissaries. His new status restricted that autonomy by which his revenues, his employees, and their establishments had remained independent of the palace. It led to a bureaucratization, under the state, of the ulema class in general, which undermined at once their effective power and their resistance to change. Deprived both of financial and administrative independence, their powers were weakened as against that of the sovereign, who progressively diminished their status and competence. He placed schools under a Ministry of Education, and transferred legal responsibilities to a Ministry of Justice, even entrusting the drafting of *fetvas* to a legal committee with a commission under its effective control. The status of the Grand Mufti, now a government office-holder, came to depend less on his traditional powers than on such influence as his personal qualities might win for him.

Finally Mahmud brought under the control of the state the old Islamic institution of the *vakf,* or pious foundation, which was based on the inalienable dedication of land and other freehold property, mostly in the cities, to religious purposes. These *evkaf,* with their substantial revenues, were usually supervised by members of the ulema, serving as administrators and collectors. The Grand Mufti and other muftis and kadis had controlled various groups of them, which were a major source of economic power for the religious institutions.

Having thus pressed home his advantage at the expense of the military and religious establishments, Mahmud now developed his own secular administration which, in its titular and organizational forms, was to have the aspect of a European government system—thus aspiring to impress Westerners with the up-to-dateness of the new Turkish state. First he abolished in its present form the office of the Grand Vezir (or Sadrazam) which for close on two centuries at the Sublime Porte had been the effective seat of Ottoman government. Formerly the Sultan's "absolute vicar," the Grand Vezir's powers were now divided between two separate ministries, those of Foreign and Civil Affairs (later the Ministry of the Interior), while the traditional office of the *defterdar* (or treasurer) was to be renamed Ministry of Finance. Above them, serving as the link between ruler and government, the Grand Vezir was renamed Prime Minister—but later his former title was restored.

Other ministries took over his various duties and prerogatives, with a new distribution of functions. Meeting together in the Privy Council, or Council of Ministers, with the Prime Minister as its president, they were in fact government departments responsible for specified affairs of state, with advisory councils to draft plans and reports and to submit decisions for the Sultan's promulgation. Of these the most important were the Council of Military Affairs and the High Council for Judicial Ordinances. At first the four ministries of Education, Commerce, Agriculture, and Industry were jointly administered by a consultative council named the Board of Useful Affairs. Whether or not, behind its facade, this new system of bureaucracy proved at once effective, it did at least break down old traditions of institutional rights and privileges, to substitute new institutions in a modernized form. They were to acquire more reality, in practical terms, when the old officials of the Porte were succeeded by a new generation of civil servants, differing from them in education, social origins, and cultural outlook.

In the provinces Mahmud's reformed administration was to depend on this central government. Intermediate sources of power, whether due to inheritance, tradition, custom, or local assent, were gradually suppressed, leaving the authority of the Sultan supreme. Two measures were introduced as a preliminary to this. One was a census of the whole male population of Rumelia and Anatolia (the Arab provinces excepted); the other was a land survey, to register all landholdings. Here the purpose was to facilitate at once the conscription for the new army, and a more accurate and effective system of taxation to finance it. Finally Mahmud abolished once and for all the system of timars, those grants of land which in the past had served as a base for the recruitment of *sipahis*. Since the end of the sixteenth century, as the feudal cavalry declined with the increase of paid regular troops, their *timars* had been converted into crown lands, then leased out to tax farmers. But in parts of Anatolia and Rumelia the old system still lingered. Mahmud, in abolishing the Janissaries, had abolished also the remnants of this feudal cavalry. Now he revoked all their surviving *timars,* which were similarly leased out as crown lands. He thus eliminated the last vestige of feudalism, and so further tightened his central control over the provinces of the Ottoman Empire as a whole.

In the field of law Sultan Mahmud made fundamental innovations. The laws of his realm consisted of the Sheriat, the Sacred Law of God, which was beyond the power of human enactment, and of *kanuns,* which were edicts of the Sultan in his capacity as caliph. Both epitomized medieval justice, which gave to each man his due in the interests of order and stability. But they did not allow him, in modern terms, equality before the law. A third concept of *adalet,* or justice, was introduced by Mahmud—who thus earned the name of Adli, "the Just." This was a body of legislation separate from that of God and the ruler. Within the secular realm, separate from both Sheriat and *kanun,* he formed a council to devise judicial codes on the basis of a new public law. These codes defined the responsibilities of judges and their powers over government officials. They laid down legal proceedings to be taken against them for dereliction of duty, with heavy penalties for bribery and other forms of corruption. This introduced for the first time the unfamiliar conception that such officials were public servants, subject not as hitherto to the arbitrary will of the sovereign, but with a responsibility of their own under the law. It reflected Mahmud's resolve to create for his administration a new tradition of public service, beyond the direct authority of government. As these new codes developed, punishment would no longer be left to the mere discretion of the judge, as hitherto, but would be closely determined, with emphasis on criminal responsibility and with increasing clarification of the differences between criminal and civil, secular and religious, private and public law.

Nonetheless, in the personal lives of the people, within the framework of their social and family institutions, the Sacred Law of Islam and its customs still reigned without challenge. There was no change in the laws of marriage and divorce, property and inheritance, the status of women and slaves. Here religion remained the basis of law, which the Sultan still was powerless to touch. At home, men still lived in the Middle Ages.

But in the broader field medieval conceptions were starting to crumble. Mahmud II, ahead of his time in the Orient, sought a new basis for Ottoman sovereignty. It was to rest with the people. His new centralized bureaucracy, with its various delegated powers, was geared toward human progress. Departing from the traditional order and discarding the panoply of sacred power, the Sultan would become no longer the Defender of the Faithful but the enlightener of the citizen. Within the framework of a benevolent despotism, Mahmud was concerned less to maintain his own absolute rights than to grant rights to his subjects, whose conditions he sought to change and improve.

Inherent in all this lay the need for a new concept of education. The Turks must in their learning become acquainted with things unknown, thus challenging the lore of the ulema, to whom all was known. As the fund of traditional knowledge, its *medresses* (religious schools) held a virtual monopoly. The learning acquired from them was confined to God and man's duties toward him and toward his own fellows. Moreover, it was largely dispensed through word of mouth, thus resulting in widespread illiteracy. In 1824 Mahmud made primary education compulsory, but still in terms of religion, since in transferring to the Sheikh-ul-Islam the whole administration of the Sacred Law, he had been obliged to exclude it from the temporal realm.

The need for higher education, as a means of progress, he saw in terms of the teaching of technical skills, and this was primarily related to the military establishment, with the building up of his new army to replace the Janissaries. At this stage higher education was in essence military education. The army urgently needed a new corps of educated and competent officers, of whom, apart from a few Western renegades, artillerymen, and engineers, there was a serious shortage.

Two schools, respectively of naval and military engineering, which dated from the end of the eighteenth century, had lately been revived, and were now firmly established, while in 1827, despite strong opposition, the Sultan took the bold step of sending small groups of students to Paris, thus following the earlier example of Mehmed Ali. Together with military and naval cadets distributed among various European capitals, they formed the advance guard of a continuous succession of Turkish students sent to Europe, who were on their return to play a significant role in the modern evolution of their country. Meanwhile, pending the formation of a permanent school for the training of officers, Mahmud established training units within the military corps, whose teachers were selected from among noncommissioned officers and soldiers, and whose pupils, when trained, could in turn pass on their instruction to others, thus forming an officer cadre for the Turkish army of the next generation.

Eventually, breaking the last links with the Janissary tradition and those between the religious and the military arm, he founded a School of Military Sciences, modelled on the lines of Napoleon's military academy of St. Cyr. Though many of its teachers were to be Frenchmen or Prussians, it represented a new army tradition, evolving from within the state with its own roots in Turkish society, and with its own progressive system of education—intellectual, social, and political—which was to serve as a positive benefit to future generations of Turks. Meanwhile, to train the drummers and trumpeters in the army bands, Mahmud had founded an imperial music school, one of whose instructors, in Western music, was Donizetti Pasha, a brother of the great Italian composer.

Most significant of all was the opening of a state school to train doctors and later surgeons for the new army. For the civil population they were still trained under the auspices of the religious establishment, in the *medresses* of the Suleimaniye Mosque, with a syllabus partly classical Greek and partly based in its essence on the writings of Galen and Avicenna.

Mahmud's medical academy was the first school in Turkey which offered the equivalent of a primary and secondary secular education. In 1838, following reorganization, it was transferred to Galatasaray in Pera, then the site of the old Palace School of pages, with some European teachers, and instruction given in both Turkish and French. At its inauguration the Sultan himself addressed the students. Explaining that Arabic as a medical language had become obsolete, he told them: "You will study scientific medicine in French . . . my purpose in having you taught French is not to educate you in the French language; it is to teach you scientific medicine and little by little to take it into our own language." Teaching medicine in French was thus regarded by Mahmud as a temporary expedient, and in fact, over the next generation, the Turkish language came to replace it as the basis for instruction, through foreign medical textbooks and other works translated by Turkish scientific scholars. Such was the end of traditional and the start of modern medicine in Turkey. In its medical field the school at Galatasaray defied the medieval Islamic tradition through the introduction into its curriculum of dissection and autopsy. Anatomy, on the ulema's insistence, had hitherto been taught from wax models. But eventually the students were granted permission to learn anatomy from human corpses—usually those of Nubian slaves, which were cheaply obtained.

As time went by the school extended its range to cover a wider field of scientific, cultural, and intellectual studies. The French language was generally used for the teaching—as never before to Moslem Turkish students—of European history and literature, that of French coming to replace the traditional study of Persian literature. Sultan Mahmud was as much concerned with civil as with military education and its auxiliary branches. There was as urgent a need for competent civil servants, to administer his new governing establishment. Here the new trend of education, directly inspired by specific influences from the West, was reflected in 1838 in a remarkably progressive and anti-traditional report by the Board of Useful Affairs:

> Religious knowledge [it read] serves salvation in the world to come but science serves the perfection of man in this world. Astronomy, for example, serves the progress of navigation and the development of commerce. The mathematical sciences lead to the orderly conduct of warfare as well as military administration. . . . In discussing every project for the recovery of agriculture, commerce and industry, the Board had found that nothing can be done without the acquisition of science, and that the means of acquiring science and remedying education lie in giving a new order to the schools.

The schools in question were the primary schools, whose reform the board at this time envisaged in secular terms. Here its recommendations were firmly rejected by the department of the Sheikh-ul-Islam, with the result that civilian primary education, until the twentieth century, continued to be a function of the religious realm. Resigned to this opposition from the ulema, the board decided to apply its proposals to schools for adolescents (*rüshdiye* schools), filling the gap between the religious education of the primaries and the "worldly" education of the schools of higher learning. Here progress was slow, but two new grammar schools, attached to the Sultan Ahmed and Suleimaniye mosques, were set up with public funds during Mahmud's reign. Their syllabus was mainly grammatical and literary, and their purpose was to prepare candidates for the civil service.

To all these plans there remained an awkward obstacle—the language barrier. Mahmud was trying to introduce a Western governmental and social system to a Moslem people who knew virtually no Western language. There were few survivors or successors of the young men whom Selim III had encouraged to pursue linguistic studies. The Greeks, as occupants of official posts, were discredited since their War of Independence, when the last Greek Dragoman of the Porte was dismissed, to be succeeded by a Moslem. A suitable occupant for the post was hard to find, and it was eventually entrusted to a teacher at the school of mathematics who was of Christian origin, and who was succeeded by one of his colleagues. Finally the Sultan himself tackled the problem of language by establishing "translation chambers" at the Sublime Porte, and these were to evolve into a school of foreign languages.

From 1834, resurrecting the short-lived and incompleted plans of Selim III, he began to establish Turkish embassies in the main European capitals. Their diplomatic staffs, now predominantly Moslem Turks and no longer Phanariot Greeks, had the opportunity not only to learn Western languages but also to absorb some of the influences of Western civilization, while non-Moslems came gradually to be debarred from the top posts in diplomacy. This developed a foreign service which during the next fifty years was to provide the Ottoman Empire with the bulk of its more enlightened leaders and statesmen.

Meanwhile, divining the importance of communications within his centralized realm, Mahmud launched the first newspaper in Istanbul in the Turkish language, with a version in French called the *Moniteur Ottoman*. It was required reading among his public officials as a means of familiarizing them with his policies and activities. This was followed in 1834 by the introduction of a postal service, under a responsible official, who in turn would appoint his own officials at appropriate places throughout the Empire to register and handle all correspondence, "so that henceforth," the Sultan explained, "no man shall dispatch letters of his own accord." He himself inaugurated the first post road from Uskudar (Scutari) to Adrianople—the forerunner of other new roads to follow.

Thus had the foundations been laid—in the realms of the army, the judiciary, and the administration—for the slow emergence of a modern Turkish state, combining the elements of Western with those of Eastern civilization. In its outward social aspects too, the Turkish manner of life was to be Westernized, with the Sultan himself leading the way. He followed no longer Ottoman but European protocol. He gave receptions at which he moved among his guests, talking with them and even showing deference to their ladies. No longer a remote, aloof figure, the Sultan appeared before his people, performing public ceremonies and addressing his audience in person. He made his ministers sit, not stand, in his presence. Their offices were furnished in the European style, no longer only with low divans and cushions but with desks and tables and upright chairs, while in defiance of Islamic inhibitions the Sultan's portrait often hung on their walls.

Mahmud discouraged the wearing of long beards and introduced significant changes of costume. He laid down for his new army European-style tunics, breeches, and boots. Twenty years earlier such a break with sartorial tradition had led directly to the mutiny which deposed Selim III. Now it was accepted, if not without reluctance. Used to loose slippers, billowing trousers and robes, which in fact impeded his movements, the Turkish soldier saw these tight-fitting uniforms as marks of the infidel, hence signs of inferiority.

Changes in headgear, in particular, were hard for him to accept, owing to their religious implications. Replacing the turban, Mahmud introduced first the *subara,* a wadded cap with a semicylindrical crown, which had been worn by Selim's new troops. But this was replaced in 1828 by the more practical fez, a red felt beret of North African and indeed ultimately European origin. Sartorial pronouncements by the Prophet himself had made headgear an especial symbol of Islamic belief. Thus the fez, before its adoption as standard military headgear, had to be vetted and approved by the ulema. The approval was given after some hesitation as to whether it were truly Islamic, and strong measures were then taken to enforce it. But Mahmud's proposal to add a leather brim to it and so protect the soldier's eyes from the sun was firmly rejected by the ulema on the grounds that this would prevent him from touching his forehead to the ground in prayer, as all true Moslems must. Civilians as well as soldiers adopted the fez, following a decree in 1829 which specified in detail the costume to be worn by the various grades of officials. The medieval robe and turban became marks of religious identity, a "uniform" confined to the clerical class of the ulema. A modern civil identity was conferred by European trousers, replacing the voluminous Turkish model, while the orthodox costume of the Turk—in the cities at least—was completed by the frock coat and black leather boots.

Acting with resolution in these various fields, Mahmud II, following his suppression of the Janissaries, had a mere thirteen years left to him in which to lay the foundations of his long-promised radical reforms, and to set them in motion—if still inevitably only on the surface. These were difficult years, facing Mahmud with problems which called into full play his inflexible willpower and sense of obstinate purpose, rivalled by few of his imperial forebears. What the Sultan was labouring to achieve was the imposition on the Ottoman Empire, as it were overnight, of a new order in place of an old, the transition of its subjects from a pattern of life deeply rooted for centuries into another still untried and unfamiliar to all but a few. Inevitably the men of the past, in the religious establishment, remained implicitly hostile to changes which they had been made impotent to reverse. Nonetheless the men of the present emerged as the products of a new officialdom, launched on a Western way of living with its heavier cost and on a Western way of working within alien and still disordered institutions. They lacked the ballast of security, and of that accustomed close-knit pattern of personal relationships and loyalties which was inherent in the old ruling hierarchy. As Westernized civil servants, with new ways and standards of living and thinking, the rulers were at first more than ever out of touch with the ways of the ruled. Moreover, as "public servants" still without public morality, they could be quite as corrupt as the old.

Throughout the first half of this period Mahmud was at least free from the threat of war from beyond his own frontiers. But this respite was no more than the time needed by Mehmed Ali, his menacing vassal, to rebuild in his shipyards the fleet which he had lost at Navarino, and to strengthen his army, which he officered largely with Frenchmen. As a reward for his intervention in the Morea, Mehmed Ali had been awarded the pashalik of Crete, but not, as he had expected, that of Syria. By 1832 he was ready to avenge this breach of the Sultan's promise, as he chose to regard it. Using the pretext of a personal quarrel with the pasha of Acre, who held the key to the province, he dispatched his son Ibrahim with a large army to take Syria by force.

Capturing Gaza and Jerusalem without trouble, and besieging Acre successfully with the aid of his fleet, Ibrahim marched onward to Aleppo and Damascus, winning successive battles against Mahmud's new troops, which were not yet a match for so practiced an enemy. He penetrated across the Taurus range to capture Konya, in the heart of Anatolia, and proceeded onward as far as Bursa. Hence he turned his eyes toward Istanbul itself, inspired by Mehmed Ali's dream of imposing his own sovereignty on the relics of an empire which he thought to be doomed.

Alarm swept through the capital, whence Mahmud dispatched an urgent plea for aid to the British government. This was strongly supported by Stratford Canning, the British ambassador, but rejected by Lord Palmerston, bent at this moment on a policy of retrenchment in his armed forces. Thus Mahmud had no choice but to call upon his old enemies the Russians for aid. Ever ready with their troops and transports, they responded with alacrity. Early in 1833 a Russian squadron from Sebastopol landed a force of six thousand troops near the mouth of the Bosporus for the city's defense. Six weeks later it was followed, from Odessa, by a second force twice as large. The troops of the Tsar thus dominated Istanbul from the Giant's Mountain at Scutari. Russians, alone among foreigners, now had access to the Sultan; their soldiers and sailors walked the streets of Istanbul; their officers were called in to help drill and command Turkish units. Ibrahim's army was ready to continue its advance toward the Bosporus. But faced with this Russian force, he prudently decided instead to negotiate on his father's behalf. Meanwhile, the British and French governments belatedly awoke to the Russian danger.

Led now by Palmerston, strong diplomatic pressure was brought to bear upon the Sultan to insist on the Russian withdrawal, in return for concessions to Mehmed Ali and an Anglo-French guarantee against his further invasion. A firman was thus issued by the Sultan, confirming Mehmed Ali not only in the pashalik of Egypt and Crete, but in those of Syria, Damascus, Tripoli, Aleppo, and Adana. He was to retain these pashaliks during his lifetime, but without guarantees of their descent, at his death, to Ibrahim or other successors. In a separate agreement, the Treaty of Hunkiar Iskelessi, the Sultan bound himself to an offensive and defensive alliance with Russia, involving her withdrawal from Istanbul, but at the same time assuring her in a secret clause the right to pass freely through the Straits at any time, with her warships. This was to be a privilege denied to other foreign powers without Russian consent, and involved the right, if considered expedient, to land Russian troops on the shores of the Bosporus.

But Mahmud could not in the long run accept the cession of so large a part of his Asiatic dominions to a rebellious vassal, whose ambition moreover was to convert them into a hereditary pashalik, virtually independent of the Porte. In 1838 Mehmed Ali made what amounted to a declaration of independence by refusing in future to pay tribute to the Porte. Determined now to crush him, Mahmud assembled an army on the Euphrates for the invasion of Syria, where

Sultan Mahmud II, 1808–39, as emperor (Padishah). Portrait in oil by Hippolyte Bertaux.

in any case much of the population resented a rule more tyrannical than the Sultan's own, and in 1839 declared war against him. He arranged also for the dispatch of a fleet to collaborate on the Syrian coast with his land force. Both expeditions ended in disaster. His army was entirely defeated, largely owing to the desertion of large numbers of troops in response to bribes in Egyptian gold. The fate of his fleet was even worse, for its treacherous commander sailed it straight to Alexandria and handed it over to Mehmed Ali.

At this, fearing a second intervention by Russia, the Western powers met together in conclave to devise terms, in a protective spirit, for the settlement of the Turco-Egyptian problem. France refused to cooperate, supporting the claims against the Sultan of Mehmed Ali, in response to what she took to be her own interests. But Russia herself did so, in a conciliatory spirit, offering for the sake of a settlement to renounce her exclusive rights to the naval passage of the Dardanelles. Lord Palmerston presided over a conference in London, at which a convention was agreed between Britain, Russia, and Austria. Under its terms Mehmed Ali was advised that, if he withdrew his troops from Syria and restored the Turkish fleet to the Porte, he would be recognized as hereditary pasha of Egypt and as pasha of Syria for his own lifetime. If he refused, the fleets of the three powers would blockade both Egypt and Syria.

When Mehmed Ali rejected this ultimatum a British fleet appeared off the Syrian coast. In two successive operations it bombarded and destroyed the forts of Beirut and Acre, then landed troops which, with the aid of a revolt by the Arabs against Mehmed Ali's harsh regime, defeated the Egyptian armies of occupation. This aroused the fury of the French, who went so far as to threaten war against Britain. But, as Louis Philippe quickly observed, there was all the difference in the world between threatening war and going to war. The British fleet, under Admiral Napier, proceeded to Alexandria, which he threatened to bombard. At this Mehmed Ali, fearing a repetition of the fate of Acre, agreed to negotiate. He restored the Sultan's fleet. He was confirmed in his position as hereditary pasha of Egypt, resuming his tribute to the Sultan and agreeing to reduce the size of his army. But he withdrew altogether from Syria, which with Crete was restored to the direct rule of the Porte.

In 1841 a convention was signed in London by which the powers, now including France, formally recognized the Dardanelles and the Bosporus as Turkish waters, to be closed to foreign warships in time of peace. Advantageous as this agreement was to Turkey, it still conflicted with her previous preferential commitments to Russia of 1883—whose consequence was indeed to prove momentous in twelve years' time.

* * *

But Sultan Mahmud had not lived to see either his humiliating defeats at the hands of his vassal or their subsequent more encouraging outcome. He died on July 1, 1839. He must rank among the greatest of Sultans. Unlike his great predecessors he was no military leader. Nor was he skilled in the crafts of diplomacy. The Ottoman Empire consistently shrank under his rule. But internally, thanks to his ability as a ruler and his foresight as a planner, it had begun perceptibly to rise from its decline, breaking the shackles of a rigid, reactionary order to move slowly ahead in the direction of a modernized, liberalized state.

Meanwhile Mahmud was succeeded as Sultan by his sixteen-year-old son, Abdul Mejid.

((32))

IF SULTAN ADBUL MEJID DID NOT INHERIT THE HIGH CAPACITIES OF his father, Mahmud, he at least showed his own good intentions. As a young man he sincerely aspired to follow Mahmud's example, to abide by his precepts and to carry his reforms to completion. So mild in manner and delicate in frame as to become known as the "gentlest of Sultans," he was nonetheless a thoughtful and serious youth. In the words of Stratford Canning, the British ambassador, who saw him from the first as a likely royal "pupil" of his own, he had "a kindly disposition, a sound understanding, a clear sense of duty, proper feelings of dignity without pride, and a degree of humanity seldom if ever exhibited by the best of his ancestors. The bent of his mind inclined him to reform conducted on mild and liberal principles. He had not energy enough to originate measures of that kind, but he was glad to sanction and promote their operation." Stratford Canning established with Abdul Mejid an intimate personal relationship unusual between ambassador and sovereign, and from the start had an unusual degree of influence over his policies.

From his youth a strong influence over him, hence over the affairs of the Empire, was that of his mother, the Sultana Valide, Circassian in origin and a woman of character. Unqualified to stand alone, as his father had consistently done, Abdul Mejid needed support from good, trusted advisers. As he confessed to Stratford, "could he but find ten pashas to cooperate he would feel sure of success." As it was he was apt to be swayed this way and that by a succession of rival *vezirs*. Outstanding among these at the outset of his reign was Mustafa Reshid Pasha, a diplomat who had served with unusual distinction as ambassador of the Porte in Paris and other posts, and who at the time of Mahmud's death was on a special mission to London as Minister of Foreign Affairs. Returning swiftly, Reshid set himself to prove to the European powers, at a time when ideas of revolution and reform were again germinating in the West, that the Ottoman Empire itself could establish a modern system of government.

He drafted a reforming decree, with a shrewd eye on European opinion, which was in essence the last testament of Mahmud II. On November 3, 1839, in a kiosk of the Grand Seraglio formerly used by the chief confectioner for the preparation of rose sweetmeats and thus known as the Chamber of Roses, the decree was dramatically proclaimed in the presence of Abdul Mejid before a concourse of foreign diplomats (never before invited to such a ceremony) together with Turkish officials. Famed henceforward as the Hatti-Sherif of Gülhane, otherwise the "Noble Rescript of the Rose Chamber," it was the first of several such instruments to become collectively known as the Tanzimat, or "Reorganization."

The earliest constitutional document in any Islamic country, it was in effect a charter of legal, social, and political rights, a Magna Carta for the subjects of the Empire, whose fundamental precepts and consequent decisions in Council the Sultan pledged himself by oath to observe. Here, crystallized and inscribed in specific form, was the embodiment of those plans and ideas which had been taking shape through the latter years of Mahmud's reign and which were now to serve as the organic basis of a planned new Ottoman regime. This, with setbacks and vicissitudes, was to evolve over the next two decades. The Tanzimat, as thus proclaimed, guaranteed freedom and security of life, honour, and property; a regular method of assessing and collecting taxes and the abolition of tax farming; an equally regular method of levying and recruiting the armed forces and fixing their duration of service; finally, fair public trial under the law, and no punishment without legal sentence.

The Sultan's councils of deliberation regarding such matters were given quasi-legislative powers, and enlarged to include ministers and other notables of the Empire. Supreme among them was the Council of Justice, organized and enlarged in 1840 to play a central role throughout the Tanzimat period. Members of the councils were free to express their opinions, and the Sultan bound himself to approve their majority decisions. In his decrees he would follow and refrain from abrogating the laws laid down under the charter. This implied, in theory, a limitation on the sovereign's absolute powers, making him an executive bound to laws made by others, and thus limiting prerogatives inherent in the medieval concept of absolute sovereignty. But the charter was no document of constitutional reform, laying down a new system of relations between ruler and ruled. Its provisions did not extend so far as popular representation. Council members were not elected but chosen and appointed by the Sultan himself, and their enactions depended on his ultimate will, through the legal sanction of his ratification. Thus his absolute sovereign authority remained in effect unimpaired.

The most radical and to the Westerner the most significant of the principles of the Tanzimat lay in the equal application of its rights to all Ottoman subjects, regardless of race or creed. This eliminated all distinction between Moslem and Christian or other non-Moslem.

It granted security and freedom to all—in terms of law and taxation and property; of education, whether in civil or military schools; of enrollment in the army and public employment in any branch of the civil service.

The decree of Gülhane, seen by the Russian representative at the Porte as a successful "theatrical stroke," excited surprise and keen speculation in the West. Here, so it seemed, in an age of growing reform in Europe, were portents of some kind of liberal metamorphosis in the declining Ottoman Empire—though still within the framework of its traditional system of government. An Islamic sovereign had opened wide the doors of his state to the Christians within it. To Lord Palmerston this was "a grand stroke of policy," which had "a great effect on public feeling both here and in France." But by Metternich and others, all too aware of the murkier aspects of the Ottoman scene, hence skeptical as to the practical prospects of reform, it was cynically dismissed as little more than an essay in window dressing.

From without there now came a new influx of Europeans, seeking to benefit from new opportunities and, it was to be hoped, new permanent advantages. On the other hand the non-Moslem subjects within the Empire itself, eager as they were for any improvement in their status, were distinctly guarded in their response to the new charter. Its much-vaunted privileges were counterbalanced by new obligations, incumbent upon them as fully qualified citizens. They were now liable for military service, from which they had hitherto earned exemption through the payment of poll tax. This faced them with the unwelcome prospect of fighting against other Christians, just as the Moslems were faced with that of fighting alongside them, perhaps under the command of Christian officers. Lacking a common sentiment of Ottoman patriotism, the Christians feared for the loss of special privileges, which furthered their educational and economic development, while their clerical leaders feared for that of their own vested interests. Mistrustful of the true intentions of the Ottoman government, they preferred still to seek foreign aid—especially from Russia—in their quest for autonomy and, in the end, independence.

As for the bulk of the Moslem population, they were outraged by this emancipation of the infidel, which struck right at the roots of their traditional conception of the absolute superiority of Islam and the inferiority of all other religions. Tolerance and protection were indeed due to the *rayas,* together with a measure of freedom in the direction of their communal affairs. But it was due to them as to a separate species. They were inferiors who in view of their disparate beliefs could never be regarded as equals, or accepted as such, morally or socially, in such a secular community as the principles of the

Tanzimat had envisaged. This opposition now provoked throughout the Empire a widespread spirit of reaction, which in the absence of a resolute Sultan was not easily checked.

It rose to a head in 1841, when Reshid Pasha, intent on the development of foreign trade, established a new court of justice in the newly created Ministry of Commerce to hear commercial disputes, and moreover prepared a new commercial code, based on those of the French, which dealt with such matters as partnership, bankruptcies, and bills of exchange. This was seen by Moslem jurists as a derogation from the Sheriat. When Reshid introduced it to the High Council, he was asked whether it conformed to the holy law. He replied, "The holy law has nothing to do with such matters." At this members of the ulema exclaimed, "Blasphemy!" The code was suspended, to the great disadvantage of foreign traders, and the Sultan, yielding to the ulema, dismissed Reshid, who was exiled to his former embassy in Paris. His reforms were interrupted and often reversed, as the reactionary Riza Pasha—the Sultana Valide's unscrupulous paramour—came to power in his place, with a Grand Vezir, Izzet Mehmed, who was notorious for his hatred of foreigners and of Western ideas.

Riza, however, as Serasker or commander-in-chief, carried out a much-needed reorganization of the army which was to stand the Empire in good stead. He divided it into two forces: the troops on active service—the *Nizam*—who served for five years; and those in the reserve—the *Redif*—who served in their respective districts for a further seven years on returning home. Recruitment was through a form of conscription; training, arms, equipment, and organization were on Western lines. A new force thus arose, quarter of a million strong, whose soldiery displayed much of the old Turkish courage and discipline, and whose officers were expected to improve in quality with the development of the military schools. It was a Moslem-Turkish army to whose ranks, despite the recent decree, Christians were not in fact recruited. Any such fusion was to be compared to the mingling of oil and water, or as Lord Palmerston expressed it, "more like that of a cat and dog shut up in the same box."

Eventually non-Moslems were relieved from the privilege of military service by the payment of an exemption tax, replacing the former poll tax. But Christians were recruited, as in the past, into the naval forces. These were reorganized by a friend of Riza's, a British naval officer named Adolphus Slade, who raised a force of ten thousand sailors but failed to increase the number of fighting ships. The creation of the new army was Riza's sole effective service to his country, through a four-year period of general injustice, insecurity, and reaction when the proud name *Gülhane,* or "Rose Chamber," became cynically but appropriately corrupted into *Gulhan,* meaning "Dust Hole."

Stratford Canning learned meanwhile that in this corrupt atmosphere Riza, with the connivance of the Finance Minister and the aid of two Christian capitalists, was engaged in large-scale peculation at the expense of the Ottoman treasury. Deeming it politic to refrain from warning the young Sultan of this, he nonetheless kept a close eye on Riza, while feigning a tacit acquiescence in his reactionary policy. Meanwhile, he quietly cultivated his personal relationship with Abdul Mejid, confessing that he found in him "more goodness than strength," but still expressing the hope "that much may be effected by European influence and example, sufficiently exerted and properly directed."

From now onward Stratford Canning, high-principled and staunch in his Protestant beliefs, emerged as the zealous champion and protector of Christians, often indeed overriding in scope his own government's specified policies. He protested insistently when in succession a young Armenian and a young Greek, who had embraced Islam, reverted to Christianity and were executed under Koranic law for their apostasy. He finally induced the Sultan in person to "give his royal word that henceforward neither should Christianity be insulted in his dominions, nor should Christians be in any way persecuted for their religion." This assurance was confirmed and spread through the provinces of the Empire in a public declaration. For the Sultan it earned a letter of congratulation from his fellow sovereign Queen Victoria. Stratford Canning himself, already respected by the Turks for the commanding dignity of his presence and the sincerity of his convictions, won enhanced prestige through this positive display of his power. Henceforward he was revered by them. To the Christians he was the Padishah of Padishahs. Eventually he achieved the fall of Riza, who was dismissed by the Sultan in 1845.

To Canning's satisfaction, Riza was succeeded by Reshid, who returned to become Grand Vezir; and the policy of reform was renewed. Initiating its next phase, the Sultan declared that, apart from the military reform, proposals for the benefit of his subjects had been misunderstood and misapplied by the ministers. Attributing this to general ignorance, he decreed the establishment of new schools, to disseminate knowledge and to facilitate, in other government departments, those improvements introduced into the Ministry of War. A committee proposed not merely a large new network of primary and secondary schools, but an Ottoman state university. So ambitious a project could only be realized, against numerous obstacles, over a long period of years. The foundations of the university were indeed laid, and a medal struck which portrayed the finished building. But for lack of funds it was never finished, the work being abandoned when its walls were no more than a few feet high.

In the field of primary education little headway could be made against the exclusive preserves of the ulema. But the number of secondary schools increased slowly, with judicious lip service by the committee to the importance of religion as an educational force, but in fact within the framework of a system of secular education, separate from the jurisdiction of the ulema. As time went on, the products of its schools were to furnish a new middle-class elite for the bureaucracy in its various branches.

Following this new edict the Sultan launched a bold experiment in provincial government, aimed against the power of the pashas and based on the principle of consultation with the people. From each province he summoned two representatives, elected from among prominent citizens for their intelligence, local knowledge, and capacity for public affairs. They were to confer with his High Council as an Assembly of Provincial Notables, giving their views on present conditions and needs for reform.

When this failed to produce a response, he sent roving commissioners to the provinces to report, for the benefit of the High Council, on the state of the reforms. For each governor, or pasha, he established a council, a *mejlis,* whose members were to be elected from the various local communities. Well-intentioned as this innovation was, in its aim to establish more responsible and representative government, it failed in practice through the Turkish tendency at once to maintain the letter and to violate the spirit of reforms. The non-Moslems were indeed represented. But the Moslem Turks, predominantly reactionary in spirit, remained in the majority. They could easily intimidate and override the minority they were meant to protect, hampering a good governor and abetting a bad one, who could lay the blame on his council and was thus seldom brought to justice. In general this was a system which not only failed to curb oppression, but could be so distorted as to give a false semblance of legality.

In two cases Stratford Canning, keeping an alert eye on the progress of the reforms, formally denounced a *mejlis* to the Sultan himself. Indeed, the foreign consuls, whose status had risen through the Tanzimat, were now in a position to intervene more effectively against corrupt pashas and on behalf of the Christian minorities, and even sometimes to secure improvement in their conditions. Canning himself, through his influence with the Sultan, could claim two further achievements: the abolition of the traffic in slaves by Turkish vessels; and the assurance that the land tax would be collected not from individuals, as through a recent abuse, but from heads of communities, as before.

In the realm of justice, mixed civil and criminal courts were established in 1847, with an equal number of Ottoman and European judges, and a procedure deriving from European rather than Islamic practice. A revised penal code was promulgated in 1851. Already, in the previous year, Reshid had secured the promulgation of his commercial code, whose attempted introduction, a decade earlier, had led to his initial downfall. Administered in the tribunals of commerce, it defined, protected, and facilitated the commercial transactions of foreigners—not only the *rayas,* but the Franks, who had for long traded as merchants within the Empire but had never yet been able to settle their commercial claims in a Turkish court. Though the Capitulations—with the right of trial in their own consular courts—protected foreigners in the civil and criminal sense, they still lacked similar protection in commercial matters.

This was now afforded to them through the formation of a court of commerce, in the form of mixed tribunals composed equally of Turkish and European members, whose function was to settle commercial cases between Turk and Frank. Promulgated in 1850, the commercial code represented the first formal recognition in Turkey—as already in certain other Islamic states—of a legal system, independent of the ulema, which dealt with matters beyond the scope of the Sacred Law. It marked a salient point in the progress, spread over the past decade, of a new economic liberalism, a wider opening of the gates of the Turkish economy to the West, in terms of a freer and closer commercial relationship.

This had originated shortly before the Tanzimat in a new Anglo-Turkish commercial convention. Founded on the principles of free trade, on the fixing at a regular rate of import and export tariffs, and on the abolition of restrictive practices, this was calculated to benefit both British and Ottoman merchants. It marked the emergence of Britain, at the expense of France, as the leading trading nation in Near Eastern waters. But its terms, amounting as they did to a complete revision and modernization of the existing commercial system, were made available to other European powers, and led immediately to revised commercial agreements with the French and the Dutch.

Foreign merchants were thus released from their previous fetters. Trade increased substantially, launching a new era of economic growth and commercial prosperity. The territories of the Empire grew in importance as a market for European industrial produce, and as a source of export for agricultural and other raw materials. Turkey saw the establishment of commercial companies, banks, insurance companies, and other such institutions of a modern economy. The urban population increased through a general migration into new and expanding towns, away from the older medieval towns and villages, whose traditional crafts and industries declined—at the expense of the artisan classes and peasantry. Within a generation the major cities had tripled and even quadrupled in size, with a large European and Levantine population, which tended to swamp the Turkish business classes, thus widening the gulf between non-Moslem and Moslem. Such were the fruits of free European economic penetration.

Merchants, businessmen, financiers the Moslem Turks were essentially not, but rather administrators, soldiers, and cultivators of the soil. A full treasury and a sound currency were assets unfamiliar to a long line of Sultans, whose machinery of government thus became stultified and its servants corrupt. It was their habit to meet a deficit by debasing the currency. During the reign of Mahmud II the form of the Ottoman coinage was frequently changed, and its rate so declined as to create chronic inflation, detrimental to the standard of living, hence to the integrity of salaried officials. In 1840 Sultan Abdul Mejid decreed the formation of an Ottoman bank, on European lines, with a guaranteed government subsidy. This was followed by the introduction of paper money in the form of treasury bonds, at fluctuating rates of interest. In 1844 the government, in conjunction with the new bank, introduced a new set of measures to safeguard the currency. The old coinage was withdrawn and a new one introduced on European lines, based on a gold pound. This stabilized the position for a while.

But the handling of finance, in the capitalist context of the nineteenth century, was to prove beyond the wit of any Ottoman government. One after the other, from 1858 onward, they came to depend on foreign loans, a dependence which was to lead them to ultimate financial collapse. In the Empire it was not the Moslem Turks who profited from banking and industrial investment. Nor any longer was it primarily the non-Moslem minorities, the resident Greeks and Armenians and Jews who had for so long amassed wealth as the middlemen. Now it was the capitalist enterprises of Europe itself which came to dominate the Turkish economy. This reinforced in financial terms the growing political hold over the Empire of the European ambassadors.

From the middle of the century onward the spirit of reform within the Empire was losing its vigour. The influence of Stratford Canning, for all his successes, had failed in its efforts to reform the prisons, to improve road communications, to suppress corruption, to ameliorate the Empire's finances. Nor, for all his preoccupation with the religious problems, had he succeeded in achieving any real degree of equality between Christians and Moslems. His noble efforts had produced more concessions in words than in deeds. Reshid, once the ardent reformer, was weakening in moral conviction and declining in spirit, discouraged by the powers of the reactionary party. He fell into debt and became prone to corruption. The Sultan himself, wearying of reform, became increasingly irresolute in public affairs, sorely trying the patience of the Great Elchi (meaning *ambassador,* or in this instance Canning) with his polite evasions and passive tactics of procrastination.

Increasingly seduced by the life of the harem, his procreative activities aroused the amazement of an English traveller and investigator, Charles MacFarlane. "Before he was twenty years old, the puny stripling was the father of *eight* children, borne to him by different women in the imperial harem, in the course of little more than *three* years." Later MacFarlane jotted down in his diary: "Very early in the morning we were startled out of our sleep by a tremendous firing of salutes. The Sultan has another son. Only last week he had another daughter!"

Oblivious of treasury deficits and dire warnings of impending bankruptcy from Stratford Canning, the Sultan, who had grown tired of the old Seraglio, crowned his extravagance with the building of the huge modern marble palace of Dolma Bahche, up the Bosporus on the European shore. This cost him a fortune. Built in a European neo-Renaissance style, with elaborate rococo ornament, its marble halls glistened with gold leaf, crystal, alabaster, and porphyry; its ceilings were painted by French and Italian artists; its throne room contained the world's largest mirrors; and in the Sultan's bedchamber the bed was made from solid silver.

Henceforward, epitomizing in its taste the Westernized trends of the court, the Dolma Bahche was to replace the old Seraglio as the permanent residence, distinct from the center of government, of all future Sultans. Here Abdul Mejid entertained with lavish ostentation in the European manner. Having a refined taste in music, he had a Turkish band trained by German and Italian masters to play the best modern compositions, which thus replaced the more primitive martial airs of the past. He imported also European actors, ballet dancers, and other performers, building a theater attached to the palace in which they staged their entertainments. Meanwhile, the finances of the Empire were heading downhill, through inertia, in the direction of chaos.

The time came when the Great Elchi grew disillusioned by the failure of the young Padishah's earlier promise. Infirmity of purpose, he realized, was the fatal weakness both of the Sultan and his Grand Vezir. Palmerston likewise feared that the Empire was "doomed to fall by the timidity and weakness and irresolution of its sovereign and of his ministers." He advised his ambassador no longer to press for major reforms. So, as Canning admitted, "the *great* game of improvement is altogether up for the present and . . . it is impossible for me to conceal that the main object of my stay here is all but gone."

Reshid had indeed failed in his main task of reform, not wholly through his own weaknesses but through the failure of Turkish popular opinion to keep pace with it, and of a still inadequate secularly educated class to support it. For even certain of those radical forces opposed to reaction feared the effects of too drastic an introduction of Western ideas into a civilization still basically Islamic in outlook. They suspected that too hasty an attempt, such as that of Stratford Canning's, to eliminate religious and racial differences would rebound to the disadvantage of the Turks without benefit to the Christians.

Thus Stratford Canning resigned his post as ambassador and left for England in the summer of 1852. He felt that he had achieved all too little, but was reassured on the eve of his departure by a flood of tributes to his labours from Armenian Protestants, Greeks, American missionaries, and the mercantile communities of Istanbul and Smyrna. He expected "perhaps never to return." But an abrupt new turn of events brought him back within a year, now ennobled as Lord Stratford de Redcliffe. The decade of peace through which he had reigned was now suddenly to end. For the Ottoman Empire was heading once more for a momentous encounter with Russia.

((33))

The Russian Tsar Nicholas I, autocratic in his rule and unrelenting in his aims as any oriental despot, had from the outset of his reign counted on the approaching fall of the Ottoman Empire, and had kept up diplomatic pressure among the Western powers for its eventual dismemberment. With Britain he first broached the subject in an official visit to London in 1844, but met only with a guarded refusal to discuss mere contingencies. Now, early in 1853, in St. Petersburg, the Tsar reverted to the topic in a series of informal but historic conversations with Sir Hamilton Seymour, the British ambassador.

Referring to the disorganized state of the Ottoman Empire and its probable fall, he considered it important that England and Russia should come to an understanding concerning it, and that neither should take any decisive step of which the other was not apprised. He concluded with the words: "We have a sick man on our hands—a man gravely ill. It will be a grave misfortune if one of these days he slips through our hands, especially before the necessary arrangements are made."

Seymour in his reply suggested that the need in this case was for a physician, not a surgeon: the invalid should be treated gently to aid his recovery. The Tsar's chancellor, Nesselrode, agreed that the patient's continued existence was precarious. It should, however, be prolonged for as long as possible. This was a view shared by the British Prime Minister, Lord Aberdeen.

A few days later the Tsar enlarged upon his theme more explicitly, assuring the ambassador that he no longer supported the "dreams and plans" of the Empress Catherine, with her designs on the city of Constantinople, since his country was so large and "so happily circumstanced" as to require no further territory. Nor was there now anything to fear from the Turks. On the other hand he was concerned with the interests of the several millions of Christians within the Empire, whose protection, secured to him by treaty, was a duty he was bound to discharge. If the Empire were to fall it would rise no more, and it was surely better to provide in advance for the contingency than to incur the chaos and the certainty of the European war which would otherwise attend such a catastrophe.

Talking to the ambassador "as a friend and as a gentleman," the Tsar spoke plainly on the future of Constantinople, which he could not cede to England. For his own part he added: "I am equally ready to promise not to establish myself there as a proprietor. As a temporary tenant I do not say I might not." A French expedition to Turkey, for example, might bring Russian troops over its border. In a further conversation the Tsar referred to the Danubian principalities of Wallachia and Moldavia as independent states under his protection. A similar protectorate could apply to Serbia and Bulgaria. As to Egypt, he would raise no objection to its occupation by Britain, together with the island of Crete. To this Seymour observed that Britain's views on Egypt extended no further than the need for "a safe and ready communication between British India and the Mother Country."

In reply to these overtures the foreign secretary, Lord John Russell, recalled, as an early eighteenth-century precedent, the treaties of the Spanish Succession, between England and France, partitioning in advance an empire whose ruler was "childless, sick in mind and body, and visibly falling into the grave." The Turkish "sick man," on the other hand, might be long a-dying: he might survive for twenty, fifty, or a hundred years longer. Thus the Turkish provinces, unlike the Spanish, could not be partitioned in advance. The revelation of any such secret convention as the Tsar envisaged "would alarm and alienate the Sultan . . . and stimulate all his enemies to increased violence and more obstinate conflict." On the subject of Constantinople, Lord John voiced misgiving as to the prospect of any Russian tenancy of the city, which might—so he hinted—lead to annexation. On behalf of England he gave the pledge that she "renounced all intention or wish to hold Constantinople."

Such, expressed with firmness and courtesy, was the attitude of Britain toward Turkey and Russia over the Eastern Question, as it came to be known. When, shortly afterward, Lord Clarendon succeeded Lord John as foreign secretary, he echoed the opinion, in sanguine terms, in a final dispatch to Sir Hamilton Seymour: "Turkey only required forbearance on the part of its allies, and a determination not to press their claims in a manner humiliating to the dignity and independence of the Sultan—that friendly support, in short, which among states as well as individuals the weak are entitled to expect from the strong—in order not only to prolong its existence but to remove all cause for alarm respecting its dissolution."

To the ambassador it was clear that the Tsar, claiming common interests with Austria, sought to cultivate the friendship of England in order to isolate France. The French were certainly his declared enemies in the negotiations with the Porte which now came to a head concerning in particular the guardianship of the holy places in

Palestine, and in general the protection of Christians in the Ottoman Empire.

Here, between the Tsar Nicholas and the Emperor Napoleon III, protectors respectively of the Orthodox Greek and the Roman Catholic Church, was a major diplomatic conflict on a religious issue, with strong political overtones, where neither of the two great powers could easily compromise, and where war now became an imminent risk. Sanctified by the gospel story, the shrines of Jerusalem and Bethlehem and the holy ground beneath and around them, trodden by the Saviour, had inspired the Christian chivalry of the Crusades and had since become a center of pilgrimage from every quarter of the Christian world. The lords of it were now the Turks, themselves reared, as Moslems, in the pilgrim tradition, with their own shrines of Mecca and Medina. They were thus respectful of the Christian shrines and of the monasteries which served as their hospices—and moreover drew from the pilgrimages a substantial annual revenue. It rested with the Ottoman authorities to apportion between the rival Christian churches the share of this revenue and of the resulting control. This allotment became a cause of perpetual strife.

In 1740 France, through her treaty of Capitulations, had obtained from the Sultan a grant confirming and enlarging the privileges of the Latin Church in Palestine. But with the decline of French religious zeal, and the rise of Russian imperial power, these privileges were usurped by the Greek Orthodox Church. Its followers were in any case more prone than the Latin Catholics to the practice of pilgrimage, and its clergy received consistent support from the Russians, winning advantages at the continual expense of the French.

At Bethlehem, by the end of the eighteenth century, the Latin monks were lamenting that the birthplace of the Saviour had been in the power of the Greeks for forty or fifty years past—through a firman which excluded the Latins. Greek influence increased steadily through the nineteenth century, with substantial acquisitions of property in the holy places, at the expense of the Latins, and the development of charitable institutions and schools under the Orthodox Patriarch. Thanks to Russian pressure his election was transferred from Constantinople to Jerusalem, thus breaking free of a dependence centuries old. Financial aid from the Russian government poured into Palestine. So did an incessant stream of pilgrims, making arduous journeys from the farthest corners of Russia in Europe and Asia. Their gold became the chief source of wealth for the Church of the Holy Sepulchre. With its other sacred sites—the waters of Jordan, the manger of Bethlehem, the Garden of Gethsemane—the Holy Land became for the Russian people a source of blessed religious experience. To their rulers it was already a serviceable channel of political influence.

* * *

It was not until the middle of the century that the French sought seriously to recover their privileges in Palestine, won while the Russians were still weak, and allowed imprudently to lapse as they grew strong. Now at last France took action to change a disturbed *status quo*. In 1850 Prince Louis Napoleon, the French president and aspiring emperor, needing political support from the Catholic party, instructed his ambassador to demand from the Porte strict execution of the grants to the Latin Church as laid down by the treaty of 1740. This would involve the annulment of conflicting grants, since given by firman to the Greek Church. It thus portended a conflict, with implied threats of armed intervention, between Russia and France—here in this very spot where, as the British foreign secretary expressed it, "the heavenly host proclaimed peace and good will towards men."

In mere practical terms the dispute boiled down to the question as to whether the Latin monks, to enable them to pass through the Church of Bethlehem into their grotto, should possess a key to its chief door, together with one of the keys of each of the two doors of the manger itself; whether they should be free to place in the sanctuary of the Nativity a silver star, with the arms of France, which had in fact been wrenched from the rock of the manger and filched by the Greeks in a recent skirmish; finally—and less emphatically—whether at Gethsemane they should retain their right to "a cupboard and a lamp in the tomb of the Virgin."

Such were the apparent trivialities which now perplexed the European diplomats and on which war or peace might depend. Was a key simply a key, in the sense of an emblem, or was it an instrument for opening or closing a door? The diplomatic answer, it seemed, was that this key, though in fact really a key, was an evil instrument in that its proposed purpose was not to keep the Greeks out but to let the Latins in.

After a long spell of equivocation at the Porte, a new, anti-Russian Grand Vezir made a token concession to the Greeks but substantial concessions to the French. These involved the solemn replacement from France of the silver star of Bethlehem, then a presentation to the Latin Patriarch of the required keys to the shrine. They were handed over at Christmas in a public ceremony of formal surrender, clearly implying that supremacy had passed from one Church to the other. Such was the final discomfiture of the Greeks—and the Russians.

It led to a sharp escalation of diplomatic conflict between the two great powers. At the end of 1852 the Tsar Nicholas, contemptuously refusing to recognize Napoleon III's recent proclamation as emperor, mobilized two army corps on the Danube, in Bessarabia, ready if need be to cross the Turkish frontier. At the same time he put at readiness his fleet at Sebastopol. Then in February, 1853, he sent an ambassador extraordinary to the Porte on a "conciliatory" mission, in the shape of Prince Menshikov. An arrogant general with a reputed contempt for the Turks and dislike for the English, he was a crude, blustering character who brought to diplomacy the rough tactics of the battlefield.

Arriving in a warship with the menacing name of *The Thunderer,* preceded and followed by a large military staff and the commander of his Black Sea fleet, Menshikov soon made it clear that he had come in a spirit of "courteous menace," not to persuade but to coerce the Turks. His mission went far beyond a mere religious settlement designed to cover, through confirmation of the Sultan's firman, the Greek rights in the holy places. It extended to a demand, essentially political in character and based on an interpretation of the Treaty of Küchük Kainarji, for a second firman, which would guarantee to Russia a protectorate over all the Orthodox subjects of the Ottoman Empire. This was to be embodied in a convention, with the force of a treaty, between Russia and the Porte, which could amount to a secret defensive alliance.

The Porte reacted with alarm and dismay to this threat by a foreign power to its internal independence, delivered as it was with a "mixture of embraces and pistol-shots." The reaction of France was to send a fleet not to the Bosporus but to Salamis in the Aegean. That of Britain was more restrained but no less effective. She rejected the request of her chargé d'affaires for the dispatch of a fleet from Malta. Instead, she sent back Lord Stratford de Redcliffe as ambassador to the Sublime Porte.

Early one glorious morning in April, 1853, with the domes and the minarets towering through the mist above the city of Istanbul, a warship was sighted sailing across the Sea of Marmara, and the Sultan and his ministers "knew who it was that was on board." By midday (as Alexander William Kinglake describes it) "there was no seeming change in the outward world. Yet all was changed. Lord Stratford de Redcliffe had entered once more the palace of the British Embassy. The event spread a sense of safety, but also a sense of awe." Prince Menshikov now met with a redoubtable adversary.

Stratford at once showed himself an adroit tactician, by separating the two demands at issue—the dispute over the holy places and the ulterior proposals for a protectorate. The first had in practice been settled at Christmas through the conversion of Latin claims into established privileges. It now remained only to deal with a few outstanding trivialities, vital to the self-esteem of the losers.

Serving as mediator between the two contending powers, the Great Elchi dealt gently with the arrogant prince, disarming him with an unexpected deference and a readiness to admit the fairness of the Russian claims over the holy places. For "French feelings of honour"

Lord Stratford showed similar deference, urging upon his French colleague a policy of moderation, in view of the forthcoming international issues involved.

Finally disagreement persisted only over the question as to whether Latins or Greeks should shoulder the burden and expense of repairing the churches, and in particular the cupola of the Church of the Holy Sepulchre. The Latins strongly contested the Greek right to do so, and it was only when the Turks stepped between the contestants to undertake the task themselves, in the name of the Sultan, that the Greeks agreed to an acceptable compromise, by which this would be done under the supervision of the Greek Patriarch. Within a mere seventeen days of his arrival the Great Elchi thus settled a thorny diplomatic dispute which had vexed the powers for close on three years past.

But Prince Menshikov had still to reach his main diplomatic objective. He lost no time in presenting to the Porte his peremptory demand for a further convention. In the guise of securing to the Orthodox religion and its clergy their traditional rights and immunities, this implied in effect the establishment of a permanent Russian protectorate over the Greek Christians. For it was made clear that it must apply not merely to the clerical elements but to the lay population, which amounted in fact to some twelve million Orthodox *rayas*. The French, quoted as a precedent, had indeed rights of protection over the Latin clerical elements and over their own Catholic nationals. But they had never aspired to protect Catholic lay subjects in general, who were in any case numbered not in millions but in thousands. Menshikov's claims were clearly for political as for religious protection.

Cautiously he revealed to the Dutch representative the true scope of these secular aims for the future political predominance of Russia at Constantinople. Hence those required "guarantees for the future" whose enforcement, as Stratford interpreted them, could "eventually prove fatal to the Porte's independence." In his eyes the convention, with its implications of a "secret alliance," was incompatible with the "desire of maintaining the integrity and independence of the Ottoman Empire as a security for the peace of Europe, which Russia had joined with England, Austria and Prussia in acknowledging in 1840," while in 1841 Russia herself, together with France, had pledged herself to the inviolability of the Sultan's sovereign rights.

Prince Menshikov, reflecting the impatient mood of the Tsar, adopted blunt, dictatorial tactics to cajole the Porte into acceptance of his "august master's" demands. He presented them in the hostile tones of an ultimatum, imposing brief time limits for a reply, threatening the rupture of diplomatic relations, with his own departure and that of his embassy, in case of delay or rejection. But the Turkish ministers had the revered Elchi at their side once more, a wise, trusted adviser who calmed their fears, stiffened their resolve, counselled an attitude combining patient moderation with firmness of purpose in defense of the Sultan's "sovereign dignity and independence." He sought to inspire in them a spirit of moral, not martial resistance, even in the event of an occupation of the Danube principalities.

Meanwhile, to the Sultan alone in private audience, he revealed his instructions, already effected, to request the British commander in the Mediterranean to hold his naval squadron in readiness, but for use only in the event of such "imminent danger" as a threat to Constantinople itself. Meanwhile, the Tsar Nicholas fumed at "the infernal dictatorship of this Redcliffe," whose name and political ascendancy at the Porte personified for him the whole Eastern Question.

After an exchange of notes, rude from the Russian and polite from the Turkish side, Prince Menshikov took action in terms of a high-handed internal coup at the Porte, by ignoring the Grand Vezir and thus precipitating his resignation. He forced on the timid Sultan a new ministry to serve his own ends, with Reshid Pasha, whom he fondly imagined to be pro-Russian in sympathy, as Minister of Foreign Affairs. In an audience with the Sultan he insisted in a hectoring manner on the need for a direct alliance between Turkey and Russia, irrespective of the European powers. He left confident of success.

Reshid was now obliged to respond to the prince's last menacing note. His old ally Lord Stratford helped him to draft an evasive reply, with a request for a few days' further delay. This was delivered to the prince, who had hitherto been counting on Reshid as an obedient servant. He angrily refused to consider it, formally broke off relations until given satisfaction, and referred ominously to the "incalculable consequences" of a failure by the Porte to agree. He put off his departure for a further two or three days. Meanwhile, the Sultan's newly formed Grand Council met to discuss the emergency, and only three out of its forty-five members voted for agreement with Russia.

Next day Reshid put verbally to Menshikov proposals which he had concocted in detail with Stratford. These offered a formal convention, virtually conceding all that Russia required with regard to the holy places. But they firmly rejected any form of protectorate over the Greek Orthodox subjects of the Ottoman Empire or such an "engagement with the force of treaty" as affected the Sultan's independence. The prince, thus deceived by his new "ally" Reshid and, to his sore humiliation, defeated by his old adversary Stratford, broke off relations, terminated his mission, threatened dire consequences of the Porte's refusal, and withdrew once and for all with his diplomatic staff to his yacht, which got up steam to advertise his immediate departure. But for four more days, in the hope of a last-minute surrender, he lingered on. "It is not easy," wrote Stratford, "to divine why."

Lord Stratford himself now assembled a meeting of the representatives of the other three European powers—Austria, France, and Prussia—thus placing the Eastern Question on the sure ground, where it belonged, of a concerted European decision. When unanimous agreement was reached on the need for the Porte to resist the extreme demands of Russia, the Austrian chargé d'affaires called upon Prince Menshikov with a joint note seeking to prevent a rupture between the two powers. Menshikov produced a revised formula for an independent agreement with the Porte, whose acceptance might induce him to suspend his departure. Though renouncing both convention and treaty for a diplomatic note, it differed in form but remained in substance identical with his previous proposals. Moreover, it specified clearly their application to the laity as to the clerical Orthodox population.

The Sultan, his dignity already compromised, now roused himself to declare the Russian demands "inadmissible." The prince refused to change them, and at long last, at midday on May 21, 1853, he steamed away up the Bosporus into the Black Sea. At the same time the Tsar's coat of arms, with its imperial eagle, was removed from the door of the palatial Russian legation. Landing at Odessa, the Prince was obliged to report in a dispatch to his "august master" the failure of his mission. The blame for this Russian discomfiture he cast, in Kinglake's words, on "the evil skill of that Antichrist, in stately English form, whom Heaven was permitting for a while to trample over the Tsar and his Church."

Here in effect was the end of peace, but not yet the beginning of war. Russian troops crossed the Pruth without resistance, to occupy the principalities of Moldavia and Wallachia, over which the Tsar already claimed a form of protectorate. British warships, with a small French squadron, moved up to the mouth of the Dardanelles, still outside the limits of the Straits as closed to other powers by the treaty of 1841. A strong British fleet thus kept watch over a strong Russian army. But their respective roles were for the present precautionary. Here by both was a show of force aimed at security, but not an act of war. The Russians still hoped to intimidate the Turks into some kind of concession, if only to salve tsarist pride. The British still hoped, in a spirit of firm moderation, for a peaceful solution through the four powers, acting in council.

The main moves in this diplomatic engagement were twofold. The first, following the polite rejection of a menacing note from St. Petersburg, which reiterated the familiar Russian demands, was a note from the Porte, inspired by Lord Stratford and consigned to the Council of the Four Powers in Vienna for delivery to St. Petersburg. Misleadingly named "the Turkish ultimatum," it transmitted copies of firmans newly and spontaneously granted by the Sultan to his religious minorities, confirming in perpetuity all privileges granted to the Greek Church, and guaranteeing them in terms of a bond to which the four other powers were witnesses.

But the note was not passed on to the Tsar. On reaching Vienna it was intercepted in transit by the four powers at the conference, who rejected it in favour of a Vienna note of their own. In the drafting of this Lord Stratford was not consulted.

It was inspired by the mediation of Austria, as an interested neighbour of the invaded principalities. It was accepted by the Tsar, but not by the Sultan. The Turkish ultimatum had been witnessed and guaranteed by the four powers alone as an undertaking, on Turkey's initiative, to Russia. The Vienna note provided for guarantees by Russia herself and France, whose preliminary consent was required for any modifications by the Porte of its obligations. Here, as the Porte saw it, and as Stratford well realized, was an implied inequality between Turkey and Russia. The terms emphasized her sense of dependence and left the door open, as in the past, to Russian interference between the Sultan and his Christian subjects. Thus the Grand Council of the Sultan, which had agreed to the Turkish ultimatum, now unanimously rejected the Vienna note, proposing amendments which were calculated to prove unacceptable to Russia.

The British government blamed Stratford for the rejection, even to the point of considering a demand for his resignation. Meanwhile, the balance now inevitably swayed toward war. In September demonstrations and riots erupted in Istanbul. The Sheikh-ul-Islam, with the encouragement of the Minister of War, sanctioned the posting of a proclamation in a mosque, urging a declaration of war against Russia, while some hundreds of members of the ulema, stiffened by a large band of theological students, drew up a manifesto which called upon the Sultan and his council for the launching, as a religious duty, of a holy war. The ministers in alarm called upon the foreign ambassadors to help maintain public order.

From the outset France, as the Emperor Napoleon sought to relieve his internal stresses through external adventures, had taken a belligerent line with regard to the Eastern Question. Now, still in pursuit of this policy, the French ambassador to the Porte, expressing concern for the safety of foreign residents, pressed for agreement by Stratford to bring up the Anglo-French fleet to the city, and received support from his Austrian colleague. Stratford, overriding them both, refused thus to violate the Straits Convention of 1841 by bringing up warships. For he knew that this could lead to war. But the terms of the convention allowed for exceptions in the form of other vessels plying between the fleet and the capital. He thus agreed to bring up four steamers, two British and two French, to join those already in the Golden Horn. Their arrival had the desired effect: the spirit of revolt died down and the guilty members of the ulema were exiled.

But the Elchi's peaceful solution was not to prevail. Before the news of it reached London, news was received in mid-September of the Tsar's refusal to accept the Turkish modifications to the Vienna note. At the same time information reached the foreign secretary, Lord Clarendon, of a private interpretation of the note by the Russian chancellor, Nesselrode, the news of which had leaked to the German press. Concerning the privileges of the Greek Church, Nesselrode declared that, under the terms of the note, the Turks must not only leave its immunities untouched but must "take account of Russia's active solicitude for her co-religious Turks." This revelation unmasked once and for all the truly aggressive intentions of Russia in the Ottoman Empire, which the British government had been slow to perceive. Clarendon condemned it as violent. He now admitted that, as Stratford had understood from the start, the Turks had been right to reject the Vienna note. The British press came out strongly against the Tsar, and demanded strong measures. The British and French governments renounced the Vienna note, with a rebuke to Russia. Here was an abrupt reversal of British policy whose balance now inevitably tilted a degree further from peace toward war.

Napoleon's ambassador intensified French pressure in London, with alarmist reports of the riots in Istanbul, and declared that his government thought it "indispensably necessary" to order up the fleets at once. Without waiting for Stratford's report on the situation, the British government gave him the order, thus in his own words "crossing the Rubicon." Aberdeen, the Prime Minister, cautiously emphasized the protective nature of his move, and disclaimed any hostile intentions against Russia. But Clarendon later emphasized that the decision was taken "not upon the demand of the French Emperor (which had twice before been refused) but because by the act of Russia a further step had been rendered inevitable." He had few illusions that peace could still be preserved.

The sole remaining hope of it, before the fleets were in fact brought up, rested in a conference of mediation between the Austrian and Russian emperors at Olmütz. The Tsar was now conciliatory, evidently concerned at the imminence of war and ready at this eleventh hour to make concessions for peace. These amounted to a new proposal, embodying assurances from the Tsar that the duty of protecting Christians should rest with the Sultan. Even the French emperor favoured acceptance of this overture. But Britain's mistrust of Russian intentions had now been aroused too far to be thus easily appeased. Therefore Stratford was given a final peremptory order to bring up the fleet. This reflected a strong wave of anti-Russian public opinion in England.

At the Porte too the feeling against Russia was hardening. The war party was strongly in the ascendant, and the Sultan was not strong enough to assert his authority against it. In a clear move toward war he made a belligerent speech to his ministers, and having girded himself with the sword of the Prophet summoned a meeting of his Grand Council. After a fanatical session it reached the unanimous decision: "A recourse to war has been declared indispensable." This was confirmed by the Sultan, the Sheikh-ul-Islam issued the requisite *fetva,* and war was officially declared against Russia on October 4, 1853, the same day on which Stratford received his instructions to call up the fleet. Aware that its arrival would inflame the warlike mood, and still working to postpone if not to prevent hostilities, he found means of delaying action for a further fortnight. But the moment came at which instructions from Paris to his French colleague prevented him from delaying any longer. Thus, on October 20, the anniversary of the battle of Navarino, he gave the necessary order to the British admiral. The Anglo-French squadrons sailed up through the Dardanelles, colours flying, into the Golden Horn.

On the day after their arrival Turkish military forces crossed the Danube, commanded by an impatient general, Omer Pasha, who a fortnight earlier had issued an ultimatum to the opposing Russian commander to evacuate the principalities. They gained four initial victories in quick succession before the winter put an end to campaigning. The Tsar gave orders to the Russian fleet in Sebastopol to make ready for action. Here, with open conflict between the Russian and Ottoman empires, was the preliminary phase of the Crimean War.

Remote as its prospects now were, the four powers of Europe still sought peace, and Lord Stratford de Redcliffe continued to work for it. Taking account of a declaration of the Tsar that Russia would remain on the defensive and "await the attack of the Turks," he prevented the dispatch of a Turkish naval squadron on a provocative cruise around the Black Sea coasts, where it hoped to "fall in with the enemy's squadron." On the other hand neither the British nor the French admiral prevented the dispatch of a Turkish flotilla to the Turkish port of Sinope, only insisting that its purpose was not aggressive but pacific. At this time the Russian fleet from Sebastopol was now staging an overt display of naval power across the center of the Black Sea. Sebastopol itself was a mere hundred miles from Sinope, whose forts were powerless against a superior force.

On arrival in its harbour, the Turkish commander sent back a message to Istanbul that six Russian ships of the line were cruising off the port, and requested reinforcements. Owing to confusion and indecision in allied counsels, British and French, diplomatic and naval, these were not authorized. The Turks, though without a single ship of the line and thus incapable of effective resistance, refused to surrender, and in fact fired the first shot. In a ferocious Russian bombardment all their ships but one were sunk, and some three thousand Turks were slaughtered.

This "massacre of Sinope," as an attack by the Russians on enemy territory, was in fact a legitimate act of war, following the Turkish land attack beyond the Danube. It was celebrated in St. Petersburg by a theatrical performance with music, *La Bataille de Sinope,* and by rejoicings and illuminations in plenty. In London it was seen as a violent and treacherous outrage, kindling a passionate upsurge of war fever against Russia. The French emperor forced militant action. Declaring that the Black Sea must be swept clear of the Russian fleet, he pressed that the allied British and French fleets should obtain complete command of its waters. The inevitable moment had indeed arrived at which action must take the place of diplomacy. Early in the new year of 1854, following Clarendon's warning dispatch, the allied fleets, under orders from London, sailed into the Black Sea.

The Russians were still assured by the British ambassadors that this was a demonstration, not an act of war. The Tsar played for time, hurrying on his final preparations for war, and sending a delegate to Vienna with counterproposals for a possible peace settlement. These were unanimously rejected by the four powers. In mid-February, having withdrawn his diplomatic representatives from London and Paris, the Tsar ordered that Sir Hamilton Seymour and his French colleague be handed their passports. At the same time he received from Britain and France, supported less actively by Austria and Prussia, a summons to withdraw all his troops from the Danubian principalities. Failure to comply with this would be regarded as a declaration of war. To these notes the Tsar returned no reply.

On March 27 the French emperor announced to his Senate a state of war with Russia, animated by no spirit of conquest, as in the past, but in ultimate alliance with Britain to "resist dangerous encroachments." Simultaneously a message from Queen Victoria, "feeling bound to give active aid to the Sultan," announced to Parliament the rupture of negotiations with Russia, and the next day war was declared. A fortnight later the Tsar declared war, fighting "not for the things of this world," but with a "divine mission" for the Orthodox faith, against which England and France were ranged with the enemies of Christianity.

Russian forces crossed the lower Danube, thus invading Turkey, which Britain and France by a new treaty had engaged themselves to defend. They signed also an Anglo-French treaty, aimed at the liberation of the Sultan's dominions and the security of Europe. This was to become, in Kinglake's phrase, a "mighty engine" of the Crimean War. Thus, thanks to the Tsar's exorbitant ambitions and to the arrogant methods of his personal diplomacy, Russia now found herself at war, without allies, against the united powers of Europe and the Ottoman Empire.

In the spring of 1854 a large Russian army crossed the Danube into Turkish territory, and laid siege to the key fortress of Silistria. Meanwhile, expeditionary forces from Britain and France, backed by their fleets, were assembling at Varna in Bulgaria, the key port of European Turkey on the Black Sea, which commanded the routes into the Balkans. The Turkish resistance to the Russian invasion provided a stout vindication of Ottoman arms. For the modernized forces of the New Order had now come of age. Though still below the standards of the West in their organization, and woefully deficient in leadership, their troops were animated in battle with a new self-confidence and self-respect, their fighting quality kindled afresh against Russia in a spirit worthy of the holy warriors of their ancestral past.

The garrison of Silistria held out courageously against a siege pressed regardless of losses. When its commander was killed, its surviving leaders were encouraged and guided in council by two young British officers. Volunteers from the Indian army, they inspired the Turkish soldiery with an unquestioning trust and devotion as they laid down new defense works, countering the burrowings of the Russian sappers, repelling assaults with ruthless slaughter, and arousing the admiration of a newly arrived British officer for "the cool indifference of the Turks to danger." While forbidding all thoughts of surrender, the young officers, in English sporting fashion, organized a sweepstake to name the date when Silistria might be relieved.

Omer Pasha, reinforcing and strengthening the Ottoman armies at Shumla, was too wary to march to the relief of Silistria and thus draw the Russian besiegers into a battle in the open field. The allied forces, short of transport, were not yet ready for a relieving operation, though they could hear from their camp the continual thunder of the guns of the fortress. But one morning late in June, after a cannonade lasting far into the night, there was a sudden, complete silence. They feared that Silistria had fallen. In fact the reverse was true. The Russians, after a five-week bombardment, had raised the siege. The road of the invading Tsar into the Sultan's dominions in Europe was thus still effectively barred.

Meanwhile, higher up the Danube, from Rustchuk on the right bank across to Giorgevo on the left, a Turkish confronted a Russian force, both of some size. Neither, at this moment, appeared to seek conflict. But once again a group of young British officers transformed the position. Seven in number, they came, proffering their services, to the camp of the Turkish commander Hassan Pasha. Early in July there were signs from across the Danube that the Russian commander had struck camp, withdrawing much of his force. Hassan Pasha authorized a reconnaissance. General Cannon, an Indian army officer who served in the Turkish army under the name of Behram Pasha, crossed the river with a battalion of Turkish infantry. Meeting with no resistance, they started to establish themselves by a mere on the opposite bank. A force of Russian infantry emerged from an earthwork to attack them, and were driven back with some slaughter. One of the young British officers, with a group of skirmishers, contained the enemy until reinforcements crossed the river and the landing force was securely entrenched.

Meanwhile, higher up the river another and larger landing force, with five British officers, crossed the stream in detached groups, and continued, despite losses from bombardment and Russian attacks, to fight along the bank. It achieved contact with the first force, which had been strengthened in the meantime, so that the Turks now had a detachment of some five thousand men beyond the Danube. For two days, without opposition, they extended and consolidated this bridgehead. Then the Russian general Prince Gortchakov appeared on the heights with a substantial body of troops, released by the raising of the siege of Silistria, and made his dispositions to drive the Turks back into the Danube next day. But toward nightfall there appeared down below him a flotilla of gunboats, which had arrived unexpectedly and was soon anchored in an inlet between the two armies. While he hesitated, perhaps overrating this naval force, the British and the Turks threw a bridge of boats across the Danube, and thus confronted him with the prospect of facing the entire Turkish force mustered at Rustchuk.

At this he called a retreat, withdrawing upon Bucharest with his whole army and thus leaving the Turks in free possession of the lower waters of the Danube. Within a month the last Russian soldier had recrossed the Pruth. A threat of war by the Austrians, in terms of a convention recently signed with the Porte, drove the Russians to evacuate their armies and their administration from the principalities of Moldavia and Wallachia. An Austrian army of occupation then took their place, barring the way to any possible Russian advance into Europe.

The purpose of the initial British ultimatum was thus fulfilled. One brief inglorious campaign had brought defeat to the Tsar's army and a swift end to his designs upon Turkey in Europe. The humiliation to his pride and the blow to his prestige were the harder to bear because they were inflicted, not by the European armies, but through the bravery and revived military prowess of the long-despised Ottoman soldiery—with the aid of a few British officers.

* * *

For the Ottoman Empire the war had fulfilled its essential defensive purpose. All Turkish aims were achieved with the expulsion of the Russians from Ottoman territory, and the successful elimination of any danger in the foreseeable future of a Russian advance into the Balkans. The Sultan and his armies had triumphed in Europe. What further action was required against Russia? From Turkey itself virtually none. For the Western powers, their objectives attained, here surely was the moment for an honourable peace. For Russia, faced on land by a Europe united as seldom in history, and at sea by the overwhelming naval power of Britain and France, there seemed to be no reasonable alternative.

But the Emperor Napoleon needed war as a means to exalt his new dynasty, while the British people craved it in a mood of fervent patriotic adventure. Their eyes were on Sebastopol, which Tsar Nicholas had transformed over the past twenty-five years into a mighty stronghold, with innumerable arsenals and fortifications on an impregnable scale. Designed for an eventual and overwhelming assault, by the fleet which it harboured, on the Ottoman Empire, it presented meanwhile a defiant challenge to British imperial aims. Thus the British Cabinet, yielding to popular pressure and overriding professional caution, instructed its commander-in-chief, Lord Raglan, "to concert measures for the siege of Sebastopol." This, with a certain reluctance, he did, to be supported, as reluctantly, by the French commander-in-chief, Marshal St. Arnaud. So the allied armies steamed eastward from Varna to occupy, without opposition, the Russian port of Eupatoria to the north of the fortress. The Danube war had been won. The Crimean War now began.

It was a war fought by Britain and France against Russia, in which Turkey, which had provided its occasion and might ultimately profit by its results, was accorded only an insignificant military part. With an army of some sixty-five thousand British and French troops, no more than a single Turkish division was landed. To Lord Lucan, their commander, its men were no more than *bashi-bazouks,* without regulation uniforms, whose fierce fighting qualities, despite their recent record and their proved amenability to allied leadership, he was slow to appreciate. In conventional British military fashion, he brushed the Turks haughtily aside as mere bandits.

Fought in part as a war for war's sake but in the long term as a further act in the classic struggle for power between Russia and the West, the Crimean campaign was the first in history to be fully covered by press correspondents. Thus for a year to come all British eyes were on the dramatic saga of the Siege of Sebastopol, with its preceding battles of Alma, Balaclava, and Inkerman and its eventual assaults on the Redan and Fort Malakhov. All was staged on a Homeric scale, bands playing and colours flying, within the compass of this small compact peninsula, with its landlocked naval harbour guarding the gates to the Tsar's Russian Empire. Patriotism took fire as the populace gloried in its heroics, bowed to its tragedies, raged at its confusions and at the blunders of its discordant Anglo-French command. Hearts glowed with pride as the cannons thundered and the Light Brigade charged into the Valley of Death; trembled with horror at the agonies of man and beast through the cruel, hard, plague-stricken winter; sighed with relief at the merciful apparition of the Lady of the Lamp, as she strove to silence the beating of the wings of the angel of death in the hospital wards of Scutari.

A Turkish force took part in the defense of Balaclava, led by incompetent officers and precipitately fleeing from the enemy. Early in the following year another force was dispatched to Eupatoria, where, under the command of Omer Pasha, it fought with courage in its natural element, the defense of earthwork fortifications. It repulsed a superior Russian force, and thus inflicted a last humiliation on the Tsar Nicholas. He died a fortnight later, to be succeeded by his son Alexander II, who was soon ready for peace. Meanwhile, on the eastern frontiers of Asia Minor, a Turkish force was achieving a noble defense, under British officers, of the fortress of Kars, which only fell to the Russians, through starvation, as a result of negligence by the Turkish authorities in the provision of supplies to relieve its blockade.

It was only at a belated stage in the war that the allies thought to enroll in the Crimea a Turkish force of some twenty thousand men, under the command of British officers. But it was not to fight. For the final capture by the French of Fort Malakhov, in September, 1855, led to the fall of Sebastopol and the end of the Crimean campaign—to the reluctance of the British, who wished to continue the fight, but on the insistence of the French, whose aims had been vindicated to the satisfaction of the Emperor Napoleon III.

This in turn led to the signature, in the spring of 1856, of the Treaty of Paris. The treaty and its accompanying convention allowed for mutual restoration of conquests by Russia in Asia and the allies in Europe. It made no territorial changes, but for the cession by the Tsar to Moldavia of southern Bessarabia and the delta of the Danube, annexed in 1812. Meanwhile both Danubian principalities were removed from their exclusive Russian protectorate and placed under joint protection of the great powers, with the recognition of the Sultan's sovereignty. Their inhabitants would benefit from an independent and national administration, subject to freedom of worship and commerce and the right to organize their own armed forces.

These provisions opened the way to the free navigation of the

Danube, which was entrusted to the authority of an international commission. The Black Sea was similarly neutralized, its waters and ports thrown open to all merchant vessels but closed to naval forces, while naval arsenals were no longer to be maintained on its shores. The Straits of the Dardanelles and the Bosporus were again to be closed to warships through a recapitulation of the treaty of 1841.

By all the Christian powers there was an undertaking, in the treaty, to respect the independence and territorial integrity of the Ottoman Empire, through the machinery of mediation and if necessary of armed intervention. In fact, whether or not the allied victory in the Crimean War justified, in the long term, its enormous cost in human life and financial expenditure, the Treaty of Paris, as signed by the Western powers and Russia, at least calmed for a further two decades the familiar conflicts inherent in the Eastern Question. This was now gradually to acquire a new emphasis. At the same time, within the Ottoman Empire itself, there was a fresh move by the Sultan toward further protection of his Christian subjects, whose disputed status had occasioned the war in the first place.

((34))

THROUGHOUT THIS INTERVAL BETWEEN THE END OF THE CRIMEAN War and the signature of the Treaty of Paris, Lord Stratford had laboured persistently with the Porte on a new Charter of Reform for the Ottoman Empire. Early in 1856 it was proclaimed in an imperial rescript, the Hatti-Humayun. Designed by the Porte to satisfy the negotiating powers in Paris as to the good intentions of the Empire and its worthiness of Western respect as a civilized state, it reaffirmed the principles and extended the scope of the Tanzimat reforms, to complete that Turkish Magna Carta of the nineteenth century.

The Charter emphasized, in terms more specific than before, the free and equal status of all Ottoman subjects, irrespective of religion, race, or language, in relation to such matters as taxation, education, justice, ownership of property, eligibility for public office, elective administration, and "the equal encouragement of good citizenship without prejudice of class or creed." In addition it envisaged concrete measures of reform for the country's financial and monetary systems, positive means of encouragement for commerce and agriculture, the construction of roads and canals. It crowned Lord Stratford's career as a reformer, setting the seal on his labours for the regeneration of the Ottoman Empire—the more so as it had been achieved in the face of widespread Moslem hostility and European indifference.

But his optimism was to be short-lived. The miracle did not materialize. The Charter was indeed incorporated in the articles of the Treaty of Paris. This implied its recognition of "the Sultan's generous intentions towards the Christian population of his Empire." But in the next breath this was nullified by a refusal to provide for its enforcement. For the powers disclaimed all right "to interfere either collectively or individually in the relations of the Sultan with his subjects or in the internal administration of the Empire."

This was generally seen as a betrayal of England by France, bent on peace at any price and the appeasement of Russia. Here, as Stratford realistically saw it, could be the deathblow to reform in the Empire. Left to itself, without foreign pressure, whether from Britain or France or the allied powers in concert, the Porte would "give way to its natural indolence and leave the firman of reform . . . a lifeless paper, valuable only as a record of sound principles."

Hence his observation on the signature of the Treaty of Paris: "I would rather have cut off my right hand than have signed that treaty." The allied powers had been in conflict from the start of the negotiations, as in the last stage of the war; the rise in the prestige of the French and their renewed influence on the Porte, as Stratford saw it, might well work against those high aspirations to which he had dedicated his Turkish career.

Nonetheless, for all his discouragement, it could justly be claimed for Stratford that he had brought East and West closer together in their respective ways of life than could have been imagined in the earlier decades of the nineteenth century. Lord Stratford's mission was soon to end. Before it did so he performed a ceremony with historic—if also ironic—implications. In the name of his sovereign, Queen Victoria, he solemnly invested Sultan Abdul Mejid with the Order of a Knight of the Garter. With the blue riband of St. George around his neck he was officially enjoined, as a sovereign of Islam, to emulate the career of a Martyr and Soldier of Christ. The Great Elchi left Turkey for the last time in October, 1858, and was succeeded as ambassador by Sir Henry Bulwer, in whose very different outlook Lord Stratford "believed he could trace the antithesis of all he had striven for, the abandonment of all he had won."

As events turned out, it was the problem of debt, not of internal reform, which henceforward preoccupied the rulers of the Ottoman Empire and conditioned its relations with the West. Turkey, whose reformers had never excelled as financiers, was slowly but surely relapsing into a state of insolvency. Continuously there was an excess of imports over exports and a failure to develop productive internal resources. The Imperial Treasury was virtually empty, the pay of the armed forces was in arrears, the cost of living rose, and an impoverished population grew increasingly hostile both to reformers and to foreigners. To help meet the cost of the Crimean War, the Porte had borrowed substantial sums from its British and French allies. Now, through the two decades following the war and in default of good management of the national economy, the insidious habit of borrowing from Europe took root to the extent of hundreds of millions of pounds. It sprouted into an escalating national debt, based on the contraction of unpaid loans and the flotation of unredeemed bonds, with high commissions to financiers and bribes to pashas who furthered the process.

In 1861 Sultan Abdul Mejid died, at the age of thirty-eight. A mild, humane ruler, with Western sympathies and good liberal intentions, he had lacked the necessary determination and energy to carry them out. Inactive by nature, inclining to self-indulgence, irresponsible in his expenditure, he had flagged as a reformer, satisfying neither his

Moslem nor his Christian subjects, failing to maintain internal unity, leaving most of the progressive measures of his father's Tanzimat charter unfulfilled.

He was succeeded by his brother Abdul Aziz, who, though on good enough terms with him personally, had meanwhile been intriguing politically with the forces of reaction. Abdul Aziz was in aspect a handsome, robust Sultan, with a muscular physique but an ill-educated mind, capricious ways, and an explosive temper. At the start of his reign he proclaimed reformist intentions, following the example of his two predecessors. He undertook to control the expenditure of the palace and husband the resources of the state. But he was soon to bely such undertakings. In the palace, having pensioned off his late brother's innumerable concubines, he came to surpass him in extravagance, accumulating a harem of his own so large as to involve the employment of three thousand eunuchs. In his policy he impeded his ministers in all plans for reform, thus gratifying the reactionaries, while the foreign powers were at first only too zealous, out of respect for the Treaty of Paris, in refraining from individual pressure on the Porte. They intervened collectively in 1867, when the French government, with the support of Britain and Austria, presented a note which urged a more active reform policy. Strongly opposed by the Sultan, it was welcomed by his two progressive ministers, Ali and Fuad Pasha, who were nonetheless able over the next three years to reorganize the High Council and introduce innovations in the fields of justice and education.

But a wholly different movement of reform was now dawning. It stemmed not from the rulers but from the ruled, and its emphasis was not merely on social but on constitutional change. Mahmud the Reformer, in the early nineteenth century, had been a paternalist Sultan, protecting and conferring benefits on his people in a spirit of benevolent despotism. From the start he had grasped the paradox that he could only succeed in his self-imposed liberal task through the patient elimination of all those checks on the Sultan's absolute authority which had in recent centuries eroded it. He had thus assumed to himself powers even more autocratic than those of his earlier Ottoman forebears. The responsible use of these powers by a strong-willed Sultan, determined to enforce his enlightened convictions, led at least to an initial stage of progress. Mahmud II had started to resolve, in positive terms, some of the inherent incompatibilities between a Westernized society and the built-in social traditions of Islam.

But the continuation of his work depended on an equally strong-willed successor, and this, for all his progressive aspirations, Abdul Mejid was not. His father, in eliminating all alternative sources of power to that of the sovereign, had left behind him a potential vacuum such as none but himself or another sovereign of his caliber could fill.

As the reforms of the Tanzimat took shape, the hollowness of its functional structure had been all too clearly exposed. For its effective application to the rights and interests of the Sultan's subjects, it could depend on no new intermediate institutions of responsible government, such as the ulema and the various sources of provincial authority had furnished. For all its machinery of consultation and its high-flown guarantees, it depended on the sole authority of the Sultan's edicts, influenced as they often were by irresponsible ministers.

In fact, if not in spirit, Abdul Mejid exercised, if in a less deliberate sense, the autocratic rule which his father, Mahmud, had bequeathed to him. After this intervening period the growing powers of an unchecked autocracy now rose to their peak with the reign of Sultan Abdul Aziz. Reactionary in his outlook and unrestrained by any liberal principles, he ruled as an absolute despot, through a strong centralized government with a close-knit bureaucracy amenable to his headstrong will. Thus in the second half of the nineteenth century the Ottoman regime reverted from a responsible to an irresponsible autocracy.

This engendered, by a sharp process of reaction, an altogether new phase of reform, more fundamentally conceived and far-reaching in scope than the old, which was based on the true constitutional principles of democracy. Mahmud II, followed by Abdul Mejid, had sought enlightenment and progress within the existing system, through Westernization in terms of science, law, education, and the machinery of government. But now, among the maturing elite which he had introduced into the administration, there was a young middle-class intelligentsia, primed with a knowledge of foreign languages and ideas and experience of life in the West, which had begun to see the reform problem ideologically, in terms of a political solution. For the West before their eyes was translating the principles of liberal democracy into the practice of constitutional and parliamentary government. As the reign of Abdul Aziz continued, it became their concern no longer to promote such limited Westernized reforms as those of the Tanzimat, but to go further and find fundamental means, in this Western context, of limiting the autocratic powers of the state.

Here, in pursuit of that ideal of freedom through nationalism to which European peoples had been actively aspiring since the revolutionary year of 1848, was an opposition group, loosely composed of young Turks, mostly with a secular education, who were oriented in a bold new direction. Their slogan was *Hürriyet,* meaning "Liberty," whereas that of the Tanzimat had been *Adalet,* meaning "Justice," and they advanced beyond the former limits of reform along a path which could lead to revolution. Their aim was to establish constitutional government for Turkey. While advocating the Western liberal conception of this, they sought still to synthesize it with all that was best in the ideas and traditions of Islam.

With their individualistic ideas, they were continually divided, ideologically and personally, as to the form in which their ends could be realized. But in 1865 a small representative group of them formed, at a historic picnic in the forest of Belgrade, up the Bosporus, a "Patriotic Alliance," which became in effect the first political party in Turkish history. They became known as the Young Ottomans, and were soon claiming some 250 adherents. A secret society, based in its organization on that of the Carbonari in Italy and another in Poland, whose members worked through a number of separate clandestine cells, had formed what in effect was a revolutionary committee. The new reformers were not politicians, imposing change from above, but intellectuals, demanding change from below. They worked through the medium of literature and above all the growing media of journalism. For a result of the Crimean War had been a widespread increase in the extent and influence of the Turkish press.

Two of the Young Ottomans had been protégés of Reshid Pasha, who died in 1858. One was Ibrahim Shinasi, who had been a student in Paris during the revolution of 1848, who edited an influential newspaper in Istanbul, and who was also a poet and dramatist. Another was Ziya Pasha, employed in the imperial household, then in other minor posts, who in 1867 fled into voluntary exile successively in Paris, London, and Geneva, to become an outspoken advocate of constitutional government and of the creation by the Sultan of an Ottoman national assembly, with gradually evolving parliamentary powers. Younger and more forceful in his radical views was Namik Kemal. Born of a line of senior Ottoman officials, he worked as a political journalist and essayist, emerging as the apostle of two allied conceptions, Freedom and Fatherland. He put forward a view of liberty and self-government under the law, with especial respect for the political rights of the citizens. His advanced revolutionary message was that of the sovereignty of the people, the idea that the powers of government should derive from the governed. This involved the principle of consultation, "whereby the legislative power is taken away from the Government."

As a sincere Moslem, Namik Kemal was at pains to reconcile his program with the principles of Islam, seeking precedents in an Islamic past, contriving to justify from a verse in the Koran the principle of consultative and representative government, and seeking to show that a form of this had been practiced in the Ottoman Empire before the days of the reform movement. Though this was hard to substantiate in terms of Moslem law and theology, it had the advantage of appealing to a new educated generation who in their attachment to Western values were no longer wholly satisfied with traditional Islam. For this proposed form of representative government, for which Islam provided no parallel, Namik Kemal drew on the liberal parliamentary constitution of England, in preference to that of France which, under Napoleon III, he considered too authoritarian. London on the other hand, with its "indomitable power of public opinion against authority," he saw as the "model of the world" in political principles.

His direct experience both of London and Paris was derived from a period of exile. His travels were furthered by a powerful ally of the Young Ottomans, the wealthy and ambitious Egyptian prince Mustafa Fazil. He had been heir to the ruling dynasty of Egypt until Ismail Pasha, his elder brother by forty days, achieved from the Sultan the title of Khedive, with a change in the Egyptian law of succession in favour of his own son. Fazil's ambition was to rule, if not as Khedive of Egypt, then as prime minister of a constitutional Turkish Empire. From Paris he sent an open letter in French to the Sultan criticizing in detail the condition of his empire and concluding with the demand for a constitution. This document was translated into Turkish by Namik Kemal with his colleagues, and distributed through the newspaper of which he had now become editor.

To this the government's reaction was sharp. Here was an infringement of their recently enacted press law, which laid down strict regulations for the conduct of the newspapers, and provided for a press commission to ensure their enforcement in the police courts. Kemal and Ziya Pasha, being government officials, were thus posted to the provinces. But instead, on the invitation of Prince Fazil, they escaped in secret to Paris, where he put them in touch with French political and official circles, allowing them to use his house as a Young Ottoman headquarters. Here, with another opposition newspaper editor, Ali Suavi, who had escaped from exile in Anatolia, they published, with type procured from Istanbul, a newspaper in Turkish named *Hürriyet,* meaning "Freedom."

In the summer of 1867 Sultan Abdul Aziz paid a state visit first to Paris, then to London—the first Ottoman sovereign to travel beyond the boundaries of his empire except at the head of an army. At the polite request of the French government, prompted by the Turkish ambassador, Namik Kemal and his group left for London, where Prince Fazil financed their activities over the next few years. When the Sultan arrived there, they mingled with the crowd at an official firework display at the Crystal Palace, where their red fezzes attracted his attention. Enquiring as to their identity, he received the laconic reply from his foreign minister: "They're your Majesty's opposition."

After a visit to Vienna, Namik Kemal, who had meanwhile been studying law and economics and translating French works into Turkish, returned to Turkey at the end of 1870. Here he wrote a patriotic drama called *Vatan,* meaning "Fatherland," which was performed in Istanbul before a rapturous audience, and as enthusiastically praised in the columns of an influential newspaper, *Ibret,* of which Kemal became the editor. Dealing with the heroic defense of Silistria against the Russians in the Crimean War, it was based on the theme of loyalty, owed not to the Sultan or to the Islamic community, but to the less familiar conception of the "nation." The press comments on this were, in official eyes, tantamount to sedition. After a defiant last editorial the newspaper was suppressed, while Namik Kemal was deported under close arrest to Cyprus. Here he was to languish in captivity for the next three years.

Meanwhile, in 1871 there died Ali Pasha, the last of the enlightened statesmen of the Tanzimat age, whose partner, Fuad Pasha, had died two years before him. Only Ali, among all his vezirs, had been able to exert some controlling influence on Sultan Abdul Aziz, who on his death remarked that he was "at last a free man." He was indeed free to assert his unfettered will against that of the Porte, to pursue his course toward Islamic reaction, anti-European chauvinism, and personal absolutism—with its perquisites of unbridled financial expenditure. Free he was too from the restraining hand of French liberal influence, thanks to the defeat of Napoleon III in the Franco-Prussian War and the resulting decline of French prestige. The reforms of the Tanzimat and of the later Charter now indeed seemed to be a dead letter, thus fulfilling the gloomy predictions of Lord Stratford de Redcliffe. From 1871 onward the Ottoman Empire was well set on a downward course heading for the depths of reaction and the brink of financial catastrophe.

In the consequent political vacuum the center of power shifted back from the Porte to the palace itself, as the Sultan boasted of his intention to rule like the Russian Tsar, with each of his ministers responsible not to a Grand Vezir but to the Sultan alone. As Grand Vezir he appointed for a start the ambitious and unprincipled Mahmud Nedim, remarking of him that he was the first of his ministers to do exactly what he, the Sultan, wanted. Nedim soon furthered administrative chaos, exiling former ministers and keeping officials "in ceaseless rotation," as he summarily dismissed them or shifted them around, determined that none should rival his own influence or offset the absolute personal rule of his master, the Sultan.

After removing Nedim from his post in 1872, Abdul Aziz appointed a succession of six Grand Vezirs over a period of three years, treating them as mere figureheads by insisting on their submission to his will, and refusing to consult them on the appointment of other ministers. The first and most notable of these was Midhat Pasha, a stout pillar of constitutional reform, who had precipitated Nedim's removal. He had risen in the service of the Porte to become an outstanding provincial administrator, giving to the provinces that he governed, under the reformed system of administration, a degree of security and prosperity which they had not enjoyed for a long time past. But Midhat soon proved too forceful and independent for the Sultan, and against manifold intrigues survived in office for a bare three months. Thus once more Nedim was recalled as Grand Vezir.

The Sultan's whims were now so capricious and singular as to suggest megalomania, and to cast doubts on his mental and emotional balance. He grew increasingly more domineering, insisting that ministers prostrate themselves before him and kiss the feet of his son; demanding that any official called Aziz, like himself, should sign another name on official documents; playing at soldiers with real ones, whom he commanded to fight mock battles; eating huge quantities of eggs; growing so obsessed with his favourite fighting cocks as to bestow orders and decorations on those that won and to exile those that lost.

On returning from his tour of the capitals of Europe, Abdul Aziz sought to emulate its luxuries, which had greatly impressed him, and indeed to surpass them on an oriental, regal scale. Returning hospitality to foreign royal guests, he staged lavish entertainments in the European-style Dolma Bahche palace, which was soon costing him some two million pounds per year to run. More constructively, impressed during his tour by the wonders of European technology, he now devoted huge sums to the building of ironclad warships and the laying down of railroads across his empire. As the state financial crisis mounted, he defiantly declared that he would build the Baghdad railway at his own personal expense.

His own Civil List came indeed to account for some 15 percent of the Imperial Treasury's total expenditure. Borrowing money from the Western bankers remained all too easy. European investors were encouraged by optimistic accounts of Turkey's great natural resources, turning a blind eye to the facts of her incapacity to develop them and to her ineptitude in the management of all financial affairs. The interest yield from the Ottoman treasury was twice as high as on most English investments. Nor did it concern the investor unduly that the interest, as it accrued, was paid by the Turks not out of increasing state revenues but out of further foreign loans and bond issues—that, as Richard Cobden expressed it, Turkey had "never paid any interest at all, because she has borrowed all the money to pay the interest." By this snowballing process the Ottoman debt rose within twenty years from four million to two hundred million pounds, unbalanced by any commensurate increase in state revenues, and the charges on it came to absorb more than 50 percent of the government's annual resources. Economic catastrophe began to loom large.

From 1873 onward the government was faced with a period of drought and famine in Anatolia, leading to widespread misery and discontent. It culminated in a winter so savage that wolves were roving the suburbs of Istanbul and devouring passers-by, sheep and oxen were perishing on a disastrous scale, men were starving in the villages and dying in their streets without burial. Agricultural shortages became such as to preclude the collection of necessary taxes. This reached the point at which the Imperial Treasury was left without adequate funds for the business of government.

The result was a major financial collapse. In October, 1875, the Ottoman government announced in the newspapers that, owing to a large budget deficit, the Porte's creditors would henceforward receive in cash only half of the interest due to them. The remaining half would be replaced over the next five years by bonds carrying 5 percent interest. Here was a default which shattered the credit and the standing of the Ottoman government abroad. At home it inflamed resentment against the Sultan and his government by Turks of the official classes, besides Armenians and Greeks, who had invested in the government bonds. Following the announcement it was said ironically that passengers on a Bosporus ferry had offered cash for half the price of their tickets and five-year bonds for the remainder.

The government's problems of financial insolvency were now aggravated by those of internal revolt. Provoked by a bad harvest and the subsequent extortions of the imperial tax farmers, an insurrection against the local authorities erupted in Herzegovina. It spread to Bosnia, where civil war soon raged between Crescent and Cross. Both Montenegro and Serbia—though as a virtually independent state the latter no longer had serious grounds for complaint against the Porte—intervened with armed bands, and in the summer of 1876 the fire of revolt spread at the instigation of the rest to Bulgaria. Here in fact was the start of a Balkan revolutionary movement which was to lead, through the next generation, to one war after another and eventually to transform the whole face of the Balkan peninsula.

In Bulgaria a rebel leader, with visions of himself as a Slav Napoleon, had pledged his followers to terrorist methods. They turned savagely on the Moslem Turks, whom they started to massacre. But within ten days their revolt was suppressed, with a savagery more terrible, by Turkish irregular forces let loose in revenge. They committed atrocities stigmatized by the British commissioner from Istanbul as "perhaps the most heinous crime of the present century." Burning innumerable villages to the ground, they spared neither age nor sex in an outbreak of indiscriminate massacre, killing in a single month no fewer than twelve thousand Christians. Their orgy of slaughter and arson and rape culminated in the mountain village of Batak. Here a thousand Christians found refuge in a church, to which the irregular troops set fire with rags soaked in petrol, burning all to death but a single old woman. In all, so it was reported, five thousand out of the seven thousand villagers of Batak perished at their hands.

The story was first told to the world, like that of the battles of the Crimean War, by the correspondent of an English newspaper, the *Daily News.* He described to his readers a churchyard which "for three feet deep was festering with dead bodies partly covered—hands, legs, arms and heads projected in ghastly confusion, while the floor of the church itself was still strewn with uncovered, putrefying corpses." Such infamies of the Middle Ages had been all too familiar through centuries of Turkish "holy" warfare. As perpetrated now in the more civilized nineteenth century by a primitive and fanatical irregular soldiery, generally Tatars, and for the first time revealed to the world by a ubiquitous press, they caused universal horror and indignation. The Liberal Mr. Gladstone took up the cause in a best-selling pamphlet on "Bulgarian Horrors," in which he demanded: "Let the Turks now carry away their abuses in the only possible manner, namely by carrying away themselves . . . bag and baggage . . . from the province they have desolated and profaned."

Coinciding as they did with the large-scale default by the Ottoman treasury on its financial commitments, these Bulgarian atrocities gave to the Turks a terrible new image, inflaming a spirit of Turcophobia throughout Britain. Though no great surprise to the British ambassador in Istanbul, Sir Henry Elliot, who explained, "We have been upholding what we know to have been a semi-civilized nation," they had a profound and enduring impact on the British public. They abruptly reversed that friendly attitude to the Turks which had prompted popular support for the Crimean War. They provoked the Tory foreign minister, Lord Derby, to assert that now "even if Russia were to declare war against the Porte Her Majesty's Government would find it practicably impossible to interfere." Indeed, following the publication of Gladstone's pamphlet, the Tsar was informed by General Ignatiev, the Russian ambassador at the Porte: "The Bulgarian massacres have brought Russia what she never had before—the support of British public opinion."

Since 1820 Russia had been assiduous in her policy of encouraging revolt among the Christian Slavs of the Balkan provinces. Concurrently she had pursued Russian interests with zeal at the Porte itself. General Ignatiev now found a ready enough accomplice in the Grand Vezir, Mahmud Nedim, who shared his hostility to any policy of reform as being a means of strengthening Western influence. When the reforming Midhat Pasha came briefly to power Ignatiev had worked craftily against him. After Midhat's dismissal—to which his intrigues doubtless contributed—Ignatiev urged upon Abdul Aziz that form of government in which, as in Russia, the sovereign was absolute master.

Now, with Nedim back in office, Ignatiev exulted in his power as "master of the situation in Constantinople, where [as a Russian colleague reported] a Grand Vezir devoted to Russia and a Sultan hostile to the West were more disposed to follow his suggestions than to listen to the advice of our adversaries." Welcoming the discomfiture of the British and French bondholders, he exulted again over the Turkish default on the loan, which he was generally suspected of instigating. But here he overplayed his hand. For it was Mahmud Nedim who now fell—and soon afterward Sultan Abdul Aziz himself.

In the early summer of 1876 some six thousand *softas,* or theological students, abandoned their studies in the *medresses* of the three principal mosques of Istanbul to assemble in a mass demonstration before the Sublime Porte. They demanded the dismissal of the Grand Vezir, Mahmud Nedim, and of the Chief Mufti. It was said that some of them were measuring the railings before the building, to test whether they were high enough on which to hang the Grand Vezir. Though riots by theological students had been, since the sixteenth century, a traditional practice in the social and political history of Turkey, these riots differed from those of the past in that they were deliberately prepaid and arranged in advance for the purpose of achieving a change in the ministry. They thus introduced into Turkey a tradition, well established in parts of Europe, which was here to set an ominous precedent for the future. They were assumed to be organized and financed by Midhat Pasha, who now led the constitutional movement of the Young Ottomans.

The Sultan gave way to the students, dismissing the Chief Mufti and Mahmud Nedim, whom he replaced with Rushdi Pasha, while Midhat returned to the government as president of the Council of State. But this was no more than a beginning. From now onward, as the British ambassador reported, "the word 'constitution' was in every mouth." What Midhat meant by it was the establishment, in terms of the principles of liberty, equality, and ministerial responsibility, of a truly national consultative assembly, representative without distinction of all classes, all races and creeds within the Empire. To this the Sultan and his ministers should henceforward be responsible. His present absolute powers would thus be limited by subjection to the counsel and will of the nation, on the model of the British system of government.

To justify this, stress was specifically laid on the more democratic prescriptions of the Koran. By an interpretation of these, the Sultan's present exercise of absolute authority usurped the rights of his people and thus infringed the Sacred Law. For under its principles their obedience was not due to a sovereign who neglected the interests of the state. Midhat's proposals reflected those made by Prince Mustafa Fazil—lately dead—in his letter to the Sultan of 1867, begging him to make such changes. Now, however, it was implied that the changes were no longer expected from above but threatened from below. The

The Dolma Bahche Palace, built by Mahmud II, was begun soon after the end in 1829 of the Greek War for Independence and was probably completed (in the form in which it appears in this engraving by Allom) before 1838. The Dolma Bahche became the full-time residence of the Sultan when Abdul Majid I (1839–61) in 1853 abandoned the Topkapi Palace, where the sultans had lived for nearly four centuries.

Allom and Walsh, *Constantinople,* Vol. 2, op. p. 2.

plan was put forward in a manifesto signed by "the Moslem Patriots," and distributed abroad to the statesmen of Europe, thus indicating Ottoman good intentions. But at this stage it was still kept secret at home. For it discussed the possible necessity of deposing the Sultan, whom it described as a "miserable madman."

This was in fact his ministers' immediate intention. First they procured a ruling from the new Grand Mufti, authorizing the Sultan's deposition. Then, before dawn on May 30, 1876, the Dolma Bahche palace was surrounded by two battalions on the landward side and by naval vessels on the side of the Bosporus, while another vessel was stationed opposite the Russian summer embassy, farther upstream, to preclude any intervention by Ignatiev. Then Midhat and his fellow ministers met at the War Ministry, where the Chief Mufti read the *fetva* of the Sultan's deposition on the grounds of "mental derangement, ignorance of political affairs, diversion of public revenues to private expenditure, and conduct generally injurious to state and community." The ministers took the oath of loyalty to his nephew and heir, Murad V, who had earlier been summoned from his private apartments.

At dawn a salvo of 101 guns from the naval vessels proclaimed a change of Sultans. Abdul Aziz offered no resistance, writing a letter of abdication and accepting his confinement in the old Seraglio across the Bosporus. This bloodless *coup d'état* was acclaimed with enthusiasm by the people of Istanbul, and welcomed by one of the ministers as another "auspicious event," like the destruction of the Janissaries. Within half a century there had emerged, in the student body, a comparable source of power in the state, but now used against tyranny and not as its instrument.

Sultan Murad's accession was welcome to the liberal elements, and palace appointments were now conferred on several Young Ottomans, notably Namik Kemal, who returned from Cyprus to become the new Sultan's private secretary. As an early adherent of their cause, Murad seemed to represent a real hope for constitutional reform in the Empire. But unhappily this was not to materialize. Murad V as a young man had shown notable intelligence. Well-educated and keenly alive to Western as to Eastern culture, he had made a favourable impression among foreigners when he accompanied Abdul Aziz to Europe. But the Sultan regarded him with suspicion when after his return he began to make contacts in secret with liberals at home and in exile. Abdul Aziz had thus condemned his nephew under strict vigilance to a life of virtual seclusion. This imposed strains on his highly strung nature, to which Murad unhappily responded with indulgence in alcohol.

He grew subject to mental disorders and had reacted with fear and trembling to his abrupt nocturnal summons to accede to the throne. A graver disturbance to his system followed a few days later when Abdul Aziz, himself in an unstable mental condition, was found dead, having committed suicide by slashing his wrists and thus severing an artery. This he did with a small pair of scissors obtained on the pretext of trimming his beard. The shock of this was too great for the new Sultan's sanity. It was worsened by the assassination, at a cabinet meeting, of his ministers of War and Foreign Affairs by an enraged Circassian army officer, avenging what he chose to interpret as their murder of Abdul Aziz.

Murad, who had still to be girded as Sultan with the sword of Osman, became incapable of appearing in public or of transacting official business. He was examined by doctors, both Turkish and foreign, whose diagnosis was in effect a severe nervous breakdown, curable only with time. In view of the urgency of the political crisis, both at home and abroad, his ministers felt bound to consider, with some reluctance, a second deposition in favour of a more active and effective sovereign. The next in line was Murad's younger brother, Abdul Hamid, still an unknown quantity, who had likewise been kept in virtual seclusion.

Midhat was delegated by his fellow ministers to call upon Abdul Hamid and to enquire whether he would consent to act as regent, pending Murad's recovery—a provision for which there was in fact no Ottoman precedent. Abdul Hamid firmly refused. He coveted the throne, but on unconditional terms, insisting first upon a medical certificate that Murad was incapable of ruling. To achieve this ambition he was ready to give certain undertakings. Midhat revisited him with a draft of the proposed new constitution, formulated earlier that year under his auspices by a committee of statesmen and members of the ulema on the lines of the nineteenth-century constitutions of Belgium and Prussia. Abdul Hamid pledged himself to abide by three conditions: he would promulgate the constitution; he would govern only through responsible advisers; he would reappoint his brother's palace secretaries.

Namik Kemal, who was one of them, pleaded with tears in his eyes for the postponement of Murad's deposition. But his pleas were in vain. A *fetva* was obtained from the Chief Mufti, deposing him, after a reign of three months, on the grounds of mental incapacity. The oath of loyalty was sworn and Abdul Hamid II proclaimed Sultan in place of him. Murad was transferred to a palace up the Bosporus where he was to survive in captivity into the first decade of the twentieth century.

A new constitution for the Ottoman Empire was finally promulgated in December, 1876, by the new Sultan, who had previously appointed Midhat Pasha as his Grand Vezir. The final document did not wholly accord with Midhat's aspirations. The Sultan had qualified the original draft in various ways, emphasizing the need for strict observance of the holy law, safeguarding his own privileges, evading certain provisions, reducing to vague generalized terms specific definitions by Midhat, finally failing to commit himself too positively to the speedy introduction of constitutional government. These imperfections portended future problems.

Nonetheless the acceptance and promulgation by the Sultan of a constitution seemed a fitting climax to a century preoccupied with the cause of reform. Here at least was an instrument for future political development, founded on the basic principle that the people of the Ottoman Empire had a right to be consulted and heard. In vibrant tones Midhat Pasha, offering thanks to the Sultan, proclaimed the inauguration of "a new era of enduring prosperity." Next day, breaking with all precedent, he called upon the Greek and Armenian patriarchs—who were themselves normally expected to call upon the Grand Vezir—with the assurance that under this constitutional regime men of all creeds would be regarded as equals. The Greek Patriarch declared in reply: "We consider you the resuscitator of the Ottoman Empire." Meanwhile, the thunder of cannon fire had proclaimed to the populace of Istanbul, both Moslem and Christian, the new liberties supposedly in store for them.

((35))

THIS RESOUNDING SALUTE TO THE CONSTITUTION WAS SHREWDLY timed by the new Sultan to disarm the European delegates at a conference of the six powers in Istanbul. For its first plenary session coincided with his decree of promulgation. The conference had arisen, on British initiative, from the situation in the Balkans and the need to concert with Russia a proposal to the Sultan for the better protection, through specified administrative changes, of his Christian subjects in Europe.

In 1876 the Balkan revolt had erupted into an open declaration of war against the Porte by Serbia and Montenegro, instigated and abetted by the Russians. Within three months the Turks had defeated the Serbs, and were only checked from a victorious march on Belgrade by the direct intervention of Russia, who insisted on an armistice. The Russian and Austrian emperors, supported by Germany, then produced the Berlin Memorandum, designed to enforce reforms on the Porte, and curtly requested British cooperation.

This was as curtly rejected by Britain, who in common with France and Italy had not previously been consulted by the three military powers, and who saw the proposals—in the words of Disraeli, then Prime Minister—as "asking us to sanction them in putting a knife to the throat of Turkey." It implied ultimately a joint military occupation of Ottoman territory, incompatible with the independence and integrity of the country, to which Britain was committed. To reassure the Porte of British support, a squadron of the Mediterranean fleet was ordered to the mouth of the Dardanelles. Then, seeking still to avert the war for which Russia was clearly preparing, Britain convened instead the "Constantinople Conference."

The announcement of the constitution took the wind out of the sails of its delegates. For it pretended that the Porte, with its own complete plan for constitutional reform, could dispense with the intervention and aid of the powers. Discounting its sincerity, in the light of previous experience, they shrugged this off as an all-too-familiar political subterfuge, a display of window dressing, as they had falsely assumed the two previous decrees of the Tanzimat to be, designed merely to secure for Turkey, in a crisis, the goodwill and support of the West against the approaching threat from Russia. But in the face of it they could now do little or nothing to achieve their own ends.

Thus in January, 1877, after an attempt at negotiation, the Conference came to an abortive close, while shortly afterward the Porte and Serbia signed a separate peace on the basis of the *status quo*. Lord Salisbury, the British delegate, left Istanbul, regarding war as certain.

In fact, his task in seeking to avert it had not been made easier, since the Bulgarian massacres, by differences of outlook in the ranks of British ministers, and by the actions of Gladstone, who had intensified his campaign against the Turkish government, following up his pamphlet with forcible speeches at meetings in all parts of the country. At these he denounced the Turks for bad government and cruelty to their Christian subjects, promoting unanimous resolutions that they be deprived of all executive power in Bulgaria, and inflaming public opinion against "the unspeakable Turk" on a widespread scale. Lord Stratford de Redcliffe himself, voicing sympathy with Gladstone, favoured the extension of British protective influence beyond Bulgaria to cover oppressed Ottoman subjects in all parts of the Balkans.

The veteran Liberal statesman had initiated a movement transcending the bounds of party politics to divide the Cabinet itself. On behalf of the government Lord Derby, the foreign secretary, though he strongly deprecated the Gladstonian conception of a crusade to turn the Turks out of Europe, informed the Sultan that these crimes had aroused the righteous indignation of the British people, and demanded punishment of the offenders and relief for the sufferers. This attitude was greatly to the satisfaction of Russia, contemplating war against Turkey and now discounting the chances of British intervention. Lord Derby provided further such encouragement in warning the Russian government that Britain, in the event of war, would not tolerate any threat to Istanbul and the Bosporus, or to Egypt and the Suez Canal. This to the Tsar was a clear indication that Britain would not interfere with Russian actions against the Porte elsewhere, and the British ambassador was assured of his pacific intentions. There was indeed a majority in the British Cabinet which opposed war against Russia on Turkey's behalf.

The Prime Minister, on the other hand, soon to be elevated to the Upper House as Lord Beaconsfield, professed a more militant attitude toward Russia, whose further expansion he dreaded and whose professions he consistently mistrusted. As a farsighted imperialist, Disraeli was still actively awake to the paramount need for maintaining the integrity and independence of the Ottoman Empire, as originally voiced by Palmerston and now guaranteed by the Treaty of Paris. This traditional approach to the Eastern Question had become all the more vital to the integrity of the British Empire since the opening of the Suez Canal, and the consequent need to guard imperial communications against any attack from the flank and any threats of Russian expansion in general.

To the Bulgarian atrocities he had reacted at first with some skepticism, rightly suspecting that the first unconfirmed reports of them, in an opposition newspaper, were exaggerated. He treated them as "coffee-house babble" and in any case a side issue in the wider perspective of the Eastern Question as a whole. Horrors there had been beyond question—though the consular investigations had shown the number of deaths to have been half the figure initially reported. But was this sufficient reason for the British Empire to denounce its treaties and change its traditional policy? What still mattered above all else to British interests was the protection of Turkey in any circumstances against invasion by Russia, as in the case of the Crimean War.

In a party political speech at Aylesbury, in his former constituency, he condemned Gladstone's agitation as "unpatriotic," at once injurious to the permanent interests of England and fatal to the peace of Europe. To Lady Bradford he wrote that Gladstone "would avenge Bulgarian atrocities by the butchery of the world." Finally, on Lord Mayor's Day at the Guildhall, he delivered a strong oration in favour of Turkish independence and against "those terrible appeals to war" which were in fact emanating from Russia.

This robust speech by Lord Beaconsfield, rather than the more qualified statements of Lords Derby and Salisbury, was interpreted by Sultan Abdul Hamid as Britain's official policy, thus convincing him of British support in any war against Russia and clinching his decision to reject any settlements proposed by the Conference. Tsar Alexander II, meanwhile, left no doubt as to his hostile intentions, through a public pronouncement in Moscow which rang throughout Europe. If, he declared, Russia could not secure adequate guarantees from the Porte, then he was firmly resolved to take independent action, sure in the conviction that the Russians would respond to his summons.

The Tsar now played for tactical advantage and time in a last attempt at a compromise settlement between the powers. But his proposals were rejected by the Porte as inconsistent with the Treaty of Paris. Russia then declared war on the Ottoman Empire. Meanwhile, she had reached an agreement, confirmed in a secret treaty, with Austria. This defined their respective spheres of Balkan influence and conceded, in return for her neutrality, the conditional right of Austria to occupy Bosnia and Herzegovina, thus securing her own flanks against attack from the west in the Russian invasion which was now to materialize.

Sultan Abdul Hamid was soon undeceived in his expectations of

British support. Lord Beaconsfield, presiding over a divided Cabinet, had to steer a middle course between the pressure of Gladstone and his Liberal crusaders to join Russia against Turkey and that of Queen Victoria, threatening to lay down her crown rather than "remain the Sovereign of a country that is letting itself down to kiss the feet of the great barbarians, the retarders of all liberty and civilization that exists." The British government, he concluded, should express disapproval of the Russian action, but could not intervene, as in the Crimean War, owing to the alienation of British popular sympathy from the Turks. The policy of his Cabinet was to be one of watchful neutrality. Sultan Abdul Hamid thus found himself obliged to fight a war against Russia alone, without allies.

In the last week of April, 1877, two Russian armies invaded his empire, one in Europe, across the Pruth, and the other in Asia, from the Caucasus, advancing on Kars, Ardahan, and Erzurum. Since the Turks still held command of the Black Sea—reinforced by the ironclads of Sultan Abdul Aziz—a land invasion of Europe was necessary. To this the key was Rumania—the two principalities of Wallachia and Moldavia, now united into one as a self-governing tributary state. Tsar Alexander's assembly approved the entry of Russian troops into Rumania. The Turks retaliated with the bombardment of a Rumanian Danube fortress. Rumania (as Serbia had done earlier) declared war against Turkey and proclaimed herself an independent state. Her territory and armed forces were a source of effective support to the Russians in their invasion of Bulgaria which followed.

On entering Bulgaria in person at the head of his army, the Tsar Alexander was rapturously received as a liberator. As the Russian troops advanced into the interior, the power of the Turk would be replaced by a new civil administration, in which native Bulgarians would be summoned to participate. "Obey the Russian authorities," the Tsar finally enjoined.

From their headquarters at Tirnovo the adventurous Russian general led a flying detachment across the Balkan range into the Thracian plain beyond, thence turned back toward the main Shipka Pass through the mountains, where he defeated a defensive Turkish force. His troops, joined by the Bulgarian Christians, then carried out raids against the Turks in the Maritza Valley, constituting a threat to Adrianople and causing some alarm in Istanbul itself.

But the tide turned, as not too infrequently in latter-day Turkish warfare, with the belated appointment by the Sultan of two competent generals. Mehmed Ali, the Prussian renegade who had been governor of Crete, became Ottoman commander in Europe, where he defeated the Russian force with its Bulgarian allies, driving it back with severe loss to the Balkan range. To the north of it the main Russian armies met with a formidable barrier to their further progress through the dispatch of a Turkish force to the Danube front under Osman Pasha, a redoubtable veteran of the Crimea.

He dug in his forces before and around Plevna, a town among vineyards in a deep rocky valley some twenty miles to the south of Nicopolis. Here, in a place hitherto defended only by the surrounding ramparts of nature, he swiftly created, with the aid of skilled engineers, a strong military fortress, raising earthworks with redoubts, digging trenches and quarrying out gun emplacements. Thus from Plevna his army soon dominated the main strategic routes into the heart of Bulgaria.

From their first assault in July, the Russians, underrating their enemy and making light, with their immensely superior forces, of the problems of siege, were surprised by the ferocious tenacity of the well-led Turkish defenders, and especially by their modern breech-loading rifles, acquired by Sultan Abdul Aziz from America, which outgunned their own slower muzzle-loading muskets. Thus by the end of the first day of the siege of Plevna the Russians were routed.

Osman Pasha now had a respite of six weeks to strengthen his defenses and build more redoubts, while the Russians sought and obtained reinforcement from the army of Prince Charles of Rumania, who made the condition that he should be given command of the joint besieging force. The next assault took place from three sides, with every expectation of a Russo-Rumanian triumph. Indeed, during the first two days of a ferocious siege both Russian and Rumanian flags flew for a spell from the redoubts. But on the third day, following as ferocious a counterattack by the Turks, the Rumanians withdrew their forces, and the Cross replaced the Russian Eagle over Plevna. Following this second defeat, the Russians accepted the impossibility of taking Plevna by storm, and under a skilled engineer of the Imperial Guard planned together with the Rumanians to encircle the fortress and thus starve out its garrison.

Realistically Osman, having won two major victories against an army twice as large as his own, and thus forced upon the Russians a hard winter campaign, would have preferred to evacuate Plevna before it was too late. But his heroic defense of it, as retailed by the press, had by now captured the imagination of Europe, reversing the current barbarous image of the Turk to glorify him as a brave fighter of the bulldog breed, and turning back the scales of public opinion in favour of the Ottoman Empire. Anxious to profit politically by this recovery of prestige in the West, Abdul Hamid ordered Osman to remain in Plevna at all costs—promising him a vast new army to march to its relief. Osman doggedly held out, bringing in supplies from the south until the last point of entry was closed by the Russians and the fortress was totally encircled. When Abdul Hamid's relieving force tardily appeared, it proved to be little more than an improvised rabble, which was soon put to flight by the Russians.

Left now, in the dead of winter, at the mercy of the Balkan snows, without prospect of relief, with ammunition diminishing and food reduced to the point at which the soldiery were scavenging for cats and dogs and rats and mice—while the Russian officers ate caviar—Osman realized that his last hope lay in a surprise breakout from the fortress with the bulk of his garrison. Thus early in December the Turks silently emerged, at dead of night, to the west. They threw bridges across the River Vid, then deployed to advance upon the surprised Russian outposts in orderly military formation. Carrying the first trenches, they swept onward against the main Russian line. Here they fought hand to hand and bayonet to bayonet, with little advantage to either side. Then Osman Pasha was wounded in the leg by a stray bullet, which killed his horse beneath him. Rumours of his own death created panic. Believing themselves leaderless, his valiant but half-starved troops broke and fled, enabling the Russians to occupy the redoubts of the fortress.

A white flag flew over Plevna, the Tsar entered the town at the head of his troops, and Osman Pasha signed terms of surrender. The Russians treated him honourably, but his troops perished in the snows by the thousand as they straggled off into captivity. The more seriously wounded were left behind in their camp hospitals, only to be atrociously butchered by the Bulgarians.

The surrender of Plevna, at the end of 1877, released some hundred thousand Russian troops which had been immobilized through the five months' siege. One army marched over the Balkan range to capture Sofia; another forced the surrender of a large Turkish army in the Shipka Pass to enter Adrianople and thus directly to threaten Istanbul. Serbia declared war once again, to capture Nish. The Montenegrins achieved conquests in Herzegovina. Slavonic armies were victorious in all parts of the Balkans. The Greeks threatened war, and supported insurrections in the Empire's Greek-inhabited provinces, Crete included. In Asia the Russians had captured the fortress of Kars from the Turks, for the third time in its history, together with those of Ardahan and Erzurum, thus occupying the bulk of eastern Armenia.

From Adrianople the Russian army of the Grand Duke Nicholas, with no effective Turkish force left to oppose him, marched onward in the direction of Istanbul, creating panic in the city itself and deep concern in London. The Turks applied unsuccessfully under the 1871 treaty for intervention by the powers, which was blocked largely by Prussia. The Porte became especially bitter against Britain for her refusal of support, and the palace-controlled press caricatured the British as "cowards."

The British Cabinet was divided, as before, between a peace party and a war party, with Lord Beaconsfield determined at all costs to prevent a Russian occupation of Istanbul. Into the city there swarmed refugees from the west in their hundreds of thousands. Men, women, and children, sick, frostbitten, and dying of starvation, they fled through the snows in the path of the advancing Russians, five thousand of them crowding for succour into the mosque of Aya Sofya alone. The *softas* (theological students) began to make trouble, and the Sultan asked the British ambassador for asylum if need be. Abdul Hamid telegraphed personally to Queen Victoria, requesting her mediation for an armistice, and his appeal was relayed to the Tsar, whose reply evaded the issue, referring it to his commanders in the field.

There the Grand Duke Nicholas was refusing armistice discussions without a preliminary acceptance of terms which amounted in effect to a dictated peace. He continued his advance to the village of San Stefano, on the shores of the Sea of Marmara, a mere ten miles from the walls of the city. To confront him Lord Beaconsfield finally overcame ministerial opposition to order five warships of the British fleet to the Sea of Marmara, where, for the ostensible purpose of protecting British life and property, they were to anchor within range of the Russians under the lee of the Princes Islands.

Russians and Turks had by now reached an armistice agreement which Beaconsfield rightly dismissed as a mere "comedy." For sure enough, the grand duke continued his advance, threatening the capital so closely as to create a near-panic on the London stock exchange. This eased Lord Beaconsfield's task of obtaining from Parliament a vote of credit for six million pounds, to place the armed forces of the crown on a war footing and, in conjunction with the naval move, to go ahead with preparations for a military landing in Gallipoli if events so required.

Amid the general excitement the Prime Minister was cheered by patriotic crowds thronging Parliament Square. For indeed British public opinion, fired by this new threat from the Russians and the new reaction toward it, had swung back in its volatile fashion to the side of the Turks, in the revived spirit of the Crimean War. In London a new imperial concept was coined as the music halls rang with the song:

> We don't want to fight:
> But, by jingo, if we do,
> We've got the men, we've got the ships,
> And we've got the money too.

Jingoism was satisfied as, in response to the British threat, the Russians refrained from entering Istanbul, and the Tsar cabled assurance to the Sultan that he had no imminent intention of occupying the city. Thus Russia could not fulfill the destiny, for which she had long hoped as "the legitimate successor of those who had reigned on the Bosporus," of dictating a treaty to the Turks in Constantinople itself. For this she had Britain to blame, and in particular—as Russians saw it—her astute ambassador, Sir Henry Layard, whom they now preferred to call Mr. Lie-Hard.

On March 3, 1878, a bilateral treaty was signed between Russia and Turkey at San Stefano. Under its terms, which were not at first disclosed to the powers, the Russians planned the virtual dismemberment of the Ottoman Empire in Europe. It was a plan conceived exclusively in the interests of its Slavonic and against those of its other populations, both Christian and Moslem. It provided for two large Balkan states, both predominantly Slav, both now to be declared fully independent and freed from all tribute to the Sultan. One was Montenegro, which was to be trebled in size and doubled in population at the expense of its neighbours; the other, with enlarged territories and new frontiers which almost adjoined it, was Serbia. Bosnia and Herzegovina were to remain subject to the Sultan, but with autonomous institutions. Rumania was confirmed in its independence but, as a Latin state, shabbily rewarded for its loyal support in the war by the loss of Bessarabia and an exchange of territories to Russia's advantage.

The chief benefits were to be conferred on its Slav neighbour, Bulgaria. This was to be enlarged on such a scale as to restore in effect the Bulgarian empire of the Middle Ages. It was to spread over the lands south of the Danube, from the Black Sea to the Aegean, with control of ports in both seas, incorporating at the expense of Greek claims much of Thrace and Macedonia, and extending westward as far as Albania. As an autonomous state, still nominally subject to the Sultan's suzerainty, the new Bulgaria would be under the rule of a prince selected by Russia, and with a Russianized administration, a large Russian enclave in the heart of the Balkans, serving still in the east as a bridgehead for an attack on Istanbul. What remained of Turkey in Europe would thus be divided into two separate parts, with a Bulgarian barrier between its two principal cities.

The Treaty of San Stefano was seen in Europe and throughout the Balkans as a flagrant violation of ethnological principles, overriding as it did the just historical claims, the religious discrepancies, and the growing national sentiments of its various non-Slav peoples. As Lord

Beaconsfield saw it: "The Sultan of Turkey is reduced to a state of absolute subjugation to Russia. . . . We therefore protest against an arrangement which practically would place at the command of Russia, and Russia alone, that unrivalled situation and the resources which the European powers placed under the government of the Porte."

He had from the outset contended that Russia must submit the terms of any treaty with Turkey to the judgment of Europe. The European powers had been responsible for the treaties of 1856 and 1871, which could not be modified without their assent. Russia had already assented in principle to the convening of a congress for the purpose, but with the proviso that she might select which articles of the treaty should be raised for discussion. The British government, however, insisted that the treaty as a whole should be so raised. When Russia refused this, Lord Beaconsfield resorted to action, calling out the reserves and ordering a force of Indian troops to proceed through the Suez Canal to Malta.

This show of force by Britain coincided with the mobilization, in defense of her own Balkan territorial interests, of Austria-Hungary, which had initially put forward the idea of a conference. Britain, moreover, was supporting the cause of the Rumanians and Greeks and their claims to be represented at the conference. To the Greeks the British government had declared that it was "prepared to exert all its influence to prevent the absorption into a Slav state of any Greek population." The Balkan Moslems appealed for justice to Queen Victoria, as the empress of a hundred million Moslem subjects. The Albanians formed a league to "resist until death" any attempt on their lands. In this atmosphere the Tsar changed his attitude. In a secret agreement, soon revealed, between the British and Russian governments, his ambassador to London modified his original plans for a "great Bulgaria." Thus the way was paved for a European congress, which opened in Berlin in the summer of 1878, with Bismarck as president.

The Treaty of Berlin, signed within a month by the six powers, effectively nullified the Treaty of San Stefano. The plan for a "great Bulgaria" was dropped by the Russians. Instead, Bulgaria was divided into two provinces. Of these the northern alone, confined within the bounds of the Danube, the Black Sea (with the port of Varna), the Serbian and Macedonian frontiers, and the Balkan range, with no outlet to the Aegean, was to have political autonomy under the suzerainty of the Sultan, with a ruling prince, not drawn from a leading dynasty, whose election should be confirmed not by Russia alone, but by the Porte, with the consent of the powers in general. A second autonomous Bulgarian province, to be named Eastern Rumelia, was to be formed south of the Balkan range and, as constituting the European frontier of the Ottoman Empire, was to be placed "under the direct political and military authority of the Sultan."

To this the Russians at first objected. But they finally bowed to Lord Beaconsfield's persistence and, as Bismarck remarked, "There is once again a Turkey in Europe." The organization of Eastern Rumelia was then entrusted to a European commission. This check to Russian encroachment in the eastern Balkans was matched in the west by the increased power of Austria-Hungary, through her occupation and administration of Bosnia and Herzegovina. This followed the lines of the secret agreement, reached before the war, between Russia and Austria, as the price of her neutrality. These two remote provinces, containing few Turks but a mixed population of Moslems, Slavs, and other Christians, were in the judgment of the congress best administered by a strong foreign power, especially one which, like the Austrian empire, already had Croats and Serbs among its own subjects. This expedient, moreover, would split up the proposed bloc of Slav states in the Balkans, through the allotment to Bosnia and Herzegovina of territories promised at San Stefano to Montenegro, whose territory was now not tripled but doubled, and to Serbia, which was compensated at the expense not of Turkey but of Bulgaria. It left, as a buffer between the two Slav states, the Turkish sanjak of Novibazar, where Austria-Hungary now had certain rights, with potential access to Albania and Macedonia.

At Berlin, as at San Stefano, the principal sufferer was Rumania, which emerged from the congress as a lasting victim of Russian injustice. Here Russia, bent on extending her own frontiers to the whole line of the Pruth, successfully persisted, as a condition for Rumanian independence, in her demand for southern Bessarabia, a land to the north of the Danube which was historically and ethnographically Rumanian. In exchange she conceded, at the expense of Bulgaria, the Dobruja, a desolate land beyond the Danube, inhabited by Bulgarians and Turks.

Finally Greece was rewarded at Berlin by no appreciable increase of territory but, thanks largely to British mediation, by certain favourable adjustments of her frontiers with the Turkish provinces of Epirus and Thessaly, while the province of Macedonia, left to Turkey, was at least spared the threat of Bulgarian rule. On the other hand Crete, which Greece had hoped to annex, remained, despite protests from its Christian subjects, under Turkish rule. No special new administration was provided for such remaining sections of the Turkish Empire in Europe as Macedonia, Thrace, Albania, and a large part of Epirus. Their Christian inhabitants, like those of Crete, had to be content with an organization of special representative commissions, as laid down ten years earlier but still a dead letter and likely to remain so.

The final Treaty of Berlin, having averted a major war through diplomacy, was hailed by Lord Beaconsfield as "peace with honour." It was a peace influenced equally by Bismarck, who had furthered the interests of Prussia in opposition to those of Russia, by strengthening the powers of Austria-Hungary in the western half of the Balkans. This was an area, moreover, where the Turks were now unable to keep effective order, and where the Austrians might well improve the conditions of its mixed population, both Christian and Moslem. At the Congress of Berlin the European powers had at least furnished the Balkans with a precarious charter which was to give it a certain measure of peace, despite constant violations, for a generation to come. At the eleventh hour they had rescued the Ottoman Empire in Europe from imminent extinction, to afford it a last but dwindling lease on life. Above all they had finally checked Russian ambitions, initially encouraged by their neutrality, to incorporate the bulk of it within the empire of the Tsar. Henceforward a degree of Russian influence in the Balkans might indeed prevail. But Russian rule could not.

The rising power to come was that of Balkan nationalism, rather than Russian imperialism. That spirit of national consciousness which had dawned earlier in the century, with the successive rebellions of the Serbs and the Greeks, was to lead, in emulation of the growing nationalist spirit of western Europe, to the struggle of their remaining minorities for freedom. The principle of the Treaty of Berlin was "the Balkans for the Balkan peoples." It sealed the evolution of a group of independent Balkan states, as a barrier against Russian imperialism less vulnerable than the weakening provinces of the Ottoman Empire. Once liberated, these *millets* becoming "nations" were unlikely again to submit passively to the domination of an imperial power.

It was Beaconsfield's hope that the new Bulgaria would serve rather as a bulwark of Turkey against Russia than of Russia against Turkey. As Bismarck later observed: "All those races have gladly accepted Russian help for liberation from the Turks; but since they have been free they have shown no tendency to accept the Tsar as successor of the Sultan." Thus in this culminating attempt to solve the Eastern Question, following the last of the Russo-Turkish wars, the Congress of Berlin had evolved for eastern Europe a political pattern differing in essence from any that had emerged from previous conflicts.

In Asia, under the Treaty of San Stefano, the Russians had restored Erzurum to the Turks, but retained Kars, Ardahan, Bayezid, and Batum, thus moving westward the Asiatic frontier of Turkey to a line drawn through the mountains between Erzurum and the Black Sea at Trebizond. Now, largely through the efforts of Beaconsfield, the Turks were to retain Bayezid, a key frontier defense post farther eastward on the transit route into Persia, while Batum, though "occupied" by the Russians, was to become, on the Tsar's undertaking, a free port, unfortified and defined as commercial. In return for this concession, Britain consented to restore the prewar *status quo* for the Dardanelles. The Turks, for the territories which they retained here in eastern Armenia, promised reforms and improvements as required for the Armenian inhabitants, and guarantees of their security against the Circassians and Kurds.

In this protective role a special responsibility was to devolve on Britain. For before the opening of the congress the British government, as an insurance against the anticipated retention by Russia of these various conquests, had secretly agreed with the Porte on a convention balancing in Asia that agreed in Europe with the Russian ambassador on the division of Bulgaria. By this Britain, to enable her to join with the Sultan in the defense of his remaining Asiatic dominions against further Russian attack, was to occupy and administer the island of Cyprus, paying to the Sultan in return an annual tribute from its surplus revenues and obtaining his promise to introduce, with British cooperation, the required reforms.

Thus here, as now revealed for the first time, was a "new Gibraltar" to help exclude Russia from the eastern Mediterranean. It was a base designed to protect not only the landmass of the Asiatic Turkish Empire but Britain's lines of communication with her own Moslem empire in India. It aimed to restore British prestige in the East, helping to neutralize other concessions to Russia. Hence now in counterpoise, on the eastern as on the western flank of the Ottoman Empire, there stood sentinel in its defense against Russian imperialism the respective imperial forces of Britain and Austria-Hungary.

Meanwhile, at the center of Ottoman government in Istanbul, the European powers had proved only too well justified—if not wholly for the right reasons—in their doubts as to the prospects of the new constitution. For all their skepticism as to Turkish motives, the convictions behind it had been wholly sincere on the part of Midhat Pasha and a maturing generation of constitutional reformers. It is indeed possible that, if the mental condition of Murad V had proved equal to the burdens and strains of the sultanate, he would have persisted in his youthful support for reform, remaining on the throne to preside over an evolving constitutional regime.

But his brother Abdul Hamid had no such intentions. By inclination and conviction an autocrat, his motives in accepting the constitution had been those of a shrewd opportunist, and his modifications of its original draft showed a determination to safeguard the rights of the sovereign rather than those of the people. He used it cynically at the Constantinople Conference, as no more than a facade behind which to forestall and prevent partition by the powers. As soon as the Conference was over, he had arbitrarily dismissed Midhat Pasha, who had inspired and framed the constitution, from his post as Grand Vezir, conveying him immediately, for fear of popular demonstrations in his favour, to the imperial yacht and banishing him into exile in Italy. This action was taken, ironically, in terms of the constitution itself, under a last-minute article on which the Sultan had insisted, against strong opposition, authorizing him "to expel from the territory of the Empire those who, as a result of trustworthy information gathered by the police administration, are recognized as dangerous to the security of the state." Three years later Midhat, brought back from exile, was tried and sentenced to death. The sentence was commuted to life imprisonment in an Arabian fortress, where he was murdered in 1884.

Such was the death knell of those individual liberties enshrined in the Tanzimat charter. In the future Ottoman state, as this assertive young Sultan envisaged it, there was no room for so assertive (and popular) a statesman as Midhat. The forceful independence of his actions and principles constituted a threat to the Sultan's prerogatives, and implied a diminution of his supreme authority. As Abdul Hamid saw it, the nation was responsible to the Sultan, not the Sultan to the nation. He alone, as its sole master, could bestow a constitution upon it. His alone was the right to command and direct the machinery of government.

Under its terms, keeping up the facade meanwhile, Abdul Hamid ordered a general election—historically the first ever held in an Islamic state. The first Ottoman Parliament met in March, 1877—a Senate composed of twenty-five nominated officials and a Chamber of 120 deputies, elected under official pressure and by a distinctly unconstitutional process. It comprised nonetheless, as Midhat had intended, Christians and Jews, Turks and Arabs, giving a voice to all sections of the community, even if not in proportion to their numbers. Abdul Hamid saw his Parliament as a puppet assembly, manufactured to give an appearance of legal validity and popular assent to such measures as he elected to impose.

Nonetheless it soon developed an identity of its own, as a diversity of representatives from all the provinces of the far-flung Ottoman Empire met together for the first time, exchanging ideas and experiences, discovering problems and grievances in common. In resulting speeches they delivered attacks, never on the Sultan himself, but often on his ministers and other pashas, accusing them of corruption and various abuses, exposing as never before the need throughout the country for radical reforms in the government. Among the deputies were men of intelligence, thoughtful in outlook and independent in mind. Their critical deliberations could have provided a reforming Sultan with valuable guidance in the formulation of a constructive internal program. In spirit if not yet in experience the Chamber thus vindicated the constitution. Its open hostility toward the rule of the pashas reached the point at which demands were made for the appearance of certain ministers before it to answer specific charges.

In response to this insubordination the Sultan dissolved the assembly after a session of three months. Six months later, on December 13, 1877, it was convoked again. The critical state of the Russian war now made it easier to manage. In his speech at the opening of Parliament, the Sultan could appeal to the "representatives of the nation" for "the cooperation and patriotism of my subjects in order to protect, with me, our legitimate rights. . . . May God bless our efforts." Then came the armistice, negotiated by the government—so the Chamber was informed—owing to the country's abandonment by Europe, and signed on January 31, 1878. Now the hostile deputies spoke up again. This time they named three ministers, bringing specific charges against them and demanding that they appear in the Chamber to answer them. This time the Sultan prorogued Parliament indefinitely. It was not to meet again for thirty years.

To a committee of senators and deputies Abdul Hamid ironically invoked the example of his grandfather, Sultan Mahmud the Reformer, as against that of his father, Abdul Mejid, who had sought reforms by permission and by liberal institutions. "I now understand," he declared, "that it is only by force that one can move the people, with whose protection God has entrusted me." Later to a European correspondent he insisted that he was no opponent to reform; "But the excess of a liberty to which one is unaccustomed is as dangerous as the absence of a liberty."

Henceforward personal rule by the Sultan replaced the infant constitution. The Young Ottomans, last apostles of the enlightened age of the Tanzimat, were soon no more, dispersed by banishment and persecution. Against the "army of spies" at home—as Namik Kemal, himself exiled, described them—they became abroad an "army of exiles turned into revolutionaries." In the words of his disillusioned friend Ziya:

> Naught but sorrows on the loyal to this Empire ever wait;
> Sheerest madness is devotion to this people and this State.

PART

VII

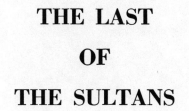

THE LAST OF THE SULTANS

((36))

ABDUL HAMID WAS AN UNHAPPY MAN AND AN INHUMAN SULTAN. After he lost, at the age of seven, his devoted Circassian mother, it was said of him that "he never loved anyone, least of all himself." From his early youth he lived within himself, shying away from the company of his contemporaries and others around him, growing up, not indeed in the Cage of his forebears—for he visited Europe as a young man with his uncle Sultan Abdul Aziz—but in an introspective cage of his own contriving.

This assumed outward and concrete form when on his accession he elected to live and to rule within the high, insurmountable walls of the park of his Yildiz Palace, on the slopes above the Bosporus. Looking inward, Abdul Hamid turned his back upon the Dolma Bahche palace, the creation of his father, which openly flaunted its splendours on the waters beneath. Instead he enlarged for his own secluded occupation a "Starry Kiosk," once built for a Sultan's favourite. Around it he demolished the houses and appropriated for his gardens the lands—including two Christian cemeteries—of his subjects, to create a haphazard, self-contained complex of pavilions and chalets, secretariats and government offices, barracks and guardhouses. This was to serve as an imperial Seraglio, the new center of power, from which the new Sultan now reigned in supreme isolation over the Ottoman Empire—an absolute autocrat hardly matched in its history.

It was likewise a center of fear—the irrational fear of Abdul Hamid himself for his own personal safety, generated through an innate distrust of all men and their motives, and in turn generating a spirit of apprehension in all those around him. Early in his reign the Sultan's nervous condition became chronic, following the outbreak in Istanbul of a liberal revolt, inspired by Ali Suavi, a leader of the Young Ottomans lately returned from exile. His aim was to dethrone Abdul Hamid and to release and enthrone once again in his place his deposed brother and predecessor, Murad V.

With a large body of armed supporters he entered the palace on the Bosporus where Murad was confined and, with his mother's complicity, urged him to gird on his sword and to follow him. But the scared prince shrank from any such prospect, and fled back into his harem. The delay had given time for a contingent of police to arrive. Their commandant felled and killed Ali Suavi with a blow of his cudgel. A number of his confederates were also killed or wounded, while a court-martial sentenced others to deportation. Murad himself, meanwhile, was removed to the safer confinement of a kiosk within the grounds of the Yildiz Palace.

This abortive coup by Ali Suavi, which the palace spies chose to interpret to the Sultan as a widespread conspiracy, so affected the balance of his mind that when Layard, the British ambassador, requested an audience on a diplomatic matter, Abdul Hamid became possessed by the delusion that he was to be borne off to a British warship and disposed of, so that Murad might ascend the throne. Sir Henry Layard, as he recounts, found the Sultan cowering with a look of terror in a corner of his large hall, with his army bodyguard at hand.

Henceforward Abdul Hamid's suspicions and fears became a neurotic obsession. Yildiz was soon virtually a fortress. Locking its gates from the inside, he built around it a second encircling wall, and against this a large barracks for his Albanian imperial guard, which was numbered in thousands. Within the walls observation posts crowned each point of vantage, with powerful telescopes to command the whole neighbourhood of the Bosporus and Golden Horn and thus help to secure the palace against possible threats from any direction. Abdul Hamid soon reached the stage when he rarely ventured beyond the walls of Yildiz. A mosque was built at its gates, where he worshipped each Friday rather than drive farther afield to the mosques of the city.

Pale, silent, and melancholy, with a "sinister and scrutinizing" look that belied his polite manners, Abdul Hamid scented danger on every side and suspected all those around him. He surrounded himself with an army of spies, *agents provocateurs,* secret police, and unofficial informers who provided him with daily reports. It thus came to be said that one-half of the population of Istanbul was employed spying on the other half.

Abdul Hamid was a ruler who kept all affairs of state strictly under his own control. He worked indefatigably from morning until night. Abstemious, from chronic dyspepsia, he paused only for a brief, light meal and a drink of water. This was drawn superstitiously from a single sacred spring, which a soothsayer declared to be free from all contamination by cholera or plague. He conducted all his own correspondence, concerning himself with the minutest details of contracts, concessions, tradesmen's accounts, and petitions, and receiving in person all with whom business had to be done.

Mistrusting all his ministers and officials as "hypocrites and parasites," he sowed and exploited mutual dissensions among them, arbitrarily appointing one for his known enmity to another, playing off all against all lest they associate for treacherous purposes. Monopolizing power in his own hands, he gave orders and instructions to them individually and directly through a staff of personal secretaries. These often contradicted instructions given to the Grand Vezir, and thus lowered his traditional status. For he no longer stood, as in the past, between the Sultan and his ministers as the chief recipient of his delegated powers.

Such was the governing pattern of an absolute despot, ruling, as he believed, by divine right. His was in effect a police state, a bureaucracy centralized within the palace of Yildiz and moreover strengthened beyond it by a new instrument of autocracy more powerful than any possessed by his forebears. This was the telegraph. First introduced by the allies in the Crimean War, then developed throughout the Empire by a French concession, it was fully exploited by Abdul Hamid under a newly formed Ministry of Posts and Telegraphs, providing courses in the schools for telegraph operators. A network of telegraphic lines and cables soon spread through all parts of the Empire, covering some twenty thousand miles, linking the capital with all its provincial centers and thus enabling Abdul Hamid directly to control his official bureaucracy, as no previous Sultan had done. A governor was no longer delegated to govern at his own discretion and risk. For with the telegraph the Sultan could now "order him about, find out what he is doing, reprimand him, recall him, instruct his subordinates to report against him, and generally deprive him of all real powers." Total autocrat as he thus was, unhampered by any semblance of political opposition or constitutional restraint upon his absolute powers, Abdul Hamid abominated all forms of liberal government. Thanks to this, as he contemptuously saw it, the rulers of the West permitted themselves to be ruled by their subjects.

Nonetheless, politics apart, he was no blind reactionary. He drew still upon the West, as his forebears of the Tanzimat had done, in his pursuit of modernization, not only for his own especial purposes in the field of technology, but in those of judicial and particularly educational reform. Here, by autocratic methods, he expanded and brought to fruition in practice much that the previous reformers had planned but only partially achieved. What the Empire still needed above all at this time was an enlarged civil service, with the competence to conduct its public affairs and to administer its laws and finances in accordance with the Sultan's will, and thus to ensure orderly and progressive development.

To keep pace with the West—and indeed with his own Christian population—the essential need, in the Sultan's eyes, was for reform and improvement in public education. He needed around him a reliable, educated class of official, to replace those now in disgrace or in exile and to augment those upon whom he could for the future rely to do his bidding and serve his state. For this purpose he reorganized the Mülkiye, the Empire's first center of higher civil education, until it had twelve times as many students as in his father's time.

In the military field the war college of the Harbiye was similarly expanded, together with the naval and military engineering and the medical schools, both military and civil. Abdul Hamid extended his educational system with eighteen new higher and professional schools, covering such subjects as finance, the fine arts, civil engineering, police, and customs. Finally he founded a University of Istanbul, the ultimate materialization of a project first mooted but never launched under the Tanzimat, half a century earlier. To provide these new colleges with students and staff, there was also a widespread expansion of primary and secondary schools and of teachers' training colleges. In the capital the eventual peak of secondary education was reached with the expansion and Turkification of the Franco-Turkish Galatasaray. Now the Imperial Ottoman Lycée, it became an elite public school for the families of the Turkish ruling class, with teachers drawn from among leading Turkish scholars and literary men.

Such, thanks to the resolute industry of Abdul Hamid, was the long-delayed consummation, in effective practical terms, of the educational ideals of the Tanzimat. Here at last was the expanding nucleus of a substantial new educated class, a civil-service elite trained professionally to staff the vast bureaucracy of the Hamidian regime—and ironically enough of the anti-Hamidian regime that was to follow it.

In the sphere of legal reform Abdul Hamid was at first less successful. Under a Ministry of Justice he designed changes so to reform Ottoman secular justice as to secure its recognition by the foreign committees, thus limiting the judicial privileges to which the Capitulations entitled them. But the foreign missions refused to accept in the mixed court the relevant new laws on civil procedure and the execution of judgments. So their extraterritorial privileges remained as entrenched as before. In the sphere of communications a further contribution to the modernization of Turkey was the spread of the printed word, through the media of newspapers, periodicals, and books. All were indeed strictly censored, often to the point of emasculation—"gelded newspapers" (as a foreign observer called them)—communicating nothing of political import. Nonetheless they had a widening circulation. In all nonpolitical subjects such as literature, science, and other branches of knowledge, a new reading public could widen its horizons.

In the sphere of finance the Ottoman Empire was now more than ever at the mercy of Europe. At the Berlin Congress, the interested powers had for the first time confronted the problem of default on the Ottoman debt. In an official protocol they provided for the establishment in Istanbul of an international financial commission, to seek means compatible with the Porte's financial situation of satisfying the claims of bondholders. Here, following losses of Ottoman territory in Europe, was the humiliating prospect of a limitation by Europe of Ottoman sovereignty at home. To Abdul Hamid it was a blow to Turkish pride which he at first found hard to swallow. But eventually, with his treasury in urgent need of funds, he recognized the need to mollify his European creditors, and in so doing to reestablish a degree of Turkish prestige abroad.

In 1881 he issued the Decree of Muharrem, which, in agreement with the European bondholders, set up a Council of the Public Debt. Composed of Ottoman and foreign representatives, it was to ensure henceforward the resumption of service on the debt. The Decree was so shrewdly framed by the Sultan as to reestablish a degree of European goodwill toward Turkey, without appearing to weaken his sovereign powers. The Council was not, as first envisaged at Berlin, an official international commission, with foreign government representatives. Instead, it was the product, more acceptable to the Sultan, of a bilateral agreement between the Porte and its creditors, semi-official in character, but freely agreed by both parties without diplomatic intervention.

Its terms favoured the Ottoman treasury in that the amount of the debt was written down by half, to just over a hundred million pounds, with a rate of interest at no more than 4 and usually as little as 1 percent. In return, the treasury ceded to the Council a large part of the government's annual revenues, for the payment of interest and the redemption of the bonds. They included those of the salt and tobacco monopolies, the tribute paid by Bulgaria and Eastern Rumelia, the Cyprus government financial surplus, and a number of indirect taxes and tithes. But any surplus from these annual revenues, after the payment of interest and redemption, was to be repaid to the Turkish treasury. The Council of the Debt, though it imposed a heavy burden on the Porte, became an institution by which the Turks, with their traditional respect for institutions, showed themselves ready to abide in an orderly and rational spirit. Forty otherwise turbulent years were indeed to pass before the Ottoman government made any attempt to disengage itself from the obligations of Abdul Hamid's Decree of Muharrem.

The Ottoman debt settlement meant in effect that henceforward the economic development of the country was financed largely by European investors, through the Council of the Public Debt. Turkey grew fast in prosperity, largely to the foreigners' benefit, but to the benefit also of the Moslem Turks, in terms of increasing employment and expanding services. Neglected agricultural and industrial resources were exploited by foreign concessionaries. The public debt revived the silk industry of Bursa. French capital exploited the coal mines of Zonguldak, on the Black Sea coast. The cultivation of tobacco became the monopoly of a Franco-Austrian company, providing employment for tens of thousands of Moslem Turkish workers from Macedonia to the Levant and northeastern Anatolia. Above all, under the impetus of the Council of the Public Debt, the Empire was opened up through the construction of railways, first initiated by Abdul Aziz, on a rapidly expanding scale. Under Abdul Hamid the principal cities of the Empire were progressively linked over some thousands of miles, often where few roads existed, to the benefit of their industries and of the rural areas around them. In 1888 Turkey was first connected by rail to western Europe, with the arrival amid a flourish of trumpets of the first through train from Vienna to Istanbul—forerunner of the Orient Express.

This dramatic breach in the barriers between East and West was not wholly welcome to Sultan Abdul Hamid. Increasingly isolationist in the foreign policy of his empire—as indeed in his own personal life—he was turning away from the Western powers, who had left him to fight his last war against Russia alone, and whose motives inspired his chronic mistrust. He was especially bitter against Britain, who had betrayed him, as he saw it, by her refusal of support in the war, who had reduced his state to bankruptcy and his own economic sovereignty to little more than a cipher, and whose consuls were continually interfering in the internal affairs of his empire by insistence on unwelcome provincial reforms. He had in particular "a kind of horror of Mr. Gladstone," who had returned to power in 1880, and who in turn saw the Sultan and his government as "a bottomless pit of fraud and falsehood."

In 1885, when the Tories returned to power, the British ambassador, Sir William White, commented to Lord Salisbury on the complete loss of influence at the Porte by the governments of London, Paris, and Vienna: "They were too much consulted formerly, now their advice is unheeded and even heard with ill-humour, if not with disdain. Their notes and applications receive evasive replies, or none at all." For Abdul Hamid had turned from his traditional allies to Russia, his traditional enemy, whose ingratiating tactics, at the artful expense of the rest, had won her increasing favour at the Porte. More momentously, the Sultan turned also to a new source of support in the increasing power of Germany, still dominated by Bismarck and now an active confederate of Russia, as of Austria, in the Triple Alliance of the "Three Emperors." German influence was soon sealed at the Porte by the dispatch of German officers to train and develop the Ottoman army.

In the aftermath of Berlin, Abdul Hamid had embarked on a delaying rear-guard action in his implementation of the terms of the treaty. His first setback, in 1880, was in Montenegro, which the treaty had recognized as an independent state, with a port on the Adriatic at Antivari. Lest this should develop into a Russian naval base, it was ceded on the condition that it should not be used by Montenegrin or foreign warships. Abdul Hamid now emphatically refused to surrender the port. His refusal provoked a naval demonstration by the European powers before it, which he still disregarded. Eventually Britain, through Gladstone's ambassador, Viscount Goschen, threatened that, if the Sultan did not yield, British ships would occupy another important Turkish port—which, as later revealed, was Smyrna. He still refused, giving way that evening to a paroxysm of rage in which he declared that he would be happy to see London destroyed. But as the British fleet made ready to sail, a boat was seen at the last moment hurrying out from the shore, with an official on board, frantically waving a paper. The Sultan had yielded.

Similar delays from the palace of Yildiz attended the settlement of the frontiers of Greece, which had been deferred by the congress, since the Greeks had abstained from the war. Here Abdul Hamid's tactics of exploiting disunity among the powers proved more effective. He rejected a proposal to cede to Greece the whole of Thessaly and Epirus. After prolonged negotiations, with the Greek army mobilized, he achieved a settlement ceding all Thessaly but only a third of Epirus, excluding districts inhabited by Moslems. But Greece still did not acquire Crete as she had hoped.

Facing Bulgaria, his nearest European neighbour, the Sultan proved less assertive. Here, following the Treaty of Berlin, a situation developed in which he had several chances for intervention, at once under the terms of the treaty and in the interests of his empire. But each time he chose, in a passive, obdurate spirit, to do nothing. In the autonomous principality of Northern Bulgaria, beyond the Balkan range, it seemed at first as though the influence of "Russia the Liberator" would surely predominate. Its prince was Alexander of Battenberg, constitutionally elected by a Bulgarian assembly which he later dissolved. He had at first the backing of the Russians, who acted as the power behind his throne, and pursued the political tactics of playing off prince against people in the name of the Tsar. But Alexander had a Germanic contempt for the Russians and resented their predominance, complaining that "all the scum of Russia has taken refuge here and has tainted the whole country." Nor did the Bulgarians long tolerate these alien taskmasters, with their tactless, domineering ways and their imperious interference with the conduct of a supposedly liberal government. Had they merely exchanged one form of bondage for another, freed from subjection to the Turks as *rayas* just to be treated by the Russians as low-grade Asiatics? They soon came to prefer the Battenberg "Alexander the Liberator," revering his portrait in their homes, while the country began to ring with the nationalist cry of "Bulgaria for the Bulgarians!"

This crystallized into a movement for union between the two Bulgarian states, North and South, as established at Berlin. South of the Balkan range lay the richer territory of Eastern Rumelia, the autonomous Bulgarian state still under the Sultan's protection. Russian troops had remained here only until its constitution was established. Then Abdul Hamid appointed as its Christian governor one Gavril Pasha, familiar to the Turks as the "Schoolmaster President" of their mixed courts. On arrival in Philippopolis he exchanged the official Turkish fez for the Bulgarian kalpak. He was tolerated by the nationalist inhabitants, only for fear that the Sultan might otherwise send troops into Rumelia, as the treaty entitled him to do, and so defeat the Bulgarian army, on which they depended.

They were nonetheless impatient for union, and the Porte precipitated demands for it by insisting on the Turkish right to veto Rumeliot legislation. Meanwhile, the Sultan issued a provocative order forbidding the display of the Bulgarian flag. Defiantly the people continued to hoist it in Philippopolis, the capital, and Bulgarian troops, unopposed, staged a "bloodless revolution" amid nationalist cries of "Long live the union." A few days later King Alexander, on the insistence of Stambulov, the leader of the rebels, marched into Philippopolis, to be acclaimed as ruler of Eastern Rumelia, while the assembly enthusiastically approved the union. Meanwhile Gavril, the Turkish governor, had been drawn through the streets in mock triumph, with an unsheathed sword by his side, to be conveyed back across the frontier into Turkey and there to resume his fez.

Here was an affront to the Ottoman Empire which was above all a flagrant breach of the Berlin Treaty. The Bulgarians made ready to defend themselves in the belief that the Sultan, having shown his opposition to the union, would now assert his treaty rights, held under mandate from the powers, by sending in Turkish troops. But no troops came. Abdul Hamid, so he let it be known, feared a repetition of the Bulgarian massacres, which had so enraged the powers, at the hands of his undisciplined soldiery. Instead he accepted the *fait accompli,* appointing Prince Alexander as governor of Eastern Rumelia for a five-year term, while from now onward the assemblies of the two states met as one body in Sofia.

This aggrandizement of Bulgaria into so large a state fired the jealous indignation of her neighbour, Serbia, whose ruler, Prince Milan, demanded territorial compensation, then launched an attack from the west across the Bulgarian frontier. The Bulgarians were caught at a disadvantage, since the Russians in their indignation at Alexander's success had withdrawn all their officer instructors from the Bulgarian army. Nonetheless, fired with nationalist zeal and with Prince Alexander to command and inspire them, they fought back stubbornly against the more experienced Serbian troops. Within three days, in a pass at Slivnitsa on the road to Sofia, they had driven them back across the Serbian frontier and were in a position to advance along the road to Belgrade. Here Austria, as the protector of Serbia, intervened to restore peace, and the *status quo* was resumed. Such, saving it from a defeat by the Serbs which might have led to the imposition upon it of an Austro-Hungarian protectorate, was the victorious baptism by fire of the Bulgarian nation.

For the second time Abdul Hamid had allowed his sovereign right of entry to go by default. He contented himself with protests and defensive measures at home. His inaction, inglorious though it was, now suited the Western powers, Britain included. Lord Salisbury came to favour a united, nationalist Bulgaria as a more effective barrier against Russia in the Balkans than a frontier left unguarded by Turks, reluctant to draw the sword since their military strength, as his ambassador saw it, was being "quietly dried up."

The Tsar had been enraged by Prince Alexander's audacious *coup d'état.* In retaliation, backed by his military attaché in Sofia, Russian officers hatched a conspiracy against Alexander. They kidnapped the prince, forced him to sign a document of abdication, and transported him across the Russian frontier. But in the resulting political confusion the rebel Stambulov so roused Bulgarian popular clamour as to achieve his return, with the subsequent arrest and imprisonment of those who had conspired against him. Alexander, however, weakened. Weary of the hazards of his equivocal position, fearing assassination or even a Russian military occupation if he remained, he confirmed his abdication, disconcerting Bulgarian opinion by a message to the Tsar: "As Russia gave me my crown I am prepared to give it back into the hands of its sovereign." Then he named a trio of regents to succeed him and left Bulgaria, never to return.

There followed a confused interregnum under the three regents, headed by Stambulov, pending elections by the assembly to choose a new ruling prince. The Russians dispatched a fleet to Varna, and intrigued diligently to reestablish their influence and prevent the elections. Despite Russian overtures, Abdul Hamid persisted in his policy of nonintervention. Meanwhile, an arrogant Russian general named Kaulbars was sent to Sofia as "adviser" to the Bulgarians. His advice was to release the imprisoned conspirators and to postpone the elections. But as he marched around the country, ranting against them, he soon alienated all sympathy from the dogged Bulgarian peasantry, merely reinforcing their belligerent nationalist spirit. When the elections were expedited and held, he announced that the Russian government refused to accept them as legal. The Tsar broke off diplomatic relations with Bulgaria, withdrawing the general and all his Russian consuls. Russia had thus suffered, at nationalist hands in the Balkans, a defeat of decisive significance.

Meanwhile, the regency had shown itself entirely capable of governing Bulgaria without foreign aid, an achievement which the powers were not slow to appreciate. This was to the credit of Stambulov, who had become in effect the country's dictator. Champion of unity and liberty for Bulgaria and the Bulgarians, he was a man of insight who understood his own people and had dedicated himself to their cause. On the threshold of nationhood, but inexperienced in political affairs, they needed at this moment of destiny a popular leader to trust and to follow. Stambulov, in confounding the Russian enemy within their gates, had roused in them a new national pride and a fierce spirit of Bulgarian patriotism.

It now remained to elect for the new nation a new ruling prince. In 1887 the assembly's unanimous choice fell on Prince Ferdinand of Coburg. Russia refused to recognize his election as valid, but he ascended the throne with the implicit consent of the other European powers under the Berlin Treaty. New elections in 1887 confirmed Ferdinand as prince. On a tour of the country the populace greeted him with polite dignity and the heroic Stambulov with unconcealed rapture. His accession, unrecognized by Russia and Turkey, was accepted by Lord Salisbury, since the "Coburger" was after all a relative of Queen Victoria. For seven years longer his prime minister, Stambulov, in continued defiance of Russia, was to win admiration from Britain as "the Bulgarian Bismarck."

Abdul Hamid, in the final resort, could not resist a sly, backhanded thrust at Bulgaria, by imposing an import duty on the entry into Turkish territory of all Bulgarian produce. But he had proved himself no warrior Sultan, ready if need be to fight for the remaining remnants of his empire. Shrinking, in the aftermath of the peace treaty, from a further act of war, with its evident risks and repercussions, he had preferred to renounce his sovereign rights over his last Bulgarian possessions. His conquering Ottoman forebears had treated Eastern Rumelia as the first stepping-stone toward a great empire in Europe. Abdul Hamid had passively refrained from treating it even as a last ditch of imperial defense. The Sick Man, in a spirit of fatalism, was indeed now turning his face away from Europe.

((37))

ALREADY, WITH NO SUCH DELIBERATE INTENT BUT IN THE SAME passive, prevaricating style of diplomacy, the Sultan was turning away also from the African continent. Here he was to lose Tunis, over which France assumed a protectorate, and above all Egypt, "the brightest jewel in the Sultan's crown." The ruling khedive of Egypt, still under his nominal sovereignty, was Ismail Pasha, whose dynasty, founded by Mehmed Ali, had reigned over the country for half a century past. Ismail, like the recent Sultans themselves, had through his extravagances run deeply into debt, contracting loans which amounted to close on a hundred million pounds. By 1876, the year of the Turkish government's own default, he was virtually bankrupt and, following a plan prepared by an international commission of the Egyptian public debt, was obliged to place the administration of his finances under the dual control of a British and a French controller-general. On their insistence a new cabinet was formed with a British minister of finance and a French minister of public works. When, in 1879, Ismail dismissed the two ministers in an attempt to form an all-Egyptian cabinet, the British and French governments officially advised him "to abdicate and to leave Egypt." They were supported in this by the other European powers.

If, on certain specified conditions, he refused to abdicate, the two governments would be obliged to address themselves to the Sultan. Hoping to gain time, Ismail himself—through an agent bearing costly bribes—referred the matter to the Sultan as an attempt by two foreign powers to override his sovereign rights. In his habitual misreading of the European mind it had not occurred to Abdul Hamid that the powers could presume to carry out such a deposition without his sovereign consent. Greatly alarmed at the consequent threat to his power and prestige, both at home and abroad, he summoned his Council of Ministers, who agreed that the step should be avoided if possible. Abdul Hamid, temporizing as usual, proposed negotiations for delay.

But one alone among his ministers, a Greek Christian named Caratheodori who had been his Minister of Foreign Affairs at Berlin, boldly insisted that, at this moment of urgency, any attempt at delay would be fatal, driving the powers to act without the Sultan's consent. It was a moment for an audacious decision, and the Sultan was finally induced to issue a firman, proclaiming the deposition of Ismail and the choice of his son Tewfik to succeed him. Thus at the eleventh hour the Sultan forestalled intervention by the powers, and so saved his sovereign face.

Two years later a new crisis developed in which his sovereignty was once again at issue. Discontent with conditions in the army among its native Egyptian officers provoked a nationalist *coup d'état* led by Ahmed Arabi, a colonel who was a *fellah* by origin, against the new Khedive Tewfik. This achieved the dismissal of his prime minister and undermined the authority of the khedive himself. Following the revolt, Gladstone and his noninterventionist ministers were at first prepared for no more than diplomatic action, insisting that any military intervention in Egypt was the responsibility of its sovereign the Sultan alone. Early in 1882, despite Gladstone's reluctance and in response to pressure from the French, whose own interests were opposed to the Sultan, the British and French governments confirmed to the khedive their support for him and the continuation of the present system of financial control.

This provoked a further explosion in Egypt, in which Arabi, with his cry of "Egypt for the Egyptians," forced on the khedive a strong nationalist government, with himself as minister of war. Britain and France now sent warships to Alexandria to keep order, and with the hope of reestablishing the khedive's authority. But in this they failed, and the military party remained firmly entrenched, unleashing new forces of public disorder. It was believed that Arabi intended the expulsion of all Christians. Army officers pressed for the deposition of the khedive. The continued presence of the foreign warships kindled the xenophobia of the Egyptian mob. Europeans were molested and spat upon in Alexandria, where large numbers had taken refuge from the confusion inland. A sheikh cried aloud in the streets: "Oh, Moslems, come and help me to kill the Christians!" The storm broke against them in a day of murderous riots, when some fifty Europeans were brutally massacred.

Clearly the time had come to suppress Arabi by force. Since France —suspected of plotting an agreement with the nationalists—now refused to cooperate, the task fell on Britain alone. This forced a reversal in the policy of Gladstone, as the more forceful elements in the British Cabinet induced him to intervene with drastic action. The British admiral Seymour was instructed to demand the cessation of work by Arabi on the erection of forts at Alexandria, which were aimed against the two fleets. On the rejection of his demand the admiral exceeded his instructions by bombarding the city. The French refused to take part in the bombardment, and withdrew their naval squadron soon afterward—to the relish of Abdul Hamid, convinced that his empire would forever be preserved through such dissensions between the major Christian powers. Meanwhile, Arabi was declared a rebel by the khedive, who proclaimed a holy war against him.

Earlier, the British and French governments had convoked a conference of the powers in Istanbul, to seek a solution to the Egyptian crisis with the Sultan's cooperation. The Sultan refused to join in the conference, evading the issue by sending two separate commissioners with contradictory instructions to Egypt, where neither achieved anything. Without his representation, the conference discussed the need for armed intervention to keep order in Egypt, and invited him to send troops for the purpose. When, after three weeks of "fatuous and occult devices," he eventually agreed to appoint a representative, it was too late to delay the planned bombardment of Alexandria—a course of action which again he could not imagine that Britain would take without his consent.

It now remained for Britain alone, without French support—hence at the eventual expense of the Anglo-French dual control—"to endeavour," in Gladstone's words, "to convert the present state of Egypt from anarchy and conflict to peace and order." His government planned only a temporary occupation of Egypt, to secure its future good government. While military preparations proceeded, over the next two months, Lord Dufferin, ambassador to the Porte, persisted in his efforts to persuade the Sultan to make it a joint occupation, through the dispatch with the British force of a Turkish detachment. This could vindicate his sovereign rights over Egypt and at the same time confirm Britain's respect for the integrity and independence of his empire. A military convention to this effect was negotiated and drawn up for the Sultan's signature. But Abdul Hamid, apparently under the illusion that Britain would not venture to act without him, delayed this agreement through persistent objections and minute alterations in the text, dragging on until the crucial moment at which Lord Granville, the British foreign secretary, was able, in a dispatch to his ambassador, to presume that "the emergency having passed, His Majesty would not now consider it necessary to send troops to Egypt."

For on that day, September 13, 1882, General Sir Garnet Wolseley, having previously reached Alexandria, transported a British expeditionary force down the Suez Canal to Ismailia, whence it moved inland, totally to destroy the Egyptian army of Arabi in the battle of Tel-el-Kebir. Next day a British cavalry force entered Cairo. Yet again Sultan Abdul Hamid had missed his chance, to his own humiliation and rage, against Britain, but to the relief of the khedive, who now made a triumphant reentry into his capital. The Sultan had yet to adjust himself to the marked differences in tempo between Eastern and Western diplomacy.

* * *

It was from the outset Britain's genuine intention, as agreed by both parties, to withdraw her forces from Egypt as soon as it became possible to establish a stable native administration, still under Turkish sovereignty. While Abdul Hamid intrigued through his agents in Cairo against British rule, Lord Dufferin drew up a plan for the introduction into the country of a measure of Egyptian self-government, while the British military authorities discussed a timetable for the evacuation within two or three years. When a Conservative government came to power in 1885, Lord Salisbury as Prime Minister dispatched Sir Henry Drummond-Wolff on a special mission to Istanbul. His task was to seek, still in a spirit of Anglo-Turkish friendship, an agreement between the two countries, to their mutual interest, which would confirm the Sultan's rights over Egypt while still preserving British influence.

A preliminary convention was soon agreed for the dispatch of British and Turkish commissioners to Egypt, to supervise the reform of its army and administration. But some time was to elapse before the start of serious negotiations. These led in 1887 to the signature of an Anglo-Turkish convention, subject to ratification by the two respective sovereigns. Under this it was agreed that, unless prevented by some serious internal or external danger to Egypt, the British government would withdraw its forces within three years, with an indefinite right to reenter the country if it were threatened by invasion or domestic disorder. The withdrawal was to be accompanied by an international guarantee of Egyptian neutrality, and thus depended on the acceptance by the European powers of the agreed terms of the convention.

In view of its implied special status in Egypt for Britain, it was now violently opposed by France, whose ambassador at the Porte put pressure on the Sultan, in menacing concert with his Russian colleague, to refuse his consent. Thus intimidated, Abdul Hamid refused —once again at the eleventh hour—to ratify the convention on Turkey's behalf. Sir Henry Drummond-Wolff left for England with his task unfulfilled, and the British occupation of Egypt continued, untroubled by plans for an early withdrawal.

Abdul Hamid, who at first seems to have prided himself on a diplomatic victory against Britain, soon came to realize that he had in fact committed a serious blunder. He thus sent a request to Lord Salisbury for the reopening of the negotiations. The Prime Minister politely but firmly declined. Attempts to secure British withdrawal by Turkey, France, and Russia over the next five years came to nothing, and the problems inherent in an Anglo-Egyptian administration of Egypt became such as to preclude it.

Control of the country, with a naval base at Alexandria, had become increasingly necessary. For the Eastern Question had changed its direction. The axis of the international struggle for power had shifted from Turkey to Egypt, from the Bosporus to the Suez Canal, from the Near to the Far East. The direct threat from the Russian to the Ottoman Empire and the consequent danger, which had persisted for a century past, of its encroachment through the Balkans or the Straits on the Mediterranean, now diminished as the Russians, in their imperial designs, looked farther eastward into Asia. This in turn shifted the hazards of an Anglo-Russian confrontation to the frontiers of India, thus giving greater importance to the sea-lanes which Egypt now commanded. Egypt was in effect now commanded by Britain. For 270 years it had been part of the Ottoman Empire. But now Sultan Abdul Hamid had relinquished the last semblance of Turkish authority over it.

In his despotic isolation the Sultan, possessed by delusions as to his own infallibility in outwitting the foreigner, had consistently denied himself the benefits of wise, trustworthy counsel. Through a combination of bad faith and obtuse diplomacy he had lost one opportunity after another in his conduct of foreign affairs. Of this Egypt had furnished a glaring example. Here, despite Britain's consistent goodwill and encouragement, Abdul Hamid had remained obdurate in his refusal to serve his own interests and those of his empire. In relinquishing his rights over Bulgaria, the gateway to his surviving Balkan possessions, his passive inclinations had doubtless been based on the more realistic conclusion that his empire in the West was doomed and its final loss could only be a matter of time. But his abandonment of Egypt was at once needless and injudicious.

Though his sovereignty over it was in secular terms now formal and largely symbolic, Egypt was in religious terms a symbol of cardinal importance to the general policy which Abdul Hamid now sought to pursue. For in turning away from the remnants of his empire in Christian Europe, he had turned, with hopes of recovery or at least of survival, toward his Moslem empire in Asia, whose widespread dominions remained largely intact. He was switching his center of gravity eastward, in the direction of Islam. Asia was the cradle not only of his race and of his dynasty, but also of his religion and that of the great mass of his people. Their Sultan was the defender not only of their lands and their lives but of their Faith.

Hence the significance of Egypt. For Cairo had for more than a thousand years been a great spiritual center of Islam, and for some centuries preceding the Turkish occupation the seat of its Caliphate. A tradition prevailed that on his entry into Cairo in 1517 the Ottoman conqueror Selim I was formally recognized as caliph, by the last heir of the Abbasid Caliphate, later receiving the homage of the sherif of Mecca to become guardian of the holy places of Islam. This implied

The Hippodrome in Istanbul, a legacy of the Byzantine Empire. By the dawn of the nineteenth century, there was little evidence of its original use. Instead the "square," forming an irregular quadrangle about 260 yards long and 150 wide, had been transformed into an informal marketplace. Note the beautiful Sultanahmet Mosque at left, the column of Constantinople (or Theodosius) and the Egyptian Obelisk, and the quaint Ottoman architecture of the buildings on the right.

Melling, *Voyage pittoresque.*

for the house of Osman the spiritual leadership of the whole Moslem world. Istanbul became widely—if questionably—acknowledged as the Abode of the Caliphate and the City of Islam, or "Islambol." Every Ottoman Sultan had, in his dual temporal and spiritual capacity, since styled himself Sultan-Caliph. Acceptance of the rights of this claim was far from general among Moslem powers. But it was through the instrument of the Caliphate that Abdul Hamid now sought to reassert the power and prestige of the house of Osman, not only in his own Asiatic dominions, but in the Islamic world as a whole. It was thus an ill-chosen moment gratuitously to sacrifice his temporal sovereignty over Egypt, the very source of that spiritual sovereignty which he derived from the Caliphate.

Abdul Hamid's reorientation of policy reflected a general reaction throughout the Islamic world against Western and Russian imperialism, with its increasing domination of Moslem territories, from North Africa to Central Asia and India. Turkey became a rallying point for its victims, who were encouraged to revere Abdul Hamid as a ruler who had broken free of the West. They saw besides that his empire was still, in the words of Arnold Toynbee, "by far and away the most powerful, efficient and enlightened Moslem state in existence." Following the failure of the Tanzimat reformers to resolve the conflict inherent in the duality of state and religion, Abdul Hamid had swept it away with his own single absolutist rule. Reinforcing it with those instruments of power which were afforded by modern technical science, he pretended to a form of "constitutional absolutism," imposing such reforms as he chose, still in the tradition of the Tanzimat, mainly at the center and for the benefit of an increasingly bureaucratic elite.

In the eyes of the mass of his subjects he had reestablished a strong, traditional Islamic regime, freed from foreign interference and influence, which they could understand and respect as their own. In their Sultan-Caliph his people recognized those personal qualities of austerity, sobriety, and piety which as Moslems, inspired by a Puritanical spirit, they were proud to respect. For the rest he was loyally supported not only by his own ministers and governing establishment but by such forces outside it as the ulema. Loyal to him too was a proliferating class of "men of religion," at various levels, respected in the name of Islamic unity whether as descendants of the Prophet or otherwise; also the scholars and mystics of the less orthodox colleges and dervish convents, several of whose orders were especially favoured throughout his dominions.

In the isolation of his capital Abdul Hamid turned all eyes away from the West, as a remote and alien world. Its misguided political views and institutions and actions were sternly ignored by his censored press. His intelligentsia were indoctrinated with a belief in the superior culture of a medieval Islamic past. The Young Ottomans, in relating their plans for reform and modernization to the institutions of Islam, had admitted that they were in fact derived from the West. Abdul Hamid admitted no such thing. The Hamidian line was that Arab civilization was the source of European civilization, which took over from Islam not only its constitutional system but Arab science and technology—algebra, chemistry, and physics; such modern inventions as the compass and gunpowder; literature and the writing of history; everything indeed that was admired in the West. What then did the Moslems require from Europe, apart from a few inventions of their own upon which Europe had since tried to improve? A book repeating this thesis opened with the words, "The bases of contemporary civilization are nothing but the actions and traditions of Mohammed."

Such was a message that appealed to the Islamic world as a whole—a message later to be rationalized in terms of the ephemeral concept of Pan-Islamism. Here in the Ottoman Empire, still unimpaired in its Asiatic dominions, was a focal power to which Moslems could turn in their quest for reassurance, inspiration, and leadership. From the earliest years of his reign Abdul Hamid had envisaged such a role for himself and for his empire. Now, withdrawing back into that Anatolian heartland from which the Turks had first crossed into Europe, he enacted it with diligence, through widening contacts with those various Islamic communities which lay both within and beyond its far-flung frontiers.

Abdul Hamid had first revealed his Islamic policy through his earlier appointment as Grand Vezir not of a Turk, as was the normal practice, or one of his own direct subjects, but a Circassian statesman, General Khair-ed-Din, who had earned distinction as chief minister of the bey of Tunis. The Sultan explained his departure from precedent by boldly proclaiming, in the relevant firman, his right as caliph to the services of all Sunni Moslems throughout Islam. He took increasing pains, in this context, to give preference in his administration and at his court to the employment not only of Moslems rather than Christians, but to Moslems of other races in his empire rather than Turks. Arab sheikhs from far afield were especially honoured with their own quarters in the imperial Seraglio. More and more the Sultan set himself to woo Moslem loyalty by concerning himself at home with the problems of Arabs, Kurds, Albanians, and other Moslems on the Christian marches of his empire, and abroad by displaying a solicitous interest in the Moslem peoples of countries farther afield. The former Sick Man of Europe, back within his Islamic frontiers, now aspired to be the Strong Man of Asia. But in so doing he was to antagonize Europe and the civilized world of the West more than ever before. For within those frontiers there still thrived a large Christian minority which he increasingly mistrusted and treated as an obstacle to all his designs—the Armenian people.

Armenia, geographically situated between East and West, at the confluence of warring imperialist tides, had lost its national independence five hundred years earlier. Now the bulk of its Christian population was divided between Turkey, Russia, and Persia, with no surviving Armenian state to which it could turn for protection. The Armenian population of the Ottoman Empire amounted to some two and a half million, of whom more than a million and a half had lands in its six eastern provinces, or vilayets. But in none of them did the Armenians enjoy a majority. Within their own homeland they lived everywhere as a religious minority among Moslems. The Armenians were no race of fighters, as the oppressed Christian minorities of the Balkans had been. Until the latter part of the nineteenth century their peasantry had remained politically quiescent, earning a reputation for sobriety and thrift, like their brethren in the business communities of the cities.

Nonetheless, as an Aryan race loyal to their religion and language and culture, they were a people of strong national pride. They felt themselves to be Europeans, and as time went on came to benefit from a Western education, not only in Catholic Europe itself but now here in the East, at the hands of American Protestant missionaries. Kindling nationalist sentiment, this prompted their dispatch to the Congress of Berlin of an Armenian delegation, requesting the appointment of a Christian governor-general—as in the Lebanon since its autonomy in 1861—to serve their interests in these eastern provinces. Though this met with no response, the European powers acknowledged the need of the Armenians for local improvements and reforms in their provinces, and for guarantees of their security against the Circassians and Kurds. Under the terms of the Berlin Treaty the Porte was obliged to carry these into effect, and periodically to report the steps it took to the powers, who would superintend their application.

But Abdul Hamid was obdurate in his refusal to implement any such promises. His sole concession was to appoint to each of the Armenian provinces a Christian subgovernor, who was in effect no more than the Sultan's puppet—obeying his orders, subject to instant dismissal if he were to venture on steps or proposals of his own, and becoming known ironically as Evet Effendi, otherwise "Mr. Yes," for his meek compliance with his master's wishes. It was soon clear that Abdul Hamid had no intention under any circumstances of carrying out any such reforms as the Berlin Treaty prescribed, certainly not at the behest of the foreign ambassadors who sought thus to interfere with his sovereignty; least of all to ameliorate the lot of the Armenians, whom he thus came to regard with obsessive fear and malevolence. It became a notorious fact that whenever representatives from a foreign ambassador achieved the dismissal of an official for such an offense as ill-treatment of Armenians, the Sultan invariably promoted him to a higher and more lucrative post.

Under the terms of the Cyprus Convention, with its similar undertakings to Britain alone, the British government sent consuls to these eastern provinces, whose reports confirmed the injustices endured by the Armenians in Turkish courts, and the gross discrimination against them in the assessment and collection of taxes and tithes by the corrupt Turkish and provincial authorities. Moreover, in those remoter districts where Turkish authority was less effective, the Armenians suffered from ruthless exactions at the hands of the powerful Kurdish chieftains and from depredations by their marauding tribesmen. Such disorder called for restraint of the Kurds through a reorganized police and gendarmerie. But British government protests were met by the Porte with a mere smoke screen of verbiage. Necessary measures, it was pretended, were in fact being taken, through the dispatch of competent officials in Kurdistan, thus ensuring security to these and other "faithful subjects of the Sultan." But it was added that "whenever misdemeanours—which naturally occur in every country of the world—happen to be committed in Armenia, some over-zealous people appear to take it upon themselves to invent imaginary crimes in addition to the real offences, and to represent them before the eyes of Europe and the consuls on the spot as having actually occurred."

This blandly evasive response provoked, in 1880, a collective note from the ambassadors of the six treaty powers, voicing criticism and demanding specific reforms "to secure the life and property of the Armenians." To this the Porte again made an equivocal reply, not even deigning to refer to the specified points at issue. Sultan Abdul Hamid, in his implacable ill will to the foreigner, was now avenging defeats in the field and at the conference table with an adamant refusal to countenance, within his own frontiers, foreign support for these remaining Christian subjects. Nor, it became clear, was there any effective step, short of armed intervention, which the powers could take on their behalf. Lord Salisbury, forced to admit the failure of the powers to implement their guarantee, expressed regret that he "could not sail the Fleet across the Taurus mountains." Gladstone, returning to power, fared no better, first reducing the special status of his military consuls, then abolishing them altogether. Measures of reform by the Turks were described in a consular report as a "perfect farce," while many of their local officials could neither read nor write.

In 1882 a further effort was made by the powers to gain acceptance for a reform plan. But this time it was thwarted from within their own ranks by Bismarck, who expressed readiness to cooperate with the British on any issue except that of pressing Armenian reforms on the Sultan. This was a refusal to which Gladstone deferred. The Armenians themselves tried in vain to achieve measures of reform by peaceful means, making it clear to the Turks that they sought no political autonomy but only personal security. They declared that they had no wish to pass under the rule of the Russians, who in any event did not encourage them to do so. For they were seeking to impose the Russian Orthodox faith on their own Armenian subjects, and so to neutralize their national consciousness. Thus for the remainder of the decade the condition of the Armenians continued to worsen, at the hands of their predatory Moslem neighbours and of the Sultan's hostile government.

Clearly the time had now come for the Armenians in Turkey to organize themselves on some kind of political basis. They began to form local nationalist groups and secret societies, gaining an impetus from their fellow Armenians in Russia, mainly in the Caucasus, whose concepts of revolution, at once socialist and anarchist, were well in advance of their own. Soon they were spreading across the frontier to such centers as Erzurum and Van, with the aim of rousing Turkish Armenians to the defense of their natural "homeland."

In 1881 an organization named the Protectors of the Fatherland was thus formed in Erzurum. Its object was to defend the Armenian population against the Kurds and Turks, and its revolutionary motto was "Liberty or Death!" The first effective Armenian political party, founded in Van in 1885, was that of the Armenagans, whose ideas were spread through liberal channels abroad, leading to the formation in London of the Armenian Patriotic Society of Europe. Their explicit objective was to "win for the Armenians the right to rule over themselves, through revolution." But their outlook was overmoderate, and they still relied, somewhat ingenuously, on the great powers to further their aims. In 1887 a more ruthless organization was formed by Armenian émigrés, on Marxist lines, in Geneva. Developing into the first revolutionary socialist party in the Ottoman Empire, its objective was the establishment through revolution of a unified Armenian socialist state, carved out of Turkish territory. Its mouthpiece was a journal, published abroad, named *Hunchak,* or "Bell," which gave to the party its resounding name.

The Hunchaks were an international movement with widespread links in the capitals of Europe, together with agents as far afield as America. But it was in practice at home here in the Caucasus that such rebel groups proved the more active, with the organization of raids into Ottoman territory and gestures of defiance by Hunchaks against Ottoman authority, not only in Erzurum, "the capital of Turkish Armenia," but as far westward as Istanbul and the other urban centers of Turkey. These activities culminated in the foundation in Tiflis, in 1890, of an Armenian Revolutionary Federation, or *Dashnaktsutium,* whose adherents became known as Dashnaks. At first they combined together the various radical groups. Soon, however, the Dashnaks, ideologically more nationalist than socialist, split with the Hunchaks, but for the overriding general aim of an armed struggle for Armenian freedom. "The Armenian," they went so far as to proclaim, "is no longer imploring. He now demands, with gun in hand." No longer prepared to await help from the powers, which was not to materialize, he took the destiny of his race into his own hands.

Alarmed at this insubordination of his Armenian subjects, whose cleverness had long aroused his mistrust, Abdul Hamid responded with the sly policy of exploiting the differences between Moslem and Christian. Using the Kurds as a deliberate instrument of division and rule, he sanctioned their attacks on the Armenians by starting, in 1891, to recruit an armed force of irregulars from among the Kurdish tribesmen. Named the Hamidiye, the "men of the Sultan," they were formed into cavalry regiments which by the end of 1892 comprised in all some fifteen thousand men, and which continued to increase year by year. In their gaudy uniforms these wild men from the east were soon attracting uneasy attention as they swaggered through the Christian quarters of Istanbul. In Armenia they spread fear through the open avowal that their official task was to suppress the Armenians, and that they were assured of legal immunity for any acts of oppression against the Christian population.

Meanwhile, in 1893 the Armenian revolutionaries went beyond mere raids with a plot to stir up a Moslem revolt, in central and western Anatolia. They launched it by posting seditious placards on the walls of the towns and by calling upon all Moslems to rise against the Sultan's oppressive rule. Of this ingenuous conspiracy the only effect was the arrest and imprisonment of large numbers of Armenians throughout Anatolia. Here was a serious setback to organized Armenian resistance. But such threats of disorder served as a pretext, in 1894, for an atrocious campaign of massacre, launched by the Sultan's orders.

In the region of Sasun, south of Mush, the exactions of the Kurdish chieftains had evolved into an organized system of tribute by blackmail, paid for their protection by the Armenian population. On top of this the Turkish authorities now chose to demand payment of arrears of government tax—which in the circumstances had for some years been tacitly remitted. When the Armenians refused to submit to this double exaction, Turkish troops were called into the area, in close concert with the Kurdish tribesmen. Soon they were indiscriminately slaughtering the helpless Armenians. The soldiers pursued them throughout the length and breadth of the region, hunting them "like wild beasts" up the valleys and into the mountains, respecting no surrender, bayoneting the men to death, raping the women, dashing their children against the rocks, burning to ashes the villages from which they had fled. For this operation the Turkish commander, Zeki Pasha, was awarded an appropriate gratuity by the Sultan.

Leakage of the news of these first Armenian massacres, which the Porte had hoped to brush aside as a trifling incident, aroused strong liberal protests throughout Europe, prompting demands by the three powers—Britain, France, and Russia—for a commission of enquiry. This was duly appointed by the Sultan, in 1895, "to enquire into the criminal conduct of Armenian brigands"—thus hoping to preempt further investigation and prove the Porte's version of events. Following this mockery of justice the powers, reinforced by mass meetings in London and Paris, put forward a scheme for Armenian reform, which the Sultan made a show of accepting in a watered-down version, with a profusion of unfulfilled paper promises.

Meanwhile, the Armenians themselves, led by the Hunchaks, staged a demonstration as they marched through the city of Istanbul to present a petition to the Porte, voicing their protests and demands for reform. Despite counsels of patience from their Patriarch, the demonstrators got out of hand when one of them (from Sasun) shouted "Liberty or Death!" The cry was taken up by the rest, breaking into a revolutionary song and provoking intervention by the police, who bludgeoned many of them to death on the spot. Meanwhile, the fanatical Moslem elements, without police intervention, ran wild through the streets, routing out Armenians and slaughtering them with clubs. There followed ten days of violence and terror, from which Armenians by the thousand took refuge in their churches, persuaded to emerge only by guarantees for their safety from the foreign embassies, on condition that they lay down their arms.

This coincided with the news, from the captain of a foreign vessel, of a great massacre in Trebizond. Powerless, he had watched as Armenian fugitives, swimming out to his ship, were knocked on the head by Moslem boatmen or forced underwater till they drowned. Nearly a thousand had been killed in the town, many of them burned in their houses, when an armed force of Turks, with indigenous Laz tribesmen from the mountains, broke into the Armenian quarter and for five hours kept up a murderous fusillade, despoiling and subsequently gutting by fire the Armenian shops in the market.

This heralded throughout eastern Turkey a series of organized massacres, coinciding with the Sultan's pretended acceptance of a new plan from the powers for Armenian reform. A telltale feature of them all was that they began and ended, as a matter of routine, with a bugle call, like any planned military operation. For such indeed they were. Here were no fortuitous police measures, forced on the authorities by outbreaks among the Sultan's Armenian subjects. Here on the contrary was an official campaign by force of arms against the Armenians as against any foreign enemy, calculated and conducted in response to his orders, closely coordinated among his military forces in the Armenian centers of the six eastern provinces.

Their tactics were based on the Sultan's principle of kindling religious fanaticism among the Moslem population. Abdul Hamid briefed agents, whom he sent to Armenia with specific instructions as to how they should act. It became their normal routine first to assemble the Moslem population in the largest mosque in a town, then to declare, in the name of the Sultan, that the Armenians were in general revolt with the aim of striking at Islam. Their Sultan enjoined them as good Moslems to defend their faith against these infidel rebels. He propounded the precept that under the holy law the property of rebels might be looted by believers, encouraging Moslems to enrich themselves in the name of their faith at the expense of their Christian neighbours, and in the event of resistance, to kill them. Hence, throughout Armenia, "the attack of an ever increasing pack of wolves against sheep."

On the other hand Abdul Hamid so perverted a further Moslem principle as to offer his enemies, at the point of the bayonet, the choice between death and forcible conversion to Islam—a practice previously renounced, under British pressure, by Sultan Abdul Mejid. It was an alternative preferred by those families in the villages who lacked the true spirit of resistance, for all the consequent sacrifice of their independent identity as members of a Christian community.

The conduct of these operations was placed in the hands of Shakir Pasha, one of the Sultan's more sinister advisers, who had once served him as ambassador in St. Petersburg. His ostensible post was that of "inspector of certain localities in the provinces of Asiatic Turkey" in connection with the Sultan's own pretended reform plans. Under this cover his actual role was the planning and execution of massacres in each specified locality. Their objective, based on the convenient consideration that Armenians were now tentatively starting to question their inferior status, was the ruthless reduction, with a view to elimination, of the Armenian Christians, and the expropriation of their lands for the Moslem Turks.

Each operation, between the bugle calls, followed a similar pattern. First into a town there came the Turkish troops, for the purpose of massacre; then came the Kurdish irregulars and tribesmen for the purpose of plunder. Finally came the holocaust, by fire and destruction, which spread, with the pursuit of fugitives and mopping-up operations, throughout the lands and villages of the surrounding province. This murderous winter of 1895 thus saw the decimation of much of the Armenian population and the devastation of their property in some twenty distinct districts of eastern Turkey. Often the massacres were timed for a Friday, when the Moslems were in their mosques and the myth was spread by the authorities that the Armenians conspired to slaughter them at prayer. Instead they were themselves slaughtered, when the Moslems emerged to forestall their design. The total number of victims was somewhere between fifty and a hundred thousand, allowing for those who died subsequently of wounds, disease, exposure, and starvation.

In each of thirteen large towns the numbers of those dead ran well into four figures. In Erzurum, the bazaar of a thousand shops was looted and wrecked by the Moslems, while some three hundred Christians were buried the next day in a single massed grave.

Cruellest and most ruinous of all were the massacres at Urfa, where the Armenian Christians numbered a third of the total population. Here in December, 1895, after a two-months siege of their quarter, the leading Armenians assembled in their cathedral, where they drew up a statement requesting Turkish official protection. Promising this, the Turkish officer in charge surrounded the cathedral with troops. Then a large body of them, with a mob in their wake, rushed through the Armenian quarter, where they plundered all houses and slaughtered all adult males above a certain age. When a large group of young Armenians were brought before a sheikh, he had them thrown down on their backs and held by their hands and feet. Then, in the words of an observer, he recited verses of the Koran and "cut their throats after the Mecca rite of sacrificing sheep."

When the bugle blast ended the day's operations some three thousand refugees poured into the cathedral, hoping for sanctuary. But the next morning—a Sunday—a fanatical mob swarmed into the church in an orgy of slaughter, rifling its shrines with cries of "Call upon Christ to prove Himself a greater prophet than Mohammed." Then they amassed a large pile of straw matting, which they spread over the litter of corpses and set alight with thirty cans of petroleum. The woodwork of the gallery where a crowd of women and children crouched, wailing with terror, caught fire, and all perished in the flames. Punctiliously, at three-thirty in the afternoon the bugle blew once more, and the Moslem officials proceeded around the Armenian quarter to proclaim that the massacres were over. They had wiped out 126 complete families, without a woman or a baby surviving, and the total casualties in the town, including those slaughtered in the cathedral, amounted to eight thousand dead.

Only in one place were the Armenians themselves the aggressors. This was in the mountain fastness of Zeitun, in the former province of Cilicia, where a force of Armenians with a strong nucleus of Hunchaks took the offensive. They defeated a Turkish force in battle, ejected the Turkish garrison from the citadel of Zeitun, captured four hundred Turkish prisoners, and changing into Turkish uniforms, looted and burned a neighbouring Turkish town, thus obtaining a wide measure of control over the district. The Turks finally advanced with a large force on Zeitun, bombarding its citadel after the Armenians had evacuated it and setting it on fire. But meanwhile the Armenian community in Istanbul had appealed for mediation by the foreign ambassadors, and it was agreed with the authorities that all in the district, whether Turk or Armenian, should surrender their arms, with a view to an amnesty.

In August, 1896, the succession of Armenian massacres culminated in Istanbul itself. Once again, as in the previous year, the Turkish authorities were presented with a pretext for action by an Armenian revolutionary group. A small body of Dashnaks was so bold as to enter the Ottoman Bank, the stronghold of European capitalist enterprise, during the lunch hour, for the ostensible purpose of changing money. Porters accompanying them carried sacks which contained, so they pretended, gold and silver coinage. Then at the blast of a whistle twenty-five armed men followed them into the bank, firing their guns and revealing that the sacks in fact were filled with bombs, ammunition, and dynamite. They declared that they were not bank robbers but Armenian patriots, and that the motive of their action was to bring their grievances, which they specified in two documents, to the attention of the six European embassies, putting forward demands for political reform and declaring that, in the absence of foreign intervention within forty-eight hours, they would "shrink from no sacrifice" and blow up the bank.

Meanwhile, its chief director, Sir Edgar Vincent, had prudently escaped through a skylight into an adjoining building. While his colleagues were held as hostages, he thence proceeded to the Sublime Porte. Here he ensured that no police attack should be made on the Dashnaks while they remained in the bank. Thus he secured for them permission to negotiate. The negotiator was the First Dragoman of the Russian embassy, who after gaining for them a free pardon from the Sultan and permission to leave the country, addressed them at length with some eloquence. Finally, with assurances of talks to come, he persuaded them to leave the bank. Retaining their arms but relinquishing their bombs, they proceeded quietly on board Sir Edgar Vincent's yacht, later to be conveyed into exile in France.

As young men of ideals inexperienced in the wiles of political agitation, they had failed to benefit their friends and had played into the hands of their enemies. For two days the streets ran with blood as gangs of undisciplined ruffians, religious fanatics, and savage irregulars raged through the Armenian quarter of the capital, brandishing murderous cudgels and knives and iron bars. Without interference from the police or the soldiery, and indeed with their evident connivance and help, they bludgeoned to death any Armenian who crossed their path, breaking into houses to kill all that hid there, and leaving, strewn everywhere, a total of some six thousand corpses. On the second day of the massacre, the representatives of the six powers delivered protests to the Porte. These were at first disregarded. But in the evening a report that the British were landing marines to protect their own nationals resulted in orders for the killing to stop. At last the ambassadors, here on their own doorsteps, could see with their own eyes the true horror of those iniquities long perpetrated through the whole of Armenia, which the double-faced Sultan, behind the deceits of his official censorship, had sought to conceal from the world. An open telegram was now sent to him by the representatives of all the six powers, publicly demanding an immediate end to the massacre, with the threat that "its continuance meant danger to his throne and dynasty."

After it had ceased they presented the first of a series of collective notes to the Sublime Porte. In a detailed recital of evidence they established the fact that the "disturbances in Istanbul" were no spontaneous fanatical outbreak but the product of a special force, "springing up under the eyes of the authorities and with the co-operation of certain of the latter's agents." Here was "an exceedingly dangerous weapon," which might at any time be used against any of the foreign colonies, or indeed "even turn against those who tolerated its creation." The representatives of the powers thus demanded of the Porte that "the origin of this organization should be sought out, and that the instigators and principal actors should be discovered and punished with the utmost vigour." They offered to facilitate such an inquiry by the submission of evidence by eyewitnesses. In diplomatic language, they were in fact implying that Abdul Hamid was the author or at least the instigator of the Istanbul massacre. Their notes thus met with evasive replies, referring to attacks by Armenians on Moslems, and promising that both would be tried by a special tribunal. They sought to placate the powers through arrests among those dregs of the population that had obediently served the Sultan's ends.

Meanwhile, Liberal opinion in Britain had been aroused once more to a pitch of fever, crying for the Sultan's dethronement. Mr. Gladstone, at the age of eighty-six, emerged from retirement to make at Liverpool a last great speech against the "unspeakable Turk," whose empire deserved to be "rubbed off the map" as a "disgrace to civilization" and a "curse to mankind." He branded the Sultan as "Abdul the Great Assassin," while the French pilloried him as "The Red

Sultan." He insisted on Britain's duty, under the Cyprus Convention, to intervene against the Sublime Porte, if necessary alone. Though at first there was talk of forcing the Dardanelles with the British fleet, it soon became evident that no power was prepared to use force on behalf of the Armenians or even to threaten it, beyond Lord Salisbury's admonitory hint to Abdul Hamid of the "ultimate fate of misgoverned countries."

Though Salisbury canvassed Russian support for the Sultan's deposition, he would not pay the price of concessions with regard to the Straits; nor did Russia relish the idea of an independent Armenia, filling in Asia Minor the role of the new Bulgaria in Europe. Austria-Hungary was too much involved in the Balkans to risk action. France, with her Ottoman investments, preferred the *status quo*. Germany, in the hope of concessions in Asia Minor, retained the role of the Sultan's protector. Ideas for a partition of the Ottoman Empire or for some form of international control of its territory thus came to nothing. After the failure of a final conference in 1897, to agree on the imposition on the Porte of a final reform scheme, no more was done to help the luckless Armenians.

Once again disunity and indecision among the European powers gave the dwindling Ottoman Empire a further brief lease of life. Abdul Hamid's implacable obstinacy had won him a negative victory over the West. But the cold inhumanity of his actions had earned for him eternal disgrace in the eyes of the civilized world.

((38))

Among the European powers only one consistent ally now courted the Sultan's favour. This was Germany. Though Bismarck had for some twenty years past kept an assiduous eye on the Ottoman Empire, this had reflected no positive designs for German expansion at Turkish expense. It was aimed rather at assuming some share of the dwindling political influence of Britain. Otherwise he had been guarded in his Eastern commitments. Having served as "honest broker" at the Berlin Congress, Bismarck saw the role of the German Empire as that of arbiter of Europe, the dominant partner in an alliance with the Austro-Hungarian empire and the Balkan states. Here its main interest lay in the maintenance of a balance of power with Russia. In such a concept the Ottoman Empire played no relevant part: the Eastern Question, as Bismarck saw it, was "not worth the bones of a single Pomeranian grenadier."

But Kaiser Wilhelm II, who succeeded to the imperial throne in 1888, had more extravagant ambitions and dreams. Encouraged by Marshal von der Goltz, who with a team of German officers had for five years past been training the Turkish army and modernizing it with arms and equipment made in Germany, the Kaiser planned further infiltration on a widespread scale. Asiatic Turkey should become a major sphere of German influence, not only in the strategic but in the economic, commercial, and technical fields. Soon, dismissing Bismarck—who deplored any such Pan-Germanic moves beyond the frontiers of Europe—Kaiser Wilhelm launched into an ambitious *Drang nach Osten*. Its chief German instrument was to be the Baghdad Railway, a line planned ultimately to link Berlin with the Persian Gulf. This fitted in with Abdul Hamid's own plans now in progress for the construction of this and of other railways in general, together with roads and telegraphic communications, linking together his far-flung Asiatic dominions and thus facilitating at once their administrative control and their economic development.

For the construction of the railway, in a series of stages, a concession was granted by the Sultan to the Deutsche Bank group. This was to lead, through the last decade of the nineteenth century, to an influx into the Ottoman Empire of German financiers, merchants, engineers, and experts in all such fields. Meanwhile, despite Bismarck's opposition, it led in the year following his accession to an official visit by Kaiser Wilhelm II to Sultan Abdul Hamid II in Istanbul. The Sultan—who had for some time past been transferring treasury bonds of his own into the neutral security of German banks—found every reason to smile upon the German race. Now he welcomed their emperor and his empress with true imperial hospitality. To house them he built, within the grounds of Yildiz, a large decorative kiosk which amounted in effect to a small palace. He entertained them at a sumptuous state banquet, regaling them with European dishes served on bejewelled gold plates from Paris. When the empress was presented by the Sultan with a bouquet of flowers from the palace garden, she found a substantial diamond nestling amid their petals.

Nine years later Kaiser Wilhelm paid a second official visit to the Sultan's dominions, where the Baghdad Railway had now reached as far as Konya, in the center of Anatolia; where a German steamship service now operated between Hamburg and Istanbul; and where everywhere German exports to Turkey and Turkish exports to Germany were booming, to the profit of all strata of the Anatolian population. To Abdul Hamid the Kaiser was now doubly welcome, since Germany, alone among the powers, had refrained from protesting against his recent Armenian massacres.

This time the Kaiser extended his visit to other parts of the Ottoman Empire. In the guise of a Christian pilgrim and crusader knight he made a spectacular entry into Jerusalem, where, after praying on his knees in the dust before the Holy City, he inaugurated a Lutheran church. Then, adroitly changing his ground and his costume, he entered the Moslem city of Damascus, where, arrayed in a turban, he paid homage at Saladin's tomb. In implied public endorsement of the Sultan-Caliph's Islamic policies, he promised to all of the three hundred million Moslems the German emperor's eternal protection. He thus readily obtained the concession for the next stage of the Baghdad Railway, from Konya in the direction of the Taurus Mountains and eventually of the Persian Gulf.

The British government, secure now in its possession and control of the Suez Canal, had hitherto shown little concern over the Anatolian railway. But the prospect of its possible extension to Mesopotamia and the Gulf now prompted Lord Curzon, as Viceroy, to negotiate an agreement between the Indian government and the sheikh of Kuwait, at the head of its waters. By this the sheikh agreed to cede no territory and to receive no foreign representative without British consent, while similar restrictions were placed on the sultan of Oman. British interests thus effectively blocked in advance the terminus of the Baghdad Railway, were it ever to be completed. Russia had meanwhile shown concern lest the railway might serve the Turks as a weapon against her in the Caucasus. She thus obliged them to accept a "Black Sea Agreement," by which railway concessions in northern Anatolia would be granted only to Russian interests and to syndicates acceptable to the Tsar.

Directly related to Abdul Hamid's aspiring leadership of the Moslem world was another such hidden project, that of the Hejaz Railway. Starting from Damascus, it was designed to serve all pilgrims to the holy shrines of Medina and Mecca, and so to make the Sultan's prestige as caliph a concrete reality, both within his own territories and beyond them—while at the same time strengthening his political hold over the Arab peoples in the Yemen and elsewhere. As a railway sacred in purpose, it was to be financed exclusively by contributions from the world of Islam and constructed by Moslem labour, including that of the Turkish army—but with the supervision and advice of foreign technicians. Started in 1901, the Hejaz Railway was completed within eight years as far as Medina, enhancing the credit of Ottoman enterprise and inspiring reverence for the caliph in the eyes of Moslems far and wide.

Germany, out of line with the other powers in the zealous pursuit of her own exclusive interests, studiously avoided condemnation of the Sultan when he flagrantly defaulted on treaty undertakings to his Christian subjects. She had refused support for the Armenians. Now she refused it successively for Crete and Macedonia, for which the rest of Europe sought the implementation of promised reforms. The island of Crete had been restive under Turkish oppression, erupting into periodic revolts from the Greek War of Independence onward. Since it was composed of a large Christian Greek-speaking majority, it might well have been incorporated into the kingdom of Greece under the Treaty of Berlin. For it was ruled in the interests of a Moslem minority which amounted to less than 10 percent of the population.

The Sultan was bent on the subjection of this Cretan Christian majority, as of his Armenian Christian minorities. But as a fighting race the Cretans resisted him stoutly. He thus found it politic to appease them at intervals through the appointment of a Christian governor. But his tenure of office was usually brief and a Moslem soon replaced him. The Cretan majority, bent on Christian government, now pressed for annexation to Greece. The Greek government, fearful of war with Turkey, treated its claims with reserve. But when in 1889 an insurrection in the island precipitated a flood of Christian refugees to Athens, popular sympathy induced it to put claims before the Porte for justice and improved government for the Cretans. The Sultan in a firman confirmed previous empty promises and introduced some reforms, which failed to satisfy the Cretans but for the time being calmed the revolt. After further disturbances the Sultan made plans to overrun the island with a force of Moslem irregular troops, as in Bulgaria twenty years earlier.

Thus in 1896 the Christians rose once more in an insurrection—which was in fact to prove their last. Following massacres by Moslems in Canea and the destruction of much of its Christian quarter, this escalated into a civil war between the Christians and the Moslem Cretans, now supported by Moslem troops. The Christians appealed to the powers and proclaimed union with Greece. At this the Greeks sent troops to Crete, first a flotilla of torpedo boats to intercept Turkish reinforcements, then a land force with orders to occupy the island. The admirals of the five powers, whose ships were in Cretan waters, occupied the port of Canea. To the east of them the Germans pressed, with the Russians, for an international blockade to force a Greek withdrawal. But British pressure helped to secure a demand by the five powers for Cretan autonomy, conditional on the withdrawal of all Greek and a large number of Turkish forces. This the Sultan had eventually to accept.

Meanwhile, in Greece itself, popular clamour was calling for war with Turkey. Neither king nor Sultan wanted war, but the hand of the Greek government was forced by its Hellenic nationalist elements. Nationalist bands crossed the frontier into Macedonia and Thessaly and in the spring of 1897 Turkey declared war against Greece. A mere Thirty Days' War, it was a disaster for the Greeks. The Greek navy, though superior to that of the Turks, achieved little—perhaps owing to pressure from the powers. On land the Greek forces fled in disorder from both Epirus and Thessaly. Panic reigned in Athens as the Turks swiftly advanced. But the powers intervened to impose an armistice. Six months later a peace treaty was signed in Istanbul. It inflicted upon the Greeks a substantial financial indemnity. But the Turks withdrew from both Thessaly and Epirus and were content with the cession of a small strip of adjoining territory. At once the Greek dynasty was saved and the prestige of the Sultan raised, after years of defeat, by a military triumph in the field which in fact he owed to the Germans.

The struggle in Crete itself dragged on for a year longer. Germany and Austria, still upholding the Sultan, defected from the concert of the powers in protest at their Philhellenic policy, and removed their own forces of occupation from the island.

The remaining powers sought an appropriate governor for an autonomous Crete, under the Sultan's suzerainty. Following Moslem disturbances which led to the death of the British vice-consul, the powers instructed the Sultan that all Turkish forces must evacuate the island, which they eventually did. Prince George of Greece was installed as governor. Abdul Hamid had effectively lost Crete. Athens rejoiced at the restoration of Cretan freedom for the first time since the Roman conquest, nineteen hundred years earlier.

Of Turkey in Europe only one major province now remained to the Ottoman Empire. This was Macedonia, a focal pivot of the Balkans. The adjoining states of Bulgaria and Serbia had achieved, since their liberation from Turkish rule, notable order and progress. Far from following their example, the province of Macedonia regressed steadily under a government which grew ever more rapacious, corrupt, and incompetent, outdoing all such flagrant misgovernment as had led to the loss of those other provinces. The Turkish troops were left unpaid, becoming a burden to the population on whom they were quartered; justice in the law courts for Christian subjects barely existed, and lawless exactions by Moslems were rife. They had appropriated lands from Christian peasants, who were denied all means of redress. Abdul Hamid did little or nothing to remedy such abuses. They resulted in a continuous emigration of Christians into the adjoining free states, particularly Bulgaria, where nearly one-half of the population of Sofia soon consisted of refugees from beyond the frontier.

Macedonia, epitomizing in miniature the Ottoman Empire itself, was compounded of a polyglot mixture of overlapping races and languages and religions, with imprecise geographical divisions among them, which were in continual conflict at once with each other and with the Turkish provincial government. Across its third frontier lay Greece, whose culture had in the past largely predominated. But the predominance, further weakened by the recent Greco-Turkish war, was now challenged by that of the Slavs, who represented the largest Christian element. Bulgarian national sentiment had lately been acknowledged in Macedonia by the creation of a Bulgarian exarchate, to counterbalance the authority of the Greek Patriarchate. This was now exploited by the Porte to encourage Bulgarian at the expense of Greek influence, and in the course of the 1890's they sanctioned the creation of seven Bulgarian bishops. Meanwhile, the Serbs secured for the first time a bishopric to represent their own Church. Such were the ingredients of a conflict in Macedonia between Greek and Slav, which intensified, with scant prospect of reconciliation, as the nineteenth century drew to a close. It was aggravated by Abdul Hamid's encouragement of the Moslem Albanians to encroach on the lands of Greeks and Slavs alike.

A Macedonian revolutionary organization was formed in Salonika, which called for the autonomy of the province; a rival committee in Sofia called for its annexation by Bulgaria, and in 1895 launched a large-scale raid into Macedonia. Bands of Bulgarian bandits roamed the mountains, attacking Turkish villages and in their turn attacked by Greek bandits, while the Turkish irregular troops fought, as suited them, for either side, with much devastation of the Macedonian countryside. The province was thus gradually relapsing into chaos and anarchy. In 1903 a series of outrages in Salonika led to an organized insurrection, which was suppressed with the aid of Turkish reinforcements from Istanbul.

This at last attracted the positive notice of the powers, as the Slav rebels had designed it to do in the hope of ending Turkish rule. It was indeed generally agreed, by Moslems and Christians alike, "that the provinces of Turkey in Europe cannot be allowed to remain in their deplorable condition," and the Sultan appointed an inspector general to deal with the problem of law and order. The powers themselves proved far from united. Neither Germany nor Austria favoured the prospect of an autonomous Macedonia, at the expense of their ally the Sultan. Austria, together with Russia, had already put forward a proposal for a modest, conservative program of administrative reforms in the province, which did little or nothing to threaten the *status quo*.

Britain on the other hand took up a more positive liberal attitude, proposing reforms which gave more power to the Christian community, under a Christian governor, and involved the withdrawal of the Turkish irregular forces. In conference at Mürzsteg, near Vienna, the Tsar and the Austrian emperor finally agreed to a modified version of the British proposals, by which the Turkish governor should be assisted, in a purely advisory capacity, by two "civil agents," one Russian and one Austrian. A European should command the gendarmerie, and each of the powers should be responsible for policing a specified part of the province, with the revision of administrative boundaries along approximate national lines, and the encouragement within them of local autonomy. In the towns a mixed commission of Moslems and Christians was to decide on local reform measures. But the withdrawal of Turkish forces was rejected by all the six powers save Britain. Otherwise they agreed in supporting the proposals, and instructed their consuls to prepare for their execution.

In view of such unanimity the Sultan could hardly do otherwise than give reluctant acceptance in principle to the Mürzsteg program. But any application of it was continuously delayed and obstructed by the Porte, with perpetual recourse to the pretext of protecting the Sultan's sovereign rights. Insofar as innovations were agreed, they were often so qualified by the Porte as to make them either inacceptable or impracticable. Two years of negotiation and attempted compromise thus passed in which little effective reform was achieved. Indeed, Austria and Germany made little or no effort to further it, acting closely together and not caring, in their own political interests, to put pressure on the Porte or to trespass too far on the Sultan's precious sovereign rights. It became all too evident that Germany and Austria were in fact opposed to any improvement in the situation of Macedonia. It suited both to prolong its survival as a backward province for as long as possible, rather than see the replacement of Turkish rule by that of some more stable international regime. The plan was evolving of an ultimate expansion of Austrian influence to the Aegean and eastward. Of this there was an ominous sign when in 1908 the Austrians demanded from the Porte economic concessions in Macedonia, and in return promised support against European pressure for aid and reform in "all problems affecting the Balkan peninsula."

The British government became all the more positive in its concern to improve conditions in Macedonia. In 1905, while the Mürzsteg program still languished, Britain proposed to the Sultan an international commission, nominated by the powers, under the presidency of the Turkish inspector general and with selected foreign representatives, to frame financial reforms for the province. The Sultan at first refused any such foreign interference, demanding instead an increase in customs duties. But when the powers—with the exception of Germany—joined in a naval demonstration, seizing the customs houses of Mytilene and Lemnos, he yielded, agreeing to recognize four European financial experts sent to cooperate with the Russian and Austrian civil agents in Salonika. But this international commission had no executive powers. In 1908 the British put forward a proposal that the governor of Macedonia, Turkish subject though he was, should be appointed only with the agreement of the powers, and that he should be served by a team of European officers paid from the revenues of the province. This proposal was accepted by both France and Russia, and sealed by an agreement between the Tsar and King Edward VII at Reval, while the provisions of the Mürzsteg program, now functioning within limits, were extended for a further six years.

Meanwhile, however, it was not only the Christian but the Moslem peoples of Macedonia who, in their growing discontent, pressed the Sultan for measures to provide for their security of life and property. His inspector general, Hilmi Pasha, was a man of repute, who formulated projects of basic reform calculated to satisfy Christians and Moslems alike. But Abdul Hamid ignored them as obstinately as he did those of the powers. In the lost province of Crete he had at least sought to further the interests of his own Moslem minority. In Macedonia he had, by his indifference to their welfare, alienated not only his Christian but his Moslem subjects.

Macedonia was a land which at this of all moments in its turbulent history cried out for decisive change, for such elements of progress as would assist it, in the Ottoman interest, to stand on a level with its evolving nationalist neighbors. But Abdul Hamid, hamstrung as it were by a deliberate inertia, adamant in his passive resistance to the foreigner, and inhuman in his neglect of the Moslem people within his own frontiers, persisted in a reactionary regime which was not merely inept but improvident. Ironically, in his fixed determination to turn his face away from Europe, Abdul Hamid was storing up among fellow Moslems in this province of Europe the fuel for an explosion which would rebound to his own undoing.

This was to spring paradoxically from his worthiest achievement—that reform and expansion of the Turkish educational system, both civil and military, which had led within the last generation to the growth of a substantial new middle class. It was among the students of the Sultan's own advanced modern schools that, in opposition to his absolutist rule, the seeds of political freedom began to take root. In 1889, the centenary year of the French Revolution, four medical students in the military medical college in Istanbul founded in secret the first organized opposition group. Forming itself into a number of cells on the model of the Italian Carbonari, as the Young Ottomans had formerly done, it quickly won adherents among cadets in the civil, military, naval, medical, and other higher schools in Istanbul. It established contact with the first organized group of liberal exiles in Paris, where they had been living since Abdul Hamid's suppression of Parliament, and where they had lately been joined by Ahmed Riza, a notable director of education in Bursa, who henceforward devoted himself to this political task.

One of them, a former member of Parliament, had started a journal called *La Jeune Turquie,* thus prompting for the conspirators the name of the Young Turks, while Riza, with other exiles, now published and smuggled through the foreign post offices into Turkey a journal called *Meshveret* (meaning "Consultation"). It was subtitled *Order and Progress,* to which the group added *Union,* envisaging that of all races and creeds, to found the Committee of Union and Progress.

An abortive plot in 1896 for a *coup d'état* against the Sultan led to the exile to remote provinces of a number of conspirators and others suspected of political agitation. Meanwhile, among the exiles abroad opposition groups spread from Paris to Cairo, Geneva, and to a lesser extent London, often divided ideologically and personally from each other. In their lack of unity some, to the discouragement of the rest, proved susceptible to blandishing overtures from the Sultan for their return to Istanbul.

But among the students of Istanbul itself the spirit of subversion continued to expand, even in the Imperial Ottoman Lycée of Galatasaray. Here the sons of the ruling elite were normally accustomed on festive occasions to shout "Long Live the Padishah!" but by 1906 they were shouting "Down with the Padishah!" Radical ferment was even more manifest in the provincial schools, beyond the range of immediate palace influence. Thus it was here, in Macedonia, that revolution was to be born. In Salonika the vigorous Committee of Union and Progress, enlisting covert support from organized groups of Freemasons, Jews, and Dönmehs (Jews turned Moslem), was more practical in its effect than the organization in Paris, with which it merged in 1907. What the Sultan in his improvidence failed to foresee was that mutinous action could spread to his own serving officers in field formations, the elite of that Ottoman army on which his power depended. Their superior intelligence and awakened political consciousness, reacting to such professional grievances as arrears of pay and deficiencies in arms and equipment, made of them a potential spearhead for any revolutionary movement.

Early in 1908 military disturbances spread through the Third Army Corps in Macedonia. In the summer of that year the meeting at Reval between the Tsar and King Edward VII was interpreted as a foreign threat to impose autonomy on the province, thus threatening the Empire from outside as it was already threatened from inside. This helped to ignite an army revolt against arbitrary rule, proclaiming the political principles of Freedom and Fatherland, the Constitution and the Nation. Abdul Hamid, underrating reports from his innumerable spies, had remained too long inactive and now found himself faced with a *fait accompli.*

The standard of freedom was raised up in the Resna Hills, behind Salonika, by two Young Turkish majors. One was Enver Bey, a man of few words with a reputation as a daring soldier. The other was Niyazi Bey, an early adherent of the Committee of Union and Progress, to which, travelling through Anatolia in various forms of disguise, he had recruited adherents from among opponents of the Sultan's rule. He now took with him to the hills troops loyal to his cause, together with arms, ammunition, and funds from the coffers of his own battalion. Here the two officers proclaimed their revolt. The Committee of Union and Progress back in Salonika supported them, formulating an explicit political demand for a revival of the constitution of 1876, the work of Midhat Pasha.

When Abdul Hamid sent a force to Monastir to confront the rebels, its commander, General Shemsi Pasha, was shot dead in broad daylight with impunity by one of his own officers, while other reactionary officers met with a similar fate. Meanwhile the Albanians, on whom the Sultan had depended hitherto as allies, came out in support of the Second Army Corps in Thrace. On July 21, 1908, a telegram was dispatched to the Sultan in the name of the committee demanding the restoration of constitutional rule, and in default threatening to proclaim his heir apparent Sultan and to march with a large army on Istanbul.

Abdul Hamid, following traditional Moslem practice, applied to the court of the Sheikh-ul-Islam for a ruling as to whether war was justifiable against Moslem soldiers in revolt against the Padishah's authority. After examining in detail the facts of the case, the Grand Mufti ruled that pleas by the troops for reforms and the redress of grievances were not contrary to the prescriptions of the Sacred Law. Abdul Hamid called a meeting of his Council of Ministers, which sat for three days. A majority of the council sympathized with the army's demands, and aware that failure to concede them would provoke civil war, it voted unanimously for the constitution. The unenviable task of imparting its decision to the Sultan was entrusted to his chief astrologer, who assured him that it was favoured also by the stars. Thus the Sultan gave way, proclaiming by telegrams to Macedonia that the constitution was once more in force and swearing accordingly on the Koran. The Parliament dissolved in 1877 was to be recalled, following a general election. Sultan Abdul Hamid had saved his throne.

On his surrender Enver Bey, in Macedonia, proclaimed Progress, with the elimination of arbitrary government, and Union, with the slogan "Henceforth we are all brothers. There are no longer Bulgars, Greeks, Roumans, Jews, Moslems; under the same blue sky we are all equal, we glory in being Ottomans." In one city the president of the Bulgarian committee embraced the Greek archbishop; in another the officers of the revolution imprisoned a Turk for insulting a Christian. A joint congregation of Turks and Armenians in a Christian cemetery echoed the prayers of their respective priests in a memorial service for the victims of the Armenian massacres. Euphoria swept through the city of Istanbul as the crowds cried "Long live the Constitution!" and "Down with the spies!"—those dreaded agents of the police state, soon to be disbanded. Newspapers burst into paeans of celebration as the censors were chased from their offices. For several days the rejoicings continued, with organized carriage processions in which Turkish mullahs, Jewish rabbis, and the prelates of discordant Christian faiths sat side by side in fraternization. Halting before the crowds at points en route, Moslem and Christian in succession would rise with hands outstretched in prayer, calling upon the One God to preserve the constitution and praising Him for its blessings of liberty.

But they invoked also blessings on the Sultan himself. Indeed, here in his own capital it was the cry of "Long Live the Sultan!" that prevailed above all. Shrewd to the end, Abdul Hamid had contrived to steal some thunder from the Young Turks by posing in the eyes of his people as the magnanimous constitutional monarch who had granted them liberty. A large crowd gathered, crying out for him in acclaim before those gates of the Yildiz Palace from which he emerged so seldom. On the next day he did so, driving amid cheers through the streets to the Friday prayer, in the great mosque of Aya Sofya, which he had not entered for a quarter of a century past. In the neighbouring Chamber, closed since 1877, he was later to open his newly elected Parliament of all races and creeds. Here for Turkey was surely the dawn of a blessed millennium.

It was nonetheless slow to materialize. The Young Turks, through their Committee of Union and Progress, were at this stage in no position to take over the government of Turkey. As a junta of patriotic young officers, with a few civilians supporting them, they had staged their coup simply to curb the powers of a despotic and incompetent Sultan, replacing them with those of a constitutional government better qualified to confront the dangers which now increasingly threatened the Empire. Essentially conservative and uninspired by ideologies, they aspired to no revolutionary social changes, but simply to an effective resumption of the reform movement of the nineteenth century.

The Young Ottomans had sprung from a ruling elite, qualified themselves to assume power and to govern under the terms of the constitution. The Young Turks could claim for themselves no such ruling capacity. As a product of Abdul Hamid's own educational, military, and civil reforms, they sprang from an emerging professional bourgeoisie, which showed promise in its various vocations, but was still largely immature and without the necessary experience to govern. Hence their role at this initial stage was that of a vigilant power behind the throne, watching alertly as guardians of the constitution while the elder Turks of the liberal establishment ruled. Power thus remained in the hands of the existing government of the Porte, cooperating closely with the committee at the expense of the palace.

Conflict soon arose over an attempt on behalf of the Sultan to assert his constitutional right to appoint not only his own Grand Vezir and Sheikh-ul-Islam, but the two service Ministers of War and Marine. The exercise of such a claim would undermine the authority of the committee and its young officers, by giving him effective control over the armed forces themselves. The committee rejected it as unconstitutional, forced the resignation of the Sultan's Grand Vezir, and secured his replacement by Kamil Pasha, an experienced elder statesman, but no adherent of the palace, who appointed an acceptable

War Minister. Pending elections to Parliament at the end of the year, he joined with the Party of Liberal Union to initiate, in the direction of progress, a traditional program of reforms.

In the direction of union the Young Turks sought at first to reassert the principle of Ottomanism, with its free integration of all races and religions in a multinational state. But such dreams were abruptly shattered from three separate directions. Austria-Hungary annexed Bosnia and Herzegovina, thus preempting any claims by their inhabitants to constitutional privileges. Bulgaria declared her complete independence, proclaiming Prince Ferdinand "Tsar of Bulgarians" in the style of the medieval Bulgarian empire. Crete proclaimed its decision to unite with Greece. The spirit of nationalism had outdated Ottomanism.

On December 17, 1908, Sultan Abdul Hamid drove through the streets, a bent, huddled figure in an overcoat, with an ashen complexion, to open the new Turkish Parliament, convoked in its original meeting place, the Fountain of Learning, on the site of the old Byzantine Senate House. Its deputies represented an approximately equal balance between his Turkish and other subjects, with the committee in a controlling majority. The president of its Senate was Ahmed Riza, its original chairman in Paris. In his opening speech, which was read aloud, the Sultan pretended that he had prorogued the previous Assembly on advice that his people were not yet ripe for constitutional government. Now that improved education had led to a general desire for its revival he had proclaimed the constitution anew without hesitation, "in spite of those who hold views and opinions opposed to this." He now affirmed "an absolute and unalterable decision to govern according to the constitution." With judicious flattery he invited all his deputies to a banquet at the Yildiz Palace, sharing the water from his own sacred spring with Ahmed Riza, who thus became almost persuaded that he honestly intended to reign as a constitutional monarch.

He was soon to be disillusioned. For the forces of reaction were mobilizing. Their political focus was the Society of Mohammed, which stood strictly for the rule of the Sacred Law and the clerical doctrines of Islam. Opposing all liberal reform, it appealed, through the pages of an organ named *Volkan,* both to the more conservative, religious elements in Parliament and to the rank and file of the army, while malcontents abounded in its support among the legions of the Sultan's dismissed spies, public servants, and court retainers.

Early in April, 1909, the troops of the First Army Corps mutinied in Istanbul, overpowering their officers and marching to the square before the Chamber of Deputies, where they called for the restoration of the Sacred Law. Their numbers were swelled by a large crowd of religious and other extremists, echoing these demands and raising also cries of "Down with the Constitution!" "Down with the Committee!" For this was their true political aim. Troops and demonstrators swarmed into the Chamber, the unionist deputies fled, the Grand Vezir resigned, and his successor formed a new ministry from which members of the committee were excluded. Abdul Hamid graciously pardoned the mutineers and acceded to their demands. Simultaneously, as though to round off his reign, disturbances in Adana and other parts of Cilicia prompted the massacre, once again, of some thousands of Armenians.

Here then was the counterrevolution. As soon as the news of it reached Salonika the committee acted sharply and swiftly in defense of the constitution. They dispatched a force of the Third Army to Istanbul as an "army of liberation" under the command of a vigorous general, Mahmud Shevket Pasha, with Niazi and Enver among his officers and as his chief of staff a young officer of promise named Mustafa Kemal. As his troops proceeded to surround the capital, deputies from both chambers came out to San Stefano, where, sitting together as a national assembly, they ratified the orders drafted by the general in person as representing the will of the nation. He was to proclaim martial law, to punish the mutineers, and to reduce the garrison of Istanbul.

On April 25 his forces marched into the capital. Its two principal barracks were held by soldiers from Salonika, who had previously replaced the Sultan's Albanian guards but had been suborned by the reactionaries. They fought hard, but thanks to the use of cannon were reduced within five hours. The Yildiz Palace was soon in the hands of the army of liberation, and that night was seen by the people to be in total darkness. Next morning the liberators marched through the streets from the palace, driving before them a long procession of the Sultan's eunuchs, spies, and slaves.

The National Assembly now met in camera to decide upon the fate of the Sultan himself. Abdul Hamid had been cunning in his avoidance of any apparent support for the counterrevolutionaries. But there was little doubt that he had distributed large sums of money, at all levels, among those who inspired it; and public opinion, which at first chose to see him as no more than a spectator, came to realize that, if not an instigator, he was at least an accomplice. Parliament thus resolved on his deposition. In strict conformity with the Sacred Law, it questioned the Sheikh-ul-Islam as to what should be done with a Commander of the Faithful who had acted against the dispositions of the Koran and the holy law: who invested public money for improper purposes; who without legal authority killed, imprisoned, and tortured his subjects and committed tyrannical acts; who "after he had bound himself by oath to amend, violates such oaths and persists in sowing discord so as to disturb the public peace, thus occasioning bloodshed." All this being so, was his deposition permissible? The answer to every question, given by the Grand Mufti, was Yes.

Following a unanimous vote, a commission from Parliament then waited upon the Sultan. They entered a large room in the palace, which was occupied by his secretaries and by thirty Black Eunuchs. Presently Abdul Hamid emerged from behind a screen, holding by the hand his small twelve-year-old son. The leader of the delegation saluted and addressed the Sultan with proper respect. He read to him a *fetva* which announced that he was unanimously and lawfully deposed, and that his brother Reshad would at once be proclaimed Sultan in his place. With dignity the Sultan replied, "This is Kismet." Then, more excitably, he asked whether his life would be spared. The deputies replied that this was a matter for Parliament, acting in the name of justice and of the Turkish people; but they were a magnanimous people. After a wailing litany of self-justification Abdul Hamid gave vent to a cry of despair: "May God punish evildoers!" Privately a commissioner echoed his words: "May He do so!" The small prince then burst into tears.

The life of the Sultan was spared. He was conveyed late at night to the railway station—which he had never before visited—and thence to Salonika, where, with two small princes and a few chosen favourites from his household and harem, he was interned in the Villa Allatini, the house of a Jew.

So was this latter-day Ottoman tyrant defeated and humbled. In first yielding to a bloodless revolution, then failing in a treacherous counterrevolution, Abdul Hamid had sealed the fate of that autocratic regime which, in defiance of its great democratic reformer, Midhat Pasha, he had imposed on the Ottoman Empire. So reactionary a rule had proved incompatible with that trend of liberal progress which, for all its setbacks and shortcomings, had been slowly taking root since the first quarter of the nineteenth century, and of which the neighbouring nation-states of the Balkans were now setting a visible example. Ironically Abdul Hamid, without counting the ultimate cost to his own regime, had himself in fact followed this trend, by bringing to fruition in his empire a reformed educational and administrative system.

For all the inhumanity of his rule Sultan Abdul Hamid has claims to be judged, in historical perspective, as a worthy successor, in a later context, of his early Ottoman forebears. He matches them as it were in reverse, no conqueror like Mehmed II and Suleiman I, but an

Sultan Abdul Hamid II, 1876–1909. Known to the Turks as Bedros (*Peter* in Armenian) because of his Armenian features, he may have had an Armenian mother.

Credit: John R. Freeman & Co. (Photographers) Ltd.

equally resolute nonconqueror. Where they were masters of action, Abdul Hamid was a master of inaction. He dedicated himself, in a defensive spirit, to the preservation of the remaining bulk of his empire through the avoidance of war and such foreign entanglements as might lead to it. Adamant in his isolationism, he would confront the foreigner no longer through positive military action but through the wiles of a negative diplomacy. His aim was to maintain peace at whatever cost, and this he virtually achieved throughout a whole generation.

Such a policy had involved consistent refusal to accept foreign intervention on behalf of his Christian minorities. But on behalf of his own Moslem subjects the reactionary Abdul Hamid was no enemy of modernization. On the contrary, he was in many respects the true heir of the Tanzimat and of the nineteenth-century reforming Sultans. Mahmud II, the great Reformer, had himself always believed that his democratic ends could be achieved only through autocratic means. The vicissitudes of the reform movement throughout the century, with its conflict of ideologies and its alternation of strong and weak Sultans, had proved this to be true. These conflicts ceased following the accession of the despot Abdul Hamid, who believed that reform—if indeed with limitations—should be imposed from above, not encouraged to grow from below.

Unhampered, in the supreme power of a monolithic regime, either by liberal or Islamic opposition, he had brought to the peak of fruition much that had been ineffectively attempted by his more liberal predecessors. He had, it is true, grossly neglected the welfare of the lower strata of his society, keeping the Turkish masses in a state of ignorance, poverty, and general backwardness. But at the upper levels he had in effect, through his educational reforms, created a new middle class. Turkey at last had the full civil-service establishment which as an aspiring modern state she had long required. This Abdul Hamid had used as an instrument of his own vaunted omnipotence as Sultan and caliph, while remaining willfully blind to the real needs of his people. But meanwhile the concurrent spread of education was bringing to maturity a new breed of Turk, comprising not only soldiers and civil servants but such professional classes as doctors, teachers, journalists, merchants, and manufacturers, whose minds willy-nilly it had awakened and broadened, through reaction against reaction, to wider and more progressive horizons. Hence the Young Turk revolution.

Such was the paradox of a generation of Hamidian despotism. Illiberal and brutal in his methods, Abdul Hamid had nonetheless opened the way to a more liberal future for Turkey. Throughout a period of peace both at home and abroad, he had filled systematically a vacuum which required to be filled. He had established in human and cultural terms, as in the technical terms of communications through the telegraph, the railroad, and the printing press, a modernized framework within which Turkey was now free to evolve as it chose. The foundations were laid, the stage was set, the cast was trained. It remained only to enact, through the next generations, the transformation scene.

((39))

THE COMMITTEE OF UNION AND PROGRESS WERE NOW MASTERS OF the Empire, effectively backed by the authority of Shevket Pasha, the army commander. Having proclaimed a state of siege which was to prevail, with martial law, for some two years to come, he ruled in effect as a military dictator. He exercised powers over all the armed forces, which overrode those of the Ministry and Cabinet, and in practice extended into the field of finance and economics. But he did not abuse these powers. As a man of patriotic intentions and a believer in the constitutional ideal, Shevket worked closely with the civil elements of the committee, which now embarked in its new situation upon a new program of legislation for the Empire.

First the recent political changes were legalized through new and amended articles written into the constitution of 1876. In confirming the supreme authority of the Chamber of Deputies, they marked an effective end to the Sultan's traditional power and prerogatives. His sovereignty became conditional on an oath before Parliament to respect the Sacred Law and the constitution and to remain faithful to country and nation. He no longer enjoyed the prerogative to nominate or dismiss ministers, and in nominating others to high office must conform to special laws. It was still his prerogative to appoint the Grand Vezir and Sheikh-ul-Islam; but it was now the Grand Vezir's own duty to make other appointments to his Cabinet, submitting his list to the Sultan for a mere formal sanction. Similarly the president and vice-presidents of the Chamber were elected, subject to this sanction, by the deputies themselves. The Sultan's former right to make treaties was now subject to the approval of Parliament. Finally his right of banishment, as a measure of security to the state—exploited by Abdul Hamid to justify the exile of Midhat Pasha and countless others—was so modified as to amount to its abrogation.

The Sultan's function in government was thus reduced to the confirmation of parliamentary decisions. As a constitutional monarch he continued to reign, but he no longer ruled. The powers of the government itself were now qualified by ministerial responsibility to the Chamber, which in the event of disagreement could oblige a Cabinet to resign. The last word thus depended on the goodwill of the deputies. These were, on paper at least, constitutional changes which, for better or for worse, strengthened the legislature at the expense of the executive.

At the same time the Chamber passed other legislation to strengthen its own position. The aim of this was to curb opposition and curtail such excess of freedom as had led, whether through individual action or meetings of public protest, to the counterrevolution. This involved, not indeed censorship, but a certain restraint on the freedom of the press. In the interests of unity and central control, a new law prohibited separatist associations based on ethnic or national groups. This led immediately to the closure of Greek, Bulgarian, and other minority clubs and societies in the Balkans. Another measure formed "pursuit battalions" from the army to disarm and suppress armed bands like the Balkan brigands. Finally, in the name of equality of race and creed, measures were taken for the first time to conscript non-Moslems into the Turkish armed forces.

But the concept of nationalism had now reached a mature stage of growth. For all Enver's rhetoric, it was too late to realize and to translate into constitutional terms the Ottoman dream of a multinational, multidenominational empire. Talaat, the most realistic of the Unionist Party leaders, admitted to a secret meeting of its Salonika committee that this was now "an unrealizable ideal. . . . We have made unsuccessful attempts to convert the Giaour into a loyal Osmanli and all such efforts must inevitably fail, as long as the small independent states of the Balkan Peninsula remain in a position to propagate ideas of Separation among the inhabitants of Macedonia." Ottomanization was thus to assume a new form. To the committee—as the British ambassador wrote to his foreign secretary, Sir Edward Grey—" 'Ottoman' inevitably means 'Turk' and their present policy of 'Ottomanization' is one of pounding the non-Turkish elements in a Turkish mortar." It had come to mean in fact Turkification, leading to the attempted imposition of the Turkish language on Arabs, Albanians, and other non-Turkish Moslems. Here, at a time of Ottoman defeat and Pan-Islamic decline, was the growth of a new Turkish nationalist consciousness akin to those of Europe in its racial and popular roots, which now gradually found expression in the political and cultural movement of Pan-Turkism.

In the nineteenth century the reforming regimes had relied for support on a small ruling elite, enlightened by Western education and imbued with a respect for European civilization. Theirs were liberal benefits conferred from above and in a broad, cosmopolitan spirit. But the political emphasis had now radically changed. The Unionists were an essentially indigenous movement, not Ottomans but Turks, not cosmopolitans but nationalists, not elitists but aspiring populists, who relied for their strength on a broad social base and a mixed class structure. They were to govern through no individual elite but ostensibly through Parliament and through the large new professional civil service which was the growing product of Abdul Hamid's reforms. Though basing their regime on the introduction into politics of the military element, the Unionists developed within it a good enough working equilibrium between military and civil.

Their effective support in the country derived largely from the new middle class, which had similarly expanded in the course of the Hamidian regime. It was moreover reinforced by that of the Turkish masses, in whom the Unionists sowed the seeds of a sense of political involvement. Theirs was a secular government which took serious notice of the man in the street, as the religious institution had done in the past, mobilizing the urban population in mass meetings and organized demonstrations for the support of its policies.

But this implied no hint of change for the direct benefit of the masses themselves. For the Young Turk revolutionaries, once armed with the magic talisman of the constitution, envisaged no new social order, no removal of old institutions, but rather the adaptation and maintenance of those that existed as a source of their own political power. Unlike the Young Ottomans and the reformists of the Tanzimat, they were more empirical than ideological in policy and method. Essentially men of action, with few theorists or intellectuals among them, they were concerned little with fundamental principles and ultimate ends, but rather with the immediate matter-of-fact task of saving at any cost what remained of the Empire.

The question still remained unanswered—What was the idea behind its salvation? What was now its identity? From this turning point in its history, to what nature of civilization was the Turk to belong—that of Islam, or that of the West, or some fusion of both? The concept of Ottomanism, that union of the elements of race, language, and creed, on which his empire had thrived for five centuries, was now outdated and—but for its remoter Asiatic provinces—doomed. It had succumbed to the European concept of nationalism. The concept of Pan-Islamism, springing from Abdul Hamid's attempt at Asiatic unity, had been a short-lived growth—little more than an abstraction which in reality had failed to materialize. What now was to be the Turk's focus of loyalty?

The answer must surely lie in the new concept of a Turkish nation, distinct from the Ottoman state and the Islamic religion, of which it remained nonetheless an integral part. As the Balkan peoples grouped into nations, the Turkish people themselves, in their wake, evolved their own sense of nationhood, seeking unity in the expression of their historical and cultural identity as a people. This had gained inspiration, since the end of the nineteenth century, from a young Turkish poet, Mehmed Emin. Writing in a folk idiom and in popular language, he imparted a new sense of dignity and pride to the name of Turk, hitherto connoting in its general usage a boorish, ignorant creature of nomadic or peasant status. Mehmed Emin now proudly proclaimed: "I am a Turk, my faith and my race are mighty." And again: "We are Turks, with this blood and with this name we live."

Such poetic revelation combined with the new European science of Turcology to awaken in Turks an awareness of their role in human history, since the days of their pre-Islamic migrations across the Asiatic steppes. This emphasized the Turanian, or "Turo-Aryan," origins of their race. It was carried too far into the realms of abstraction through the visionary concept of Pan-Turanianism. This nourished dreams of unity through ethnical kinship and in eventual political terms between all Turkish-speaking peoples, not only across Central Asia as far as Mongolia and China, but across Russia into Europe, through Hungary and kindred states.

What in fact took root among the Young Turks was the more realistic and limited concept of Pan-Turkism, or simply Turkism. This insisted on the essential Turkishness of all that remained of the Ottoman Empire. Limited at first to cultural and social but extending to political terms, it was expressed through the influential periodicals of Turkish societies and through the foundation in 1912 of a quantity of nonpolitical clubs named Turkish Hearths, whose aims were "to advance the national education and raise the scientific, social and economic level of the Turks, who are the foremost of the peoples of Islam, and to strive for the betterment of the Turkish race and language."

Meanwhile, as time went on dissension grew both within and without the ranks of the dominant group of the Committee of Union and Progress. But it was not until 1911 that a serious opposition party presented a threat to it. Named the New Party and inclining to conservative views, it openly criticized the committee's constitutional procedures and its political and social policies. It put forward demands which insisted on the maintenance, within the constitutional framework, of "historic Ottoman traditions"; on the amendment of certain clauses in the constitution to reinforce the "sacred rights of the Caliphate and Sultanate"; but also, while preserving "religious and national ethics and morals," the increased use, within the Empire, of "the advances and products of Western civilization." There were, one of its leaders maintained, three tendencies in the country: to reactionary fanaticism, to overrapid progress, and to cultural progress compatible with the preservation of existing customs and traditions. It was this that the party required. The contentions of this and other dissident groups were discussed with some heat at the Party Congress—the last to be held in Salonika. Its resolutions boiled down to an ineffectual compromise.

Soon afterward the Party of Liberal Union emerged under the

leadership of Damad Ferid Pasha, to combine most of the elements opposed to the Committee of Union and Progress. At a by-election—the first such genuine electoral contest in Turkey between two opposing candidates—its liberal candidate was elected by a landslide vote. In response to this and other hostile intimations, the committee procured the dissolution of Parliament, which led in the spring of 1912 to a general election. The first to be held under pressure of the ruling party, it was so shamelessly manipulated, through bribes, concessions, and the restriction of opposition meetings, as to ensure for itself a landslide, with the election of a mere six liberal candidates. Notorious in Turkish history as the "big-stick election," it aroused against the committee an illegal movement of opposition far more menacing than the legal movement which they had so imprudently smothered.

Cast ironically in their own past Macedonian image as liberators from oppression, this opposition movement was the product of a military conspiracy in which a group of young officers took to the hills to support a rebellion in Albania. They stemmed from a liberal organization of "Saviour Officers" in Istanbul, who aimed to break the power of the Committee of Union and Progress, now turned oppressors as the government of the Sultan had been, and to restore constitutional government through free and legal elections. At the same time they insisted on the withdrawal of the army from politics as soon as it had achieved its objectives; nor would its officers meanwhile accept government appointments.

On the issue of Albania, Mahmud Shevket Pasha resigned as Minister of War. There followed in the Chamber a near-unanimous vote of confidence which totally failed to appease the malcontents. The Saviour Officers moved into action. A manifesto in the press and a declaration to the Sultan were accompanied by evident military preparations and movements. The Cabinet resigned. The Saviours dictated their terms, namely the appointment of two ministers of their choice under a Grand Vezir to be chosen by the Sultan. His choice was Ahmed Mukhtar Pasha, a man known to be above politics and held in repute for his military record, who later gave way to the former holder of the office, the liberal Kamil Pasha. The state of siege was lifted—though soon reimposed. All serving officers swore on oath neither to join any political societies nor to interfere in the affairs of the state. Parliament was dissolved and the Sultan called for new elections.

But already, amid the strain of these internal party conflicts, the Empire was once again at war with the foreigner. The new agent of its dismemberment was Italy. The theater of war was North Africa. Here the Ottoman territory of Tunisia had fallen as a protectorate to the French. Now the Italians, coveting a share of the imperial spoils for themselves, claimed in "compensation" the territory of Libya. Its two historic Roman provinces of Tripolitania and Cyrenaica were the last African lands to remain in Ottoman possession as integral parts of the Empire. For some time past Italians had been infiltrating into Tripoli, ostensibly in the interests of trade and with declared peaceful intentions. But according to press speculation in Istanbul, Italy now regarded Tripoli as its "promised land" which, through the inability of the Turks to defend it, would at any moment "fall of its own weight like an overripe fruit."

The moment came on September 28, 1911, with an abrupt ultimatum from the Italian government. It declared Italy's intention to occupy the province, whose "state of disorder and neglect" under the Turkish authorities endangered its own Italian subjects. To this it demanded the consent of the Porte within twenty-four hours. The Porte played for time with a conciliatory reply, declaring readiness to discuss Italian claims and afford economic privileges within the bounds of that Ottoman sovereignty which the Italian government had hitherto publicly respected.

But now nationalist aspirations in Italy were roused, with financial interests behind them, and on the next day she declared war against the Ottoman Empire. The Turks were in no state to defend the province, which was made largely inaccessible to troops and munitions through the inadequacy of their naval forces. These might in earlier times have prevented an Italian landing. But now, thanks to the decline under Abdul Hamid of the Ottoman navy, the Italian navy had command of the Adriatic, and was thus able to send to Tripoli an army of some fifty thousand men. Since Egypt, proclaiming its neutrality through Britain, forbade the dispatch of Turkish forces overland, all that the Porte could do to reinforce its occupying troops was to send to Tripoli a group of Turkish officers, which included Enver and Mustafa Kemal, lately chief of staff to the army of liberation in Istanbul.

The Italians were soon in occupation of the coast, with its ports, from which they could not easily be dislodged. But the Turks had the support of the Arab tribesmen of the desert, whom their officers now organized into military formations, so instructing them in guerrilla tactics as to harass the enemy with raids on his outposts and communications, and to make it impossible for him to advance through the waterless hinterland. The result, within two months, was a stalemate.

Thus in the spring of 1912 the Italians turned aside with their fleet to bombard such Turkish ports of the Levant as Beirut and Smyrna; they occupied Rhodes, Kos, and other islands, while avoiding Greek islands protected by Austria-Hungary; they bombarded the two forts that guarded the Dardanelles. This led the Turks to close the Straits for fear of an attempt on the Bosporus by Russia. Nonetheless, by the autumn the Italians had effectively won their war, and on October 18, 1912, the Turks signed a peace treaty at Ouchy, near Lausanne, ceding Tripolitania to Italy and, pending their own evacuation of the rest of Libya, leaving her in "temporary" possession of the Dodecanese Islands.

Peace in Africa for the Turks had now become an urgent necessity. For on the very next day the Ottoman Empire was at war in the Balkans with Greece, Serbia, and Bulgaria. Uniting for the first and only time in their history, these states had formed—with the adhesion of Montenegro—a Balkan League for military intervention in Macedonia, where conditions under the Young Turks were little better than before. The aim of the League was the liberation of its Christian populations from Turkish rule—and the gratification of their own territorial ambitions at Turkish expense. At this well-chosen moment of Turkish military preoccupation abroad and political confusion at home, they based their alliance on two treaties, respectively between Bulgaria and Serbia and between Greece and Bulgaria. They demanded from the Porte the appointment of a neutral Christian governor-general of the province, local legislative assemblies, local gendarmeries, and detailed reforms to be introduced under their supervision and that of the powers. The Porte agreed in principle but refused guarantees until Parliament, lately dissolved, should meet and provide its sanction.

Public opinion, as reflected in the Turkish press, hardened in favour of war, which it preferred to the humiliation of any such concessions. The powers strove to avert it, reviving the proposals for reform embodied in the Treaty of Berlin. But the Balkan governments, skeptical now of all promises of reform, refused to respond to their pressure. Among their own populations the clamour for war was so strong that it could only be ignored at the risk of revolution. Thus war it now was.

It was to prove a catastrophe for the Ottoman Empire. The Turkish army in Europe was greatly outnumbered by that of the Balkan states, which were said to have seven hundred thousand men under arms. It was now, moreover, caught unprepared in this theater of war, and required time to mobilize. The involvement of the army in politics had not furthered its military organization as a fighting force. Its leadership had been weakened by the dismissal of officers for political motives, and by the present absence of Enver and other high-grade officers in North Africa.

The army had modern weapons in plenty from the Germans, but lacked a staff competent to make the best use of them. Its commissariat had been grossly neglected. Nor were the troops, in their light summer uniforms, equipped with clothing fit for a Balkan winter campaign. Finally, there were divisions within their own ranks, through the recent conscription of Christians sympathetic to the enemy's cause. The Balkan armies, on the other hand, were to astonish Europe by their self-evident military progress over the past few years, trained on a Westernized basis and fired by the inspiration of a newly won nationhood. The old myth of the invincible Turk was once and for all to be scotched, not by the powers of Europe but by his own former despised subjects.

The First Balkan War was a blitzkrieg, from three separate directions, which the Turkish armies, one defeat following another, survived for a bare six weeks. The Greeks, advancing from the south under the command of their German-educated Crown Prince Constantine, overcame a strong Turkish force, which they then trapped in a ravine to capture all its artillery and transport. When the Turks, reinforced, took up a stronger position, the Greek guns mowed them down, putting them to flight like a disorderly rabble. Then the Greeks pursued the rest of the Turkish army across the border to liberate Salonika, marching into the city on the feast day of its patron saint, Demetrios, to be pelted with roses by delirious Greek crowds in the streets. After almost five hundred years of Turkish domination, the blue-and-white Greek national flag flew from its windows and rooftops, while the Star and Crescent vanished forever.

Meanwhile from the north, down the valley of the Vardar, came the Serbs, to defeat a large Turkish army at Kumanovo, then another at Monastir, whose remnants, after a loss of ten thousand prisoners, fled across the frontier into Albania. In the east the Bulgarians invaded Thrace in strength, to defeat the Turks in a two-day battle at Kirk-Kilissa, then to confront the main Turkish army at Lule Burgas and to drive it back to the Chatalja Lines, between the Black Sea and the Marmara, whose fortifications were the last line of defense before Istanbul. Here with the aid of Krupp guns and of reinforcements from Asia the Turks, forever tenacious under siege, were able to regain confidence and to halt the advance while the Bulgarians were hampered by their extended supply lines. Thus on December 3, 1912, an armistice was agreed with the Serbs and Bulgarians, but not yet with the Greeks.

This led to a conference in London at which the great powers sought to reassert their influence against any attempt by the Balkan states to make a peace on their own. On January 1, 1913, the Porte put forward its peace proposals. These related especially to the status of Adrianople, the former imperial capital, which alone among its European cities of the Empire—apart from Scutari, in Albania, and Janina in Epirus—still withstood its besiegers. While ready to cede Thracian territories to the west of it, the Turkish delegates insisted that the vilayet of Adrianople, with agreed ratifications of frontiers, should remain in Ottoman possession as an autonomous tributary state. This was rejected by the powers, who in a note to the Porte required the cession of Adrianople to Bulgaria.

To forestall any such ignominious surrender by the liberal regime of Kamil Pasha, the Young Turks of the committee, who from the start of the war had vainly sought his cooperation on a national, nonparty basis, struck out at him on January 23, 1913, in a revolutionary *coup d'état*. Led by Enver, now back from North Africa, a small group of their officers launched a spectacular raid on the Sublime Porte. Bursting into the gilded Cabinet Chamber they shot dead the War Minister, Nazim Pasha, whom they blamed for the Turkish defeat; forced at gunpoint the resignation of Kamil Pasha; and triumphantly secured from the Sultan the restoration as Grand Vezir of Mahmud Shevket Pasha. Back now in office, the committee rejected the demands of the powers, the Balkan states denounced the Armistice, and war broke out once again.

After a long, resolute resistance Adrianople eventually fell to a joint Serbo-Bulgarian assault. Meanwhile, Janina fell to the Greeks and later Scutari to the Montenegrins. The London conference reassembled and under the resulting treaty nothing was left to the Empire of its European possessions, beyond the walls of Istanbul and its Chatalja defenses, but a small part of Thrace, within a line drawn from the Black Sea to the Marmara. Meanwhile, the future of Albania and of the Turkish islands in the Aegean was left for later discussion and settlement. Thanks to the allied forces of European nationalism Turkey had ceased, so it seemed, to be a power in Europe.

But they did not remain allied for long. When it came to dividing the spoils of their swift, unforeseen victories, the rival Balkan states fell back into jealous recrimination and conflict. The triumphs of the Bulgarians at the expense of the Turks reawakened in them arrogant dreams from the past of a greater Bulgaria. The Russians sought to restrain them, with warnings that any renewal of war in the Balkans could provoke the intervention of Rumania and rouse the Turks once again. But their militant government, swollen with confidence in Bulgarian arms and contemptuous of those of the Greeks and the Serbians, swept aside all counsels of compromise in the conviction that their forces could confront and defeat both former allies at once.

Bulgaria from the start had made no secret of her resentment at the Greek capture of Salonika. She had indeed tried to forestall it by dispatching a force of her own, which arrived too late but remained to provide a joint garrison for the city. Since then, even before the Treaty of London, the two powers had been in dispute over the city and its Macedonian coastline, while there had been clashes between them in the Struma Valley beyond. Greece, having acquired Salonika, with the southern portion of Macedonia, by force of conquest, was determined to hold it at any cost.

Serbia, for her part, whose forces in the Vardar Valley had contributed so largely, without Bulgarian aid, to the Turkish defeat, resented the smallness of her share of Macedonia, as formerly agreed in the prewar Serbo-Bulgarian Treaty. The imbalance of Balkan power threatened her the more now that Bulgaria, besides her own larger share of Macedonia, had acquired with Serbian aid Eastern Thrace, with Adrianople; moreover, Serbia would now be deprived of an outlet to the Adriatic through the proposed independence of Albania. Thus Greece and Serbia formed an alliance. Each power agreed to support the other, with reciprocal military aid, against possible attack by Bulgaria; defined the new frontiers which it would demand in the event of a successful war; and made overtures to Turkey for support. But Bulgaria, in her obstinate belligerence, rejected Russian arbitration, threatened to occupy the whole of Macedonia, and at midnight on June 30, 1913, without provocation or declaration of war, launched a dual attack from Macedonia, with the initial aim of separating the allied Greek and Serbian forces. Thus the Second Balkan War began.

Described as "the shortest and most sanguinary campaign on record," it lasted barely a month, confounding all expectations with a dramatic sequence of Bulgarian defeats, and wholly reversing the balance of power between the Balkan states. The Serbs and Greeks, at first taken by surprise, soon rallied to win resounding victories in the river valleys to the north and in the mountains to the east of Salonika. The Greeks, under the command of King Constantine, hailed in a Byzantine spirit as a new "Basil the Bulgar-Slayer," advanced eastward through Serres. Spreading fire and massacre, they drove the Bulgarians before them in a devastating scorched-earth retreat. While their fleet captured the ports of Kavalla in Macedonia, and Dedeagach in Eastern Thrace, their land forces overran the Thracian coast as far as the River Maritza, the traditional frontier. Rumania, as the Russians had foretold, joined in the conflict. Dissatisfied with her miserly spoils under the Treaty of London and with the Bulgarian hegemony in the Balkans, she sent an army across the Danube, which occupied the fortress of Silistria and marched westward without opposition to Plevna (of gallant Rumanian memory) to halt within twelve miles of Sofia itself. From the west Serbia crossed the Bulgarian frontier to threaten the Danube fortress of Vidin. Finally, the Turks themselves avenged their treaty when a Young Turk army under Enver's command advanced from the Chatalja Lines to recapture Adrianople and reassert Turkish mastery of Eastern Thrace.

Encircled by victorious enemies, Bulgaria was compelled, through the mediation of Russia, to sue for peace. In the Treaty of Bucharest her pretensions were humbled by the surrender of territory to all. Of her conquests in the previous war she retained only the Strumitsa Valley and a stretch of the Thracian coastline. Serbia obtained at her expense a large share of Macedonia; Greece an even larger share of it, with a coastline which included Kavalla in Western Thrace. Rumania was awarded the Dobruja, with a strategic frontier from the Danube to the Black Sea. Turkey, by a separate treaty, recovered Adrianople together with Kirk-Kilissa, the scene of her former defeat, and a share of Eastern Thrace which included Demotika and thus cut the railway to Sofia. Bulgaria had impulsively thrown away in as many days a commanding position in the Balkans built up—thanks to the Treaty of Berlin—over the past thirty-five years.

((40))

The Ottoman Empire now entered upon the last fateful phase of its history, which was to culminate in the First World War. In June, 1913, Mahmud Shevket Pasha, the Unionist Grand Vezir, was assassinated, in reprisal for the assassination of Nazim Pasha, in the earlier revolutionary coup at the Sublime Porte. From now onward, the Young Turks of the Committee of Union and Progress reigned supreme over the Empire, establishing an authority as absolute in effect as that of Abdul Hamid himself had been. They reigned without opposition, through an efficient and ruthless triumvirate, drawn from the more radical elements in the Union and Progress Party.

At the head of it was Enver, the youngest of the three. A popular hero of the revolution while still in his twenties, he was still the living symbol of Young Turkish freedom. He saw himself as a man of destiny in the Napoleonic tradition. He was now Minister of War, general, and pasha, and was soon to seal his ambitions by marrying an Ottoman princess, thus acquiring the noble title of Damad. As his prestige grew it came to be said of him, in his flamboyant vanity, "Enver Pasha has killed Enver Bey." Obscure in his family origins—the son perhaps of a railway porter, perhaps of a railway official—Enver had graduated through the School of Military Science into the new middle class of the army. Among his fellow soldiers he inspired loyal admiration. Cool and imperturbable, with his bland good looks, he was reckless in decision, impulsive in action, and fearless in battle. In office he devoted his energies to the reform and above all the rejuvenation of the Turkish army.

The second of the triumvirs—nine years older than Enver—was Jemal Pasha, who came of an Ottoman military family and was himself a highly competent professional soldier. Black-bearded and short in stature but dynamic in energy, he took in all around him through his dark, piercing eyes, to act always with swift resolution. As military governor of Istanbul, following the *coup d'état,* he showed skill in the organization of the police force and in its relentless use for his party's ends. Later he was successively Minister of Marine and army commander in Syria, where he ruled in the autocratic style of a dynastic prince. Polite in his manners, with an assured air of authority, he was cool in his intelligence and often ruthless to the point of cruelty in the discharge of his responsibilities and the pursuit of his interests.

The ablest of the three triumvirs was a civilian, Talaat Pasha, a man of the people from the region of Adrianople, who took pride in his peasant origins and was believed to have gypsy blood in his veins. After a local education he became a postman, then a telegraph operator, then he rose to a position in the Directorate of Posts and Telegraphs in Salonika. This enabled him to give practical assistance to his adopted political cause, that of the Committee of Union and Progress. After the revolution he played a dominant part in the organization and management of the party machine, rising rapidly in its councils to become Minister of the Interior and maintaining a strong hold over the provincial administration. Talaat was a man of virility and gusto, powerful in frame, humorous in talk, warm and genial in manner, with a rough, frank simplicity which masked a swift supple mind and a realistic ruthless outlook. Forceful in action, he was a patriot to the point of chauvinism, wedded to his country's interests, who had come, through his apparent moderation, to be known as "the Danton of the Turkish Revolution."

Outside the triumvirate but influential in its councils was Javid, a shrewd Dönmeh, Jewish by ancestry but Moslem by religion, with a quick financial brain, who was an expert Minister of Finance. The Grand Vezir was Prince Said Halim, of the Egyptian Khedivial dynasty, who had succeeded Mahmud Shevket. A gentlemanly figurehead from an older liberal regime and an orthodox Moslem, he was ready enough to become a captive of the Unionist cause, serving the committee as an appropriate contact at once with the Moslem peoples of the Empire and with the foreign ambassadors to the Porte.

In one important appointment, that of the Sheikh-ul-Islam, the Unionists made a radical departure from precedent. Traditionally this powerful dignitary, the chief religious authority in the land through his mastery of Islamic theology and law, was appointed directly by the Sultan and stood outside the parliamentary hierarchy. Hitherto he had been drawn from the strictest ranks of the ulema. As such he had, in his conservatism, recurrently served as a hindrance to liberal reform. Determined to rid themselves of this obstacle, the Unionists chose for the post Mustafa Hayri Bey, one who no longer identified himself with this religious elite, and who ceased to wear its symbol, the turban, as he came to play a more directly political role. He had become a member of Parliament, serving on secular tribunals as Minister of Justice and of the religious foundations. The Unionists, thus using a traditional religious institution to further their plans for social and political modernization, now appointed him Sheikh-ul-

Islam. The appointment was accepted with favour not only by the ulema but by conservative elements in general. It amounted to a new element of potential secular control over the religious arm.

Such control was applied also to the palace. With the counter-revolution it had served as the rallying point for forces opposed to the Unionists, and the Chief Eunuch of the imperial household was among its officials court-martialled and hanged after the mutiny. With its Damads and royal princes it had since continued to play an opposition role. From January, 1914, it was deprived of all such influence. Members of the imperial family were debarred from any part in politics and from membership in any political party, while their freedom of circulation was limited. At the same time many members of the Sultan's entourage were replaced by adherents of the committee, which thus now held the court under its effective control.

Administratively the Unionist triumvirate, for all its ruthless, repressive methods, embarked on such constructive projects as the country required. They established a new system of provincial and local administration. They modernized that of Istanbul itself, through a new municipal organization with an energetic program of public works, equipping it with such amenities as fire brigades and public transport services. They reorganized its police, together with that of the provinces, where the new-style gendarmerie, introduced into Macedonia under Abdul Hamid, was extended to other parts of the Empire. In much of this they benefitted from the experience of foreign advisers. They tackled judicial reform. They expanded public education at all levels, and for the first time opened the schools and the University of Istanbul to women. This move toward feminine emancipation was to lead, during the years ahead, to their entry into professional life and to new legislation with regard to the rights of the female sex.

Finally, as a token of ostensible respect for normal constitutional practice, parliamentary elections were held throughout the Empire in the course of the winter of 1913, and the third Ottoman Parliament met in the spring of 1914. The British ambassador dismissed it as the "entirely obedient machine" of a "more or less intelligent despotism." In fact, though it represented only one organized political party, it was composed of a consensus of diverse elements, generally representative of progressive public opinion and not always obedient without question to party control. It still involved some representation, though on a more limited scale than before, of the dissident Christian communities. But the Moslem Turks were now, since the loss of Europe, by far the largest element in the population of the Empire, and the Turkish parliamentary deputies represented a wide ground of patriotic concern for its future, combined with a common awareness of the radical improvements required to achieve its salvation.

The outstanding need for reform was in the army. This was the province of Enver. Trained as a young officer under the auspices of the German military mission, he had gone after the revolution as Turkish military attaché to Berlin, where his War Minister, Izzet Pasha, had received his own military training. Enver soon fell under the spell of direct German influence, coming to admire the strength and efficiency of the German military system, and now seeking to emulate its methods at home, where the Turkish army was at a low ebb, following the two Balkan wars.

He sought especially its rejuvenation. The junior officers of the army were in conflict with their seniors, for the most part conservatives of the former regime, who had shown in the two wars a hesitant and even defeatist spirit. Thus it was the younger officers under Enver, ignoring their overcautious advice, who had recaptured Adrianople. Izzet Pasha, as War Minister, now recognized the need for a purge of the old officer corps, but refused himself to carry it out, since "all those to be purged are my friends." Thus Enver, ostensibly on a temporary basis, replaced him as War Minister early in January, 1914. The Sultan himself first read of the appointment in a newspaper, and remarked on it: "That is unthinkable, he is much too young."

Aged thirty-two, he was received in audience a few hours later, and the purge was at once introduced through an imperial decree. This placed on the retired list many hundreds of officers, including "the commanders responsible for the dreary series of defeats in Macedonia, along with most generals over fifty-five." Expounding it, Enver recalled that in the past the Ottoman army had consisted of officers suitable for peacetime activity and officers suitable for war. From now onward these latter alone would be retained in the services.

A more momentous step was the arrival from Germany, at the request of the Turkish government, of a new and substantial military mission, with widely extended powers, composed of some forty officers. It was commanded by a German major-general, Liman von Sanders. This created an immediate diplomatic crisis. For it involved the stipulation that he be given the command of the Turkish First Army Corps, which provided the garrison for Istanbul and its surroundings. Whatever the intentions of the German government, Von Sanders himself, essentially a soldier, had no political motives in mind. He was concerned simply with the military argument that, in training the Turkish army, he would find it easier here in the capital to overcome resistance to the required reforms. But for Russia this meant that a German general would be in command of the Straits, thus putting Germany in a position to establish a political predominance at Istanbul.

Sazonov, her foreign minister, protested strongly. The German government replied that an effective defense of the Straits by the Turks was surely in the interests of Russia. But Sazonov, hinting at reprisals against the Turks and the possibility of war with the Germans, demanded that Von Sanders and his mission be transferred to some less strategic position, and the British and French governments, though belittling his objections, felt obliged to support him in a joint note of protest. Thus in a face-saving compromise Von Sanders was promoted to the rank of full general in the German army, hence automatically to field marshal in the Turkish army. This made him too senior to command a mere army corps, and he was elevated to the position of inspector general of the Turkish army.

Nonetheless, in a climate of growing antagonism between German and Slav there was realistic good sense behind the Russian misgivings. Opinion in Russia reacted to the incident with gloomy forebodings of a lasting disturbance in the relations between Russia and Germany. Haunted by the specter of a German domination in Istanbul, like that of the British domination in Cairo, Sazonov worked with persistence from now onward for some agreement on the Straits which would suit the interests of Russia and Turkey alike.

Here Britain, however, maintained a policy of caution. Through the preceding decades she had remained foremost among the powers in her efforts to keep alive the Sick Man of Europe, largely through the encouragement of internal reforms and support for the minorities in his European provinces. During the Macedonian crisis this had led in 1907 to a "diplomatic revolution" in the form of that Anglo-Russian entente which had been confirmed between the Tsar and King Edward VII at Reval. Though concerned primarily with Anglo-Russian interests in Persia, this combined with the Anglo-French entente of 1904 to create a Triple Entente for the preservation of a balance of power in Europe, which was at risk through the growing ascendancy of the central powers with their Triple Alliance. Britain's new relationship with Russia was in the eyes of her foreign secretary, Sir Edward Grey, so delicate as to involve a modification of her traditional policy of support for the integrity of the Ottoman Empire. For this had been conceived largely as a safeguard against Russian expansion toward Istanbul and the Straits. As Grey commented in 1908 on a minute from his ambassador in Istanbul: "We cannot revert to the old policy of Lord Beaconsfield; we have now to be pro-Turkish without giving rise to any suspicion that we are anti-Russian."

But Grey had given a warm initial welcome to the constitutional revolution of the Young Turks—despite his own reservations as to its possible example to Britain's Moslem subjects in Egypt, as in India. On the other hand, rather than antagonize his two allies with their respective Turkish interests—Russia in the Straits, France in Syria and the Levant—he was careful to avoid any undue British intervention on a "most favoured nation" basis. As a result of his policy, the new regime became distinctly pro-British, revering Britain in constitutional terms as "the mother of Parliaments," and responding to British advice.

British policy, however, still remained that of a benevolent but aloof neutrality. In November, 1908, the Young Turks sent two high-level emissaries to London to propose an Anglo-Turkish alliance, which they hoped would be joined by France. Grey replied with expressions of goodwill to the new government and offers of British advisers, who were in fact to materialize in several ministries. But he insisted that it was Britain's policy to keep her hands free in terms of alliances.

A similar approach was made in July, 1909, after the counter-revolution, through a Turkish parliamentary delegation concerned to counterbalance German influence. This met with a similar reception. With Turkey's defeat in the First Balkan War, the Sick Man of Europe was evidently dead and as such beyond saving. At the London conference Grey impressed upon the Turkish delegation the hard fact that if the Young Turks could not maintain Turkey in Europe, no other power had sufficient motive to maintain it for them.

The eyes of the Western powers now rested on Europe itself, on that new Balkan bloc which replaced European Turkey and must in itself be supported, whether in Turkish interests or otherwise, to contain any threat from the central powers. The Young Turks thus came to see that they could no longer expect western European intervention to save them if they could not save themselves. At the same time, weakened and insolvent as they were, isolated and at the mercy of acquisitive neighbours, they saw that their survival depended, as never before, on the protection and support of a great power.

In June, 1913, Tewfik Pasha, as Grand Vezir, reopened with Grey the question of an Anglo-Turkish alliance. Once more it was rejected, with the argument that, in the words of the new British ambassador, Sir Louis Mallet, "an alliance with Turkey would in present circumstances unite Europe against us and be a source of weakness and danger to ourselves and Turkey." Were it to involve, as Tewfik proposed, some understanding with the Triple Entente as a whole, this would be interpreted by Germany, Austria, and Italy as a challenge from the Triple Entente to their Triple Alliance. "We alone," noted Grey, "can certainly not put Turkey on her feet: she would when her fears subsided resist efforts at reform and play off one Power against the other unless all were united."

Turkey, as he saw it, was now the "Sick Man of Asia," and it was in his Asiatic dominions that the European powers should now combine, as formerly in Europe, for the sake of their mutual interests. Through 1913 Britain, Germany, Austria, France, and Italy, without Russia, held talks with the Turks and with one another which amounted in effect to the establishment in Asiatic Turkey of zones of economic influence—and could indeed, if events so materialized, amount to a blueprint for the ultimate political partition of Asiatic, as already of European, Turkey. Most significant of all, as August approached, these resulted in the signature of a satisfactory Anglo-German agreement with regard to the Baghdad Railway. Germany retained the right to exploit it, with all its accompanying commercial implications, in the Anatolian and Cilician sectors. But it was agreed that it should not proceed beyond the planned terminus of Basra. This safeguarded Britain's imperial interests in the river valleys of Mesopotamia and in the Persian Gulf.

But still no such agreement was broached with regard to the more crucial channel between Asia and Europe. Russia, for her part, was concerned with the threat to the Straits in the event of a war more vital to Britain and Russia now as allies than in the past as rival powers. It was here, as the Russians saw it, that the greatest danger—from Germany—lay. But it was a danger which Britain, beyond cherishing hopes of Turkish neutrality, was doing little or nothing to forestall.

In Istanbul, Germany was flaunting her power and prestige through her ambassador, Baron von Wangenheim, who now dominated the diplomatic as Von Sanders came to dominate the military scene. His new rank as field marshal and inspector general gave him in fact wider powers than before and encouraged him to claim precedence, like the ambassador himself, as a "personal representative" of the Kaiser. It was increasingly evident that Germany planned eventual control of the Straits, which were still, as in the past, the essential key to the Eastern Question. Here was a situation which called for a bolder diplomatic confrontation with Germany in the interests of Turkey than Britain, overcautious in her diplomacy and overconfident in Turkish neutrality, was disposed to support.

But if British action was inclined to be negative, Russian action was vigorously positive. In the spring of 1914 the Russian ambassador in Istanbul, firmly supported by Sazonov in St. Petersburg, discussed with the Turkish ministers proposals for such an agreement between Russia and Turkey as should solve the problem of the Straits in the interests of both. Russia would provide Turkey with the protection she needed. In the event of war, Turkey, as the ally of Russia, would close the Straits to all enemy powers. In the event of victory (as it was later to be specified) Turkey would receive the German concessions in Asia and a guarantee of her own frontiers.

The Russian proposals were eagerly welcomed by Talaat, who went to St. Petersburg in May, 1914, to propose a formal Turco-Russian alliance. In the following month Jemal went to Paris, where he proposed, as more effective, an alliance with all three powers of the Triple Entente. He received the cautious reply—which amounted to a veiled refusal—that this must depend on agreement among them, and that France could not on her own take the initiative. In fact, no agreement materialized. The French rejected outright territorial guarantees required by the Turks at the expense of the Balkan states. The British agreed with them, insisting still on a policy of Turkish neutrality and remaining sanguine in their hope that it would be adopted as being in Turkish self-interest.

For the sixth and last time Turkey's plea for an alliance with the Western powers had failed. Talaat and Jemal returned to Istanbul empty-handed and disconsolate at its failure. Soon they were to be turning with reluctance to the last resort of the triumvirate's militant War Minister, Enver Pasha. This was the hazardous gamble of an alliance with Germany. It was a situation which boded ill for the ultimate fate of both the Russian and the Ottoman empires. For a European war now became virtually certain.

On June 28, 1914, the heir to the Austrian throne, the Archduke Francis Ferdinand, was assassinated with his wife as they drove through the streets of Sarajevo, in Bosnia. His assassin was a student from a secret terrorist organization in Serbia, which had protested against Austria's annexation of Bosnia and Herzegovina and now aimed at the creation at her expense of a Pan-Serb, South Slav nationalist state. At first it was hoped by the central powers to localize the resulting conflict. Austria, given a blank check by Germany, delivered an ultimatum to Serbia, demanding the disbandment of the South Slav societies, and going so far as to propose Austrian collaboration for this purpose on Serbian territory. Appalled at the nature of the ultimatum, Sir Edward Grey protested strongly against it as "the most formidable document I had ever seen addressed by one state to another that was independent." He saw in it a danger to European peace, and foresaw that "a great European war under modern conditions would be a catastrophe for which previous wars afforded no precedent." But Austria rejected a conciliatory reply from Belgrade and declared war on Serbia on July 28.

Germany had not at first anticipated the intervention of Russia, which she knew to be unprepared, at this stage, for war. The Kaiser had failed to grasp, until it was too late to restrain Austria, that any subjugation of Serbia to the central powers must inevitably be resisted by Russia, as fatal to her influence among the Slavs of the Balkan peninsula. It was useless for Germany to insist, in response to Grey's further efforts at mediation, that "Austria's quarrel with Serbia was a purely Austrian concern with which Russia had nothing to do." On July 31 Russia, after a preliminary warning to Germany, declared general mobilization. On August 1 Germany declared war against Russia. France rejected a German demand for her neutrality and entered the war on August 3. The German armies invaded Belgium, and Britain, pledged to defend Belgian neutrality, declared war against Germany on August 4. Thus began, as Grey defined it, "one of the greatest catastrophes that have ever befallen the human race."

Two days earlier, largely on Enver's initiative, an alliance had been agreed in secret between Turkey and Germany. Under its terms the Turkish government promised to enter the war on the side of the central powers if Russia intervened in the Austro-Serbian conflict. On August 4, still unaware of this agreement but aware that Turkey was mobilizing, Grey instructed his chargé d'affaires in Istanbul to press for Turkish neutrality. "You must however," he added, "be careful to give your communication the character of good advice from Turkey's oldest friend, and avoid giving rise to an impression that we are threatening."

Nonetheless Grey, belatedly aware of the extent of German influence in Istanbul, had come to realize "that Enver Pasha wished to bring Turkey out on the side of Germany; and that nothing but the assassination of Enver would keep Turkey from joining Germany." The other two members of the triumvirate now came to support Enver. After Germany had proposed the alliance, Talaat enquired of Jemal: "You can see for yourself that we have nothing to hope for from France. As France has declined, would you decline Germany's suggestion too?" To this Jemal replied: "I should not hesitate to accept any alliance which rescued Turkey from her present position of isolation." On the other hand he preferred to postpone her entry into the war for as long as possible, to allow time to complete the long process of mobilization. To this the Germans agreed, and the Turkish government—whose alliance still remained secret—proclaimed neutrality, which general mobilization would enforce.

Meanwhile, Turkish public opinion turned indignantly against Britain when, on the outbreak of the European War, her government requisitioned two warships, the *Sultan Osman* and the *Reshadiye,* which were being built or reconditioned for Turkey in English shipyards. Britain, now herself at war, could claim every right to commandeer the ships, which in Turkish hands threatened to disturb the balance of naval power in the Black Sea, and for which the substantial sum of seven and a half million pounds would be offered in compensation. But their purchase had been much aided by public subscription in a nationwide campaign to stimulate enthusiasm for the Turkish navy, officials had submitted for this patriotic purpose to cuts in their salaries, and the final installment had lately been paid. The Porte accused Britain of a breach of international law, the public accused her of plain theft, and a pro-German newspaper invoked upon her "A Thousand Curses."

The incident made the task of the triumvirate easier in deflecting public sympathy from Britain to Germany, and in reconciling the Turkish people to mobilization. Their task was made easier still when, on August 10, two German warships, the *Goeben* and the *Breslau,* cruising in the Mediterranean on the outbreak of war, evaded a British naval force in pursuit of them, and appeared before the entrance to the Dardanelles, requesting permission to enter. Under pressure from the German military mission, this was granted by Enver, and the two ships took refuge in the Straits. He further agreed to order the forts to open fire if the pursuing British warships tried to follow them. Announcing the news to his colleagues, Enver exclaimed: "Unto us a son is born!"

The allied ambassadors protested at this breach of their international treaties. But on the following day it was announced that the ships had been "sold" to Turkey, Jemal informing the press that they were to take the place of the two ships of which perfidious Britain had robbed her. A condition of the "sale" was that their German commander, Admiral Souchon, should replace the British admiral Limpus as commander of the Turkish fleet. So the two German ships, now renamed the *Yavuz* and *Medilli,* their crews donning Turkish fezzes, sailed into the Sea of Marmara with the Turkish ensign at their mastheads to anchor off Istanbul. Here a few days later they were ceremonially reviewed by the Sultan, with the rest of the Turkish fleet, and an ensuing regatta off the Princes Islands aroused enthusiasm from the crowds of Istanbul.

Lacking the authority to resist such political pressure from the Ministry of Marine, the British admiral Limpus withdrew from his flagship, and soon no British officers remained on board any Turkish vessel. Admiral Souchon was officially named naval commander-in-chief. Germany had scored a spectacular success as the overt friend of the Turkish people. In the ensuing weeks the foreign ambassadors had no success in pressing for the internment and repatriation of the German naval crews, who were in fact now incorporated in the Turkish navy, while the British naval mission was dismissed a few weeks later. When Javid Bey broke the bad news to a distinguished Belgian friend that the Germans had captured Brussels, the Belgian, pointing to the two ships, retorted in sympathy with the equally bad news: "The Germans have captured Turkey."

Anticipating that the Turks would not now for long remain neutral, Winston Churchill, the First Lord of the Admiralty, had wanted the British squadron to shoot its way through the Straits and to sink the two German ships in the Marmara. But he was overruled by his colleagues. Now, after consultations with Lord Kitchener (the new secretary of state for war) he put forward a plan for the seizure of the Gallipoli peninsula, with the support of a force promised by the Greeks, and urged Grey to obtain similar support from the Russians. But they had no such troops to spare. King Constantine (whose wife was a sister of the Kaiser) now declared that the Greeks would attack only if the Turks attacked first, and Churchill was convinced by advisers that a naval attack, without land forces, must fail. So for the present the project lapsed.

There ensued a twilight phase which was neither peace nor war. The Turks were now in a strong position to carry on a diplomatic flirtation with both sides, playing off the powers of the Triple Alliance against those of the Triple Entente. On August 16 Russia, fearing a closure of the Straits in the event of Turkish hostility, joined with Britain and France in a proposed guarantee of Turkish neutrality and territorial integrity. But this came to nothing. For the Turks, emboldened as they now were, demanded in return for neutrality such guarantees and concessions as the allies could not accept—the total abolition of the Capitulations, the restoration by Britain of the commandeered Turkish warships, the recovery of the Aegean islands and of territories in Western Thrace. When a revised proposal was made a fortnight later, reports of a major German victory in France precluded any such settlement.

Undoubtedly a majority of the Turkish Cabinet, and indeed of the Turkish Chamber, still favoured and mistrusted or indeed underrated the militant minority with its pro-German policy. But over the next two months the drift toward war became unmistakable. It was clear enough to Sir Edward Grey, whose diplomacy was now reduced to a twofold limited objective. First, Turkey's entry into the war, regardless of whether or not it could be ultimately prevented, must at any cost be delayed for as long as possible. Lord Kitchener insisted that she be kept neutral or at least still at peace with Britain, until the Indian imperial troops could be brought safely through the Suez Canal. Secondly, Grey sought to make sure, if the worst had to come, that it came by the unprovoked aggression of Turkey, and through no fault of Britain. Both his ends were to be realized. The Indian forces reached Egypt and the Mediterranean, en route for France, in safety.

On September 27 the British naval squadron at the mouth of the Dardanelles ordered a Turkish torpedo boat to turn back. This unjustified action gave the Germans a welcome pretext to press for the closure of the Straits against foreign shipping. This was duly ordered by Enver, to be followed by the laying of mines. By now there were several thousand Germans in the capital. The German and Austrian ambassadors began to press strongly for Turkish action against the powers of the Triple Entente. On October 11 Enver and Talaat pledged themselves to armed intervention in return for a substantial loan from Germany. The former *Goeben* and *Breslau,* under the command of Admiral Souchon, took to cruising in the Black Sea "in maneuvers," as though seeking to provoke the Russians with a *casus belli.*

Finally, on October 28, the German admiral led a powerful Turkish squadron into the Black Sea, under secret orders from Enver which he had concealed from his ministerial colleagues: "The Turkish fleet should gain the mastery of the Black Sea by force. Seek out the Russian fleet and attack her wherever you find her, without declaration of war." Without warning he bombarded the Russian ports of Odessa, Sebastopol, and Novorossisk, and in the process sank a number of Russian ships. "Never," was Grey's verdict, "was there a more wanton, gratuitous and unprovoked attack by one country on another." By November 5 Britain, Russia, and France had declared war on the Ottoman Empire.

So disastrous an outcome had now become inevitable. At an earlier stage Britain might have impressed upon Turkey, through more vigorous diplomacy, the alternative policy of neutrality. Logically such a policy was in Turkey's self-interest, as in that of the allies. After the disastrous defeats in the recent Balkan Wars she needed above all things a period of peace in which to recuperate and build up her military strength, to maintain a balance between the allied and the central powers, to watch events before deciding whether or not to intervene and if so on which side. Such was the argument vainly put to Enver in mid-July by Mustafa Kemal, whom he had relegated to Bulgaria as military attaché. He strongly opposed any German alliance on the grounds that if Germany won the war she would make a satellite of Turkey, and if she lost it—as he believed that she would—Turkey would lose everything. Such rational views were held by others in the Unionist ranks. But the mood of Turks in general, exploited by Enver and underrated by the British ambassador, who still believed in the moderates, was no longer disposed toward reason.

Humiliated in her pride by recent defeats, apprehensive in her weakness of enemies old and new, Turkey had a deep, psychological fear of isolation. Moreover, she believed that a policy of neutrality could lead only to the eventual partition of her territories between the great powers. Deserted, as it now seemed clear, by their former Western allies, the Turkish people were ready to turn with resignation, if not with universal enthusiasm, to the new alliance with Germany.

Such was the climate of feeling in which Enver Pasha now embarked on his reckless gamble. On hearing the news of it, Javid Bey, always a moderate, resigned from the Young Turk government, with the prophetic valedictory words: "It will be our ruin, even if we win."

Here indeed, after six centuries of life, was the last fateful phase in the decline and fall of the Ottoman Empire. The war started badly for the Ottomans. First, in 1914, the impulsive Enver Pasha lost almost a whole Turkish army in an improvident winter campaign against the Russians in the Caucasus. Then Jemal Pasha, governor of Syria and bent on the conquest of Egypt, sent an expeditionary force across the waterless Sinai Desert to the Suez Canal. Checked on the banks by forewarned British forces, it was obliged to withdraw across the desert, back to his army headquarters in Beersheba.

Early in 1915 the Russians, short of ammunition and now cut off from Mediterranean supply lines by Turkish control of the Bosporus, applied to Britain through the Grand Duke Nicholas for aid, in the form of relief from Turkish pressure. This led to the revival of Winston Churchill's earlier plan for an expedition against the Dardanelles. To ensure Russian military survival, it was proposed to force a passage through the Straits to the Sea of Marmara and so to Istanbul. Churchill planned this as a wholly naval operation, with a land force held in reserve. At this prospect consternation fell upon the Turks, with their traditional respect for British sea power, who now feared a third and final defeat following so swiftly on those of the Caucasus and Suez.

But, following staff disagreements and owing largely to Lord Kitchener, the emphasis of the campaign shifted from the naval into the military dimension, ceasing to be an assault on the narrows by sea, to become a land invasion of the Gallipoli peninsula. By the end of 1915 this had failed in two costly offensives, leading to a British withdrawal and providing the Turks with a decisive and unforeseen victory. For this the credit was due largely to the leadership of Mustafa Kemal, who now proved to be a commander fit to rank with those of the Ottoman imperial past.

The British failure at Gallipoli gave a breathing space to the Young Turk triumvirate, leaving it free to pursue, without external interference, a premeditated internal policy for the final elimination of the Armenian race. Their proximity to the Russians on the Caucasus front furnished a convenient pretext for their persecution, on a scale far exceeding the atrocities of Abdul Hamid, through the deportation and massacre of one million Armenians, more than half of whom perished.

In 1916 the Russians returned to the offensive on the Caucasus front, capturing the stronghold of Erzurum, as a base for the invasion of Anatolia, and the port of Trebizond, with its command of the Black Sea supply routes. Their advance was only checked by the outbreak of the Russian Revolution in March, 1917. This saved the Turks from defeat in Asia and granted them a further reprieve. But their armies were becoming depleted by desertions amounting to hundreds of thousands, while their supply sources were near to a state of collapse.

Baghdad fell to the allies, and the British forces advanced up the valley of the Tigris into the interior of Iraq. Meanwhile, an enemy within the Ottoman ranks had arisen in the shape of the Arabs, who proclaimed a revolt in the Hejaz, in the name of Arab independence, against Ottoman rule. This was to spread to all Arab lands and to exercise a profound influence on the outcome of the war and its aftermath.

Now in the autumn of 1918 the eleventh hour dawned, as the allied forces, having captured Jerusalem, prepared for their final lightning offensive under General Allenby on the Palestine front—destined, in the words of an Arab historian, to sweep the Turks out of Syria "like thistledown before the wind." Once again the Turkish hero of the campaign was Mustafa Kemal, who, after a masterly strategic retreat to the heights above Aleppo, found himself in command of the remnants of the Ottoman forces now defending the soil of Turkey itself, of which this was the natural frontier. They were still undefeated when news was received of the signature on October 30, 1918, of an armistice between Britain and Turkey—leaving him, at the end of the struggle, the sole Turkish commander without a defeat to his name. Behind him were those Anatolian homelands of the Turkish race, where his future destiny and that of his people lay.

The leaders of the Young Turk triumvirate fled into exile, where all three were to meet with violent deaths. The allies, soon in occupation of Istanbul, drafted plans at the Paris Peace Conference not only for the dismemberment of the Ottoman Empire, but for the partitioning of its Anatolian homeland between France, Italy, and Greece, with a Turkish state reduced to a rump of a few inland provinces.

Roused to fight once again for his country's rights, Mustafa Kemal contrived to obtain an official post in Anatolia. Here with the support of the commanders of two Turkish armies he launched a movement of national resistance against the allies and the peace terms they sought to dictate. Within three years, victorious first in a civil war against the Sultan's forces, then in a war of independence to drive out those of the Greeks, he freed Turkish home territory from foreign occupation. He established his own nationalist Parliament in Angora.

Finally, in a new peace conference at Lausanne, he obtained from the allies the new frontiers he had demanded for Turkey, thus preserving intact the Anatolian homelands and a strip of Turkey in Europe which included Adrianople (now Edirne).

Having abolished the sultanate and dispatched the last Sultan, Mehmed VI, into exile, Mustafa Kemal proclaimed, on October 29, 1923, a Turkish republic. So was Turkey, following its ruin as a universal empire, now to survive—and indeed to thrive—as a national state.

Thus did a new phase begin, following on from the old, in the history of the Turkish race.

EPILOGUE

THE TURKS WERE AMONG THE GREAT IMPERIAL POWERS OF HISTORY. Theirs was the last in time and the greatest in extent of four Middle Eastern empires, following those of the Persians, the Romans, and the Arabs, to achieve a long period of unity over this wide focal area where seas meet and continents converge. As a new life-force from the East their contribution to history was twofold. First, through their early successor-sultanates they revived and reunited Islam in its Asiatic lands; then through the imperial Ottoman dynasty they regenerated the European lands of Eastern Christendom. As agents of continuity, uniting East with West, they filled a void left by the disintegration of the Arab Empire in Asia and of the Byzantine Empire in Europe, to evolve within it a new and creative Ottoman civilization.

There were three distinct aspects to the Ottoman Empire. First it was in essence a Turkish state. Its loyalty was to a Turkish family dynasty; its language was Turkish; its roots lay in the tribal societies of Turkestan, with their spirit of ethnical solidarity and their own distinct symbols and customs. It cohered through a natural spirit of authority, a strict sense of order and discipline, a skill and adaptability in the organization of government which reflected the innate resources of the Turks as a nomadic community.

But theirs was, as essentially, an Islamic state, depending on no racial distinction but on a sense of community between Moslems and a respect for their shared institutions. The Ottoman Sultan ruled within the bounds of the Sacred Law and with reverence for the high principles of Islam, through the official hierarchy of a ulema, whose duties and responsibilities were defined with a strict Turkish sense of order and clarity.

But for all its Turkish solidarity and Moslem structure, the Ottoman state was above all else a universal empire. The wide span of its rule was so all-embracing as to cover, in its contrasting cities and plains, river valleys, mountains, and deserts, countless disparate racial, social, and especially religious communities. For long the Byzantine Empire had been fatally torn by religious strife between Catholic and Orthodox, Latin and Greek, Pope and Emperor. With the Fall of Constantinople it was the Ottoman conqueror who, for all his alien faith and culture, restored order and peace to Orthodox Christendom, serving not merely as its master but as its avowed and active protector, leading its devotees to prefer the rule of a Moslem Padishah to the "thralldom of a Latin Pope." For the minority populations were formed, through a degree of delegation from the central authority, into separate ethnical, social, and religious communities, all free to direct, within the framework of the state, their own especial affairs, and to preserve in harmonious coexistence their respective identities.

Here, thanks to the enlightened system of the Ottoman invader, was the long-sought restoration of Orthodox Christian society. The Greek Oecumenical Patriarch, with implied ascendancy over other Orthodox churches, came nearer to universal religious authority under the Ottoman than ever under the Byzantine Empire. Here, in the relations between Moslem and Christian, lay Pax Ottomanica, whose principles marked the affinity between the Ottoman and the Roman empires. For the sake of their own Pax Romana, the Romans had practiced similar tolerance to the foreigner within their own frontiers, often granting him Roman citizenship, and encouraging him to turn his abilities both to his own and to the Empire's advantage.

Just such a tradition, which had likewise prevailed throughout Islam, was now inherited and turned to practical account by the family of Osman. His became in no sense a national but a dynastic and multiracial empire, whose varied populations, whether Turkish or otherwise, Moslem or Christian or Jewish, were above all else Ottomans, members of a single body politic which transcended such conceptions as nationhood, religion, and race. Alone in its time it thus gave recognition to all three monotheistic faiths.

To draw the more effectively on the services of its conquered Christian population, the Ottomans evolved the unique system of a civil service based on the Sultan's Slave Household. Reflecting those principles of slavery to which the Turks, in other lands, had themselves in their earlier history submitted and under which they had thrived, it became a ruling institution composed of Christian slaves. Whether captured in battle, recruited through drafts, purchased in the market, presented as gifts to the Sultan, or enlisting voluntarily in his service, they accepted conversion to Islam, celibacy, separation from their families, and renunciation of all property. For this their reward was a comprehensive course of education and training on Spartan lines, in the Palace School for pages. This led to a discerning selection for that career in the public service which best suited their talents, with opportunities for promotion to the highest offices of state. It meant in effect rule through the conquered in the interests of the conqueror. Unnatural as such enslavement might appear in the eyes of the West, it proved in its own context to be an enlightened and practical formula for using to the full the qualities and skills of the Sultan's young Christian subjects, to the benefit of the Empire and indeed of the slaves themselves. For they soon came not to resent but to value their enforced status, for the privileges which it brought to them and which were denied to the Moslem-born. Deprived of their own families to become part of the Sultan's "family," they developed into a nonhereditary ruling class, reared on the principles of meritocracy alone.

Here was an elite which, through the first centuries of the Empire, helped to secure the power and to ensure the stability of the Ottoman dynasty, relieving the state from the disruptive rivalries and nepotist forces of any hereditary aristocracy, Moslem-born. Moreover, the Sultans themselves ceased as a rule to contract legal and dynastic marriages, breeding their progeny instead through women of the Slave Household, reared in the harem, and thus, for better or worse, introducing mixed blood into the veins of the Ottoman dynasty.

In its earlier stages this Ottoman slave force had been confined to the military arm, with the recruitment of young Christian captives for the corps of the Janissaries. Handpicked for their physical qualities, they were trained and disciplined as a force to serve the Sultan in person, first as a bodyguard, then, growing in numbers, as an infantry arm which became the hard core of the Ottoman army and of its resistance in battle. It supplemented the Moslem-born force of cavalry, the *sipahis,* recruited on a feudal basis from the land, which served as the spearhead of the Ottoman army's advance into battle. It was completed by a force of artillery fired by gunpowder—as never before in the East—and by bands of irregular levies. Together these units made of the Ottoman army a large modern military force, well trained, well armed, well organized, and rigidly disciplined, which outclassed in the unity of its command, in the strength of its armaments, and in the tenacity of its fighting spirit any European army of its time.

Always under the personal leadership of a Sultan of innate military capacity, commanding and inspiring his own troops in the field, its conquests continued through two and a half centuries, building up on two fronts and in three continents an empire which came to extend eastward over Asia as far as the Persian Gulf; southward into Africa through Egypt, to the Red Sea and beyond; westward over the Balkans and across the Danube through much of eastern Europe, to be checked only at the frontiers of central Europe itself. Finally at sea it came to command the entire Mediterranean and a long stretch of the North Africa coast, thus linking through its sea-lanes the Atlantic with the Indian Ocean.

For the first time in history the East, with its institutions, had penetrated deep into the West, to make a true impact as a unifying power upon an important part of Europe. Where the Persians and Arabs before them had failed, the Ottomans had triumphed, rising through their mastery of arms and their innate qualities of order and organization to be an imperial power of high stature in the world of their age. Respected and valued furthermore for their mastery of the arts of diplomacy, they became an integral force in the balance of power of the imperial Europe of the Renaissance, adept in their unity at manipulating the divided forces of the West. Such was the Empire of Osman at the peak of its power under Suleiman—the Magnificent, the Lawgiver—the last and greatest of a line of ten great ruling Sultans.

But its peak became all too quickly a watershed. For twenty-five successive Sultans of lesser breeds followed Suleiman. Under their fluctuating rule an Ottoman Empire was indeed to survive, with varying fortunes, for a further three and a half centuries. But it was an empire in the continual throes of a decline which, despite periods of respite and glimpses of momentary recovery, was to prove irreversible. In the past it had depended essentially on the absolute sovereign authority of a Sultan with the will and capacity to rule. This its Sultans now generally lacked, prone rather to the distractions of the harem, whose ladies, the Sultanas, often developed into the ruling force behind them.

No longer was an heir to the throne sent to gain experience in public affairs as the governor of a province. No longer—with rare exceptions—did a Sultan command his own troops in battle. Seldom indeed did he emerge from the walls of his Seraglio, while his heirs, from one generation to another, were generally denied all contact with the outside world by an incarceration in the Cage, which rendered them ultimately unfit to reign. This weakness coincided with a swing in the historic pendulum of military power.

The Ottoman armies, after an unrelieved spell of warfare on two fronts against enemies whom they could defeat but no longer subjugate, had reached their limits of expansion with few new fields to conquer. The military tide, after three centuries, was turning once more against the East and in favour of the West, with its growing industrial and economic power, and its technical progress in warfare. With this the East, fatally conservative in habit, moreover now lacking in leadership, failed to compete, falling back from an offensive to a defensive role.

Furthermore, the Ottoman Empire, with its treasury already depleted by overexpenditure on armaments, both military and naval, was hit soon after Suleiman's death by a major economic crisis, which afflicted much of the Mediterranean world. Arising from the influx, across the Atlantic, of Spanish-American bullion, it caused a depreciation of the Ottoman silver currency and a high rate of inflation, which doubled prices, leading to the debasement of coinage and increased rates of taxation.

Since the Empire had doubled its population in the course of the past century, this led, in the absence of new conquests, to a shortage of land for settlement, and to large-scale unemployment. It not only created a deprived landless peasantry, but aroused discontent among the army irregulars, unpaid in peacetime, who would often now turn for a living to banditry. It affected also the landed cavalry themselves, the *sipahis,* who were becoming an obsolete force through the technical developments of modern warfare and the greater need for armed infantry. Often deprived of their lands, they were ready enough to join with other landless malcontents in a sequence of revolts in Anatolia led by local chieftains.

These, in the absence of a strong central authority, drove out much of the peasantry and laid waste large areas of land, while much of the rest of it was appropriated by a new class of hereditary landlords, often absentees living in the cities. The development of such landed estates involved a radical change in the traditional Ottoman system of land distribution. It created an ominous imbalance in the social and administrative structure of the Empire, as Suleiman's forebears had conceived and developed it. It involved a shift of power from the center to the landed classes, and to such local forces as the lords of the valleys and the tribal sheikhs of the mountains. This was the process which a sequence of Sultans proved powerless to redress.

More fundamental in its effects was a major dilution, at the center, of the ruling institution itself. Hitherto the Sultan's Slave Household had been strictly closed to all Moslem subjects, thus remaining free from the infection of inherited privilege. But as time went by, and as the Empire grew in size and population, so exclusive a system had come inevitably to arouse the resentment of the Moslem-born gentry. As first-class citizens, faithful adherents of the state and loyal fighters for the faith, they had claimed the right to be treated as a privileged community, eligible for a share in the business of government through admission to the Sultan's household.

The result, through pressure on a line of irresolute Sultans, was the opening of official posts in the Sultan's service to all free Moslems, with the right to bequeath their posts to their own sons. This led to the gradual erosion and ultimate disappearance of the Slave Household, which had provided the Empire, through the centuries of conquest, with an administration of dedicated public servants. But dating back as it did to the Middle Ages, this system had in its inherent rigidity outlived its time. A stronger and more discerning Sultan than Suleiman's successors might well, with due thought and discrimination, have adapted it to a more flexible process of change, thus seeking to preserve its more valuable qualities. In the event the administration soon swelled into an inflated and unwieldy bureaucracy, fraught with intrigue and corruption and—within its negative, self-interested limits—becoming as rigid as the more positive, disinterested regimes of the past.

More momentous was the accompanying dilution and inflation of the corps of the Janissaries. To its ranks free Moslems were likewise admitted, with the freedom to marry and to procure the enlistment of their sons. Through the last quarter of the sixteenth century the corps expanded in numbers from twelve thousand to more than a hundred thousand. Many of these now earned their living through commerce, supplementing their pay with the sale, together with the civilian artisan population, of manufactured commodities.

This change in their exclusive composition undermined, in war, their spirit of team solidarity and self-discipline. In periods of peace, which now grew more frequent, they were to become a subversive, mutinous force in the state, which the central government often failed to control. They became besides a continual threat to the Christian peasant population, whom it was their duty to protect but whom they now often plundered at will. Through the next two centuries they grew progressively more turbulent, disturbing in a succession of revolts the internal security of the state, while in the field they declined sharply in cohesion and discipline.

During the second half of the seventeenth century the Empire, while Europe was at war within itself, enjoyed a period of internal rehabilitation under the Köprülü family—a "dynasty" of Grand Vezirs, Albanian in origin, to which three successive Sultans delegated much of their power. This enabled them to stamp out corruption and injustice and restore solvency to the treasury, to suppress revolts in Anatolia and elsewhere, and to attempt some regeneration of the armed forces. Though the continuity of the rule of the Köprülüs was not to recur, the periodic emergence of a single Grand Vezir of their stamp, usually under a relatively responsible Sultan and with the backing of the higher bureaucracy, could still for a spell vindicate, for the benefit of the state, the authority of the ruling institution. Just so, through the religious institution, could a wise Grand Mufti reassert with effect the authority of Islam. With the survival in whatever form of these two traditional pillars, the structure of the Ottoman state, whatever its condition of decline, died hard. Even the increase of corruption furthered a wide vested interest in its continued survival.

In the eyes of Europe, meanwhile, its prestige in the field suffered an inescapable blow toward the end of the seventeenth century, through the humiliating failure of the Ottoman armies in the second siege of Vienna, and in the campaigns that followed it. Undertaken by a vain and incompetent Grand Vezir who was the son-in-law of an irresponsible Sultan and who aspired in his vanity to surpass Suleiman, the siege failed through such a series of military blunders as to bring shame on the Ottoman imperial memory. Following the rout of the Janissaries, his army broke before that of his more disciplined enemy, disintegrating into such a fugitive rabble as to recall those of the West itself in the crusading wars of the past. Europe rejoiced at this palpable turn of the tide, seeing in it the death knell of the Moslem Turks as a threat to the peoples of Christendom. Once and for all the mighty were fallen. Their fall marked the first of a succession of territorial losses which, after further defeats followed by unfavourable treaties, were at regular intervals to continue right into the twentieth century.

For now, from the start of the eighteenth century onward, a new imperial power was threatening both East and West. This was the Russia of Peter the Great. As absolute a sovereign as the Sultans in the prime of their empire, the Tsar had by his own personal efforts created, as they were now failing to do, a modern professional army equipped with Western armaments, with which he aspired to little short of world conquest. But paradoxically this new threat of aggression was to prolong the Ottoman Empire's survival.

As in its former strength it had provided a balance of power within Europe itself, now in its weakness it became essential to the balance of power between the European powers and Russia. The Empire of the Sultan must at any cost be upheld as a buffer against that of the Tsar. This led to a profound change as the Ottomans, dependent no longer on force of arms but on negotiation at the conference table, drew closer to those Western powers upon whose support, in a spirit of mutual interest, it now depended, thus becoming a key element in diplomacy as once in war.

Traditionally aloof in their attitude to the foreigner, they were now obliged to organize a foreign service, composed of officials skilled in diplomacy. Few Turks at this time, whether Moslem or Christian-born, had any knowledge of European languages or indeed any appreciable experience of the outside world. Thus the Sultan was now obliged to draw on his Greek Christian subjects, mostly the Phanariots. They alone had a wide experience, through navigation and commerce, of the Western world, becoming familiar with its languages and usages and habits of life. Now the ablest among them were appointed by the Sultan to high offices of state, thus acquiring a share of political power in the direction and control of the Empire.

First among these was the Dragoman, or interpreter, to the Porte, who in effect acted as Minister of Foreign Affairs. Other Greek Christians became ambassadors or governors of autonomous provinces, providing an effective substitute for the earlier Christian converts in the Sultan's household. In these and other posts, the administration now included free Christians, working in partnership with free Moslems. So did the Ottomans, in their adaptable fashion, continue to uphold those flexible principles by which the services of all subjects, regardless of race or religion, could be turned to the benefit of the state.

Toward the end of the eighteenth century the Empire suffered a second humiliating defeat in the field, this time in a long war with the Russians, who in the course of it penetrated with their fleet into the eastern Mediterranean, to make landings in Greece and Beirut. Then came Napoleon's invasion of Egypt and a Turkish alliance with Britain and Russia to drive his troops out of this prosperous province. Henceforward European influence at the Porte was active and paramount. In the first place it helped to arrest the disintegration of the Empire; in the second place its pressure drove the Ottoman government to reform itself and to improve the condition of its Christian subjects.

So the nineteenth century became an age of reform. The first reforming Sultan, with the example before him of the French Revolution and its military aftermath, was Selim III, who experimented with a new model army, armed on Western lines, and trained by Western officers. But he was overthrown and deposed through the vested interests of the Janissaries, finally losing his life. Twenty years later their corps was itself eliminated by the ruthless planned action of his ultimate successor, Mahmud II, who thus emerged as the great reformer in modern Ottoman history.

The objects of his work, and that of his reforming associates, were to create a modern army, thus to restore the power of the central government in the provinces; then to establish new institutions of administration and secular law; finally to guarantee equal rights and the benefits of a modern Westernized "civilization," both rational and progressive, to all the Sultan's subjects. Its fruits were a great charter of reorganization, the Tanzimat, which was to serve as a model for such internal reforms through the nineteenth century.

Its aim was to transform the Ottoman state, within little more than half a century, from a medieval society five centuries old into a modern liberal state, founded on the principles of the constitutional West. Seeking to temper absolutism with the regulations of justice, the restraints of a responsible bureaucracy, and the benefits of representative rule, the growth of the Tanzimat was fraught with vicissitudes, torn between the good intentions of one Sultan and the ill intentions of another, as it strove to achieve a balance between the hidebound religious institutions of the ulema and the progressive secular aspirations of a growing intellectual elite.

But in these fifty years, it achieved manifest changes in administration and justice, general reforms in many provinces, and some improvements in the situation of the non-Moslem communities. In the 1870's it culminated in a short-lived period of constitutional rule, on a parliamentary basis. Then came a reversion to absolute despotism under Sultan Abdul Hamid. It was nonetheless to the credit of this autocrat that he greatly extended and improved education, enabling new ideas and new social conceptions to take root for the benefit of future generations and ironically to the misfortune of the Sultan himself, through his deposition in the next generation by the Young Turk revolutionaries.

Meanwhile, the Empire was breaking up the more rapidly before the mounting forces of European nationalism. Here was a concept alien to the principles of a dynastic multinational empire, which was actively to threaten the Sultan's dominions from the Greek War of Independence onward. Encouraged by the West for liberal motives and exploited for their own ends by the Russians, it culminated in the Balkan Wars of the early twentieth century, and the consequent loss, with the conversion of Ottoman provinces into independent nation-states, of virtually all Turkey in Europe. Hitherto the Ottomans, notably at the Congress of Berlin, had been supported by the Western powers—at the expense of the Russians—as the Sick Man of Europe. But now no longer. Hence their contraction of an alliance with Germany in the First World War, which was to seal the end of their empire.

But Turkey, extinct as an empire, was to endure as a nation. The greatest of all Middle Eastern nationalist leaders was Kemal Atatürk, who, ahead of his Young Turk contemporaries, had adhered from his youth to the realistic belief that the days of empires were doomed and the days of nation-states had arrived. Now that his fellow Turks had proved themselves once again ready to fight under his leadership for the survival of their race in the soil of their forebears, he was able to found a successor-state to the Ottoman Empire in the form of the Turkish Republic. His aim was the regeneration of a strong, healthy body through the amputation of its outlying limbs and its final renunciation of imperial expansion. Covering an area of Asia Minor comparable to that of its ancestral Seljuks, the Turkey of today has proved, over a confused half-century, to be the most stable of all such incipient successor-states of the last Middle Eastern empire.

Within its more compact compass there remains indeed a high degree of continuity between the Republic and the Empire that fathered it. No longer an Islamic or a universal but an essentially Turkish state, it is built on those principles of liberal and constitutional change born of the Tanzimat, but now carried to its logical conclusion through secularization, which progressive generations of Turks had sought to implement from the nineteenth century onward.

Its modern rulers are living products of that age of reform, grown to maturity through the evolution of a professional and military middle-class ruling establishment, with the final impetus of a regained pride in their racial heritage. The Turkish nation combines, in its new secular identity, the traditional cultures of both East and West to maintain an element of relative stability and balance in this disturbed focal area of the Middle East. Initiating it, the new "Father of the Turks," Kemal Atatürk, justly honoured with his title of Gazi, was a worthy heir to that earlier and holier warrior, the paternal Sultan Osman.

SELECT BIBLIOGRAPHY

Cahen, Claude, *Pre-Ottoman Turkey,* London, 1968.

Cantemir, Dimitrie, *The History of the Growth and Decay of the Ottoman Empire* (trans. by N. Tindal), London, 1734 (extracts reprinted Bucharest, 1973).

Creasy, Edward S., *History of the Ottoman Turks,* London, 1854 (reprinted Beirut, 1963).

Eliot, Sir Charles, *Turkey in Europe,* London, 1900 (reprinted London, 1965).

Encyclopaedia of Islam, new edit., Leiden, 1954 (proceeding).

Eton, W., *Survey of the Turkish Empire,* 2 vols., London, 1799.

Forster, Charles Thornton, and Blackburn Danniell, F. H., *The Life and Letters of Ogier Ghiselen de Busbecq,* 2 vols., London, 1881.

Ganem, Halil, *Les sultans ottomans,* 2 vols., Paris, 1901–2.

Gibb, H. A. R., and Bowen, Harold, *Islamic Society and the West,* 2 vols., London and New York, 1956–57.

Gibbon, Edward, *The Decline and Fall of the Roman Empire,* edited by J. B. Bury, 7 vols., London, 1896–1900.

Gibbons, Herbert Adams, *The Foundation of the Ottoman Empire,* Oxford, 1916 (reprinted London, 1968).

Hammer-Purgstall, J. von, *Geschichte des Osmanischen Reiches,* 10 vols., Pest, 1827–35. (French trans. by B. Hellert, *Histoire de l'empire ottoman,* 18 vols., Paris, 1835–46.)

Hasluck, F. W., *Christianity and Islam under the Sultans,* 2 vols., Oxford, 1929.

Inalcik, Halil, *The Ottoman Empire: the Classical Age 1300–1600,* London, 1973.

Karpat, Kemal H. (ed.), *The Ottoman State and its Place in World History,* Leiden, 1974.

Knolles, Richard, *A Generall Historie of the Ottoman Empire,* London, 1603, and subsequent editions.

Lane-Poole, Stanley, *The Life of Stratford Canning,* London and New York, 1888.

Lewis, Bernard, *The Emergence of Modern Turkey,* 2nd edit., London and New York, 1968.

Lewis, Raphaela, *Everyday Life in Ottoman Turkey,* London and New York, 1971.

Lyber, Albert Howe, *The Government of the Ottoman Empire in the Time of Suleiman the Magnificent,* Cambridge, 1913 (reprinted New York, 1966).

Miller, William, *The Ottoman Empire and its Successors, 1801–1927,* Cambridge, 1927 (reprinted London, 1966).

d'Ohsson, Mouradgea, *Tableau général de l'empire ottoman,* Paris, 1788–1824.

Pears, Sir Edwin, *Life of Abdul Hamid,* London, 1917 (reprinted New York, 1973).

Penzer, N. M., *The Harem,* London, 1936 (reprinted London, 1965).

Ranke, Leopold, *The Ottoman and Spanish Empires in the Sixteenth and Seventeenth Centuries,* London, 1843.

Runciman, Steven, *The Fall of Constantinople, 1453,* Cambridge, 1965.

Rycaut, Sir Paul, *History of the Turkes to 1699,* London, 1700.

Tott, Baron F. de, *Mémoires sur les Turcs et les Tatares,* 4 vols., Amsterdam, 1784.

Wittek, Paul, *The Rise of the Ottoman Empire,* London, 1938.

Young, G., *Corps de droit ottoman,* 7 vols., Oxford, 1905–6.

INDEX